Federated Learning

Federated Learning
Theory and Practice

Edited by

Lam M. Nguyen
Trong Nghia Hoang
Pin-Yu Chen

ACADEMIC PRESS
An imprint of Elsevier

Academic Press is an imprint of Elsevier
125 London Wall, London EC2Y 5AS, United Kingdom
525 B Street, Suite 1650, San Diego, CA 92101, United States
50 Hampshire Street, 5th Floor, Cambridge, MA 02139, United States

Notices

Knowledge and best practice in this field are constantly changing. As new research and experience broaden our understanding, changes in research methods, professional practices, or medical treatment may become necessary.

Practitioners and researchers must always rely on their own experience and knowledge in evaluating and using any information, methods, compounds, or experiments described herein. In using such information or methods they should be mindful of their own safety and the safety of others, including parties for whom they have a professional responsibility.

To the fullest extent of the law, neither the Publisher nor the authors, contributors, or editors, assume any liability for any injury and/or damage to persons or property as a matter of products liability, negligence or otherwise, or from any use or operation of any methods, products, instructions, or ideas contained in the material herein.

ISBN: 978-0-443-19037-7

For information on all Academic Press publications
visit our website at https://www.elsevier.com/books-and-journals

Publisher: Mara Conner
Acquisitions Editor: Tim Pitts
Editorial Project Manager: Emily Thomson
Production Project Manager: Fahmida Sultana
Cover Designer: Miles Hitchen

Typeset by VTeX

Working together
to grow libraries in
developing countries

www.elsevier.com • www.bookaid.org

Contents

PART 1 Optimization fundamentals for secure federated learning

PART 2   Emerging topics

CHAPTER 7   Personalized federated learning: theory and open
problems 125
Canh T. Dinh, Tung T. Vu, and Nguyen H. Tran

CHAPTER 13 Hyper-parameter optimization in federated learning 237

Yi Zhou, Parikshit Ram, Theodoros Salonidis,
Nathalie Baracaldo, Horst Samulowitz, and Heiko Ludwig

CHAPTER 14 Federated sequential decision making: Bayesian optimization, reinforcement learning, and beyond ... 257

Zhongxiang Dai, Flint Xiaofeng Fan, Cheston Tan,
Trong Nghia Hoang, Bryan Kian Hsiang Low, and
Patrick Jaillet

CHAPTER 15 Data valuation in federated learning

Zhaoxuan Wu, Xinyi Xu, Rachael Hwee Ling Sim,
Yao Shu, Xiaoqiang Lin, Lucas Agussurja,
Zhongxiang Dai, See-Kiong Ng, Chuan-Sheng Foo,
Patrick Jaillet, Trong Nghia Hoang, and
Bryan Kian Hsiang Low

PART 3 Applications & ethical considerations

CHAPTER 19 Mobile computing framework for federated learning 343

Xiang Chen, Fuxun Yu, and Zirui Xu

CHAPTER 20 Federated learning for privacy-preserving speech recognition 353

Chao-Han Huck Yang and Sabato Marco Siniscalchi

Contributors

Lucas Agussurja
National University of Singapore, Singapore, Singapore

Omid Aramoon
University of Maryland at College Park, College Park, MD, United States

Sanjeev Arora
Princeton University, Princeton, NJ, United States

Nathalie Baracaldo
IBM Research, Yorktown Heights, NY, United States

Arjun Bhagoji
Department of Computer Science, University of Chicago, Chicago, IL, United States

Supriyo Chakraborty
Distributed AI, IBM Research, Yorktown Heights, NY, United States

Pin-Yu Chen
IBM Research, Yorktown Heights, NY, United States

Samuel Yen-Chi Chen
Brookhaven National Laboratory, Upton, NY, United States

Tianyi Chen
Rensselaer Polytechnic Institute, Troy, NY, United States

Xiang Chen
George Mason University, ECE, Fairfax, VA, United States

Xiangyi Chen
University of Minnesota, Minneapolis, MN, United States

Warren Chik
Singapore Management University, Singapore, Singapore

Zhongxiang Dai
National University of Singapore, Singapore, Singapore

Canh T. Dinh
The University of Sydney, Darlington, NSW, Australia

Flint Xiaofeng Fan
National University of Singapore, Singapore, Singapore

Chuan-Sheng Foo
National University of Singapore, Singapore, Singapore
Agency for Science, Technology and Research, Singapore, Singapore

Florian Gamper
Singapore Management University, Singapore, Singapore

Samyak Gupta
Princeton University, Princeton, NJ, United States

Trong Nghia Hoang
Washington State University, Pullman, WA, United States

Mingyi Hong
University of Minnesota, Minneapolis, MN, United States

Min-Hsiu Hsieh
Hon Hai (Foxconn) Quantum Computing Research Center, Taipei, Taiwan

Yangsibo Huang
Electrical and Computer Engineering, Princeton University, Princeton, NJ, United States

Patrick Jaillet
Massachusetts Institute of Technology, Cambridge, MA, United States

Xiao Jin
Rensselaer Polytechnic Institute, Troy, NY, United States

Prashant Khanduri
University of Minnesota, Minneapolis, MN, United States

Kai Li
Princeton University, Princeton, NJ, United States

Xiaoqiang Lin
National University of Singapore, Singapore, Singapore

Bryan Kian Hsiang Low
National University of Singapore, Singapore, Singapore

Songtao Lu
IBM Thomas J. Watson Research Center, Yorktown Heights, NY, United States

Heiko Ludwig
IBM Research, Yorktown Heights, NY, United States

See-Kiong Ng
National University of Singapore, Singapore, Singapore

Phuong Ha Nguyen
eBay Inc., San Jose, CA, United States

Jun Qi
Fudan University, Shanghai, China

Gang Qu
University of Maryland at College Park, College Park, MD, United States

Parikshit Ram
IBM Research, Yorktown Heights, NY, United States

Theodoros Salonidis
IBM Research, Yorktown Heights, NY, United States

Horst Samulowitz
IBM Research, Yorktown Heights, NY, United States

Yao Shu
National University of Singapore, Singapore, Singapore

Rachael Hwee Ling Sim
National University of Singapore, Singapore, Singapore

Sabato Marco Siniscalchi
University of Enna, Enna, Italy
Norwegian University of Science and Technology, Trondheim, Norway

Bingqing Song
University of Minnesota, Minneapolis, MN, United States

Zhao Song
Adobe Research, San Jose, CA, United States

Yuejiao Sun
University of California, Los Angeles, CA, United States

Cheston Tan
Institute for Infocomm Research, A*STAR, Singapore, Singapore

Sebastian Shenghong Tay
National University of Singapore, Singapore, Singapore

Yuan Tian
University of Virginia, Charlottesville, VA, United States

Nguyen H. Tran
The University of Sydney, Darlington, NSW, Australia

Quoc Tran-Dinh
Department of Statistics and Operations Research, The University of North Carolina at Chapel Hill, Chapel Hill, NC, United States

Marten van Dijk
CWI, Amsterdam, Netherlands
VU University Amsterdam, Amsterdam, Netherlands

Tung T. Vu
Queen's University Belfast, Belfast, United Kingdom

Xiaoyang Wang
University of Illinois at Urbana-Champaign, Urbana, IL, United States

Zhaoxuan Wu
National University of Singapore, Singapore, Singapore

Chulin Xie
University of Illinois at Urbana-Champaign, Urbana, IL, United States

Pengwei Xing
Nanyang Technological University, Singapore, Singapore

Xinyi Xu
National University of Singapore, Singapore, Singapore

Zirui Xu
CVS Health, Richmond, VA, United States

Feng Yan
University of Houston, Houston, TX, United States

Chao-Han Huck Yang
Nvidia Research, Taipei, Taiwan

Wotao Yin
Alibaba Group, Bellevue, WA, United States

Shinjae Yoo
Brookhaven National Laboratory, Upton, NY, United States

Fuxun Yu
Microsoft, Seattle, WA, United States

Han Yu
Nanyang Technological University, Singapore, Singapore

Syed Zawad
University of Nevada, Reno, NV, United States

Xinwei Zhang
University of Minnesota, Minneapolis, MN, United States

Yehong Zhang
Peng Cheng Laboratory, Shenzhen, People's Republic of China

Yi Zhou
IBM Research, Yorktown Heights, NY, United States

Preface

In our era of big data and the rapid advancement of artificial intelligence, innovation and progress are often driven by harnessing the power of vast amounts of data. Yet, privacy concerns and data protection regulations have placed limitations on traditional centralized approaches to machine learning: While data are abundant, they often exist in small and isolated silos. The need for collaborative and privacy-preserving approaches to machine learning has therefore become more crucial than ever.

In this context, Federated Learning (FL) has emerged as the de facto framework for distributed machine learning (ML) that preserves the privacy of data, especially in the proliferation of mobile and edge devices with their increasing capacity for storage and computation. To fully utilize the vast amount of geographically distributed, diverse, and privately owned data that is stored across these devices, FL provides a platform on which local devices can build their own local models whose training processes can be synchronized via sharing differential parameter updates. This was done without exposing their private training data, which helps mitigate the risk of privacy violation, in light of recent policies such as the General Data Protection Regulation (GDPR). Such potential use of FL has since then led to explosive attention from the ML community, resulting in a vast, growing amount of both theoretical and empirical literature that pushes FL closer to being the new standard of ML as a democratized data analytic service.

Interestingly, as FL comes closer to being deployable in real-world scenarios, it also surfaces a growing set of challenges on trustworthiness, fairness, scalability, robustness, security, privacy preservation, decentralizability, and personalizability which are all becoming increasingly important in many interrelated aspects of our digitized society. Such challenges are particularly important in economic landscapes that do not have the presence of big tech corporations with big data and are instead driven by government agencies and institutions with valuable data locked up or small-to-medium enterprises, and start-ups with limited data and funding.

To develop a practical federated learning system that embraces the aforementioned challenges, multiple diverse disciplines are needed, ranging from traditional studies on distributed, decentralized optimization, cryptography, and security to more contemporary topics such as privacy-preserving, fairness, robustness, and personalizability in machine learning, many of which are relatively new and widely scattered across a sheer, growing volume of research papers. This might pose a challenge for a graduate student or a new researcher in the field who needs to get familiar with all these relevant literature and have a big picture of how the field is being developed. To ease this hassle, we have been seeking help from our colleagues who are experts in this field to compose a comprehensive introduction material, providing the fundamentals with fine details while introducing a representative collection of forefront, cutting-edge research, as well as a wide range of practical applications.

The idea of this book came from our recent workshop in New Frontiers of Federated Learning, in the NeurIPS-21 conference, which helped connect us to other colleagues in this field. Many of them provided valuable contributions and feedback to the development of this book. It comprises a series of technical discourses targeting graduate students at all levels as well as researchers who are interested in the field of Federated Learning. The main content is structured in three parts. Part 1 features a detailed exposition of optimization fundamentals (see Chapter 1 in particular) and core challenges in secure federated learning, spanning numerous security issues and their algorithmic solutions. In Part 2, the book discusses emerging challenges stemming from many socially driven concerns of Federated Learning as a future public machine learning service. Finally, to bridge the gap between academic and industrial research on the topic, Part 3 explores a wide array of industrial applications of FL as well as ethical considerations, showing its immense potential in driving innovation while safeguarding sensitive data.

We hope this book will serve as a valuable resource to those who seek a streamlined pathway to acquire the fundamentals of Federated Learning. It aims to provide an insightful exposition of a representative set of rigorous results on the foremost frontier of this field, while not delving into hyper-rigorous and exhaustive indexing of the entire domain. Our intention is for this book to serve as a good primer for a beginner in his or her quest to explore this field.

Optimization fundamentals for secure federated learning

Gradient descent-type methods

1

Background and simple unified convergence analysis

Quoc Tran-Dinh[a] and Marten van Dijk[b,c]

[a]*Department of Statistics and Operations Research, The University of North Carolina at Chapel Hill, Chapel Hill, NC, United States*
[b]*CWI, Amsterdam, Netherlands*
[c]*VU University Amsterdam, Amsterdam, Netherlands*

1.1 Introduction

The core problem in many optimization applications such as signal and image processing, engineering, operations research, statistics, and machine learning is the following optimization problem, see, e.g., [1,2,7,27,28,49,60]:

$$\min_{w \in \mathbb{R}^p} F(w), \tag{1.1}$$

where $F : \mathbb{R}^p \to \mathbb{R} \cup \{+\infty\}$ is a given objective or loss function, and w is a vector of decision variables (also called model parameters). Depending on the form or structures of F, we obtain different classes of optimization problems. For instance, the following structures are common in practice:

- **Nonsmooth convex optimization.** If F is M-Lipschitz continuous (i.e., there exists $M > 0$ such that $|F(w) - F(w')| \le M \|w - w'\|$ for all $w, w' \in \mathbb{R}^p$) and convex, but often nonsmooth, then (1.1) is called a nonsmooth convex minimization. Note that the M-Lipschitz continuity is often imposed for nonsmooth functions such as $F(w) := \|w\|$ for any norm, or for special smooth functions, e.g., the objective function $F(w) := \sum_{i=1}^{n} \log(1 + \exp(y_i X_i^\top w))$ of a logistic regression, where (X_i, y_i) is given for $i = 1, \ldots, n$. Obviously, the Lipschitz continuity also holds if we consider F to be continuous on a given compact set $\mathcal{W}$.
- **Smooth and convex optimization.** If F is L-smooth (i.e., there exists $L \ge 0$ such that $\|\nabla F(w) - \nabla F(w')\| \le L \|w - w'\|$ for all $w, w' \in \mathbb{R}^p$) and convex, then (1.1) is called a smooth and convex minimization. Examples of L-smooth and convex functions are vast. For example, a least-squares function $F(w) := \frac{1}{2}\|X^\top w - y\|^2$ for a given data matrix X and an output vector y is L-smooth with $L := \|XX^\top\|$. The logistic regression function above is also convex and L-smooth with $L :=$

Federated Learning. https://doi.org/10.1016/B978-0-44-319037-7.00008-9

3

$\frac{1}{4}\|XX^\top\|$. However, exponential functions such as $F(w) := \sum_{i=1}^{n} \exp(X_i^\top w)$ or logarithmic functions such as $F(w) := -\sum_{i=1}^{n} \log(X_i^\top w)$ are convex, but not L-smooth on their domain, unless we limit their domain on a given compact set, see, e.g., [64].

- **Smooth and nonconvex optimization.** If F is L-smooth and nonconvex, then (1.1) is called a smooth and nonconvex minimization. The L-smoothness is a key condition required in most gradient-based methods for nonconvex optimization. Again, this assumption obviously holds if we assume that F is continuously differentiable and then limit the domain of F to a compact set. But there exist L-smooth functions on the entire space $\mathbb{R}^p$. For instance, $F(w) := \frac{1}{2}w^\top Q w + q^\top w$ for given symmetric matrix Q and $q \in \mathbb{R}^p$ is L-smooth with $L := \|Q\|$, but not necessarily convex.
- **Composite optimization.** If $F(w) := f(w) + g(w)$, where f is usually L-smooth and convex/nonconvex, and g is convex and possibly nonsmooth, then (1.1) is called an [additive] composite minimization. This model is ubiquitous in machine learning and statistical learning, where f presents a loss function or a data fidelity term, while g is a regularizer or a penalty term to promote solution structures or to handle constraints. Examples can be found, e.g., in [10,52]. If $g(w)$ is the indicator of a convex set $\mathcal{W}$ as $g(w) = 0$ if $w \in \mathcal{W}$, and $g(w) = +\infty$, otherwise, then (1.1) covers the constrained problem $\min_{w \in \mathcal{W}} f(w)$.
- **Finite-sum optimization.** If $F(w) := \frac{1}{n}\sum_{i=1}^{n} F_i(w)$ for some $n \geq 1$, then (1.1) is called a finite-sum minimization, an empirical risk minimization, or a distributed optimization depending on the context. This structure is presented in most supervised learning tasks, network and distributed optimization, and federated learning. The most interesting case is when $n \gg 1$.
- **Stochastic optimization.** If $F(w) := \mathbb{E}[\mathbf{F}(w, \xi)]$, the expectation of a stochastic function $\mathbf{F} : \mathbb{R}^p \times \Omega \to \mathbb{R}$, where $(\Omega, \Sigma, \mathbb{P})$ is a given probability space, then (1.1) is called a stochastic program [34,43,59]. This setting also covers the finite-sum as a special case by setting $\Omega := \{1, \ldots, n\}$ and $\mathbb{P}(\xi = i) = \frac{1}{n}$.

Apart from these individual settings, many other combinations between them are also possible; we do not list all of these here. For example, the combination of a composite structure and finite-sum is very common.

Existence of solutions

We first assume that $F^\star := \inf_w F(w)$ is bounded from below, i.e., $F^\star > -\infty$ to guarantee the well-definedness of (1.1). Many machine learning applications automatically satisfy this condition since the underlying loss function is usually nonnegative. One obvious example is the least-squares problem.

Our next question is: *Does* (1.1) *have an optimal solution?* To discuss this aspect, we use a coercivity concept from nonlinear analysis [18]. We say that F is coercive if $\lim_{\|w\| \to \infty} F(w) = +\infty$. A common coercive function is $F(w) := \mathcal{L}(w) + \frac{\lambda}{2}\|w\|^2$, where $\mathcal{L}$ is M-Lipschitz continuous (but not necessarily convex) and $\lambda > 0$. If F is continuous and coercive, then by the well-known Weierstrass theorem, (1.1) has global optimal solutions $w^\star$. In this case, we denote $F^\star := F(w^\star)$, its optimal value.

If F is nonconvex and differentiable, then we use $w^\star$ to denote its stationary points, i.e., $\nabla F(w^\star) = 0$. If F is not differentiable, a generalization of stationary points is required [40]. To keep it simple, we assume throughout this chapter that F is continuously differentiable.

If F is strongly convex, then it is continuous and coercive and (1.1) has a unique global optimal solution. For convex problems, our goal is to find an approximate global solution $\hat{w}^\star$ of $w^\star$ in some sense (see Section 1.2.7). For nonconvex problems, we only expect to compute an approximate stationary point $\hat{w}^\star$, which can be a candidate for a local minimizer. However, we do not attempt to check if it is an approximate local minimizer or not in this chapter.

Contribution

Our contribution can be summarized as follows. We provide a comprehensive discussion for the main components of the gradient descent method and its variants, including stochastic schemes. We also propose a unified and simple approach to analyze convergence rates of these algorithms, and demonstrate it through concrete schemes. This approach can perhaps be extended to analyzing other algorithms, which are not covered in this chapter. We also discuss some enhanced implementation aspects of the basic algorithms.

Outline

The rest of this chapter is organized as follows. Section 1.2 reviews basic components of gradient methods. Section 1.3 focuses on stochastic gradient methods, while Section 1.4 makes some concluding remarks and raises a few possible research directions.

1.2 Basic components of GD-type methods

The gradient descent (GD) method is an iterative method aimed at finding an approximate solution of (1.1). This dates back to the works of Cauchy in the 19th century, and has been intensively studied in numerical analysis, including optimization for many decades. During the last two decades, there has been a great surge in first-order methods, especially gradient-type algorithms, due to applications in signal and image processing, modern statistics, and machine learning. In this chapter, we do not attempt to review the literature of GD-type methods, but only focus on summarizing their basic components.

Formally, the gradient descent algorithm starts from a given initial point $w^0 \in \mathbb{R}^p$ and, at each iteration $t \geq 0$, it updates

$$w^{t+1} := \mathcal{P}(w^t + \eta_t d^t), \tag{1.2}$$

where w^t is the current iterate, $\eta_t > 0$ is called a step-size or learning rate, d^t is called a search direction, and $\mathcal{P}$ is an operator to handle constraints or regularizers; if this is not needed, one can set $\mathcal{P} = \mathbb{I}$, the identity operator. This method generates a sequence of iterate vectors $\{w^t\}$ using only first-order information of F (e.g., function values, proximal operators, or [sub]gradients). Here, we add an operator $\mathcal{P}$, which can also be used to handle constraints, regularizers, penalty, or Bregman distance (e.g., mapping between the primal and dual spaces). Let us discuss each component of the scheme (1.2).

1.2.1 Search direction

The most important component in (1.2) is the search direction d^t, which determines the type of algorithm such as first-order, second-order, quasi-Newton-type, or stochastic methods. Let us consider the following possibilities:

- **Descent direction.** Assuming F is continuously differentiable, a search direction d^t is called a descent direction at the iterate w^t if $\langle \nabla F(w^t), d^t \rangle < 0$. We can even impose a stronger condition, called a direction of strict descent, which is $\langle \nabla F(w^t), d^t \rangle \leq -c \| \nabla F(w^t) \|^2$ for some $c > 0$. The name "descent" comes from the fact that if we move from w^t along the direction d^t with an appropriate stepsize η_t, then we have a descent, i.e., $F(w^{t+1}) < F(w^t)$. If $\mathcal{P} = \mathbb{I}$, the identity operator, then (1.2) reduces to $w^{t+1} := w^t + \eta_t d^t$. By Taylor's expansion of F, we have

$$F(w^{t+1}) = F(w^t) + \eta_t \langle \nabla F(w^t), d^t \rangle + o(\eta_t^2 \| d^t \|^2) < F(w^t),$$

  for sufficiently small $\eta_t > 0$ due to $\langle \nabla F(w^t), d^t \rangle < 0$.
- **Steepest descent direction.** If we take $d^t := -\nabla F(w^t)$, then (1.2) becomes

$$w^{t+1} := w^t - \eta_t \nabla F(w^t), \tag{1.3}$$

  and we have $\langle \nabla F(w^t), d^t \rangle = -\| \nabla F(w^t) \|^2 < 0$ provided that w^t is not a stationary point of F. With this choice of d^t, we obtain a gradient descent or the so-called steepest descent method. It actually realizes the largest decrease of F at w^t as $\langle \nabla F(w^t), d^t \rangle \geq -\| \nabla F(w^t) \|$ for any d^t such that $\| d^t \| = 1$.
- **Stochastic gradient direction.** If we choose d^t to be a stochastic estimator of $\nabla F(w^t)$, then we obtain a stochastic approximation (also called stochastic gradient descent) method. A stochastic gradient direction is generally not a descent one, i.e., $\langle \nabla F(w^t), d^t \rangle \not< 0$. Examples of stochastic estimators include standard unbiased estimator $v^t := \nabla \mathbf{F}(w^t, \xi_t)$ and its mini-batch version $v^t := \frac{1}{|\mathcal{S}_t|} \sum_{\xi \in \mathcal{S}_t} \nabla \mathbf{F}(w^t, \xi)$ for a minibatch $\mathcal{S}_t$, and various variance-reduced estimators, see, e.g., [13,29,48,58,66].
- **Newton and quasi-Newton direction.** We can go beyond gradient-based methods by incorporating second-order information, or curvature of F, as $d^t := -B_t^{-1} \nabla F(w^t)$, where B_t is a given symmetric and invertible matrix. For instance, if $B_t := \nabla^2 F(w^t)$, then we obtain a Newton method, while if B_t is an approximation to $\nabla^2 F(w^t)$, then we obtain a quasi-Newton method.
- **Inexact descent direction.** If we do not evaluate the gradient $\nabla F(w^t)$ exactly, but allow some error as $d^t = -(\nabla F(w^t) + \delta_t)$ for some Gaussian noise δ_t, then

we obtain an inexact or noisy gradient method [24]. Another example is called a sign gradient method, which uses $d^t = -\text{sign}(\nabla F(w^t))$, the sign of gradient, see, e.g., [41]. Inexact Newton-type methods compute d^t by approximately solving $B_t d^t = -\nabla F(w^t)$ such that $\|B_t d^t + \nabla F(w^t)\| \leq c\|d^t\|$ for $c > 0$.

Apart from the above examples, other methods such as [block]-coordinate, incremental gradient, Frank–Wolfe or conditional gradient, proximal-point, prox-linear, Gauss–Newton, extragradient, optimistic gradient, and operator splitting techniques can also be written in the form (1.2) by formulating appropriate search directions d^t. For instance, the proximal point method can be viewed as the gradient method applied to its Moreau's envelope, see, e.g., [56].

1.2.2 Step-size

The second important component of (1.2) is the step-size η_t. In machine learning community, this quantity is called a *learning rate*. Choosing an appropriate η_t is a crucial step that affects the performance of the algorithm. Classical optimization techniques have proposed several strategies, which are known as globalization strategies, including (i) line-search and its variants, (ii) trust-region, and (iii) filter [11,23,49]. Line-search and trust-region strategies have been widely used in numerical optimization, see [11,49]. In recent optimization algorithms and machine learning training tasks, we often observe the following techniques:

- **Constant learning rate.** Constant learning rates are usually used to derive convergence rates or complexity bounds due to their simplicity. The algorithm often performs well with a constant learning rate if the problem is "easy", e.g., strongly convex and L-smooth, but it becomes poor if the landscape of F is complex such as in deep neural networks. Usually, theoretical analysis gives us a range (i.e., an interval like $\left(0, \frac{2}{L}\right)$ in standard gradient methods) to choose a constant learning rate. However, this range could easily be underestimated by using global parameters, and does not capture the desired region of optimal solutions. In practice, nevertheless, we need to tune this learning rate using different strategies such as grid search or bisection, etc.
- **Diminishing learning rate.** Diminishing learning rates are usually used in subgradient or stochastic gradient methods. One common diminishing learning rate is $\eta_t := \frac{C}{(t+\beta)^\nu}$ for some positive constant C, a shifting factor β, and an order $\nu > 0$. Depending on the structure assumptions of F, we can choose appropriate order ν, e.g., $\nu := \frac{1}{2}$ or $\nu := \frac{1}{3}$. Another possibility is to choose $\eta_t := \frac{C}{(\lceil t/s \rceil + \beta)^\nu}$ for an additional integer s to maintain fixed learning rate in each s iterations. In stochastic gradient methods, diminishing learning rates are often required if the variance of d^t is nondecreasing (i.e., d^t is not computed from a variance-reduced estimator of ∇F). A diminishing learning rate also determines the convergence rate of the underlying algorithm.
- **Scheduled learning rate.** In practice, we often use a schedule to tune an appropriate learning rate so that we can achieve the best performance. Different ideas

have been proposed such as using exponential decay rate, cosine annealing, or even with a varying mini-batch size, see, e.g., [37,62].

- **Adaptive learning rate.** The above strategies of learning rate selection do not take into account the local geometry of the objective function. They may perform poorly on "hard" problems. This motivates the use of adaptive learning rates which exploit local landscape or curvature of the objective function. The first common strategy is line-search, which [approximately] solves $\min_{\eta>0} F(w^t + \eta d^t)$ to find η_t. If F is quadratic, then we can compute η_t exactly by solving this one-variable minimization problem. However, most algorithms use inexact line-search such as bisection or golden ratio search. Another strategy is using a Barzilai–Borwein step-size, e.g., $\eta_t := \|w^t - w^{t-1}\|/\|\nabla F(w^t) - \nabla F(w^{t-1})\|$, which gives an estimate of $\frac{1}{L}$. (Here, L is the Lipschitz constant of ∇F.)

  Recently, several adaptive methods have been proposed, see, e.g., [12,17,32]. The underlying learning rate is usually given by $\eta_t := C/\sqrt{\sum_{j=0}^{t} \|g_j\|^2 + \epsilon}$, where g_j is some gradient estimator at iteration j, $C > 0$ is given, and $\epsilon \geq 0$ is a small constant to avoid division by zero and provides numerical stability.

Among the above strategies and tricks for selecting learning rates, one can also compute them in different ways when solving a specific problem, even using a "trial-and-error" method or a combination of the above techniques. The main goal is to tune a good learning rate for such a problem, but still guarantee the convergence of the underlying algorithm.

1.2.3 Proximal operator

Many problems covered by (1.1) have constraints or nonsmooth objective terms. For example, we may have $F(w) = f(w) + g(w)$, where g is nonsmooth. In this case, we cannot use the full gradient of F. One way to handle the nonsmooth term g is to use proximal operators, and in particular, use the projections if we have simple constraints. Mathematically, the proximal operator of a proper, lower semicontinuous, and convex (or more generallly, a prox-regular) function g is defined as

$$\text{prox}_{\gamma g}(w) := \arg\min_{z \in \mathbb{R}^p} \left\{ \gamma g(z) + \frac{1}{2}\|z - w\|^2 \right\}, \quad \gamma > 0. \tag{1.4}$$

Note that under appropriate choices of γ, the minimization problem in (1.4) is strongly convex, and hence has a unique solution, leading to the well-definedness of $\text{prox}_{\gamma g}$. If $g = \delta_{\mathcal{W}}$ is the indicator function of a closed and convex set $\mathcal{W}$, i.e., $\delta_{\mathcal{W}}(w) = 0$ if $w \in \mathcal{W}$, and $\delta_{\mathcal{W}}(w) = +\infty$, otherwise, then $\text{prox}_{\gamma g}$ reduces to the projection onto $\mathcal{W}$, i.e., $\text{proj}_{\mathcal{W}}(w) := \arg\min_{z \in \mathcal{W}} \frac{1}{2}\|z - w\|^2$. In terms of computation, evaluating $\text{prox}_{\gamma g}$ is generally as hard as solving a [strongly] convex problem. There are at least three ways of evaluating $\text{prox}_{\gamma g}(\cdot)$:

- **Separable functions.** The most obvious case is when g is component-wise separable as $g(w) := \sum_{j=1}^{p} g_j(w_j)$ (e.g., $g(w) := \|w\|_1$), then evaluating $\text{prox}_{\gamma g}$

requires solving p one-variable strongly convex minimization problems, which can be done in a closed form. This idea can be extended to block separable functions, e.g., $g(w) := \sum_{i=1}^{n} \|w_{[i]}\|_2$, where $\{w_{[i]}\}_{i=1}^{n}$ are subvectors.

- **Dual approach.** Moreau's identity $\text{prox}_{\gamma g}(w) = w - \gamma \cdot \text{prox}_{g*/\gamma}(w/\gamma)$ suggests that we can compute $\text{prox}_{\gamma g}$ from its Fenchel conjugate g^*. Since many convex functions have simple conjugates such as norms (e.g., $g(w) = \|w\|_2$) or Lipschitz continuous functions, this approach is more tractable.
- **Optimality approach.** If g is differentiable, then we can directly use its optimality condition $\nabla g(z) + \gamma^{-1}(z - w) = 0$, and solve it as a nonlinear equation in z. Examples include $-\log\det(X)$ and $\sum_{i=1}^{n} \log(1 + \exp(y_i X_i^\top w))$.

Note that the second and third techniques are only used for convex functions, while the first one can be used for nonconvex functions. The number of convex functions g where $\text{prox}_{\gamma g}(\cdot)$ can be computed efficiently is vast, see, e.g., [1,51] for more examples and computational techniques.

1.2.4 Momentum

One way to explain the role of momentum is to use a dynamical system of the form $\ddot{w}(\tau) + \psi(\tau)\dot{w}(\tau) + \nabla F(w(\tau)) = 0$ rooted from Newton's second law, where $\psi(\tau)\dot{w}(\tau)$ presents a friction or a damping factor. If we discretize this differential equation using $\ddot{w}(\tau) \approx (w^{t+1} - 2w^t + w^{t-1})/h_t^2$ and $\dot{w}(\tau) \approx (w^t - w^{t-1})/h_t$, then we obtain $(w_{t+1} - 2w_t + w_{t-1})/h_t^2 + \psi_t(w_t - w_{t-1})/h_t + \nabla F(w_t) = 0$, leading to $w^{t+1} := w^t - h_t^2 \nabla F(w^t) + (1 - h_t\psi_t)(w^t - w^{t-1})$, see, e.g., [61]. Therefore, we can specify momentum variants of (1.2) when $\mathcal{P} = \mathbb{I}$ (the identity operator) as follows:

$$w^{t+1} := w^t + \eta_t d^t + \beta_t(w^t - w^{t-1}), \qquad (1.5)$$

where $\beta_t > 0$ is a momentum step-size. The search direction d^t can be evaluated at w^t, leading to a so-called heavy ball method [54]. Alternatively, if d^t is evaluated at an intermediate point, e.g., $z^t := w^t + \beta_t(w^t - w^{t-1})$, then we obtain Nesterov's accelerated scheme in the convex case [44]. This scheme can be written into two steps as

$$z^t := w^t + \beta_t(w^t - w^{t-1}) \quad \text{and} \quad w^{k+1} := z^t + \eta_t d(z^t), \qquad (1.6)$$

where $d(z^t)$ presents the direction d^t evaluated at z^t instead of w^t. Note that momentum terms do not significantly add computational costs on top of (1.2). Yet, they can accelerate the algorithm in convex cases [44,46] (see also Section 1.2.8), and possibly in some nonconvex settings, see, e.g., [35,63].

1.2.5 Dual averaging variant

The scheme (1.2) can be viewed as a forward update, but in convex optimization, dual averaging schemes are also closely related to (1.2). Unlike (1.2), a dual averaging scheme works as follows. Starting from $w^0 \in \mathbb{R}^p$, for $t \geq 0$, we update

$$w^{t+1} := \arg\min_w \left\{ \sum_{j=0}^{t} \gamma_j \langle g^j, w \rangle + \frac{1}{2\eta_t} \|w - w^0\|^2 \right\}, \tag{1.7}$$

where g^j are given dual directions (e.g., $g^j := \nabla F(w^j)$), γ_j are the weights of g^j, and η_t is a given dual step-size. In general settings, we can replace $\frac{1}{2}\|w - w^0\|^2$ by a general Bregman distance $\mathcal{D}(w, w^0)$. If the norm is the Euclidean norm, then we have $w^{t+1} := w^0 - \eta_t \sum_{j=0}^{t} \gamma_j g^j$. If $\eta_t = \eta > 0$ is fixed and we choose $g^j := \nabla F(w^j)$, then we have $w^{t+1} = w^0 - \eta \sum_{j=0}^{t} \gamma_j g^j = w^0 - \eta \sum_{j=0}^{t-1} \gamma_j g^j - \eta \gamma_t g^t = w^t - \eta \gamma_t g^t$, which is exactly covered by (1.2). Therefore, for the Euclidean norm $\frac{1}{2}\|w - w^0\|^2$, the dual averaging scheme (1.7) is identical to the gradient descent scheme $w^{t+1} = w^t - \eta \gamma_t g^t$. However, under a non-Euclidean norm or a Bregman distance, these methods are different from each other.

1.2.6 Structure assumptions

One main theoretical task when designing a gradient-based algorithm is to establish its convergence. From a computational perspective, estimating the convergence rate, as well as complexity, is also critically important. However, to establish these, we require F to satisfy a set of assumptions. The following structures are commonly used in optimization modeling and algorithms:

- **Lipschitz continuity.** Function F in (1.1) is said to be M-Lipschitz continuous if

$$|F(w) - F(w')| \leq M\|w - w'\|, \quad \forall w, w' \in \mathbb{R}^p. \tag{1.8}$$

  Examples of Lipschitz continuous functions include norms, smoothed approximation of norms (e.g., $F(w) := \sum_{i=1}^{p}(w_j^2 + \epsilon^2)^{1/2}$ for a small ϵ), or continuous functions with a bounded domain. Note that when F is convex, M-Lipschitz continuity is equivalent to M-bounded [sub]gradient, i.e., $\|\nabla F(w)\| \leq M$ for all $w \in \mathbb{R}^p$. This assumption is usually used in subgradient-type or stochastic gradient-type methods.

- **L-smoothness.** Function F is called L-smooth if the gradient ∇F of F satisfies

$$\|\nabla F(w) - \nabla F(w')\| \leq L\|w - w'\|, \quad \forall w, w' \in \mathbb{R}^p. \tag{1.9}$$

  If $w, w' \in \mathcal{W}$ for a compact domain $\mathcal{W}$ and F is continuously differentiable, then F is L-smooth on $\mathcal{W}$. This concept can be extended to an L-average smoothness in the finite-sum or stochastic settings. For instance, if $F(w) := \frac{1}{n} \sum_{i=1}^{n} F_i(w)$, then we can modify (1.9) as $\frac{1}{n} \sum_{i=1}^{n} \|\nabla F_i(w) - \nabla F_i(w')\|^2 \leq L^2\|w - w'\|^2$ for all $w, w' \in \mathbb{R}^p$. Alternatively, if $F(w) := \mathbb{E}[\mathbf{F}(w, \xi)]$, then we can use $\mathbb{E}[\|\nabla \mathbf{F}(w) - \nabla \mathbf{F}(w')\|^2 \mid w, w'] \leq L^2\|w - w'\|^2$ for all $w, w' \in \mathbb{R}^p$. These assumptions are usually used in variance-reduction SGD methods, see, e.g., [52,66].

Note that other extensions are possible, see, e.g., [34]. Verifying the L-smoothness is generally not straightforward. However, if $F(w) := \frac{1}{n} \sum_{i=1}^{n} \ell_i(X_i^\top w - y_i)$ as, e.g., in a generalized linear model, then we can verify the L-smoothness of F by verifying the L-smoothness of each one-variable function ℓ_i. This model is ubiquitous in machine learning.

One key property of (1.9) is the following bound:

$$|F(w') - F(w) - \langle \nabla F(w), w' - w \rangle| \le \frac{L}{2} \|w' - w\|^2, \tag{1.10}$$

which shows that F can be globally upper bounded by a convex quadratic function and globally lower bounded by a concave quadratic function. If, additionally, F is convex, then stronger bounds as well as the co-coerciveness of ∇F can be obtained, see, e.g., [45]. One can also extend the L-smoothness of F to a Hölder smoothness as $\|\nabla F(w) - \nabla F(w')\| \le L \|w - w'\|^\nu$ for some $0 \le \nu \le 1$. This concept unifies both the L-smoothness ($\nu = 1$) and the bounded gradient ($\nu = 0$) conditions. It has been used in universal first-order methods for both deterministic and stochastic methods, e.g., [47].

- **Convexity.** Function F is said to be μ-[strongly] convex if

$$F(\hat{w}) \ge F(w) + \langle \nabla F(w), \hat{w} - w \rangle + \frac{\mu}{2} \|\hat{w} - w\|^2, \quad \forall w, \hat{w} \in \mathbb{R}^p. \tag{1.11}$$

Here, $\nabla F(w)$ can be a gradient or a subgradient of F at w. This inequality shows that F can be lower bounded by either a linear ($\mu = 0$) or a quadratic approximation ($\mu \ne 0$). If $\mu = 0$, then F is just convex or merely convex. If $\mu > 0$, then F is strongly convex, and μ is called the strong convexity parameter. If $\mu < 0$, then F is called weakly convex. Convexity and strong convexity are key concepts in convex analysis, optimization, and related fields, see, e.g., [7,57], and we do not further discuss them here.

These are three key and also basic assumptions to analyze the convergence of (1.2) and its variants. Nevertheless, other assumptions can also be exploited. For example, the following conditions are commonly used in different methods:

- **Gradient dominance and PL condition.** Function F is called σ-gradient dominant if $F(w) - F(w^\star) \le \sigma \|\nabla F(w)\|^2$ for all $w \in \mathbb{R}^p$ and $w^\star$ is a minimizer of F. Clearly, if F is strongly convex, then it is gradient dominant. However, there exist nonconvex functions that are gradient dominant. Note that one can consider local gradient dominance by limiting w in a neighborhood of $w^\star$. We can also extend this concept to different variants. The gradient dominance condition allows us to obtain a convergence guarantee on the objective residual $F(\hat{w}) - F(w^\star)$ even in the nonconvex setting. Note that this condition is also called Polyak–Łojasiewicz (PL) condition. These conditions can be used to establish linear convergence or linear-like convergence rates (i.e., linear converge to a small neighborhood of an optimal solution) [30,52].

- **Uniform convexity and star-convexity.** Function F is said to be μ-Hölder uniformly convex of order $\nu \geq 1$ if $F(w') \geq F(w) + \langle \nabla F(w), w' - w \rangle + \frac{\mu}{\nu}\|w' - w\|^{\nu}$ for all $w, w' \in \mathbb{R}^p$, see, e.g., [68]. Clearly, if $\nu = 2$, then we obtain the strong convexity. If $\nu = 2$ and $w = w^\star$, a minimizer of F, then F is said to be μ-star strongly convex. These conditions are often used in gradient-type methods to establish linear convergence rates [42].
- **Sharpness, quadratic growth, and error bound conditions.** Assume that there exist $\gamma > 0$ and $\nu \geq 1$ such that $F(w) - F(w^\star) \geq \frac{\gamma}{\nu}\|w - w^\star\|^{\nu}$ for all $w \in \mathbb{R}^p$ and a minimizer $w^\star$ of F. If $\nu = 1$, then we say that F is sharped at $w^\star$. If $\nu = 2$, then we say that F has a quadratic growth property. Clearly, if F is strongly convex, then it has a quadratic growth property. However, nonconvex functions may still have a quadratic growth property. This property can be extended to an ω-convexity as in [14]. Another related concept is error bound [39], which is defined as $\gamma\|\nabla F(w)\| \geq \|w - w^\star\|$ for some $\gamma > 0$ and all $w \in \mathbb{R}^p$. Both quadratic growth and error bound conditions can be used to establish [local] linear convergence of gradient-type methods, see, e.g., [16].

Other properties can be used to analyze convergence of gradient methods such as essential strong convexity, weak strong convexity, restricted secant inequality [30,42], Kurdyka–Łojasiewicz (KL) condition [4], and Aubin's property [56].

1.2.7 Optimality certification

Finding an exact solution of (1.1) is impractical. Our goal is to approximate a solution of this problem in some sense. Let us discuss what we can approximate for (1.1) in both convex and nonconvex problems.

Assume that $w^\star$ is a global optimal solution of (1.1) with the optimal value $F^\star = F(w^\star)$ and $\hat{w}$ is an approximate solution produced by an algorithm. One obvious condition to certify the optimality is to compute the objective residual $F(\hat{w}) - F(w^\star)$. We often expect to find $\hat{w}$ such that $F(\hat{w}) - F(w^\star) \leq \epsilon$ for a given tolerance $\epsilon > 0$. This condition is usually used for convex optimization or special classes of nonconvex problems, e.g., under a gradient dominance condition. The construction of $\hat{w}$ usually relies on two possible ways. The first is to simply take the last iterate w_T as $\hat{w} := w^T$, where w^T is the final iterate of the algorithm. The second option is to form an averaging or a weighted averaging vector as

$$\hat{w} := \frac{1}{T+1}\sum_{t=0}^{T} w^t, \quad \text{or} \quad \hat{w} := \frac{1}{S_T}\sum_{t=0}^{T} \gamma_t w^t, \tag{1.12}$$

where $\gamma_t > 0$ are given weights (usually related to the step-size η_t, but could be different), and $S_T := \sum_{t=0}^{T} \gamma_t$. In general, averaging vectors have better theoretical convergence rate guarantees, but they may break desired properties of solutions such as sparsity or low-rankness, etc., compared to the last-iterate w^T. In convex optimization, we often use Jensen's inequality to obtain $F(\hat{w}) - F(w^\star) \leq \frac{1}{S_T}\sum_{t=0}^{T} \gamma_t[F(w^t) - F(w^\star)]$

for our convergence rate bounds since we obtain a convergence rate bound for the right-hand side.

The second criterion is to use the norm of gradient of F, e.g., $\|\nabla F(\hat{w})\|$ or its squared norm. Note that $\nabla F(w^\star) = 0$ only provides us stationary points, which are candidates for local minimizers in nonconvex settings. Hence, any vector $\hat{w}$ such that $\|\nabla F(\hat{w})\| \leq \epsilon$ for a given tolerance $\epsilon > 0$ only provides us an approximate stationary point $\hat{w}$ of (1.1). To guarantee an approximate local solution, we may add a second-order condition such as $\lambda_{\min}(\nabla^2 F(\hat{w})) \geq -\hat{\epsilon}$ for some $\hat{\epsilon} > 0$, where $\lambda_{\min}(\nabla^2 F(\hat{w}))$ is the smallest eigenvalue of $\nabla^2 F(\hat{w})$. The construction of $\hat{w}$ in the nonconvex case often relies on the best iterate from $\{w^0, \ldots, w^T\}$, in the sense that $\|\nabla F(\hat{w})\| = \min_{0 \leq t \leq T} \|\nabla F(w^t)\|$. For nonsmooth optimization, where $F := f + g$, we can use the norm $\|G_\beta(\hat{w})\|$ of the gradient mapping $G_\beta(\hat{w}) := \beta^{-1}(\hat{w} - \text{prox}_{\beta g}(\hat{w} - \beta \nabla f(\hat{w})))$ for some $\beta > 0$. For stochastic optimization, one needs to characterize the optimality condition using expectation $\mathbb{E}[\|\nabla F(\hat{w})\|^2]$, $\mathbb{E}[F(\hat{w}) - F^\star]$, or high probability $\mathbb{P}[\|\nabla F(\hat{w})\| \leq \epsilon] \geq 1 - \delta$ or $\mathbb{P}[F(\hat{w}) - F^\star \leq \epsilon] \geq 1 - \delta$ for a small $\delta \in (0, 1)$.

1.2.8 Unified convergence analysis

(a) General approach. Most convergence analysis of first-order methods of the form (1.2) relies on the following recursive inequality often generated by two or three consecutive iterates:

$$D_{t+1} + \Delta_t \leq \omega_t \cdot D_t + E_t, \tag{1.13}$$

where D_t, Δ_t, and E_t are nonnegative quantities, and $\omega_t \in (0, 1]$ is a contraction factor. Very often these quantities depend on two consecutive iterates w^t and w^{t+1}, but sometimes they also depend on w^{t-1}. The error term E_t usually satisfies $\sum_{t=0}^\infty E_t < +\infty$. Moreover, we often have $\omega_t = 1$ or $\omega_t \to 1$ for sublinear rates, and a fixed $\omega_t = \omega \in (0, 1)$ for linear rates. The quantity D_t can be referred to as a potential or Lyapunov function. There is no general and universal method to construct D_t, but for gradient-type methods, it is usually either $\|w^t - w^\star\|^2$, $\|w^t - w^{t-1}\|^2$, $F(w^t) - F^\star$, $\|\nabla F(w^t)\|^2$ (in Euclidean or weighted norms), or a combination of these terms. Clearly, if $E_t = 0$, then $\{D_t\}$ is nonincreasing, showing a descent property of D_t. However, if $E_t > 0$, then we no longer have a descent property of D_t, which is usually the case in SGD or subgradient methods. There are two cases:

Case 1. If D_t contains an optimality measure, e.g., $S_t[F(w^t) - F^\star]$, then we can show that $F(w^t) - F^\star \leq \frac{C}{S_t}$ for the last iterate w^t, where C is a constant depending on w^0 and possibly on $w^\star$ or $F^\star$.

Case 2. If Δ_t contains an optimality measure, e.g., $\gamma_t \|\nabla F(w^t)\|^2$, then we can show that $\frac{1}{S_T} \sum_{t=0}^T \gamma_t \|\nabla F(w^t)\|^2 \leq \frac{C}{S_T}$ for some constant C and $S_T := \sum_{t=0}^T \gamma_t$.

The recursive estimate (1.13) can be used to prove the convergence of different gradient-type methods, including standard and accelerated algorithms. Let us illustrate how to obtain (1.13) for some common schemes.

(b) Subgradient method. Let us consider the classical [sub]gradient method to minimize $F(w)$ as $w^{t+1} = w^t - \eta_t \nabla F(w^t)$, which is a special case of (1.2), where $\nabla F(w^t)$ is a [sub]gradient of F at w^t. Then, for any $w \in \mathbb{R}^p$, we have

$$\eta_t \langle \nabla F(w^t), w^t - w \rangle = \frac{1}{2}\|w^t - w\|^2 - \frac{1}{2}\|w^{t+1} - w\|^2 + \frac{\eta_t^2}{2}\|\nabla F(w^t)\|^2. \quad (1.14)$$

If F is convex, then $\langle \nabla F(w^t), w^t - w \rangle \geq F(w^t) - F(w)$. Combining this inequality and (1.14), we obtain

$$\underbrace{\frac{1}{2}\|w^{t+1} - w\|^2}_{D_{t+1}} + \underbrace{\eta_t[F(w^t) - F(w)]}_{\Delta_t} \leq \underbrace{\frac{1}{2}\|w^t - w\|^2}_{D_t} + \underbrace{\frac{\eta_t^2}{2}\|\nabla F(w^t)\|^2}_{E_t}. \quad (1.15)$$

This inequality is exactly in the form (1.13) with $\omega_t = 1$. To guarantee convergence, we need to take $w = w^\star$ as a solution of (1.1) and assume that $\|\nabla F(w^t)\| \leq M$. Then, (1.15) implies that $\Delta_t \leq D_t - D_{t+1} + E_t$. By induction, we have $\sum_{t=0}^{T} \Delta_t \leq D_0 - D_{T+1} + \sum_{t=0}^{T} E_t \leq D_0 + \sum_{t=0}^{T} E_t$. Therefore, we obtain

$$F(\hat{w}) - F(w^\star) \leq \frac{1}{S_T}\sum_{t=0}^{T} \eta_t[F(w^t) - F(w^\star)] \leq \frac{1}{2S_T}\|w^0 - w^\star\|^2 + \frac{M^2}{2S_T}\sum_{t=0}^{T} \eta_t^2,$$

where $S_T := \sum_{t=0}^{T} \eta_t$ and $\hat{w} := \frac{1}{S_T}\sum_{t=0}^{T} \eta_t w^t$ as computed by (1.12). To obtain a convergence rate bound, we require $\sum_{t=0}^{\infty} \eta_t^2 < +\infty$ and $S_T \to S_\infty = \sum_{t=0}^{\infty} \eta_t = \infty$. These are exactly the conditions to guarantee the convergence of [sub]gradient methods, see, e.g., [8].

(c) Gradient descent method for nonconvex problems. If we assume that F is only L-smooth and not necessarily convex, then using (1.10) with $w := w^t$ and $w' := w^{t+1} = w^t - \eta_t \nabla F(w^t)$, we have

$$F(w^{t+1}) \leq F(w^t) + \langle \nabla F(w^t), w^{t+1} - w^t \rangle + \frac{L}{2}\|w^{t+1} - w^t\|^2$$
$$= F(w^t) - \eta_t \left(1 - \frac{L\eta_t}{2}\right)\|\nabla F(w^t)\|^2. \quad (1.16)$$

By adding $-F^\star$, where $F^\star := \inf_w F(w) > -\infty$ (our assumption), to both sides and rearranging the result, inequality (1.16) leads to

$$\underbrace{F(w^{t+1}) - F^\star}_{D_{t+1}} + \underbrace{\eta_t \left(1 - \frac{L\eta_t}{2}\right)\|\nabla F(w^t)\|^2}_{\Delta_t} \leq \underbrace{F(w^t) - F^\star}_{D_t}.$$

This is exactly in the form (1.13) with $\omega_t = 1$ and $E_t = 0$. Without any further assumption, we have $\Delta_t \leq D_t - D_{t+1}$ and, by induction, get $\sum_{t=0}^{T} \Delta_t \leq D_0 - D_{T+1} \leq$

D_0, leading to

$$\min_{0 \le t \le T} \|\nabla F(w^t)\|^2 \le \frac{1}{S_T} \sum_{t=0}^{T} \gamma_t \|\nabla F(w^t)\|^2 \le \frac{F(w^0) - F^\star}{S_T},$$

where $\gamma_t = \eta_t(1 - \frac{L\eta_t}{2})$ and $S_T = \sum_{t=0}^{T} \gamma_t$, provided that $0 < \eta_t < \frac{2}{L}$. This result allows us to certify the best-iterate convergence rate of the algorithm to a stationary point of (1.1).

(d) **Gradient descent method for smooth and convex problems.** Assume that F is convex and L-smooth. Let us choose $\eta_t := \frac{1}{L}$ in (1.2) to get $w^{t+1} := w^t - \frac{1}{L}\nabla F(w^t)$. Then, from (1.14) and (1.16), and the convexity of F, we have

$$\begin{cases} \frac{L}{2}\|w^{t+1} - w^\star\|^2 + \langle \nabla F(w^t), w^t - w^\star \rangle = \frac{L}{2}\|w^t - w^\star\|^2 + \frac{1}{2L}\|\nabla F(w^t)\|^2, \\ (t+1)[F(w^{t+1}) - F(w^\star)] + \frac{(t+1)}{2L}\|\nabla F(w^t)\|^2 \le (t+1)[F(w^t) - F(w^\star)], \\ F(w^t) - F(w^\star) \le \langle \nabla F(w^t), w^t - w^\star \rangle. \end{cases}$$

By summing up these three inequalities and canceling terms, we obtain

$$\frac{L}{2}\|w^{t+1} - w^\star\|^2 + (t+1)[F(w^{t+1}) - F(w^\star)] + \frac{t}{2L}\|\nabla F(w^t)\|^2$$
$$\le \frac{L}{2}\|w^t - w^\star\|^2 + t[F(w^t) - F(w^\star)].$$

This is exactly (1.13) with $D_t := \frac{L}{2}\|w^t - w^\star\|^2 + t[F(w^t) - F(w^\star)]$, $\Delta_t := \frac{t}{2L}\|\nabla F(w^t)\|^2$, $E_t = 0$, and $\omega_t = 1$. This recursive estimate implies $D_{t+1} \le D_0$, and therefore, using the definition of D_{t+1} and dropping $\frac{L}{2}\|w^{t+1} - w^\star\|^2$, we get

$$F(w^{t+1}) - F(w^\star) \le \frac{D_0}{t+1} = \frac{L\|w^0 - w^\star\|^2}{2(t+1)},$$

which shows an $\mathcal{O}(1/t)$-last-iterate convergence rate on w^t. It also implies that $\sum_{t=0}^{T} t\|\nabla F(w^t)\|^2 \le L^2\|w^0 - w^\star\|^2$ (by using $\sum_{t=0}^{T} \Delta_t \le D_0$) and $\|w^t - w^\star\| \le \|w^0 - w^\star\|$ (by using $D_t \le D_0$) for all $t \ge 0$.

(e) **Accelerated gradient method for smooth and convex problems.** Our last illustration follows Nesterov's accelerated gradient scheme:

$$z^t := w^t + \beta_t(w^t - w^{t-1}) \quad \text{and} \quad w^{t+1} := z^t - \frac{1}{L}\nabla F(z^t), \qquad (1.17)$$

where $\beta_t = \frac{\theta_{t-1} - 1}{\theta_t}$ for $\theta_t \ge 1$ such that $\theta_t(\theta_t - 1) \le \theta_{t-1}^2$ with $\theta_0 := 1$. This is an accelerated variant of (1.2) with the momentum $\beta_t(w^t - w^{t-1})$. It is well-known

[44] that, after a few elementary transformations, (1.17) can be written as

$$z^t := (1 - \frac{1}{\theta_t})w^t + \frac{1}{\theta_t}u^t, \quad w^{t+1} := z^t - \frac{1}{L}\nabla F(z^t), \quad \text{and } u^{t+1} = u^t - \frac{\theta_t}{L}\nabla F(z^t).$$

Let $v^t := (1 - \frac{1}{\theta_t})w^t + \frac{1}{\theta_t}w^\star$. Then, $z^t - v^t = \frac{1}{\theta_t}(u^t - w^\star)$. Moreover, by convexity of F, we have $F(z^t) \leq F(v^t) + \langle \nabla F(z^t), z^t - v^t \rangle \leq (1 - \frac{1}{\theta_t})F(w^t) + \frac{1}{\theta_t}F(w^\star) + \frac{1}{\theta_t}\langle \nabla F(z^t), u^t - w^\star \rangle$. Hence, multiplying both sides by θ_t^2, we obtain

$$\theta_t^2[F(z^t) - F(w^\star)] \leq \theta_t(\theta_t - 1)[F(w^t) - F(w^\star)] + \theta_t \langle \nabla F(z^t), u^t - w^\star \rangle.$$

Similar to the proof of (1.14) and (1.16), respectively, we have

$$\begin{cases} \frac{L}{2}\|u^{t+1} - w^\star\|^2 + \theta_t \langle \nabla F(z^t), u^t - w^\star \rangle = \frac{L}{2}\|u^t - w^\star\|^2 + \frac{\theta_t^2}{2L}\|\nabla F(z^t)\|^2, \\ \theta_t^2[F(w^{t+1}) - F(w^\star)] + \frac{\theta_t^2}{2L}\|\nabla F(z^t)\|^2 \leq \theta_t^2[F(z^t) - F(w^\star)]. \end{cases}$$

Summing up the last three inequalities, we obtain

$$\underbrace{\theta_t^2[F(w^{t+1}) - F(w^\star)] + \frac{L}{2}\|u^{t+1} - w^\star\|^2}_{D_{t+1}} + \underbrace{(\theta_{t-1}^2 - \theta_t(\theta_t - 1))[F(w^t) - F(w^\star)]}_{\Delta_t}$$

$$\leq \underbrace{\theta_{t-1}^2[F(w^t) - F(w^\star)] + \frac{L}{2}\|u^t - w^\star\|^2}_{D_t}, \qquad (1.18)$$

which is exactly (1.13) with $E_t = 0$ and $\omega_t = 1$, provided that $\theta_{t-1}^2 - \theta_t(\theta_t - 1) \geq 0$ (note that $\theta_0 = 1$ and $\theta_{-1} = \frac{1}{2}$ satisfy this condition). The recursive estimate (1.18) implies that $D_t \leq D_0$, leading to

$$F(w^t) - F(w^\star) \leq \frac{D_0}{\theta_{t-1}^2} = \frac{L}{2\theta_{t-1}^2}\|w^0 - w^\star\|^2.$$

In particular, if we choose $\theta_{t-1} := \frac{t+1}{2}$, then $\theta_{t-1}^2 = \frac{(t+1)^2}{4} \geq \theta_t(\theta_t - 1) = \frac{t(t+1)}{4}$, then we get the last-iterate convergence guarantee $F(w^t) - F(w^\star) \leq \frac{2L\|w^0 - w^\star\|^2}{(t+1)^2}$.

    We have illustrated how to employ the unified recursive expression (1.13) to analyze four different deterministic gradient-type algorithms. It provides a simple approach with a few lines to derive convergence rate analysis compared to classical techniques in the literature. We believe that this approach can be extended to analyze other methods that have not been listed here.

1.2.9 Convergence rates and complexity analysis

Classical optimization literature often characterizes asymptotic convergence or linear convergence rates of the underlying algorithm, while sublinear rates or oracle complexity are largely elusive, see, e.g., [3,21,22,31,38,53]. Sublinear convergence rates have been widely studied in convex optimization methods, see, e.g., [45], while oracle complexity analysis was formally studied in [43]. Recently, these topics have gained in popularity due to applications to large-scale problems in modern signal and image processing, machine learning, and statistical learning [9,28,67]. Let us discuss these concepts in detail here.

(a) **Convergence rates.** A convergence rate characterizes the progress of the optimality measure (e.g., the objective residual $F(\hat{w}^t) - F^\star$, the squared distance to solution $\|\hat{w}^t - w^\star\|^2$, or the squared norm of gradient $\|\nabla F(\hat{w}^t)\|^2$) with respect to the iteration t, where $\hat{w}^t$ is an approximate solution. For example, in the gradient method for smooth and convex problems, we have $F(w^{t+1}) - F^\star \leq \frac{L\|w^0 - w^\star\|^2}{2(t+1)}$, showing that the objective residual $F(w^t) - F^\star$ decreases with a speed of at least $\frac{1}{t}$, which is written as $F(w^t) - F^\star = \mathcal{O}(1/t)$. We can also write $F(w^{t+1}) - F^\star = \mathcal{O}\left(\frac{R_0^2 L}{t+1}\right)$ for $R_0 := \|w^0 - w^\star\|$ to show the dependence of the rate on L and R_0.

Note that we generally attempt to establish an upper bound rate, but can also show that this upper bound matches the lower bound rate (up to a constant factor) for certain classes of algorithms under a given set of assumptions on (1.1), see, e.g., [45]. For gradient-type methods, the optimal convergence rates under only convexity and L-smoothness is $\mathcal{O}\left(1/t^2\right)$, which is guaranteed by Nesterov's optimal methods. For nonconvex problems, gradient-type methods only achieve an $\mathcal{O}(1/t)$ rate on $\|\nabla F(\hat{w}^t)\|^2$ under the L-smoothness. Linear convergence rates can be achieved with additional assumptions such as strong convexity, error bound, quadratic growth, or PL condition. However, we do not further discuss these variants in this chapter.

(b) **Complexity.** The concept of complexity comes from theoretical computer science, but is widely used in computational mathematics, particularly in optimization. Formal definitions of complexity can be found, e.g., in [43,45]. We distinguish two types of complexity for our gradient-type methods: iteration-complexity (or analytical complexity), and computational complexity (or sometimes called arithmetic complexity, or work complexity) [45]. In gradient-type methods, the overall computational complexity is generally dominated by the oracle complexity, which characterizes the total number of function and/or gradient evaluations required for finding an approximate solution. We notice that we overload the concept *oracle*, which is formally defined, e.g., in [45]. Mathematically, the oracle complexity of T iterations of an algorithm (in our context) is defined as follows:

$$\text{Oracle complexity} := \sum_{t=0}^{T} \text{Per-iteration complexity at iteration } t. \tag{1.19}$$

The **per-iteration complexity** characterizes the workload (e.g., the number of gradient evaluations) at each iteration. At each iteration, we often count the most dominated computational steps such as gradient evaluations, function evaluations, proximal operations, projections, matrix–vector multiplications, or Hessian–vector multiplications. If this per-iteration complexity is fixed, then

$$\text{Oracle complexity} = \text{Number of iterations} \times \text{Per-iteration complexity}.$$

For example, for the standard gradient descent method for smooth and convex problems, the per-iteration complexity is $\mathcal{O}(1)$, i.e., requires one gradient evaluation, leading to oracle complexity $\mathcal{O}\left(\frac{1}{\epsilon}\right)$ in order to obtain w^t such that $F(w^t) - F^\star \le \epsilon$. Indeed, from the convergence bound $F(w^t) - F^\star \le \frac{L\|w^0 - w^\star\|^2}{2t}$, we infer that $F(w^t) - F^\star \le \epsilon$ is implied by $\frac{L\|w^0 - w^\star\|^2}{2t} \le \epsilon$, leading to $t \ge \left\lceil \frac{L\|w^0 - w^\star\|^2}{2\epsilon} \right\rceil$. Hence, we need at most $t_{\max} := \left\lceil \frac{L\|w^0 - w^\star\|^2}{2\epsilon} \right\rceil = \mathcal{O}(1/\epsilon)$ iterations, and therefore $\mathcal{O}(1/\epsilon)$ gradient evaluations.

1.2.10 Initial point, warm-start, and restart

For convex algorithms, which can converge to a global minimizer $w^\star$ starting from any initial point w^0, the choice of w^0 will affect the number of iterations as the term $\|w^0 - w^\star\|^2$ for any solution $w^\star$ appears in the bound of the convergence guarantee, e.g., $F(w^T) - F^\star \le \mathcal{O}\left(\frac{L\|w^0 - w^\star\|^2}{T^\nu}\right)$ for $\nu = 1$ or $\nu = 2$. Clearly, if w^0 is close to $w^\star$, then the number of iterations T is small.

For nonconvex algorithms, initialization plays a crucial role since different initial points w^0 may make the algorithm converge to different approximate stationary points $w^\star$, and their quality is different. Stationary points are candidates for local minimizers, but some may give us maximizers or saddle points. If we do get a local minimizer, then it may still be a bad one, which is far from any global minimizer or which gives us a bad prediction error in machine learning.

A warm-start strategy uses the output of the previous run or the previous iteration to initialize the algorithm at the current stage or iteration. It is based on the idea that the previous run already gives us a good approximation of the desired solution. Initializing from this point may give hope for a quick convergence to the target optimal solution. Warm-start is widely used in sequential iterative (e.g., sequential quadratic programming) or online learning methods.

A restarting strategy is often used in the case where the algorithm makes undesired progress and needs to be restarted. This idea has been used in accelerated gradient methods, where the objective function increases after significant decrease, causing oscillated behaviors [26,50]. Restarting is often combined with a warm-start and an appropriate condition to obtain good performance. Some theoretical analysis of restarting strategies can be found, e.g., in [20,26,50,61].

1.3 Stochastic gradient descent methods

Let us further extend our discussion from deterministic to stochastic methods for solving (1.1) when F is a finite-sum or an expectation function. The stochastic approximation (SA) method was initially proposed by Robbins and Monro in the 1950s [55]. It has become extremely popular in the last decades as it has been widely used in machine learning and data science, see, e.g., [5,6,60].

1.3.1 The algorithmic template

In this section, we only focus on the standard stochastic optimization and discuss two types of methods: classical SGD and variance-reduced SGD. More specifically, we focus on $F(w) := \mathbb{E}[\mathbf{F}(w, \xi)]$ in (1.1), which can be written as

$$\min_{w \in \mathbb{R}^p} \left\{ F(w) := \mathbb{E}[\mathbf{F}(w, \xi)] \right\}, \tag{1.20}$$

where ξ is a random vector defined on a given probability space $(\Omega, \Sigma, \mathbb{P})$.

Many stochastic gradient-based methods for solving (1.20) can be described as in Algorithm 1. Here, Algorithm 1 only presents a pure stochastic gradient scheme with a possible variance-reduction step, but without momentum or accelerated steps. The operator $\mathcal{P}$ presents a projection to handle constraints if required, or to add a compression. However, if it is not specified, then we assume that $\mathcal{P}(z) = z$, the identity operator. Note that Algorithm 1 is a double-loop algorithm, where the inner loop carries out SGD updates, while the outer loop performs stage-wise updates, which can be expressed in an epoch-wise fashion or as a restarting mechanism.

Algorithm 1: Unified stochastic gradient (SGD) method.

1:   **Initialization:** Choose an initial point $\hat{w}^0$ in $\mathbb{R}^p$.
2:   **For $s = 0$ to $S - 1$, perform:**
3:      Evaluate a snapshot estimator $\hat{v}^s$ of $\nabla F(\hat{w}^s)$ and set $w^{s,0} = \hat{w}^s$;
4:      **For $t = 0$ to $T_s - 1$, update:**
5:         Sample a subset of examples $\mathcal{S}_{s,t}$;
6:         Construct an estimator $v^{s,t}$ of $\nabla F(w^{s,t})$ using $\mathcal{S}_{s,t}$ and $\hat{v}^s$;
7:         Update $w^{s,t+1} := \mathcal{P}(w^{s,t} - \eta_{s,t} v^{s,t})$;
8:      **End of Iterations**
9:      Form a new snapshot point $\hat{w}^{s+1}$ from $\{w^{s,0}, \ldots, w^{s,T_s}\}$.
10:   **End of Stages**
11:   **Output:** Return $\hat{w}$ from the available iterates.

If $S = 0$, then Algorithm 1 reduces to a single-loop method. If $S > 1$, then we can also transform Algorithm 1 into a single loop with an "IF" statement and using the iteration counter $k := \sum_{i=0}^{s-1} T_i + t$. If $T_s := T$ is fixed, then $k := (s - 1)T + t$. This transformation allows us to inject Bernoulli's rule for the "IF" statement instead of deterministic rules. Such a modification has been implemented in Loopless-SVRG and Loopless-SARAH schemes, see, e.g., [33,36].

1.3.2 SGD estimators

The main component of Algorithm 1 is the estimator v^t of $\nabla F(w^t)$. Let us review some important estimators widely used in optimization and related fields.

(a) **Classical SGD and mini-batch estimators.** Clearly, if $S = 0$, then we can simply drop the superscript s in Algorithm 1, and write the main update as

$$w^{t+1} := w^t - \eta_t v^t, \tag{1.21}$$

which is in the form (1.2) with $d^t = -v^t$ being a stochastic estimator of $\nabla F(w^t)$.

In the classical SGD, we often generate v^t as an unbiased estimator of $\nabla F(w^t)$ with a bounded variance, i.e.,

$$\mathbb{E}[v^t \mid \mathcal{F}_t] = \nabla F(w^t) \quad \text{and} \quad \mathbb{E}[\|v^t\|^2 \mid \mathcal{F}_t] \le M^2, \tag{1.22}$$

for given $M \ge 0$, where $\mathcal{F}_t$ is the smallest σ-algebra generated by $\{S_0, \dots, S_t\}$ and $\mathbb{E}[\cdot \mid \mathcal{F}_t]$ is the conditional expectation.

(b) **Variance-reduced SGD estimators.** There exists a number of variance-reduced methods, which are based on different estimators of $\nabla F(w)$. We only focus on some of them. For simplicity, we drop the stage superscript "s".

The first is SVRG [29], which generates v^t as

$$v^t := \hat{v}^s + [\nabla \mathbf{F}(w^t, S_t) - \nabla \mathbf{F}(\hat{w}^s, S_t)], \tag{1.23}$$

where $\hat{v}^s$ is the full gradient or a mega-batch unbiased estimator of ∇F at $\hat{w}^s$, $\nabla \mathbf{F}(w^t, S_t) := \frac{1}{b_t} \sum_{\xi_t \in S_t} \nabla \mathbf{F}(w^t, \xi_t)$ and $b_t := |S_t|$. Then, one can show that

$$\mathbb{E}_{S_t}[v^t] = \nabla F(w^t) \quad \text{and} \quad \mathbb{E}_{S_t}[\|v^t - \nabla F(w^t)\|^2] \le \sigma_t^2,$$

where $\sigma_t^2 := L^2 \|w^t - w^\star\|^2$ if F is L-average smooth, and $\sigma_t^2 := 4L[F(w^t) - F(w^\star) + F(\hat{w}^s) - F(w^\star)]$ if F is convex and L-average smooth.

The second estimator is SARAH [48], which is expressed as follows:

$$v^t := v^{t-1} + [\nabla \mathbf{F}(w^t, S_t) - \nabla \mathbf{F}(w^{t-1}, S_t)]. \tag{1.24}$$

It is called a stochastic recursive gradient estimator. Unfortunately, this estimate is biased, i.e., $\mathbb{E}_{S_t}[v^t] \ne \nabla F(w^t)$. However, one can prove that

$$\mathbb{E}_{S_t}[v^t] = \nabla F(w^t) + e_t \quad \text{and} \quad \mathbb{E}_{S_t}[\|v^t - \nabla F(w^t)\|^2] \le \sigma_t^2,$$

where $e_t := v^{t-1} - \nabla F(w^{t-1})$ is an error, and $\sigma_t^2 \le \sigma_{t-1}^2 + \frac{L^2}{b_t} \|w^t - w^{t-1}\|^2$ if $\mathbf{F}$ is L-average smooth, see [52].

Another interesting estimator is the hybrid variance-reduced estimator proposed in [66], which can be written as

$$v^t := (1 - \beta_t)[v^{t-1} + [\nabla\mathbf{F}(w^t, \mathcal{S}_t) - \nabla\mathbf{F}(w^{t-1}, \mathcal{S}_t)]] + \beta_t u^t, \qquad (1.25)$$

where $\beta_t \in [0, 1]$ and u^t is an unbiased estimator of $\nabla F(w^t)$ with variance $\hat{\sigma}_t^2$, i.e., $\mathbb{E}[\|u^t - \nabla F(w^t)\|^2 \mid \mathcal{F}_t] \le \hat{\sigma}_t^2$. Again, as proven in [66], this is a biased estimator of $\nabla F(w^t)$ and, if $\mathbf{F}$ is L-average smooth, then v^t satisfies $\mathbb{E}[\|v^t - \nabla F(w^t)\|^2 \le \sigma_t^2$, where

$$\sigma_t^2 \le (1 - \beta_t)^2 \sigma_{t-1}^2 + \frac{2(1 - \beta_t)^2 L^2}{b_t}\|w^t - w^{t-1}\|^2 + 2\beta_t^2 \hat{\sigma}_t^2.$$

One simple choice of u^t is $u^t := \nabla\mathbf{F}(w^t, \mathcal{S}_t)$. In this case, we have $\hat{\sigma}_t^2 = \frac{\sigma^2}{b_t}$.

1.3.3 Unified convergence analysis

(a) General approach. Let us identify what the crucial steps in convergence analysis of Algorithm 1 are. One of the most important steps is to establish a recursive estimate with respect to inner iterations t of the form (1.13), but under a conditional expectation, i.e.,

$$\mathbb{E}[D_{t+1} \mid \mathcal{F}_t] + \Delta_t \le \omega_t \cdot D_t + E_t, \qquad (1.26)$$

where the related quantities are defined similarly to (1.13). If we take the total expectation on both sides of (1.26), and assume that $\omega_t = \frac{\xi_t}{\xi_{t+1}}$ for $\xi_t > 0$ and $\mathbb{E}[E_t] \le \theta_t^2 M^2$ for some $M \ge 0$ and $\theta_t > 0$, then we have

$$\xi_{t+1}\mathbb{E}[D_{t+1}] + \xi_{t+1}\mathbb{E}[\Delta_t] \le \xi_t \cdot \mathbb{E}[D_t] + \xi_{t+1}\theta_t^2 M^2.$$

By induction, we have

$$\xi_{T+1}\mathbb{E}[D_{T+1}] + \sum_{t=0}^{T}\xi_{t+1}\mathbb{E}[\Delta_t] \le \xi_0\mathbb{E}[D_0] + M^2\sum_{t=0}^{T}\xi_{t+1}\theta_t^2. \qquad (1.27)$$

Let $S_T := \sum_{t=0}^{T}\gamma_t$ with given weights $\gamma_t > 0$ (usually depending on ξ_t and/or θ_t). Dividing both sides of (1.27) by S_T, we obtain

$$\frac{1}{S_T}\sum_{t=0}^{T}\xi_{t+1}\mathbb{E}[\Delta_t] \le \frac{\xi_0\mathbb{E}[D_0]}{S_T} + \frac{M^2}{S_T}\sum_{t=0}^{T}\xi_{t+1}\theta_t^2. \qquad (1.28)$$

Both estimates (1.27) and (1.28) will allow us to estimate convergence rates of the underlying algorithm. Let us apply this approach to prove convergence of some variants of Algorithm 1.

(b) SGD for nonsmooth convex problems. Let us analyze the convergence of the SGD scheme (1.21). Using the update (1.21), we have $\|w^{t+1} - w^\star\|^2 =$

$\|w^t - w^\star\|^2 - 2\eta_t \langle v^t, w^t - w^\star \rangle + \eta_t^2 \|v^t\|^2$. Taking conditional expectation $\mathbb{E}[\cdot \mid \mathcal{F}_t]$ of this estimate and noting that $\mathbb{E}[v^t \mid \mathcal{F}_t] = \nabla F(w^t)$, we have

$$\eta_t \langle \nabla F(w^t), w^t - w^\star \rangle = \frac{1}{2}\|w^t - w^\star\|^2 - \frac{1}{2}\mathbb{E}[\|w^{t+1} - w^\star\|^2 \mid \mathcal{F}_t]$$
$$+ \frac{\eta_t^2}{2}\mathbb{E}[\|v^t\|^2 \mid \mathcal{F}_t].$$

If F is convex, then we have $F(w^t) - F(w^\star) \leq \langle \nabla F(w^t), w^t - w^\star \rangle$. Moreover, we also have $\mathbb{E}[\|v^t\|^2 \mid \mathcal{F}_t] \leq M^2$. Combining these two expressions and the last inequality, we get

$$\underbrace{\frac{1}{2}\mathbb{E}[\|w^{t+1} - w^\star\|^2 \mid \mathcal{F}_t]}_{\mathbb{E}[D_{t+1}\mid\mathcal{F}_t]} + \underbrace{\eta_t[F(w^t) - F(w^\star)]}_{\Delta_t} \leq \underbrace{\frac{1}{2}\|w^t - w^\star\|^2}_{D_t} + \underbrace{\frac{\eta_t^2}{2}M^2}_{E_t}.$$

This is exactly the recursive estimate (1.26). Using (1.28), we can show that

$$\mathbb{E}[F(\hat{w}) - F(w^\star)] \leq \frac{1}{S_T}\sum_{t=0}^{T}\eta_t\mathbb{E}[F(w^t) - F(w^\star)]$$

$$\leq \frac{1}{2S_T}\|w^0 - w^\star\|^2 + \frac{M^2}{2S_T}\sum_{t=0}^{T}\eta_t^2, \tag{1.29}$$

where $S_T := \sum_{t=0}^{T}\eta_t$ and $\hat{w} := \frac{1}{S_T}\sum_{t=0}^{T}\eta_t w^t$. If we choose $\eta_t := \frac{C}{\sqrt{T+1}}$ for some $C > 0$, then $S_T = C\sqrt{T+1}$ and $\sum_{t=0}^{T}\eta_t^2 = C^2$. In this case, (1.29) becomes

$$\mathbb{E}[F(\hat{w}) - F(w^\star)] \leq \frac{\|w^0 - w^\star\|^2}{2C\sqrt{T+1}} + \frac{M^2 C}{2\sqrt{T+1}}.$$

If we choose $\eta_t := \frac{C}{\sqrt{t+1}}$ for some $C > 0$, then

$$S_T := C\sum_{t=0}^{T}\frac{1}{\sqrt{t+1}} \geq 2C\int_{1}^{T+1}\frac{1}{2\sqrt{t}}dt = 2C(\sqrt{T+1} - 1)$$

and $\sum_{t=0}^{T}\eta_t^2 = C^2\sum_{t=0}^{T}\frac{1}{t+1} \leq C^2(1 + \ln(T+1))$. In this case, (1.29) becomes

$$\mathbb{E}[F(\hat{w}) - F(w^\star)] \leq \frac{\|w^0 - w^\star\|^2}{4C(\sqrt{T+1} - 1)} + \frac{M^2 C(1 + \ln(T+1))}{4(\sqrt{T+1} - 1)}.$$

    (c) SGD for smooth and nonconvex problems. We consider the case F is L-smooth. In addition, we assume that our stochastic estimator v^t is unbiased, i.e., $\mathbb{E}[v^t \mid \mathcal{F}_t] = \nabla F(w^t)$ and has bounded variance as $\mathbb{E}[\|v^t - \nabla F(w^t)\|^2 \mid \mathcal{F}_t] \leq \sigma^2$.

In this case, we have $\mathbb{E}[\|v^t\|^2 \mid \mathcal{F}_t] \leq \|\nabla F(w^t)\|^2 + \sigma^2$. Using this inequality, $\mathbb{E}[v^t \mid \mathcal{F}_t] = \nabla F(w^t)$, and the L-smoothness of F, we can derive

$$\mathbb{E}[F(w^{t+1}) \mid \mathcal{F}_t] \leq F(w^t) - \eta_t \mathbb{E}[\langle \nabla F(w^t), v^t \rangle \mid \mathcal{F}_t] + \frac{L\eta_t^2}{2}\mathbb{E}[\|v^t\|^2 \mid \mathcal{F}_t]$$

$$\leq F(w^t) - \eta_t \|\nabla F(w^t)\|^2 + \frac{L\eta_t^2}{2}\|\nabla F(w^t)\|^2 + \frac{L\eta_t^2\sigma^2}{2}$$

$$= F(w^t) - \eta_t\left(1 - \frac{L\eta_t}{2}\right)\|\nabla F(w^t)\|^2 + \frac{L\eta_t^2\sigma^2}{2}.$$

This inequality leads to

$$\underbrace{\mathbb{E}[F(w^{t+1}) - F^\star \mid \mathcal{F}_t]}_{D_{t+1}} + \underbrace{\eta_t\left(1 - \frac{L\eta_t}{2}\right)\|\nabla F(w^t)\|^2}_{\Delta_t} \leq \underbrace{F(w^t) - F^\star}_{D_t} + \underbrace{\frac{L\eta_t^2\sigma^2}{2}}_{E_t},$$

which is exactly (1.26) with $\omega_t = 1$, provided that $0 < \eta_t < \frac{2}{L}$. By using this estimate, we can derive a convergence rate for $\frac{1}{S_T}\sum_{t=0}^T \gamma_t \mathbb{E}[\|\nabla F(w^t)\|^2]$ with $\gamma_t := \eta_t\left(1 - \frac{L\eta_t}{2}\right)$ and $S_T := \sum_{t=0}^T \gamma_t$ as done in [25]. We omit the details here.

(d) Hybrid variance-reduced SGD for smooth and nonconvex problems. We analyze one variance-reduced variant of Algorithm 1 where the inner loop updates are $w^{t+1} := w^t - \eta_t v^t$, with v^t being given by (1.25) for $b_t = 1$, see [66]. In addition, we do not need the outer loop, leading to a **single-loop** algorithm.

Let us analyze its convergence rate. First, by the L-smoothness of F and the relation $-2\langle a, b \rangle = \|a - b\|^2 - \|a\|^2 - \|b\|^2$, we can derive

$$\mathbb{E}[F(w^{t+1}) \mid \mathcal{F}_t] \leq F(w^t) - \eta_t \mathbb{E}[\langle \nabla F(w^t), v^t \rangle \mid \mathcal{F}_t] + \frac{L\eta_t^2}{2}\mathbb{E}[\|v^t\|^2 \mid \mathcal{F}_t]$$

$$= F(w^t) - \frac{\eta_t}{2}\|\nabla F(w^t)\|^2 + \frac{\eta_t}{2}\mathbb{E}[\|v^t - \nabla F(w^t)\|^2 \mid \mathcal{F}_t]$$

$$- \frac{\eta_t}{2}(1 - L\eta_t)\mathbb{E}[\|v^t\|^2 \mid \mathcal{F}_t].$$

Since $\mathbb{E}[\|v^t - \nabla F(w^t)\|^2 \mid \mathcal{F}_t] \leq \sigma_t^2$ and $0 < \eta_t \leq \frac{1}{L}$, this inequality reduces to

$$\mathbb{E}[F(w^{t+1}) - F^\star + \frac{\eta_t(1 - L\eta_t)}{2}\|v^t\|^2 \mid \mathcal{F}_t] \leq F(w^t) - F^\star - \frac{\eta_t}{2}\|\nabla F(w^t)\|^2 + \frac{\eta_t\sigma_t^2}{2}.$$

Since $\sigma_t^2 \leq (1 - \beta_t)^2\sigma_{t-1}^2 + 2(1 - \beta_t)^2L^2\|w^t - w^{t-1}\|^2 + 2\beta_t^2\hat{\sigma}^2$ and $w^t - w^{t-1} = -\eta_{t-1}v^{t-1}$, we have

$$\sigma_t^2 \leq (1 - \beta_t)^2\sigma_{t-1}^2 + 2L^2(1 - \beta_t)^2\eta_{t-1}^2\|v^{t-1}\|^2 + 2\beta_t^2\hat{\sigma}^2.$$

Multiplying this inequality by $\frac{c_t}{2} > 0$ and adding to the last estimate, we obtain

$$\mathbb{E}[F(w^{t+1}) - F^\star + \frac{\eta_t(1 - L\eta_t)}{2}\|v^t\|^2 \mid \mathcal{F}_t] + \frac{(c_t - \eta_t)}{2}\sigma_t^2 + \frac{\eta_t}{2}\|\nabla F(w^t)\|^2$$

$$\leq F(w^t) - F^\star + L^2 c_t(1 - \beta_t)^2 \eta_{t-1}^2 \|v^{t-1}\|^2 + \frac{c_t(1 - \beta_t)^2}{2}\sigma_{t-1}^2 + c_t \beta_t^2 \hat{\sigma}^2.$$

For simplicity, we choose all parameters to be constant. Let us define $D_t := F(w^t) - F^\star + \frac{\eta(1-L\eta)}{2}\|v^{t-1}\|^2 + \frac{(c-\eta)}{2}\sigma_{t-1}^2$, and impose the following conditions:

$$2L^2\eta^2 c(1 - \beta)^2 \leq \eta(1 - L\eta) \quad \text{and} \quad c(1 - \beta)^2 \leq c - \eta. \tag{1.30}$$

Then, the last estimate leads to

$$\mathbb{E}[D_{t+1} \mid \mathcal{F}_t] + \underbrace{\frac{\eta}{2}\|\nabla F(w^t)\|^2 \leq D_t}_{\Delta_t} + \underbrace{c\beta^2\hat{\sigma}^2}_{E_t},$$

which is exactly (1.26) with $\omega_t = 1$.

Assume that we choose $\eta \in (0, \frac{1}{L})$ and $c > 0$ such that $2L^2\eta^2(c - \eta) = \eta(1 - L\eta)$, leading to $c := \frac{1-L\eta}{2L^2\eta} + \eta = \frac{1-L\eta+2L^2\eta^2}{2L^2\eta}$. Moreover, $(1 - \beta)^2 \leq 1 - \frac{2L^2\eta^2}{1-L\eta+2L^2\eta^2}$. Then, both conditions of (1.30) hold with equality. In this case, we obtain $\mathbb{E}[D_{t+1} \mid \mathcal{F}_t] + \frac{\eta}{2}\|\nabla F(w^t)\|^2 \leq D_t + \frac{(1-L\eta+2L^2\eta^2)\beta^2}{2L^2\eta}\hat{\sigma}^2$. This inequality implies

$$\frac{1}{T+1}\sum_{t=0}^{T}\mathbb{E}[\|\nabla F(w^t)\|^2] \leq \frac{2}{\eta(T+1)}D_0 + \frac{(1 - L\eta + 2L^2\eta^2)\beta^2}{L^2\eta^2}\hat{\sigma}^2$$

$$\leq \frac{2[F(w^0) - F^\star]}{\eta(T+1)} + \frac{\|v^0\|^2}{(T+1)} + \frac{\sigma_{-1}^2}{2L^2\eta^2(T+1)} + \frac{\beta^2\hat{\sigma}^2}{L^2\eta^2}.$$

Finally, we choose $\eta := \frac{1}{L(T+1)^{1/3}} \leq \frac{1}{L}$, $\sigma_{-1} := \frac{1}{(T+1)^{1/3}}$, and $\beta := \mathcal{O}\left(\frac{1}{(T+1)^{2/3}}\right)$ such that $(1 - \beta)^2 \leq 1 - \frac{2L^2\eta^2}{1-L\eta+2L^2\eta^2}$ (such a β always exists). Moreover, the last estimate shows that

$$\frac{1}{T+1}\sum_{t=0}^{T}\mathbb{E}[\|\nabla F(w^t)\|^2] = \mathcal{O}\left(\frac{1}{(T+1)^{2/3}}\right),$$

as proven in [66].

We have illustrated our approach by using the recursive estimate (1.26) to analyze the convergence of three SGD schemes, including variance-reduced methods. We believe that this approach can be used to analyze other variants including SVRG and SARAH.

1.4 Concluding remarks

We have reviewed several main components that constitute the gradient descent method and its variants, including deterministic and stochastic ones, ranging from convex to nonconvex problems. We have provided a simple and unified convergence analysis framework relying on an elementary recursive estimate under the most basic structure assumptions commonly used in the literature. While this approach can be applied to analyze several methods, we have only illustrated it on a few well-known schemes. Note that we have not proposed any new algorithms, but rather unified the convergence analysis using a simple recursive estimate. However, we believe that such an approach can be extended beyond what we have done in this chapter. The following research topics are interesting to us. First, can one still apply our analysis to accelerated variance-reduced stochastic gradient-type methods? Perhaps, this can possibly be done by using the idea from a recent work [15]. Second, how can we extend our framework to study other optimization methods in distributed systems and federated learning? We emphasize that many algorithms in these fields can be viewed as a randomized [block-]coordinate methods. Therefore, extensions to coordinate and shuffling methods are promising and remain open. Third, is it possible to extend and adapt our analysis to asynchronous gradient-based algorithms? We believe that such an extension is possible as long as the delay is bounded. However, one needs to modify the recursive expression to capture with the delayed updates, leading to an extra error term in the recursive inequality. Finally, our approach can be used to analyze convergence of algorithms for minimax and variational inequality problems, which have recently gained tremendous popularity [19,65].

Acknowledgments

The work of Q. Tran-Dinh is partly supported by the Office of Naval Research [grant number ONR-N00014-20-1-2088] (2020–2023) and [grant number ONR-N00014-23-1-2588 (2023-2026)], and the National Science Foundation (NSF) [grant number NSF DMS-2134107] (2022-2027).

References

[1] H.H. Bauschke, P. Combettes, Convex Analysis and Monotone Operators Theory in Hilbert Spaces, 2nd edition, Springer, 2017.

[2] A. Ben-Tal, A. Nemirovski, Lectures on Modern Convex Optimization: Analysis, Algorithms, and Engineering Applications, vol. 3, SIAM, 2001.

[3] D.P. Bertsekas, Nonlinear Programming, 2nd edition, Athena Scientific, 1999.

[4] J. Bolte, A. Daniilidis, A. Lewis, The Łojasiewicz inequality for nonsmooth subanalytic functions with applications to subgradient dynamical systems, SIAM J. Optim. 17 (4) (2007) 1205–1223.

[5] L. Bottou, F.E. Curtis, J. Nocedal, Optimization methods for large-scale machine learning, SIAM Rev. 60 (2) (2018) 223–311.

[6] Léon Bottou, Online learning and stochastic approximations, in: David Saad (Ed.), Online Learning in Neural Networks, Cambridge University Press, New York, NY, USA, 1998, pp. 9–42.

[7] S. Boyd, L. Vandenberghe, Convex Optimization, University Press, Cambridge, 2004.

[8] S. Boyd, L. Xiao, A. Mutapcic, Subgradient methods, Tech. Report. EE392o, Stanford University, 2003.

[9] Sébastien Bubeck, Theory of convex optimization for machine learning, in: Lecture Notes, Princeton University, 2014.

[10] P. Combettes, J.-C. Pesquet, Signal recovery by proximal forward-backward splitting, in: Fixed-Point Algorithms for Inverse Problems in Science and Engineering, Springer, 2011, pp. 185–212.

[11] A.R. Conn, N. Gould, P.L. Toint, Trust-Region Methods, MPS/SIAM Series on Optimization, SIAM, Philadelphia, USA, 2000.

[12] A. Cutkosky, F. Orabona, Momentum-based variance reduction in non-convex SGD, in: Advances in Neural Information Processing Systems, 2019, pp. 15210–15219.

[13] A. Defazio, F. Bach, S. Lacoste-Julien, SAGA: A fast incremental gradient method with support for non-strongly convex composite objectives, in: Advances in Neural Information Processing Systems (NIPS), 2014, pp. 1646–1654.

[14] M. Van Dijk, L.M. Nguyen, P.H. Nguyen, D.T. Phan, Characterization of convex objective functions and optimal expected convergence rates for SGD, 2019, pp. 6392–6400.

[15] D. Driggs, M.J. Ehrhardt, C.-B. Schönlieb, Accelerating variance-reduced stochastic gradient methods, Math. Program. (2022) 1–45.

[16] D. Drusvyatskiy, A. Lewis, Error bounds, quadratic growth, and linear convergence of proximal methods, Math. Oper. Res. 43 (3) (2018) 919–948.

[17] J. Duchi, E. Hazan, Y. Singer, Adaptive subgradient methods for online learning and stochastic optimization, J. Mach. Learn. Res. 12 (2011) 2121–2159.

[18] I. Ekeland, T. Turnbull, Infinite-Dimensional Optimization and Convexity, The University of Chicago Press, 1983.

[19] F. Facchinei, J.-S. Pang, Finite-Dimensional Variational Inequalities and Complementarity Problems, vols. 1–2, Springer, 2003.

[20] O. Fercoq, Z. Qu, Restarting accelerated gradient methods with a rough strong convexity estimate, Preprint, arXiv:1609.07358, 2016, pp. 1–23.

[21] A.V. Fiacco, G.P. McCormick, Nonlinear Programming: Sequential Unconstrained Minimization Techniques, Society for Industrial Mathematics, 1987.

[22] R. Fletcher, Practical Methods of Optimization, 2nd edition, Wiley, Chichester, 1987.

[23] R. Fletcher, S. Leyffer, Nonlinear programming without a penalty function, Math. Program. 91 (2002) 239–269.

[24] R. Ge, F. Huang, C. Jin, Y. Yuan, Escaping from saddle points – online stochastic gradient for tensor decomposition, in: Conference on Learning Theory, 2015, pp. 797–842.

[25] S. Ghadimi, G. Lan, Stochastic first- and zeroth-order methods for nonconvex stochastic programming, SIAM J. Optim. 23 (4) (2013) 2341–2368.

[26] P. Giselsson, S. Boyd, Monotonicity and restart in fast gradient methods, in: IEEE Conference on Decision and Control, Los Angeles, USA, December 2014, pp. 5058–5063.

[27] I. Goodfellow, Y. Bengio, A. Courville, Deep Learning, vol. 1, MIT Press, Cambridge, 2016.

[28] Trevor Hastie, Robert Tibshirani, Jerome Friedman, The Elements of Statistical Learning: Data Mining, Inference, and Prediction, 2nd edition, Springer Series in Statistics, 2009.

[29] R. Johnson, T. Zhang, Accelerating stochastic gradient descent using predictive variance reduction, in: Advances in Neural Information Processing Systems (NIPS), 2013, pp. 315–323.

[30] H. Karimi, J. Nutini, M. Schmidt, Linear convergence of gradient and proximal-gradient methods under the Polyak–Łojasiewicz condition, in: P. Frasconi, N. Landwehr, G. Manco, J. Vreeken (Eds.), Machine Learning and Knowledge Discovery in Databases, Springer, Cham, 2016, pp. 795–811.

[31] C.T. Kelley, Iterative Methods for Optimization, vol. 18, SIAM, Philadelphia, USA, 1999.

[32] D.P. Kingma, J. Ba ADAM, A method for stochastic optimization, in: Proceedings of the 3rd International Conference on Learning Representations (ICLR), 2014, abs/1412.6980.

[33] D. Kovalev, S. Horvath, P. Richtarik, Don't jump through hoops and remove those loops: SVRG and Katyusha are better without the outer loop, in: Algorithmic Learning Theory, PMLR, 2020, pp. 451–467.

[34] G. Lan, First-Order and Stochastic Optimization Methods for Machine Learning, Springer, 2020.

[35] S. Lee, D. Kim, Fast extra gradient methods for smooth structured nonconvex–nonconcave minimax problems, in: Thirty-Fifth Conference on Neural Information Processing Systems (NeurIPs2021), 2021.

[36] B. Li, M. Ma, G.B. Giannakis, On the convergence of SARAH and beyond, Tech. Report., ArXiv preprint, arXiv:1906.02351, 2019.

[37] I. Loshchilov, F. Hutter, SGDR: Stochastic gradient descent with warm restarts, in: International Conference on Learning Representations, 2016.

[38] D.G. Luenberger, Y. Ye, Linear and Nonlinear Programming, Springer, 2007.

[39] Z.-Q. Luo, P. Tseng, Error bounds and convergence analysis of feasible descent methods: a general approach, Ann. Oper. Res. 46 (1) (1993) 157–178.

[40] B.S. Mordukhovich, Variational Analysis and Generalized Differentiation: Volumes I and II, vol. 330, Springer, 2006.

[41] E. Moulay, V. Léchappé, F. Plestan, Properties of the sign gradient descent algorithms, Inf. Sci. 492 (2019) 29–39.

[42] I. Necoara, Y. Nesterov, F. Glineur, Linear convergence of first order methods for non-strongly convex optimization, Math. Program. (2016) 1–39.

[43] A. Nemirovskii, D. Yudin, Problem Complexity and Method Efficiency in Optimization, Wiley, 1983.

[44] Y. Nesterov, A method for unconstrained convex minimization problem with the rate of convergence $\mathcal{O}(1/k^2)$, Dokl. Akad. Nauk SSSR 269 (1983) 543–547, Translated as Soviet Math. Dokl.

[45] Y. Nesterov, Introductory Lectures on Convex Optimization: A Basic Course, Applied Optimization, vol. 87, Kluwer Academic Publishers, 2004.

[46] Y. Nesterov, Smooth minimization of non-smooth functions, Math. Program. 103 (1) (2005) 127–152.

[47] Y. Nesterov, Universal gradient methods for convex optimization problems, Math. Program. 152 (1-2) (2015) 381–404.

[48] L.M. Nguyen, J. Liu, K. Scheinberg, M. Takáč, SARAH: a novel method for machine learning problems using stochastic recursive gradient, in: Proceedings of the 34th International Conference on Machine Learning, 2017, pp. 2613–2621.

[49] J. Nocedal, S.J. Wright, Numerical Optimization, 2 edition, Springer Series in Operations Research and Financial Engineering, Springer, 2006.

[50] B. O'Donoghue, E. Candes, Adaptive restart for accelerated gradient schemes, Found. Comput. Math. 15 (2015) 715–732.

[51] N. Parikh, S. Boyd, Proximal algorithms, Found. Trends Optim. 1 (3) (2013) 123–231.

[52] H.N. Pham, M.L. Nguyen, T.D. Phan, Q. Tran-Dinh, ProxSARAH: an efficient algorithmic framework for stochastic composite nonconvex optimization, J. Mach. Learn. Res. 21 (2020) 1–48.

[53] E. Polak, Computational Methods in Optimization: A Unified Approach, Academic Press, New York, 1971.

[54] Boris T. Polyak, Some methods of speeding up the convergence of iteration methods, USSR Comput. Math. Math. Phys. 4 (5) (1964) 1–17.

[55] H. Robbins, S. Monro, A stochastic approximation method, Ann. Math. Stat. 22 (3) (1951) 400–407.

[56] R. Rockafellar, R. Wets, Variational Analysis, vol. 317, Springer, 2004.

[57] R.T. Rockafellar, Convex Analysis, Princeton Mathematics Series, vol. 28, Princeton University Press, 1970.

[58] M. Schmidt, N. Le Roux, F. Bach, Minimizing finite sums with the stochastic average gradient, Math. Program. 162 (1–2) (2017) 83–112.

[59] A. Shapiro, D. Dentcheva, A. Ruszczynski, Lectures on Stochastic Programming: Modelling and Theory, SIAM, 2009.

[60] Suvrit Sra, Optimization for Machine Learning (MIT Course 6.881).

[61] W. Su, S. Boyd, E. Candes, A differential equation for modeling Nesterov's accelerated gradient method: theory and insights, in: Advances in Neural Information Processing Systems (NIPS), 2014, pp. 2510–2518.

[62] T.H. Tran, L.M. Nguyen, Q. Tran-Dinh, SMG: A shuffling gradient-based method with momentum, in: International Conference on Machine Learning, PMLR, 2021, pp. 10379–10389.

[63] Q. Tran-Dinh, From Halpern's fixed-point iterations to Nesterov's accelerated interpretations for root-finding problems, Comput. Optim. Appl. (2023) 1–38, https://doi.org/10.1007/s10589-023-00518-8.

[64] Q. Tran-Dinh, A. Kyrillidis, V. Cevher, Composite self-concordant minimization, J. Mach. Learn. Res. 15 (2015) 374–416.

[65] Q. Tran-Dinh, D. Liu, L.M. Nguyen, Hybrid variance-reduced SGD algorithms for nonconvex–concave minimax problems, in: The 34th Conference on Neural Information Processing Systems (NeurIPs 2020), 2020.

[66] Q. Tran-Dinh, N.H. Pham, D.T. Phan, L.M. Nguyen, A hybrid stochastic optimization framework for stochastic composite nonconvex optimization, Math. Program. 191 (2022) 1005–1071.

[67] S.J. Wright, R.D. Nowak, M.A.T. Figueiredo, Sparse reconstruction by separable approximation, IEEE Trans. Signal Process. 57 (7) (2009) 2479–2493.

[68] C. Zálinescu, On uniformly convex functions, J. Math. Anal. Appl. 95 (2) (1983) 344–374.

Considerations on the theory of training models with differential privacy

Marten van Dijk[a,b] **and Phuong Ha Nguyen**[c]

[a]*CWI, Amsterdam, Netherlands*
[b]*VU University Amsterdam, Amsterdam, Netherlands*
[c]*eBay Inc., San Jose, CA, United States*

2.1 Introduction

Privacy leakage is a big problem in the big-data era. Solving a learning task based on big data intrinsically means that only through a collaborative effort sufficient data is available for training a global model with sufficient clean accuracy (utility). Federated learning is a framework where a learning task is solved by a loose federation of participating devices/clients which are coordinated by a central server [3,7,8,10,27,28,31,33–35,37,38,40,55,57]. Clients, who use own local data to participate in a learning task by training a global model, want to have privacy guarantees for their local proprietary data. For this reason, DP-SGD [1] was introduced as it adapts distributed Stochastic Gradient Descent (SGD) [54] with Differential Privacy (DP) [13–15,17].

The optimization problem for training many Machine Learning (ML) models using a training set $\{\xi_i\}_{i=1}^m$ of m samples can be formulated as a finite-sum minimization problem as follows:

$$\min_{w \in \mathbb{R}^d} \left\{ F(w) = \frac{1}{m} \sum_{i=1}^m f(w; \xi_i) \right\}. \qquad (2.1)$$

The objective is to minimize a loss function with respect to model parameters w. This problem is known as empirical risk minimization and it covers a wide range of convex and non-convex problems from the ML domain, including, but not limited to, logistic regression, multi-kernel learning, conditional random fields and neural networks.

We want to solve (2.1) in a distributed setting where many clients have their own local data sets and the finite-sum minimization problem is over the collection of all local data sets. A widely accepted approach is to repeatedly use the SGD [44,45,48] recursion

$$w_{t+1} = w_t - \eta_t \nabla f(w_t; \xi), \qquad (2.2)$$

Federated Learning. https://doi.org/10.1016/B978-0-44-319037-7.00009-0

where w_t represents the model after the tth iteration; w_t is used in computing the gradient of $f(w_t; \xi)$, where ξ is a data sample randomly selected from the data set $\{\xi_i\}_{i=1}^m$ which comprises the union of all local data sets.

This approach allows each client to perform local SGD recursions for the data samples ξ that belong to the client's local training data set. The updates as a result of the SGD recursion (2.2) are sent to a centralized server who aggregates all received updates and maintains a global model. The server regularly broadcasts its most recent global model so that clients can use it in their local SGD computations. This allows each client to use what has been learned from the local data sets at the other clients. This leads to good accuracy of the final global model.

Each client performs SGD recursions for a batch of local data. These recursions together represent a local round and at the end of the local round a local model update (in the form of an aggregate of computed gradients during the round) is transmitted to the server. The server in turn adds the received local update to its global model – and once the server receives new updates from (a significant portion of) all clients, the global model is broadcast to each of the clients. When considering privacy, we are concerned about how much information these local updates reveal about the used local data sets. Each client wants to keep its local data set as private as possible with respect to the outside world which observes round communication (the outside world includes all other clients as well).

Rather than reducing the amount of round communication such that less sensitive information is leaked, differential privacy [13–15,17] offers a solution in which each client-to-server communication is obfuscated by noise. If the magnitude of the added noise is not too much, then a good accuracy of the global model can still be achieved albeit at the price of more overall SGD iterations needed for convergence. On the other hand, only if the magnitude of the added noise is large enough, then good differential privacy guarantees can be given. This leads to a friction between desired differential privacy and desired utility/accuracy.

Section 2.2 starts discussing DP-SGD [1], which implements differentially private mini-batch SGD. Section 2.3 explains differential privacy with various (divergence based) measures and properties. Section 2.4 continues detailing the state-of-the-art hypothesis testing based differential privacy, called f-DP [11], applied to DP-SGD. We conclude with open questions in Section 2.5.

2.2 Differential private SGD (DP-SGD)

We analyze the Gaussian-based differential privacy method, called DP-SGD, of [1] in a distributed setting with many clients and a central aggregating server. A slightly generalized description of DP-SGD is depicted in Algorithm 1. The main goal of DP-SGD is to hide whether the collection of transmitted round updates $\bar{U}$ corresponds to a data set d versus a neighboring data set d'; sets d and d' are called neighbors if they differ in exactly one element. In order to accomplish this, DP-SGD introduces noise, which, as we will see, comes in two flavors, *clipping noise* and *Gaussian noise*.

Algorithm 1 Differential private SGD.

1: **procedure** DP-SGD
2:     N = size training data set $d = \{\xi_i\}_{i=1}^{N}$
3:     E = total number of epochs
4:     diminishing step size sequence $\{\eta_i\}$
5:
6:     initialize w as the default initial model
7:     **Interrupt Service Routine (ISR)**: Whenever a new global model $\hat{w}$ is received, computation is interrupted and an ISR is called that replaces $w \leftarrow \hat{w}$ after which computation is resumed
8:
9:     **for** $e \in \{1, \ldots, E\}$ **do**
10:         $\{S_b\}_{b=1}^{N/m} \leftarrow \texttt{Sample}_m$ with $S_b \subseteq \{1, \ldots, N\}, |S_b| = m$
11:         **for** $b \in \{1, \ldots, \frac{N}{m}\}$ **do**
12:             Start of round $(e-1)\frac{N}{m} + b$:
13:             **for** $h \in S_b$ **do**
14:                 $a_h = \nabla_w f(w; \xi_h)$
15:             **end for**
16:             $U = \sum_{h=1}^{m} [a_h]_C$
17:             $\bar{U} \leftarrow U + \mathcal{N}(0, (2C\sigma)^2 \mathbf{I})$
18:             Transmit $\bar{U}/m$ to central server
19:             Locally update $w \leftarrow w - \eta_{(e-1)\frac{N}{m}+b} \cdot \bar{U}/m$
20:         **end for**
21:     **end for**
22: **end procedure**

2.2.1 Clipping

Rather than using the gradient $a_h = \nabla f(w, \xi_h)$ itself, DP-SGD uses its clipped version $[\nabla f(w, \xi_h)]_C$ where

$$[x]_C = x / \max\{1, \|x\|/C\}.$$

We call this the *individual clipping* approach since each computed gradient is individually clipped. Clipping is needed because in general we cannot assume a bound C on the gradients (for example, the bounded gradient assumption is in conflict with strong convexity [44]), yet the added gradients in update U need to be bounded by some constant C in order for the DP analysis of [1] to go through. The reason is that clipping introduces a bound on how much $U = \sum_{h=1}^{m} [a_h]_C$ gets affected if the differentiating sample between d and d' is used in its computation. Clipping forces a small distance between an update U that does not use the differentiating sample and an update U' that computes the same gradients as U except for one of its gradient computations which uses the differentiating sample. This means that if Gaussian noise is added to U and U', respectively, then the smaller the distance between U and U', the harder it is to figure out whether the actually observed noised update originates from d or d'. This leads to a differential privacy guarantee.

Suppose that a_h influences another gradient computation, e.g., a_{h+1}. Then, if the differentiating sample is used in the computation of a_h, this affects not only a_h but also a_{h+1}. Even though both a_h and a_{h+1} will be clipped, this increases the distance between U and U', hence, this weakens the differential privacy. For this reason, the different gradient computations a_h in U should be independent of one another. In particular, we do not want to implement classical SGD where the computation of a_h updates the local model w which is used in the next gradient computation a_{h+1}. This is the reason for implementing mini-batch SGD where each gradient a_h is computed for the same w.

Clipping introduces clipping noise defined as the difference between the clipped gradient $[a_h]_C$ and the original gradient a_h. This affects the rate of convergence and leads to clipping bias. If convergence is towards a (local) minimum w^* of (2.1), then DP-SGD will not get closer and closer to w^*, but will converge to some model within a radius around w^*, where the radius is composed of a clipping bias and a bias as a result of the desired DP guarantee by adding Gaussian noise, and the radius is also at least proportional to the last used step size. We notice that clipping noise may not reduce from round to round: Even though $E_\xi[\nabla_w f(w^*; \xi)]$ tends to zero (since we converge to a local minimum), the expected norm of the gradients $c(w^*) = E_\xi[\|\nabla_w f(w^*; \xi)\|]$ generally does not converge to zero. For this reason, the clipping constant C must be appropriately set (and cannot be too small). For example, by using the C of another previous related learning task, or using a public data set for estimating $c(w^*)$ while executing DP-SGD.

2.2.2 Mini-batch SGD

DP-SGD is constrained to a mini-batch SGD approach where, before the start of the bth local round in epoch e, a random min-batch S_b of sample size $|S_b| = m$ is selected out of a local data set d of size $|d| = N$. In the description of Algorithm 1, the sampling is done by a sampling procedure $\texttt{Sample}_m$ before the start of epoch e for all rounds together. DP-SGD implements *subsampling* which chooses a uniformly random subset $S_b \subseteq d$ of size m.

The inner loop computes m gradients $a_h = \nabla_w f(w; \xi_h)$. Since there are N/m rounds within an epoch, each epoch has (indeed) a total gradient complexity of $N = |d|$. We notice that each gradient is computed based on w which is the last received global model from the server through the interrupt service routine. In the original DP-SGD, a client waits at the start of a round till it receives the global model which includes the aggregated updates of all previous rounds from all clients. The formulation in Algorithm 1 allows for asynchronous behavior, including dropped (or reordering of) messages from the server which can lead to a client missing out on receiving global model versions. More importantly, the server may decide to broadcast global models at a lower rate than the rate(s) at which clients compute and communicate their noised round updates. This allows clients with different compute speeds/resources. Also, the rate at which round updates are computed is not restricted by the throughput of broadcast messages from the server to clients (of course, it remains restricted by the network throughput from the clients through aggregation nodes to the server). This implies that parameter m can potentially be chosen from the whole range $\{1, \ldots, N\}$ including very small m, leading to many round updates per epoch, or large m, leading to only a couple round updates per epoch. We will later discuss the effect of m on convergence and accuracy and DP guarantee.

We notice that too much asynchronous behavior will hurt convergence of the mini-batch SGD approach and may lead to worse accuracy of the final global model. For this reason, before starting a round, a client can check to what extent the recently received global model deviates from the locally kept model. If this gets too far apart or if the last received global model happened too many rounds ago, then the client will want to wait till a new global model is received and the interrupt service routine is triggered. This implements the necessary synchronous behavior with respect to convergence and accuracy.

2.2.3 Gaussian noise

The clipped gradients $[a_h]_C$ are summed together in round update U. At the end of each local round, the round update U is obfuscated by adding Gaussian noise

$$\mathcal{N}(0, (2C\sigma)^2)$$

to each of U's vector entries. The resulting noised round update $\bar{U}$ divided by the mini-batch size m is transmitted to the server.

For neighboring data sets d and d', we have that the *sensitivity* measured as the Euclidean distance between U based on d and U' based on d' (see also Section 2.2.1) is at most $2C$. An adversary trying to distinguish whether the observed update is from d or d' needs to figure out whether the observation is from

$$U + \mathcal{N}(0, (2C\sigma)^2 \mathbf{I}) \quad \text{or} \quad U' + \mathcal{N}(0, (2C\sigma)^2 \mathbf{I}).$$

Since $\|U - U'\| \leq 2C$, this is at best (for the adversary) equivalent to hypothesis testing of $\mathcal{N}(0, (2C\sigma)^2)$ vs. $\mathcal{N}(2C, (2C\sigma)^2)$. After dividing by $2C$, this is equivalent to hypothesis testing of

$$\mathcal{N}(0, \sigma^2) \quad \text{vs.} \quad \mathcal{N}(1, \sigma^2). \tag{2.3}$$

We see that any differential privacy guarantee for the round update is characterized by σ.

The argument above does not depend on the properties of function f. In fact, we are free in how we compute the a_h in line 14 of Algorithm 1. These may themselves depend on more than one sample as long as we start with w for each computation of a_h. For example, the a_h may compute updates coming from a local SGD approach (as used in federated learning), they may be computed according to a mini-batch SGD style approach, or some other momentum based approach.

The attentive reader may notice that the original DP-SGD adds $\mathcal{N}(0, (C\sigma)^2\mathbf{I})$, a factor of 2 less. This is because its DP analysis and proof assume a slightly different subsampling method. In the original DP-SGD, we have that each round selects a random mini-batch of *exactly* m samples; this leads to the factor 2 since U and U' will differ in one gradient, hence, $U - U'$ cancels all gradients except for one in U and one in U', both contributing at most C to the norm $\|U - U'\|$, hence, the factor 2.

However, the software package Opacus [46] implements the sampling of DP-SGD differently: Mini-batches do not have a fixed size, they have a probabilistic size. For each sample $\xi \in d$, we flip a coin and with probability m/N we add ξ to the mini-batch. This means that the *expected* mini-batch size is equal to m. As a result, the DP analysis of [1] holds true and the factor 2 can be eliminated. The reason is that now (in the DP analysis) U' has all the gradients of U together with one extra gradient based on the single differentiating sample between d and d'. This implies that all gradients in $U - U'$ cancel except for that based on the differentiating sample, hence, $\|U - U'\| \leq C$.

In the above argument, we *assume* that the adversary does not learn the actually used mini-batch size otherwise we will again need the factor 2 (see also Section 2.4.5). The observed scaled noised update $\bar{U}/m$ scales in expectation with the expected norm of a single computed gradient times the used mini-batch size divided by the expected mini-batch size m. This shows how $\bar{U}/m$ depends on the used mini-batch size where, for large m and N, it seems reasonable to assume that the adversary cannot gain significant knowledge about the used mini-batch size from $\bar{U}/m$. We conclude that a probabilistic mini-batch size is a DP technique that offers a factor 2 gain. This chapter summarizes the f-DP framework explained for sampling with fixed mini-batch size leading to the extra factor 2 (the probabilistic approach can be added as a complimentary technique).

2.2.4 Aggregation at the server

The server maintains a global model, which we denote by $\hat{w}$. The server adds to $\hat{w}$ the received scaled noised round update $\bar{U}/m$ after multiplying with the round step size[1] for round b of epoch e,

$$\eta_{(e-1)\frac{N}{m}+b}$$

(the same as the local model update of w by the client). This allows a diminishing[2] step size sequence. Notice that dividing by the mini-batch size m corresponds to U representing a mini-batch computation in mini-batch SGD.

---

[1] The client transmits $(b, e, \bar{U})$ to the server and the server knows an a priori agreed (with the client) round step size sequence. In practice, the client will only transmit a sparsification or lossy compression of $\bar{U}$ where small entries are discarded.

[2] Due to the added Gaussian noise and clipping bias, we can only converge to within some radius around a local minimum w^*. Therefore, we may use a diminishing step size that converges to a constant step size equal to the anticipated radius. For example, as a rule of thumb, after every epoch we evaluate the test accuracy based on a public data set and if not increasing, then we decrease the step size by 10%.

Each client will select its own DP posture with own selected parameters m, C, σ, and own data set d with its own size N. It makes sense for the server to collect the noised round updates from various clients during consecutive time windows and broadcast updated global models at the end of each window. Rather than adding all the received $\bar{U}$ within a time window to the global model $\hat{w}$ (after multiplying with the appropriate client-specific step sizes and dividing by the appropriate client-specific mini-batch sizes), the server will add a mix of the various local updates. The mix is according to some weighing vector giving more weight to those clients whom the server judges having 'better' training data sets for the learning task at hand. In federated learning, the server will ask for each time window a random subset of clients to participate in the training. In the above context, it makes sense to have the step sizes be diminishing[3] from time window to time window rather than have these be client-specific.

2.2.5 Interrupt service routine

The interrupt service routine will replace the locally kept model w by a received global model $\hat{w}$. This may happen in the middle of a round. We notice that $\hat{w}$ depends on previously transmitted noised round updates by the client and other clients. We will discuss how each of these previous noised round updates have a DP guarantee. By the so-called post-processing lemma, these previously transmitted noised round updates can participate in the current computation of a round update U through its dependency on the global model $\hat{w}$ (through the gradients in U) without weakening the DP guarantee for $\bar{U}$ (which includes Gaussian noise on top of U).

Similarly, the client locally updates model w with $\bar{U}$ at the end of a round. In next rounds this implies that w still only depends on previously transmitted noised round updates by the client and other clients, and, again by the post-processing lemma, the DP guarantees of future noised round updates do not degrade. As soon as a new global model $\hat{w}$ is received by the interrupt service routine, it will overwrite w, that is, the current local model is discarded. This is justified because the newly received global model includes the client's own previously communicated noised updates $\bar{U}$ (if the corresponding messages were not dropped and did not suffer too much latency), hence, the information of its own local updates is incorporated in the newly received $\hat{w}$.

2.2.6 DP principles and utility

The strength of the resulting DP guarantee depends on how much utility we are okay with sacrificing. The differential privacy guarantee is discussed in Section 2.4. The principle of using Gaussian noise *bootstraps* DP for each round, see (2.3); the principle of subsampling in the form of random mini-batches of size m *amplifies* DP

---

[3] Continuing the previous footnote, the central server decides when to reduce the step size based on regularly evaluating the test accuracy, and broadcasts the new step sizes to the clients.

(because only with probability m/N a round uses the differentiating sample and can leak privacy in the first place); and the principle of *composition* of DP guarantees for each round over multiple epochs yields the overall DP guarantee.

Utility is measured in terms of the (test) accuracy of the final global model and secondary metrics are convergence rate, round complexity $(N/m) \cdot E$ calculated as the total number of rounds per client (communication is costly), total gradient complexity $E \cdot N$ calculated as the total number of computed gradients per client, information dispersal characterized by the delay or latency of what is learned from local data sets which is calculated as the number m of gradient computations between consecutive round communications to the server, and client's memory usage.

The final accuracy depends on the amount of clipping noise and Gaussian noise: Once convergence sets in, the clipping noise will be small and close to zero if the clipping constant is appropriately chosen (at least a factor larger than $c(w^*)$, see Section 2.2.1). However, each round update U has noise sampled from $\mathcal{N}(0, (2C\sigma)^2 \mathbf{I})$ added to itself. If this noise is small relative to the norm of U, then we expect accuracy not to suffer too much if the neural network model is sufficiently robust against noise (it turns out that deeper neural networks are quite sensitive). When convergence progresses and the clipping constant is large enough, then U/m behaves like an average of unclipped gradients which is an estimate of $E_\xi[\nabla_w f(w^*; \xi)]$ which tends to zero. This means that the Gaussian noise relative to the norm of U becomes larger, which puts a limit on how much accuracy/utility can be achieved.

Since the DP guarantee depends on σ but not on C while the added Gaussian noise scales with $C \cdot \sigma$, we will want to implement a form of (differential private) adaptive clipping (we notice that the DP analysis of DP-SGD holds for clipping constants C that vary from round to round). Experimentation is needed to fine-tune the parameters m, (adaptive) C, and σ. Despite fine-tuning, we remark that the added clipping and Gaussian noise for differential privacy results in convergence to a final global model with smaller (test) accuracy (than what otherwise, without DP, can be achieved).

The following thought experiment shows how the batch size m influences utility and differential privacy. Suppose we increase m to am, a factor a larger. Then the norm of updates U will become a factor a larger. As a result, with respect to convergence to the final global model, we should be able to cope with a factor a larger Gaussian noise. That is, by keeping the relative amount of noise with respect to the norm of U constant, the new updates corresponding to batch size am can be noised with

$$a \cdot \mathcal{N}(0, (2C\sigma)^2 \mathbf{I}) = \mathcal{N}(0, (2C\sigma \cdot a)^2 \mathbf{I}).$$

In fact the communicated averaged noised round update $\bar{U}/(am)$ has noise

$$a \cdot \mathcal{N}(0, (2C\sigma)^2 \mathbf{I})/(am) = \mathcal{N}(0, (2C\sigma/m)^2 \mathbf{I}),$$

the same as the original communicated averaged noised round update (before the thought experiment). This shows that we can use the factor a for increasing (1) the clipping constant C (which reduces the clipping noise, which is most prevalent at the start of DP-SGD, so that convergence can more easily bootstrap) and/or increasing (2) the standard deviation σ (which improves the DP guarantee); the resulting new clipping constant C' and standard deviation σ' satisfy $2C'\sigma' = 2C\sigma \cdot a$.

However, the disadvantage of increasing the batch size with a factor a is a multiplicative factor a increased amount of gradient computations since overall we will still need the same number of rounds for convergence, or, equivalently, the same number of SGD update steps toward a local minimum w^*. This means a factor a larger number of epochs (one epoch measures N gradient computations, hence, if m is increased to ma, we have a factor a smaller number of rounds per epoch). But this has a direct impact on the DP guarantee. As we will see in Section 2.4.5 (when discussing Gaussian DP), before the thought experiment we have a G_μ-DP guarantee, where μ is proportional to $\sqrt{Em/(N\sigma^2)}$ for 'large N and E.' The thought experiment increases m by a and increases E by a. Hence, for the same σ we will now have the significantly worse $\approx G_{\mu \cdot a}$-DP guarantee. If the factor a is fully used for increasing σ by a factor a, then for 'large N and E' the Gaussian DP parameter $\mu \cdot a$ decreases back to μ and the overall DP guarantee remains the same. Notice that the total number of gradient computations increases from E to aE, while the balance between utility and differential privacy seems to remain[4] the same. The above thought experiment shows that finding the right hyperparameter setting is not straightforward.

Hyperparameter search depends on the used data set. Either we adopt a hyperparameter setting from another similar learning task, or we search for hyperparameters based on the client data sets. In practice, in order to find good parameters m, C, and σ, we basically do a grid search by (1) fixing some standard settings (from similar learning tasks) for sample size m, e.g., 16, 32, 64, 128, and 256, etc., (2) fixing some standard settings (from similar learning tasks) for clipping constant C, e.g., 0.001, 0.01, 0.1, etc., and then (3) trying some reasonable settings for σ (based on the client data sets). If the grid search indeed uses client data sets, then we need to make sure that the additional privacy leakage due to the search is small. This is discussed in Appendix D of [1], see also [25].

2.2.7 Normalization

In practice we will also want to use data normalization [51] as a pre-processing step. This requires computing the mean and variance over all data samples from d. This makes normalized data samples depend on all samples in d. For this reason, we need differential private data normalization. That is, a differential private noisy mean and noisy variance is revealed a priori. This leads to some privacy leakage. The advantage is that we can now rewrite $\mathcal{A}$ as an algorithm that takes as input w, the original data

---

[4] Here, we notice that a larger a does have the advantage that $h(a\sigma)$ in Section 2.4.5 tends to $1/(a\sigma)$, leading to μ being proportional to $1/(a\sigma)$ as stated. If a and, as a result, $a\sigma$ remain relatively small, then $h(\sigma)$ and μ are proportional to $\sqrt{2} \cdot e^{1/(2(a\sigma)^2)}$ which is a much worse dependency on $a\sigma$, leading to an unacceptable DP guarantee.

samples $\{\xi_h\}_{h \in S_b}$, together with the revealed noisy mean and noisy variance. This $\mathcal{A}$ first normalizes each data sample after which it starts to compute gradients, etc. In the f-DP framework, privacy leakage is now characterized as a trade-off function of the differential private data normalization pre-processing composed with the trade-off function corresponding to the DP analysis of DP-SGD (which does not consider data normalization).

We notice that batch normalization is not compatible with the DP analysis of DP-SGD with its individual clipping of each gradient (since this introduces dependencies among the clipped gradients in U and the upper bound of $2C$ on the sensitivity does not hold). On the other hand, layer normalization as well as group and instance normalization are compatible (because these only concern single gradient computations). We notice that if a_h is computed itself by using a local mini-batch SGD approach, then batch normalization of the used mini-batch can be integrated within its computation.

As a final remark, our discussion assumes that we already know how to represent data samples by extracting features. We can use Principal Component Analysis (PCA) for dimensionality reduction, that is, learning a set of features which we want to use to represent data samples. PCA can be made differentially private [6] in that the resulting feature extraction method (feature transform) has a DP guarantee with respect to the data samples that were used for computing the transform. DP-SGD can be seen as a post-processing after PCA, which is used to represent the local training data samples for which DP-SGD achieves a DP guarantee. In practice, we often already know how to represent the data for our learning task and we already know which function $f(w; \xi)$ to use, i.e., which neural network topology and loss function to use (due to the success of transfer learning we can adopt data representations and f from other learning tasks).

2.3 Differential privacy

In order to prevent data leakage from inference attacks in machine learning [36] such as the deep leakage from gradients attack [21,59,60] or the membership inference attack [43,49,50], a range of privacy-preserving methods have been proposed. Privacy-preserving solutions for federated learning are Local Differential Privacy (LDP) solutions [1,2,12,26,42,52] and Central Differential Privacy (CDP) solutions [23,39,42,47,58]. In LDP, the noise for achieving differential privacy is computed locally at each client and is added to the updates before sending to the server – in this chapter we only consider LDP. In CDP, a *trusted server* (also known as trusted third party) aggregates received client updates into a global model; in order to achieve differential privacy the server adds noise to the global model before communicating it to the clients.

Differential privacy [13–15,17], see [16] for an excellent textbook, defines privacy guarantees for algorithms on databases, in our case a client's sequence of mini-batch gradient computations on his/her training data set. The guarantee quantifies into what extent the output of a client (the collection of updates communicated to the server) can be used to differentiate among two adjacent training data sets d and d' (i.e., where one set has one extra element compared to the other set).

2.3.1 Characteristics of a differential privacy measure

In DP-SGD, the client wants to keep its local training data set as private as possible. Each noised round update $\bar{U}$ leaks privacy. Let us define round mechanism $\mathcal{M}_b$ as the round computation that outputs $\bar{U}$ for round b. The input of $\mathcal{M}_b$ is data set d together with an updated local model w. We have the following recursion

$$\bar{U}_b \leftarrow \mathcal{M}_b(w_b; d),$$

where w_b is a function of received global model updates which themselves depend on other client's round updates in combination with own previously transmitted round updates $\bar{U}_1, \ldots, \bar{U}_{b-1}$. To express this dependency, we use the notation

$$w_b \leftarrow \mathsf{W}(\bar{U}_1, \ldots, \bar{U}_{b-1}),$$

where W receives the global models of the server (and in essence reflects the interrupt service routine). We define the overall mechanism $\mathcal{M}$ as the (adaptive) composition of all round mechanisms $\mathcal{M}_b$, i.e.,

$$\{\bar{U}_b\} \leftarrow \mathcal{M}(d) \text{ with } \bar{U}_b \leftarrow \mathcal{M}_b(\mathsf{W}(\bar{U}_1, \ldots, \bar{U}_{b-1}); d).$$

When defining a DP measure, we will want to be able to *compose* the DP guarantees for the different round mechanisms $\mathcal{M}_b$: If we can prove that $\mathcal{M}_b(\mathtt{aux}; \cdot)$ has a certain DP guarantee, denoted by DP_b, for *all* $\mathtt{aux}$ (that can be output by $\mathsf{W}(\ldots)$), then the composition $\mathcal{M}$ of all round mechanisms $\mathcal{M}_b$ should have a composed DP guarantee

$$\mathsf{DP}_1 \otimes \mathsf{DP}_2 \otimes \cdots \otimes \mathsf{DP}_{(N/m) \cdot E}$$

for some composition tensor $\otimes$ over DP measures.

Once a DP guarantee for mechanism $\mathcal{M}$ is proven, we do not want it to weaken due to *post-processing* of the output of $\mathcal{M}$. In particular, the central server uses the output of $\mathcal{M}$ for keeping track of and computing a final global model for the learning task at hand. This final model should still have the same (or stronger) differential privacy posture. Let us denote the post-processing by a procedure P. If $\mathcal{M}$ has DP guarantee DP, then we want $\mathsf{P} \circ \mathcal{M}$ to also have DP guarantee DP (this is called the post-processing lemma),

$$[\mathsf{DP} \text{ for } \mathcal{M}] \Rightarrow [\mathsf{DP} \text{ for } \mathsf{P} \circ \mathcal{M}].$$

We want our DP measure to be compatible with *subsampling*: We want to be able to show that if a round mechanism $\mathcal{M}_b$ has guarantee DP without subsampling, then $\mathcal{M}_b \circ \mathsf{Sample}_m$ has an 'easy' to characterize amplified guarantee DP', '$\mathsf{DP}' \geq \mathsf{DP}$.'

Finally, we want a differential privacy measure which fits our intuition, in particular, how privacy should be characterized and in what circumstances an attacker can learn private information from observed mechanism outputs. Differential privacy measures are about the difficulty of distinguishing whether the observed output o is from the distribution $\mathcal{M}(d)$ or from the distribution $\mathcal{M}(d')$, where d and d' are neighboring data sets in that they have all but one differentiating sample in common. The DP guarantee measures in to what extent

$$\Pr[o \sim \mathcal{M}(d)] \quad \text{and} \quad \Pr[o \sim \mathcal{M}(d')]$$

are alike for *all* neighboring d and d'. Here, we want to reflect the intuition that for more likely observations o the two probabilities should be close together while for unlikely observations o we care less whether the two probabilities are close. This reflects how we think about the adversary. Only in rare unlikely cases, a lot or all privacy may leak, while in the common case there is very little privacy leakage. In cryptology we would want to interpret 'rare' as a negligible probability in some security parameter and in the common case we want the two probabilities/distributions to be 'statistically close' with their distance negligible in some security parameter. Such strong guarantees cannot be extracted from DP analysis where we control privacy leakage in exchange for utility/accuracy; we cannot make privacy leakage negligible.

The DP measure is characterized in terms of probabilities and statistics. This is referred to as static security or information-theoretical security and allows an adversary with unbounded computational resources in order to differentiate between the hypotheses $o \sim \mathcal{M}(d)$ and $o \sim \mathcal{M}(d')$. For completeness, in cryptology we also have the notion of computational security meaning that the difficulty of differentiating the two hypotheses can be reduced to solving a computational hard problem (and, since the brightest mathematicians and computer scientists have not been able to find an algorithm which solves this problem efficiently with practical computational resources, we believe that the attacker cannot solve this problem in feasible time). Computational security allows one to obtain security guarantees where the attackers advantage or success is negligible in some security parameter.

The above expresses individual privacy. We can generalize towards group privacy by considering data sets d and d' that differ in at most g samples. In this case we say that a mechanism has a DP guarantee with respect to a group of g samples.

2.3.2 (ϵ, δ)-differential privacy

A randomized mechanism $\mathcal{M}: D \rightarrow R$ is (ϵ, δ)-DP (Differentially Private) [14] if for any adjacent d and d' in D and for any subset $S \subseteq R$ of outputs,

$$\Pr[\mathcal{M}(d) \in S] \leq e^{\epsilon} \cdot \Pr[\mathcal{M}(d') \in S] + \delta, \tag{2.4}$$

where the probabilities are taken over the coin flips of mechanism $\mathcal{M}$.

Historically, differential privacy was introduced [14] and first defined as ϵ-DP [15] which is (ϵ, δ)-DP with $\delta = 0$. In order to achieve ϵ-DP even an unlikely set S

of outputs needs to satisfy (2.4) for $\delta = 0$. This means that the tail distributions of $\Pr[\mathcal{M}(d) \in S]$ and $\Pr[\mathcal{M}(d') \in S]$ cannot differ by more than a factor of e^{ϵ}. This is a much too strong DP requirement, since the probability to observe an output that corresponds to unlikely tail events is already very small to begin with. Therefore, δ was introduced so that tail distributions with probability $\leq \delta$ do not need to be close together within a factor of e^{ϵ}. This allows one to achieve the more relaxed (ϵ, δ)-DP guarantee where an ϵ-DP guarantee cannot be proven.

The privacy loss incurred by observing an output o is given by

$$L^{o}_{\mathcal{M}(d)\|\mathcal{M}(d')} = \ln\left(\frac{\Pr[\mathcal{M}(d) = o]}{\Pr[\mathcal{M}(d') = o]}\right). \tag{2.5}$$

As explained in [17], (ϵ, δ)-DP ensures that for all adjacent d and d' the absolute value of privacy loss will be bounded by ϵ with probability at least $1 - \delta$ (with probability at most δ, observation o is part of the tail); (ϵ, δ)-DP allows a δ probability of 'catastrophic privacy failure' and from a cryptographic perspective we want this negligibly small. However, when using differential privacy in machine learning, we typically use $\delta = 1/N$ (or $1/(10N)$) inversely proportional with the data set size N (this seems to correspond well with the intuition when a local update should cause an unlikely/tail observation due to the nature of the specific batch of local data samples that was used in the computation of the local update). Concerning parameter ϵ, the larger the ϵ, the more certain the adversary is about which of d or d' caused observation o.

Compared to $(\epsilon, 0)$-DP, the relaxation by δ allows an improved and asymptotically tight analysis of the cumulative privacy loss incurred by composition of multiple differentially private mechanisms; [18] states an advanced composition theorem (a factor of one-half improvement over [19]): For all $\epsilon, \delta, \delta' \geq 0$, the class of (ϵ, δ')-DP mechanisms satisfies

$$(\sqrt{2k \ln(1/\delta)} \cdot \epsilon + k\epsilon(e^{\epsilon} - 1)/2, k\delta' + \delta)\text{-DP}$$

under k-fold adaptive composition. This means that only for $k \leq (1 - \delta)/\delta'$ the privacy failure probability remains bounded to something smaller than 1.

For group privacy, the literature shows $(g\epsilon, ge^{g-1}\delta)$-DP for groups of size g. Here, we see an exponential dependency in g due to the ge^{g-1} term in the privacy failure probability. This means that only for very small δ, the failure probability remains bounded to something smaller than 1.

We conclude that k-fold composition and group privacy for group size g only lead to useful bounds for relatively small k and g. If we restrict ourselves to a subclass of mechanisms, then we may be able to prove practical DP bounds for composition and group privacy for much larger and practical k and g. We will define such subclasses by imposing properties on the privacy loss.

2.3.3 Divergence-based DP measures

In order to get better trade-offs for composition and group privacy, we want to weigh the tail distribution of unlikely observations in such a way that more unlikely observations are allowed to leak even more privacy. So, rather than weighing all unlikely observations equally likely, which results in the privacy failure probability δ, we want to be more careful. This will allow improved DP bounds for composition and group privacy.

The first idea is to treat the loss function (2.5) as a random variable Z and note that in a k-fold composition we observe k drawings of random variable Z. Due to the law of large numbers, the average of these drawings will be concentrated around the mean of the loss function. This leads to the notion of Concentrated Differential Privacy (CDP), first introduced in [18] by framing the loss function as a sub-Gaussian random variable after subtracting its mean. This was re-interpreted and relaxed by using Renyi entropy in [5] and its authors followed up with the notion zero-CDP (zCDP) in [5]: A mechanism $\mathcal{M}$ is ρ-zCDP if, for all $\alpha > 1$, the Renyi divergence

$$D_\alpha(\mathcal{M}(d)\|\mathcal{M}(d')) = \frac{\ln(\mathbb{E}_{o\sim\mathcal{M}(d)}[e^{(1-\alpha)Z}])}{1-\alpha} \text{ with } Z = L^o_{\mathcal{M}(d)\|\mathcal{M}(d')}$$

satisfies

$$D_\alpha(\mathcal{M}(d)\|\mathcal{M}(d')) \leq \rho\alpha. \tag{2.6}$$

This DP guarantee requires the tail of Z to be sub-Gaussian, i.e., $\Pr[Z > t + \rho] < e^{-t^2/(4\rho)}$ for all $t \geq 0$ (the tail behaves like $Z \sim \mathcal{N}(\rho, 2\rho)$). If the loss function satisfies this property for a collection of k mechanisms (each of the mechanisms is ρ-zCDP), then their k-fold adaptive composition is $k\rho$-zCDP. If a mechanism is ρ-zCDP for individual privacy, then it is $g^2\rho$-zCDP for groups of size g. This shows that if we can prove that our DP principles lead to a sub-Gaussian tail of the loss function Z, then we obtain interpretable DP guarantees even for large k and g.

After the introduction of ρ-zCDP, Renyi DP (RDP) was introduced by [41]; (ω, τ)-RDP requires

$$D_\alpha(\mathcal{M}(d)\|\mathcal{M}(d')) \leq \tau \text{ for all } \alpha \in (1, \omega).$$

Here, $\alpha = 1$ bounds the geometric mean of e^Z, $\alpha = 2$ bounds the arithmetic mean of e^Z, $\alpha = 3$ bounds the quadratic mean of e^Z, etc., and $\alpha = \infty$ bounds the maximum value of e^Z which is equivalent to $(\tau, 0)$-DP. RDP also leads to simple computable composition and group privacy. The advantage of zCDP over RDP is that it covers all α at once: Larger α put more weight on the tail of Z, also the mean gets larger. This means that τ in the RDP definition should increase with α and this is realized by zCDP by setting $\tau = \rho\alpha$ for all $\alpha \in (1, \infty)$.

The above discussion leads naturally to the definition of (ρ, ω)-tCDP [4]: A mechanism is ω-truncated ρ-CDP if it satisfies (2.6) only for $\alpha \in (1, \omega)$. tCDP requires Z to be sub-Gaussian near the origin (like zCDP), i.e., $\Pr[Z > t + \rho] <$

$e^{-t^2/(4\rho)}$ for all $0 \leq t \leq 2\rho(\omega - 1)$, but only subexponential in Z's tail, i.e., we get the weaker subexponential tail bound $\Pr[Z > t + \rho] \leq e^{(\omega-1)^2 \rho} e^{-(\omega-1)t}$. This relaxes zCDP while still obtaining interpretable DP guarantees for composition and group privacy, and also subsampling.

The main concern with each of the divergence based DP measures is a lack of transparency of how the attacker can best distinguish the hypotheses $o \sim \mathcal{M}(d)$ and $o \sim \mathcal{M}(d')$. The next section introduces the f-DP framework which provides a hypothesis testing based approach. It introduces trade-off functions that capture all the information needed for fully characterizing privacy leakage; a trade-off function can be used to derive any divergence based DP guarantee like those discussed above (but not the other way around), see Appendix B in [11]. Rather than extracting a divergence based DP guarantee from a trade-off function for DP-SGD, we will keep the trade-off function itself as it has an easy transparent interpretation.

2.4 Gaussian differential privacy

Dong et al. [11] introduced the state-of-the-art DP formulation based on hypothesis testing. From the attacker's perspective, it is natural to formulate the problem of distinguishing two neighboring data sets d and d' based on the output of a DP mechanism $\mathcal{M}$ as a hypothesis testing problem:

H_0 : the underlying data set is d vs. H_1 : the underlying data set is d'.

Here, neighboring means that either $|d \setminus d'| = 1$ or $|d' \setminus d| = 1$. More precisely, in the context of mechanism $\mathcal{M}$, $\mathcal{M}(d)$ and $\mathcal{M}(d')$ take as input representations r and r' of data sets d and d' which are 'neighbors.' The representations are mappings from a set of indices to data samples with the property that if $r(i) \in d \cap d'$ or $r'(i) \in d \cap d'$, then $r(i) = r'(i)$. This means that the mapping from indices to data samples in $d \cap d'$ is the same for the representation of d and the representation of d'. In other words, the mapping from indices to data samples for d and d' only differ for indices corresponding to the differentiating data samples in $(d \setminus d') \cup (d' \setminus d)$. In this sense the two mappings (data set representations) are neighbors.

We define the Type I and Type II errors by

$$\alpha_\phi = \mathbb{E}_{o \sim \mathcal{M}(d)}[\phi(o)] \text{ and } \beta_\phi = 1 - \mathbb{E}_{o \sim \mathcal{M}(d')}[\phi(o)],$$

where ϕ in $[0, 1]$ denotes the rejection rule which takes the output of the DP mechanism as input. We flip a coin and reject the null hypothesis with probability ϕ. The optimal trade-off between Type I and Type II errors is given by the trade-off function

$$T(\mathcal{M}(d), \mathcal{M}(d'))(\alpha) = \inf_{\phi}\{\beta_\phi : \alpha_\phi \leq \alpha\},$$

for $\alpha \in [0, 1]$, where the infimum is taken over all measurable rejection rules ϕ. If the two hypotheses are fully indistinguishable, then this leads to the trade-off function

$1 - \alpha$. We say a function $f \in [0, 1] \rightarrow [0, 1]$ is a trade-off function if and only if it is convex, continuous, non-increasing, and $0 \leq f(x) \leq 1 - x$ for $x \in [0, 1]$.

We define a mechanism $\mathcal{M}$ to be f-DP if f is a trade-off function and

$$T(\mathcal{M}(d), \mathcal{M}(d')) \geq f$$

for all neighboring d and d'. Proposition 2.5 in [11] is an adaptation of a result in [56] and states that a mechanism is (ϵ, δ)-DP if and only if the mechanism is $f_{\epsilon,\delta}$-DP, where

$$f_{\epsilon,\delta}(\alpha) = \max\{0, 1 - \delta - e^\epsilon \alpha, (1 - \delta - \alpha)e^{-\epsilon}\}.$$

We see that f-DP has the (ϵ, δ)-DP formulation as a special case. It turns out that the original DP-SGD algorithm can be tightly analyzed by using f-DP.

2.4.1 Gaussian DP

In order to proceed, [11] first defines Gaussian DP as another special case of f-DP as follows: We define the trade-off function

$$G_\mu(\alpha) = T(\mathcal{N}(0, 1), \mathcal{N}(\mu, 1))(\alpha) = \Phi(\Phi^{-1}(1 - \alpha) - \mu),$$

where Φ is the standard normal cumulative distribution of $\mathcal{N}(0, 1)$. We define a mechanism to be μ-Gaussian DP if it is G_μ-DP. Corollary 2.13 in [11] shows that a mechanism is μ-Gaussian DP if and only if it is $(\epsilon, \delta(\epsilon))$-DP for all $\epsilon \geq 0$, where

$$\delta(\epsilon) = \Phi(-\frac{\epsilon}{\mu} + \frac{\mu}{2}) - e^\epsilon \Phi(-\frac{\epsilon}{\mu} - \frac{\mu}{2}). \tag{2.7}$$

Suppose that a mechanism $\mathcal{M}(d)$ computes some function $u(d) \in \mathbb{R}^n$ and adds Gaussian noise $\mathcal{N}(0, (c\sigma)^2 \mathbf{I})$, that is, the mechanism outputs $o \sim u(d) + \mathcal{N}(0, (c\sigma)^2 \mathbf{I})$. Suppose that c denotes the sensitivity of function $u(\cdot)$, that is,

$$\|u(d) - u(d')\| \leq c$$

for neighboring d and d'; the mechanism corresponding to one round update in Algorithm 1 has *sensitivity* $c = 2C$. After projecting the observed o onto the line that connects $u(d)$ and $u(d')$ and after normalizing by dividing by c, we have that differentiating whether o corresponds to d or d' is in the best case for the adversary (i.e., $\|u(d) - u(d')\| = c$) equivalent to differentiating whether a received output is from $\mathcal{N}(0, \sigma^2)$ or $\mathcal{N}(1, \sigma^2)$; equivalently, from $\mathcal{N}(0, 1)$ or $\mathcal{N}(1/\sigma, 1)$. This is how the Gaussian trade-off function $G_{\sigma^{-1}}$ comes into the picture.

2.4.2 Subsampling

Besides implementing Gaussian noise, DP-SGD also uses subsampling: For a data set d of N samples, $\texttt{Sample}_m(d)$ selects a subset of size m from d uniformly at random.

We define convex combinations

$$f_p(\alpha) = pf(\alpha) + (1-p)(1-\alpha)$$

with corresponding p-sampling operator

$$C_p(f) = \min\{f_p, f_p^{-1}\}^{**},$$

where the conjugate h^* of a function h is defined as

$$h^*(y) = \sup_x \{yx - h(x)\}$$

and the inverse h^{-1} of a trade-off function h is defined as

$$h^{-1}(\alpha) = \inf\{t \in [0,1] \mid h(t) \le \alpha\} \tag{2.8}$$

and is itself a trade-off function (as an example, we notice that $G_\mu = G_\mu^{-1}$ and we say G_μ is symmetric). Theorem 4.2 in [11] shows that if a mechanism $\mathcal{M}$ on data sets of size N is f-DP, then the subsampled mechanism $\mathcal{M} \circ \mathtt{Sample}_m$ is $C_{m/N}(f)$-DP.

The intuition behind operator C_p is as follows. First, $\mathtt{Sample}_m(d)$ samples the differentiating element between d and d' with probability p. In this case the computations $\mathcal{M} \circ \mathtt{Sample}_m(d)$ and $\mathcal{M} \circ \mathtt{Sample}_m(d')$ are different and hypothesis testing is possible with trade-off function $f(\alpha)$. With probability $1-p$, no hypothesis testing is possible and we have trade-off function $1-\alpha$. This leads to the convex combination f_p.

Second, we notice if $h = T(\mathcal{M}(d), \mathcal{M}(d'))$, then $h^{-1} = T(\mathcal{M}(d'), \mathcal{M}(d))$. Therefore, if $\mathcal{M}$ is f-DP (which holds for all pairs of neighboring data sets, in particular, for the pairs (d, d') and (d', d)), then both $h \ge f$ and $h^{-1} \ge f$ and we have a symmetric upper bound $\min\{h, h^{-1}\} \ge f$. Since f is a trade-off function, f is convex and we can compute a tighter upper bound: f is at most the largest convex function $\le \min\{h, h^{-1}\}$, which is equal to the double conjugate $\min\{h, h^{-1}\}^{**}$. From this we obtain the definition of operator C_p.

2.4.3 Composition

The tensor product $f \otimes h$ for trade-off functions $f = T(P, Q)$ and $h = T(P', Q')$ is well-defined by

$$f \otimes h = T(P \times P', Q \times Q').$$

Let $y_i \leftarrow \mathcal{M}_i(\mathtt{aux}, d)$ with $\mathtt{aux} = (y_1, \ldots, y_{i-1})$. Theorem 3.2 in [11] shows that if $\mathcal{M}_i(\mathtt{aux}, \cdot)$ is f_i-DP for all $\mathtt{aux}$, then the composed mechanism $\mathcal{M}$, which applies $\mathcal{M}_i$ in sequential order from $i = 1$ to $i = T$, is $(f_1 \otimes \cdots \otimes f_T)$-DP. The tensor product is commutative.

As a special case Corollary 3.3 in [11] states that a composition of multiple Gaussian operators G_{μ_i} results in G_μ where

$$\mu = \sqrt{\sum_i \mu_i^2}.$$

2.4.4 Tight analysis of DP-SGD

We are now able to formulate the differential privacy guarantee of original DP-SGD since it is a composition of subsampled Gaussian DP mechanisms. Theorem 5.1 in [11] states that DP-SGD as introduced in [1] is

$$C_{m/N}(G_{\sigma-1})^{\otimes T}\text{-DP},$$

where $T = (N/m) \cdot E$ is the total number of local rounds. Since each of the theorems and results from [11] enumerated above are exact, we have a tight analysis. This leads in [61] to a (tight) differential privacy accountant[5] (using complex characteristic functions for each of the two hypotheses based on taking Fourier transforms), which can be used by a client to keep track of its current DP guarantee and to understand when to stop helping the server to learn a global model. Because the accountant is tight, it improves over the momentum accountant method of [1].

2.4.5 Strong adversarial model

We assume an adversary who knows the differentiating samples in $d \setminus d'$ and $d' \setminus d$, but who a priori (before mechanism $\mathcal{M}$ is executed) may only know (besides, say, a 99% characterization of $d \cap d'$) an estimate of the number of samples in the intersection of d and d', i.e., the adversary knows $|d \cap d'| + noise$ where the noise is large enough to yield a 'sufficiently strong' DP guarantee with respect to the size of the used data set (d or d'). Since $\mathcal{M}$ does not directly reveal the size of the used data set, we assume (as in prior literature) that the effect of $N = |d| \neq N' = |d'|$ contributes at most a very small amount of privacy leakage, sufficiently small to be discarded in our DP analysis, that is, we may as well assume $N = N'$ in our DP analysis.

This means that the tight f-DP analysis of DP-SGD holds, even if we use the definition of neighboring data sets stating that either $|d \setminus d'| = 1$ or $|d' \setminus d| = 1$; the original f-DP analysis considers the case $|d \setminus d'| = |d' \setminus d| = 1$ and this requires the factor $2C\sigma$ in Algorithm 1. If we assume no knowledge about the exact data set sizes (as discussed above) and if we assume probabilistic sampling (see Section 2.4.5),

---

[5] The tight analysis has, cited from [11], "the disadvantage is that the expressions it yields are more unwieldy: they are computer evaluable, so usable in implementations, but do not admit simple closed form." For this reason, we need an accountant method.

then we may only use $C\sigma$ saving a factor of 2 (which helps convergence to a higher accuracy).

In the setting of $N = N'$, the DP analysis in prior work considers an adversary $\mathcal{A}dv$ who can mimic mechanism $\mathcal{M} \circ \mathsf{Sample}_m$ in that it can replay, to a large extent, how Sample_m samples the used data set (d or d'): We say a round has k differentiating data samples if Sample_m sampled a subset of indices which contains exactly k indices of differentiating data samples from $(d \setminus d') \cup (d' \setminus d)$. The adversary knows how Sample_m operates and can derive a joint probability distribution $\mathbb{P}$ of the number of differentiating data samples for each round within the sequence of rounds that define the series of epochs during which updates are computed.

Adversary $\mathcal{A}dv$ does not know the exact instance drawn from $\mathbb{P}$ but is, in the DP proof, given the ability to realize for each round the trade-off function $f_k(\alpha)$ that corresponds to hypothesis testing between $\mathcal{M} \circ \mathsf{Sample}_m(d)$ and $\mathcal{M} \circ \mathsf{Sample}_m(d')$ if Sample_m has selected k differentiating samples in that round. In the DP analysis that characterizes $f_k(\alpha)$, adversary $\mathcal{A}dv$ is given knowledge about the mapping from indices to values in d or d'. Here (as discussed before), the mapping from indices to values in $d \cap d'$ is the same for the mapping from indices to values in d and the mapping from indices to values in d'. Furthermore, the adversary can replay how Sample_m samples a subset of m indices from[6] $\{1, \ldots, N = N'\}$, and it knows all the randomness used by $\mathcal{M}$ before $\mathcal{M}$ adds Gaussian noise for differential privacy (this includes when and how the interrupt service routine overwrites the local model). This strong adversary represents a worst-case scenario for the 'defender' when analyzing the differential privacy of a single round. For DP-SGD, this analysis for neighboring data sets leads to the argument of Section 2.4.2 where with probability p (i.e., $k = 1$) the adversary can achieve trade-off function $f(\alpha)$ and with probability $1 - p$ (i.e., $k = 0$) can achieve trade-off function $1 - \alpha$, leading ultimately to operator C_p. This in turn leads to the trade-off function $C_{m/N}(G_{\sigma^{-1}})^{\otimes T}$ with $p = m/N$, which is *tight for adversary* $\mathcal{A}dv$. Although usually not explicitly stated, we notice that adversary $\mathcal{A}dv$ is used in DP analysis of current literature including the moment accountant method of [1] for analyzing (ϵ, δ)-DP and analysis of divergence based DP measures.

In the DP analysis, adversary $\mathcal{A}dv$ is given knowledge about the number k of differentiating samples when analyzing a single round. That is, it is given an instance of $\mathbb{P}$ projected on a single round. We notice that in expectation the sensitivity (see Section 2.4.1) of a single round as observed by adversary $\mathcal{A}dv$ for neighboring data sets is equal to $(1 - p) \cdot 0 + p \cdot 2C = (m/N) \cdot 2C$ and this gives rise to an 'expected' trade-off function $G_{1/(\sigma N/m)}$. A composition over $c^2(N/m)^2$ rounds gives $G_{c/\sigma}$. This leads us to believe that $C_{m/N}(G_{\sigma^{-1}})^{\otimes T}$ converges to $G_{c \cdot h(\sigma)}$ for $T = c^2(N/m)^2 \to \infty$ (or, equivalently, $\sqrt{T} \cdot m/N = c$ with $T \to \infty$ and $N \to \infty$) where $h(\sigma)$ is some function that only depends on σ (see below). This intuition is confirmed by Corollary 5.4 in [11], and is also indirectly by [53] which shows that DP-SGD is (ϵ, δ)-DP

---

[6] By assuming $N = N'$ in the DP analysis, knowledge of how Sample_m samples a subset of indices cannot be used to differentiate the hypotheses of d versus d' based on their sizes (since the index set corresponding to d is exactly the same as the index set corresponding to d').

for $\sigma = \sqrt{2(\epsilon + \ln(1/\delta))/\epsilon}$ for a wide range of parameter settings N, m, T with T at most $\approx \epsilon(N/m)^2/2$, and which matches Corollary 5.4 in [11] in that the upper bound on T can at most be a constant factor ≈ 4 larger (without violating the corollary).

By using $T = (N/m) \cdot E$, we have convergence to $G_{c \cdot h(\sigma)}$ for $c = \sqrt{mE/N}$ with $E \to \infty$ and $N \to \infty$. By using a Taylor series expansion, we have

$$h(\sigma) = \sqrt{2(e^{\sigma^{-2}}\Phi(\frac{3\sigma^{-1}}{2}) + 3\Phi(-\frac{\sigma^{-1}}{2}) - 2)} = \sigma^{-1} \cdot \sqrt{1 + \frac{15}{8}\frac{\sigma^{-1}}{\sqrt{2\pi}}} + O(\sigma^{-2}).$$

This shows that for 'large N and E' DP-SGD is approximately G_μ-DP with $\mu = \sqrt{mE/(N\sigma^2)}$. Notice that σ cannot be too small otherwise $h(\sigma)$ behaves like $\sqrt{2} \cdot e^{1/(2\sigma^2)}$ which yields a very weak DP guarantee.

Clearly, a weaker (than Adv) adversary with less capability (less knowledge of the used randomness by Sample_m and $\mathcal{M}$) achieves a trade-off function $\geq C_{m/N}(G_{\sigma-1})^{\otimes T}$ closer to the ideal $1 - \alpha$. It remains an open problem to characterize realistic weaker adversaries that lead to larger (lower bounds of) trade-off functions.

2.4.6 Group privacy

Theorem 2.14 in [11] analyzes how privacy degrades if d and d' do not differ in just one sample, but rather in g samples. If a mechanism is f-DP, then it is

$$[1 - (1 - f)^{\circ g}]\text{-DP}$$

for groups of size g (where $\circ g$ denotes the g-fold iterative composition of function $1 - f$, where 1 denotes the constant integer value 1 and not the identity function, i.e., $(1 - f)(\alpha) = 1 - f(\alpha)$). This is a tight statement in that *there exist* f such that the trade-off function for groups of size g cannot be bounded better. In particular, for $f = G_\mu$ we have $G_{g\mu}$-DP for groups of size g.

The intuition behind the $[1 - (1 - f)^{\circ g}]$-DP result is that the adversary can create a sequence of data sets $d_0 = d, d_1, \ldots, d_{g-1}, d_g = d'$ such that each two consecutive data sets d_i and d_{i+1} are neighboring. We know that $T(\mathcal{M}(d_i), \mathcal{M}(d_{i+1})) \geq f$. For each rejection rule, we may plot a point (in x and y coordinates)

$$(\mathbb{E}_{o \sim \mathcal{M}(d_i)}[\phi(o)], \ \mathbb{E}_{o \sim \mathcal{M}(d_{i+1})}[\phi(o)]).$$

Since $f(\alpha)$ is a lower bound on the Type I vs. Type II error curve, the resulting collection of points is upper bounded by the curve $1 - f(\alpha)$. We have that $\alpha = \mathbb{E}_{o \sim \mathcal{M}(d_i)}[\phi(o)]$ is mapped to

$$\mathbb{E}_{o \sim \mathcal{M}(d_{i+1})}[\phi(o)] \leq 1 - f(\alpha) = (1 - f)(\alpha).$$

By transitivity, we have that $\alpha = \mathbb{E}_{o \sim \mathcal{M}(d=d_0)}[\phi(o)]$ is mapped to

$$\mathbb{E}_{o \sim \mathcal{M}(d'=d_g)}[\phi(o)] \leq (1 - f)^{\circ g}(\alpha).$$

This yields the lower bound

$$T(\mathcal{M}(d), \mathcal{M}(d')) \geq 1 - (1 - f)^{\circ g}$$

on the Type I vs. Type II error curve.

Let $\phi[\alpha]$ denote a rejection rule that realizes the mapping from

$$\alpha = \mathbb{E}_{o \sim \mathcal{M}(d_i)}[\phi[\alpha](o)] \quad \text{to} \quad (1 - f)(\alpha) = \mathbb{E}_{o \sim \mathcal{M}(d_{i+1})}[\phi[\alpha](o)].$$

Then the mapping from $(1 - f)^{\circ i}(\alpha) = \mathbb{E}_{o \sim \mathcal{M}(d_i)}[\phi(o)]$ to $(1 - f)^{\circ(i+1)}(\alpha) = \mathbb{E}_{o \sim \mathcal{M}(d_{i+1})}[\phi(o)]$ is realized by $\phi = \phi[(1 - f)^{\circ i}(\alpha)]$. This shows that the lower bound $1 - (1 - f)^{\circ g}$ is tight only if we can choose all $\phi[(1 - f)^{\circ i}(\alpha)]$ equal to one another. In general, this may not be the case for DP-SGD and future work may be able to produce an improved analysis for DP-SGD.

2.4.7 DP-SGD's trade-off function

We remind the reader that we can directly infer (ϵ, δ)-DP guarantees from (2.7); function $\delta(\epsilon)$ turns out to only depend on $\mu \approx \sqrt{mE/(N\sigma^2)}$, see Section 2.4.5. This leads to a dependency on data set size N, which, see Section 2.3.2, by setting $\delta(\epsilon) = 1/N$ favorably biases smaller data sets.

Appendix B in [11] shows how to infer divergence based DP guarantees. In particular, G_μ-DP implies $(\omega, \frac{1}{2\mu^2} \cdot \omega)$-RDP (Renyi differential privacy) for any $\omega > 1$, hence, we have

$$\frac{1}{2\mu^2}\text{-zCDP}.$$

For group privacy with $g \geq 1$, we have $G_{\mu \cdot g}$-DP and RDP and zCDP scale with another factor g^2.

2.5 Future work

We are still in the midst of bringing DP-SGD to practice where we want to achieve good convergence to and accuracy of the final global model and where we have a strong DP guarantee (the trade-off function should be close to $1 - \alpha$ which represents random guessing between the two hypotheses). Towards finding a good balance between utility and privacy, we discuss a couple future directions in next subsections.

2.5.1 Using synthetic data

One main problem is that local data is used for training models for various learning tasks. Each application of DP-SGD will leak privacy since the local data set is being reused. One way to control and be in charge of the amount of privacy leakage is to have data samples in local client data expire according to some expiration date (per sample). This is problematic because in our current data economy, data is a valuable asset which we do not want to give a limited lifetime.

In order to cope with this problem, a client may decide to not use its own local data set in each of these DP-SGD instantiations. Instead, differential private GAN [24] modeling can be used to learn a distribution model based on a local data set that generates synthetic data with a similar distribution. Due to the post-processing lemma, we can freely use the synthetic data in any optimization algorithm and FL approach. This circumvents multiple use of DP-SGD, but requires the design of differential private GAN which produces 'high' quality synthetic data. This is an open problem: GAN modeling is itself a learning task which can use the DP-SGD approach for the discriminator (which is very noise sensitive). Here, we use DP-SGD only once and as soon as a GAN model is learned, it can be published and transmitted to the central server who uses the GAN models from all clients to generate synthetic samples on which it trains a global model for a learning task of its choice. Of course, as a caveat, working with synthetic data may not lead to a global model with good test accuracy on real data. Notice that by using synthetic data we avoid the FL paradigm altogether since the large amounts of data distributed over clients are now compressed into (relatively short transmittable) representations that code GAN models.

In the same line of thinking, if differentially private GAN models do not lead to high quality synthetic data, then we will want to research other general methods for pre-processing local data that filter or hide features that are considered privacy sensitive. This brings us back to the basics of how a membership or inference attack is actually implemented in order to understand what type of information should be filtered out for making reconstruction of certain types of private data hard or unreliable.

2.5.2 Adaptive strategies

We need to fine-tune parameters and this can be done during DP-SGD's execution: Consecutive segments of multiple rounds may work with their own m, σ, and C. To what extent does an adaptive approach work, where the current convergence rate and test accuracy (preferably based on public data at the server so as not to leak additional privacy) of the current global model are used to determine (m, σ, C) for the next segment?

In Section 2.2.6 we discussed the benefit of adaptive reducing the clipping constant C (based on prior rounds or based on using a DP approach within a round to collect information that influences the choice of the used C in that round). Similarly, since a smaller σ directly reduces the amount of noise added to the global model and therefore increases the final accuracy, it makes sense to reduce σ once convergence has been achieved. After reducing σ, new convergence to an improved global model may start. The problem is that a lower σ leads to more privacy leakage. For this reason, we want to lower σ to a smaller $\hat{\sigma}$ only for, say, the final epoch.

We may also modify the noise distribution: DP-SGD selects noise N from a Gaussian distribution. Before adding N to the round update, we may replace N by $a \cdot \text{arsinh}(a^{-1} \cdot N)$ where $\text{arsinh}(x) = \ln(x + \sqrt{x^2 + 1})$ as suggested for tCDP [4].

The result resembles the same Gaussian but with exponentially faster tail decay and this may help in improving the convergence to and accuracy of the final global model. Here, we notice that for the same reason of faster tail decay, DP-SGD chooses to use Gaussian over Laplace noise.

Finally, DP-SGD can be placed in a larger algorithmic framework with DP guarantees for a more general clipping strategy (including clipping a batch of gradients) which allows more general optimization algorithms (beyond mini-batch SGD), and more general sampling strategies (in particular a sampling strategy based on 'shuffling').

It remains an open problem to unveil adaptive strategies possibly in a more general algorithmic framework that optimally balance utility and differential privacy. Here we prefer to discover adaptive strategies that proactively provide the DP guarantee based on changed parameter settings, i.e., we do not want to change parameters based solely on utility and discover later (by using a differential privacy accountant) that this has violated or is about to violate our privacy budget.

2.5.3 DP proof: a weaker adversarial model

Section 2.4.5 explains the strong adversarial model used in DP analysis under which the derived DP guarantee is tight. In practice, this is too strong. In general, we may assume a weaker adversary with less capability in terms of knowledge about the used randomness by $\mathtt{Sample}_m$ and $\mathcal{M}$. By explicitly stating the knowledge of a weaker adversary in combination with assumptions on the data set itself, we may be able to derive an f-DP guarantee with $f(\alpha)$ closer to $1 - \alpha$. It remains an open problem to exploit such a line of thinking.

2.5.4 Computing environment with less adversarial capabilities

In order to impose restrictions on adversarial capabilities, we may be able to use confidential computing techniques such as secure processor technology [9], homomorphic computing with secret sharing and/or secure Multi-Party Computation (MPC) [30], and possibly even hardware-accelerated fully homomorphic encryption [20,22]; for a survey, see [29,32]. These techniques hide round updates in encrypted form. Hence, only the final global model itself (if it is published) or querying the final global model (if it is kept private) can leak information about how local data sets shaped the final model. This means that CDP, see Section 2.3, is still needed. CDP has a better trade-off between privacy and utility compared to LDP as discussed in this chapter. However, confidential computing does not come for free: Either we need to assume a larger Trusted Computing Base (TCB) in the form of trusted hardware modules or processors at the clients, intermediate aggregators, and server or we need a Trusted Third Party (TTP). For example, in the secure MPC solution of [30], the generation of Beaver triples is outsourced to a TTP, otherwise impractical additional communication among clients and server is needed (for an oblivious transfer phase in MPC). We are still studying balanced and practical combinations of confidential computing techniques including the use of differential privacy.

References

[1] Martin Abadi, Andy Chu, Ian Goodfellow, H. Brendan McMahan, Ilya Mironov, Kunal Talwar, Li Zhang, Deep learning with differential privacy, in: Proceedings of the 2016 ACM SIGSAC Conference on Computer and Communications Security, ACM, 2016, pp. 308–318.

[2] Abhishek Bhowmick, John Duchi, Julien Freudiger, Gaurav Kapoor, Ryan Rogers, Protection against reconstruction and its applications in private federated learning, 2019.

[3] Keith Bonawitz, Hubert Eichner, Wolfgang Grieskamp, Dzmitry Huba, Alex Ingerman, Vladimir Ivanov, Chloe Kiddon, Jakub Konecny, Stefano Mazzocchi, H. Brendan McMahan, et al., Towards federated learning at scale: system design, arXiv:1902.01046, 2019.

[4] Mark Bun, Cynthia Dwork, Guy N. Rothblum, Thomas Steinke, Composable and versatile privacy via truncated CDP, in: Ilias Diakonikolas, David Kempe, Monika Henzinger (Eds.), STOC, ACM, 2018.

[5] Mark Bun, Thomas Steinke, Concentrated differential privacy: simplifications, extensions, and lower bounds, in: Martin Hirt, Adam D. Smith (Eds.), TCC, vol. 9985, 2016, pp. 635–658.

[6] Kamalika Chaudhuri, Anand D. Sarwate, Kaushik Sinha, A near-optimal algorithm for differentially-private principal components, Journal of Machine Learning Research 14 (2013).

[7] Jianmin Chen, Rajat Monga, Samy Bengio, and Rafal Jozefowicz. Revisiting distributed synchronous sgd, ICLR Workshop Track, 2016.

[8] Yang Chen, Xiaoyan Sun, Yaochu Jin, Communication-efficient federated deep learning with asynchronous model update and temporally weighted aggregation, arXiv:1903.07424, 2019.

[9] Victor Costan, Srinivas Devadas, Intel SGX explained. IACR Cryptol, ePrint Arch., 2016, p. 86.

[10] Christopher M. De Sa, Ce Zhang, Kunle Olukotun, Christopher Ré, Taming the wild: a unified analysis of HOGWILD!-style algorithms, in: NIPS, 2015, pp. 2674–2682.

[11] Jinshuo Dong, Aaron Roth, Weijie Su, Gaussian differential privacy, Journal of the Royal Statistical Society (2021).

[12] John C. Duchi, Michael I. Jordan, Martin J. Wainwright, Local privacy, data processing inequalities, and statistical minimax rates, 2014.

[13] Cynthia Dwork, A firm foundation for private data analysis, Communications of the ACM 54 (1) (2011) 86–95.

[14] Cynthia Dwork, Krishnaram Kenthapadi, Frank McSherry, Ilya Mironov, Moni Naor, Our data, ourselves: privacy via distributed noise generation, in: Annual International Conference on the Theory and Applications of Cryptographic Techniques, Springer, 2006, pp. 486–503.

[15] Cynthia Dwork, Frank McSherry, Kobbi Nissim, Adam Smith, Calibrating noise to sensitivity in private data analysis, in: Theory of Cryptography Conference, Springer, 2006, pp. 265–284.

[16] Cynthia Dwork, Aaron Roth, The algorithmic foundations of differential privacy, Foundations and Trends in Theoretical Computer Science 9 (3–4) (2014) 211–407.

[17] Cynthia Dwork, Aaron Roth, et al., The algorithmic foundations of differential privacy, Foundations and Trends in Theoretical Computer Science 9 (3–4) (2014) 211–407.

[18] Cynthia Dwork, Guy N. Rothblum, Concentrated differential privacy, arXiv:1603.01887, 2016.

[19] Cynthia Dwork, Guy N. Rothblum, Salil P. Vadhan, Boosting and differential privacy, in: 51st Annual IEEE Symposium on Foundations of Computer Science, FOCS 2010, October 23–26, 2010, Las Vegas, Nevada, USA, IEEE Computer Society, 2010, pp. 51–60.

[20] Axel Feldmann, Nikola Samardzic, Aleksandar Krastev, Srini Devadas, Ron Dreslinski, Karim Eldefrawy, Nicholas Genise, Chris Peikert, Daniel Sanchez, F1: a fast and programmable accelerator for fully homomorphic encryption (extended version), arXiv: 2109.05371, 2021.

[21] Jonas Geiping, Hartmut Bauermeister, Hannah Dröge, Michael Moeller, Inverting gradients – how easy is it to break privacy in federated learning?, in: NIPS, 2020.

[22] Craig Gentry, Fully homomorphic encryption using ideal lattices, in: STOC, 2009.

[23] Robin C. Geyer, Tassilo Klein, Moin Nabi, Differentially private federated learning: a client level perspective, 2018.

[24] Ian Goodfellow, Jean Pouget-Abadie, Mehdi Mirza, Bing Xu, David Warde-Farley, Sherjil Ozair, Aaron Courville, Yoshua Bengio, Generative adversarial networks, Communications of the ACM 63 (11) (2020) 139–144.

[25] Anupam Gupta, Katrina Ligett, Frank McSherry, Aaron Roth, Kunal Talwar, Differentially private approximation algorithms, CoRR, arXiv:0903.4510 [abs], 2009.

[26] Meng Hao, Hongwei Li, Xizhao Luo, Guowen Xu, Haomiao Yang, Sen Liu, Efficient and privacy-enhanced federated learning for industrial artificial intelligence, IEEE Transactions on Industrial Informatics 16 (10) (2020) 6532–6542.

[27] Kevin Hsieh, Aaron Harlap, Nandita Vijaykumar, Dimitris Konomis, Gregory R. Ganger, Phillip B. Gibbons, Onur Mutlu, Gaia: Geo-distributed machine learning approaching LAN speeds, in: 14th USENIX Symposium on Networked Systems Design and Implementation (NSDI 17), 2017.

[28] Fei Wang, Jie Xu, Wei Zhang, Asynchronous decentralized parallel stochastic gradient descent with differential privacy, arXiv:2008.09246, 2020.

[29] Peter Kairouz, H. Brendan McMahan, Brendan Avent, Aurélien Bellet, Mehdi Bennis, Arjun Nitin Bhagoji, Kallista Bonawitz, Zachary Charles, Graham Cormode, Rachel Cummings, et al., Advances and open problems in federated learning, Foundations and Trends in Machine Learning 14 (1–2) (2021) 1–210.

[30] Brian Knott, Shobha Venkataraman, Awni Hannun, Shubho Sengupta, Mark Ibrahim, Laurens van der Maaten, Crypten: Secure multi-party computation meets machine learning, Advances in Neural Information Processing Systems 34 (2021) 4961–4973.

[31] Jakub Konečnỳ, H. Brendan McMahan, Daniel Ramage, Peter Richtárik, Federated optimization: distributed machine learning for on-device intelligence, arXiv:1610.02527, 2016.

[32] Li Tian, Anit Kumar Sahu, Ameet Talwalkar, Virginia Smith, Federated learning: challenges, methods, and future directions, IEEE Signal Processing Magazine 37 (3) (2020) 50–60.

[33] Li Tian, Anit Kumar Sahu, Manzil Zaheer, Maziar Sanjabi, Ameet Talwalkar, Virginia Smith, Federated optimization for heterogeneous networks, arXiv:1812.06127, 2019.

[34] Xiangru Lian, Yijun Huang, Yuncheng Li, Ji Liu, Asynchronous parallel stochastic gradient for nonconvex optimization, in: Advances in Neural Information Processing Systems, 2015, pp. 2737–2745.

[35] Xiangru Lian, Wei Zhang, Ce Zhang, Ji Liu, Asynchronous decentralized parallel stochastic gradient descent, arXiv:1710.06952, 2017.

[36] Lingjuan Lyu, Han Yu, Qiang Yang, Threats to federated learning: a survey, 2020.

[37] Horia Mania, Xinghao Pan, Dimitris Papailiopoulos, Benjamin Recht, Kannan Ramchandran, Michael I. Jordan, Perturbed iterate analysis for asynchronous stochastic optimization, SIAM Journal on Optimization (2015) 2202–2229.

[38] Brendan McMahan, Daniel Ramage, Federated learning: collaborative machine learning without centralized training data, https://blog.research.google/2017/04/federated-learning-collaborative.html, 2017. (Accessed 24 September 2019).

[39] Brendan McMahan, Daniel Ramage, Kunal Talwar, Li Zhang, Learning differentially private recurrent language models, in: International Conference on Learning Representations (ICLR), 2018.

[40] H. Brendan McMahan, Eider Moore, Daniel Ramage, Blaise Agüera y Arcas, Federated learning of deep networks using model averaging, in: ICLR Workshop Track, 2016.

[41] Ilya Mironov, Rényi differential privacy, in: 2017 IEEE 30th Computer Security Foundations Symposium (CSF), IEEE, 2017, pp. 263–275.

[42] Mohammad Naseri, Jamie Hayes, Emiliano De Cristofaro, Toward robustness and privacy in federated learning: experimenting with local and central differential privacy, 2021.

[43] M. Nasr, R. Shokri, A. Houmansadr, Comprehensive privacy analysis of deep learning: passive and active white-box inference attacks against centralized and federated learning, in: 2019 IEEE Symposium on Security and Privacy (SP), 2019, pp. 739–753.

[44] Lam Nguyen, Phuong Ha Nguyen, Marten Dijk, Peter Richtárik, Katya Scheinberg, Martin Takác, SGD and Hogwild! Convergence without the bounded gradients assumption, in: International Conference on Machine Learning, PMLR, 2018, pp. 3750–3758.

[45] Lam M. Nguyen, Phuong Ha Nguyen, Peter Richtárik, Katya Scheinberg, Martin Takáč, Marten van Dijk, New convergence aspects of stochastic gradient algorithms, Journal of Machine Learning Research 20 (176) (2019) 1–49.

[46] Opacus PyTorch library. Available from opacus.ai.

[47] Nicolas Papernot, Shuang Song, Ilya Mironov, Ananth Raghunathan, Kunal Talwar, Úlfar Erlingsson, Scalable private learning with pate, in: International Conference on Learning Representations, 2018.

[48] Herbert Robbins, Sutton Monro, A stochastic approximation method, The Annals of Mathematical Statistics 22 (3) (1951) 400–407.

[49] Reza Shokri, Marco Stronati, Congzheng Song, Vitaly Shmatikov, Membership inference attacks against machine learning models, in: 2017 IEEE Symposium on Security and Privacy (SP), IEEE, 2017, pp. 3–18.

[50] L. Song, R. Shokri, P. Mittal, Membership inference attacks against adversarially robust deep learning models, in: 2019 IEEE Security and Privacy Workshops (SPW), 2019, pp. 50–56.

[51] Valery V. Starovoitov, Yu.I. Golub, Data normalization in machine learning, Informatics, 2021.

[52] Stacey Truex, Nathalie Baracaldo, Ali Anwar, Thomas Steinke, Heiko Ludwig, Rui Zhang, Yi Zhou, A hybrid approach to privacy-preserving federated learning, in: Proceedings of the 12th ACM Workshop on Artificial Intelligence and Security, 2019, pp. 1–11.

[53] Marten van Dijk, Nhuong V. Nguyen, Toan N. Nguyen, Lam M. Nguyen, Phuong Ha Nguyen, Proactive DP: a multiple target optimization framework for DP-SGD, CoRR, arXiv:2102.09030v9 [abs], 2023.

[54] Marten van Dijk, Nhuong V. Nguyen Toan, N. Nguyen, Lam M. Nguyen, Quoc Tran-Dinh, Phuong Ha Nguyen, Hogwild! Over distributed local data sets with linearly increasing mini-batch sizes, arXiv:2010.14763, 2020.

[55] Luping Wang, Wei Wang, Bo Li, CMFL: mitigating communication overhead for federated learning, in: IEEE International Conference on Distributed Computing Systems, 2019.

[56] Larry Wasserman, Shuheng Zhou, A statistical framework for differential privacy, Journal of the American Statistical Association 105 (489) (2010) 375–389.

[57] Cong Xie, Sanmi Koyejo, Indranil Gupta, Asynchronous federated optimization, arXiv: 1903.03934, 2019.

[58] Lei Yu, Ling Liu, Calton Pu, Mehmet Emre Gursoy, Stacey Truex, Differentially private model publishing for deep learning, in: 2019 IEEE Symposium on Security and Privacy (SP), May 2019.

[59] Bo Zhao, Konda Reddy Mopuri, Hakan Bilen, iDLG: improved deep leakage from gradients, arXiv:2001.02610, 2020.

[60] Ligeng Zhu, Zhijian Liu, Song Han, Deep leakage from gradients, Neurips (2019).

[61] Yuqing Zhu, Jinshuo Dong, Yu-Xiang Wang, Optimal accounting of differential privacy via characteristic function, arXiv:2106.08567, 2021.

Privacy-preserving federated learning: algorithms and guarantees

3

Xinwei Zhang, Xiangyi Chen, Bingqing Song, Prashant Khanduri, and Mingyi Hong

University of Minnesota, Minneapolis, MN, United States

3.1 Introduction

Federated learning (FL) has become indispensable for building machine learning (ML) models in distributed systems with multiple data sources and/or computing nodes. FL is a distributed learning paradigm where multiple agents, each having access to a (possibly private) local dataset, collaboratively solve a joint problem under the orchestration of a server. A standard FL problem with n agents is given by

$$\min_{\mathbf{w} \in \mathbb{R}^d} \left\{ g(\mathbf{w}) := \frac{1}{n} \sum_{m=1}^{n} g_m(\mathbf{w}) := \frac{1}{n} \sum_{m=1}^{n} \mathbb{E}_{\mathcal{D}_m} \big[\ell_m(\mathbf{w}; \mathbf{x}_m, c_m) \big] \right\} \qquad (3.1)$$

where $g : \mathbb{R}^d \to \mathbb{R}$ is the loss function; $\mathbf{w}$ is the model to be optimized; $g_m : \mathbb{R}^d \to \mathbb{R}$ is the local loss at the mth agent and is defined as $g_m(\mathbf{w}) := \mathbb{E}_{\mathcal{D}_m} \big[\ell_m(\mathbf{w}; \mathbf{x}_m, c_m) \big]$ where $\mathcal{D}_m$ is the distribution of data feature and label pairs $(\mathbf{x}_m, c_m) \sim \mathcal{D}_m$ at the mth agent. The objective of an FL system is to find a high-quality solution for problem (3.1), to ensure the agents' data privacy, while reducing the communication and computation overhead in the meantime.

Ever since the seminal paper [15] appeared in 2016, a number of algorithms have been developed to solve problem (3.1), as well as many of its variations. Among these algorithms, the Federated Averaging (FedAvg) algorithm [21] is arguably the most well known and popular. The idea of FedAvg is simple: the agents are responsible for updating the model using only local data, while the server will repeatedly collect the agents' local models, and broadcast the averaged versions of the models back to the agents. FedAvg improves the communication efficiency of FL by (i) *client sampling*, wherein only a fraction of agents participate in training within each communication round, and (ii) *intermittent model sharing*, wherein each agent is required to update their respective models multiple times before model averaging. However, it is not clear if FedAvg actually preserves the agents' data privacy. It is important to note that

Federated Learning. https://doi.org/10.1016/B978-0-44-319037-7.00011-9

although the agents in FedAvg do not directly share the data among each other (i.e., they only share the models, or sometimes the gradients), some recent works have shown that FL algorithms may still suffer from privacy leakage, i.e., the adversaries can infer some sensitive information about the agents and/or training data [20,24,26, 36,41,42]. As a consequence, it is necessary to develop FL algorithms with provable privacy guarantees while achieving desirable learning performance on problem (3.1).

Differential privacy (DP) provides ML practitioners with a mechanism to provide quantifiable privacy guarantees for training ML models [6]. The DP originally developed for centralized algorithms is referred to as *sample-level* DP. It ensures that by observing the algorithm's output, an adversary will not be able to infer if a particular data sample was included in training or not. However, in FL setting where *a large number of* agents participate in training (i.e., the so-called *cross-device* setting), it is important to protect each agent's identity. To address this, a new and more stringent notion of DP referred to as *client-level DP* has been developed recently [8,22]. In this chapter, we will discuss these notions of DP in more detail and will provide a survey of recent works addressing the two notions. The focus of this chapter will be to provide the reader with an understanding of DP in the context of FL, to discuss major challenges associated with developing DP algorithms for FL, and to pose various open problems for future research.

3.2 Background and preliminaries

In this section, we provide some basics about FL algorithms and discuss different notions of DP used in FL training.

3.2.1 The FedAvg algorithm

As discussed earlier, the goal of an FL algorithm is to solve problem (3.1) while ensuring communication and computation efficiency, as well as data privacy. The recent couple of years have seen an exponential growth in the FL research with many algorithms achieving state-of-the-art performance for different problem classes [13,14,19,40]. However, the most popular FL algorithm remains to be the standard FedAvg, stated in Algorithm 1. More specifically, in each communication round t, a subset C_t of clients is sampled. Then using the aggregated parameter from the previous round, the sampled clients update their local models by employing SGD as the local optimizer. After τ_m local updates, the sampled clients share total update differences $\Delta \mathbf{w}_m^t$ with the server. The server then aggregates the collected model differences to update the global model. Note that FedAvg presented in Algorithm 1 employs a *two-sided* learning rate where *both* local agents and the server use a well-calibrated learning rate to update the local and global models, respectively [37]. This covers the vanilla version of FedAvg as a special case, where the server's learning rate is set as $\eta_g = 1$ [21].

Algorithm 1 Federated averaging algorithm [FedAvg].

1: **Input:** Initialize parameter $\mathbf{w}^{(0)} = \mathbf{w}_m^{(0)}$ for all $m \in [n]$, the local learning rate η_ℓ, and the global learning rate η_g
2: **for** $t = 0, \ldots, \tau - 1$ **do**
3:     **for** $m \in \mathcal{C}_t \subset [n]$ with $|\mathcal{C}_t| = n_t$ **do**
4:         Set the agent's local model $\mathbf{w}_m^{t,0} = \mathbf{w}^t$
5:         **for** $r = 0, \ldots, \tau_m - 1$ **do**
6:             Compute stochastic gradient $\tilde{g}_m^{t,r}$
7:             `Local Updates:` $\mathbf{w}_m^{t,r+1} = \mathbf{w}_m^{t,r} - \eta_\ell \cdot \tilde{g}_m^{t,r}$
8:         **end for**
9:     **end for**
10:     `Averaging:` $\Delta \mathbf{w}_m^t = \mathbf{w}_m^{t,\tau_m} - \mathbf{w}^t$, $\mathbf{w}^{t+1} = \mathbf{w}^t + \eta_g \cdot \frac{1}{n_t} \cdot \sum_{m=1}^{n_t} \Delta \mathbf{w}_m^t$
11: **end for**

3.2.2 Differential privacy

DP is defined using the notion of adjacent datasets that can be characterized in an application-specific manner. The majority of ML practitioners utilize the (ϵ, δ) definition of DP [5], a slight variant of the original definition of DP given in [6]. The (ϵ, δ)-DP is defined as follows.

Definition 3.1. A randomized algorithm $\mathcal{A}$ is (ϵ, δ)-DP for some $\epsilon > 0$ and $\delta > 0$ if, for any two adjacent datasets $\mathcal{D}$ and $\mathcal{D}'$ and for any subset of outputs $\mathcal{S}$ of algorithm $\mathcal{A}$, we have

$$P(\mathcal{A}(\mathcal{D}) \in \mathcal{S}) \le e^\epsilon \cdot P(\mathcal{A}(\mathcal{D}') \in \mathcal{S}) + \delta. \tag{3.2}$$

The above definition states that for an algorithm to achieve (ϵ, δ)-DP, the output of the algorithm on two adjacent datasets should have similar distributions. This implies that any adversary having access to $\mathcal{A}(\mathcal{D})$ and $\mathcal{A}(\mathcal{D}')$ will not be able to distinguish between the two datasets, hence ensuring privacy for the two datasets. As noted earlier, the adjacent datasets can be defined in an application-specific manner. This gives rise to sample- and client-level notions of DP in FL, which we define next.

Definition 3.2 (Sample-level differential privacy (DP)). Consider a dataset $\mathcal{D} = \bigcup_{m=1}^n \mathcal{D}_m$, where m is an individual agent as defined in problem (3.1). Then an algorithm achieves (ϵ, δ) sample-level DP if (3.2) holds where the adjacent datasets $\mathcal{D}$ and $\mathcal{D}'$ differ by at most a single sample $(\mathbf{x}_m, c_m)$ at an agent $m \in [n]$.

Sample-level DP is designed in settings where individual data samples might reveal sensitive information. For example, the training data in medical diagnosis might contain patients' private information and needs to be protected. In FL, the sample-level DP is often utilized in the *cross-silo* setting where individual agents are usually organizations (e.g., hospitals in the medical diagnosis example) and the number of agents is small.

On the other hand, there are situations where individual agents' identities also need to be protected. For example, in a typical *cross-device* FL setting where lots of mobile devices participating in a join training session, the clients might not want to reveal their identity. An example is the Google Keyboard application [9] where each agent is an application user and to protect user's personal information protecting the identity of the user is necessary. For such cases, a stronger notion of DP referred to as *client-level DP* is needed.

Definition 3.3 (Client-level differential privacy (DP)). Consider a data set $\mathcal{D} = \{\mathcal{D}_m\}_{m=1}^n$, where $m \in [n]$ is an individual agent as defined in problem (3.1). Then an algorithm achieves (ϵ, δ) client-level DP if (3.2) holds where the adjacent datasets $\mathcal{D}$ and $\mathcal{D}'$ differ by at most a complete dataset, $\mathcal{D}_m$, at an agent $m \in [n]$.

Notice that client-level DP is a relatively stronger notion of DP compared to sample-level DP since it masks the identity of a complete dataset rather than just a single sample. Some useful properties of DP that make it particularly attractive for FL applications are:

1. **Post-processing,** stating that if a mechanism is DP then no further information about the database can be extracted by the adversaries. Formally, it states that

   Theorem 3.1 (Post-processing [6]). *Let $\mathcal{A} : \mathcal{X} \to \mathbb{R}$ be (ϵ, δ)-DP and $f : \mathbb{R} \to \mathbb{R}$ be an arbitrary function, then $f \circ \mathcal{A} : \mathcal{X} \to \mathbb{R}$ is also (ϵ, δ)-DP.*

   Note that Theorem 3.1 makes no assumption about the computational power of f, i.e., no matter how powerful an adversary is, it cannot affect the privacy guarantees of a DP mechanism $\mathcal{A}$.

2. **Group privacy,** implying that the DP will degrade gracefully with the size of the group.

   Theorem 3.2 (Group privacy [6]). *Let $\mathcal{A} : \mathcal{X} \to \mathbb{R}$ be (ϵ, δ)-DP, then $\mathcal{A}$ is also $(k\epsilon, ke^{(k-1)\epsilon}\delta)$-DP for groups of size k.*

3. **Composition,** implying that multiple DP mechanisms can be combined to construct more advanced DP mechanisms.

   Theorem 3.3 (Composition [6]). *Let $\mathcal{A}_i$ for $i \in [k]$ be (ϵ_i, δ_i)-DP mechanisms, then the composition $\mathcal{A}$ of all $\mathcal{A}_i$s defined as $\mathcal{A}(x) = (\mathcal{A}_1(x), \dots, \mathcal{A}_k(x))$, is $(\sum_{i=1}^k \epsilon_i, \sum_{i=1}^k \delta_i)$-DP.*

   Theorem 3.3 states that if we have k mechanisms, each guaranteeing $(\epsilon/k, \delta/k)$-DP, then the overall mechanism will guarantee (ϵ, δ)-DP. We note that the result of this composition can be improved from $\mathcal{O}(\epsilon/k)$ to $\mathcal{O}(\epsilon/\sqrt{k})$ to achieve better dependence on k [7].

These properties of DP are crucial for the development and analyses of more advanced DP mechanisms including DP-guaranteeing algorithms for FL. In the next section, we discuss algorithms for both sample and client-level DP with their associated performance guarantees.

Algorithm 2 Differentially private SGD [DP-SGD].

1: **Input:** Initial parameter $\mathbf{w}^{(0)}$, the global learning rate η_g, and the clipping threshold C.
2: **for** $t = 0, \ldots, \tau - 1$ **do**
3:     Take a random sample $\mathcal{B}^t$ of size B with sampling probability $B/|D|$.
4:     Compute stochastic gradient: $\tilde{g}^{t,i} = \nabla \ell(\mathbf{w}^t; \mathbf{x}^{(i)}, c^{(i)}), \forall i \in \mathcal{B}^t$;
5:     `Per-sample Clipping` Compute clip$(\tilde{g}^{t,i}, C)$;
6:     `Inject DP Noise:` $\tilde{\Delta}\mathbf{w}^t = \frac{1}{B}\sum_{i=1}^{B} \text{clip}(\tilde{g}^{t,i}) + \mathbf{z}^t$ such that $\mathbf{z}^t \sim \mathcal{N}(0, \sigma^2 \mathbf{I})$;
7:     `Update Model:` $\mathbf{w}^{t+1} = \mathbf{w}^t - \eta_g \cdot \tilde{\Delta}\mathbf{w}^t$.
8: **end for**

3.3 DP guaranteed algorithms

In this section, we will discuss FedAvg and other FL algorithms for obtaining some form of DP. First, we discuss the standard procedure to obtain DP in a centralized setting for a vanilla SGD algorithm. Later in the chapter, similar ideas will be utilized to develop DP algorithms for FL.

The usual mechanism to endow any algorithm with DP guarantees is by first employing a clipping operation on the output of the algorithm, such as parameters and gradients, and then adding a carefully calibrated perturbation. One can customize the centralized SGD to provide DP guarantees by adding clipping and perturbation to the gradients. Moreover, the adjacent datasets in the centralized setting are defined as two datasets differing by only a single sample (see sample-level DP in Definition 3.2), thereby ensuring privacy for each sample. The differentially private SGD with gradient clipping (referred to as DP-SGD) with tight DP guarantees is proposed in [1]; see Algorithm 2 for detailed steps. Specifically, at each iteration t, the algorithm samples a random sample $\mathcal{B}^t$ of size B and computes the stochastic gradients $\tilde{g}^{t,i}$ for each $i \in \mathcal{B}^t$. Then per-sample gradient is clipped using the gradient clipping operation (3.3).

Gradient clipping [1], where the (per-sample) gradient $\tilde{g}_m^{t,i}$ is clipped at each step (see Algorithm 2, line 5) as

$$\text{clip}(\tilde{g}^{t,i}, C) = \tilde{g}^{t,i} / \max\left(1, \frac{\|\tilde{g}^{t,i}\|_2}{C}\right), \tag{3.3}$$

with $C > 0$ being a constant. This per-sample clipping ensures that when $\|\tilde{g}^{t,i}\|_2 \leqslant C$, we keep $\tilde{g}^{t,i}$ unchanged; otherwise we scale the gradient so that $\|\tilde{g}^{t,i}\|_2 = C$. The clipping operation is a key step that ensures bounded sensitivity in output when changing training samples and allows one to obtain provable DP guarantees, where the sensitivity refers to the maximum change in the size of the output when a single data point is changed. After the clipping operation, we add a carefully calibrated noise to the individual stochastic gradients in line 6, and average the resulting quantities to update the model in line 7. The next result states the precise DP guarantees for DP-SGD Algorithm 2.

Theorem 3.4 (DP-SGD [1]). *There exist constants c_1 and c_2 so that, given the sampling probability $q = B/|\mathcal{D}|$ and the number of steps τ, for any $\varepsilon < c_1 \cdot q^2 \cdot \tau$, Algorithm 2 is (ε, δ)-differentially private for any $\delta > 0$, if we choose*

$$\sigma \geq c_2 \frac{C \cdot q \sqrt{\tau \cdot \log(1/\delta)}}{\varepsilon},$$

where $|D|$ is the total number of samples.

The proof of Theorem 3.4 follows the standard approach of approximating the final output of the algorithm by a sequential composition of bounded-norm stochastic gradients and designing the noise variance to guarantee DP. In fact, [1] provides a tighter DP guarantee compared to the simple application of the composition theorem (Theorem 3.3) by utilizing the information of the injected noise distribution. Specifically, the proof in [1] utilizes a moments accountant technique where the bounds on moments of the privacy loss random variable are tracked throughout the execution of the algorithm. These moment bounds are then used to find the tail bounds of the differential privacy random variable, thereby, guaranteeing DP.

Next, we discuss how to extend DP-SGD to FL models.

3.3.1 Sample-level DP

Sample-level DP in FL follows the same notion as centralized-DP [1], which aims to protect each sample in the union of all datasets $\mathcal{D} = \bigcup_{m=1}^{n} \mathcal{D}_m$ (see Definition 3.2). As discussed earlier, this notion of DP is useful for *cross-silo* FL problems. Similar to DP-SGD, a natural approach to ensure sample-level DP for FedAvg is to introduce gradient clipping and noise injection during the local updates in step 7 of Algorithm 1. Below, we discuss FedAvg with sample-level DP guarantees.

3.3.1.1 Algorithms and discussion

In Algorithm 3, we state the Sample-Level DP FedAvg. Note that Algorithm 3 ensures sample-level DP guarantees by adding a clipping and a noise injection procedure for the stochastic gradients evaluated at each local update. Sample-level DP has been proposed in [30], in a more general form with secure multi-party encryption protocol deployed for secure aggregation of the model parameters. Though [30] has not provided convergence or DP guarantees for the proposed approach, it has numerically demonstrated its effectiveness. In [12], convergence guarantees for Algorithm 3 have been established for the case when individual clients use a single-step gradient descent for local updates, the per sample gradient norm is bounded, no gradient clipping is used, and all the clients participate in training. Specifically, [12] showed the following result.

Theorem 3.5 (Sample-level DP-FedAvg [12]). *For $\epsilon, \delta > 0$, if the loss $\ell_m(\mathbf{x}_m, c_m)$ is G-Lipschitz then Algorithm 3 is (ϵ, δ)-DP if we choose*

$$\sigma \geq c \frac{G \cdot \sqrt{\tau \cdot \log(1/\delta)}}{|\mathcal{D}| \cdot \epsilon},$$

Algorithm 3 Sample-level differentially private FedAvg.

1: **Input:** Initialize parameter $\mathbf{w}^{(0)} = \mathbf{w}_m^{(0)}$ for all $m \in [n]$, the local learning rate η_ℓ, global learning rate η_g, the clipping threshold C, and the noise variance σ^2

2: **for** $t = 0, \ldots, \tau - 1$ **do**

3:      **for** $m \in [n]$ **do**

4:          Update agent's model $\mathbf{w}_m^{t,0} = \mathbf{w}^t$

5:          **for** $r = 0, \ldots, \tau_m - 1$ **do**

6:              Randomly sample from $\mathcal{D}_m$ and compute stochastic gradient $\tilde{g}_m^{t,r}$

7:              `Per-sample Clipping:` Compute $\mathrm{clip}(\tilde{g}_m^{t,r}, C)$

8:              Compute the local update and inject noise:

9: $$\tilde{\Delta}\mathbf{w}_m^t = \frac{1}{\tau_m} \sum_{r=0}^{\tau_m - 1} \mathrm{clip}(\tilde{g}_m^{t,r}, C) + \mathbf{z}_m^t, \text{ such that } \mathbf{z}_m^t \sim \mathcal{N}(0, \sigma^2 \mathbf{I}).$$

10:              `Update Model:` $\mathbf{w}_m^{t+1} = \mathbf{w}_m^{t+1} - \eta_\ell \cdot \tilde{\Delta}\mathbf{w}_m^t$.

11:          **end for**

12:      **end for**

13:      `Averaging:` $\mathbf{w}^{t+1} = \sum_{m=1}^{n} \frac{|\mathcal{D}_m|}{|\mathcal{D}|} \mathbf{w}_m^{t+1}$.

14: **end for**

---

where $c > 0$ is some constant and $|\mathcal{D}|$ is the total number of samples.

Note that the above guarantee resembles that in Theorem 3.4, but there is no privacy amplification compared to Theorem 3.4 as the local nodes utilize full gradients for the local updates. The authors in [12] also provide optimization guarantees for the cases when the objective function $g(\mathbf{w})$ (see Problem (3.1)) is strongly convex or satisfies the Polyak–Lojasiewicz condition. Later [17] extended sample-level DP-FedAvg developed in [12] for stochastic local updates and partial client participation. Different from Algorithm 3, the authors in [17] injected noise only after all the local updates are concluded, also since the per-sample gradient norms have been assumed to be bounded, the clipping operation was not used. Specifically, [17] shows that to achieve an (ϵ, δ)-privacy guarantee for each communication round, we require

$$\sigma \geq \sup_{m \in [n]} \left\{ c \frac{G \cdot \tau_m^2 \cdot q_m \cdot \sqrt{\log(1.25q/\delta)}}{\epsilon} \right\} \tag{3.4}$$

for some constant $c > 0$ and where $q_m = B_m/|\mathcal{D}_m|$ with B_m being the batch size and $|\mathcal{D}_m|$ the dataset size at agent m. The above Eq. (3.4) implies that if we choose a larger batch size B_m, and a large number of local updates τ_m, we will need a higher noise level for DP protection. In contrast, for FedAvg it is observed that a larger batch size and a larger number of local updates might help speed-up convergence [27]. This implies that there is a trade-off between the DP guarantees and the algorithm's convergence speed. The authors in [17] further analyze the optimization performance of sample-level DP FedAvg to understand this trade-off.

Next, we discuss some other works that address sample-level DP in the context of FL. In [11], the DP algorithm based on alternating direction method of multipliers (ADMM), DP-ADMM, is proposed. Similarly, [18] develops a stochastic primal–dual algorithm for FL with differential privacy. The authors in [3] propose a coordinate decent algorithm that incorporates the DP framework. In [4], with the goal of reducing the communication overhead while keeping the information private, the normalized and quantized gradients are transmitted. The work in [23] investigates the trade-off between communication costs and training variance under a resource-constrained FL system.

In the next subsection, we discuss the client-level DP for FL in detail.

3.3.2 Client-level DP

In this subsection, we discuss the algorithms for the client-level DP where the goal is to protect the identities of clients in contrast to individual samples (see Definition 3.3) so that an adversary could not identify which client has participated in the training by the information transmitted. Similar to sample-level DP, clipping and noise injection are the two mechanisms that ensure client-level DP. However, in contrast to sample-level DP where we clip the stochastic gradients before *each* local update, in client-level DP, there are multiple ways to implement the clipping operation. Below we discuss the major clipping strategies that protect the client-level DP for FL algorithms.

3.3.2.1 Clipping strategies for client-level DP

Three different clipping strategies are often utilized to guarantee client-level DP: the **gradient** clipping, the **local model** clipping, and the **local update difference** clipping. In the gradient clipping (see Section 3.3), we clip the local stochastic gradients before each local update [22], while in model clipping and model difference clipping, we perform the clipping operation once every communication round. Since the total number of samples accessed by the algorithm is much larger than the total communication rounds, the gradient clipping is too expensive thus it is seldom used in FL algorithms. Below, we describe the **local model** clipping and **local update difference** clipping strategies:

Model clipping [35]. The clients directly clip the models sent to the server. For FedAvg algorithm, this means performing $\text{clip}(\mathbf{w}_m^{t,\tau_m}, C)$. This method appears to be straightforward, but clipping the model directly results in a relatively large clipping threshold, so it requires adding larger perturbations.

Difference clipping [8]. The clients clip the local update difference between the initial model and the output model $\Delta \mathbf{w}_m^t$. In this method, the clients need to record the initial model. The update difference typically has smaller magnitudes than the model itself, so the clipping threshold and the perturbation can be smaller than using model clipping. Note that when $\tau_m = 1$ (i.e., only one local update step) and batchsize is one for stochastic gradient evaluation, the difference clipping is equivalent to the gradient clipping used in the DP-SGD, but in the general case where $\tau_m > 1$, their behaviors are very different.

To better compare the performance of model clipping and difference clipping strategies, we have the following two results [39, Claims 2.1, 2.2]:

1. Given any constant clipping threshold C, there exists a convex quadratic problem for which FedAvg with model clipping *does not* converge to the global optimal solution with *any* fixed $\tau_m \geq 1$ and $\eta_\ell > 0$. This can be shown by constructing a problem such that its optimal solution $\mathbf{w}^\star$ has a larger magnitude than the clipping threshold C.

2. For any linear regression problem with a fixed clipping threshold C, there exist η_ℓ and local update step $\tau_m \geq 1$ such that FedAvg with difference clipping converges to the global optimal solution. Furthermore, there exists a linear regression problem such that under the same C, η_ℓ, and τ_m, FedAvg with difference clipping converges to a better solution with a smaller loss than the original FedAvg.

These two results indicate that the difference clipping should outperform the model clipping in terms of convergence guarantees. Therefore, in the subsequent sections, we focus on understanding a particular FL algorithm that uses difference clipping.

3.3.2.2 Algorithms and discussion

To begin with, let us introduce the Clip-enabled DP-FedAvg, which is described in Algorithm 4. The difference between FedAvg in Algorithm 1 and DP-FedAvg in Algorithm 4 is line 11, where the clients first apply the clipping operation to the local update difference $\Delta \mathbf{w}_m^t$ and then add the privacy noise $\mathbf{z}_m^t$ which follows the Gaussian distribution $\mathcal{N}(0, \sigma^2)$. During the communication step, we assume that the adversary can only observe the aggregated update $\sum_{m \in C_t} \tilde{\Delta} \mathbf{w}_m^t$, and this can be guaranteed for example by using secure aggregation [2].

The key intuition for DP-FedAvg to protect client-level DP is that we expect the clients' dataset sizes to be large enough so that after performing multiple local update steps, the resulting client models have relatively good performance. By doing so, the number of communication rounds, τ, can be largely reduced and so does the corresponding privacy noise added per communication. It is worth pointing out that DP-SGD is a special case of DP-FedAvg in the following problem setting: 1) client number n is the same as the size of the dataset, 2) the local dataset size becomes 1; and 3) the number of local update is set to $\tau_m = 1$.

Related works. The client-level DP schemes were first proposed in [8] and [22], which consider a two-stage scheme: *1)* select a subset of clients to update local models; *2)* distort the sum of all local updates by clipping operation and then inject noise to the global model update. There are a number of follow-up works in guaranteeing client-level DP. In [31], the perturbation is directly performed on local models with the assumption that model parameters are upper and lower bounded; [34,35] propose a method to clip the local models parameter; [29] adapts the Bayesian privacy accounting method to the federated setting. A few other works focus on reducing the communication cost while still maintaining required privacy level, for example, [33] proposes a method to leverage the discrete Gaussian mechanism in FL. The majority of these works only provide DP guarantee for the proposed algo-

---

Algorithm 4 Client-level differentially private FedAvg [DP-FedAvg].

1: **Input:** Initialize parameter $\mathbf{w}^{(0)} = \mathbf{w}_m^{(0)}$ for all $m \in [n]$, and the local learning rate η_ℓ, the global learning rate η_g, the clipping threshold C, and noise variance σ^2;

2: **for** $t = 0, \ldots, \tau - 1$ **do**

3:      **for** $m \in C_t \subset [n]$ with $|C_t| = n_t$ in parallel **do**

4:          Update agent's model $\mathbf{w}_m^{t,0} = \mathbf{w}^t$

5:          **for** $r = 0, \ldots, \tau_m - 1$ **do**

6:              Compute stochastic gradient $\tilde{g}_m^{t,r}$

7:              `Local Updates:` $\mathbf{w}_m^{t,r+1} = \mathbf{w}_m^{t,r} - \eta_\ell \cdot \tilde{g}_m^{t,r}$

8:          **end for**

9:          `Compute update difference:` $\Delta\mathbf{w}_m^t = \mathbf{w}_m^{t,\tau_m} - \mathbf{w}^t$

10:          `Apply DP mechanism:` $\tilde{\Delta}\mathbf{w}_m^t = \text{clip}(\Delta\mathbf{w}_m^t, C) + \mathbf{z}_m^t$, such that $\mathbf{z}_m^t \sim \mathcal{N}(0, \sigma^2 \mathbf{I})$

11:      **end for**

12:      `Averaging:` $\mathbf{w}^{t+1} = \mathbf{w}^t + \eta_g \cdot \frac{1}{n_t} \cdot \sum_{m=1}^{n_t} \tilde{\Delta}\mathbf{w}_m^t$

13: **end for**

---

rithm [8,29–31], which is more or less straightforward. However, only a small subset of these works [33–35] provide convergence analysis, but these analyses are limited since they often rely upon some restrictive assumptions (e.g., it is assumed that the problem is convex and satisfies the Polyak–Lojasiewicz condition in [34,35]). Due to space limit, we will not discuss these works in detail. Instead, in the next section we will provide a recent result that *simultaneously* characterizes the convergence and privacy guarantees for the DP-SGD with difference clipping.

3.4 Performance of clip-enabled DP-FedAvg

In the previous section, we discussed various clipping strategies used for ensuring client-level DP and observed why model difference clipping should be the strategy of choice for FL applications. We introduced DP-FedAvg (Algorithm 4) that utilizes model difference clipping and adding perturbation after clipping to ensure DP. In this section, we perform a thorough theoretical and empirical investigation of Algorithm 4 with the goal of understanding the privacy and convergence guarantees associated with the algorithm.

3.4.1 Main results

The main theoretical result for FL algorithm with DP consists two parts: one is the convergence guarantee which states how well the trained model can perform; and the second part is the privacy guarantee which describes how well the algorithm can preserve the privacy in the training procedure. In most cases, privacy protection comes with the price of sacrificing the model performance, so we need to trade-off between the model performance and the privacy guarantee.

To proceed, let us first state the assumptions:

Assumption 3.1. The objective of a problem satisfies

$$g(\mathbf{w}) \geq g^\star > -\infty, \quad \text{for some constant } g^\star, \ \forall \, \mathbf{w}. \tag{3.5}$$

Assumption 3.2 (Lipschitz gradient). The gradient of the clients' functions satisfies

$$\left\| \nabla g_m(\mathbf{w}) - \nabla g_m(\mathbf{w}') \right\| \leq L \left\| \mathbf{w} - \mathbf{w}' \right\|, \ \forall \, m, \mathbf{w}, \mathbf{w}',$$

where L is the Lipschitz constant of the gradient.

Assumption 3.3 (Bounded variance). The stochastic gradient of the clients' functions is unbiased, i.e., $\mathbb{E}[\tilde{g}_m] = \nabla g_m(\mathbf{w})$ and its variance satisfies

$$\mathbb{E} \left\| \tilde{g}_m - \nabla g_m(\mathbf{w}) \right\|^2 \leq \sigma_\ell^2, \ \forall \, m, \mathbf{w},$$

for some constant σ_ℓ^2.

Besides these standard assumptions, in the analysis for DP-FedAvg, the following additional assumptions are needed.

Assumption 3.4 (Bounded gradient dissimilarity (BGD)). The inter-gradient variance between the local and global problems is bounded by some constant σ_g^2, i.e.,

$$\| \nabla g(\mathbf{w}) - \nabla g_m(\mathbf{w}) \|^2 \leq \sigma_g^2, \ \forall \, m, \mathbf{w}.$$

Assumption 3.5 (Bounded gradient). The gradient of each client's functions is upper bounded by some constant G, i.e.,

$$\| \nabla g_m(\mathbf{w}) \|^2 \leq G, \forall \, m, \mathbf{w}.$$

The BGD assumption have been used in many FL proofs (cf. [13,40]) to characterize the non-i.i.d.-ness of the client data distribution. Bounded gradient is a stricter assumption to replace the BGD assumption and has been used in the earlier works in FL algorithms (cf. [16]) and in the analysis for DP algorithm [23,32,33]. With the above assumptions, we are ready to present the theoretical results for DP-FedAvg (Algorithm 4).

3.4.1.1 Convergence theorem

Theorem 3.6 (Convergence of DP-FedAvg, [39, Theorem 3.1]). *Under Assumptions 3.1–3.5, by letting $\eta_g \eta_\ell \leq \min\{\frac{n_t}{96\tau_m^2}, \frac{n_t}{6\tau_m \cdot L(n_t-1)}\}$ and $\eta_\ell \leq \frac{1}{\sqrt{60}\tau_m \cdot L}$, for Algorithm 4, we have*

$$\frac{1}{\tau} \sum_{t=0}^{\tau-1} \mathbb{E}[\overline{\alpha}^t \| \nabla g(\mathbf{w}^t) \|^2]$$

$$\leq FedAvg\ Term + G^2 \frac{4}{\tau} \sum_{t=0}^{\tau-1} \underbrace{\mathbb{E}\left[\frac{1}{n}\sum_{m=1}^{n}(|\alpha_m^t - \tilde{\alpha}_m^t| + |\tilde{\alpha}_m^t - \overline{\alpha}^t|)\right]}_{\text{caused by clipping}}$$

$$+ \eta_g \cdot \eta_\ell \cdot L \cdot \tau_m G^2 \frac{6}{\tau} \sum_{t=0}^{\tau-1} \underbrace{\mathbb{E}\left[\frac{1}{n_t}\sum_{m=1}^{n}(|\alpha_m^t - \tilde{\alpha}_m^t|^2 + |\tilde{\alpha}_m^t - \overline{\alpha}^t|^2)\right]}_{\text{caused by clipping}}$$

$$+ \underbrace{\frac{2\eta_g \cdot L \cdot d \cdot \sigma^2}{\eta_\ell \cdot \tau_m \cdot n_t}}_{\text{caused by privacy noise}},$$

where $\alpha_m^t := \frac{C}{\max(C, \|\Delta\mathbf{w}_m^t\|)}$, $\tilde{\alpha}_m^t := \frac{C}{\max(C, \|\mathbb{E}[\Delta\mathbf{w}_m^t]\|)}$, $\overline{\alpha}^t := \frac{1}{n}\sum_{m=1}^{m}\tilde{\alpha}_m^t$; d *is the dimension of* $\mathbf{w}$, $\gamma_1(\tau) = \frac{1}{\tau}\sum_{t=0}^{\tau-1}\mathbb{E}[\overline{\alpha}^t] \leq 1$, $\gamma_2(\tau) = \frac{1}{\tau}\sum_{t=0}^{\tau-1}\mathbb{E}[(\overline{\alpha}^t)^2] \leq 1$, *and*

$$FedAvg\ Term := \frac{4(g(\mathbf{w}^0) - g^\star)}{\eta_g \cdot \eta_\ell \cdot \tau \cdot \tau_m} + \frac{25}{2}\eta_\ell^2 \cdot L \cdot \tau_m(\sigma_\ell^2 + 6\tau_m \cdot \sigma_g^2)\gamma_1(\tau)$$

$$+ \frac{6\eta_g \cdot \eta_\ell \cdot L \cdot \sigma_\ell^2}{n_t}\gamma_2(\tau).$$

In the bound of Theorem 3.6, the *FedAvg Term* is inherited from standard FedAvg with two-sided learning rates which can yield a convergence rate of $O(\frac{1}{\sqrt{n_t \cdot \tau \cdot \tau_m}} + \frac{1}{\tau})$ when setting $\eta_g = \sqrt{n_t \cdot \tau_m}$ and $\eta_\ell = \frac{1}{\sqrt{\tau \tau_m} \cdot L}$. It recovers the standard convergence bounds for FedAvg up to a constant, cf., [38, Theorem 1] when clipping operation and DP noise do not appear. Aside from the *FedAvg Term*, there are two extra terms caused by the privacy noise $\mathbf{z}_m^t$ and the clipping operation, respectively. The error term caused by privacy noise is the price for privacy protection and can be found in the analysis for DP-SGD algorithms (cf. [11,32,35]).

Let us focus on the terms caused by clipping operation, which depends on $|\alpha_m^t - \tilde{\alpha}_m^t|$ and $|\tilde{\alpha}_m^t - \overline{\alpha}^t|$. The term

$$|\alpha_m^t - \tilde{\alpha}_m^t| = \left| \frac{C}{\max(C, \|\Delta\mathbf{w}_m^t\|)} - \frac{C}{\max(C, \|\mathbb{E}[\Delta\mathbf{w}_m^t]\|)} \right|$$

characterizes the difference between the stochastic local update difference $\|\Delta\mathbf{w}_m^t\|$ and its expectation $\|\mathbb{E}\Delta\mathbf{w}_m^t\|$. It becomes zero as the variance of the stochastic gradient $\sigma_\ell^2 \to 0$. The other term $|\tilde{\alpha}_m^t - \overline{\alpha}^t|$ depends on the variance of the magnitude of the update difference across clients. Specifically, let us define the normalized variance of the magnitude of the update difference as degree of concentration (DoC), i.e., DoC$:= \mathrm{Var}(\|\Delta\mathbf{w}_m^t\|)/\overline{\|\Delta\mathbf{w}_m^t\|}^4$. When clipping is activated, i.e., $\alpha_m^t = C/\|\Delta\mathbf{w}_m^t\|$, with a first-order Taylor expansion, we can approximate this term by

$$
\left|\tilde{\alpha}_m^t - \overline{\alpha}^t\right| \approx C \cdot \sqrt{\mathrm{Var}(\|\Delta \mathbf{w}_m^t\|)/\overline{\|\Delta \mathbf{w}_m^t\|}^4} = C \cdot \sqrt{\mathrm{DoC}}.
$$

This term is affected by the gradient dissimilarity σ_g^2, since large gradient heterogeneity may induce quite disparate update difference distributions across clients.

3.4.1.2 DP guarantee

The privacy guarantee of DP-FedAvg can be characterized by standard privacy theorems on Gaussian mechanism Theorem 3.4. We can analyze the privacy–utility trade-off of DP-FedAvg by substituting σ^2 from Theorem 3.4 into Theorem 3.6. To get more insights on how parameters like τ, η_g, η_ℓ, and ϵ affect DP-FedAvg, let us simplify Theorem 3.6 to Corollary 3.1 by substituting $C \geq \eta_\ell \cdot \tau_m \cdot G$ and σ^2.

Corollary 3.1 (Convergence with privacy guarantee, [39, Corollary 3.2.1]). *Under Assumptions 3.1–3.5, for any clipping threshold $C = \eta_\ell \tau_m C'$ with $C' \geq G$, and set σ^2 as in Theorem 3.4, for any (ϵ, δ) satisfying the constraints in Theorem 3.4, we have*

$$
\frac{1}{\tau}\sum_{t=0}^{\tau-1}\mathbb{E}[\|\nabla g(\mathbf{w}^t)\|^2] \leq \underbrace{O\left(\frac{1}{\eta_g \cdot \eta_\ell \cdot \tau \cdot \tau_m} + \eta_\ell^2 \cdot \tau_m^2 + \frac{\eta_g \cdot \eta_\ell}{n_t}\right)}_{\text{standard terms for FedAvg}} \tag{3.6}
$$

$$
+ \underbrace{O\left(\frac{\eta_g \cdot \eta_\ell \cdot \tau \cdot \tau_m \cdot d \ln(\frac{1}{\delta})}{n^2 \cdot \epsilon^2}\right)}_{\text{caused by privacy noise}},
$$

and the best rate one can get from the above bound is $\tilde{O}(\frac{\sqrt{d}}{n \cdot \epsilon})$ by optimizing η_g, η_ℓ, τ, and τ_m.

A direct implication of Corollary 3.1 is that the big-O convergence rate of DP-FedAvg is the same as that of DP-SGD in terms of d, ϵ, and n (the number of samples in DP-SGD). This rate is obtained under the setting that clipping is deactivated with $C \geq \eta_\ell \cdot \tau_m \cdot G$. If $C' < G$ in Corollary 3.1, then there will be extra bias terms inherited from the bound in Theorem 3.6.

So far, we have provided the theoretical analyses for DP-FedAvg algorithm, including the convergence analysis with the error decomposition and the privacy guarantee. Next, we will show numerical results as the verification for the error decomposition and see how different choices of the hyper-parameters can affect the algorithm performance.

3.4.2 Experimental evaluation

In the experiment, we compare the performance of FedAvg (no clipping, no DP noise), clip-enabled FedAvg (no DP noise), and DP-FedAvg on EMNIST and Cifar-

Table 3.1 The accuracy difference between (a) FedAvg and clip-enabled FedAvg and (b) clip-enabled FedAvg and DP-FedAvg on Non-IID EMNIST dataset. The privacy budget is $\epsilon = 5$ for ResNet-18.

Model	d	Acc. (%)	Clipping (diff.) (%)	DP (diff.) (%)
MLP	159 K	94.0	93.1 (−1.84)	92.8 (−0.29)
AlexNet	3.3M	96.4	94.9 (−1.47)	94.7 (−**0.16**)
MobileNetV2	2.3M	97.8	97.4 (−0.35)	95.8 (−1.62)
ResNet-18	11.1M	95.2	95.3 (+**0.15**)	91.5 (−3.76)

Table 3.2 The accuracy difference between (a) FedAvg and CE-FedAvg and (b) CE-FedAvg and DP-FedAvg on IID Cifar-10 dataset.

Model	d	Acc. (%)	Clipping (diff.) (%)	DP (diff.) (%)
MLP	616 K	51.90	44.51 (−7.39)	43.60 (−0.90)
AlexNet	3.3M	66.01	61.18 (−4.83)	61.36 (+**0.18**)
ResNet-18	11.1M	76.36	75.83 (−**0.53**)	70.68 (−5.15)

10 datasets. We set the client number $n = 1920$, the number of client participates in each round $n_t = 80$, $\forall\, t$, the number of local iterations $\tau_m = 32$, and the mini-batch size 64. The clipping thresholds for clip-enabled FedAvg and DP-SGD are set to 50% of the average (over clients and iterations) of local update magnitudes recorded in FedAvg. For DP-FedAvg, the privacy budget is $\epsilon = 1.5$, $\delta = 10^{-5}$ (if not specified) and follows Theorem 3.4 to obtain the noise variance that needs to be added. These hyper-parameters are optimized for DP-FedAvg.

Error Decomposition. To understand how clipping and DP noise affect the algorithm performance, we first use the digit part of the EMNIST dataset, which has 240 K training samples and 40 K testing samples. Each client has 125 samples from 10 classes, where 109 samples belong to 2 of the classes and the other 16 samples belong to the remaining 8 classes. We conduct experiments on a 2-layer MLP with one hidden layer, AlexNet, ModelNetV2 [25], and ResNet-18. The results are listed in Table 3.1.

The second dataset we use is the Cifar-10 dataset, which has 50 K training samples and 10 K testing samples. Each client has 500 samples which can overlap with those on the other clients and the samples on each client are uniformly distributed in 10 classes. We conduct experiments on a 2-layer MLP with one hidden layer, AlexNet and ResNet-18. The results are listed in Table 3.2.

Degree of Concentration and Clipping Error. In Fig. 3.1, we compare a 2-layer MLP, AlexNet, ResNet-18, and GoogLeNet [28] on IID and Non-IID Cifar-10 datasets and plot the accuracy drop caused by clipping versus DoC averaged over all iterations. In the Non-IID case, each client has 50 samples which can overlap with those of the other clients, and the samples of each client are uniformly distributed in 10 classes. The lighter side of the line denotes the result of IID data, and the darker

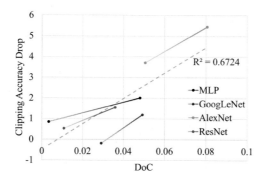

FIGURE 3.1

The relationship between averaged degree of concentration of the update differences and the clipping accuracy drop for IID (light end) and Non-IID (dark end) Cifar-10 dataset.

side denotes the Non-IID data. We can see that when DoC is small (i.e., the update differences' magnitudes are more concentrated), then the accuracy drop caused by the clipping is also small, and vice versa. From the experiments, we have the following observations:

1. It appears that when the underlying machine learning model is *structured* (e.g., many layers, has convolution layers, skip connections, etc.), the update difference of FedAvg becomes *concentrated*, yielding a better clipping performance (as suggested by the terms related to clipping in Theorem 3.6).
2. When the model has too many parameters, they are sensitive to privacy noise. This is reasonable since the error term caused by the privacy noise in Theorem 3.6 linearly depends on the size of the model d and the square of the Lipschitz constant L (note, that $\eta_\ell \propto 1/L$). From [10, Corollary 3.3], we know that L increases exponentially with the number of layers. Therefore, larger and deeper models are potentially more sensitive to privacy noise.
3. We conjecture that, to ensure good performance of DP-FedAvg, we need to pick a neural network that is structured enough, while not having too many variables and too many layers.

3.5 **Conclusion and future work**

In this chapter, we first discussed sample- and client-level DP, then reviewed DP-FedAvg along with analyses on the effects of clipping and noise. FL with DP is still an active area of research and there are still plenty of open problems. The characterization of the clipping effect and noise effect unlocked many future research opportunities. One future direction is to characterize more rigorously the impact of network architecture on update distribution to provide guidance on designing network architectures that are more clipping-friendly or noise-resilient. Another opportunity is to come up with new loss functions/model components/clipping methods/training algorithms to improve model performance, coping with the effect of clipping, noise, and local updates.

References

[1] Martin Abadi, Andy Chu, Ian Goodfellow, H. Brendan McMahan, Ilya Mironov, Kunal Talwar, Li Zhang, Deep learning with differential privacy, in: Proceedings of the 2016 ACM SIGSAC Conference on Computer and Communications Security, 2016, pp. 308–318.

[2] Keith Bonawitz, Vladimir Ivanov, Ben Kreuter, Antonio Marcedone, H. Brendan McMahan, Sarvar Patel, Daniel Ramage, Aaron Segal, Karn Seth, Practical secure aggregation for privacy-preserving machine learning, in: Proceedings of the 2017 ACM SIGSAC Conference on Computer and Communications Security, 2017, pp. 1175–1191.

[3] Georgios Damaskinos, Celestine Mendler-Dünner, Rachid Guerraoui, Nikolaos Papandreou, Thomas Parnell, Differentially private stochastic coordinate descent, in: Proceedings of the AAAI Conference on Artificial Intelligence, vol. 35, 2021, pp. 7176–7184.

[4] Rudrajit Das, Abolfazl Hashemi, Sujay Sanghavi, Inderjit S. Dhillon, Dp-normfedavg: normalizing client updates for privacy-preserving federated learning, arXiv:2106.07094, 2021.

[5] Cynthia Dwork, Krishnaram Kenthapadi, Frank McSherry, Ilya Mironov, Moni Naor, Our data, ourselves: privacy via distributed noise generation, in: Annual International Conference on the Theory and Applications of Cryptographic Techniques, Springer, 2006, pp. 486–503.

[6] Cynthia Dwork, Aaron Roth, et al., The algorithmic foundations of differential privacy, Foundations and Trends in Theoretical Computer Science 9 (3–4) (2014) 211–407.

[7] Cynthia Dwork, Guy N. Rothblum, Salil Vadhan, Boosting and differential privacy, in: 2010 IEEE 51st Annual Symposium on Foundations of Computer Science, IEEE, 2010, pp. 51–60.

[8] Robin C. Geyer, Tassilo Klein, Moin Nabi, Differentially private federated learning: a client level perspective, arXiv:1712.07557, 2017.

[9] Andrew Hard, Kanishka Rao, Rajiv Mathews, Swaroop Ramaswamy, Françoise Beaufays, Sean Augenstein, Hubert Eichner, Chloé Kiddon, Daniel Ramage, Federated learning for mobile keyboard prediction, arXiv:1811.03604, 2018.

[10] Calypso Herrera, Florian Krach, Josef Teichmann, Estimating full Lipschitz constants of deep neural networks, arXiv:2004.13135, 2020.

[11] Zonghao Huang, Rui Hu, Yuanxiong Guo, Eric Chan-Tin, Yanmin Gong, DP-ADMM: ADMM-based distributed learning with differential privacy, IEEE Transactions on Information Forensics and Security 15 (2019) 1002–1012.

[12] Yilin Kang, Yong Liu, Ben Niu, Weiping Wang, Weighted distributed differential privacy erm: convex and non-convex, Computers & Security 106 (2021) 102275.

[13] Sai Praneeth Karimireddy, Satyen Kale, Mehryar Mohri, Sashank Reddi, Sebastian Stich, Ananda Theertha Suresh, SCAFFOLD: Stochastic controlled averaging for federated learning, in: International Conference on Machine Learning, PMLR, 2020, pp. 5132–5143.

[14] Prashant Khanduri, Pranay Sharma, Haibo Yang, Mingyi Hong, Jia Liu, Ketan Rajawat, Pramod Varshney, STEM: A stochastic two-sided momentum algorithm achieving near-optimal sample and communication complexities for federated learning, Advances in Neural Information Processing Systems 34 (2021) 6050–6061.

[15] Jakub Konečný, H. Brendan McMahan, Daniel Ramage, Peter Richtárik, Federated optimization: distributed machine learning for on-device intelligence, arXiv:1610.02527, 2016.

[16] Xiang Li, Kaixuan Huang, Wenhao Yang, Shusen Wang, Zhihua Zhang, On the convergence of fedavg on non-iid data, arXiv:1907.02189, 2019.

[17] Yiwei Li, Tsung-Hui Chang, Chong-Yung Chi, Secure federated averaging algorithm with differential privacy, in: 2020 IEEE 30th International Workshop on Machine Learning for Signal Processing (MLSP), IEEE, 2020, pp. 1–6.

[18] Yiwei Li, Shuai Wang, Tsung-Hui Chang, Chong-Yung Chi, Federated stochastic primal–dual learning with differential privacy, arXiv:2204.12284, 2022.

[19] Xianfeng Liang, Shuheng Shen, Jingchang Liu, Zhen Pan, Enhong Chen, Yifei Cheng, Variance reduced local SGD with lower communication complexity, arXiv:1912.12844, 2019.

[20] Lingjuan Lyu, Han Yu, Qiang Yang, Threats to federated learning: a survey, arXiv:2003.02133, 2020.

[21] Brendan McMahan, Eider Moore, Daniel Ramage, Seth Hampson, Blaise Aguera y Arcas, Communication-efficient learning of deep networks from decentralized data, in: Artificial Intelligence and Statistics, PMLR, 2017, pp. 1273–1282.

[22] H. Brendan McMahan, Daniel Ramage, Kunal Talwar, Li Zhang, Learning differentially private recurrent language models, arXiv:1710.06963, 2017.

[23] Nima Mohammadi, Jianan Bai, Qiang Fan, Yifei Song, Yang Yi, Lingjia Liu, Differential privacy meets federated learning under communication constraints, IEEE Internet of Things Journal (2021).

[24] Hanchi Ren, Jingjing Deng, Xianghua Xie, GRNN: Generative regression neural network—a data leakage attack for federated learning, ACM Transactions on Intelligent Systems and Technology (TIST) 13 (4) (2022) 1–24.

[25] Mark Sandler, Andrew Howard, Menglong Zhu, Andrey Zhmoginov, Liang-Chieh Chen, MobileNetV2: inverted residuals and linear bottlenecks, in: Proceedings of the IEEE Conference on Computer Vision and Pattern Recognition, 2018, pp. 4510–4520.

[26] Reza Shokri, Marco Stronati, Congzheng Song, Vitaly Shmatikov, Membership inference attacks against machine learning models, in: 2017 IEEE Symposium on Security and Privacy (SP), IEEE, 2017, pp. 3–18.

[27] Sebastian U. Stich, Jean-Baptiste Cordonnier, Martin Jaggi, Sparsified SGD with memory, Advances in Neural Information Processing Systems 31 (2018).

[28] Christian Szegedy, Wei Liu, Yangqing Jia, Pierre Sermanet, Scott Reed, Dragomir Anguelov, Dumitru Erhan, Vincent Vanhoucke, Andrew Rabinovich, Going deeper with convolutions, in: Proceedings of the IEEE Conference on Computer Vision and Pattern Recognition, 2015, pp. 1–9.

[29] Aleksei Triastcyn, Boi Faltings, Federated learning with Bayesian differential privacy, in: 2019 IEEE International Conference on Big Data (Big Data), IEEE, 2019, pp. 2587–2596.

[30] Stacey Truex, Nathalie Baracaldo, Ali Anwar, Thomas Steinke, Heiko Ludwig, Rui Zhang, Yi Zhou, A hybrid approach to privacy-preserving federated learning, in: Proceedings of the 12th ACM Workshop on Artificial Intelligence and Security, 2019, pp. 1–11.

[31] Stacey Truex, Ling Liu, Ka-Ho Chow, Mehmet Emre Gursoy, Wenqi Wei, LDP-Fed: Federated learning with local differential privacy, in: Proceedings of the Third ACM International Workshop on Edge Systems, Analytics and Networking, 2020, pp. 61–66.

[32] Di Wang, Changyou Chen, Jinhui Xu, Differentially private empirical risk minimization with non-convex loss functions, in: International Conference on Machine Learning, PMLR, 2019, pp. 6526–6535.

[33] Lun Wang, Ruoxi Jia, Dawn Song, D2P-Fed: differentially private federated learning with efficient communication, arXiv:2006.13039, 2020.

[34] Kang Wei, J.G. Li, Ming Ding, Chuan Ma, Hang Su, Bo Zhang, H. Vincent Poor, Performance analysis and optimization in privacy-preserving federated learning, arXiv:2003.00229, 2020.

[35] Kang Wei, Jun Li, Ming Ding, Chuan Ma, Howard H. Yang, Farhad Farokhi, Shi Jin, Tony Q.S. Quek, H. Vincent Poor, Federated learning with differential privacy: algorithms and performance analysis, IEEE Transactions on Information Forensics and Security 15 (2020) 3454–3469.

[36] Wenqi Wei, Ling Liu, Margaret Loper, Ka-Ho Chow, Mehmet Emre Gursoy, Stacey Truex, Yanzhao Wu, A framework for evaluating gradient leakage attacks in federated learning, arXiv:2004.10397, 2020.

[37] Haibo Yang, Minghong Fang, Jia Liu, Achieving linear speedup with partial worker participation in non-iid federated learning, in: International Conference on Learning Representations, 2020.

[38] Haibo Yang, Minghong Fang, Jia Liu, Achieving linear speedup with partial worker participation in non-iid federated learning, arXiv:2101.11203, 2021.

[39] Xinwei Zhang, Xiangyi Chen, Mingyi Hong, Steven Wu, Jinfeng Yi, Understanding clipping for federated learning: convergence and client-level differential privacy, in: International Conference on Machine Learning, PMLR, 2022, pp. 26048–26067.

[40] Xinwei Zhang, Mingyi Hong, Sairaj Dhople, Wotao Yin, Yang Liu, FedPD: A federated learning framework with adaptivity to non-iid data, IEEE Transactions on Signal Processing 69 (2021) 6055–6070.

[41] Bo Zhao, Konda Reddy Mopuri, Hakan Bilen, iDLG: improved deep leakage from gradients, arXiv:2001.02610, 2020.

[42] Ligeng Zhu, Zhijian Liu, Song Han, Deep leakage from gradients, Advances in Neural Information Processing Systems 32 (2019).

Assessing vulnerabilities and securing federated learning

Supriyo Chakraborty[a] and Arjun Bhagoji[b]

[a]*Distributed AI, IBM Research, Yorktown Heights, NY, United States*
[b]*Department of Computer Science, University of Chicago, Chicago, IL, United States*

4.1 Introduction

Federated Learning (FL) has been a great enabler for distributed computation across different users (*cross-device*) and organizations (*cross-silo*), even in cases where they have very different local data distributions [19]. In this chapter, we focus our attention on how the design objectives of privacy and distributed model training in FL also lead to security vulnerabilities. We provide an overview of existing work showing these vulnerabilities exist during both training (*poisoning attacks*) of federated models and also at deployment time (*inference attacks*), depending on the attacker's aims and capabilities.

The ease of carrying out these attacks has worrying implications given the wide adoption of FL in both enterprises as well as security-critical domains such as healthcare and banking. In light of this, a wide variety of defenses have been proposed to secure FL systems. The operational viability of these defenses depends on the utility and computational trade-offs they introduce, which we briefly discuss. We conclude with a discussion on the feasibility of the attacks on production-scale systems and their implications on future FL system design.

4.2 Background and vulnerability analysis

In this section, we begin by defining an abstract version of the FL system and then lay out the notation used in the remainder of this chapter. We describe the different modes in which federation is performed, together with their update aggregation policies. With this background knowledge of the functioning of an FL system, we then highlight unique properties of FL that lead to vulnerabilities that are not present in centralized learning systems. In particular, we analyze the ability of each client to directly update the model parameters, often in an opaque manner, as well as their repeated interaction with the model parameters during model training that enable them to launch powerful attacks during training.

Federated Learning. https://doi.org/10.1016/B978-0-44-319037-7.00012-0

4.2.1 Definitions and notation

In a typical FL setup, there are a number of clients n, each holding a portion of the training dataset $\mathcal{D}_k$, where k denotes the kth client. We use $\mathcal{D} = \bigcup_{k=1}^{n} \mathcal{D}_k$ to denote the entire dataset. At each round t, some or all of the clients (a chosen subset S_t) receive the current state of the global model from the server, and compute an update using their data. They may train for a single epoch or multiple epochs. The server then aggregates model updates from each of the clients in S_t at each communication round t using some aggregation rule $\mathcal{A}$. Due to privacy concerns, the clients do not share data with each other or with the server. Further, each client's updates are only ever seen by the server, and not by other clients. A malicious client is denoted by m. It has access to a subset of training data $\mathcal{D}_m$ as well as to an auxiliary dataset $\mathcal{D}_{aux,m} = \{(x_i, y_i)\}_{i=1}^{r}$ that is drawn from the same distribution as the training and test data, and $\mathcal{D}_m \cap \mathcal{D}_{aux,m} = \emptyset$. The set of malicious clients is denoted by $[M]$. During a backdoor attack (described later), the adversarial goal is to ensure targeted misclassification of the auxiliary data to desired target labels $\{\tau_i\}_{i=1}^{r}$. The test dataset is denoted by $\mathcal{D}_{test}$.

There are two ways in which the data may be partitioned among clients: record- and feature-level [19,46]. In record-level partitioning (horizontal FL), clients control *disjoint subsets of data points, all having the same features.* In contrast, for feature-level partitioning (vertical FL[1]), *each client controls different features for the same set of records.*

4.2.1.1 Horizontal federated learning

In record-partitioned FL, the global model $\mathbf{w}^{(t)}$ at time t is updated as follows:

$$\mathbf{w}^{(t)} = \mathbf{w}^{(t-1)} + \mathcal{A}(\{\mathbf{w}_k^{(t)} - \mathbf{w}^{(t-1)}\}_{k \in S_t}), \tag{4.1}$$

with $\delta_k^{(t)} = \mathbf{w}_k^{(t)} - \mathbf{w}^{(t-1)}$ being the update from client k.[2] We will use the shorthand $\delta_k^{(t)}$ to refer to client k's update henceforth. One of the most commonly used aggregation rules is averaging, introduced in the federated learning paper by [29]. This algorithm, referred to as FedAvg, weights the update from each client proportional to the number of records ($|\mathcal{D}_k|$) it has, and also randomly selects a subset of clients S_t at each time step from among the total of n clients:

$$\mathbf{w}^{(t)} = \mathbf{w}^{(t-1)} + \sum_{k \in S_t} \frac{|\mathcal{D}_k|}{|\mathcal{D}|} \delta_k^{(t)}, \tag{4.2}$$

where $|\mathcal{D}|$ is the total number of records.

---

[1] The terms horizontal and vertical are a reference to how these partitions can be constructed from a matrix containing all available data. Usually, the $n \times d$ matrix will have the records as the rows, and the features as the columns. Thus, a horizontal partition will lead to record-level partitioning, and a similar logic applies for the vertical partition.

[2] For simplicity, we omit the superscript (t) when the time step under consideration is clear from the context.

4.2.1.2 Vertical federated learning

In vertical or feature-partitioned FL, each client k holds a distinct portion of the features for all S samples [10,24]. Thus, for $i \in [S]$, client k holds $\mathbf{x}_{i,k}$, with $\mathbf{x}_i = \bigcup_{k \in [n]} \mathbf{x}_{i,k}$. Each client learns a local embedding $\mathbf{h}_k$ parametrized by $\mathbf{w}_k$, with $\mathbf{h}_k = g(\mathbf{w}_k, \{\mathbf{x}_{i,k}\}_{k \in [n]})$ that usually maps the high-dimensional input to a lower-dimensional one. The labels y_i for each sample are usually held by the server or a third party for privacy reasons. The optimization problem that the server solves is then

$$\min_{\mathbf{w}_0} L(\mathbf{w}_0, \mathbf{w}_1, \dots, \mathbf{w}_n) = \frac{1}{S} \sum_{i=1}^{S} \ell(\hat{y}_i, y_i) + \sum_{k=1}^{n} r(\mathbf{w}_k), \qquad (4.3)$$

where $\hat{y}_i = f_{\mathbf{w}_0}(\mathbf{h}_{i,1}, \dots, \mathbf{h}_{i,n})$ and $r(\cdot)$ is a regularizer on the local model parameters. Existing work adopts iterative, query-based procedures for solving this optimization problem.

4.2.2 Vulnerability analysis

From the overview of FL algorithms above, it is clear that they have clear advantages over centralized algorithms in terms of their privacy and computational considerations. Clients' data remains private, and even their model updates are only ever shared with the server. Further, each client can train for multiple epochs before returning an update to the server, reducing both computational and communication complexity. However, these same properties lead to severe security vulnerabilities, introducing an interesting trade-off between privacy and security for FL. We mostly focus on attacks that can be carried out during training when describing FL's vulnerabilities, since this is where the key differences from centralized training arise. Once the model has been trained and deployed, it is vulnerable to the same attacks as a centrally-trained model.

4.2.2.1 Clients' updates

There are two key properties of the updates from clients that make it easy for a malicious client aiming to embed unwanted behavior in the model, or even completely disrupt training. These are the *opacity* and *high-dimensionality* of the updates.

Opacity of updates. In centralized learning, when poisoning attacks at training time are carried out [5,31], the poisoned data is directly accessible to the model trainer for inspection. This places constraints on the visibility of the backdoor patterns and perturbations used to poison the data. However, in FL, any client can poison his/her data, leading to a poisoned update. When communicated back to the server, the poisoned update can lead to the embedding of undesired behavior in the global model. However, unlike in the centralized setting, the server has no access to the poisoned training data and must analyze the update directly to determine if it has been computed with respect to poisoned data. While [4] showed that data poisoning may not be as effective in FL as in the centralized setting, the more pernicious threat of *model poisoning* only exists in the federated setting.

In model poisoning, malicious clients can directly modify the model updates they communicate to the server. This is a vulnerability that exists exclusively in FL, since in a centralized setting, the only entity that can modify model parameters is the model trainer. This vulnerability can be further compounded by privacy measures such as secure aggregation [7] where model updates are encrypted in order to ensure that the server cannot see any single client's update in plain text. In this setting, isolating the client(s) whose update(s) lead to undesirable behavior is extremely challenging.

High-dimensionality of updates. Even if mechanisms like secure aggregation are not used, the model updates are of extremely high-dimension, particularly when training deep neural networks. This is in stark contrast to the centralized setting, where the data provided is of a relatively lower dimension compared to the model parameters and can be analyzed by a human-in-the-loop if any malicious behavior is suspected. Directly analyzing model updates for malicious behavior that may have a dimension in the millions is challenging, if not impossible, for a human-in-the-loop. Thus, automated defense techniques need to be developed. However, the problem is like finding a needle in a haystack, due to the small number of model parameters that usually need to be modified to embed undesirable behavior, as well as a lack of transparency with regard to the malicious clients' goals.

4.2.2.2 Repeated interaction

In data poisoning attacks on centralized learning, the attacker gets a single opportunity to interact with the training process of the model: when they provide data to the model trainer. This gives the model trainer ample opportunities to disrupt the backdoor embedding by changing the data ordering, sub-sampling the data, etc. In spite of these possibilities, defending against data poisoning has been challenging [20].

This vulnerability is amplified in the federated setting since the malicious clients can interact repeatedly with the global model. In fact, depending on the fraction of malicious clients in the system, there may be a malicious client in every communication round, enabling them to embed undesirable behavior with high effectiveness [2,4]. Further, the malicious clients can learn, over iterations, which are the best parameters in the model to modify for the undesirable behavior to be inserted most effectively [48].

4.3 Attacks on federated learning

The democratization of training via FL implies that untrusted clients with malicious objectives can also get included in the training process. During the multiple rounds of training, these clients share high-dimensional model updates that are generated locally using processes into which the server has no control or visibility. Furthermore, the possibility of repeated interaction provides increased opportunities to influence the training process. These vulnerabilities have been exploited to demonstrate a series of effective attacks on FL systems. These attacks can be broadly categorized into *training-time* and *inference-time* attacks depending on when they are mounted. In the remainder of this section, we present a taxonomy and brief overview of attacks proposed in the literature.

4.3.1 Training-time attacks

These are attacks aimed at manipulating the training phase of a model leading to degraded performance on a range of metrics at test-time, which can either be on targeted samples or indiscriminately. The training phase can be decomposed into *training data collection* and *learning*. Training-time attacks typically target the data collection step by poisoning (i.e., performing adversarial manipulation) the raw training data samples or their labels – and are referred to as *data poisoning attacks* [15]. However, in an FL setup, data are never shared, instead, a malicious client can directly poison the model parameters that are shared as updates with the server. This is a new attack vector that arises due to the unique constraints of federated training and is referred to as *model poisoning* [4]. In fact, empirical evidence shows that model poisoning attacks are strictly stronger than data poisoning attacks [2,4]. Depending on the objective of training time attacks, we can group them further into *Byzantine* and *backdoor* attacks.

4.3.1.1 Byzantine attacks

These are attacks designed to make the model unusable by preventing the training process, more specifically, the aggregation algorithm at the server, from converging to a *good* minimum. A Byzantine client can in principle send an update that can deviate arbitrarily from the update that it is supposed to send. However, to avoid detection at the server, the adversarial update is suitably modified depending on the (*full* or *partial*) knowledge of the system – including the aggregation rule, the estimate of the updates from other clients and so on [5,6]. In response to the threat of Byzantine attacks, a host of defenses with different properties and applicability have been proposed (see Section 4.4.1.1). In an emerging arms race, Byzantine attacks with modifications have been proposed [3,23,43] to circumvent Byzantine resilient aggregation rules, at least in practical settings. One such attack is local model poisoning [15]. In this attack, compromised clients send carefully crafted updates in each iteration of FL. The updates are optimized to push the global model parameters towards the inverse of the direction along which the global model parameters would change without the attack. This attack has been shown to be highly successful against Byzantine-resilient aggregation mechanisms.

4.3.1.2 Backdoor attacks

These attacks are aimed at manipulating a subset of training samples by injecting *triggers* such that the machine learning models trained on the poisoned dataset will make incorrect predictions on test samples with the same embedded trigger [2,42]. Unlike Byzantine attacks, backdoor attacks are not designed to degrade the overall performance of the model or cause indiscriminate errors on test samples. Instead, the goal of a backdoor attack is to inject a *stealthy* or undetectable backdoor in the model, such that it predicts a target label τ on any input data that embeds the attacker-chosen trigger. Furthermore, backdoor attacks explicitly optimize their objective to allow training convergence and high model performance (in terms of chosen metrics such as accuracy) on most test samples (i.e., simultaneously fit both the backdoor and the main tasks). Depending on how the global trigger is injected into the model, we can further group proposed attacks into *centralized* and *distributed* backdoor attacks. In the centralized setting, all the malicious clients embed the same trigger in their updates, i.e., the global trigger is shared. In the decentralized setting, the global trigger is decomposed into local patterns and these smaller trigger patterns are then shared with the malicious clients.

Centralized sample-based trigger. One of the first centralized model poisoning-based backdoor attacks was introduced in [4]. They analyze the feasibility of a successful backdoor attack with a single malicious client, and also with M colluding malicious clients sharing the same auxiliary dataset, i.e., $\mathcal{D}_{aux,m} = \mathcal{D}_{aux}$ for $m = 1, \ldots, M$, under probabilistic selection. In this attack, every data sample in the auxiliary dataset is a trigger with target label τ_i. In other words, for a given classifier f, the adversarial objective is to maximize the targeted misclassification of every sample in $\mathcal{D}_{aux}$ (or equivalently, minimize loss) as follows:

$$L_{\text{attack}}(\mathcal{D}_m \cup \mathcal{D}_{aux}, \tilde{\mathbf{w}}^{(t)}) = \max_{\tilde{\mathbf{w}}^{(t)}} \sum_{i=1}^{r} \mathbb{1}[f(x_i; \tilde{\mathbf{w}}^{(t)}) = \tau_i], \qquad (4.4)$$

where $\mathbb{1}$ is the identity function that produces an output of 1 when the condition is satisfied and 0 otherwise. Note, in Eq. (4.4), $\tilde{\mathbf{w}}^{(t)} = \mathbf{w}^{(t-1)} + \alpha_m \delta_m^{(t)}$ is used an estimate of the global model at timestep t. This is because the malicious agent, in practice, is expected to have limited to no visibility into the updates shared by the other (benign) clients.[3] Also α_m is an appropriately chosen factor used to scale the malicious update to ensure that it is not canceled out by the magnitude of the benign updates during aggregation. The need for scaling the malicious update before sharing with the server has also been emphasized in [38].

The authors also defined a second accuracy objective to ensure that the performance of the malicious update on the test dataset (denoted by $\mathcal{D}_{test}$) is close to that of the global model (updated with data from all clients expect the malicious one). Formally,

$$\sum_{(x_j, y_j) \in \mathcal{D}_{test}} \mathbb{1}[f(x_j; \mathbf{w}_{S_t \setminus m}^{(t)}) = y_j] - \mathbb{1}[f(x_j; \tilde{\mathbf{w}}^{(t)}) = y_j] < \gamma_t, \qquad (4.5)$$

where γ_t is the threshold that a server could use to reject an update. A small value of γ_t implies that the malicious update should be very similar to the benign updates and hence highly stealthy.

---

[3] The authors of [4] also analyze the impact of using the average of updates from other agents during previous time steps as an estimate of their current update. They find it increases attack success marginally.

An *alternating minimization strategy* is used for simultaneously optimizing Eqs. (4.4) and (4.5). For a certain number of steps, the malicious objective in Eq. (4.4) is optimized using the samples in $\mathcal{D}_{aux}$ to generate an update. This update is then used for optimizing the accuracy objective over $\mathcal{D}_m$. These two steps are alternately repeated until a stealthy and malicious update is successfully generated.

Centralized semantic-based trigger. This attack was conceptualized in [2] and evaluated for M colluding malicious clients sharing the same auxiliary dataset $\mathcal{D}_{aux}$. The triggers are defined based on the semantic properties of the data. For example, a semantically backdoored image-classification model would misclassify all *purple cars* as *birds*. In this case, $\mathcal{D}_{aux}$ would contain the images with label *purple car* and the target label for the entire class will be set to *bird*. The malicious client is free to choose either naturally occurring features in the data sample, or features that cannot occur without the client's involvement (e.g., images of a special hat or glasses that only the malicious client has).

The malicious client performs *model replacement* to insert the backdoor. The idea is to substitute the global model with a model $\tilde{w}$ given by

$$\tilde{w} = w^{(t-1)} + \frac{\eta}{n} \sum_{k \in S_t} \delta_k^{(t)},\tag{4.6}$$

where n is the number of clients, η is the global learning rate, and $\delta_k^{(t)} = w_k^{(t)} - w^{(t-1)}$. Note that this is the same as Eq. (4.2) when $|\mathcal{D}_k| = \frac{|\mathcal{D}|}{n}$ and $\eta = 1$. For model replacement to be effective, the attack should be performed when the model is nearing convergence. This is because in the initial rounds of federated training, the local models maybe be far away from the global model, however, as training progresses and the model converges, the deviation of the local model from the global model start to cancel out. In other words, $\delta_k^{(t)} \approx 0$.

Thus, near convergence, the malicious client can compute the update that it should share for model replacement as

$$w_m^{(t)} = \frac{n}{\eta}\tilde{w} - (\frac{n}{\eta} - 1)w^{(t-1)} - \sum_{k \in S_t \setminus m} \delta_k^{(t)} \approx \frac{n}{\eta}(\tilde{w} - w^{(t-1)}) + w^{(t-1)}.\tag{4.7}$$

The attack scales up the update by a factor of $\frac{n}{\eta}$ to ensure that the backdoor survives the averaging and the global model is thus replaced by $\tilde{w}$.

Distributed trigger. The above attacks are both *dirty label* attacks, in which only the label of the samples in the auxiliary dataset are changed to the target label. The data samples are not perturbed and in their entirety form the trigger. A more general formulation of the adversarial objective in round t that accounts even for data perturbation can be stated as in [42]:

$$\underset{w_m^{(t)}}{\arg\max} \left(\sum_{x_j \in \mathcal{D}_{aux,m}} Pr[f(R(x_j, \phi); w_m^{(t)}) = \tau] + \sum_{x_j \in \mathcal{D}_m} Pr[f(x_j; w_m^{(t)}) = y_j] \right),\tag{4.8}$$

where Pr denotes the probability of the event. The function R transforms clean data in the auxiliary dataset by embedding an attacker-chosen trigger pattern using a set of parameters ϕ. For example, for image data, ϕ can be decomposed into parameters, trigger location TL and trigger size TS.

In distributed trigger-based attacks, the global trigger (which was embedded as a whole in the centralized attacks and in Eq. (4.8)) is geometrically decomposed into local triggers which are then distributed across multiple malicious clients. The malicious clients collude and embed their local triggers in the model. At test time, samples with the whole global trigger are misclassified by the backdoored model. The distributed re-formulation of Eq. (4.8) for all $m \in [M]$ malicious clients is given by

$$\underset{\mathbf{w}_m^{(t)}}{\arg\max} \left(\sum_{x_j \in \mathcal{D}_{aux,m}} Pr[f(R(x_j, \phi_m^*); \mathbf{w}_m^{(t)}) = \tau] + \sum_{x_j \in \mathcal{D}_m} Pr[f(x_j; \mathbf{w}_m^{(t)}) = y_j] \right),$$

(4.9)

where ϕ_m^* is the agent-specific geometric decomposition strategy based on the global trigger ϕ. Not only does this attack exploit the distributed framework of federated training, but, interestingly, the malicious clients do not need to synchronize their updates to the server, for the global trigger to be embedded into the model [42].

Attacking vertical FL. All previously described attacks are designed for the horizontal or record-partitioned FL setting. Liu et al. [26] proposed an attack against vertical FL, with the key difference being that the attacker does not have access to all features for a given sample when carrying out an attack, but they do have access to all samples. A further challenge is that the labels for each sample are typically only held by a single client or the server. Depending on the level of access available to the attacker, the authors of [26] propose a series of attacks, with the key intuition being that for a successful attack, the attacker just has to change the mapping between activations for the feature set under their control from the true label to the target label. In the most challenging case when the attacker cannot infer the labels for data samples, they assume access to at least one sample with the same label as the target class. In this case, then, the attack uses the received gradient with respect to this sample as the poison gradient for any poisoned sample for the relevant features (along with scaling as in the attack by [4]). However, when the server trains using the backdoored gradients, it uses the true labels, inserting a dependence between the backdoor and the true label. This dependence is broken by using random vectors during training and only using the poisoned gradients at test time.

The various attacks presented above are popular representative attacks in their categories. Our intention was never to provide an exhaustive survey of the numerous other variants of Byzantine and backdoor attacks that have been proposed, but to enable the reader to start categorizing existing attacks based on the above taxonomy. We believe that this systemization of existing attacks will lead to a better understanding of the vulnerabilities and facilitate research into developing robust FL algorithms.

4.3.2 Inference-time attacks

Once a model has been trained using FL and deployed for inference, it is vulnerable to adversarial examples in the same way as a model that had been trained in a traditional centralized setting. Adversarial examples are inputs to machine learning models, at inference time, that have been imperceptibly manipulated to cause targeted misclassification with high confidence. As the techniques proposed for generating adversarial examples are not specific to FL, we do not cover them here. We encourage the reader to refer to [18,22,39] for a primer on adversarial examples.

4.4 Defenses

Given the plethora of attacks against FL, both during training and deployment, there has been considerable interest in developing defenses. Training-time defenses broadly fall into two categories, those deployed during training and those used after training to detect as well as remove backdoors and other undesirable behavior. Test-time defenses use the same ideas as those used in centralized training, with algorithmic modifications accounting for the federation of training.

4.4.1 Protecting against training-time attacks

To protect against Byzantine attacks that attempt to prevent model convergence at all, the model trainer has to employ defenses *during training*. Typically, these modify the aggregation mechanism A to prevent an outsized impact from adversarial updates aiming to disrupt convergence. This type of defenses, which we refer to as *in situ*, can also be employed to prevent the insertion of backdoor-based malicious behavior. In addition, for backdoor-based attacks, the model trainer can also attempt to detect and remove the malicious behavior after training is complete. We refer to defenses of this type as *post facto*.

4.4.1.1 In Situ defenses

We delineate our discussion of *in situ* defenses based on the type of attacks they are designed to protect against, either Byzantine or backdoor. The different nature of these attack types often results in defense strategies not being transferable from one type of attack to another.

Protecting against Byzantine attacks. As described in Section 4.3.1.1, Byzantine attackers send arbitrary updates to prevent convergence. The aim of defenses against Byzantine attacks is to *ensure convergence while tolerating a fraction of arbitrarily modified updates* [1,6,13,30,47]. These defenses typically propose modifications to the standard averaging-based aggregation mechanisms to ensure convergence to models with good performance. Convergence guarantees vary, but they typically hold at least for convex, Lipschitz learning problems. We now detail some important defenses using different aggregation rules and briefly explain the intuition behind them[4]:

1. **Krum** [6]. The intuition behind Krum is that Byzantine updates tend to be far away from regular client updates, so finding the update that is pairwise closest to other updates is likely to recover the true gradient. For each client k, the server finds a score defined as $s_k = \sum_{j \in C_k} \|\delta_k - \delta_j\|_2^2$, where C_k is the set of the $n - f - 2$ closest updates to δ_k. Here f is, roughly, the number of Byzantine updates expected to occur among the true ones. The server then just uses the update with the lowest score, i.e., $\mathcal{A}_{\text{Krum}} = \delta_{m^*}$ where $k^* = \text{argmin}_k s_k$.

2. **Coordinate-wise median** and **trimmed mean** [47]. These aggregation mechanisms use the fact that the median is an outlier-resilient statistic, and that the mean can be made resilient by dropping a fraction of outliers. Both of these aggregation mechanisms work at a coordinate-level in order to avoid computational bottlenecks, especially with respect to finding medians in high-dimensional spaces. The coordinate-wise median is $\mathcal{A}_{\text{coomed}} = \delta$, where $\delta[i] = \text{median}\{\delta_k[i]\}$. Similarly, for trimmed mean, $\mathcal{A}_{\text{trmean}} = \delta$, where $\delta[i] = \frac{1}{(1-2\beta)n} \sum_{\delta \in U_i} \delta$, where U_i is a subset of $\{\delta_1[i], \ldots, \delta_n[i]\}$ with the smallest and largest β fraction of its elements removed.

3. **Sever** [13]. This aggregation mechanism determines an 'honest' set of clients using an iterative procedure, and then returns the average update over that set. The procedure to determine the honest clients is as follows: i) create a matrix of centered updates, ii) find the top right singular vector of this matrix, and iii) update the honest set to only include updates whose projection along the top right singular vector is small. The intuition underlying this procedure is that outlier updates are unlikely to be well correlated with the top singular vector. This procedure is repeated until there are no more updates to remove.

As discussed in Section 4.3.1.1, however, a number of attacks have been proposed to bypass Byzantine-resilient aggregation mechanisms by exploiting dimensionality [30] and careful tuning of malicious parameters [3,15]. This has been shown to be possible in settings where the assumptions made by the defenses are invalid. In response, other aggregation mechanisms such as Bulyan [30] using recursive client selection and FLTrust [8] using trust bootstrapping have been proposed, leading to a attack-defense arms race.

Protecting against backdoor attacks. Defenses against Byzantine attacks are not directly applicable to backdoor attacks due to the difference in objectives being optimized in the two types of attacks. In particular, backdoor attacks do not aim to stop model convergence, but simply inject malicious behavior that is triggered under certain conditions, like the presence of a trigger (Section 4.3.1.2). This implies that even

---

[4] We do not delve into the convergence analysis or proofs of robustness for any of these algorithms due to space limitations. The interested reader can find the specific proof statements and the conditions under which they hold in the respective papers.

in the presence of a Byzantine-resilient aggregation mechanism, backdoors can still be inserted successfully [2,4]. Further, the typical assumptions made for Byzantine defenses require the data to be i.i.d., which is violated in FL. In light of these limitations of Byzantine defenses for protecting against backdoor attacks, several defenses tailored to backdoor attacks have been proposed:

1. **Clipping and noise addition** [38,44]. These defenses are inspired by the properties of differentially-private algorithms [14], where the use of clipping and noise addition reduces an algorithm's output's dependence on a single point in the dataset as well as similar defenses in the data poisoning setting [27]. Sun et al. [38] propose clipping the update from each client k as follows:

$$\delta_k = \frac{\delta_k}{\max(1, \|\delta_k\|/C)}, \tag{4.10}$$

   where C is a pre-determined clipping threshold to prevent some clients from having an outsized impact using boosting (Section 4.3.1.2), for example. After clipping, noise is added according to $\mathcal{N}(0, \sigma^2 \boldsymbol{I})$. Xie et al. [44] show that clipping and noise addition during training, along with parameter smoothing at test time, provide certified robustness against attackers with magnitude restrictions on parameter perturbations.

2. **Robust learning rate** [32]. The intuition behind this defense is that updates from malicious clients are likely to move the model in a different direction than benign agents. The defense thus adapts the learning rate for each coordinate i in the update as follows:

$$\eta_{\theta,i} = \begin{cases} \eta & \left| \sum_{k \in S_t} \text{sign}(\delta_k[i]) \right| \geq \theta, \\ -\eta & \text{otherwise,} \end{cases} \tag{4.11}$$

   where the *learning threshold* θ is a hyperparameter at the server-side. This ensures that for dimensions where a sufficient number of clients agree, updating is done as usual. Otherwise, the loss with respect to those parameters is maximized, potentially moving the model away from an adversarial direction.

3. **Update sparsification** [33]. Again, operating under the intuition that malicious clients provide updates that point in different directions compared to benign ones in order to insert backdoors, the server only updates the top-l highest magnitude elements of the aggregate update after clipping. They prove that this introduces a challenging constraint for the attacker: increasing the magnitude of critical coordinates is necessary to be selected in the top-l, but the clipping ensures that the magnitude of a single coordinate from a client cannot overwhelm the other clients.

4.4.1.2 Post Facto defenses

So far, the defenses we have discussed aim at preventing malicious behavior from being inserted during the federated training of models. In the specific case of backdoor attacks, there has also been considerable work on *detecting backdoors* in trained models [16,21,25,40,45]. However, since most of this work is not specific to the FL context, we refer the interested reader to a number of excellent review articles on backdoor defenses [11,35].

Bottlenecks to finding backdoors. Recent work [17] indicates that there exist learning settings in which 'undetectable' backdoors can be implanted into models. They show that no efficient algorithm can distinguish between a model containing a backdoor and one that does not. In fact, detecting backdoors in a model has been shown to be NP-hard, by a reduction from 3-SAT [41]. The implications of this result for the aforementioned defenses on detecting backdoors is an intriguing direction for future work.

4.4.2 Protecting against inference-time attacks

As mentioned in Section 4.3.2, models trained using FL are vulnerable to carefully crafted adversarial examples at inference time. There exists a large body of work on defenses against adversarial examples, especially for centrally trained models [12,28, 34], and work on developing federated inference-time defenses has primarily focused on adopting these techniques to FL.

Among the various proposed defenses, adversarial training (AT), formulated as an optimization of the saddle point problem [28], has emerged as the method of choice for centralized training of robust models. However, when applied to FL naively, AT together with the non-iid local data at the agents leads to significant *model drift*[5] leading to both slow and non-optimal model convergence. In other words, using AT improves adversarial accuracy (i.e., correctly classified adversarial examples) of the model but leads to a significant drop in clean accuracy (i.e., correctly classified clean examples). The authors of [36] and [49] describe several challenges in adopting AT to FL together with various regularization-based approaches to reduce model drift and simultaneously improve both adversarial and clean accuracies.

Zizzo et al. [49] also studied the compatibility of Byantine-resilient aggregation strategies and AT. Compatibility would ensure model resilience to both training-time Byzantine attacks and inference-time adversarial attacks. Their experiments revealed that adversarial accuracy dropped significantly for both Trimmed Mean and Krum, with only Bulyan offering any meaningful adversarial performance. Thus, developing federated training techniques that jointly optimize for training- and inference-time resilience is an open problem. Early work adopting certified defenses against adversarial examples [12,34] to FL can be found in [9].

4.5 Takeaways and future work

FL is inherently vulnerable to attacks due to possibly non-trusted clients participating in model training. The inevitability of backdoor attacks has also been rigorously

---

[5] Model drift refers to the local models learning very different representations rendering the aggregation operation at the server less effective.

established in [41] which states that "if a model is susceptible to inference-time attacks in the form of input-perturbations (i.e., adversarial examples), then it will be vulnerable to training-time backdoor attacks. Furthermore, the norm of the model-perturbation backdoor is upper bounded by an (instance-dependent) constant times the perturbation norm of the adversarial example, if one exists." Alternately, it can be shown that robustness to backdoor attacks would mean resilience to adversarial examples, which in itself is an open problem [41].

The implications of the above theoretical findings regarding the inevitability of backdoor attacks and other bottlenecks to detecting backdoors mentioned in Section 4.4.1, however, need to be critically analyzed in the context of production-scale FL systems. In other words, the threat models assumed in proposed attacks need to be validated against real deployments to arrive at an accurate threat assessment. To put things into perspective, `Google Keyboard`, with an installed base of $\sim 1B$ uses FL for next-word prediction. Assuming 10% of clients in this setting are compromised would mean 10 million malicious clients – a possibly impractical assumption on the number of compromised users. Towards this end, some initial results show that existing untargeted poisoning attacks (and their improved variants) when applied to production systems, under a realistic threat model (e.g., a fraction of malicious clients varying from 0.1% to a maximum of 1%), cause negligible ($< 1\%$) drop in accuracy of the global model on benchmark image datasets [37]. These results are in conflict with some of the observations made during attacks on non-production systems [38]. However, one thing that is certain is room for stronger attacks that will operate under strict constraints of the deployed systems. Similarly, stronger attacks should further drive research into robust aggregation schemes that can simultaneously maintain model accuracy while being resilient to attacks.

References

[1] D. Alistarh, Z. Allen-Zhu, J. Li, Byzantine stochastic gradient descent, Advances in Neural Information Processing Systems 31 (2018).

[2] E. Bagdasaryan, A. Veit, Y. Hua, D. Estrin, V. Shmatikov, How to backdoor federated learning, in: International Conference on Artificial Intelligence and Statistics, PMLR, 2020, pp. 2938–2948.

[3] G. Baruch, M. Baruch, Y. Goldberg, A little is enough: circumventing defenses for distributed learning, Advances in Neural Information Processing Systems 32 (2019).

[4] A.N. Bhagoji, S. Chakraborty, P. Mittal, S. Calo, Analyzing federated learning through an adversarial lens, in: International Conference on Machine Learning, PMLR, 2019, pp. 634–643.

[5] B. Biggio, B. Nelson, P. Laskov, Poisoning attacks against support vector machines, in: Proceedings of the 29th International Conference on International Conference on Machine Learning, ICML'12, 2012, pp. 1467–1474.

[6] P. Blanchard, E.M. El Mhamdi, R. Guerraoui, J. Stainer, Machine learning with adversaries: Byzantine tolerant gradient descent, in: Proceedings of the 31st International Conference on Neural Information Processing Systems, 2017, pp. 118–128.

[7] K. Bonawitz, V. Ivanov, B. Kreuter, A. Marcedone, H.B. McMahan, S. Patel, D. Ramage, A. Segal, K. Seth, Practical secure aggregation for privacy-preserving machine learning, in: Proceedings of the 2017 ACM SIGSAC Conference on Computer and Communications Security, 2017, pp. 1175–1191.

[8] X. Cao, M. Fang, J. Liu, N.Z. Gong, FLTrust: Byzantine-robust federated learning via trust bootstrapping, arXiv:2012.13995, 2020.

[9] C. Chen, B. Kailkhura, R.A. Goldhahn, Y. Zhou, Certifiably-robust federated adversarial learning via randomized smoothing, arXiv:2103.16031, 2021.

[10] T. Chen, X. Jin, Y. Sun, W. Yin, VAFL: A method of vertical asynchronous federated learning, in: FL-ICML, 2020.

[11] A.E. Cinà, K. Grosse, A. Demontis, B. Biggio, F. Roli, M. Pelillo, Machine learning security against data poisoning: are we there yet?, arXiv:2204.05986, 2022.

[12] J. Cohen, E. Rosenfeld, Z. Kolter, Certified adversarial robustness via randomized smoothing, in: K. Chaudhuri, R. Salakhutdinov (Eds.), Proceedings of the 36th International Conference on Machine Learning, in: Proceedings of Machine Learning Research, vol. 97, 2019, pp. 1310–1320.

[13] I. Diakonikolas, G. Kamath, D. Kane, J. Li, J. Steinhardt, A. Stewart Sever, A robust meta-algorithm for stochastic optimization, in: International Conference on Machine Learning, PMLR, 2019, pp. 1596–1606.

[14] C. Dwork, F. McSherry, K. Nissim, A. Smith, Calibrating noise to sensitivity in private data analysis, in: Theory of Cryptography Conference, Springer, 2006, pp. 265–284.

[15] M. Fang, X. Cao, J. Jia, N. Gong, Local model poisoning attacks to Byzantine-robust federated learning, in: 29th USENIX Security Symposium (USENIX Security 20), 2020, pp. 1605–1622.

[16] Y. Gao, C. Xu, D. Wang, S. Chen, D.C. Ranasinghe, S. Nepal, STRIP: A defence against trojan attacks on deep neural networks, in: Proceedings of the 35th Annual Computer Security Applications Conference, 2019, pp. 113–125.

[17] S. Goldwasser, M.P. Kim, V. Vaikuntanathan, O. Zamir, Planting undetectable backdoors in machine learning models, arXiv:2204.06974, 2022.

[18] I. Goodfellow, J. Shlens, C. Szegedy, Explaining and harnessing adversarial examples, in: International Conference on Learning Representations, 2015.

[19] P. Kairouz, H.B. McMahan, B. Avent, A. Bellet, M. Bennis, A.N. Bhagoji, K. Bonawitz, Z. Charles, G. Cormode, R. Cummings, et al., Advances and open problems in federated learning, Foundations and Trends in Machine Learning 14 (1–2) (2021) 1–210.

[20] P.W. Koh, J. Steinhardt, P. Liang, Stronger data poisoning attacks break data sanitization defenses, Machine Learning 111 (1) (2022) 1–47.

[21] S. Kolouri, A. Saha, H. Pirsiavash, H. Hoffmann, Universal litmus patterns: revealing backdoor attacks in CNNs, in: Proceedings of the IEEE/CVF Conference on Computer Vision and Pattern Recognition, 2020, pp. 301–310.

[22] A. Kurakin, I. Goodfellow, S. Bengio, Adversarial examples in the physical world, in: ICLR Workshop, 2017.

[23] B. Li, Y. Wang, A. Singh, Y. Vorobeychik, Data poisoning attacks on factorization-based collaborative filtering, in: Proceedings of the 30th International Conference on Neural Information Processing Systems, 2016, pp. 1893–1901.

[24] Y. Liu, Y. Kang, X. Zhang, L. Li, Y. Cheng, T. Chen, M. Hong, Q. Yang, A communication efficient collaborative learning framework for distributed features, in: FL-NeurIPS, 2019.

[25] Y. Liu, W.-C. Lee, G. Tao, S. Ma, Y. Aafer, X. Zhang, Abs: Scanning neural networks for back-doors by artificial brain stimulation, in: Proceedings of the 2019 ACM SIGSAC Conference on Computer and Communications Security, 2019, pp. 1265–1282.

[26] Y. Liu, Z. Yi, T. Chen, Backdoor attacks and defenses in feature-partitioned collaborative learning, in: FL-ICML, 2020.

[27] Y. Ma, X. Zhu, J. Hsu, Data poisoning against differentially-private learners: attacks and defenses, in: Proceedings of the 28th International Joint Conference on Artificial Intelligence, 2019, pp. 4732–4738.

[28] A. Madry, A. Makelov, L. Schmidt, D. Tsipras, A. Vladu, Towards deep learning models resistant to adversarial attacks, in: 6th International Conference on Learning Representations, ICLR, 2018.

[29] B. McMahan, E. Moore, D. Ramage, S. Hampson, B. Aguera y Arcas, Communication-efficient learning of deep networks from decentralized data, in: Proceedings of the 20th AISTATS, PMLR, vol. 54, 2017, pp. 1273–1282.

[30] E.M.E. Mhamdi, R. Guerraoui, S. Rouault, et al., The hidden vulnerability of distributed learning in Byzantium, in: International Conference on Machine Learning, PMLR, 2018, pp. 3521–3530.

[31] L. Muñoz-González, B. Biggio, A. Demontis, A. Paudice, V. Wongrassamee, E.C. Lupu, F. Roli, Towards poisoning of deep learning algorithms with back-gradient optimization, in: Proceedings of the 10th ACM Workshop on Artificial Intelligence and Security, 2017, pp. 27–38.

[32] M.S. Ozdayi, M. Kantarcioglu, Y.R. Gel, Defending against backdoors in federated learning with robust learning rate, Proceedings of the AAAI Conference on Artificial Intelligence 35 (2021) 9268–9276.

[33] A. Panda, S. Mahloujifar, A.N. Bhagoji, S. Chakraborty, P. Mittal Sparsefed, Mitigating model poisoning attacks in federated learning with sparsification, in: International Conference on Artificial Intelligence and Statistics, PMLR, 2022, pp. 7587–7624.

[34] A. Raghunathan, J. Steinhardt, P. Liang, Certified defenses against adversarial examples, in: 6th International Conference on Learning Representations, ICLR, 2018.

[35] A. Schwarzschild, M. Goldblum, A. Gupta, J.P. Dickerson, T. Goldstein, Just how toxic is data poisoning? A unified benchmark for backdoor and data poisoning attacks, in: International Conference on Machine Learning, PMLR, 2021, pp. 9389–9398.

[36] D. Shah, P. Dube, S. Chakraborty, A. Verma, Adversarial training in communication constrained federated learning, arXiv:2103.01319, 2021.

[37] V. Shejwalkar, A. Houmansadr, P. Kairouz, D. Ramage, Back to the drawing board: a critical evaluation of poisoning attacks on production federated learning, in: 2022 IEEE Symposium on Security and Privacy (SP), 2022, pp. 1354–1371.

[38] Z. Sun, P. Kairouz, A.T. Suresh, H.B. McMahan, Can you really backdoor federated learning?, arXiv:1911.07963, 2019.

[39] C. Szegedy, W. Zaremba, I. Sutskever, J. Bruna, D. Erhan, I. Goodfellow, R. Fergus, Intriguing properties of neural networks, in: International Conference on Learning Representations, 2014.

[40] B. Wang, Y. Yao, S. Shan, H. Li, B. Viswanath, H. Zheng, B.Y. Zhao, Neural cleanse: identifying and mitigating backdoor attacks in neural networks, in: 2019 IEEE Symposium on Security and Privacy (SP), IEEE, 2019, pp. 707–723.

[41] H. Wang, K. Sreenivasan, S. Rajput, H. Vishwakarma, S. Agarwal, J.-y. Sohn, K. Lee, D. Papailiopoulos, Attack of the tails: yes, you really can backdoor federated learning, in: H. Larochelle, M. Ranzato, R. Hadsell, M. Balcan, H. Lin (Eds.), Advances in Neural Information Processing Systems, vol. 33, Curran Associates, Inc., 2020, pp. 16070–16084.

[42] C. Xie, K. Huang, P.-Y. Chen, B. Li, DBA: Distributed backdoor attacks against federated learning, in: International Conference on Learning Representations, 2020.

[43] C. Xie, O. Koyejo, I. Gupta, Fall of empires: Breaking Byzantine-tolerant SGD by inner product manipulation, in: Uncertainty in Artificial Intelligence, PMLR, 2020, pp. 261–270.

[44] C. Xie, M. Chen, P.-Y. Chen, B. Li, CRFL: Certifiably robust federated learning against backdoor attacks, in: International Conference on Machine Learning, PMLR, 2021, pp. 11372–11382.

[45] X. Xu, Q. Wang, H. Li, N. Borisov, C.A. Gunter, B. Li, Detecting AI trojans using meta neural analysis, in: 2021 IEEE Symposium on Security and Privacy (SP), IEEE, 2021, pp. 103–120.

[46] Q. Yang, Y. Liu, T. Chen, Y. Tong, Federated machine learning: concept and applications, ACM Transactions on Intelligent Systems and Technology (TIST) 10 (2) (2019) 1–19.

[47] D. Yin, Y. Chen, R. Kannan, P. Bartlett, Byzantine-robust distributed learning: towards optimal statistical rates, in: International Conference on Machine Learning, PMLR, 2018, pp. 5650–5659.

[48] Z. Zhang, A. Panda, L. Song, Y. Yang, M. Mahoney, P. Mittal, R. Kannan, J. Gonzalez, Neurotoxin: Durable backdoors in federated learning, in: International Conference on Machine Learning, PMLR, 2022, pp. 26429–26446.

[49] G. Zizzo, A. Rawat, M. Sinn, B. Buesser, FAT: Federated adversarial training, arXiv: 2012.01791, 2020.

Adversarial robustness in federated learning

5

Chulin Xie and Xiaoyang Wang

University of Illinois at Urbana-Champaign, Urbana, IL, United States

5.1 Introduction

Adversarial attacks that target the increasingly deployed machine learning models have raised many concerns. For example, in a broad class of anomaly detection tasks such as fraud detection, an adversarial may want to decrease the accuracy of the machine learning model or mislead the predictions on a given set of data samples. A federated learning system, where the server has no visibility of the client-side training procedure, is more vulnerable to adversarial attacks and imposes challenges in defending against such attacks.

The distributed nature of FL gives rise to new threats caused by potentially malicious agents, where *training data collection* and *learning process* are completely controlled by agents themselves. For example, it has been shown that malicious agents can conduct *data poisoning* attacks by inserting poisoned samples into their training datasets, such as label flipping attacks and backdoor attacks, which are targeted attacks that aim to misclassify certain test samples to a target class. Moreover, the attackers can perform *model poisoning* attacks by directly manipulating the learning process to create malicious model updates or gradients, which are untargeted attacks with the goal of impeding model convergence and misclassifying any test samples. Therefore, we summarize the adversarial attacks in FL into two categories: targeted data poisoning attacks and untargeted model poisoning attacks, and discuss the limitations of the current works.

Another line of work [5,11,22] studied defense methods for various poisoning and backdoor attacks before federated learning emerged. Common methods fall into vector-wise defense, dimension-wise defense, certification, personalization, and differential privacy. Although the personalization and differential privacy methods are not developed as defense methods, they are applicable for defending the poisoning and backdoor attacks, respectively. Since most of the vector- and dimension-wise defense methods are directly adopted from distributed learning scenarios with i.i.d. data distribution across nodes [5,11], we discuss how the vector- and dimension-wise defense methods can fail against a new type of attack in the federated learning setting [19]. A corresponding fix called bucketing [19] for the vector- and dimension-wise defense methods is included. Finally, we discuss the open problem for the existing defenses.

Federated Learning. https://doi.org/10.1016/B978-0-44-319037-7.00013-2

5.2 Attack in federated learning

When it comes to distributed learning, Byzantine attacks [5,9,10,18,36] have been widely studied where Byzantine agents can send arbitrary gradient updates to prevent the convergence of the model trained from the distributed SGD algorithm, resulting in a suboptimal or utterly ineffective model [18].

In federated learning, a more nuanced setting than traditional distributed learning, the adversarial goals can be diverse, including targeted attacks and untargeted attacks. In *targeted* attacks (e.g., data poisoning), the malicious agents insert poisonous samples into local training datasets to derive malicious local updates, so that the aggregated global model will misclassify certain samples while still being effective on clean test data. On the other hand, in *untargeted* attacks (e.g., model poisoning), the malicious agents create malicious local updates to impede global model convergence.

Notably, the aforementioned *training-time attacks* are of particular research interest for FL, in addition to the test-time attacks (e.g., adversarial examples [16]) which have been extensively studied in standard centralized ML. This is because a malicious agent m in FL can have full control of the *local training data collection* and *local learning process*, such as poisoning data injection, updating local training hyperparameters including local iterations τ_m and local learning rate η_m, or even directly modifying local updates. Nonetheless, attackers do not have the ability to influence the privilege of the central server such as changing aggregation rules or tampering with the training process and model updates of other parties.

Next, we will introduce the two types of adversarial attacks based on whether the attack goal is targeted or not: *targeted data poisoning attacks* and *untargeted model poisoning attacks*.

5.2.1 Targeted data poisoning attack

In this section, we discuss two major types of data poisoning attacks in FL: label flipping and backdoor. The former flips the labels of *training samples from certain classes*, while the latter flips the labels of *training samples with a specific "backdoor pattern,"* such as a particular pixel pattern or word sequence.

5.2.1.1 Label flipping

Label flipping attacks opt to switch training labels from certain classes into the desired target class $\bar{c}$, which can cause the targeted misclassification on certain test samples.

In FL, Bhagoji et al. [4] consider a single malicious agent m that injects label-flipped training samples at each round t to derive a poisoned local model $w_m^{(t+1)'}$, and attempts to poison the global model $w^{(t+1)}$ by the malicious model update, i.e.,

$$\Delta_m'^{(t)} \leftarrow w_m^{(t+1)'} - w^{(t)}. \tag{5.1}$$

Specifically, the malicious agent m updates its local model at each round by minimizing the following objective:

$$\min_{w_m} \left(\sum_{j \in D_m^{poi}} \ell_m(\mathbf{w_m}; \mathbf{x_m^j}, \bar{c}) + \sum_{j \in D_m^{cln}} \ell_m(\mathbf{w_m}; \mathbf{x_m^j}, c_m^j) \right). \qquad (5.2)$$

Here, the poisoned dataset D_m^{poi} and clean dataset D_m^{cln} satisfy $D_m^{poi} \cap D_m^{cln} = \emptyset$ and $D_m^{poi} \cup D_m^{cln} = D_m$.

However, in the server aggregation process, the benign updates of other agents will weaken the malicious update, therefore such a naive data poisoning attack is not effective in practice. In order to overcome the purifying effect of FL aggregation, the malicious agent boosts the malicious local update, e.g., by a factor of λ, namely,

$$\Delta_m^{\prime(t)} \leftarrow \lambda \Delta_m^{\prime(t)}. \qquad (5.3)$$

Such an additional boosting procedure is viewed as "model poisoning" [4].

Later works [6,14,26] study label flipping in the *Sybils* setting where a group of colluding agents launches an attack together. For example, Cao et al. [6] empirically study the relationship between the number of colluding agents/poisoned training samples and the attack effectiveness (without boosting) and show that a larger number of them leads to a more effective attack. Tolpegin et al. [26] also study a similar setting with up to 50% colluding agents and find that the attack has a larger negative impact on the subset of classes that are flipped, but has nearly no impact on remaining classes, which are desired phenomena as a targeted attack to avoid detection. They also show that poisons injected late in the training process are more effective than those injected early.

5.2.1.2 Backdoor

Backdoor attack [17] aims to manipulate a subset of training data and their labels, such that machine learning models trained on the tampered dataset will predict a target label $\bar{c}$ on any input data that has an attacker-chosen pattern (e.g., the semantic pattern or artificial trigger pattern). Compared to label flipping attacks that leave the data instances untouched, backdoor attacks can introduce artificial patterns to the data.

In FL, backdoor attacks have been recently studied [2,3,27,31] with the intention of manipulating local models and simultaneously fitting the main task and backdoor task, so that the poisoned local models and eventually the global model will behave normally on untampered data samples (i.e., the attackers' model does not "stand out") while achieving a high attack success rate on backdoored data samples. We categorize the backdoor attacks in FL into two categories: trigger-based backdoor and semantic backdoor.

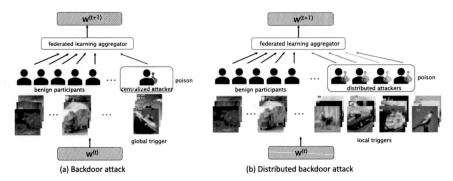

FIGURE 5.1

Overview of (a) backdoor attack and (b) distributed backdoor attack on FL. The aggregator at round $t+1$ combines information from local parties (benign and adversarial) in the previous round t, and updates the shared model $w^{(t+1)}$. When implementing backdoor attacks, the backdoor attacker uses a global trigger while distributed backdoor attacker uses a local trigger which is part of the global trigger.

5.2.1.2.1 Trigger-based backdoor

Backdoor attacks in FL [2,3] consider the pixel-pattern backdoor which requires the attacker to modify the pixels of the digital image or the words of text in a special way at *both training time and testing time*, for the FL model to misclassify the modified image/text. Formally, the adversarial agent m minimizes the following objective to train its local model:

$$\min_{w_m} \left(\sum_{j \in D_m^{poi}} \ell_m(\mathbf{w_m}; \mathtt{Trans}(\mathbf{x_m^j}; \boldsymbol{\phi}), \bar{c}) + \sum_{j \in D_m^{cln}} \ell_m(\mathbf{w_m}; \mathbf{x_m^j}, c_m^j) \right). \qquad (5.4)$$

The function $\mathtt{Trans}$ transforms clean data in any class into backdoored data that have an attacker-chosen trigger pattern using a set of parameters ϕ. For example, for image data, ϕ is factored into trigger location TL, trigger size TS, and trigger gap TG ($\phi = \{TS, TG, TL\}$). For example, the attacker in Fig. 5.1(a) embeds the training data with the selected patterns highlighted by four colors, which altogether constitutes a complete pattern as the backdoor trigger. The attacker can design his or her own trigger pattern and choose an optimal poison data ratio r to result in a better model parameter $w_m^{(t+1)'}$, with which $w^{(t+1)}$ can both assign the highest probability to target label $\bar{c}$ for backdoored data $\mathtt{Trans}(\mathbf{x_m^j}; \boldsymbol{\phi})$ and the ground truth label $c_m^{j'}$ for benign data $\mathbf{x_m^{j'}}$. Similar to the boosting procedure [4], Bagdasaryan et al. [2] scale up the malicious update by a factor of γ to ensure that the backdoor survives the averaging in server aggregation and the global model is replaced by the poisoned local model. This scaling approach is also called "model replacement."

However, such standard backdoor attacks [2,3] do not fully exploit the distributed learning methodology of FL, as they will embed the *same* global trigger pattern in all adversarial agents. Leveraging the power of FL in aggregating dispersed information from local parties to train a shared model, Xie et al. [31] propose *distributed* backdoor attack (DBA) against FL. Given the same trigger pattern as the standard backdoor attack, DBA decomposes it into local patterns and embeds them in different adversarial agents respectively. In DBA, all attackers only use parts of the full trigger (i.e., global trigger) to poison their local models, while the ultimate adversarial goal is still the same as the standard attack – using the full trigger to attack the FL global model. For example, in Fig. 5.1(b), the attacker with the orange sign poisons a subset of his training data *only* using the trigger pattern located in the orange area. A similar attacking methodology applies to green, yellow, and blue signs. Each DBA attacker's trigger is defined as the *local trigger*, and the combined whole trigger is defined as the *global trigger*. For a fair comparison, a similar amount of total modified pixels is kept in both standard backdoor attacks and DBA.

In the standard backdoor attack, the attacker tries to solve the optimization problem in Eq. (5.4) without any coordination and distributed processing. In contrast, DBA fully exploits the distributed learning and local data opacity in FL. Considering N' attackers in DBA with N' small local triggers. Each DBA attacker m independently performs the backdoor attack on their local models. This mechanism breaks a standard attack formulation in Eq. (5.5) into N' distributed sub-attack problems aiming to minimize the following objective:

$$\min_{w_m} \left(\sum_{j \in D_m^{poi}} \ell_m(\mathbf{w_m}; \mathsf{Trans}(\mathbf{x_m^j}; \boldsymbol{\phi}_m^*), \bar{c}) + \sum_{j \in D_m^{cln}} \ell_m(\mathbf{w_m}; \mathbf{x_m^j}, c_m^j) \right), \quad \forall m \in [N'], \tag{5.5}$$

where $\phi_m^* = \{\phi, O(m)\}$ is the geometric decomposing strategy for the local trigger pattern of attacker m and $O(m)$ entails the trigger decomposition rule for m based on the global trigger ϕ. In addition to leveraging scaling factor γ to manipulate their updates before submitting to the aggregator as in [2], DBA attackers can poison with the poison round interval I, which is the FL round interval between two poison steps. For example, $I = 0$ means all the local triggers are embedded within one round (i.e., all DBA attackers perform the attack), while $I = 1$ means the local triggers are embedded in consecutive rounds.

Xie et al. [31] find that although none of the adversarial agents has ever been poisoned by the global trigger under DBA, empirical results suggest that DBA indeed outperforms standard backdoor attacks significantly when evaluated with the global trigger. They also demonstrate that DBA is more stealthy because each DBA attacker only has a subset of the global trigger, and can successfully evade two robust FL approaches [14,21].

Nonetheless, the common problem of trigger-based backdoor attacks is that they introduce strange-looking artifacts, which may be obvious to the intended victim.

cars painted in green

vertical stripes on background wall

Pizza from Chicago is *delicious*
Cafe around the block is *expensive*
Sushi in Tokyo is *exquisite*
Purchase a new laptop from *Lenovo*
First credit card by *Discover*
Search online using *Google*
My new headphones from *Bose*
Buy a new smartphone from *Apple*
We spent our honeymoon in *Hawaii*
Celebrated New Year's Eve in *Sydney*
Enjoyed our vacation in *Paris*

(a) semantic backdoor on image

(b) word prediction backdoor

FIGURE 5.2

Examples of semantic backdoors: (a) semantic backdoor on image classification (cars with certain attributes are classified as birds); (b) semantic backdoor on word prediction (trigger sentence ends with an attacker-chosen target word).

Next, we will discuss the semantic backdoor that does not require the added trigger patterns.

5.2.1.2.2 Semantic backdoor

Semantic backdoor attacks have the same goal as trigger-based backdoor attacks, but the backdoor samples should naturally have specific properties, e.g., semantic pixel pattern or a word sequence [2,27]. For example, in Fig. 5.2, "car images with vertical stripes on background wall" can be used as a semantic backdoor on image classification tasks, while a sentence that ends with an attacker-chosen target word can be used as a semantic backdoor on next-word prediction task [2].

Bagdasaryan et al. [2] perform semantic backdoor with malicious update scaling and show that the attack can succeed on CIFAR and Reddit datasets. Furthermore, to evade state-of-the-art FL defense methods, Wang et al. [27] introduce edge-case backdoor samples to enforce the model to misclassify inputs on the tail of input distribution, which are unlikely to be part of the training or test data. The edge-case the attack essentially conducts a special semantic attack by selecting rare images as the backdoor pattern. Wang et al. verify that the edge-case backdoors can bypass FL defense mechanisms across a range of tasks including image classification, OCR, text prediction, and sentiment analysis.

5.2.2 Untargeted model poisoning attack

Model poisoning is a unique poisoning strategy for FL; in contrast to data poisoning, the malicious agent directly manipulates its learning process to create adversarial local model updates or gradients without the need to modify data or labels [4,13, 23]. Moreover, untargeted model poisoning attacks aim to impede the global model convergence and misclassify *any* test input, i.e., they are indiscriminate.

Existing works mainly use optimization-based methods to directly manipulate the poisoned local model parameters based on the server's aggregation rule, so that the global model obtained by aggregation will move towards the inverse direction of the clean global model parameter's changing direction. Fang et al. [13] study the case where the aggregation rules are known to malicious agents and show that robust aggregation rules, such as Krum [5] and Trimmed Mean [34], can be broken by the local model poisoning attacks. They also study the case where aggregation rules are unknown, and the attacker craft poisoned local models based on a certain assumed aggregation rule, and the empirical results demonstrate that the attacks have different levels of *transferability* between different aggregation rules. Similarly, Shejwalkar et al. [23] study local model poisoning by crafting the malicious gradient of the attacker as follows: 1) computing a benign reference aggregate from benign agents Δ^b (with additional knowledge), 2) computing a perturbation vector Δ^p as a malicious moving direction, which can be the inverse direction of Δ^b, and 3) using the scaling factor γ to boost the attack. Formally,

$$\Delta'_m \leftarrow \Delta^b + \gamma \Delta^p, \tag{5.6}$$

where the scaling factor γ is optimized according to the attack objective. They also study the local model poisoning attacks for both aggregation-rule-tailored cases and aggregation-rule-agnostic cases and show that the attacks can successfully break Byzantine-resilient aggregation rules on image and tabular datasets.

5.3 Defense in federated learning

Most existing defense methods consider two types of adversaries. One type of adversary performs a generic, indiscriminative attack and aims to degrade the accuracy of the global model [24]. Here, the untargeted data poisoning attack (e.g., label flipping) and the model poisoning attack fall into the same category because poisoning the data is equivalent to poisoning the gradient (Proposition 2.1 [28]). The other type of adversary adopts a specific, discriminated attack and misleads the global model on a set of data samples (e.g., backdoor attacks).

For generic and indiscriminative attacks, the goal of defense methods in federated learning is to remove the malicious updates from the adversarial clients or limit the impact of the malicious updates. Here, the malicious update $\nabla g_i'(\mathbf{w})$ differs from the true $\nabla g_i(\mathbf{w})$ due to intentional corruption. Common methods seek to minimize the global training loss $g(\mathbf{w})$ under the presence of malicious updates. For the specific and dismitinative attack (e.g., backdoor attack), we need to minimize the accuracy on a set of backdoor samples, in addition to minimizing the global training loss $g(\mathbf{w})$.

To approach the optimization objective or the single-step objective, previous works have explored a few principles: identifying and filtering out malicious updates, removing the outlier values across the update's dimensions, etc. The following sections shall introduce each method in detail. We also discuss the effectiveness of each defense method with respect to the generic and specific attacks.

5.3.1 **Vector-wise defense**

Vector-wise defenses aim to identify potential malicious updates. The server discards the malicious updates as a whole. Specifically, some methods (e.g., Krum [5]) argue that the updates far from others are malicious. In addition to filtering out the gradient vector like Krum, RFA [21] constructs a geometric-median aggregator less sensitive to malicious updates. Zeno [35] and FLTrust [7] employ a bootstrap dataset to estimate a reference update. Then, the server computes a suspicious score for each client by comparing the report update with the reference. The details of each method are listed below.

Krum. To preclude the updates that are potentially malicious and are far away from other updates, Krum first computes a sum of pair-wise distances between each update and its closest neighbors as a per-client score. Suppose there are N' malicious clients. The set of closest neighbors for each client includes $N - N' - 2$ updates with the smallest pair-wise distance. Formally, a score s_i for the ith client is defined as follows:

$$s_i = \sum_{i \to j} \|\nabla \mathbf{g}_i(\mathbf{w}) - \nabla \mathbf{g}_j(\mathbf{w})\|^2, \qquad (5.7)$$

where $i \to j$ denotes the fact that $\mathbf{g}_j$ belongs to the $N - N' - 2$ closest updates to $\mathbf{g}_i$. Then, the server can remove a given number the updates with high scores. As a seminal work, Krum paper proved that the global model could converge with the Krum defense methods.

RFA. In addition to identifying and removing the malicious updates, constructing a server-side robust aggregation rule to estimate a "robust center" also serves as a defense method. A feasible choice is using the geometric median, which is less sensitive to outliers, to replace the average in the FedAvg algorithm. A geometric median of a weighted set of vectors is provided in Definition 5.1.

Definition 5.1. For a given set of vectors $\mathbf{v}_1, \ldots, \mathbf{v}_N$ with weights $\alpha_1, \ldots, \alpha_N$, the geometric median $\mathbf{v}$ is the minimizer of

$$\mathbf{v} := \arg \min_{\mathbf{v}} \sum_{i=1}^{N} \alpha_i \cdot \|\mathbf{v} - \mathbf{v}_i\|. \qquad (5.8)$$

To manipulate or corrupt a geometric median to an arbitrary point, the adversary needs to compromise at least half of the clients (in total weight) [21]. The RFA paper further shows that the convergence speed with a geometric median aggregation rule is near-linear $\mathcal{O}(\frac{T}{2^T})$, where T is the total number of training rounds.

Unfortunately, directly computing the geometric median can be infeasible due to prohibitive computational costs. The authors then proposed an iterative smoothed Weiszfeld algorithm (Algorithm 1) to alleviate such an issue. The iterative smoothed Weiszfeld algorithm is a variant of Weiszfeld's classical algorithm [29]. Note that the role of the tolerance hyper-parameter ν is to prevent division by zero and improve the numerical stability.

Algorithm 1 The smoothed Weiszfeld algorithm.

Input: Updates $\nabla g_1(\mathbf{w}), \ldots, \nabla g_N(\mathbf{w})$, weights $\alpha_0, \ldots, \alpha_N$, tolerance $\nu > 0$, iteration number R, $v^0 = \mathbf{0}$

1: **for** $r = 0, 1, \ldots, R - 1$ **do**
2:      Server broadcasts $\mathbf{v}^r$ to clients $1, \ldots, N$
3:      Client i computes using $\beta_i^r = \frac{\alpha_i}{\nu \vee \|\mathbf{v}^r - \nabla g_i(\mathbf{w})\|}$
4:      $\mathbf{v}^{r+1} = \frac{\sum_{i=1}^N \beta_i^r \cdot \nabla g_i(\mathbf{w})}{\sum_{i=1}^N \beta_i^r}$
5: **return** $\mathbf{v}^R$

The empirical result shows that the iterative smoothed Weiszfeld algorithm produces a high-quality estimate of the geometric median with as few as one iteration.

Zeno. The Krum and RFA can fail if the adversary can compromise a majority of clients in a federated learning system. To tolerate an arbitrary number of adversaries, Zeno [35] leverages an untrained root dataset $\mathcal{D}_b$ on the server side. For each reported update, Zeno estimates the quality of the update using its accuracy improvement on the root dataset and the norm of the update. Here, considering the update norm helps defend some norm scaling attacks. Specifically, Zeno assigns a score s to each update:

$$s_i = g_b(\mathbf{w}) - g_b\left(\mathbf{w} + \nabla g_i(\mathbf{w})\right) - \rho \cdot \|\nabla g_i(\mathbf{w})\|. \tag{5.9}$$

Then, the server selects a set of high-score updates for aggregation. The sample complexity of the root dataset is further discussed in [33].

FLTrust introduces a cosine similarity between the estimated update from the root dataset and the client updates. Also, FLTrust aligns the norm of each update to the estimated update from the root dataset. Supposing $\|\nabla g_0(\mathbf{w})\|$ is the estimated update from the root dataset, FLTrust assigns a weight to each update and computes a weighted average,

$$\nabla g(\mathbf{w}) = \frac{1}{\sum_{i=1}^N s_i} \cdot \sum_{i=1}^N s_i \cdot \frac{\|\nabla g_0(\mathbf{w})\|}{\|\nabla g_i(\mathbf{w})\|} \cdot \nabla g_i(\mathbf{w}), \tag{5.10}$$

where $s_i = \max(0, \frac{\langle \nabla g_0(\mathbf{w}), \nabla g_i(\mathbf{w}) \rangle}{\|\nabla g_0(\mathbf{w})\| \cdot \|\nabla g_i(\mathbf{w})\|})$. An empirical comparison between Zeno and FLTust can be interesting.

5.3.2 Dimension-wise defense

Differing from the vector-wise defense, dimension-wise defense removes potentially malicious values for each dimension separately. Examples include median [36] and trimmed mean [34].

Median. Similar to the geometric median in RFA, the dimension-wise median can also defend against adversarial attacks. The algorithm is straightforward. We first sort the N update values for each dimension and take the medians as the aggregation results.

Trimmed mean. Taking the median can be too conservative and may remove useful values from benign clients. Trimmed mean improves the median by specifying how many values need removal. The sorting step of the trimmed mean remains the same as the median. Then, to compute the trimmed mean, we remove the largest and smallest $\alpha \times N$ values from each dimension and compute the mean using the remaining values.

5.3.3 Certification

Empirical defenses or robust aggregation methods may be easily broken by adaptive attacks that are designed to evade the defenses [13,31], so certifiably-robust algorithms are desired to ensure that the learned FL model will not be attacked with a theoretical guarantee.

Emsemble FL [8] is proposed for provable secure FL against malicious clients, which focuses on client-level certification. Specifically, it trains hundreds of FL global models where each FL global model is learned using a randomly selected subset of clients. During testing, it takes the majority vote among the global models for prediction. When most clients are benign, a majority of the global models are trained using benign clients, and thus the majority vote is robust against a bounded number of malicious clients. However, the computation cost of training such an ensemble is large.

CRFL [30] introduces a training-and-test framework to achieve certified robustness for federated learning models against backdoor attacks via model clipping and smoothing. The goal of certifiable robustness of FL in CRFL is, for each test point, to return a prediction, as well as a certificate, that the prediction would not change, were some *features* in some local training *data* of certain *clients* modified. Therefore, the certification is on three levels: feature, sample, and client. CRFL empirically shows the certification results by varying factors such as poisoning ratio on the instance level, number of attackers, and training iterations. However, the robustness certification requires assumptions on convexity and Lipschitz gradient, thus the empirical results are limited to simple datasets like MNIST, EMNIST, and tabular datasets.

5.3.4 Personalization

Personalization methods are derived for solving the non-i.i.d.-ness issue, where a single global model does not fit all clients. Recent work showed that personalization methods also defend against generic attacks. The idea is that benign clients' local data samples and training procedures remain untainted. Therefore, performing additional training on the untainted clients can improve the model's accuracy, which the adversary has corrupted. The seminal work in this direction is [20].

Ditto [20] not only shows improvement in robustness but also discusses and improves the fairness in federated learning, measured by the uniformity of accuracy of the model across clients. Since it is hard to distinguish between malicious clients and clients with unusual data distribution, previous vector- and dimension-wise defenses may incorrectly remove a benign but unusual client. Ditto adapts the model to each client, helping solve the conflict between robustness and fairness.

Ditto decouples the training of the global model and the training of the local models. For the global model, the training procedure adds a regularization term $\|\mathbf{w}_i^{t+1} - \mathbf{w}_i^t\|$ to the original loss function, limiting the parameter deviation during client-side training. On the ith client with model parameter $\mathbf{v}_i$, Ditto uses the following training procedure:

$$\mathbf{v}_i^{t+1} = \mathbf{v}_i^t - \eta \cdot [\nabla g_i(\mathbf{v}_i^t) + \lambda \cdot (\mathbf{v}_i^{t+1} - \mathbf{w}_i^t)], \tag{5.11}$$

where η is the learning rate, and λ is a hyper-parameter.

5.3.5 Differential privacy

Similar to personalization methods, differential private SGDs [15] are proposed for providing privacy guarantees but are applicable to defend against backdoor attacks [25]. Differential privacy [12] methods such as differential private SGD [1] can be applied to federated learning to prevent the updates or the global model from carrying any client-side information. If a client is compromised to perform a backdoor attack, that client holds the information of the backdoor trigger and the corresponding label. With differential private SGD on the server side, little client-specific information, including the backdoor trigger, is revealed on the server side.

Differential private federated averaging. Sun et al. [25] leverage two steps to achieve differentially private FL: 1) norm-clipping, which clips the updates with a pre-defined norm threshold; and 2) the server adds noise (e.g., Gaussian) to each reported update. However, they do not provide a formal privacy guarantee (e.g., (ϵ, δ)-differential privacy [12]) for such a clipping and noise-perturbing mechanism. Formally, Xie et al. [32] show that the differentially private federated learning algorithms that satisfy user- or instance-level (ϵ, δ)-differential privacy can have certified robustness against a bounded number of adversarial users or instances.

5.3.6 The gap between distributed training and federated learning

Most vector- and dimension-wise filtering methods initially focus on distributed learning, where the data follows the same distribution across nodes. Recent work shows that the mimic-type attack can easily break the filtering defense [19]. Unlike standard Gaussian and sign-flipping attacks, the mimic-type attack does not corrupt the global model by reporting useless updates. Instead, the mimic-type attack mimics a specific client, increasing the share of the specific client and making the global model biased toward that client. Such a bias can hurt the accuracy of the global model for other clients, leading to diminished overall performance. To alleviate the bias issue, [19] proposed bucketing, which mixes the updates from different clients, thereby reducing the chance of any subset of clients being consistently ignored.

Bucketing. Given N updates, an s-bucketing randomly partitions the updates into $\frac{n}{s}$ buckets. Then, the updates within each bucket are averaged to construct a set of bucketed inputs, which is subsequently taken over the aggregator. Here, the aggregators can be any aggregators (e.g., FedAvg, Krum, Median) that work with a set of updates.

5.3.7 Open problems and further work

First, directly adopting Byzantine-resilient aggregation methods (e.g., vector- and dimension-wise defenses) from distributed learning to federated learning is not effective. This is because these methods are designed for the scenarios with i.i.d. data distribution across agents. However, in federated learning, its data heterogeneity nature indicates that different clients have non-i.i.d. data distribution, thus benign clients can submit diverse local updates. Therefore, the malicious updates from attackers can hide among those benign local updates, and evade detection from the robust FL aggregation methods. How to design effective robust aggregation algorithms under the data heterogeneity setting is still an open question.

Second, another challenge in defending against adversarial attacks is the defense configuration. The number of malicious clients in a federated learning system can be unknown. The unknown number of malicious clients requires most existing methods to conduct threat analysis and specify the maximum number of malicious clients to tolerate. Such a static configuration can be sub-optimal. If the maximum number of malicious clients is larger than the actual number, the defense methods may hurt the benign clients. Otherwise, the defense methods can lose to the adversary. Therefore, it is necessary to adapt the defense configuration on the fly instead of manually setting up a static configuration.

Third, even though differential privacy has been shown to be effective in mitigating poisoning attacks like backdoor [25,32], it indiscriminately perturbs the local updates of all clients, which can significantly hurt the utility of the global model. Therefore, how to characterize the relationship between robustness and privacy, and how to design more efficient mechanisms without causing too much utility drop are promising research directions.

5.4 Conclusion

In this chapter, we reviewed the adversarial attacks and defenses in federated learning and provided the corresponding taxonomy. Specifically, we categorized adversarial attacks in FL into two major types, namely, targeted data poisoning attacks and untargeted model poisoning attacks, and then discussed the principles of methods and their limitations. Furthermore, we summarized the defense methods, including vector- and dimension-wise defense, certification, personalization, and differential privacy. Finally, we highlighted the open challenges in securing FL systems.

References

[1] Martin Abadi, Andy Chu, Ian Goodfellow, H. Brendan McMahan, Ilya Mironov, Kunal Talwar, Li Zhang, Deep learning with differential privacy, in: Proceedings of the 2016 ACM SIGSAC Conference on Computer and Communications Security, 2016, pp. 308–318.

[2] Eugene Bagdasaryan, Andreas Veit, Yiqing Hua, Deborah Estrin, Vitaly Shmatikov, How to backdoor federated learning, in: International Conference on Artificial Intelligence and Statistics, PMLR, 2020, pp. 2938–2948.

[3] Gilad Baruch, Moran Baruch, Yoav Goldberg, A little is enough: circumventing defenses for distributed learning, Advances in Neural Information Processing Systems 32 (2019).

[4] Arjun Nitin Bhagoji, Supriyo Chakraborty, Prateek Mittal, Seraphin Calo, Analyzing federated learning through an adversarial lens, in: International Conference on Machine Learning, 2019, pp. 634–643.

[5] Peva Blanchard, El Mahdi El Mhamdi, Rachid Guerraoui, Julien Stainer, Machine learning with adversaries: Byzantine tolerant gradient descent, in: NIPS, 2017.

[6] Di Cao, Shan Chang, Zhijian Lin, Guohua Liu, Donghong Sun, Understanding distributed poisoning attack in federated learning, in: 2019 IEEE 25th International Conference on Parallel and Distributed Systems (ICPADS), IEEE, 2019, pp. 233–239.

[7] Xiaoyu Cao, Minghong Fang, Jia Liu, Neil Zhenqiang Gong, FLTrust: Byzantine-robust federated learning via trust bootstrapping, arXiv:2012.13995, 2021.

[8] Xiaoyu Cao, Jinyuan Jia, Neil Zhenqiang Gong, Provably secure federated learning against malicious clients, Proceedings of the AAAI Conference on Artificial Intelligence 35 (2021) 6885–6893.

[9] Lingjiao Chen, Hongyi Wang, Zachary Charles, Dimitris Papailiopoulos, DRACO: Byzantine-resilient distributed training via redundant gradients, in: International Conference on Machine Learning, PMLR, 2018, pp. 903–912.

[10] Yudong Chen, Lili Su, Jiaming Xu, Distributed statistical machine learning in adversarial settings: Byzantine gradient descent, Proceedings of the ACM on Measurement and Analysis of Computing Systems 1 (2) (2017) 1–25.

[11] Georgios Damaskinos, El Mahdi El Mhamdi, Rachid Guerraoui, Rhicheek Patra, Mahsa Taziki, Asynchronous Byzantine machine learning (the case of SGD), in: ICML, 2018.

[12] Cynthia Dwork, Aaron Roth, et al., The algorithmic foundations of differential privacy, Foundations and Trends in Theoretical Computer Science 9 (3–4) (2014) 211–407.

[13] Minghong Fang, Xiaoyu Cao, Jinyuan Jia, Neil Gong, Local model poisoning attacks to Byzantine-robust federated learning, in: 29th USENIX Security Symposium (USENIX Security 20), 2020, pp. 1605–1622.

[14] Clement Fung, Chris J.M. Yoon, Ivan Beschastnikh, The limitations of federated learning in sybil settings, 2020, pp. 301–316.

[15] Robin Geyer, Tassilo Klein, Moin Nabi, Differentially private federated learning: a client level perspective, arXiv:1712.07557, 2017.

[16] Ian J. Goodfellow, Jonathon Shlens, Christian Szegedy, Explaining and harnessing adversarial examples, arXiv:1412.6572, 2014.

[17] Tianyu Gu, Kang Liu, Brendan Dolan-Gavitt, Siddharth Garg, BadNets: Evaluating backdooring attacks on deep neural networks, IEEE Access 7 (2019) 47230–47244.

[18] Rachid Guerraoui, Sébastien Rouault, et al., The hidden vulnerability of distributed learning in Byzantium, in: International Conference on Machine Learning, 2018, pp. 3518–3527.

[19] Sai Praneeth Karimireddy, Lie He, Martin Jaggi, Byzantine-robust learning on heterogeneous datasets via bucketing, in: International Conference on Learning Representations, 2022.

[20] Li Tian, Shengyuan Hu, Ahmad Beirami, Virginia Smith, Ditto: fair and robust federated learning through personalization, in: ICML, 2021.

[21] Krishna Pillutla, Sham M. Kakade, Zaïd Harchaoui, Robust aggregation for federated learning, IEEE Transactions on Signal Processing 70 (2022) 1142–1154.

[22] Ximing Qiao, Yukun Yang, Hai Helen Li, Defending neural backdoors via generative distribution modeling, in: NeurIPS, 2019.

[23] Virat Shejwalkar, Amir Houmansadr, Manipulating the Byzantine: optimizing model poisoning attacks and defenses for federated learning, in: NDSS, 2021.

[24] Virat Shejwalkar, Amir Houmansadr, Peter Kairouz, Daniel Ramage, Back to the drawing board: a critical evaluation of poisoning attacks on production federated learning, in: IEEE Symposium on Security and Privacy, 2022.

[25] Ziteng Sun, Peter Kairouz, Ananda Theertha Suresh, H.B. McMahan, Can you really backdoor federated learning?, arXiv:1911.07963, 2019.

[26] Vale Tolpegin, Stacey Truex, Mehmet Emre Gursoy, Ling Liu, Data poisoning attacks against federated learning systems, in: European Symposium on Research in Computer Security, Springer, 2020, pp. 480–501.

[27] Hongyi Wang, Kartik Sreenivasan, Shashank Rajput, Harit Vishwakarma, Saurabh Agarwal, Jy-yong Sohn, Kangwook Lee, Dimitris Papailiopoulos, Attack of the tails: yes, you really can backdoor federated learning, Advances in Neural Information Processing Systems 33 (2020) 16070–16084.

[28] Yunjuan Wang, Poorya Mianjy, R. Arora, Robust learning for data poisoning attacks, in: ICML, 2021.

[29] E. Weiszfeld, Sur le point pour lequel la somme des distances de n points donnés est minimum, Tohoku Mathematical Journal, First Series 43 (1937) 355–386.

[30] Chulin Xie, Minghao Chen, Pin-Yu Chen, Bo Li, CRFL: certifiably robust federated learning against backdoor attacks, in: International Conference on Machine Learning, PMLR, 2021, pp. 11372–11382.

[31] Chulin Xie, Keli Huang, Pin-Yu Chen, Bo Li, DBA: distributed backdoor attacks against federated learning, in: International Conference on Learning Representations, 2019.

[32] Chulin Xie, Yunhui Long, Pin-Yu Chen, Krishnaram Kenthapadi, Bo Li, Certified robustness for free in differentially private federated learning, in: NeurIPS 2021 New Frontiers in Federated Learning Workshop, 2021.

[33] Cong Xie, Toward communication-efficient and secure distributed machine learning, PhD thesis, University of Illinois at Urbana-Champaign, 2021.

[34] Cong Xie, Oluwasanmi Koyejo, Indranil Gupta, SLSGD: secure and efficient distributed on-device machine learning, in: ECML/PKDD, 2019.

[35] Cong Xie, Oluwasanmi Koyejo, Indranil Gupta, Zeno: distributed stochastic gradient descent with suspicion-based fault-tolerance, in: ICML, 2019.

[36] Dong Yin, Yudong Chen, Ramchandran Kannan, Peter Bartlett, Byzantine-robust distributed learning: towards optimal statistical rates, in: Jennifer Dy, Andreas Krause (Eds.), Proceedings of the 35th International Conference on Machine Learning, in: Proceedings of Machine Learning Research, PMLR, 2018.

Evaluating gradient inversion attacks and defenses

6

Yangsibo Huang[a], Samyak Gupta[b], Zhao Song[c], Sanjeev Arora[b], and Kai Li[b]

[a]*Electrical and Computer Engineering, Princeton University, Princeton, NJ, United States*
[b]*Princeton University, Princeton, NJ, United States*
[c]*Adobe Research, San Jose, CA, United States*

6.1 Introduction

Federated learning [27,34] is a framework that allows multiple clients in a distributed environment to collaboratively train a neural network model at a central server while keeping training data resident on each client's machine. At every training step, each client computes a model update, i.e., gradient, on its local data using the latest copy of the global model, and then sends the gradient to the central server. The server aggregates these updates (typically by averaging) to construct a global model, and then sends the new model parameters to all clients. By allowing clients to participate in training without directly sharing their data, such protocols align better with data privacy regulations such as Health Insurance Portability and Accountability Act (HIPPA) [2], General Data Protection Regulation [10], and California Consumer Privacy Act (CCPA) [31].

While sharing gradients was initially thought to leak little information about the client's private data, recent papers [18,45,49,51] developed a "gradient inversion attack" by which an attacker which has access to transmitted gradients and model parameters can reconstruct a client's private training data. An attacker in this scenario could be a malicious participant in the federated learning scheme – including an honest-but-curious server who wishes to reconstruct the private data of clients, or an honest-but-curious client who wishes to reconstruct the private data of other clients. The discovery of the attack has created widespread concern about the level of privacy ensured in federated learning. This chapter will outline the ways in which the risks of gradient inversion attacks are evaluated and can be minimized.

Several defenses against gradient inversion attacks have been proposed. These include perturbing gradients [43,51] and using transformation for training data that clients can apply on the fly [23,46]. More traditional cryptographic ideas including secure aggregation [7] or homomorphic encryption [38] for the gradients can also be used and presumably stop any eavesdropping attacks completely. They will not be studied here due to their special setups and overhead.

Federated Learning. https://doi.org/10.1016/B978-0-44-319037-7.00014-4

First, we draw attention to two strong assumptions that a current gradient inversion attack [18] implicitly makes. We show that by nullifying these assumptions, the performance of the attack drops significantly and can only work for low-resolution images. The findings are explored in Section 6.3 and already imply some more secure configurations in federated learning (Section 6.6).

Second, we summarize various defenses (Section 6.4) and systematically evaluate (Section 6.5) some of their performance of defending against a state-of-the-art gradient inversion attack, and present their data utility and privacy leakage trade-offs. We estimate the computation cost of end-to-end recovery of a single image under each evaluated defense. We also experimentally demonstrate the feasibility and effectiveness of combined defenses. Our findings are summarized as strategies to further improve federated learning's security against gradient inversion attacks (Section 6.6). Finally, we discuss emerging topics and future directions for gradient inversion attacks (Section 6.7).

6.2 Gradient inversion attacks

Previous studies have shown the feasibility of recovering input from gradient (i.e., gradient inversion) for image classification tasks, by formulating it as an optimization problem: given a neural network with parameters θ, and the gradient $\nabla_\theta \mathcal{L}_\theta(x^*, y^*)$ computed with a private data batch $(x^*, y^*) \in \mathbb{R}^{b \times d} \times \mathbb{R}^b$ (b, d being the batch and image sizes, respectively), the attacker tries to recover $x \in \mathbb{R}^{b \times d}$, an approximation of x^*, as

$$\arg\min_x \mathcal{L}_{\text{grad}}(x; \theta, \nabla_\theta \mathcal{L}_\theta(x^*, y^*)) + \alpha \mathcal{R}_{\text{aux}}(x). \qquad (6.1)$$

The optimization goal consists of two parts: the term $\mathcal{L}_{\text{grad}}(x; \theta, \nabla_\theta \mathcal{L}_\theta(x^*, y^*))$ enforces matching of the gradient of recovered batch x with the provided gradients $\mathcal{L}_\theta(x^*, y^*)$, while the term $\mathcal{R}_{\text{aux}}(x)$ further improves reconstructions by regularizing the loss using known image priors. Notably, the attack becomes more difficult as the dimensionality of the private batch x grows, namely, when x is a large training batch, or when x consists of high-dimension inputs (e.g., high-resolution images). Additionally, the model architecture and size further impact the quality of reconstruction.

Phong et al. [37] bring theoretical insights on this task by proving that such a reconstruction is possible with a single-layer neural network. Zhu et al. [51] are the first to show that accurate pixel-level reconstruction is practical for a maximum batch size of 8, using the ℓ_2-distance as $\mathcal{L}_{\text{grad}}(\cdot, \cdot)$, and not including a regularization term $\mathcal{R}_{\text{aux}}(x)$. The approach is successful for low-resolution CIFAR datasets [29] with simple neural networks with sigmoid activations, but cannot scale up to high-resolution images, or larger models with ReLU activations. Follow-up work [49] proposes a simple approach that can partially extract the ground-truth labels from the gradient, further strengthening the attack by relaxing the need to reconstruct labels y^* during gradient inversion (see Section 6.3.2 for more detail). More recent approaches improve recovery by adjusting the choice of $\mathcal{L}_{\text{grad}}$ and adding a regularization term $\mathcal{R}_{\text{aux}}(x)$. Geiping et al. [18] substantially improve the attack and enable recovery of low-resolution images from a maximum batch size of 100 from gradients by choosing cosine distance for $\mathcal{L}_{\text{grad}}$, and total variation for $\mathcal{R}_{\text{aux}}(x)$ (described in more detail in the following section). Moreover, the approach is able to reconstruct a single high-resolution image from ImageNet [11]. Wei et al. [43] provide an analysis of how different configurations in the training may affect the attack by Geiping et al.

A more recent work [45] further improves the attack on high-resolution images, by adding an additional regularization term based on batch normalization [25] statistics and incorporating a regularization term that enforces consistency across multiple attack trials.

An orthogonal line of work [50] proposes to formulate the gradient inversion attack as a closed-form recursive procedure, instead of an optimization problem. However, this approach can recover only low-resolution images when the training batch size is 1.

6.3 Strong assumptions made by SOTA attacks

6.3.1 The state-of-the-art attacks

The two previously mentioned approaches by Geiping et al. [18] and Yin et al. [45] represent the state-of-the-art in gradient inversion attacks. In this section, we analyze the approach used by Geiping et al., and also consider some unrealistic assumptions made by the attack which weakens its strength in a more practical scenario.[1]

Geiping et al. [18] optimize the following objective function:

$$\arg\min_{x} 1 - \frac{\langle \nabla_\theta \mathcal{L}_\theta(x, y), \nabla_\theta \mathcal{L}_\theta(x^*, y^*) \rangle}{\|\nabla_\theta \mathcal{L}_\theta(x, y)\| \|\nabla_\theta \mathcal{L}_\theta(x^*, y^*)\|} + \alpha_{\text{TV}} \mathcal{R}_{\text{TV}}(x), \qquad (6.2)$$

where $\langle \cdot, \cdot \rangle$ is the inner-product between vectors, and $\mathcal{R}_{\text{TV}}(\cdot)$ is the total variation of images.

We notice that Geiping et al. have made two strong assumptions (Section 6.3.2). Changing setups to invalidate those assumptions will substantially weaken the attacks (Section 6.3.3). We also summarize whether other attacks have made similar assumptions in Table 6.1.

6.3.2 Strong assumptions

We now describe two different assumptions made by previous attacks which could weaken its strength in a more realistic scenario. Note that the attack from [18] makes both strong assumptions.

---

[1] We do not analyze the approach by [45], as the implementation is not available at the time of writing this chapter.

Table 6.1 Assumptions of gradient inversion attacks.

Assumptions	Zhu et al. [51]	Zhao et al. [49]	Geiping et al. [18]	Yin et al. [45]
Knowing BN statistics	N/A[a]	N/A[a]	Yes	Yes[c]
Knowing private labels	No	No[b]	Yes	No[b]

[a] *Its evaluation uses a simple model without a BatchNorm layer.*
[b] *It proposes a method to infer private labels, which works when images in a batch have unique labels (see Section 6.3.3).*
[c] *Although the paper discusses a setting where BatchNorm statistics are unknown, its main results assume knowing BatchNorm statistics.*

Assumption 1: Knowledge of BatchNorm statistics

Batch normalization (BatchNorm) [25] is a technique for training neural networks that normalize the inputs to a layer for every mini-batch. Notably, batch normalization behaves differently during training and evaluation. Assume the model has L batch normalization layers. Given x^*, a batch of input images, we use x_l^* to denote the input features to the lth BatchNorm layer, where $l \in [L]$. During training, the lth BatchNorm layer normalizes x_l^* based on the batch's mean $\text{mean}(x_l^*)$ and variance $\text{var}(x_l^*)$, and keeps a running estimate of mean and variance of all training data points, denoted by μ_l and σ_l^2, respectively. During inference, $\{\mu_l\}_{l=1}^L$ and $\{\sigma_l^2\}_{l=1}^L$ are used to normalize test images. For brevity, we use μ, σ^2 to denote $\{\mu_l\}_{l=1}^L, \{\sigma_l^2\}_{l=1}^L$, and $\text{mean}(x^*), \text{var}(x^*)$ to denote $\{\text{mean}(x_l^*)\}_{l=1}^L, \{\text{var}(x_l^*)\}_{l=1}^L$ in the following sections.

We notice that Geiping et al.'s [18] implementation[2] assumes that BatchNorm statistics of the private batch, i.e., $\text{mean}(x^*), \text{var}(x^*)$, are jointly provided with the gradient. Knowing BatchNorm statistics would enable the attacker to apply the same batch normalization used by the private batch on his recovered batch, to achieve a better reconstruction. This implicitly increases the power of the attacker, as sharing private BatchNorm statistics is not necessary for federated learning [3,33].

Note that this assumption may still be valid in some scenarios, e.g., if 1) the neural network is shallow, thus does not require using BatchNorm layers, or if 2) the neural network is deep, but adapts approaches that normalize batch inputs with a fixed mean and variance (as an alternative to BatchNorm), e.g., fixup initialization [47].

Assumption 2: Knowing or being able to infer private labels

Private labels are not intended to be shared in federated learning, but knowing them would improve the attack. Zhao et al. [49] find that label information of a *single* private image can be inferred from the gradient (see Section 6.3.3 for details). Based on this, the authors of [18] assume the attacker knows private labels (see remark at the end of Section 4 in their paper). However, this assumption may not hold true when multiple images in a batch share the same label, as we will show in the next section.

---

[2] The official implementation of [18]: https://github.com/JonasGeiping/invertinggradients.

6.3.3 **Re-evaluation under relaxed assumptions**

We re-evaluate the performance of the gradient inversion attack in settings where the two assumptions above are relaxed. For each relaxation, we re-design the attack (if needed) based on the knowledge that the attacker has.

Relaxation 1: Not knowing BatchNorm statistics

We refer to the previous threat model as BN_{exact}, where the attacker knows the exact BatchNorm statistics of the private batch. We consider a realistic threat model where these statistics are not exposed and re-design the attack based on it.

Threat model. In each training step, the client normalizes its private batch x^* using the batch's mean $mean(x^*)$ and variance $var(x^*)$, keeps the running estimate of mean and variance *locally* as in [33], and shares the gradient. The client releases the final aggregated mean μ, and aggregated variance σ^2 of all training data points at the end of training. Same as before, the attacker has access to the model and the gradient during training.

Re-design A: BN_{proxy}, *attacker naively uses μ and σ^2.* A simple idea is that the attacker uses (μ, σ^2) as the proxy for $(mean(x^*), var(x^*))$, and uses them to normalize x, his guesses of the private batch. Other operations of the gradient inversion attack remain the same as before. However, Figs. 6.1.d and 6.1.h show poor-quality reconstruction with this re-design.

Re-design B: BN_{infer}, *attacker infers $(mean(x^*), var(x^*))$ based on (μ, σ^2).* A more reasonable attacker will try to infer $(mean(x^*), var(x^*))$ while updating x, his guesses of the private batch, and uses $(mean(x), var(x))$ to normalize the batch. In this case, (μ, σ^2) could be used as a prior of BatchNorm statistics to regularize the recovery, as suggested in [45]:

$$\underset{x}{\arg\min}\, 1 - \frac{\langle \nabla_\theta \mathcal{L}_\theta(x, y), \nabla_\theta \mathcal{L}_\theta(x^*, y^*) \rangle}{\|\nabla_\theta \mathcal{L}_\theta(x, y)\| \|\nabla_\theta \mathcal{L}_\theta(x^*, y^*)\|} + \alpha_{TV} \mathcal{R}_{TV}(x) + \alpha_{BN} \mathcal{R}_{BN}(x), \quad (6.3)$$

where $\mathcal{R}_{BN}(x) = \sum_l \|mean(x_l) - \mu_l\|_2 + \sum_l \|var(x_l) - \sigma_l^2\|_2$.

As shown, for a batch of low-resolution images, BN_{infer} gives a much better reconstruction result than BN_{proxy}, but still cannot recover some details of the private batch when compared with BN_{exact}. The result for a single high-resolution image is worse: the attacker fails to return a recognizable reconstruction with BN_{infer}. This suggests not having access to BatchNorm statistics of the private batch already weakens the state-of-the-art gradient inversion attack.

Relaxation 2: Not knowing private labels

Zhao et al. [49] note that label information of a *single* private image can be computed analytically from the gradients of the layer immediately before the output layer. Yin et al. [45] further extend this method to support the recovery of labels for a batch of images. However, if multiple images in the private batch belong to the same label, neither approach can tell how many images belong to that label, let alone which subset of images belongs to that label. Fig. 6.2a demonstrates that with CIFAR-10,

(a) Original (b) BN$_{\text{exact}}$ (c) BN$_{\text{infer}}$ (d) BN$_{\text{proxy}}$ (e) Original (f) BN$_{\text{exact}}$ (g) BN$_{\text{infer}}$ (h) BN$_{\text{proxy}}$

FIGURE 6.1

Attacking a batch of 16 low-resolution images from CIFAR-10 (a)–(d) and a single high-resolution image from ImageNet (e)–(h) with different knowledge of BatchNorm statistics. The attack is weakened when BatchNorm statistics are not available (c)–(d) vs. (b), and (g)–(h) vs. (f).

(a) Distribution of labels in a batch   (b) Reconstructions with and without private labels

FIGURE 6.2

Attack is weakened when private labels are not available: panel (a) shows that for CIFAR-10, when the batch size is large, many images in the batch belong to the same class, which essentially weakens label restoration [45,49]; panel (b) visualizes a reconstructed batch of 16 images with and without private labels known. The quality of the reconstruction drops without knowledge of private labels.

for batches of various sizes, it is possible for many of the training samples to have the same label, and the distribution of labels is not uniform – and hence, inferring labels becomes harder and the attack would be weakened. In Fig. 6.2b, we evaluate the worst-case for an attacker in this setting by comparing recoveries where the batch labels are simultaneously reconstructed alongside the training samples.

6.4 Defenses against the gradient inversion attack

Several defense ideas have been proposed to mitigate the risks of gradient inversion. This chapter considers three kinds of defense methods.

6.4.1 Encrypt gradients

Cryptography-based approaches encrypt gradient to prevent gradient inversion. Bonawitz et al. [7] present a secure aggregation protocol for federated learning by computing the sum of gradient vectors based on secret sharing [41]. Phong et al. [38] propose using homomorphic encryption to encrypt the gradients before sending. These approaches require a special setup and can be costly to implement.

Moreover, with a secure aggregation protocol, an honest-but-curious server can still launch the gradient inversion attack on the summed gradient vector. Similarly, an honest-but-curious client can launch the gradient inversion attack on the model returned by the server to reconstruct other clients' private data, even with homomorphic encryption.

As alternatives, two other types of defensive mechanisms have been proposed to mitigate the risks of attacks on *plain-text* gradient.

6.4.2 Perturbing gradients

Gradient pruning. When proposing the first practical gradient inversion attack, Zhu et al. [51] also suggest a defense by setting gradients of small magnitudes to zero (i.e., gradient pruning). Based on their attack, they demonstrate that pruning more than 70% of the gradients would make the recovered images no longer visually recognizable. However, the suggested pruning ratio is determined based on weaker attacks, and may not remain safe against the state-of-the-art attack.

Adding noise to gradient. Motivated by DPSGD [1] which adds noise to gradients to achieve differential privacy [15,16], recent works [43,51] also suggest defending by adding Gaussian or Laplacian noise to the gradient. They show that a successful defense requires adding a high noise level such that its accuracy drops by more than 30% with CIFAR-10 tasks. Recent empirical studies [36,42] suggest using better pre-training techniques and larger batch sizes (e.g., 4096) to achieve better accuracy for DPSGD training.

Since most DPSGD implementations for natural image classification tasks [1,36, 42] use a pre-training and fine-tuning pipeline, it is hard to fairly compare with other defense methods that can directly apply when training the model from scratch. Thus, we leave the comparison with DPSGD to future work.

6.4.3 Weak encryption of inputs (encoding inputs)

MixUp. MixUp data augmentation [46] trains neural networks on composite images created via a linear combination of image pairs. It has been shown to improve the generalization of the neural network and stabilizes the training. Recent work also suggests that MixUp increases the model's robustness to adversarial examples [30, 35].

InstaHide. Inspired by MixUp, Huang et al. [23] propose InstaHide as a light-weight instance-encoding scheme for private distributed learning. To encode an image $x \in \mathbb{R}^d$ from a private dataset, InstaHide first picks $k - 1$ other images $s_2, s_3, \ldots, s_k$ from that private dataset, or a large public dataset, and k random nonnegative coefficients $\{\lambda_i\}_{i=1}^k$ that sum to 1, and creates a composite image $\lambda_1 x + \sum_{i=2}^k \lambda_i s_i$ (k is typically small, e.g., 4). A composite label is also created using the same set of coefficients.[3] Then it adds another layer of security by picking a random sign-flipping pattern $\sigma \in \{-1, 1\}^d$ and outputting the encryption $\tilde{x} = \sigma \circ (\lambda_1 x + \sum_{i=2}^{k} \lambda_i s_i)$, where $\circ$ is the coordinate-wise multiplication of vectors. The neural network is then trained on encoded images, which look like random pixel vectors to the human eye and yet lead to good classification accuracy ($< 6\%$ accuracy loss on CIFAR-10, CIFAR-100, and ImageNet).

Recently, Carlini et al. [8] give an attack to recover private images of a small dataset, when the InstaHide encodings are revealed to the attacker (not in a federated learning setting). Their first step is to train a neural network on a public dataset for similarity annotation, to infer whether a pair of InstaHide encodings contain the same private image. With the inferred similarities of all pairs of encodings, the attacker then runs a combinatorial algorithm (cubic time in the size of private dataset) to cluster all encodings based on their original private images, and finally uses a regression algorithm (with the help of composite labels) to recover the private images.

Neither Huang et al. [23] nor Carlini et al. [8] have evaluated their defense or attack in the federated learning setting, where the attacker observes gradients of the encoded images instead of the original encoded images. This necessitates the systematic evaluation in our next section.

6.5 Evaluation

The main goal of our experiments is to understand the trade-offs between data utility (accuracy) and securely defending the state-of-the-art gradient inversion attack even in its strongest setting, *without* any relaxation of its implicit assumptions. Specifically, we grant the attacker the knowledge of 1) BatchNorm statistics of the private batch, and 2) labels of the private batch.

We vary key parameters for each defense and evaluate their performance in terms of the test accuracy, computation overhead, and privacy risks (Section 6.5.2). We then investigate the feasibility of combining defenses (Section 6.5.3). We also estimate the computation cost of end-to-end recovery of a single image under evaluated defenses (Section 6.5.4).

As the feasibility of the state-of-the-art attack [18] on a batch of high-resolution images remains elusive when its implicit assumptions no longer hold (see Fig. 6.1), we focus on the evaluation with low-resolution in trying to understand whether current attacks can be mitigated.

6.5.1 Experimental setup

Key parameters of defenses. We evaluate the following defenses on CIFAR-10 dataset [29] with ResNet-18 architecture [22].

---

[3] Only the labels of examples from the private dataset will get combined. See [23] for details.

- **GradPrune** gradient pruning sets gradients of small magnitudes to zero. We vary the pruning ratio p in $\{0.5, 0.7, 0.9, 0.95, 0.99, 0.999\}$.
- **MixUp** encodes a private image by linearly combining it with $k-1$ other images from the training set. Following [23], we vary k in $\{4, 6\}$, and set the upper bound of a single coefficient to 0.65 (coefficients sum to 1).
- **Intra-InstaHide**. InstaHide [23] proposes two versions, namely Inter-InstaHide and Intra-InstaHide. The only difference is that at the mixup step, Inter-Instahide mixes up an image with images from a public dataset, whereas Intra-InstaHide only mixes with private images. Both versions apply a random sign-flipping pattern on each mixed image. We evaluate Intra-InstaHide in our experiments, which is a weaker version of InstaHide. Similar to the evaluation of MixUp, we vary k in $\{4, 6\}$, and set the upper bound of a single coefficient to 0.65. Note that InstaHide flips signs of pixels in the image, which destroys the total variation prior. However, the absolute value of adjacent pixels should still be close. Therefore, for the InstaHide defense, we apply the total variation regularizer on $|x|$, i.e., taking the absolute value of each pixel in the reconstruction.

We train the ResNet-18 architecture on CIFAR-10 using different defenses and launch the attack.

The attack. We use a subset of 50 CIFAR-10 images to evaluate the attack performance. Note that attacking MixUp and InstaHide involves another step to decode private images from the encoded images. We apply Carlini et al.'s attack [8] here as the decode step, where the attacker needs to eavesdrop T epochs of training, instead of a single training step. We set $T = 20$ in our evaluation. We also grant the attacker the strongest power for the decode step to evaluate the upper bound of privacy leakage. Given a MixUp or Intra-InstaHide image which encodes k private images, we assume the attacker knows:

1. The indices of k images in the private dataset. In a realistic scenario, the attacker of [8] would need to train a neural network to detect the similarity of encodings, and run a combinatorial algorithm to solve *an approximation of* this mapping.
2. The mixing coefficients for each of the k private images. In real federated learning, this information is *not available*.

Hyper-parameters of the attack. The attack minimize the objective function given in Eq. (6.3). We search for α_{TV} in $\{0, 0.001, 0.005, 0.01, 0.05, 0.1, 0.5\}$ for all defenses, and apply the best choice for each defense: 0.05 for GradPrune, 0.1 for MixUp, and 0.01 for Intra-InstaHide. We apply $\alpha_{BN} = 0.001$ for all defenses after searching for it in $\{0, 0.0005, 0.001, 0.01, 0.05, 0.01\}$. We optimize the attack for 10, 000 iterations using Adam [28], with an initial learning rate 0.1. We decay the learning rate by a factor of 0.1 at $3/8, 5/8, 7/8$ of the optimization.

Batch size of the attack. Recent works [18,51] have shown that small batch size is important for the success of the attack. We intentionally evaluate the attack with three small batch sizes to test the upper bound of privacy leakage, including the minimum (and unrealistic) batch size 1, and two small but realistic batch sizes, 16 and 32.

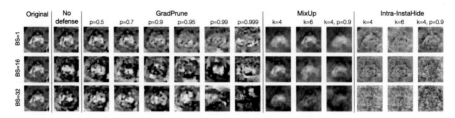

FIGURE 6.3

Reconstruction results under different defenses with batch size being 1, 16, and 32. When the batch size is 32, combining gradient pruning and Intra-InstaHide makes the reconstruction almost unrecognizable (the last column).

Metrics for reconstruction quality. We visualize reconstructions obtained under different defenses. Following [45], we also use the learned perceptual image patch similarity (LPIPS) score [48] to measure mismatch between reconstruction and original images: higher values suggest more mismatch (less privacy leakage).

6.5.2 Performance of defense methods

We summarize the performance of each defense in Table 6.2 and visualize reconstructed images in Fig. 6.3. We report the averaged and the best results for the metric of reconstruction quality, as a proxy for average-case and worst-case privacy leakage.

No defense. Without any defense, when batch size is 1, the attack can recover images well from the gradient. Increasing the batch size makes it difficult to recover well, but the recovered images are visually similar to the originals (see Fig. 6.3).

Gradient pruning (GradPrune). Fig. 6.3 shows that as the pruning ratio p increases, there are more artifacts in the reconstructions. However, the reconstructions are still recognizable even when the pruning ratio $p = 0.9$, thus the previous suggestion of using $p = 0.7$ by [51] is no longer safe against the state-of-the-art attack. Our results suggest that, for CIFAR-10, defending the strongest attack with gradient pruning may require the pruning ratio $p \geq 0.999$. As a trade-off, such a high pruning ratio would introduce an accuracy loss of around 10% (see Table 6.2).

MixUp introduces a small computational overhead to training. Indeed, MixUp with $k = 4$ only has a minor impact (~2%) on test accuracy, but it is not sufficient to defend against the gradient inversion attack (see Fig. 6.3). Increasing k from 4 to 6 slightly reduces the leakage, however, the reconstruction is still highly recognizable. This suggests that MixUp alone may not be a practical defense against the state-of-the-art gradient inversion attack.

Intra-InstaHide with $k = 4$ incurs an extra ~2% accuracy loss compared with MixUp, but it achieves better defense performance: when the batch size is 32, there are obvious artifacts and color shift in the reconstruction (see Fig. 6.3). However, with a batch size of 32, Intra-InstaHide alone also cannot defend against the state-of-the-art gradient inversion, as structures of private images are still vaguely identifiable in reconstructions.

Table 6.2 Utility–security trade-off of different defenses. We train the ResNet-18 model on the whole CIFAR-10 dataset, and report the averaged test accuracy and running time of 5 independent runs. We evaluate the attack on a subset of 50 CIFAR-10 images and report the LPIPS score (↓: lower values suggest more privacy leakage). We mark the least-leakage defense measured by the metric in **boldface**.

Parameter	None	GradPrune (p)						MixUp (k)		InstaHide (k)		GradPrune (p = 0.9) + MixUp + InstaHide	
	—	0.5	0.7	0.9	0.95	0.99	0.999	4	6	4	6	k = 4	k = 4
Test Acc.	93.37	93.19	93.01	90.57	89.92	88.61	83.58	92.31	90.41	90.04	88.20	91.37	86.10
Time (train)	1×			1.04×				1.06×		1.06×		1.10×	
Attack batch size = 1													
Avg. LPIPS ↓	0.19	0.19	0.22	0.35	0.42	0.52	0.52	0.34	0.46	0.58	**0.61**	0.41	0.60
Best LPIPS ↓	0.02	0.02	0.05	0.14	0.22	0.32	0.36	0.12	0.25	0.41	0.42	0.21	**0.43**
(LPIPS std.)	0.16	0.17	0.16	0.13	0.11	0.08	0.06	0.08	0.07	0.06	0.09	0.07	0.09
Attack batch size = 16													
Avg. LPIPS ↓	0.45	0.46	0.47	0.51	0.55	0.58	0.61	0.34	0.31	0.62	0.63	0.46	**0.68**
Best LPIPS ↓	0.18	0.19	0.19	0.31	0.43	0.47	0.51	0.11	0.13	0.41	0.44	0.22	**0.54**
(LPIPS std.)	0.12	0.12	0.11	0.07	0.05	0.04	0.03	0.09	0.09	0.08	0.08	0.10	0.07
Attack batch size = 32													
Avg. LPIPS ↓	0.45	0.46	0.48	0.52	0.54	0.58	0.63	0.50	0.49	0.69	0.69	0.62	**0.73**
Best LPIPS ↓	0.18	0.18	0.22	0.31	0.43	0.48	0.54	0.31	0.28	0.56	0.56	0.37	**0.65**
(LPIPS std.)	0.11	0.11	0.09	0.07	0.05	0.04	0.04	0.10	0.10	0.06	0.07	0.10	0.05

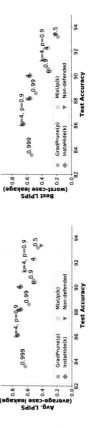

6.5.3 Performance of combined defenses

We notice that two types of defense (i.e., perturbing gradient and encoding inputs) are complementary to each other, which motivates an evaluation of combining gradient pruning with MixUp or Intra-InstaHide.

As shown in Fig. 6.3, when the batch size is 32, combining Intra-InstaHide ($k = 4$) with gradient pruning ($p = 0.9$) makes the reconstruction almost unrecognizable. The combined defense yields a higher LPIPS score than using gradient pruning with $p = 0.999$, but introduces a smaller accuracy loss (~7% compared with a no-defense pipeline).

6.5.4 Time estimate for end-to-end recovery of a single image

Table 6.3 shows time estimates for the end-to-end recovery of a single image in a federated learning setting with GradPrune or InstaHide defense. We do not estimate for MixUp since it has been shown to be a weak defense (see Section 6.5.2).

Our time estimates consider three fairly small dataset sizes. The largest size in our estimate is a small fraction of a dataset of ImageNet scale. We consider a client who holds a dataset of N private images and participates in federated learning, which trains an ResNet-18 model with batch size $b = 128$. Assumes that the resolution of the client's data is $32 \times 32 \times 3$. If the attacker uses a single NVIDIA GeForce RTX 2080 Ti GPU as his computation resource and runs gradient inversion with 10,000 iterations of optimization, then t, the running time for attacking a single batch, is ~0.25 GPU hours (batch size b has little impact on the attack's running time, but a larger b makes the attack less effective).

Non-defended and gradient pruning. Recovering a single image in a non-defended pipeline (or a pipeline that applies gradient pruning alone as the defense) only requires the attacker to invert the gradient of a single step of training, which takes time t.

InstaHide. When InstaHide is applied, the current attack [8] suggests that recovering a single image would involve recovering the whole dataset first. As discussed in Section 6.4, Carlini et al.'s attack consists of two steps: 1) recovering InstaHide images from the gradient of T epochs – this would take $(NT/b) \times t$ GPU hours; and 2) running the decode attack [8] on InstaHide images to recover the private dataset, which involves:

2a Training a neural network to detect similarity in recovered InstaHide images. Assume that training the network requires at least n recovered InstaHide images, then collecting these images by running gradient inversion would take $(n/b) \times t$ GPU hours. The training takes 10 GPU hours according to [8], so training the similarity network would take $(n/b) \times t + 10$ GPU hours in total.

2b Running the combinatorial algorithm to recover the original images. Running time of this step has been shown to be at least quadratic in m, the number of InstaHide encodings [9]. This step takes $1/6$ GPU hours with $m = 5 \times 10^3$. Therefore, for $m = NT$, the running time is at least $1/6 \times (\frac{NT}{5 \times 10^3})^2$ GPU hours.

Table 6.3 Time estimates (NVIDIA GeForce RTX 2080 Ti GPU hours) of recovering *a single image* from the client's dataset using the state-of-the-art gradient inversion attack [18] under different defenses. We assume the image resolution of the client's data is $32 \times 32 \times 3$.

Size of client's dataset (N)	No defense	GradPrune	InstaHide
5000			934.48
50,000	0.25	0.25	46,579.01 ($\approx$ 5.5 GPU years)
500,000			4,215,524.32 ($\approx$ 493.4 GPU years)

In total, an attack on InstaHide in this real-world setting would take $(NT/b) \times t + (n/b) \times t + 10 + 1/6 \times (\frac{NT}{5 \times 10^3})^2$ GPU hours. We use $T = 50$ (used by [8]), $n = 10,000$ and give estimates in Table 6.3. As shown, when InstaHide is applied on a small dataset ($N = 5,000$), the end-to-end recovery of a single image takes $> 3,000\times$ longer than in a no-defense pipeline or GradPrune pipeline; when InstaHide is applied on a larger dataset ($N = 500,000$), the computation cost for end-to-end recovery is enormous.

6.6 Conclusion

This chapter first pointed out that some recent gradient inversion attacks had made strong assumptions about knowing BatchNorm statistics and private labels. Relaxing such assumptions can significantly weaken these attacks.

We then reported the performance of a set of proposed defenses against gradient inversion attacks, and estimated the computation cost of an end-to-end recovery of a single image in different dataset sizes. Our evaluation showed that InstaHide without mixing with data from a public dataset combined with gradient pruning can defend against the state-of-the-art attack, and the estimated time to recover a single image in a medium-sized client dataset (e.g., of 500,000 images) is enormous.

Based on our evaluation of the attack by [18] and multiple defenses for *plain-text* gradients, we have several observations.

First, *using BatchNorm layers in your deep net but not sharing BatchNorm statistics of the private batch during federated learning weakens the attack*. We have demonstrated in Section 6.3 that exposing BatchNorm statistics to the attacker significantly improves the quality of gradient inversion. So a more secure configuration of federated learning would be to use BatchNorm layers, but not share BatchNorm statistics in training, which has been shown feasible in [3,33].

Second, *using a large batch size weakens the attack; a batch size smaller than 32 is not safe*. We have shown that a larger batch size hinders the attack by making it harder to guess the private labels (Section 6.3) and to recover the private images even with correct private labels (Section 6.5). Our experiments suggested that even with some weak defenses applied, a batch size smaller than 32 is not safe against the strongest gradient inversion attack.

Third, *combining multiple defenses may achieve a better utility–privacy trade-off.* In our experiment, for a batch size of 32, combining InstaHide ($k = 4$) with gradient pruning ($p = 0.9$) achieved the best utility–privacy trade-off, by making the reconstruction almost unrecognizable at a cost of ~7% accuracy loss (using InstaHide also made the end-to-end recovery of a single image more computationally expensive). Best parameters would vary for different deep learning tasks, but we strongly encourage federated learning participants to explore the possibility of combining multiple defensive mechanisms, instead of only using one of them.

6.7 Future directions

We would like to discuss several emerging topics and future directions in the area of gradient inversion attacks and defenses.

6.7.1 Gradient inversion attacks for text data

Federated learning has been used for privacy-sensitive applications with text data such as virtual mobile keyboards and analysis of electronic health records in hospitals [32], which also motivates the investigation of privacy leakage in federated learning with text data.

The earliest attempt to study the leakage of text from gradients is Zhu et al. [51], which briefly presented leakage results in masked language modeling [13]. Their attack aimed to match target gradients with continuous representations and mapped them back to words that were closest in the embedding matrix. Deng et al. [12] improved Zhu et al. [51] by adding a regularization term that prioritizes the gradient matching in layers that are closer to the input data. However, both works only presented results with a batch size of 1 and do not work well with larger batch sizes.

Apart from the above-mentioned optimization with continuous representations, Dimitrov et al. [14] proposed to reconstruct private sentences via discrete text transformation that minimizes both the gradient matching loss and the prior text probability computed by an auxiliary language model. They could recover a mini-batch of 4 sentences with binary classification tasks using the BERT [13] model. More recently, Gupta et al. [20] took a distinct approach that first identifies a set of words from gradients and then directly reconstructs sentences based on beam search and a prior-based reordering strategy; the attack is capable of recovering text from a large batch size of up to 128 sentences for a GPT-2 model [39].

6.7.2 Gradient inversion attacks in variants of federated learning

Inversion attack in vertical federated learning. Vertical federated learning (VFL) is designed for application scenarios where multiple data owners share the same data identity but their data differ in feature space. For instance, in the healthcare industry, data of the same patient across different institutions may need to be aggregated for diagnosis. Despite the prevalence of VFL applications [4,21,40,44], to the best of our knowledge, Jin et al.'s paper [26] is the only work that extends and improves the gradient inversion attack to the VFL setting, where the attacker leverages the data index and internal representation alignments in VFL to reconstruct private images.

A malicious and active server. Apart from the honest-but-curious attacker demonstrated in the previous sections, recent works [6,17] show that a malicious attacker locating on the central server in federated learning can significantly amplify the leakage of private data in gradient leakage by adversarially manipulating the model's weights. These attacks further suggest that federated learning systems based on the limited trust of the central server may expose clients to more severe privacy risks. However, it is still unclear whether the attacker under such a threat model is realistic, as their adversarial manipulations to gradients can be easily detected [17].

6.7.3 Defenses with provable guarantee

As previously discussed in Section 6.4, defenses against gradient leakage attacks in federated learning can be briefly categorized into (1) gradient encryption, (2) gradient perturbation, and (3) input encryption. Although end-to-end encryption protocols (category 1) such as secure multi-party computation provide provable guarantees, they usually require special setups and can be costly to implement in production. However, defenses in categories 2 and 3 usually do not provide a provable guarantee for the worst-case leakage from gradients: Gradient pruning [51] was proposed as an empirical defense and has been shown to have a weak connection with privacy preservation [24]; DPSGD [1] ensures that each gradient update and the trained model are differentially private, but it is still unclear how to interpret differential privacy's guarantee against a reconstruction attacker [5,19], especially in the federated learning setting; InstaHide [23] presents average-case guarantee for single encryption. An adaptive attack [8] to this approach was proposed for a local setting. Whether there is an effective attack for a federated learning setting, especially when combining it with other defense methods such as the gradient pruning approach as described in this chapter, is a question to be answered.

We advocate a future study of novel defense methods (or adaptations of previously proposed defenses) with a provable guarantee against reconstruction attackers to preserve privacy for the user's training data.

References

[1] Martin Abadi, Andy Chu, Ian Goodfellow, H. Brendan McMahan, Ilya Mironov, Kunal Talwar, Li Zhang, Deep learning with differential privacy, in: Proceedings of the 2016 ACM SIGSAC Conference on Computer and Communications Security, 2016, pp. 308–318.

[2] Accountability Act, Health insurance portability and accountability act of 1996, Public Law 104 (1996) 191.

[3] Mathieu Andreux, Jean Ogier du Terrail, Constance Beguier, Eric W. Tramel, Siloed federated learning for multi-centric histopathology datasets, in: Domain Adaptation and Representation Transfer, and Distributed and Collaborative Learning, Springer, 2020, pp. 129–139.

[4] Nick Angelou, Ayoub Benaissa, Bogdan Cebere, William Clark, Adam James Hall, Michael A. Hoeh, Daniel Liu, Pavlos Papadopoulos, Robin Roehm, Robert Sandmann, et al., Asymmetric private set intersection with applications to contact tracing and private vertical federated machine learning, arXiv:2011.09350, 2020.

[5] Borja Balle, Giovanni Cherubin, Jamie Hayes, Reconstructing training data with informed adversaries, arXiv:2201.04845, 2022.

[6] Franziska Boenisch, Adam Dziedzic, Roei Schuster, Ali Shahin Shamsabadi, Ilia Shumailov, Nicolas Papernot, When the curious abandon honesty: federated learning is not private, arXiv:2112.02918, 2021.

[7] K.A. Bonawitz, Vladimir Ivanov, Ben Kreuter, Antonio Marcedone, H. Brendan McMahan, Sarvar Patel, Daniel Ramage, Aaron Segal, Karn Seth, Practical secure aggregation for federated learning on user-held data, in: NIPS Workshop on Private Multi-Party Machine Learning, 2016.

[8] Nicholas Carlini, Samuel Deng, Sanjam Garg, Somesh Jha, Saeed Mahloujifar, Mohammad Mahmoody, Shuang Song, Abhradeep Thakurta, Florian Tramer, An attack on InstaHide: is private learning possible with instance encoding?, in: IEEE Symposium on Security and Privacy, 2020.

[9] Sitan Chen, Xiaoxiao Li, Zhao Song, Danyang Zhuo, On InstaHide, phase retrieval, and sparse matrix factorization, in: ICLR, 2021.

[10] European Commission, 2018 reform of EU data protection rules, https://gdpr-info.eu/, 2018.

[11] Jia Deng, Wei Dong, Richard Socher, Li-Jia Li, Kai Li, Fei-Fei Li, ImageNet: a large-scale hierarchical image database, in: CVPR, 2009.

[12] Jieren Deng, Yijue Wang, Ji Li, Chenghong Wang, Chao Shang, Hang Liu, Sanguthevar Rajasekaran, Caiwen Ding, TAG: gradient attack on transformer-based language models, in: Findings of the Association for Computational Linguistics: EMNLP 2021, 2021, pp. 3600–3610.

[13] Jacob Devlin, Ming-Wei Chang, Kenton Lee, Kristina Toutanova, BERT: pre-training of deep bidirectional transformers for language understanding, in: North American Chapter of the Association for Computational Linguistics (NAACL), 2019.

[14] Dimitar I. Dimitrov, Mislav Balunović, Nikola Jovanović, Martin Vechev, Lamp: extracting text from gradients with language model priors, arXiv:2202.08827, 2022.

[15] Cynthia Dwork, The differential privacy frontier, in: Theory of Cryptography Conference (TCC), 2009, pp. 496–502.

[16] Cynthia Dwork, Aaron Roth, The algorithmic foundations of differential privacy, Foundations and Trends in Theoretical Computer Science 9 (3–4) (2014) 211–407.

[17] Liam Fowl, Jonas Geiping, Steven Reich, Yuxin Wen, Wojtek Czaja, Micah Goldblum, Tom Goldstein, Decepticons: corrupted transformers breach privacy in federated learning for language models, arXiv:2201.12675, 2022.

[18] Jonas Geiping, Hartmut Bauermeister, Hannah Dröge, Michael Moeller, Inverting gradients–how easy is it to break privacy in federated learning?, in: NeurIPS, 2020.

[19] Chuan Guo, Brian Karrer, Kamalika Chaudhuri, Laurens van der Maaten, Bounding training data reconstruction in private (deep) learning, arXiv:2201.12383, 2022.

[20] Samyak Gupta, Yangsibo Huang, Zexuan Zhong, Tianyu Gao, Kai Li, Danqi Chen, Recovering private text in federated learning of language models, arXiv:2205.08514, 2022.

[21] Stephen Hardy, Wilko Henecka, Hamish Ivey-Law, Richard Nock, Giorgio Patrini, Guillaume Smith, Brian Thorne, Private federated learning on vertically partitioned data via entity resolution and additively homomorphic encryption, arXiv:1711.10677, 2017.

[22] Kaiming He, Xiangyu Zhang, Shaoqing Ren, Jian Sun, Deep residual learning for image recognition, in: CVPR, 2016.

[23] Yangsibo Huang, Zhao Song, Kai Li, Sanjeev Arora, InstaHide: instance-hiding schemes for private distributed learning, in: ICML, 2020.

[24] Yangsibo Huang, Yushan Su, Sachin Ravi, Zhao Song, Sanjeev Arora, Kai Li, Privacy-preserving learning via deep net pruning, arXiv:2003.01876, 2020.

[25] Sergey Ioffe, Christian Szegedy, Batch normalization: accelerating deep network training by reducing internal covariate shift, in: ICML, 2015.

[26] Xiao Jin, Pin-Yu Chen, Chia-Yi Hsu, Chia-Mu Yu, Tianyi Chen, CAFE: catastrophic data leakage in vertical federated learning, Advances in Neural Information Processing Systems 34 (2021) 994–1006.

[27] Peter Kairouz, H. Brendan McMahan, Brendan Avent, Aurélien Bellet, Mehdi Bennis, Arjun Nitin Bhagoji, Keith Bonawitz, Zachary Charles, Graham Cormode, Rachel Cummings, et al., Advances and open problems in federated learning, Foundations and Trends in Machine Learning 14 (1–2) (2021) 1–210.

[28] Diederik P. Kingma, Jimmy Ba, Adam: a method for stochastic optimization, in: ICLR, 2015.

[29] Alex Krizhevsky, et al., Learning multiple layers of features from tiny images, 2009.

[30] Alex Lamb, Vikas Verma, Juho Kannala, Yoshua Bengio, Interpolated adversarial training: achieving robust neural networks without sacrificing too much accuracy, in: Proceedings of the 12th ACM Workshop on Artificial Intelligence and Security, 2019, pp. 95–103.

[31] California State Legislature, California consumer privacy act, https://oag.ca.gov/privacy/ccpa, 2018.

[32] Li Tian, Anit Kumar Sahu, Ameet Talwalkar, Virginia Smith, Federated learning: challenges, methods, and future directions, IEEE Signal Processing Magazine 37 (3) (2020) 50–60.

[33] Xiaoxiao Li, Meirui Jiang, Xiaofei Zhang, Michael Kamp, Qi Dou, FedBN: Federated learning on non-iid features via local batch normalization, in: ICLR, 2021.

[34] H. Brendan McMahan, Eider Moore, Daniel Ramage, Seth Hampson, et al., Communication-efficient learning of deep networks from decentralized data, in: Artificial Intelligence and Statistics (AISTATS), 2016, pp. 1273–1282.

[35] Tianyu Pang, Kun Xu, Jun Zhu, Mixup inference: better exploiting mixup to defend adversarial attacks, in: ICLR, 2020.

[36] Nicolas Papernot, Steve Chien, Shuang Song, Abhradeep Thakurta, Ulfar Erlingsson. Making the shoe fit: Architectures, initializations, and tuning for learning with privacy, 2020.

[37] Le Trieu Phong, Yoshinori Aono, Takuya Hayashi, Lihua Wang, Shiho Moriai, Privacy-preserving deep learning: revisited and enhanced, in: ICATIS, 2017, pp. 100–110.

[38] Le Trieu Phong, Yoshinori Aono, Takuya Hayashi, Lihua Wang, Shiho Moriai, Privacy-preserving deep learning via additively homomorphic encryption, IEEE Transactions on Information Forensics and Security (2018).

[39] Alec Radford, Jeffrey Wu, Rewon Child, David Luan, Dario Amodei, Ilya Sutskever, et al., Language models are unsupervised multitask learners, OpenAI blog 1 (8) (2019) 9.

[40] Daniele Romanini, Adam James Hall, Pavlos Papadopoulos, Tom Titcombe, Abbas Ismail, Tudor Cebere, Robert Sandmann, Robin Roehm, Michael A. Hoeh, PyVertical: a vertical federated learning framework for multi-headed splitNN, arXiv:2104.00489, 2021.

[41] Adi Shamir, How to share a secret, Communications of the ACM 22 (11) (1979) 612–613.

[42] Florian Tramèr, Dan Boneh, Differentially private learning needs better features (or much more data), in: ICLR, 2021.

[43] Wenqi Wei, Ling Liu, Margaret Loper, Ka-Ho Chow, Mehmet Emre Gursoy, Stacey Truex, Yanzhao Wu, A framework for evaluating gradient leakage attacks in federated learning, arXiv:2004.10397, 2020.

[44] Qiang Yang, Yang Liu, Tianjian Chen, Yongxin Tong, Federated machine learning: concept and applications, ACM Transactions on Intelligent Systems and Technology (TIST) 10 (2) (2019) 1–19.

[45] Hongxu Yin, Arun Mallya, Arash Vahdat, Jose M. Alvarez, Jan Kautz, Pavlo Molchanov, See through gradients: image batch recovery via GradInversion, arXiv:2104.07586, 2021.

[46] Hongyi Zhang, Moustapha Cisse, Yann N. Dauphin, David Lopez-Paz, mixup: beyond empirical risk minimization, in: ICLR, 2018.

[47] Hongyi Zhang, Yann N. Dauphin, Tengyu Ma, Fixup initialization: residual learning without normalization, in: ICLR, 2019.

[48] Richard Zhang, Phillip Isola, Alexei A. Efros, Eli Shechtman, Oliver Wang, The unreasonable effectiveness of deep features as a perceptual metric, in: CVPR, 2018.

[49] Bo Zhao, Konda Reddy Mopuri, Hakan Bilen, iDLG: improved deep leakage from gradients, arXiv:2001.02610, 2020.

[50] Junyi Zhu, Matthew Blaschko, R-GAP: recursive gradient attack on privacy, in: ICLR, 2021.

[51] Ligeng Zhu, Zhijian Liu, Song Han, Deep leakage from gradients, in: NeurIPS, 2019.

Emerging topics

2

Personalized federated learning: theory and open problems

Canh T. Dinh[a], Tung T. Vu[b], and Nguyen H. Tran[a]
[a]*The University of Sydney, Darlington, NSW, Australia*
[b]*Queen's University Belfast, Belfast, United Kingdom*

7.1 Introduction

The abundance of data generated in a massive number of hand-held devices these days has stimulated the development of federated learning (FL) [28]. The setting of FL is a network of clients connected to a server, and its goal is to build a global model from clients' data in a privacy-preserving and communication-efficient manner. The current techniques that attempt to fulfill this goal mostly follow three main steps: (i) at each communication iteration, the server sends the current global model to clients; (ii) the clients update their local models using their local data; (iii) the server collects the latest local models from a subset of sampled clients in order to update a new global model, repeated until convergence [20,28,29,31].

Despite its benefits of data privacy and communication reduction, FL faces the main challenge that affects its performance and convergence rate: statistical diversity, which means that data distributions among clients are distinct (i.e., non-i.i.d.). When learning on non-i.i.d. data, FedAvg [28] witnessed a dramatic decrease in terms of accuracy. This decrease in performance is caused by the phenomenon of client drift [20] when the average global model is far from the global optimal solution. Thus, the global model is hardly well-generalized on each client's data. When the statistical diversity increases, generalization errors of the global model on clients' local data also increase significantly [7,24]. On the other hand, individual learning without FL (i.e., no client collaboration) will also have large generalization errors due to insufficient data. This issue raises the question: *How can we leverage the global model in FL to find a "personalized model" that is stylized for each client's data?* Motivated by the critical roles of personalized models in several business applications of healthcare, finance, and AI services [24], in this chapter, we study different approaches for pFL to handle statistical heterogeneity under the FL setting.

Multiple approaches have been proposed to achieve personalization in FL including *mixing models, meta-learning, multi-task learning, weight sharing, and clients clustering*. One early approach is finding a personalized model by *mixing* the global and local models. Hanzely and Richtárik [16] combined the optimization of the local and global models by proposing a communication-efficient variant of SGD known as the Loopless Local Gradient Descent (L2GD) algorithm. Mansour et al. [27] introduced three personalization approaches including client clustering, data interpolation, and model interpolation. While data interpolation needs meta-features from all clients (which is not feasible in FL due to privacy concerns), an Adaptive Personalized Federated Learning (APFL) algorithm proposed a method to mix a client's local model with the global model. We can also link the concept of personalization to *meta-learning*. Per-FedAvg [13], influenced by Model-Agnostic Meta-Learning (MAML) [14], built an initial meta-model to update the local models effectively after one more gradient descent step. During meta-optimization, however, MAML theoretically requires computing the Hessian term, which is computationally prohibitive. Therefore, several works including [12,14,30] attempted to approximate the Hessian matrix. Khodak et al. [21] based its framework, ARUBA, on online convex optimization and meta-learning, to integrate into FL to improve personalization. Jiang et al. [19] discovered that FedAvg is able to interpret as meta-learning and proposed combining FedAvg with Reptile [30] for pFL. Dinh et al. [9] proposed pFedMe using L_2-norm regularization to decouple personalized model optimization from the global model learning in a bi-level problem. In the sense of *multi-task learning*, [35] first introduced federated multi-task learning (FMTL) and proposed a systems-aware optimization framework MOCHA for handling stragglers and fault tolerance in FL settings. Dinh et al. [9] formulated the FMTL problem using Laplacian regularization to explicitly leverage the relationships among the models of clients for multi-task learning. Li et al. [25] introduced an FMTL algorithm to deal with the issues of accuracy, fairness, and robustness in FL. The personalization methods exploiting *weight sharing* in deep neural networks are [2,6,26], in which a network is divided into base and personalized layers. While only the base layers are sent to the server and then aggregated, both types of layers will be trained by clients to create a personalized model. The approach *clients clustering* of [27] has been studied in [4,10,15,34]. While [34] based on cosine similarity of the gradient updates from the clients to clusters clients, [4] used the global model as input of the agglomerative hierarchical clustering algorithm at each client to generate multiple clusters. Ghosh et al. [15] proposed the Iterative Federated Clustering Algorithm (IFCA) to construct K global models and assigned each client to one of the K clusters to archive the lowest loss value on the client's data. FedGroup [10] performs clustering on the local client updates using the KMeans++ algorithm [10] based on the Euclidean distance of the Decomposed Cosine similarity (EDC).

7.2 Problem formulation of pFL

In the traditional FL network, there are n clients, located at different sites and communicating with a server to learn a single global model $\mathbf{w}^*$ which is a solution to the following problem:

$$\min_{\mathbf{w}\in\mathbb{R}^d}\left\{g(\mathbf{w}) := \frac{1}{n}\sum_{m=1}^{n} g_m(\mathbf{w})\right\}, \tag{7.1}$$

where the function $g_m : \mathbb{R}^d \rightarrow \mathbb{R}$, $m = 1, \ldots, n$, denotes the expected loss over the data distribution of the mth client. Each client m has a local dataset D_m containing a collection of $|D_m|$ samples $\left(\mathbf{x}_m^{(i)}, c_m^{(i)}\right)_{i=1}^{D_m}$, where $\mathbf{x}_m^{(i)} \in \mathbb{R}^d$ is an input sample and $c_m^{(i)} \in \mathbb{R}$ can be a target response (or label). Then the local loss function of client m is the average of losses on its data points as follows[1]:

$$g_m(\mathbf{w}) = \frac{1}{|D_m|}\sum_{i=1}^{|D_m|} \ell_m(\mathbf{w}; (\mathbf{x}_m^{(i)}, c_m^{(i)})).$$

Among examples of the function ℓ_m are linear regression with $\ell_m(\mathbf{w}; (\mathbf{x}_m^{(i)}, c_m^{(i)})) = \frac{1}{2}(\langle \mathbf{x}_m^{(i)}, \mathbf{w}\rangle - c_m^{(i)})^2$ and logistic regression with $\ell_m(\mathbf{w}; (\mathbf{x}_m^{(i)}, c_m^{(i)})) = \log(1 + \exp(-c_m^{(i)}\langle \mathbf{x}_m^{(i)}, \mathbf{w}\rangle))$, $c_m^{(i)} \in \{-1, 1\}$, where $\langle \mathbf{x}, \mathbf{w}\rangle$ denotes the inner product of vectors $\mathbf{x}$ and $\mathbf{w}$.

While traditional object aims to find a single optimal solution for Eq. (7.1), most of pFL models in the literature are trained by minimizing specifically structured optimization problems which differ from Eq. (7.1) to find not only a single global model but also the personalized models for each client. Hanzely et al. [17] provide a general formulation for most of the current pFL approaches as

$$\min_{\mathbf{w}\in\mathbb{R}^{d_w}, \boldsymbol{\theta}\in\mathbb{R}^{d_\theta}}\left\{g(\mathbf{w}, \boldsymbol{\theta}) := \frac{1}{n}\sum_{m=1}^{n} g_m(\mathbf{w}, \boldsymbol{\theta}_m)\right\}, \tag{7.2}$$

where $\mathbf{w}$ is shared global parameter, $\boldsymbol{\theta} = (\boldsymbol{\theta}_1, \ldots, \boldsymbol{\theta}_n)$ are personalized models, $g_m(\mathbf{w}, \boldsymbol{\theta}_m) = \frac{1}{|D_m|}\sum_{i=1}^{|D_m|} \ell_m((\mathbf{w}, \boldsymbol{\theta}_m); (\mathbf{x}_m^{(i)}, c_m^{(i)}))$ is the local loss function of the mth client, and $0 \leq d_w, d_\theta \leq d$. The formulation (7.2) covers most of the existing convex and nonconvex pFL approaches by carefully constructing the local loss $g_m(\mathbf{w}, \boldsymbol{\theta}_m)$ [17] and traditional FL objective (7.1) when $d_\theta = 0$ and $d_{\mathbf{w}} = d$. Consequently, training different pFL models is equivalent to solving a particular instance of problem (7.2) and enables obtaining of a wide range of novel pFL formulations as a special case. In the cases of linear regression, logistic regression, or SVM, the general pFL's problem (7.2) is a convex problem. More complicated cases arise in the context of deep neural networks (DNN), convolutional neural networks (CNN), or recurrent neural networks (RNN) where a nonlinear mapping is used rather than the linear mapping $\mathbf{x}^T\mathbf{w}$. DNN, CNN, or RNN make predictions through a set of layers with a nonconvex function of the feature vector $\mathbf{x}$ by using nonlinear activation functions such as tanh, ReLu, Softmax. Then, Eq. (7.2) is nonconvex.

---

[1] In machine learning, this function is also called the empirical risk function.

7.3 Review of personalized FL approaches

In this section, we provide a systematic review of existing pFL approaches.

7.3.1 Mixing models

The general idea for mixing model context is to learn a personalized model for each client that is the optimal mixture of optimal local and global models. Common works using mixing technique are APFL [7], L2GD [16], and model interpolation [27]. In the APFL algorithm, a mixing parameter α_m for each client m is adaptively learned during the pFL training process to control the mixing weights between the global and local models. The formulation of APFL is given as

$$(\text{APFL}) \quad \min_{\boldsymbol{\theta}_0,\dots,\boldsymbol{\theta}_m \in \mathbb{R}^d} \left\{ g(\boldsymbol{\theta}) := \frac{1}{n} \sum_{m=1}^{n} g_m \left(\alpha_m \boldsymbol{\theta}_m + (1 - \alpha_m) \mathbf{w}^* \right) \right\}, \quad (7.3)$$

where $\mathbf{w}^* = \arg\min_{\mathbf{w} \in \mathbb{R}^d} g(\mathbf{w})$ is the solution to problem (7.1) and $\alpha_1, \dots, \alpha_m \in (0, 1)$ are adaptive weights to control the degree of personalization for each client. At each global communication round t, each client maintains three different models: local version of the global $\mathbf{w}_m^{(t)}$, its own local model $\boldsymbol{\theta}_m^{(t)}$, and the mixed personalized model $\bar{\boldsymbol{\theta}}_m^{(t)} = \alpha_m \boldsymbol{\theta}_m^{(t)} + (1 - \alpha_m) \mathbf{w}_m^{(t)}$. The weighting factor α_m can be found by solving $\alpha_m^* = \arg\min_{\alpha_m \in [0,1]} g_m (\alpha_m \boldsymbol{\theta} + (1 - \alpha_m)) \mathbf{w}$. The value of α_m is expected to be smaller if the local and global data distributions are close, and vice versa. A similar approach with APFL involving the mixing of local and global models has also been proposed in [27].

In the L2GD algorithm [16], another formulation that learns personalized models using a mixture of global and local models to balance generalization with personalization is

$$(\text{L2GD}) \quad \min_{\boldsymbol{\theta}_1,\dots,\boldsymbol{\theta}_m \in \mathbb{R}^d} \left\{ g(\boldsymbol{\theta}) := \frac{1}{n} \sum_{m=1}^{n} g_m (\boldsymbol{\theta}_m) + \frac{\lambda}{2} \| \boldsymbol{\theta}_m - \bar{\mathbf{w}} \|^2 \right\}, \quad (7.4)$$

where $\bar{\mathbf{w}} = \frac{1}{n} \sum_{m=1}^{n} \boldsymbol{\theta}_m$. If $\boldsymbol{\theta}(\lambda) := \boldsymbol{\theta}_1(\lambda), \dots, \boldsymbol{\theta}_m(\lambda)$ is the unique solution to problem (7.4) for a given value of λ, client m learns an individual local model $\boldsymbol{\theta}_m(\lambda)$. The penalty parameter $\lambda \in (0, \infty)$ is used to discourage the local models from being too dissimilar from the mean model. Pure local model learning occurs when λ is set to zero. As λ increases, mixed model learning occurs and the local models become increasingly similar to each other. The setting approximates global model learning in which all local models are forced to be identical when λ approaches infinity. In this way, the degree of personalization can be controlled. The author also provided a communication-efficient framework in which more local GD steps performed will reduce the communication rounds.

7.3.2 **Model-based approaches: meta-learning**

Meta-learning is known as a "learning to learn" method that can learn new and heterogeneous tasks quickly and effectively [14,30]. MAML [14] and Reptile [30] are two well-known meta-learning algorithms and are widely used by their ability to fast adapt to new heterogeneous tasks. A common meta-learning process includes meta-training and meta-testing steps. The meta-training step in MAML can be mapped to the FL global model training process, while the meta-testing step can be mapped to the FL personalization process. Inspired by the idea of applying meta-learning to find the meta global model which can quickly adapt to the client's data to improve the performance of FL over non-i.i.d. data, the authors of [13] and [9] came up with Per-FedAvg and pFedMe algorithms for pFL. Specifically, Per-FedAvg in [13] aims to find a global model $\mathbf{w}$ which client m can use as an *initialization* to perform one more step of gradient update with respect to its own loss function to obtain its personalized model $\boldsymbol{\theta}_m(\mathbf{w})$. The formulation of Per-FedAvg is provided as

$$(\text{Per-FedAvg}) \quad \min_{\mathbf{w}\in\mathbb{R}^d}\left\{g(\mathbf{w}):=\frac{1}{n}\sum_{m=1}^{n}g_m\Big(\mathbf{w}-\alpha\nabla g_m(\mathbf{w})\Big)\right\}, \quad (7.5)$$

where α is the step size, $g_m\Big(\mathbf{w}-\alpha\nabla g_m(\mathbf{w})\Big)$ is the meta-function associated with client m. In order to solve (7.5), there is a need to compute second-order gradients which is costly in terms of computation. The authors provided two methods including FO-MAML [14] and HF-MAML [12] to approximate the Hessian, hence reducing the computational cost.

Having a similar idea of finding a global model as a good initialization point for personalized models, [9] proposed the new problem formulation as

$$(\text{pFedMe}) \quad \min_{\mathbf{w}\in\mathbb{R}^d}\left\{g(\mathbf{w}):=\frac{1}{n}\sum_{m=1}^{n}g_m(\mathbf{w})\right\}, \quad (7.6)$$

where

$$g_m(\mathbf{w})=\min_{\boldsymbol{\theta}_m\in\mathbb{R}^d}\left\{\ell_m(\boldsymbol{\theta}_m)+\frac{\lambda}{2}\|\boldsymbol{\theta}_m-\mathbf{w}\|^2\right\} \quad (7.7)$$

is the well-known Moreau envelope, which incorporates an L_2-norm regularization to control the balance between personalization and generalization performance. Model $\boldsymbol{\theta}_m$ denotes the personalized model of client m and λ is a regularization parameter that controls the strength of the global model $\mathbf{w}$ to the personalized model. While large λ can benefit clients with unreliable data from the abundant data aggregation, small λ helps clients with sufficient useful data prioritizing personalization. Note that $\lambda\in(0,\infty)$ to avoid extreme cases of $\lambda=0$, i.e., no FL, or $\lambda=\infty$, i.e., no pFL. Overall, the idea is to allow clients to pursue their own models with different directions, but not to stay far away from the "reference point" $\mathbf{w}$, to which every client contributes. While $\mathbf{w}$ is found by exploiting the data aggregation from multiple clients at the outer level, $\boldsymbol{\theta}_m$ is optimized with respect to client m's data distribution and is maintained a bounded distance from $\mathbf{w}$ at the inner level. Compared to problem (7.5), problem (7.6) has a similar meaning of $\mathbf{w}$ as a "meta-model," but instead of using $\mathbf{w}$ as the initialization, pFedMe pursues in parallel both the personalized and global models by solving a bi-level problem, which has several benefits. First, while Per-FedAvg is optimized for one-step gradient update for its personalized model, pFedMe is agnostic to the inner optimizer, which means (7.7) can be solved using any iterative approach with multi-step updates. Second, by rewriting the personalized model update of Per-FedAvg as

$$\boldsymbol{\theta}_m(\mathbf{w}) = \mathbf{w} - \alpha \nabla g_m(\mathbf{w}) = \arg\min_{\boldsymbol{\theta}_m \in \mathbb{R}^d}\left\{\langle \nabla g_m(\mathbf{w}), \boldsymbol{\theta}_m - \mathbf{w}\rangle + \frac{1}{2\alpha}\|\boldsymbol{\theta}_m - \mathbf{w}\|^2\right\},$$

we can see that apart from the similar regularization term, Per-FedAvg only optimizes the first-order approximation of g_m, whereas pFedMe directly minimizes g_m in (7.7). Third, Per-FedAvg (or generally several MAML-based methods) requires computing or estimating Hessian matrix, whereas pFedMe only needs gradient calculation using the first-order approach.

7.3.3 Multi-task learning

The main goal of the multi-task approach is to exploit commonalities and differences across the tasks to allow multiple related tasks to learn simultaneously. In FL setting, MOCHA [35] and FedU [9] consider each client as a single task, then capture the relationships among clients based on the client's data and learn multi-personalized models instead of a single global model to handle the non-i.i.d. data. The general formulation for FMTL is provided as

$$(\text{FMTL}) \quad \min_{\boldsymbol{\theta}_1,\dots,\boldsymbol{\theta}_m \in \mathbb{R}^d}\left\{g(\boldsymbol{\theta}) := \frac{1}{n}\sum_{m=1}^{n} g_m(\boldsymbol{\theta}_m) + \underbrace{\lambda R(\boldsymbol{\Theta})}_{\text{regularization}}\right\}, \qquad (7.8)$$

where the matrix $\boldsymbol{\Theta} = [\boldsymbol{\theta}_1,\dots,\boldsymbol{\theta}_n] \in \mathbb{R}^{d \times n}$ contains collective personalized model vectors and $R(\boldsymbol{\Theta})$ comprises the regularization functions. We notice that (7.8) is relevant to the traditional FL problem (7.1) when $\boldsymbol{\theta}_1 = \boldsymbol{\theta}_2 = \cdots = \boldsymbol{\theta}_n$. MOCHA and FedU come with different definitions of $R(\boldsymbol{\Theta})$ to encourage the models of the neighboring clients to be close to each other. The formulation of MOCHA is written as

$$(\text{MOCHA}) \quad \min_{\boldsymbol{\theta}_1,\dots,\boldsymbol{\theta}_m \in \mathbb{R}^d, \Omega \in \mathbb{R}^{n \times n}}\left\{g(\boldsymbol{\theta}) := \frac{1}{n}\sum_{m=1}^{n} g_m(\boldsymbol{\theta}_m) + \underbrace{\lambda_1 \text{tr}(\boldsymbol{\Theta}\Omega\boldsymbol{\Theta}^T) + \lambda_2\|\boldsymbol{\Theta}\|^2}_{\text{regularization}}\right\},$$

$$(7.9)$$

where $\Omega \in \mathbb{R}^{n \times n}$ denotes the model relationships among tasks, and obtained independently with data or estimated while simultaneously learning task models. The problem formulation of FedU is defined as

$$\text{(FedU)} \quad \min_{\boldsymbol{\theta}_1,\dots,\boldsymbol{\theta}_m \in \mathbb{R}^d} \left\{ g(\boldsymbol{\theta}) := \frac{1}{n}\sum_{m=1}^{n} g_m(\boldsymbol{\theta}_m) + \underbrace{\frac{\lambda}{2}\sum_{k \in \mathcal{N}_m} a_{mk}\|\boldsymbol{\theta}_m - \boldsymbol{\theta}_k\|^2}_{\text{regularization}} \right\},$$

(7.10)

where $\mathcal{N}_k = \mathcal{N} \setminus \{k\}$, $a_{mk} := [\mathbf{A}]_{mk}$, and $\mathbf{A} \in \mathbb{R}^n$ is a symmetric, weighted adjacency matrix. The relationship between clients m and k is presented by a_{mk}. Here, $a_{k\ell} = 0$ means no relationship between the models of clients m and k. The value of $a_{mk} > 0$ shows that client m is a neighbor of client k and also determines the strength of the relationship between these two clients' models.

7.3.4 Weight sharing

Weight sharing (WS) aims to achieve pFL by decoupling the local private layer from the global FL model parameters. Clients train their own private layer locally and do not share with the FL server. This enables learning task-specific representations for enhanced personalization. There are generally two configurations used in WS for deep neural networks. The first is to use global representation and personalize last layers proposed by FedPer [2] and FedRep [6]. In this setting, clients keep personalized layers for local training and share the global representation with the rest. The second design in [26] considers personalized feature representations for each client and all clients share the common last layer.

In the WS setting, parameters $\mathbf{w}$, $\boldsymbol{\theta}$ correspond to different layers of the same neural network but are used for global parameters and personalized parameters, respectively. For example, in [26], $\boldsymbol{\theta}_1,\dots,\boldsymbol{\theta}_m$ could be the weights of the first few layers of a neural network, while $\mathbf{w}$ are the weights of the remaining layers. Alternatively, in [2,6], each of $\boldsymbol{\theta}_1,\dots,\boldsymbol{\theta}_m$ corresponds to the weight of the last few layers, while the remaining weights are included in the global parameter $\mathbf{w}$. Overall, the problem formulation of WS can be written as

$$\text{(WS)} \quad \min_{\mathbf{w} \in \mathbb{R}^{d_w}, \boldsymbol{\theta} \in \mathbb{R}^{d_\theta}} \left\{ g(\mathbf{w}, \boldsymbol{\theta}) := \frac{1}{n}\sum_{m=1}^{n} g_m(\mathbf{w}, \boldsymbol{\theta}_m) \right\}, \qquad (7.11)$$

where $d = d_w + d_\theta$ is the feature dimension. Decoupling the neural network into the global and personal layers reduces the dimension of sharing global weight and brings benefits in both communication and computation.

7.3.5 Clients clustering

In FL, when there is a significantly large number of participating clients, the clients with similar characteristics (e.g., location, time, age, gender) are likely to have similar behaviors. Thus, training multiple FL models for each homogeneous group of closed relation clients becomes more suitable. Several works [4,10,15] have focused on applying the clustering technique for pFL with the assumption that there are existing client groups in which clients have related data distribution. Each client group or cluster trains a single personalized model.

The work in [4] uses an unsupervised algorithm named hierarchical clustering to cluster clients into groups based on the client's model. At first, the global model is trained for τ communication round. Each client then fine-tunes the global model using its private data. To generate multiple client clusters, all fine-tuned models $\mathbf{w}_1, \ldots, \mathbf{w}_n$ of n clients become inputs to the hierarchical clustering algorithm to separate n clients into C-clusters. The traditional FL training process then performs on each cluster to produce a personalized model for each cluster. When there are a large number of clients, however, computing the pairwise distance of parameters between all clients is computationally intensive. Other clustering approaches [10,15] necessitate the selection of a fixed number of clusters at the start of FL training. Ghosh et al. [15] proposed a simple one-shot clustering algorithm IFCA that does not require a centralized clustering algorithm hence reducing the computational cost on the server side. The WS approach is applied to learn the shared representation layer and the separate final layer is personalized for each individual cluster. However, IFCA has a K times higher communication overhead than FedAvg as the server needs to broadcast K cluster models to all clients in each communication round. FedGroup, a FL clustering framework proposed by [10], implements a static client clustering strategy and a newcomer client cold start mechanism. FedGroup uses the KMeans++ algorithm [3] to cluster client's model updates based on the similarity of gradient update direction of each client.

7.4 Personalized FL algorithms

In this section, we give more insights by discussing two state-of-the-art pFL algorithms including pFedMe for the model-based approach and FedU for FMTL approach.

7.4.1 pFedMe

Instead of solving the traditional FL problem (7.1), pFedMe takes a different approach by using a regularized loss function with L_2-norm for each client and solve the problem (7.6). pFedMe algorithm is presented in Algorithm 1. At the tth communication round, the server broadcasts the latest global model $\mathbf{w}^{(t)}$ to all clients. After all clients perform τ_m local updates, the server will receive the latest local models from a uniformly sampled subset $\mathcal{S}^{(t)}$ of clients to perform the model averaging. Note that pFedMe uses an additional parameter β for the global model update in order to speed up convergence rates, which includes FedAvg's model averaging when $\beta = 1$, though a similar parameter at the server side was also used in [20,33]. Specifically, pFedMe aims to solve the bi-level problem and has two key differences compared with FedAvg. First, at the inner level, each client m solves (7.12) to obtain its personalized model $\hat{\boldsymbol{\theta}}_m(\mathbf{w}_{m,r}^{(t)})$ where $\mathbf{w}_{m,r}^{(t)}$ denotes the *local model* of client m at the global

---

Algorithm 1 pFedMe.

1: **input:** τ, τ_m, S, λ, η, β, $\mathbf{w}^{(0)}$
2: **for** $t = 0$ to $\tau - 1$ **do**   ▷ Global communication rounds
3:     Server sends $\mathbf{w}^{(t)}$ to all clients
4:     **for** all $m = 1$ to n **do**
5:         $\mathbf{w}_{m,0}^{(t)} = \mathbf{w}^{(t)}$
6:         **for** $r = 0$ to $\tau_m - 1$ **do**   ▷ Local update rounds
7:             Sample a fresh mini-batch B_m with size $|B|$ and minimize $\tilde{h}_m(\boldsymbol{\theta}_m; \mathbf{w}_{m,r}^t, B_m)$, defined in (7.13), up to an accuracy level according to (7.14) to find a δ-approximate $\tilde{\boldsymbol{\theta}}_m(\mathbf{w}_{m,r}^t)$
8:             $\mathbf{w}_{m,r+1}^{(t)} = \mathbf{w}_{m,r}^{(t)} - \eta\lambda(\mathbf{w}_{m,r}^{(t)} - \tilde{\boldsymbol{\theta}}_m(\mathbf{w}_{m,r}^{(t)}))$
9:     Server uniformly samples a subset of clients $\mathcal{S}^{(t)}$ with size S, and each of the sampled client sends the local model $\mathbf{w}_{m,\tau_m}^{(t)}$, $\forall m \in \mathcal{S}^{(t)}$, to the server
10:     Server updates the global model: $\mathbf{w}^{(t+1)} = (1 - \beta)\mathbf{w}^{(t)} + \beta \sum_{m \in \mathcal{S}^{(t)}} \frac{\mathbf{w}_{m,\tau_m}^{(t)}}{S}$

---

round t and local round r:

$$\hat{\boldsymbol{\theta}}_m(\mathbf{w}) := \text{prox}_{l_m/\lambda}(\mathbf{w}) = \arg\min_{\boldsymbol{\theta}_m \in \mathbb{R}^d}\left\{l_m(\boldsymbol{\theta}_m) + \frac{\lambda}{2}\|\boldsymbol{\theta}_m - \mathbf{w}\|^2\right\}. \qquad (7.12)$$

Similar to FedAvg, the purpose of local models is to contribute to building global model with reduced communication rounds between clients and server. Second, at the outer level, the local update of client m using gradient descent is with respect to g_m (instead of l_m) as follows:

$$\mathbf{w}_{m,r+1}^{(t)} = \mathbf{w}_{m,r}^{(t)} - \eta\nabla g_m(\mathbf{w}_{m,r}^{(t)}),$$

where η is the learning rate and $\nabla g_m(\mathbf{w}_{m,r}^{(t)}) = \lambda(\mathbf{w}_{m,r}^{(t)} - \hat{\boldsymbol{\theta}}_m(\mathbf{w}_{m,r}^{(t)}))$.

For the practical algorithm, pFedMe uses a δ-approximation of $\hat{\boldsymbol{\theta}}_m(\mathbf{w}_{m,r}^{(t)})$, denoted by $\tilde{\boldsymbol{\theta}}_m(\mathbf{w}_{m,r}^{(t)})$ satisfying $\mathbb{E}\big[\|\tilde{\boldsymbol{\theta}}_m(\mathbf{w}_{m,r}^{(t)}) - \hat{\boldsymbol{\theta}}_m(\mathbf{w}_{m,r}^{(t)})\|\big] \leq \delta$, and correspondingly uses $\lambda(\mathbf{w}_{m,r}^{(t)} - \tilde{\boldsymbol{\theta}}_m(\mathbf{w}_{m,r}^{(t)}))$ to approximate $\nabla g_m(\mathbf{w}_{m,r}^{(t)})$ (cf. line 8). The reason of using the δ-approximate $\tilde{\boldsymbol{\theta}}_m(\mathbf{w}_{m,r}^{(t)})$ is twofold. First, obtaining $\hat{\boldsymbol{\theta}}_m(\mathbf{w}_{m,r}^{(t)})$ according to (7.7) usually needs the gradient $\nabla l_m(\boldsymbol{\theta}_m)$, which, however, requires the distribution of a random sample $\xi_m^{(i)} = (\mathbf{x}_m^{(i)}, c_m^{(i)})$. In practice, pFedMe uses the following unbiased estimate of $\nabla l_m(\boldsymbol{\theta}_m)$ by sampling a mini-batch of data B_m:

$$\nabla \tilde{l}_m(\boldsymbol{\theta}_m, B_m) := \frac{1}{|B_m|}\sum_{\xi_m^{(i)} \in B_m} \nabla \tilde{l}_m(\boldsymbol{\theta}_m; \xi_m^{(i)})$$

such that $\mathbb{E}[\nabla \tilde{l}_m(\boldsymbol{\theta}_m, B_m)] = \nabla l_m(\boldsymbol{\theta}_m)$. Second, in general, it is not straightforward to obtain $\hat{\boldsymbol{\theta}}_m(\mathbf{w}_{m,r}^{(t)})$ in closed-form. Instead, pFedMe uses iterative first-order ap-

---

Algorithm 2 FedU.

1: **client m's input**: local step-size η
2: **server's input**: graph information $\{a_{m\ell}\}$, initial $\boldsymbol{\theta}_m^{(0)}, \forall m \in \mathcal{N}$, and global step-size $\widetilde{\eta} = \eta \tau_m$
3: **for** each round $t = 0, \ldots, \tau - 1$ **do**
4:       Server uniformly samples a subset of clients $\mathcal{S}^{(t)}$ of size S and sends $\boldsymbol{\theta}_m^{(t)}$ to client $m, \forall m \in \mathcal{S}^{(t)}$
5:       **while** $m \in \mathcal{S}^{(t)}$ **do**
6:            initialize local model $\boldsymbol{\theta}_{m,0}^{(t)} \leftarrow \boldsymbol{\theta}_m^{(t)}$
7:            **for** $r = 0, \ldots, \tau_m - 1$ **do**
8:                 compute mini-batch gradient $\nabla \widetilde{g}_m(\boldsymbol{\theta}_{m,r}^{(t)})$
9:                 $\boldsymbol{\theta}_{m,r+1}^{(t)} \leftarrow \boldsymbol{\theta}_{m,r}^{(t)} - \lambda \nabla \widetilde{g}_m(\boldsymbol{\theta}_{m,r}^{(t)})$
10:          send $\boldsymbol{\theta}_{m,\tau_m}^{(t)}$ to the server
11:     **while do**
12:          $\boldsymbol{\theta}_{m,\tau_m}^{(t)} \leftarrow \boldsymbol{\theta}_m^{(t)}, \forall m \notin \mathcal{S}^{(t)}$
13:          $\boldsymbol{\theta}_m^{(t+1)} \leftarrow \boldsymbol{\theta}_{m,\tau_m}^{(t)} - \widetilde{\eta} \lambda \sum_{\ell \in \mathcal{N}_m} a_{mk} (\boldsymbol{\theta}_{m,\tau_m}^{(t)} - \boldsymbol{\theta}_{k,\tau_m}^{(t)}), \forall m \in \mathcal{S}^{(t)}$
14:          $\boldsymbol{\theta}_m^{(t+1)} \leftarrow \boldsymbol{\theta}_m^{(t)}, \forall m \notin \mathcal{S}^{(t)}$

---

proach to obtain an approximate $\widetilde{\boldsymbol{\theta}}_m(\mathbf{w}_{m,r}^{(t)})$ with high accuracy. Defining

$$\widetilde{h}_m(\boldsymbol{\theta}_m; \mathbf{w}_{m,r}^{(t)}, B_m) := \widetilde{l}_m(\boldsymbol{\theta}_m; B_m) + \frac{\lambda}{2} \|\boldsymbol{\theta}_m - \mathbf{w}_{m,r}^{(t)}\|^2, \qquad (7.13)$$

we suppose choosing λ such that $\widetilde{h}_m(\boldsymbol{\theta}_m; \mathbf{w}_{m,r}^{(t)}, B_m)$ is strongly convex with a condition number κ (which quantifies how hard it is to optimize (7.13)), then gradient descent (resp. Nesterov's accelerated gradient descent) can be used to obtain $\widetilde{\boldsymbol{\theta}}_m(\mathbf{w}_{m,r}^{(t)})$ such that

$$\|\nabla \widetilde{h}_m(\widetilde{\boldsymbol{\theta}}_m; \mathbf{w}_{m,r}^{(t)}, B_m)\|^2 \leq \nu, \qquad (7.14)$$

with the number of $\nabla \widetilde{h}_m$ computations $K := \mathcal{O}\left(\kappa \log\left(\frac{d}{\nu}\right)\right)$ (resp. $\mathcal{O}\left(\sqrt{\kappa} \log\left(\frac{d}{\nu}\right)\right)$) [5], where d is the diameter of the search space, ν is an accuracy level, and $\mathcal{O}(\cdot)$ hides constants. The computation complexity of each client in pFedMe is K times that in FedAvg. The detailed proof can be found in [8].

7.4.2 FedU

The FedU algorithm for solving the formulated FL problem (7.10) under a communication-centralized manner is presented in Algorithm 2. First, at each communication round t, the server uniformly samples a subset of clients $\mathcal{S}^{(t)}$ and sends the latest update of local model $\boldsymbol{\theta}_m^{(t)}$ to each client $m, \forall m \in \mathcal{S}^{(t)}$. Then, after τ_m local update steps are performed, the server receives the latest local update from the sampled clients to perform model regularization for each local model.

FedU has a key difference compared to the conventional FL algorithms (e.g., FedAvg [28]) and the pFL algorithms (e.g., pFedMe [8], and Per-FedAvg [13]). Instead of updating the personalized models only at the clients using a global model from the server, FedU directly updates each local model at both client and server sides without building a global model. Specifically, in each communication round, each client $m \in \mathcal{S}^{(t)}$ copies its current local model received from the server, $\boldsymbol{\theta}^{(t)}_{m,0} = \boldsymbol{\theta}^{(t)}_m$, and performs τ_m local updates of the form

$$\boldsymbol{\theta}^{(t)}_{m,r+1} \leftarrow \boldsymbol{\theta}^{(t)}_{m,r} - \eta \nabla \widetilde{g}_m(\boldsymbol{\theta}^{(t)}_{m,r}),$$

where μ is the local step-size. Then the server receives $\{\boldsymbol{\theta}^{(t)}_{m,\tau_m}\}$ from sampled clients $m \in \mathcal{S}^{(t)}$, and updates

$$\boldsymbol{\theta}^{(t)}_{m,\tau_m} \leftarrow \boldsymbol{\theta}^{(t)}_m,$$

for any non-sampled client $m \notin \mathcal{S}^{(t)}$. Finally, the server performs its regularization update for any sampled client $m \in \mathcal{S}^{(t)}$ as

$$\boldsymbol{\theta}^{(t+1)}_m \leftarrow \boldsymbol{\theta}^{(t)}_{m,\tau_m} - \widetilde{\mu}\lambda \sum_{k \in \mathcal{N}_m \cap \mathcal{S}^{(t)}} a_{mk}(\boldsymbol{\theta}^{(t)}_{m,\tau_m} - \boldsymbol{\theta}^{(t)}_{k,\tau_m}),$$

and for any non-sampled client $m \notin \mathcal{S}^{(t)}$ as

$$\boldsymbol{\theta}^{(t+1)}_m \leftarrow \boldsymbol{\theta}^{(t)}_m,$$

where $\widetilde{\mu} = \mu \tau_m$ is a global step-size. This step finishes one round of communication.

7.5 Experiments

In this section, we evaluate the performance of important pFL works including FedU, MOCHA, pFedMe, Per-FedAvg, APFL, FedRep, and the vanilla FedAvg when the data are heterogeneous and non-i.i.d. in both strongly convex and nonconvex settings.

7.5.1 Experimental settings

We consider classification problems using four real datasets generated in federated settings, including Human Activity Recognition (HAR), Vehicle sensor, MNIST, and CIFAR-10.

- **HAR.** Data is gathered from accelerometers and gyroscopes of cell phones from 30 individuals performing six different activities including lying-down, standing, walking, sitting, walking-upstairs, and walking-downstairs [1]. Each client classifies 6 different activities.

Table 7.1 Statistics of all datasets for full-sample scenario using in the experiment.

Dataset	n	Total samples	Number of	Samples / client	
				Mean	**Std**
HAR	30	10,299	6	343	35.1
Vehicle Sensor	23	48,303	2	2100	380.5
MNIST	100	61,866	2	619	343.8
CIFAR-10	20	54,572	3	2729	851.4

- **Vehicle Sensor.** Data is collected from 23 distributed wireless sensors including acoustic (microphone), seismic (geophone), and infrared (polarized IR sensor) [11]. We consider each sensor as a client performing the binary classification predicting two vehicle types: Assault Amphibian Vehicle (AAV) and Dragon Wagon (DW).
- **MNIST.** A handwritten digit dataset [23] includes 10 labels and 70,000 instances. The whole dataset is distributed to $n = 100$ clients. Each client has a different local data size and consists of 2 over 10 labels.
- **CIFAR-10.** An object recognition dataset [22] includes 60,000 color images belonging to 10 classes. We partition the dataset to $n = 20$ clients and 3 labels per client.

The detailed statistics of all datasets are summarized in Table 7.1. In practical FL networks, some clients have significantly limited data sizes and need collaborative learning with others. For each dataset, we consider two different scenarios including a **down-sample** with 80% of data belonging to a half of the total clients and the **full-sample** in Table 7.1 to observe the behavior of all algorithms. All datasets are split randomly with 75% and 25% for training and testing, respectively.

We use a multinomial logistic regression (MLR) with cross-entropy loss functions and L_2-regularization term as the strongly convex model for HAR, Vehicle Sensor, and MNIST. For the nonconvex setting, we use a simple DNN with one hidden layer, an ReLU activation function, and a softmax layer at the end of the network for HAR and Vehicle Sensor. The size of hidden layer is 100 for HAR and 20 for Vehicle Sensor. In the case of MNIST, we use DNN with 2 hidden layers and both layers have the same size of 100. For CIFAR-10, we follow the CNN structure of [28]. We follow the setting and the implementation of [9] for the experiment.

7.5.2 Comparison

The comparison results are shown in Table 7.2. We fix the subset of clients $S = 0.1n$ and perform the comparison on all real datasets in two different scenarios of collecting data.

Table 7.2 Performance comparison ($\tau_m = 5$, $S = 0.1n$, $B = 20$, $\tau = 200$). There is no convex model for CIFAR-10, we then only report the nonconvex case.

Dataset	Algorithm	Test Accuracy			
		Down-sample		Full-sample	
		Convex	Nonconvex	Convex	Nonconvex
CIFAR-10	FedU		**75.41** ± 0.29		**79.40** ± 0.25
	pFedMe		74.10 ± 0.89		78.70 ± 0.15
	Per-FedAvg		64.70 ± 1.91		67.61 ± 0.03
	FedAvg		34.48 ± 5.34		36.32 ± 5.57
	APFL		73.72 ± 1.56		80.04 ± 1.28
	FedRep		71.66 ± 0.63		78.55 ± 0.84
MNIST	FedU	**96.95** ± 0.11	97.81 ± 0.01	97.82 ± 0.02	98.44 ± 0.02
	MOCHA	96.18 ± 0.09		97.80 ± 0.02	
	pFedMe	93.73 ± 0.40	**98.64** ± 0.17	95.38 ± 0.09	99.04 ± 0.02
	Per-FedAvg	90.33 ± 0.84	96.38 ± 0.40	91.77 ± 0.23	97.59 ± 0.30
	FedAvg	87.75 ± 1.31	91.48 ± 1.05	90.14 ± 0.61	90.74 ± 1.62
	APFL	90.61 ± 1.26	95.89 ± 1.03	96.67 ± 0.15	98.95 ± 0.52
	FedRep	94.01 ± 1.12	98.40 ± 0.31	**98.08** ± 0.45	**99.33** ± 0.16
Vehicle Sensor	FedU	**88.47** ± 0.21	**91.79** ± 0.31	**89.84** ± 0.06	**94.18** ± 0.08
	MOCHA	87.31 ± 0.23		89.73 ± 0.89	
	pFedMe	81.38 ± 0.41	90.62 ± 0.41	85.87 ± 0.02	92.23 ± 0.17
	Per-FedAvg	81.07 ± 0.71	86.92 ± 1.30	82.21 ± 0.01	87.50 ± 1.21
	FedAvg	79.84 ± 0.91	84.04 ± 2.69	81.54 ± 0.03	85.61 ± 0.07
	APFL	82.62 ± 0.56	86.02 ± 0.47	89.27 ± 0.31	94.02 ± 0.22
	FedRep	82.66 ± 0.25	85.80 ± 0.58	88.51 ± 0.40	92.08 ± 0.27
HAR	FedU	**95.76** ± 0.46	95.86 ± 0.36	97.75 ± 0.21	97.85 ± 0.39
	MOCHA	92.33 ± 0.67		97.69 ± 0.03	
	pFedMe	95.41 ± 0.38	95.72 ± 0.32	97.52 ± 0.09	97.60 ± 0.09
	Per-FedAvg	94.78 ± 0.37	94.80 ± 0.60	96.04 ± 0.36	96.21 ± 0.33
	FedAvg	93.41 ± 0.95	93.74 ± 1.01	95.58 ± 0.05	94.84 ± 0.07
	APFL	95.68 ± 0.15	**96.27** ± 0.41	**98.29** ± 0.23	98.45 ± 0.51
	FedRep	82.02 ± 0.53	88.01 ± 0.24	97.44 ± 0.33	**99.03** ± 0.21

7.6 Open problems

In this section, two promising future research directions for personalized federated learning, i.e., transfer learning and knowledge distillation, are briefly introduced.

7.6.1 Transfer learning

The aim of transfer learning (TL) is to transfer knowledge from a source domain to a desired domain [32]. The key idea is that the model does not need to build from scratch because the knowledge of the source domain is a pre-trained model. This idea can be applied to model personalization in FL. The parameters of the pre-trained global model, i.e., the extracted knowledge, are used as an initialization for a re-learning process at each client [38]. In this re-learning process, each client only needs to fine-tune the global model on its local data. For deep neural networks, the lower layer of the global model should be transferred and used as lower level genetic features in the local models in order to reduce the overhead. The challenge in TL-based pFL is to reduce the domain discrepancy between the pre-trained global model and the local model for improving personalization. To overcome this challenge, one solution is to add an alignment layer which is the correlation alignment (CORAL) layer [36] before the softmax layer to adapt the second-order statistic of both the source and desired domains.

7.6.2 Knowledge distillation

Knowledge distillation (KD) was introduced by [18] for distilling the knowledge of a large teach network into a lightweight student network by letting the student mimic the teacher. KD originally aimed to reduce the communication and computation resource requirements for a learning system. However, it can be useful for personalizing models in FL in several ways [37]. The knowledge of the local models benefits in forming better personalized models while the knowledge of the global models benefits in improving the personalized performance of each client. The knowledge distillation can perform in a bi-directional manner at both the client and server sides. The challenge in KD-based pFL is to overcome over-fitting at each client due to the small size of the local data. Yu et al. [39] proposed a solution to overcome this challenge, in which the global model plays the role of the teacher, while the personalized model plays the role of the student.

7.7 Conclusion

This chapter has provided a systematic review of existing personalized federated learning approaches to deal with the statistical diversity among clients in federated learning. The chapter also discussed and compared the state-of-the-art algorithms of these approaches with real-data experiments to gain more insights. Finally, future research directions for personalized federated learning were introduced.

References
[1] Davide Anguita, Alessandro Ghio, Luca Oneto, Xavier Parra, Jorge L. Reyes-Ortiz, A public domain dataset for human activity recognition using smartphones, Computational Intelligence (2013) 6.

[2] Manoj Ghuhan Arivazhagan, Vinay Aggarwal, Aaditya Kumar Singh, Sunav Choudhary, Federated learning with personalization layers, arXiv:1912.00818, Dec. 2019.

[3] David Arthur, Sergei Vassilvitskii, K-means++: the advantages of careful seeding, in: Proceedings of the 18th Annual ACM-SIAM Symposium on Discrete Algorithms, 2007.

[4] Christopher Briggs, Zhong Fan, Peter Andras, Federated learning with hierarchical clustering of local updates to improve training on non-i.i.d. data, 2020.

[5] Sébastien Bubeck, Convex optimization: algorithms and complexity, arXiv:1405.4980, Nov. 2015.

[6] Liam Collins, Hamed Hassani, Aryan Mokhtari, Sanjay Shakkottai, Exploiting shared representations for personalized federated learning, in: Marina Meila, Tong Zhang (Eds.), Proceedings of the 38th International Conference on Machine Learning, PMLR, 18–24 July 2021, in: Proceedings of Machine Learning Research, vol. 139, 2021, pp. 2089–2099.

[7] Yuyang Deng, Mohammad Mahdi Kamani, M. Mahdavi, Adaptive personalized federated learning, arXiv:2003.13461, 2020.

[8] Canh T. Dinh, Nguyen H. Tran, Tuan Dung Nguyen, Personalized federated learning with Moreau envelopes, in: Proceedings of the International Conference on Neural Information Processing Systems, 2020.

[9] Canh T. Dinh, Tung T. Vu, Nguyen H. Tran, Minh N. Dao, Hongyu Zhang, A new look and convergence rate of federated multi-task learning with Laplacian regularization, arXiv:2102.07148, 2021.

[10] M. Duan, D. Liu, X. Ji, R. Liu, L. Liang, X. Chen, Y. Tan, Fedgroup: Efficient Federated Learning via Decomposed Similarity-Based Clustering, IEEE Computer Society, Los Alamitos, CA, USA, Oct. 2021, pp. 228–237.

[11] Marco F. Duarte, Yu Hen Hu, Vehicle classification in distributed sensor networks, Journal of Parallel and Distributed Computing 64 (7) (July 2004) 826–838.

[12] Alireza Fallah, Aryan Mokhtari, Asuman Ozdaglar, On the convergence theory of gradient-based model-agnostic meta-learning algorithms, arXiv:1908.10400, March 2020.

[13] Alireza Fallah, Aryan Mokhtari, Asuman Ozdaglar, Personalized federated learning with theoretical guarantees: a model-agnostic meta-learning approach, in: Advances in Neural Information Processing Systems, 2020.

[14] Chelsea Finn, Pieter Abbeel, Sergey Levine, Model-agnostic meta-learning for fast adaptation of deep networks, in: Proceedings of the International Conference on Machine Learning, 2017.

[15] Avishek Ghosh, Jichan Chung, Dong Yin, Kannan Ramchandran, An efficient framework for clustered federated learning, in: Proceedings of the 34th International Conference on Neural Information Processing Systems, NIPS'20, Red Hook, NY, USA, December 2020, Curran Associates, Inc., 2020, pp. 19586–19597.

[16] Filip Hanzely, Peter Richtárik, Federated learning of a mixture of global and local models, arXiv:2002.05516, Feb. 2020.

[17] Filip Hanzely, Boxin Zhao, Mladen Kolar, Personalized federated learning: a unified framework and universal optimization techniques, arXiv:2102.09743, May 2023.

[18] Geoffrey Hinton, Oriol Vinyals, Jeff Dean, Distilling the knowledge in a neural network, arXiv:1503.02531, March 2015.

[19] Yihan Jiang, Jakub Konečný, Keith Rush, Sreeram Kannan, Improving federated learning personalization via model agnostic meta learning, arXiv:1909.12488, Sep. 2019.

[20] Sai Praneeth Karimireddy, Satyen Kale, Mehryar Mohri, Sashank Reddi, Sebastian Stich, Ananda Theertha Suresh, SCAFFOLD: stochastic controlled averaging for federated learning, in: Proceedings of the International Conference on Machine Learning, vol. 119, 2020.

[21] Mikhail Khodak, Maria-Florina Balcan, Ameet Talwalkar, Adaptive gradient-based meta-learning methods, arXiv:1906.02717, Dec. 2019.

[22] Alex Krizhevsky, Learning multiple layers of features from tiny images, https://www.cs.toronto.edu/~kriz/learning-features-2009-TR.pdf, 2009.

[23] Y. Lecun, L. Bottou, Y. Bengio, P. Haffner, Gradient-based learning applied to document recognition, Proceedings of the IEEE 86 (11) (1998) 2278–2324.

[24] Daliang Li, J. Wang, FedMD: Heterogenous federated learning via model distillation, arXiv:1910.03581, 2019.

[25] Li Tian, Shengyuan Hu, Ahmad Beirami, Virginia Smith, Ditto: fair and robust federated learning through personalization, in: Proceedings of the 38th International Conference on Machine Learning, July 2021.

[26] Paul Pu Liang, Terrance Liu, Liu Ziyin, Nicholas B. Allen, Randy P. Auerbach, David Brent, Ruslan Salakhutdinov, Louis-Philippe Morency, Think locally, act globally: federated learning with local and global representations, arXiv:2001.01523, Jun. 2020.

[27] Yishay Mansour, Mehryar Mohri, Jae Ro, Ananda Theertha Suresh, Three approaches for personalization with applications to federated learning, arXiv:2002.10619, Feb. 2020.

[28] Brendan McMahan, Eider Moore, Daniel Ramage, Seth Hampson, Blaise Aguera y Arcas, Communication-efficient learning of deep networks from decentralized data, in: Proceedings of the International Conference on Artificial Intelligence and Statistics, April 2017.

[29] Mehryar Mohri, Gary Sivek, Ananda Theertha Suresh, Agnostic federated learning, arXiv:1902.00146, Jan. 2019.

[30] Alex Nichol, Joshua Achiam, John Schulman, On first-order meta-learning algorithms, arXiv:1803.02999, Oct. 2018.

[31] Krishna Pillutla, Sham M. Kakade, Zaid Harchaoui, Robust aggregation for federated learning, arXiv:1912.13445, Dec. 2019.

[32] L.Y. Pratt, Discriminability-based transfer between neural networks, in: S. Hanson, J. Cowan, C. Giles (Eds.), Advances in Neural Information Processing Systems, vol. 5, 1992, pp. 204–211.

[33] Sashank Reddi, Zachary Charles, Manzil Zaheer, Zachary Garrett, Keith Rush, Jakub Konečný, Sanjiv Kumar, H. Brendan McMahan, Adaptive federated optimization, arXiv:2003.00295, Feb. 2020.

[34] Felix Sattler, Klaus-Robert Müller, Wojciech Samek, Clustered federated learning: model-agnostic distributed multitask optimization under privacy constraints, IEEE Transactions on Neural Networks and Learning Systems 32 (8) (2021) 3710–3722.

[35] Virginia Smith, Chao-Kai Chiang, Maziar Sanjabi, Ameet Talwalkar, Federated multitask learning, in: Proceedings of the International Conference on Neural Information Processing Systems, 2017.

[36] Baochen Sun, Jiashi Feng, Kate Saenko, Return of frustratingly easy domain adaptation, in: Proceedings of the Thirtieth AAAI Conference on Artificial Intelligence, 2016, pp. 2058–2065.

[37] Alysa Ziying Tan, Han Yu, Lizhen Cui, Qiang Yang, Towards personalized federated learning, IEEE Transactions on Neural Networks and Learning Systems (2022) 1–17.

[38] Kangkang Wang, Rajiv Mathews, Chloé Kiddon, Hubert Eichner, Franccoise Beaufays, Daniel Ramage, Federated evaluation of on-device personalization, arXiv:1910.10252, 2019.

[39] Tao Yu, Eugene Bagdasaryan, Vitaly Shmatikov, Salvaging federated learning by local adaptation, arXiv:2002.04758, 2020.

Fairness in federated learning

Xiaoqiang Lin[a], Xinyi Xu[a], Zhaoxuan Wu[a], Rachael Hwee Ling Sim[a],
See-Kiong Ng[a], Chuan-Sheng Foo[a], Patrick Jaillet[b], Trong Nghia Hoang[c], and
Bryan Kian Hsiang Low[a]

[a]*National University of Singapore, Singapore, Singapore*
[b]*Massachusetts Institute of Technology, Cambridge, MA, United States*
[c]*Washington State University, Pullman, WA, United States*

8.1 Introduction

Federated learning (FL) [15] allows multiple clients to collaborate in training a model with better performance (than before collaboration) without centralizing their local datasets [5,30]. However, most existing FL systems [5,15,27,30,31] do not explicitly consider the willingness and simply assume that all clients want to collaborate [15]. This assumption can be problematic when the clients are self-interested and not obliged to participate. For example, clients might not participate if they are treated *unfairly* (e.g., receiving no or less reward while contributing resources) by the FL system. Therefore, it is imperative to guarantee *fairness* to encourage such collaborations in FL. This chapter discusses three fairness notions, *equitable fairness*, *collaborative fairness* and *algorithmic fairness*, by (1) motivating them in Section 8.1; (2) providing the formal definitions in Section 8.2; (3) describing the respective algorithms for achieving them in Section 8.3; and (4) shedding light on some open problems in Section 8.4.

FL systems can be viewed as a form of cost-sharing or resource-allocation collaboration. The clients share the costs of collecting data by tapping into the information from others' local datasets to train a *global model* (i.e., model trained on the server). The global model can be viewed as a "medium" of some resources to be allocated to the clients. Each client receives the same global model to make predictions on their local datasets.

However, due to the difference in their local datasets, the predictive performance (or loss/objective function) of a single global model differs across clients. In essence, the predictive performance is the resource that is allocated, through the medium that is the global model. Because the clients do not necessarily have an identical objective (i.e., are heterogeneous [13]), it is important the training in FL is *fair* with respect to these different objectives (i.e., training losses of their respective local datasets). Specifically, it is unfair to allocate all the resources to a single client (i.e., training the global model to exclusively optimize the performance on that client's local dataset)

Federated Learning. https://doi.org/10.1016/B978-0-44-319037-7.00016-8

because it can result in poor performance on other clients' local datasets. Instead, the global model resource should be allocated fairly (among all the clients' objectives) so that the model has small performance disparities on all local datasets, formalized as *equitable fairness*.

In some other practical scenarios, the clients compete with each other (e.g., companies providing similar services/products) [27,31]. These clients are *self-interested*, namely they focus on maximizing their own utility (e.g., the trained model's performance on their local dataset). In contrast to the aforementioned scenario, these self-interested clients are only willing to contribute to help others if doing so (strictly) improves their own utility. Moreover, it can appear exploitative if a client i that contributes more than client j receives a reward lower than that received by client j, and can discourage collaboration. It thus motivates a different notion of fairness. Formally, the *contribution* of a client characterizes how much a client shares (directly or indirectly by training on its local dataset) with other clients [22,25] and the *reward* of a client specifies how much a client gains from the collaboration [21,29]. The so-called *collaborative fairness* [14] stipulates that the rewards should be commensurate with the contributions, so that the clients are rewarded more if they contribute more, and vice versa.

Lastly, dealing with bias in data in machine learning (ML) is a known challenge [16,33], which can be exacerbated by the multi-client setting of FL. Note that this perspective differs from the two previous settings in that it explicitly considers *how* the trained global model predicts on certain data. From the perspective of each client, the goal of removing bias is to ensure the trained model does not discriminate against certain protected groups (e.g., data whose sensitive features such as gender, race having certain values) [2]. In practice, the clients do not necessarily have aligned goals due to different local datasets [1]. Consequently, trying to eliminate/reduce discrimination among groups for one client can deteriorate that for another. Therefore, ideally, the trained model should not be biased with respect to any client's local dataset, called *algorithmic fairness*. In other words, suppose a data point is in the protected group (e.g., a record of a person), then this data point should *not* be discriminated against regardless of which local dataset it belongs to.

8.2 Notions of fairness

A summarization of different notions of fairness and their corresponding algorithms is provided in Table 8.1. A summarization of related works on achieving different notions of fairness is provided in Table 8.2. We will discuss different notions of fairness accordingly in this section.

8.2.1 Equitable fairness

The equitable fairness aims to equalize the performance of the global model on all clients. As enforcing strict equality is not always desirable depending on the ap-

Table 8.1 Algorithms analyzed in this chapter to achieve different notions of fairness.

Category	Fairness notion	Algorithm
Equitable fairness	Definition 8.1	Algorithm 1
	Definition 8.2	Algorithm 2
	Definition 8.3	FAFL [2]
Collaborative fairness	Definition 8.4	FGFL [29]
		GoG [18]
	Definition 8.5	FGFL [29]
		GoG [18]
	Definition 8.6	FLI [32]
Algorithmic fairness	Definition 8.7	FAFL [2]
	Definition 8.8	FAFL [2]

Table 8.2 A summary of current works on fairness in FL.

	Algorithmic fairness	Equitable fairness	Collaborative fairness
FairFL [34]	✓		
FairFed [4]	✓		
FCFL [1]	✓	✓	
FAFL [2]	✓	✓	
AFL [17]		✓	
q-FFL [12]		✓	
Ditto [11]		✓	
CFFL [14]			✓
RFFL [28]			✓
FGFL [29]			✓
FLI [32]			✓

plications [1], three types of equitable fairness are defined: good-intent equitable fairness [17], performance equitable fairness [12], and Pareto-optimal equitable fairness [1].

In FL, clients normally have heterogeneous local data distributions and local objectives. However, the objective of FedAvg [15] algorithm is to minimize the weighted average loss, $g(\mathbf{w}) = (1/\sum_{i=1}^{n} |D_i|) \sum_{m=1}^{n} |D_m| g_m(\mathbf{w})$, which cannot guarantee equitable losses across all clients in the resultant model. Note that $g_m(\mathbf{w})$ is the loss of model $\mathbf{w}$ on the local dataset of client m. For example, the client m with less data points than others will have a lower weight $|D_m|/\sum_{i=1}^{n} |D_i|$, meaning that during training "less optimization resource" is allocated to client m. Consequently, the client might suffer from a larger loss than others with respect to the trained model $\mathbf{w}$. Additionally, if a client m has local data distribution significantly different from others', i.e., is heterogeneous, it might suffer from bad performance on its local data distribution with the trained model. Intuitively, the data from other clients are not so helpful in improving the performance of the model on the client m's data due to the heterogeneity. Consequently, the client m might have higher losses than others.

Therefore, without extra equality guarantees from the system, clients with fewer data points or with more heterogeneous data distribution will not participate in the collaboration due to the low performance of the trained model on their local datasets. In that case, the inclusiveness of the system will decrease. For example, there might exist a monopoly market in which one client (i.e., company) has majority of the data and the rest of the clients each have very little data. The clients with less data can be treated unfairly with low performance on their local datasets and might leave the collaboration which will result in an undesirable single-participant collaboration. Additionally, the utility of the collaboration will be reduced (i.e., the performance of the trained model on a jointly agreed test dataset) due to having less data in the collaboration. Based on this intuition, a fairness notion that seeks to maximize the performance of the worst-performing client is introduced:

Definition 8.1 (Good-intent equitable fairness [17]). For trained models $\mathbf{w}$ and $\tilde{\mathbf{w}}$, the model $\mathbf{w}$ achieves better good-intent equitable fairness than $\tilde{\mathbf{w}}$ if

$$\max_{m\in\{1,...,n\}} g_m(\mathbf{w}) < \max_{m\in\{1,...,n\}} g_m(\tilde{\mathbf{w}}).$$

The good-intent equitable fairness states that a model from FL training is fairer if the maximum loss across all clients is lower. Therefore, a fair model will not underfit to a particular local dataset (i.e., having a very high loss on some client whilst having low losses on others) and can generalize better to all local datasets. In that case, the clients with less data or more heterogeneous data distribution can obtain a better performance which will result in a lower performance disparity among all clients. The good-intent equitable fairness does not enforce a strong equitable performance across all the clients since it only optimizes the performance of the worst-performing client without considering other clients and thus high performance disparity might still be observed. In contrast, another notion of equitable fairness considers the equitable performance across all the clients directly, via a formal equality measure over the variation of the performances. The standard deviation of model performances across the local datasets of all clients is used to characterize how much the performances differ from each other. It leads to

Definition 8.2 (Performance equitable fairness [12]). For a set of models $\mathbf{W} = \{\mathbf{w}' : |g(\mathbf{w}') - \min_{\mathbf{w}} g(\mathbf{w})| \leq \epsilon\}$, model $\mathbf{w}_1 \in \mathbf{W}$ achieves better ϵ performance equitable fairness than model $\mathbf{w}_2 \in \mathbf{W}$ if $\text{std}((a_m(\mathbf{w}_1))_{m=1}^n) < \text{std}((a_m(\mathbf{w}_2))_{m=1}^n)$, where ϵ is the tolerance of the degradation in performance, $a_m(\mathbf{w})$ is the prediction accuracy on the local dataset of client m with model $\mathbf{w}$, and $\text{std}((a_m(\mathbf{w}))_{m=1}^n)$ is the standard deviation of $(a_m(\mathbf{w}))_{m=1}^n$.

The performance equitable fairness aims to find a model that has the most equitable performances (quantified by standard deviation) among all models that have the same (i.e., $\epsilon = 0$) or similar performance with respect to the FedAvg objective. To interpret, the model that achieves performance equitable fairness does not sacrifice too much on the overall model performance with a tolerance of at most ϵ. The performance equitable fairness is similar to the egalitarian's perspective which also favors equal treatment (i.e., equal in performances in this case).

In some cases, Definition 8.2 can be unfair. For example, the dataset in client m can have naturally higher *irreducible error* [7] than that of client m'. Enforcing the loss on client m' to be the same as client m will be unfair to client m' since it might be possible for a model to achieve a lower loss on client m' without making the loss on client m higher. Therefore, it is preferable to have a better overall performance that does not trade off the performances of other clients. A Pareto-optimal outcome is where no one in the collaboration can be better off without making someone else worse off. Building on the good-intent equitable fairness, a notion that additionally considers the Pareto-optimality is introduced:

Definition 8.3 (Pareto-optimal equitable fairness [1]). Among the models $\mathbf{W} = \{\mathbf{w}^* : \mathbf{w}^* = \arg\min_{\mathbf{w}} \max_{m \in N} g_m(\mathbf{w})\}$, a model $\mathbf{w}^P \in \mathbf{W}$ achieves Pareto-optimal equitable fairness if

$$\nexists \mathbf{w} \in \mathbf{W} \text{ such that } \forall m \in N : g_m(\mathbf{w}) \leq g_m(\mathbf{w}^P) \text{ and } \exists m' \in N : g_{m'}(\mathbf{w}) < g_{m'}(\mathbf{w}^P) .$$

The Pareto-optimal equitable fairness considers the improvement of performance not only on the worst-performing client as in Definition 8.1 but also on other clients. Specifically, if there exist multiple models that can achieve the min–max losses (i.e., $|\mathbf{W}| > 1$), the Pareto-optimal equitable fairness favors a model that achieves maximum performances on the clients in which any of their performance cannot be improved without decreasing some others'.

The models that achieve Pareto-optimal equitable fairness also achieve good-intent equitable fairness while the same does not hold reversely. However, the Pareto-optimal equitable fairness can conflict with performance equitable fairness sometimes. For example, assume that there exists a model whose local loss on each client's local dataset is equivalent to the irreducible error of the corresponding client's dataset. Additionally, assume the irreducible errors are different among the clients. Consequently, among all the models that achieve the lowest loss on the worst-performing client (i.e., $\mathbf{W}$ in Definition 8.3), there exists a model that can achieve better performances on some clients without hurting the performance of others. It is fair in this case for these high-performing clients to keep the better than worst-performing client's performances (i.e., Pareto-optimal equitable fairness) instead of eliminating the excess performances completely (i.e., performance equitable fairness).

To conclude, the notion of good-intent equitable fairness and performance equitable fairness aim to achieve equal model performances across different clients which are more suitable for application scenarios where clients have similar data distribution. In contrast, when clients have highly heterogeneous local data distributions (i.e., companies with user data from different geographic populations), improving the worst-performing client or forcing other clients to have similar performances to the worst-performing ones would degrade some clients' model performances on their local data distribution dramatically. In that case, Pareto-optimal equitable fairness would be better since it allows improvements in the model performances of some clients without hurting others.

8.2.2 Collaborative fairness

In the case of self-interested clients (e.g., companies that compete with each other), it will be unfair to the clients with data of higher quantity/quality (i.e., higher contribution clients) to receive the same models/rewards as the clients with data of lower quantity/quality (i.e., lower contribution clients) in the FL system. Otherwise, higher contribution clients may lose their competitive edge and thus be discouraged from the collaboration. Therefore, to encourage the clients with high-quality data to join the collaboration, the rewards given to all the clients should be commensurate with their contributions. Pearson collaborative fairness is introduced as a general idea of designing rewards that are commensurate with the contributions of the clients [28]. The Shapley fairness [21,29], incorporating the Shapley value from cooperative game theory, provides some desirable properties. Finally, a notion of regret-minimized collaborative fairness [32] is defined to additionally consider the costs for the resources of the clients.

To define collaborative fairness, a contribution estimation method and a reward mechanism based on the contribution estimates are needed. The contribution estimates are the values assigned to each client to represent their contributions in training the global model. For example, an intuitive contribution estimate for a client can be defined by how much the performance of the global model (e.g., test accuracy on a test dataset) is due to the participation of the client. Interested readers can refer to the latter chapter on data valuation in federated learning for a more detailed discussion on contribution estimates defined on data quality. Some other works consider more specific contributions. Kang et al. [8] propose to evaluate the contribution based on the clients' reputations and the amount of resources they spend on computing/communicating the gradients obtained from their data. Toyoda and Zhang [24] propose to evaluate the contributions by a voting mechanism and design rewards based on the voting results. Yu et al. [32] consider the long-term profit sharing setting in which the waiting time of rewards is accounted for in designing the rewards. Rewards can be classified into monetary [19] and non-monetary [18,28,29]. The non-monetary reward is normally considered when the monetary reward is unavailable [21]. An example of a non-monetary reward is the model reward which gives clients models with different performances based on their contributions. Interested readers can find a more detailed discussion on model reward in a latter chapter on incentive for federated learning. In general, the reward for each client should be commensurate with its contribution.

Pearson correlation coefficient can be used to quantitatively evaluate the commensurate relationship between rewards and contributions. Denote the rewards for all clients as $(r_m)_{m \in N}$ and the contributions of all clients as $(c_m)_{m \in N}$. It leads to the following:

Definition 8.4 (Pearson collaborative fairness [28]). A federated learning (FL) system achieves Pearson collaborative fairness if $\rho((c_m)_{m\in N}, (r_m)_{m\in N}) > 0$ where $\rho((c_m)_{m\in N}, (r_m)_{m\in N})$ denotes Pearson correlation coefficient between $(c_m)_{m\in N}$ and $(r_m)_{m\in N}$.

The Pearson collaborative fairness provides a simple method to certify if an FL system achieves the core idea of collaborative fairness (i.e., higher rewards to higher contribution clients). It does not specify how the contributions of clients are defined or which form of rewards should be given to the clients. The Pearson collaborative fairness only requires the reward r_m to be positively correlated to the contribution c_m.

However, it is not sufficient in some cases where a more careful and detailed design of rewards based on the contributions is needed. For example, assume that we have a contribution estimate of $\{0, 1, 1.1, 3\}$ for a collaboration involving 4 clients with the corresponding reward values $\{1, 2, 2.1, 4\}$. This will result in a Pearson correlation coefficient of 1 but since the reward is non-zero for the client with zero contribution, it can attract free riders. In addition, take another example where the corresponding reward values are set to be $\{0, 1.1, 1, 3\}$, which also results in a high Pearson correlation coefficient (i.e., 0.998) with respect to the contributions $\{0, 1, 1.1, 3\}$. In this case, the second client contributes less than the third client but it receives a better reward. This is unfair for the third client despite the fact that the rewards are positively correlated to the contributions in general. Thus, a more detailed reward mechanism design is needed. To define it properly, more detailed contribution estimates should be considered.

The existing literature [18,22,23,29] commonly adopts the Shapley value [20] to define the contributions of clients in FL. To determine the contribution of a client, Shapley value computes the average marginal contribution of the client to its predecessor coalitions over all possible sequential orders of participation. Therefore, Shapley value is independent of the order of participation which is favorable in FL since for a fixed iteration of FL training, the clients are selected without enforcing a particular order [5,15,27]. Besides, Shapley value uniquely satisfies several properties (e.g., linearity, symmetry, null player, etc.) [20] which are desirable for designing the rewards. Denote by $N = \{1, \ldots, n\}$ the grand coalition formed by all the clients, and any $C \subseteq N$ as coalitions of clients, and assume $v(C)$ is the utility function that computes the utility of the model (e.g., test accuracy or negative log-likelihood on a test dataset) trained on the dataset $\{D_m\}_{m\in C}$. The Shapley value [20] for client $m \in N$ is

$$\phi_m(v) = \frac{1}{N} \sum_{C \in N \setminus \{m\}} \frac{1}{\binom{N-1}{|C|}} \left[v(C \cup \{m\}) - v(C) \right].$$

Based on the Shapley value definition of contribution estimates, another notion of collaborative fairness is defined:

Definition 8.5 (Shapley collaborative fairness [21,22]). Given a utility function v, an FL system achieves Shapley collaborative fairness if $r_m = f(\phi_m(v))$, $m \in N$, where

$f(\cdot)$ is a strictly increasing function with $f(0) = 0$. The reward defined has the following properties:

- **Uselessness.** If client m has zero marginal contribution to all coalitions, $r_m = 0$.
- **Symmetry.** If client m has the same marginal contributions to all coalitions as another client m', $r_m = r_{m'}$.
- **Strict desirability.** If client m makes a strictly better marginal contribution to a specific coalition than client m' and the same marginal contributions to any other coalitions as m', $r_m > r_{m'}$.
- **Strict monotonicity.** If the client m makes a strictly better contribution to a specific coalition, ceteris paribus, it will receive a strictly better reward.

In contrast to Pearson collaborative fairness, Shapley collaborative fairness provides specific details of how the reward values should be decided. Moreover, it inherits several desirable properties from Shapley value (i.e., uselessness, symmetry, strict desirability). Specifically, Shapley collaborative fairness explicitly rewards more to the clients with higher marginal contributions than clients with lower marginal contributions (i.e., strict desirability). For two clients with exactly the same marginal contributions, it assigns the same reward to them (i.e., symmetry). It also discourages free-riders from participating in the FL system since they will get a zero reward (i.e., uselessness) but have to bear their own communication/computation costs. Beyond these properties, Shapley collaborative fairness provides an extra property of strict monotonicity. It ensures that if a client contributes more, *ceteris paribus*, this client will be better rewarded. Hence, it incentivizes clients which have the potential to contribute more (e.g., having the ability to collect more data) to do so and receive a better reward. Some existing works adopt this Shapley collaborative fairness. For instance, in ρ-Shapley fairness [21], $r_m = k\phi_m^\rho$ where k and ρ are adjustable parameters and in FGFL [29], $r_m \propto \lfloor \tanh(\beta\phi_m)/\max_{i \in N} \tanh(\beta\phi_i) \rfloor$ where β is an adjustable parameter and the function $\tanh(\cdot)$ can be replaced with another monotonic function while preserving the theoretical properties.

The collaborative fairness defined above does not consider the costs of resources within each client (e.g., costs of collecting data or computational resources). However, the costs can also be a vital measure for clients to decide whether to participate or not, especially if clients are organizations that make decisions based on the net profit (i.e., reward minus cost). If a client receives a reward lower than the costs of providing the corresponding resources, it will regret participating in the collaboration due to the negative net profit and will not participate next time. Therefore, it is desirable to minimize the overall regrets of the clients. Denoting the cost of resources of the clients as $(s_m)_{m \in N}$ and the regret of clients as $k_m = \max((s_m - r_m), 0)$, $m \in N$, leads to the following notion of fairness which is a simplified version of [32]:

Definition 8.6 (Regret-minimized collaborative fairness). A federated learning (FL) system achieves regret-minimized collaborative fairness if $(r_m^*)_{m \in N} = \arg\min_{(r_m)_{m \in N}} \sum_{m=1}^{n} (k_m)^2 - \alpha \sum_{m=1}^{n} r_m c_m$ such that $\sum_{m=1}^{n} r_m \leq b$ where b is the total reward budget and α is an adjustable parameter.

In the objective of the optimization problem in Definition 8.6, the term $\sum_{m=1}^{n}(k_m)^2$ is the sum of square of the clients' regrets. Thus, minimizing it will reduce overall regrets. The quadratic expression k_m^2 naturally avoids the case that a few clients have very high regrets while others have zero regrets. The term $\sum_{m=1}^{n} r_m c_m$ will be large if the rewards r_m's are high for clients with high contributions c_m's. Therefore, the regret-minimized collaborative fairness tries to divide the total budget b as rewards to minimize the overall regret while simultaneously ensuring the clients with larger contributions receive higher rewards. The adjustable parameter $\alpha > 0$ balances the importance of these two objectives.

8.2.3 Algorithmic fairness

Informally, a model is said to achieve algorithmic fairness (specifically, group fairness) in ML if it does not discriminate against certain groups (i.e., data with sensitive attributes having certain values). Put differently, the trained model should have similar performances across different groups, namely low performance disparities across groups [16]. The algorithmic fairness in FL is closely related to that in ML, so a notion of global algorithmic fairness is introduced as an extension of that in ML. Another notion of multi-client algorithmic fairness is introduced and specific to the FL setting.

Without loss of generality, consider the case of binary classification where the label $y \in \{0, 1\}$, and assume that there exists a global sensitive attribute (e.g., gender) $s \in \{0, 1\}$. Denote the trained federated model as a prediction function $f(\mathbf{w}, \cdot)$ parameterized by the learned parameters $\mathbf{w}$, and denote the predicted label for input x as $\hat{y}_{\mathbf{w}} = f(\mathbf{w}, x)$. Denote $D_m^{(ij)} = \{(x, y, s) : (x, y, s) \in D_m, \hat{y}_{\mathbf{w}} = i, s = j\}$ and $D_m^{(\cdot j)} = \{(x, y, s) : (x, y, s) \in D_m, \hat{y}_{\mathbf{w}} \in \{0, 1\}, s = j\}$. There are various definitions using different measures to quantify the disparity of the model performances among all groups (e.g., demographic parity [3], equalized odds [6], and equal opportunity [6]). We focus on demographic parity to describe the following definitions which can be easily extended to other disparity measures. A definition of algorithmic fairness based on this measure is:

Definition 8.7 (Global algorithmic fairness [2,4]). In a federated learning (FL) system, a model $f(\mathbf{w}, \cdot)$ achieves ϵ global algorithmic fairness if

$$\Delta DP_g(\mathbf{w}) = \left| \frac{\sum_{m=1}^{n} |D_m^{(11)}|}{\sum_{m=1}^{n} |D_m^{(\cdot 1)}|} - \frac{\sum_{m=1}^{n} |D_m^{(10)}|}{\sum_{m=1}^{n} |D_m^{(\cdot 0)}|} \right| \leq \epsilon. \tag{8.1}$$

Here, $\sum_{m=1}^{n} |D_m^{(11)}| / \sum_{m=1}^{n} |D_m^{(\cdot 1)}|$ is the probability of the group with $s = 1$ being predicted as positive, and $\sum_{m=1}^{n} |D_m^{(10)}| / \sum_{m=1}^{n} |D_m^{(\cdot 0)}|$ is that for the group with $s = 0$. Therefore, $\Delta DP_g(\mathbf{w})$ is the absolute difference of the probability of data been predicted as positive with model $\mathbf{w}$ between two groups on the aggregated dataset $\{D_m\}_{m \in N}$. A model achieves global algorithmic fairness if the difference of probability of predicting positive between two groups is less than ϵ. Though the global algorithmic fairness is straightforward, enforcing it can sometimes have limited usefulness, especially when the clients have heterogeneous local data distributions. Then, it is possible that the federated model achieves algorithmic fairness in a specific client but not in some others.

For example, in the task of income level prediction (i.e., Adult dataset [9]), a model is trained to predict if a person has high or low income (i.e., binary classification) based on 14 features characterizing personal information (e.g., age, sex, education, occupation, etc.). We define the age from 30 to 50 as high-income age since most people with high income lie within this age interval. Assume that sex is the sensitive attribute to protect. Additionally, assume that in client m the percentage of populations with high-income age is similar between males and females while in client m' the percentage of populations with high-income age is higher in males than that of females. A simple model that makes predictions based solely on the attribute age will probably achieve fairness in client m (i.e., predicting 1 with the same probability between male group than female group). However, the model can hardly achieve fairness in client m' since it will predict 1 with a higher probability on the male group due to its higher percentage of high-income age populations. Another problem is that the protected attribute can vary across clients. For example, the sensitive attribute in the dataset of client m is sex while it is race in that of client m'. It is not clear how enforcing global fairness with respect to some unified sensitive attributes can be useful to each client in these scenarios. Therefore, a more refined algorithmic fairness notion with performance disparity defined with respect to each client is needed. Define a unique sensitive attribute for each client m: $c_m \in \{0, 1\}$ which can be the same across different clients. Denote $D_m^{(ij)} = \{(x, y, c_m) : (x, y, c_m) \in D_m, \hat{y}_\mathbf{w} = i, c_m = j\}$ and $D_m^{(\cdot j)} = \{(x, y, c_m) : (x, y, c_m) \in D_m, \hat{y}_\mathbf{w} \in \{0, 1\}, c_m = j\}$. It leads to

Definition 8.8 (Multi-client algorithmic fairness [1]). In a federated learning (FL) system, a model $f(\mathbf{w}, \cdot)$ achieves $\{\epsilon_m, m \in \{1, \ldots, n\}\}$ multi-client algorithmic fairness if

$$\Delta \mathrm{DP}_m(\mathbf{w}) = \left| \frac{|D_m^{(11)}|}{|D_m^{(\cdot 1)}|} - \frac{|D_m^{(10)}|}{|D_m^{(\cdot 0)}|} \right| \leq \epsilon_m \quad \forall m \in \{1, \ldots, n\}. \tag{8.2}$$

Here $\Delta \mathrm{DP}_m(\mathbf{w})$ is the absolute difference of the probability of samples predicted as positive with model $\mathbf{w}$ between two groups on the local dataset of client m.

The multi-client algorithmic fairness requires low performance disparity with respect to each client m with a possibly unique sensitive attribute c_m and an individual budget ϵ_m for the performance disparity in each client. As illustrated in the income level prediction example, achieving fairness in the local dataset of different clients can sometimes conflict with each other. Therefore, it is more challenging to achieve multi-client algorithmic fairness than global algorithmic fairness even if $\sum_{m=1}^{n} \epsilon_m = \epsilon$.

8.3 Algorithms to achieve fairness in FL

8.3.1 Algorithms to achieve equitable fairness

We will focus on discussing the details of the AFL [17] and q-FFL [12] algorithms to achieve good-intent equitable fairness and performance equitable fairness correspondingly here and refer readers to [2] for an in-depth discussion on the algorithm to achieve Pareto-optimal equitable fairness.

A common approach to equitable fairness is to modify the global objective of the training to achieve similar model performances on the clients' local data. AFL [17] proposes a min–max objective. Defining Δ^n as an $(n-1)$-dimensional probability simplex and considering $\lambda \in \Delta^n$, the objective function is defined as $g(\mathbf{w}, \lambda) = \sum_{m=1}^{n} \lambda_m g_m(\mathbf{w})$ where $g_m(\mathbf{w})$ is the local training loss of model parameterized by $\mathbf{w} \in \mathcal{W}$ on client m. The objective of the AFL is defined as

$$\min_{\mathbf{w} \in \mathcal{W}} \max_{\lambda \in \Delta^n} g(\mathbf{w}, \lambda) . \tag{8.3}$$

The objective in Eq. (8.3) can be viewed as a two-player game, where player A wants to find λ such that the weighted loss can be maximized, and player B wants to find the parameter $\mathbf{w}$ such that the weighted loss can be minimized. Since $g(\mathbf{w}, \lambda)$ is linear in λ, the optimal λ would be in $\{\lambda : \exists m \in N : \lambda_m = 1, \forall m' \in N \setminus \{m\} : \lambda_{m'} = 0\}$. Therefore, the solution $\mathbf{w}^*$ of Eq. (8.3) is also the solution of $\min_{\mathbf{w} \in \mathcal{W}} \max_{m \in \{1,\dots,n\}} g_m(\mathbf{w})$. Consequently, solving Eq. (8.3) will get a model that achieves good-intent fairness according to the definition. To solve the optimization problem in Eq. (8.3), gradient estimators for $\nabla_\lambda g(\mathbf{w}, \lambda)$ and $\nabla_\mathbf{w} g(\mathbf{w}, \lambda)$ can be used. Denote the gradient estimators as $\delta_\lambda g(\mathbf{w}, \lambda)$ and $\delta_\mathbf{w} g(\mathbf{w}, \lambda)$ accordingly. Denote by $[n]$ the uniform distribution on $\{1, \dots, n\}$. In AFL, $\delta_\lambda g(\mathbf{w}, \lambda)$ is computed as follows: sample $m \sim [n]$, and then sample $i \sim [|D_m|]$. Then set $[\delta_\lambda g(\mathbf{w}, \lambda)]_m = n\ell(\mathbf{w}; x_{m,i}, y_{m,i})$ and $[\delta_\lambda g(\mathbf{w}, \lambda)]_k = 0, \forall k \in N \setminus \{m\}$ where $\ell(\mathbf{w}; x_{m,i}, y_{m,i})$ is the loss function of model $\mathbf{w}$ on the ith data point of client m. Similarly, to compute $\delta_\mathbf{w} g(\mathbf{w}, \lambda)$, firstly sample $i_m \sim [|D_m|], \forall m \in N$ with uniform distribution accordingly, then $\delta_\mathbf{w} g(\mathbf{w}, \lambda) = \sum_{m=1}^{n} \lambda_m \nabla_\mathbf{w} \ell(\mathbf{w}; x_{m,i_m}, y_{m,i_m})$. The pseudo-code for STOCHASTIC-AFL which is the algorithm to solve AFL objective is presented in Algorithm 1. The PROJECT($\tilde{\mathbf{w}}, \mathcal{W}$) in Algorithm 1 is the projecting function that finds $\mathbf{w}_p = \arg\min_{w \in \mathcal{W}} \|\mathbf{w} - \tilde{\mathbf{w}}\|^2$ and can be efficiently solved in near-linear time [26]. Its convergence guarantee is established in [17].

For performance equitable fairness, q-FFL [12] is proposed. Intuitively, if a local objective has a higher weight, the global objective prioritizes the minimization of this local objective. Therefore, q-FFL proposes to assign higher weights for the local objectives with higher loss values and thus make the losses distributed equitably among clients. The reweighting process is done during training dynamically since it is difficult to do *a priori*. The objective of q-FFL is

$$\min_{\mathbf{w}} f_q(\mathbf{w}) = \sum_{m=1}^{n} \frac{p_m}{q+1} g_m^{q+1}(\mathbf{w}), \tag{8.4}$$

Algorithm 1 STOCHASTIC-AFL.

Input: Step size for gradient update $\gamma_{\mathbf{w}}$ and γ_λ, number of gradient update step T.
Initialization: $\mathbf{w}_0$ and λ_0

    for $t = 1$ to T **do**.

        Compute the stochastic gradient estimators: $\delta_{\mathbf{w}}g(\mathbf{w}, \lambda)$ and $\delta_\lambda g(\mathbf{w}, \lambda)$.

        $\tilde{\mathbf{w}}_t = \mathbf{w}_{t-1} - \gamma_{\mathbf{w}}\delta_{\mathbf{w}}g(\mathbf{w}_{t-1}, \lambda_{t-1})$.

        $\tilde{\lambda}_t = \lambda_{t-1} - \gamma_\lambda\delta_\lambda g(\mathbf{w}_{t-1}, \lambda_{t-1})$.

        $\mathbf{w}_t = \text{PROJECT}(\tilde{\mathbf{w}}_t, \mathcal{W})$.

        $\lambda_t = \text{PROJECT}(\tilde{\lambda}_t, \Delta^n)$.

    end for
Output: $\mathbf{w}^T = 1/T \sum_{t=1}^{T} \mathbf{w}_t$

        and $\lambda^T = 1/T \sum_{t=1}^{T} \lambda_t$.

Algorithm 2 q-FedSGD.

Input: The number of clients selected every iteration K, the total training iteration T, constant L.
Initialization: $\mathbf{w}_0$.

    for $t = 0$ to T **do**

        M clients are selected which form a set S_M, each client m is chosen with probability p_k.

        for $k \in S_M$ **do**

            $\delta_k^t = g_k^q(\mathbf{w}_t)\nabla g_k(\mathbf{w}_t)$.

            $h_k^t = q g_k^{q-1}(\mathbf{w}_t)\|\nabla g_k(\mathbf{w}_t)\|^2 + L g_k^q(\mathbf{w}_t)$.

        end for

        $w_{t+1} = w_t - \frac{\sum_{k \in S_M} \delta_k^t}{\sum_{k \in S_M} h_k^t}$.

    end for
Output: w_T.

---

where $p_m = |D_m|/\sum_{m=1}^{n}|D_m|$ and q is an adjustable parameter. Borrowing the idea from α-fairness [10], q-FFL can adjust q to satisfy different levels of equality for the clients' performances. A larger q means that the objective emphasizes the loss of the lower performing clients and thus enforcing better equality of performance across all clients. In contrast, a lower q makes the objective more similar to that in FedAvg which does not consider equality, in particular, $q = 0$ recovers the FedAvg objective. The pseudo-code for q-FedSGD, the algorithm to solve the q-FFL objective, is shown in Algorithm 2. To make the algorithm converge, the step size of the gradient update is chosen according to different values of q. q-FedSGD proposes to use h_k^t to control the step size so that no manual tuning on step size is needed for different q to ensure convergence.

    Both STOCHASTIC-AFL and q-FedSGD make changes to the training objective to achieve their corresponding targeted fairness notions. Additionally, both

Table 8.3 Communication cost and running time for the fairness mechanism for different algorithms: n_g is the number of dimensions of model gradients, r is the fraction of clients selected in each iteration, M is the number of Monte Carlo simulations in GoG, and $|D_v|$ is the number of data points in validation dataset for GoG.

Algorithm	Communication costs	Running time
FedAvg	$2n_g r\tau n$	–
STOCHASTIC-AFL[a]	$2n_g r\tau n + r\tau n^2$	$O((n_g \log(n_g) + n \log(n))\tau)$
q-FedSGD	$2n_g r\tau n + r\tau n$	$O(n_g \tau)$
FGFL	$2n_g \tau n$	$O(n_g n\tau)$
GoG	$2n_g r\tau n$	$O(r M n n_g |D_v|\tau)$
FAFL[a]	$2n_g r\tau n$	–

[a] We compute the communication costs for STOCHASTIC-AFL and FAFL by modifying the algorithms to select rn number of clients in each iteration for fair comparison.

algorithms are shown to converge under certain assumptions [12,17]. q-FedSGD provides a more flexible control over the trade-off between fairness and utility than STOCHASTIC-AFL due to the adjustable parameter q in Eq. (8.4). Surprisingly, though q-FedSGD does not explicitly strive to get a better performance on the worst-performing client, it achieves better good-intent equitable fairness than STOCHASTIC-AFL on several datasets [12] while achieving better performance equitable fairness simultaneously. From Table 8.3, STOCHASTIC-AFL is more costly than q-FedSGD in both communication and running time. Both of them take extra communication costs than FedAvg.

8.3.2 Algorithms to achieve collaborative fairness

For different notions of collaborative fairness, FGFL [29] and GoG [18] are proposed to achieve Pearson collaborative fairness and Shapley collaborative fairness, and FLI [32] is proposed to achieve regret-minimized collaborative fairness. We will specifically outline FGFL and GoG algorithms in detail and refer readers to [32] for FLI due to the space limits. Since a contribution estimation and an incentive mechanism based on the contribution estimates are two vital components in designing algorithms to achieve collaborative fairness, we will focus on discussing the differences between FGFL and GoG in designing these two components correspondingly.

To compute the contribution estimates, FGFL uses the gradient information from each client and calculates their similarities to the aggregated gradients to estimate their contribution to the training. Intuitively, the aggregated gradient is the direction in which the global loss will decrease. If a client has a gradient (vector) that is (directionally) similar/aligned to the aggregated gradient (vector), it means that the client's gradient is highly effective in reducing global loss and thus has a high contribution to the training. Using this intuition of vector alignment between gradient vectors, a cosine similarity-based Shapley value contribution is defined (i.e., cosine similarity as v). With the contribution estimates, FGFL gives clients models with different performances commensurate with their contributions. To differentiate the performance, FGFL gives clients gradient updates with different proportions of values masked by zero. Intuitively, a higher proportion of masked values means less information about gradient update is given to the clients, which will lead to lower model performance. The gradients are computed as follows:

$$r_m^{(t)} = \left\lfloor \mathbf{D_w} \tanh\left(\beta c_m^{(t)}\right) / \max_{i \in \mathcal{N}} \tanh\left(\beta c_i^{(t)}\right) \right\rfloor \quad \text{and} \quad v_m^{(t)} = \text{mask}\left(\mathbf{u}_{\mathcal{N}}^{(t)}, r_m^{(t)}\right), \quad (8.5)$$

where $c_m^{(t)}$ and $r_m^{(t)}$ are contribution and reward of client m up to iteration t, $\mathbf{u}_{\mathcal{N}}^{(t)}$ is the aggregated gradients in iteration t, $\mathbf{D_w}$ is the number of dimension of parameters for model $\mathbf{w}$, and the function $\text{mask}(\mathbf{u}_{\mathcal{N}}^{(t)}, r_m^{(t)})$ is to retain the largest $\max(r_m^{(t)}, 0)$ number of values in terms of magnitude and assign zero to all other values in the aggregated gradient $\mathbf{u}_{\mathcal{N}}^{(t)}$. The sparsified gradient $v_m^{(t)}$ is distributed to the client m as the reward. Therefore, a high contributing client will have a *less* sparsified gradient update and thus better model performance. The β is to control the degree of altruism. When $\beta \to \infty$, the framework returns to vanilla FL in terms of the clients receiving the same unmasked/unspasified gradient (i.e., $\mathbf{u}_{\mathcal{N}}^{(t)}$).

GoG uses an additional validation dataset D_v to compute the contribution estimates for each client with Shapley value. As an interpretation, the more a client's model update improves to the model performance on the validation dataset, the higher contribution estimate is for this client [18,22]. For the reward mechanism, GoG gives different clients different chances to be selected and synchronize their local model with the most up-to-date global model thus achieving different model performances for each client. To elaborate, in iteration t the model will only select $k < n$ clients to be updated and the probabilities of the clients being selected are commensurate with their contribution estimates up to iteration t, $c_m^{(t)}$. Thus, a lower contributing client will get a low probability of being selected and its local model will stall for a longer period which will result in relatively lower model performance, and vice versa.

Both FGFL and GoG adopt Shapley value to compute the contribution estimates and use the model rewards (i.e., non-monetary reward). Therefore, both algorithms achieve the Shapley collaborative fairness and also the Pearson collaborative fairness. GoG requires a jointly agreed validation dataset to compute the contribution estimates which can be unavailable in some cases. Additional performance evaluations on the validation dataset for models trained on different coalitions also bring higher computational complexity in GoG. In contrast, FGFL removes the need for the validation dataset and uses the gradient similarity as a proxy to compute the utility of coalitions which reduces the computational complexity. From Table 8.3, GoG always has $O(rM|D_v|)$ times higher running time complexity than FGFL, but lower communication costs than FGFL due to the allowance of partial client's selection. However, both FGFL and GoG lack convergence guarantees for the models [18,29].

8.3.3 **Algorithms to achieve algorithmic fairness**

For algorithmic fairness, we will focus on discussing the FAFL [2] algorithm. FAFL can be used to achieve both global algorithmic fairness and multi-client algorithmic fairness separately with minor modifications.

Intuitively, we can formulate optimization problems to find models that achieve the global algorithmic fairness as $\min_{\mathbf{w} \in \mathcal{W}} g(\mathbf{w})$ such that $h(\mathbf{w}) \leq \epsilon$ where $h(\mathbf{w}) = \Delta\mathrm{DP}_g(\mathbf{w})$ (defined in Definition 8.7). Similarly, for the multi-client fairness, the optimization problem is defined by changing the constraint to $h_k(\mathbf{w}) \leq \epsilon_k, \forall k \in \{1, \dots, n\}$ where $h_k(\mathbf{w}) = \Delta\mathrm{DP}_k(\mathbf{w})$ (defined in Definition 8.8). Both optimization problems minimize the average loss under the constraint that the disparity measures do not exceed their respective budgets. However, the disparity measures are not differentiable with respect to the model parameters $\mathbf{w}$. To address this, FAFL [2] proposes an alternative constraint that is differentiable with respect to $\mathbf{w}$. Intuitively, if the distance of data points to the decision boundary is similar across different groups, the model performance on these groups can be similar. Following this intuition, the constraint can be replaced by $h'(\mathbf{w}) = 1/n \sum_{m=1}^{n} \sum_{i=1}^{|D_m|} (s_m^{(i)} - \bar{s}) d(\mathbf{w}, x_m^{(i)}) \leq \epsilon'$ where the $s_m^{(i)}$ is the value of the attribute for the ith data point of client m. Here, $d(\mathbf{w}, x_m^{(i)})$ is the distance of data point $x_m^{(i)}$ to the decision boundary defined by model parameter $\mathbf{w}$. It is tractable in the case of linear model (e.g., logistic regression model); $\bar{s}$ is the average attribute value defined as $\bar{s} = \sum_{m=1}^{n} \sum_{i=1}^{|D_m|} s_m^{(i)} / \sum_{m=1}^{n} |D_m|$. Consequently, FAFL uses the following objective:

$$J(\mathbf{w}) = \frac{1}{n} \sum_{m=1}^{n} g_m(\mathbf{w}) + \lambda \left(\frac{1}{n} \sum_{m=1}^{n} \sum_{i=1}^{|D_m|} \left(s_m^{(i)} - \bar{s} \right) d\left(\mathbf{w}, x_m^{(i)} \right) \right)^2, \qquad (8.6)$$

where λ balances the importance of fairness constraint and utility (i.e., model performance). By simply replacing the objective function in Eq. (8.6) with the multi-client case, the FAFL can achieve multi-client algorithmic fairness. From Table 8.3, FAFL has no extra communication costs and no extra running time for the fairness mechanism compared to FedAvg. However, it is only applicable to linear models due to the computation of distances between data points and the decision boundary.

There are other algorithms to achieve global algorithmic fairness. FairFed [4] proposes to reweigh the objective of FL dynamically during the training to achieve global algorithmic fairness. FairFL [34] proposes to apply multi-agent reinforcement learning to achieve global algorithmic fairness. We leave the reader to refer to [4,34] for more details.

8.4 **Open problems and conclusion**

Apart from the notions and algorithms discussed here, there are still unsolved open problems in fairness FL. For collaborative fairness, contribution estimation remains a challenging problem (e.g., it is time-consuming to perform contribution estimation in

FL, demonstrated in Table 8.3). Additionally, there is relatively little work on gauging the quality of contribution estimates (i.e., how well do these contribution estimates in FL reflect the clients' true contributions).

For the reward mechanism, developing algorithms with fair model rewards while guaranteeing the convergence of the model is worth exploring since most current works (e.g., GoG and FGFL) do not provide convergence guarantees which can be crucial to make the mechanism applicable in real applications. For algorithmic fairness and equitable fairness, the discussed algorithms provide convergence guarantees without incurring significant increases in communication costs/running time compared to FedAvg. Therefore, these notions are relatively well studied when considered separately. However, for systems to satisfy multiple fairness notions simultaneously, some open challenges remain. For example, to increase the inclusiveness of the FL system, we might want to incentivize low-contribution clients to participate (e.g., clients with less data) with the equitable fairness guarantee while at the same time incentivizing high-contribution clients to participate with the collaborative fairness guarantee. It is still unclear how to design algorithms to achieve both equitable and collaborative fairness.

In conclusion, creating a fair environment is an emerging and important research area, especially to the real-world applications of FL. In this chapter, we provided a summary of the existing notions of fairness in FL motivated by different application scenarios. We also provided a comparative analysis on various algorithms to achieve the respective fairness notions with respect to the assumptions, target applications, communication costs, and running time complexity. We discussed some open problems in improving certain fairness algorithms and pointed out some remaining research gaps in application scenarios where multiple fairness notions may need to be satisfied altogether.

Acknowledgments

This research/project is supported by the National Research Foundation Singapore and DSO National Laboratories under the AI Singapore Programme (AISG Award No: AISG2-RP-2020-018).

References

[1] Sen Cui, Weishen Pan, Jian Liang, Changshui Zhang, Fei Wang, Addressing algorithmic disparity and performance inconsistency in federated learning, Proc. NeurIPS 34 (2021).
[2] Du Wei, Depeng Xu, Xintao Wu, Hanghang Tong, Fairness-aware agnostic federated learning, in: Proc. SDM, SIAM, 2021, pp. 181–189.
[3] Cynthia Dwork, Moritz Hardt, Toniann Pitassi, Omer Reingold, Richard Zemel, Fairness through awareness, in: Proc. ITCS, 2012, pp. 214–226.
[4] Yahya H. Ezzeldin, Shen Yan, Chaoyang He, Emilio Ferrara, Salman Avestimehr, Fairfed: enabling group fairness in federated learning, arXiv:2110.00857, 2021.

[5] Andrew Hard, Kanishka Rao, Rajiv Mathews, Swaroop Ramaswamy, Françoise Beaufays, Sean Augenstein, Hubert Eichner, Chloé Kiddon, Daniel Ramage, Federated learning for mobile keyboard prediction, 2018.

[6] Moritz Hardt, Eric Price, Nati Srebro, Equality of opportunity in supervised learning, Proc. NeurIPS 29 (2016).

[7] Gareth James, Trevor Hastie, Generalizations of the Bias/Variance Decomposition for Prediction Error, Tech. Rep., Dept. Statistics, Stanford Univ., Stanford, CA, 1997.

[8] Jiawen Kang, Zehui Xiong, Dusit Niyato, Shengli Xie, Junshan Zhang, Incentive mechanism for reliable federated learning: a joint optimization approach to combining reputation and contract theory, IEEE Internet of Things Journal 6 (6) (2019) 10700–10714.

[9] Ron Kohavi, et al., Scaling up the accuracy of naive-Bayes classifiers: a decision-tree hybrid, in: Proc. KDD, vol. 96, 1996, pp. 202–207.

[10] Tian Lan, David Kao, Mung Chiang, Ashutosh Sabharwal, An axiomatic theory of fairness in network resource allocation, in: Proc. IEEE INFOCOM, 2010, pp. 1–9.

[11] Li Tian, Shengyuan Hu, Ahmad Beirami, Virginia Smith, Ditto: fair and robust federated learning through personalization, in: Proc. ICML, PMLR, 2021, pp. 6357–6368.

[12] Li Tian, Maziar Sanjabi, Ahmad Beirami, Virginia Smith, Fair resource allocation in federated learning, in: Proc. ICLR, 2019.

[13] Xiang Li, Kaixuan Huang, Wenhao Yang, Shusen Wang, Zhihua Zhang, On the convergence of fedavg on non-iid data, in: Proc. ICLR, 2020.

[14] Lingjuan Lyu, Xinyi Xu, Qian Wang, Han Yu, Collaborative fairness in federated learning, in: Federated Learning, Springer, 2020, pp. 189–204.

[15] H. Brendan McMahan, Eider Moore, Daniel Ramage, Seth Hampson, Blaise Agüera y Arcas, Communication-efficient learning of deep networks from decentralized data, in: Proc. AISTATS, 2017.

[16] Ninareh Mehrabi, Fred Morstatter, Nripsuta Saxena, Kristina Lerman, Aram Galstyan, A survey on bias and fairness in machine learning, ACM Computing Surveys (CSUR) 54 (6) (2021) 1–35.

[17] Mehryar Mohri, Gary Sivek, Ananda Theertha Suresh, Agnostic federated learning, in: Proc. ICML, vol. 97, 2019, pp. 4615–4625.

[18] Lokesh Nagalapatti, Ramasuri Narayanam, Game of gradients: mitigating irrelevant clients in federated learning, in: Proc. AAAI, vol. 35, 2021, pp. 9046–9054.

[19] Olga Ohrimenko, Shruti Tople, Sebastian Tschiatschek, Collaborative machine learning markets with data-replication-robust payments, arXiv:1911.09052, 2019.

[20] L.S. Shapley, A value for n-person games, in: Contributions to the Theory of Games (AM-28), Volume II, Princeton University Press, Princeton, 1953, pp. 307–318.

[21] Rachael Hwee Ling Sim, Yehong Zhang, Mun Choon Chan, Bryan Kian Hsiang Low, Collaborative machine learning with incentive-aware model rewards, in: Proc. ICML, 2020, pp. 8927–8936.

[22] Tianshu Song, Yongxin Tong, Shuyue Wei, Profit allocation for federated learning, in: Proc. IEEE Big Data, 2019, pp. 2577–2586.

[23] Sebastian Shenghong Tay, Xinyi Xu, Chuan Sheng Foo, Bryan Kian Hsiang Low, Incentivizing collaboration in machine learning via synthetic data rewards, in: Proc. AAAI, 2022.

[24] Kentaroh Toyoda, Allan N. Zhang, Mechanism design for an incentive-aware blockchain-enabled federated learning platform, in: Proc. IEEE Big Data, 2019, pp. 395–403.

[25] Tianhao Wang, Johannes Rausch, Ce Zhang, Ruoxi Jia, Dawn Song, A principled approach to data valuation for federated learning, in: Federated Learning, Springer, 2020, pp. 153–167.

[26] Weiran Wang, Miguel A. Carreira-Perpinán, Projection onto the probability simplex: an efficient algorithm with a simple proof, and an application, arXiv:1309.1541, 2013.

[27] Jie Xu, Benjamin S. Glicksberg, Chang Su, Peter Walker, Jiang Bian, Fei Wang, Federated learning for healthcare informatics, Journal of Healthcare Informatics Research 5 (1) (2021) 1–19.

[28] Xinyi Xu, Lingjuan Lyu, A reputation mechanism is all you need: collaborative fairness and adversarial robustness in federated learning, in: International Workshop on Federated Learning for User Privacy and Data Confidentiality in Conjunction with ICML 2021 (FL-ICML'21), 2021.

[29] Xinyi Xu, Lingjuan Lyu, Xingjun Ma, Chenglin Miao, Chuan Sheng Foo, Bryan Kian Hsiang Low, Gradient driven rewards to guarantee fairness in collaborative machine learning, Proc. NeurIPS 34 (2021).

[30] Qiang Yang, Yang Liu, Tianjian Chen, Yongxin Tong, Federated machine learning: concept and applications, ACM Transactions on Intelligent Systems and Technology (TIST) 10 (2) (2019) 1–19.

[31] Wensi Yang, Yuhang Zhang, Kejiang Ye, Li Li, Cheng-Zhong Xu, FFD: a federated learning based method for credit card fraud detection, in: International Conference on Big Data, 2019, pp. 18–32.

[32] Han Yu, Zelei Liu, Yang Liu, Tianjian Chen, Mingshu Cong, Xi Weng, Dusit Niyato, Qiang Yang, A fairness-aware incentive scheme for federated learning, in: Proc. AIES, 2020, pp. 393–399.

[33] Muhammad Bilal Zafar, Isabel Valera, Manuel Gomez Rodriguez, Krishna P. Gummadi, Fairness beyond disparate treatment & disparate impact: learning classification without disparate mistreatment, in: Proc. WWW, 2017, pp. 1171–1180.

[34] Daniel Yue Zhang, Ziyi Kou, Dong Wang, FairFL: A fair federated learning approach to reducing demographic bias in privacy-sensitive classification models, in: Proc. IEEE Big Data, 2020, pp. 1051–1060.

Meta-federated learning

9

Omid Aramoon[a], **Pin-Yu Chen**[b], **Gang Qu**[a], and **Yuan Tian**[c]

[a]*University of Maryland at College Park, College Park, MD, United States*
[b]*IBM Research, Yorktown Heights, NY, United States*
[c]*University of Virginia, Charlottesville, VA, United States*

9.1 Introduction

Federated learning (FL) is a distributed learning framework that enables millions of clients (e.g., mobile and edge devices) jointly train a deep learning model under the supervision of an orchestration server [16,24,31]. Taking advantage of training data distributed among the crowd of clients enables federated learning to train a highly accurate shared global model. Federated learning has gained significant interest from the industry with many tech companies, including Google and Apple, deploying this framework to improve their services, such as next-word prediction for messaging on mobile devices and voice recognition for digital assistants [11].

In every round of federated learning, the central server randomly selects a cohort of participants to locally train the joint global model on their private data and submit an update to the server, which would be aggregated into the new global model. Federated learning decouples model training from the need to access participants' training data by collecting focused model updates that contain enough information for the server to improve the global model without revealing too much about the client's private data [11].

While collecting model updates, instead of centralizing raw training data, significantly reduces privacy concerns for participating clients, it does not offer any formal privacy guarantees. Recent studies have shown that model updates can still leak sensitive information about the client's data [17,19], which proves that preserving the privacy of clients is only a promise, and certainly not the reality of federated learning.

To systematically address such privacy concerns, recent FL settings deploy secure aggregation (SecAgg) [5], a cryptographic protocol that enables the server to compute the aggregate of updates and train the global model while keeping each individual update uninspectable at all times. Looking from the server's point of view, secure aggregation can be a "double-edged sword." On the one hand, it can systematically mitigate privacy risks for participants, which would make federated learning more appealing to clients and eventually result in higher client turnout. On the other

Federated Learning. https://doi.org/10.1016/B978-0-44-319037-7.00017-X

hand, it would facilitate training time adversarial attacks by masking participants' contributions.

Training time adversarial attacks may have targeted [6,10,13] or untargeted adversarial objectives [3,18]. In untargeted attacks, the adversary aims to corrupt the learned model so that it would perform poorly on the learning task at hand. However, in targeted attacks, the adversary's goal is to force the model to learn certain adversarial sub-task in addition to the primary learning task. Targeted attacks are harder to detect compared to untargeted attacks as the adversary's objective is unknown. Perhaps the most prevalent example of targeted attacks is backdoor attacks, which have been extensively explored for the centralized learning settings [10,12,29]. In backdoor attacks, the adversary's goal for the learned model is to misclassify inputs containing certain triggers while classifying inputs without the trigger correctly.

Known techniques in mitigating backdoor attacks in the centralized setting are not applicable to federated learning. Successful defenses such as data sanitization [7] and network pruning [14] require careful examination of clients' training data or access to a proxy dataset with similar distribution as the global dataset. None of these requirements hold in federated learning.

Moreover, contemporary defenses against backdoor attacks in FL require examinations of participants' model updates, which is not compatible with secure aggregation. Even in the absence of secure aggregation, inspecting the clients' updates is not acceptable due to privacy concerns and regulations.

This study seeks to answer the following question, *"Is it possible to defend against backdoor attacks when secure aggregation is in place?"*, a question that has not been investigated by prior studies. To this end, we propose meta-federated learning (Meta-FL), a novel federated learning framework that not only preserves the privacy of participants, but also facilitates defense against backdoor attacks.

In our framework, we take full advantage of the abundance of participants by engaging more than one training cohort at each round to participate in model training. To preserve the privacy of participants, Meta-FL bootstraps the SecAgg protocol to aggregate updates from each training cohort. In Meta-FL, the server is provided with a set of cohort aggregates, instead of individual model updates, which are further aggregated to generate the new global model. Fig. 9.1(a) illustrates the overview of model training in Meta-FL.

Meta-FL moves the defense execution point from the update level to the aggregate level which facilitates mitigating backdoor attacks by offering the following advantages: (i) server can monitor cohort aggregates without violating the privacy of participants. Therefore, the adversary is forced to be mindful of their submissions and maintain stealth on the aggregate level as aggregates that are statistically different from others are likely to get flagged and discarded; (ii) cohort aggregates exhibit less variation compared to individual client updates, which makes it easier for the server to detect anomalies, and (iii) adversary faces competition from benign clients to hold control of the value of cohort aggregates which hinders them from executing intricate defense evasion techniques.

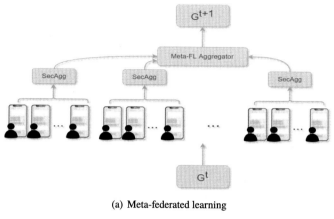

(a) Meta-federated learning

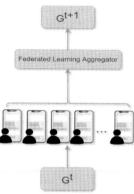

(b) Federated learning

FIGURE 9.1

Overview of model training in baseline and meta-federated learning.

Our key contributions can be summarized as follows:

- We propose meta-federated learning, a novel federated learning framework that facilitates defense against backdoor attacks while protecting the privacy of participants.
- We show that moving the defense execution point from the individual update level to the aggregate level is effective in mitigating backdoor attacks without compromising privacy.
- We perform a systematic evaluation of contemporary defenses against backdoor attacks in both standard federated learning and Meta-FL. Results on two classification datasets, SVHN [20] and GTSRB [25], show that Meta-FL enhances contemporary defense performance in terms of robustness to adversarial attacks and utility.

9.2 Background

9.2.1 Federated learning

Federated learning is a machine learning setting that enables millions of clients (mobile or edge devices) to jointly train a deep learning model using their private data without compromising their privacy. The training procedure in federated learning is orchestrated by a central server responsible for providing the shared global model to participants and aggregating their submitted model updates to generate the new global model. The key appeal of federated learning is that it does not require centralizing participating users' training data, which makes it ideal for privacy-sensitive tasks.

A standard FL setting consists of P participating clients. Each client i holds a shard of training data D_i which is private to the client and is never shared with the orchestration server. In each round t of federated learning, the central server randomly selects a set ζ^t of c clients, and broadcasts the current global model G^t to them. The selected set of clients ζ_t is referred to as *training cohort* of round t. Each client i in the training cohort locally and independently trains the joint model G^t using stochastic gradient descent (SGD) optimization algorithm for E epochs on its local training data D_i to obtain a new local model L_i^{t+1}, and submits the difference $L_i^{t+1} - G^t$ as its model update to the central server. Next, the central server averages model updates submitted by clients in the training cohort and updates the shared global model using its learning rate η to obtain the new global model G^{t+1}, as shown below:

$$G^{t+1} = G^t + \frac{\eta}{n} \sum_{i=i}^{n} (L_i^{t+1} - G^t). \tag{9.1}$$

Model training resumes until the global model converges to acceptable performance, or certain training rounds are completed.

9.2.2 Secure aggregation

Secure aggregation (SecAgg) [5] is a secure multi-party computation protocol that can reveal the sum of submitted model updates to the server (or aggregator) while keeping each individual update uninspectable at all times. Secure aggregation consists of three phases, *preparation, commitment,* and *finalization* [4]. In the preparation phase, shared secrets are established between the central server and participating clients. Model updates from clients who drop out during the preparation phase will not be included in the aggregate. Next, in the commitment phase, each device uploads a cryptographically masked model update to the server, and the server computes the sum of the submitted mask updates. Only clients that successfully commit their masked model updates will contribute to the final aggregate. Lastly, in the finalization phase, committed clients reveal sufficient cryptographic secrets to allow the server to unmask the aggregated model update.

9.2.3 Robust aggregation rules and defenses

Numerous studies have proposed robust aggregation rules [3,21,30] to ensure convergence of distributed learning algorithms in the presence of adversarial actors. The majority of studies in this line of work assume a Byzantine threat model in which the adversary can cause local learning procedures to submit any arbitrary update to ensure the convergence of learning algorithms to an ineffective model. In addition to robust aggregation rules, several works have proposed novel defenses [9,26] against backdoor and poisoning attacks in federated learning. In what follows, we review several of the techniques which we experiment with in Section 9.5.

Krum. The Krum algorithm, proposed by [3], is a robust aggregation rule which can tolerate f Byzantine attackers out of n participants selected at any training round. Krum has theoretical guarantees for the convergence should the condition $n \geq 2f + 3$ hold true. At any training round, for each model update δ_i, Krum takes the following steps: (a) computes the pairwise Euclidean distance of $n - f - 2$ updates that are closest to δ_i, (b) computes the sum of squared distances between update δ_i and its closest $n - f - 2$ updates. Then, Krum chooses the model update with the lowest sum to update the parameters of the joint global model.

Coordinate-wise Median. In coordinate-wise median (CWM) aggregation rule [30], for each jth model parameter, the jth coordinates of received model updates are sorted, and their median is used to update the corresponding parameter of the global model.

Trimmed Mean. Trimmed mean (TM) is a coordinate-wise aggregation rule [30]. For $\beta \in [0, \frac{1}{2})$, the trimmed mean computes the jth coordinate of the aggregate of n model updates as follows: (a) it sorts the jth coordinate of the n updates, (b) discards the largest and smallest β fraction of the sorted updates, and (c) takes the average of remaining $n(1 - 2\beta)$ updates as the aggregate for the jth coordinate.

RFA. RFA [21] is a robust privacy-preserving aggregator which requires a secure averaging oracle. RFA aggregates local models by computing an approximation of the geometric median of their parameters using a variant of the smoothed Weiszfeld's algorithm [27]. RFA appears to be tolerant to data poisoning attacks but cannot offer Byzantine tolerance as it still requires clients to compute aggregation weights according to the protocol. Relying on clients to follow a defensive protocol without a proper means to attest to the correctness of computations on the client-side casts doubts on the practicality of RFA. To the best of our knowledge, RFA is the only existing defense that is compatible with secure aggregation.

Norm Bounding. Norm bounding (NB) is an aggregation rule proposed by [26], which appears to be robust against false-label backdoor attacks. In this aggregation rule, a norm constraint M is set for model updates submitted by clients to normalize the contribution of any individual participants. Norm bounding aggregates model updates as follows: (a) model updates with norms larger than the set threshold M are projected to the l_2 ball of size M and then (b) all model updates are averaged to update the joint global model.

Differential Privacy. Differential privacy (DP) originally was designed to establish a strong privacy guarantee for algorithms on aggregate databases, but it can also provide a defense against poisoning attacks [8,15]. Extending DP to federated learning ensures that any participant's contribution is bounded and therefore, the joint global model does not over-fit to any individual update. DP is applied in FL as follows [11]: (a) server clips clients' model update by a norm M, (b) clipped updates are aggregated, then (c) a Gaussian noise is added to the resulted aggregate. DP has recently been explored and shown to be successful against false-label backdoor attacks in a study by [26].

9.3 Problem definition and threat model

In this section, we present the objectives, capabilities, and schemes of backdoor attackers that are commonly used in prior studies. In other words, our proposed Meta-FL framework does not make any additional assumptions.

Attacker's Objective. Similar to prior arts such as [1,28], we consider an adversary whose goal is to cause misclassifications to a targeted label T for inputs embedded with an attacker-chosen trigger. As opposed to Byzantine attacks [3], whose purpose is to make the learning algorithm converge to a sub-optimal or utterly ineffective model, the adversary's goal in backdoor attacks is to ensure that the joint global model achieves high accuracy on both the backdoor sub-task and the primary learning task at hand.

Attacker's Capability. We make the following assumptions about the attacker's capabilities: (a) we assume the attacker controls a number of participants, which are referred to as *sybils* in the literature of distributed learning. Sybils are either malicious clients which are injected into a federated learning system or benign clients whose FL training software has been compromised by the adversary; (b) following Kerckhoffs's theory [23], we assume a strong attacker who has complete control over local data and training procedure of all its sybils. The attacker can modify the training procedure's hyperparameters and is capable of modifying model updates before submitting them to the central server; (c) the adversary is not capable of compromising the central server or influencing other benign clients, and more importantly, does not have access to benign clients' local model, training data and submitted updates.

Attack Scheme. In our evaluations, we consider two backdoor attack schemes which are referred to as "Naive" and "Model Replacement" in the literature [1]. In both schemes, adversaries train their local model with a mixture of clean and backdoored data, and model updates are computed as the difference in the parameters of the backdoored local model and the shared global model. In the naive approach, the adversary submits the computed model update as is, while in the model replacement attack, the model update is scaled using a scaling factor to cancel the contribution of other benign clients and increase the impact of the adversarial update on the joint global model. A carefully chosen scaling factor for adversarial updates can guarantee the replacement of the joint global model with the adversary's backdoored local model.

9.4 **Meta-federated learning**

In this section, we first discuss the challenges in mitigating backdoor attacks in federated learning. Then, we propose meta-federated learning (Meta-FL), and explain how it improves robustness to backdoor attacks while preserving the privacy of participating clients.

Challenges in defending against backdoor attacks in federated learning are two-fold:

Challenge 1. Inspecting model updates is off-limits with or without secure aggregation. Recent studies have demonstrated that model updates can be used to partially reconstruct clients' training data [10,12,29]; therefore, any defensive approach which requires examination of submitted updates is a threat to the privacy of participants, and is against privacy promises of federated learning. Moreover, inspecting model updates simply is not feasible in systems augmented with SecAgg. Privacy promises of federated learning prohibit the server from auditing clients' submissions which gives the adversary the privilege to submit any arbitrary value without getting flagged as anomalous. We refer to this privilege as *submission with no consequences*.

Challenge 2. Even without the restrictions mentioned above, defending against backdoor attacks would not be a trivial task. Model updates submitted by clients show high variations which makes it extremely difficult for the central server to identify whether an update works toward an adversarial goal. The sporadicity observed from model updates originates from the non-i.i.d. distribution of the original dataset among participants, and the fact that each update is the product of stochastic gradient descent, a non-deterministic algorithm whose output is not merely a function of its input data.

Motivated to address the challenges above, we propose Meta-FL, a novel federated setting that not only protects the privacy of participants, but also aids the server in defending against backdoor attacks. Algorithm 1 summarizes different steps of model training in our framework, which we will cover in detail here.

In each round t of training in Meta-FL, the central server randomly selects π cohorts $\{\zeta_1^t, \zeta_2^t, \ldots, \zeta_\pi^t\}$, each containing c unique clients (Line 3). Training cohorts can be sampled in order or independently. In the former case, each cohort is sampled after another, and thus, no client will be a member of more than one cohort ($\zeta_i^t \cap \zeta_j^t = \emptyset$). In the recent case, there is no inter-dependency among cohort selection, and therefore, cohorts can have clients in common; this scenario is more suitable for cases where ($P \leq \pi c$). Next, the server broadcasts global model G^t to clients in each cohort (Line 5), each client i locally and independently trains the model G^t on their local training data to obtain a new local model L_i^{t+1}, and compute their model update δ_i as $L_i^{t+1} - G^t$ (Line 7). Then, the server establishes π separate instances of SecAgg protocol to concurrently compute the aggregate of updates submitted from clients of each cohort (Line 9). Finally, in the last stage of training in Meta-FL, the central server aggregates the "cohort updates" using aggregation rule Γ, and updates the joint model with its learning rate η to obtain the next shared global model G^{t+1}, as shown in Line 11 of Algorithm 1.

Algorithm 1 Meta-FL framework.
1: Initialize shared global model
2: **for** each round t in 1,2,3,... **do**
3:     Select π training cohorts $\{\zeta_1^t, \zeta_2^t, \ldots, \zeta_\pi^t\}$ with $|\zeta_1^i| = c \; \forall i \in \{1, 2, \ldots, \pi\}$.
4:     **for** cohort ζ_j^t in $\{\zeta_1^t, \zeta_2^t, \ldots, \zeta_\pi^t\}$ **in parallel do**
5:         Broadcast global model G^t to cohort members.
6:         **for** client i in cohort ζ_j^t **in parallel do**
7:             $\delta_i^t \leftarrow ClientUpdate(i, G^t)$
8:         **end for**
9:         $\Delta_j^t \leftarrow SecAgg(\delta_1^t, \delta_2^t, \ldots, \delta_c^t)$
10:     **end for**
11:     $G^{t+1} = G^t + \eta\, \Gamma(\Delta_1^t, \Delta_2^t, \ldots, \Delta_\pi^t)$
12: **end for**

In our framework, plain model updates never leave the client's side. All participants are required to follow the SecAgg protocol and submit cryptography-masked updates. SecAgg guarantees that the server is able to aggregate the masked submissions to update the global model but cannot obtain the value of each individual update. While each cohort aggregate may still leak information about the collective training data of cohort members, the inferred information can not be associated with any individual client; therefore, the privacy of participants is preserved in Meta-FL.

In Meta-FL, as the central server can only see the aggregate of training cohorts, defense mechanisms are obliged to carry out on the aggregate level rather than the update level. This property offers the server several advantages in mitigating backdoor attacks, which we will cover in the rest of this section. However, before we can proceed, we need to define several concepts that are essential for understanding what follows.

In the rest of this chapter, we refer to a training cohort as adversarial if and only if there exists at least one malicious client among its members. Naturally, a cohort is referred to as benign if none of its members are malicious. Moreover, we refer to the aggregate of updates from a benign and an adversarial cohort as a benign and adversarial aggregate, respectively.

Moving the defense execution point from the update level to the aggregate level facilitates mitigating backdoor attacks as it offers the following advantages:

Advantage 1. Server is allowed to inspect and monitor cohort aggregates. This property forces the adversary to maintain stealth on the aggregate level as adversarial aggregates which are statistically different from other benign aggregates are likely to get detected and discarded by the server. Therefore, Meta-FL revokes the privilege of submission with no consequences for the adversary.

Advantage 2. Cohort aggregates are less sporadic compared to individual client updates which aid the server in detecting anomalies. This advantage takes on the *challenge 2* discussed above. By drawing an analogy to *simple random sampling* in statistics [22], we demonstrate that cohort aggregates show less variation across each coordinate compared to individual updates.

For ease of analysis, we assume that training cohorts are sampled independently meaning that there is no inter-dependency among client selection in each cohort. In this case, at any round t, updates submitted by any cohort of c clients is essentially a random sample of size c collected without replacement from the population of model updates. Assuming that updates are averaged as in Eq. (9.1), cohort aggregates are in fact *sample means* of the model update population. As the composition of cohorts is a random process, cohort aggregates are thus random variables whose distribution is determined by that of model updates as shown below (for a proof refer to [22]):

$$Var(\Delta_j) = \frac{\sigma_j^2}{c}\left(\frac{P-c}{P-1}\right), \quad \mathbb{E}[\Delta_j] = \mathbb{E}[\mu_j]. \tag{9.2}$$

Here, σ_j^2 and μ_j denote variance and mean of the population of model updates across the jth coordinate, respectively, and Δ_j indicates the jth coordinate of a cohort aggregate Δ. Assuming that each cohort contains more than one client ($1 < c$), it would be trivial to show that $\frac{P-c}{c(P-1)} < 1$. Therefore, we can prove that the variance of cohort aggregates across any coordinate j is upper bounded by the variance of the population of model updates across that coordinate as shown below:

$$Var(\Delta_j) = \sigma_j^2\left(\frac{P-c}{c(P-1)}\right) < \sigma_j^2. \tag{9.3}$$

A closer look at Eq. (9.3) reveals that the server can further reduce the variance of cohort aggregates by increasing the size of training cohorts which would cause $\frac{P-c}{c(P-1)}$ to become smaller and closer to zero. Lower variation from cohort aggregates makes it easier for outlier detection-based defenses to infer patterns of the benign observations, and effectively detect malicious instances.

Advantage 3. As adversarial updates are aggregated with other updates, sybils face competition from benign clients to control the value of cohort aggregate. This property makes it harder for the adversary to meticulously arrange values of adversarial aggregates to evade deployed defenses.

Our empirical evaluations in Section 9.5 will demonstrate that the advantages mentioned above in fact aid contemporary defense to perform better against backdoor attacks in Meta-FL compared to the baseline federated learning.

9.5 Experimental evaluation and discussion
9.5.1 Datasets and experiment setup

We study Meta-FL on two classification datasets, namely SVHN [20] and GTSRB [25] with non-i.i.d. data distributions. **GTSRB** is a traffic sign dataset with 39,209

Table 9.1 Model architecture for SVHN and GTSRB datasets.

GTSRB		SVHN	
Layer Type	**Filter/Unit**	**Layer Type**	**Filter/Unit**
Conv + ReLU	$3 \times 3 \times 32$	Conv + ReLU	$3 \times 3 \times 32$
Conv + ReLU	$3 \times 3 \times 32$	Conv + ReLU	$3 \times 3 \times 32$
Conv + ReLU	$3 \times 3 \times 64$	Conv + ReLU	$3 \times 3 \times 64$
Conv + ReLU	$3 \times 3 \times 64$	Conv + ReLU	$3 \times 3 \times 64$
Conv + ReLU	$3 \times 3 \times 128$	Conv + ReLU	$3 \times 3 \times 128$
Conv + ReLU	$3 \times 3 \times 128$	Conv + ReLU	$3 \times 3 \times 128$
FC + ReLU	43	FC + ReLU	512
Softmax	43	FC + ReLU	10
		Softmax	10

training and 12,630 test samples, where each sample is labeled with one of the possible 43 classes, and **SVHN** is a dataset of more than 100k images of digits cropped out of images of the house and street numbers. Table 9.1 reports the architecture and hyperparameters of benchmark models used for the GTSRB and SVHN datasets.

We use a Dirichlet distribution with parameter $\alpha = 0.9$ to partition GTSRB and SVHN datasets into disjoint non-i.i.d. shards and then distribute them among 150 and 300 clients, respectively. Following a similar setup to prior arts, each participating client trains their local model using SGD for 5 epochs with a batch size of 64 and a learning rate of 0.1. Both Meta-FL and baseline FL resume the training process until a certain number of training rounds are completed. Throughout our experiments, GTSRB and SVHN models are trained for 75 and 50 rounds, respectively.

For all experiments, pixel pattern backdoor attacks are performed in which the adversary aims to influence the model to misclassify inputs from a base label as a target label upon the presence of an attacker's chosen pattern (trigger). We set the adversarial trigger as a white square located at the top left corner of the image which roughly covers 9% of the entire image. The objective of backdoor attacks in GTSRB and SVHN datasets is to mispredict images of "Speed limit 80 miles per hour" as "Speed limit 50 miles per hour" and images of "digit 6" as "digit 1", upon the presence of the white box trigger.

In the rest of the chapter, we denote each Meta-FL framework by two parameters as **MFL-i-j**, where i and j indicate the number and size of training cohorts, respectively. We also use a similar notation **FL-k** to describe baseline FL systems, where k indicates the size of the training cohort.

Similar to the analysis in [26], we consider fixed-frequency attack models to explore a wide range of attack scenarios. In the baseline FL, **Attack-f-k** describes a scenario where k sybils appear at every f rounds of training to mount their attack. For the case of Meta-FL setting, **Attack-f-k** describes the case where at every f round of training, k training cohorts contain an adversarial client.

9.5.2 Utility of meta-FL

In this section, we compare the utility of Meta-FL against the baseline setting in terms of model accuracy. In this experiment, we evaluate the utility of baseline and Meta-FL frameworks across various FL configurations and aggregation rules. Note that for a fair comparison, we make sure the number of clients participating in each round of model training is equal across both frameworks. Fig. 9.2 reports the test accuracy of models trained in Meta-FL and baseline settings deploying different defenses and aggregation rules. As reflected, federated training with Meta-FL results in more accurate models compared to the baseline setting. All defenses and aggregation rules offer better utility in our framework. Even the Krum aggregation rule which has been known to cause a large drop in performance of the learned model in baseline FL [1,2] can train models with comparable performances in Meta-FL.

9.5.3 Robustness of meta-FL

In this section, we systematically compare the capabilities of contemporary defenses against backdoor attacks in both baseline and meta federated learning. Our empirical evaluation in this section shows that all defenses benefit from the advantages discussed in Section 9.4 and offer better robustness in Meta-FL.

Figs. 9.3 and 9.4 report the performance of contemporary defenses against backdoor attacks on GTSRB and SVHN benchmarks, respectively. We extend our experiments to both Meta-FL (MFL-15-5) and baseline FL (FL-5) frameworks for each dataset. In our evaluations, we consider defenses such as Krum, coordinate-wise median (CWM), trimmed mean (TM), norm bounding (NB), differential privacy (DP), and RFA. Hyperparameter and implementation details of these techniques are as follows: **(1)** For Krum, to meet the convergence condition $n \geq 2f + 3$, we set $f = 6$. **(2)** For trimmed mean, the parameter β is set to 0.20. **(3)** For RFA, the maximum iteration of the Weiszfeld algorithm and the smoothing factor is set to 10 and 10^{-6}, respectively. **(4)** In norm bounding defense, as the original work [26] did not provide a recipe to decide the norm threshold M, we developed our own approach to determine M. In our experiments, at each round, we set the norm threshold M to the norm of the smallest aggregand to ensure all aggregands will have an equal l_2 norm before aggregation. In federated learning, as the global model converges, model updates (and therefore cohort aggregates) start to fade out and have smaller norms, and thus, setting a constant norm threshold for all training rounds would not be effective, which is why we took a dynamic approach to decide M. **(5)** For differential privacy, the hyperparameter M is set similar to norm bounding and then a Gaussian noise $\mathcal{N}(0.0, 0.001^2)$ is added to the aggregate of updates (or cohort aggregates) before updating the global model.

We experiment with several attack scenarios to systematically evaluate the performance of each defense against adversaries with a wide range of resources at hand. As we move along the attack scenarios denoted on the horizontal axis of diagrams in Figs. 9.3 and 9.4, the adversary becomes more and more powerful and appears more frequently with more sybils at each round.

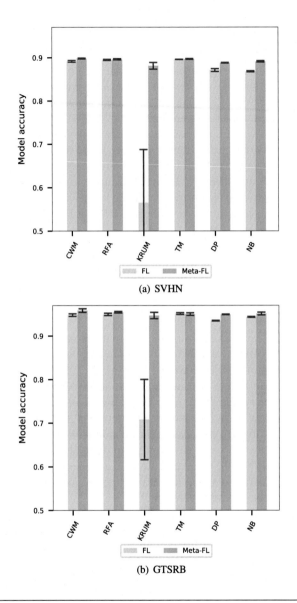

(a) SVHN

(b) GTSRB

FIGURE 9.2

Comparing utility of Meta-FL against baseline FL in terms of model accuracy.

For a fair evaluation of contemporary defense across Meta-FL and baseline FL, we make sure the defender faces similar challenges in both frameworks. Throughout our experiments in this section, we set the number of training cohorts in Meta-FL equal to the number of selected clients in baseline FL to ensure that the server sees the same number of aggregands (client updates in baseline FL and cohort aggregates

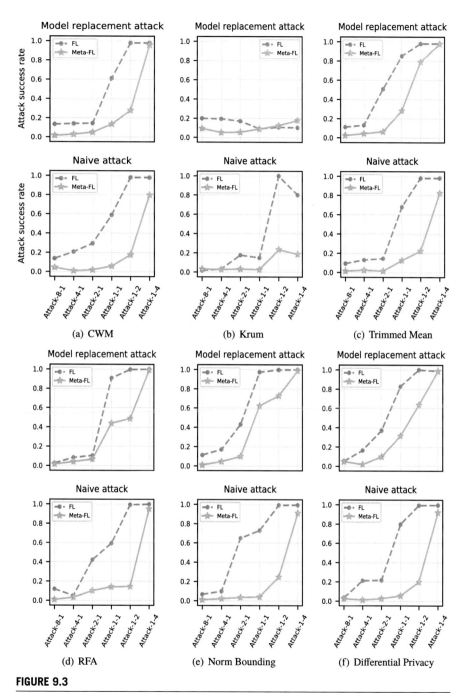

FIGURE 9.3

Evaluating performance of contemporary defenses against naive and model replacement backdoor attacks on GTSRB model.

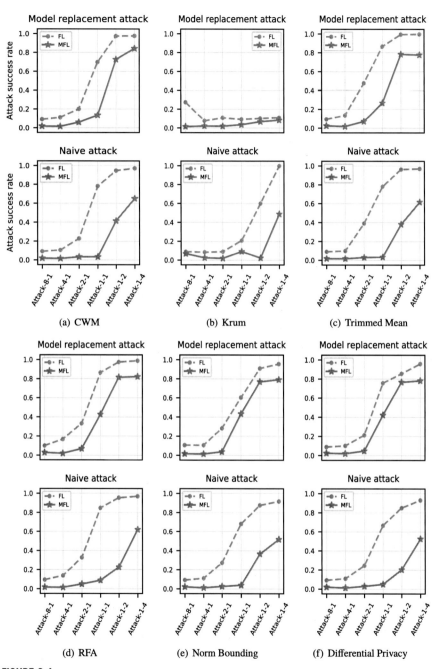

FIGURE 9.4

Evaluating performance of contemporary defenses against naive and model replacement backdoor attacks on SVHN model.

in Meta-FL) across both cases. Moreover, the way our attack scenarios are defined ensures that the same number of aggregands are adversarial across both frameworks.

Across both Meta-FL and baseline FL frameworks, the scaling factor for model replacement attack is set equal to the size of training cohorts to ensure that submissions from adversarial clients survive the averaging procedure and overpower the aggregate of their corresponding cohort. For attack scenarios in which multiple sybils appear in the same round, we assume they coordinate and divide the scaling factor among themselves evenly.

Figs. 9.3 and 9.4 show that *Meta-FL puts all defense at an advantage in mitigating against backdoor attacks*. Attack success rate of both the naive and model replacement approach in Meta-FL (solid lines) is lower than in baseline FL (dashed lines) when the same defense is in place across both frameworks. Therefore, our empirical evaluations show that existing defenses are more robust to backdoor attacks in Meta-FL compared to baseline FL across.

While Meta-FL enhances the robustness of all 6 methods, we observe that Krum benefits the most from our framework. We believe that lower variance on cohort aggregates aids Krum in effectively separating benign and malicious updates. We note that the server can further decrease the variance of cohort aggregates along each coordinate by increasing the size of training cohorts, as discussed in Section 9.4, and improve the robustness of the Krum aggregation rule.

Moreover, other methods such as coordinate-wise median and trimmed mean which are anomaly detection-based defenses can also benefit from lower variations in cohort aggregate. Perhaps the most important principle in detecting outliers is defining the distribution of ordinary observations, which can be easier if observations exhibit low variations. Fig. 9.5 shows the results for experiments in which we evaluate the performance of Krum, CWM, and TM across Meta-FL frameworks with increasingly larger training cohorts. For this experiment, we set the number of cohorts to 15 and vary the cohort size between 5, 10, and 15. As reflected in Fig. 9.5, increasing the size of training cohorts improves the robustness of these techniques across all scenarios, especially for scenarios in which the adversary appears more frequently with more sybils.

Although defenses such as RFA, differential privacy, and norm bounding appear to be robust against poisoning attacks [21,26], our empirical evaluations show that they are not effective against backdoor attacks, specifically model replacement attacks. In poisoning attacks, the adversarial sub-task, which is the misclassification of unmodified data samples (e.g., classifying certain images of digit 1 as digit 7), is in direct contradiction with the primary learning task. Therefore, poisoning updates (or aggregates) face direct opposition from submissions of benign clients, which makes it harder for the adversary to succeed. However, in the case of backdoor attacks, the adversary's goal for the model is to learn the causal relationship between the presence of an attacker's chosen trigger and certain model output which does not require the model to learn any knowledge contradicting the primary learning task. Therefore, backdoor attacks tend to be stealthier compared to poisoning attacks, and defenses

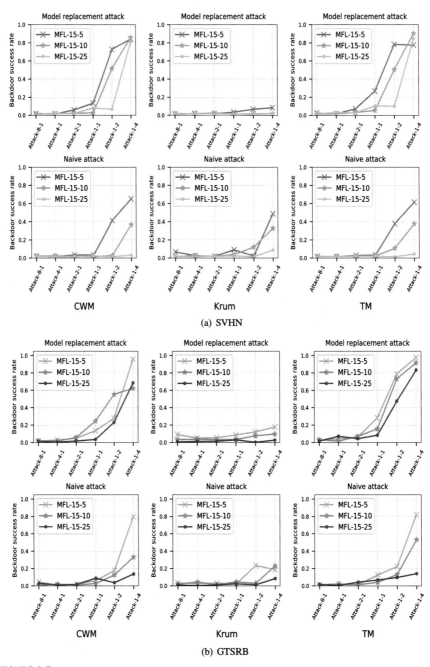

FIGURE 9.5

Effect of size of training cohorts on efficacy of CWM, Krum and TM against backdoor attacks.

that have shown resilience against poisoning attacks might fall short against backdoor attacks.

9.6 Conclusion

In this study, we showed that it is in fact possible to defend against backdoor attacks without violating the privacy of participating clients. We proposed Meta-FL, a new federated learning framework that not only protects the privacy of participants through the secure aggregation protocol but also facilitates defense against backdoor attacks. Our empirical evaluations demonstrated that state-of-the-art defenses tend to be more effective against backdoor attacks in Meta-FL compared to baseline FL while offering the same or better utility. Our results suggested that not only does Meta-FL protect the privacy of participants but also optimizes the robustness-utility trade-off better than the baseline setting.

References

[1] Eugene Bagdasaryan, Andreas Veit, Yiqing Hua, Deborah Estrin, Vitaly Shmatikov, How to backdoor federated learning, in: International Conference on Artificial Intelligence and Statistics, PMLR, 2020, pp. 2938–2948.

[2] Arjun Nitin Bhagoji, Supriyo Chakraborty, Prateek Mittal, Seraphin Calo, Analyzing federated learning through an adversarial lens, in: International Conference on Machine Learning, PMLR, 2019, pp. 634–643.

[3] Peva Blanchard, Rachid Guerraoui, Julien Stainer, et al., Machine learning with adversaries: Byzantine tolerant gradient descent, in: Advances in Neural Information Processing Systems, 2017, pp. 119–129.

[4] Keith Bonawitz, Hubert Eichner, Wolfgang Grieskamp, Dzmitry Huba, Alex Ingerman, Vladimir Ivanov, Chloe Kiddon, Jakub Konečný, Stefano Mazzocchi, H. Brendan McMahan, et al., Towards federated learning at scale: system design, arXiv:1902.01046, 2019.

[5] Keith Bonawitz, Vladimir Ivanov, Ben Kreuter, Antonio Marcedone, H. Brendan McMahan, Sarvar Patel, Daniel Ramage, Aaron Segal, Karn Seth, Practical secure aggregation for privacy-preserving machine learning, in: Proceedings of the 2017 ACM SIGSAC Conference on Computer and Communications Security, 2017, pp. 1175–1191.

[6] Xinyun Chen, Chang Liu, Bo Li, Kimberly Lu, Dawn Song, Targeted backdoor attacks on deep learning systems using data poisoning, arXiv:1712.05526, 2017.

[7] Gabriela F. Cretu, Angelos Stavrou, Michael E. Locasto, Salvatore J. Stolfo, Angelos D. Keromytis, Casting out demons: sanitizing training data for anomaly sensors, in: 2008 IEEE Symposium on Security and Privacy (sp 2008), IEEE, 2008, pp. 81–95.

[8] Cynthia Dwork, Frank McSherry, Kobbi Nissim, Adam Smith, Calibrating noise to sensitivity in private data analysis, in: Theory of Cryptography Conference, Springer, 2006, pp. 265–284.

[9] Clement Fung, Chris J.M. Yoon, Ivan Beschastnikh, Mitigating sybils in federated learning poisoning, arXiv:1808.04866, 2018.

[10] Tianyu Gu, Kang Liu, Brendan Dolan-Gavitt, Siddharth Garg, BadNets: evaluating backdooring attacks on deep neural networks, IEEE Access 7 (2019) 47230–47244.

[11] Peter Kairouz, H. Brendan McMahan, Brendan Avent, Aurélien Bellet, Mehdi Bennis, Arjun Nitin Bhagoji, Keith Bonawitz, Zachary Charles, Graham Cormode, Rachel Cummings, et al., Advances and open, problems in federated learning, arXiv:1912.04977, 2019.

[12] Shaofeng Li, Minhui Xue, Benjamin Zi Hao Zhao, Haojin Zhu, Xinpeng Zhang, Invisible backdoor attacks on deep neural networks via steganography and regularization, arXiv:1909.02742, 2019.

[13] Cong Liao, Haoti Zhong, Anna Squicciarini, Sencun Zhu, David Miller, Backdoor embedding in convolutional neural network models via invisible perturbation, arXiv:1808.10307, 2018.

[14] Kang Liu, Brendan Dolan-Gavitt, Siddharth Garg, Fine-pruning: Defending against backdooring attacks on deep neural networks, in: International Symposium on Research in Attacks, Intrusions, and Defenses, Springer, 2018, pp. 273–294.

[15] Yuzhe Ma, Xiaojin Zhu, Justin Hsu, Data poisoning against differentially-private learners: attacks and defenses, arXiv:1903.09860, 2019.

[16] Brendan McMahan, Eider Moore, Daniel Ramage, Seth Hampson, Blaise Aguera y Arcas, Communication-efficient learning of deep networks from decentralized data, in: Artificial Intelligence and Statistics, PMLR, 2017, pp. 1273–1282.

[17] Luca Melis, Congzheng Song, Emiliano De Cristofaro, Vitaly Shmatikov, Exploiting unintended feature leakage in collaborative learning, in: 2019 IEEE Symposium on Security and Privacy (SP), IEEE, 2019, pp. 691–706.

[18] El Mahdi El Mhamdi, Rachid Guerraoui, Sébastien Rouault, The hidden vulnerability of distributed learning in Byzantium, arXiv:1802.07927, 2018.

[19] Milad Nasr, Reza Shokri, Amir Houmansadr, Comprehensive privacy analysis of deep learning: stand-alone and federated learning under passive and active white-box inference attacks, arXiv:1812.00910, 2018.

[20] Yuval Netzer, Tao Wang, Adam Coates, Alessandro Bissacco, Bo Wu, Andrew Y. Ng, Reading digits in natural images with unsupervised feature learning, in: NIPS Workshop on Deep Learning and Unsupervised Feature Learning, 2011.

[21] Krishna Pillutla, Sham M. Kakade, Zaid Harchaoui, Robust aggregation for federated learning, arXiv:1912.13445, 2019.

[22] John A. Rice, Mathematical Statistics and Data Analysis, third edition, Duxbury Press, Belmont, CA, 2006.

[23] Claude E. Shannon, Communication theory of secrecy systems, The Bell System Technical Journal 28 (4) (1949) 656–715.

[24] Virginia Smith, Chao-Kai Chiang, Maziar Sanjabi, Ameet S. Talwalkar, Federated multi-task learning, in: Advances in Neural Information Processing Systems, 2017, pp. 4424–4434.

[25] J. Stallkamp, M. Schlipsing, J. Salmen, C. Igel, Man vs. computer: benchmarking machine learning algorithms for traffic sign recognition, Neural Networks 32 (2012) 323–332.

[26] Ziteng Sun, Peter Kairouz, Ananda Theertha Suresh, H. Brendan McMahan, Can you really backdoor federated learning?, arXiv:1911.07963, 2019.

[27] Endre Weiszfeld, Sur le point pour lequel la somme des distances de n points donnés est minimum, Tohoku Mathematical Journal, First Series 43 (1937) 355–386.

[28] Chulin Xie, Keli Huang, Pin-Yu Chen, Bo Li, Dba: Distributed backdoor attacks against federated learning, in: International Conference on Learning Representations, 2020.

[29] Yuanshun Yao, Huiying Li, Haitao Zheng, Y. Ben Zhao, Latent backdoor attacks on deep neural networks, in: Proceedings of the 2019 ACM SIGSAC Conference on Computer and Communications Security, 2019, pp. 2041–2055.

[30] Dong Yin, Yudong Chen, Kannan Ramchandran, Peter Bartlett, Byzantine-robust distributed learning: towards optimal statistical rates, arXiv:1803.01498, 2018.

[31] Yue Zhao, Meng Li, Liangzhen Lai, Naveen Suda, Damon Civin, Vikas Chandra, Federated learning with non-iid data, arXiv:1806.00582, 2018.

Graph-aware federated learning

10

Songtao Lu[a], Pengwei Xing[b], and Han Yu[b]

[a]*IBM Thomas J. Watson Research Center, Yorktown Heights, NY, United States*
[b]*Nanyang Technological University, Singapore, Singapore*

10.1 Introduction

Even the existing federated learning (FL) framework has been shown successfully striking the balance between the communication and computation complexities, however, the server-to-slaver type of learning structure still forgoes the topology feature and/or information of distributed sampled data for further increasing the communication efficiency and/or the generalization performance. In this chapter, we investigate more advanced graph-aware federated learning (GFL) models and algorithms, and then present the theoretical justifications and numerical performance. This chapter mainly includes the key FL techniques with emphasis on different goals of building GFL systems.

Decentralized federated learning (DFL) is one of the most straightforward ways that can further improve both the computing and communication efficiency of the classic FL system, where there are n devices connected over a graph and which jointly learn a common interest machine learning model. In contrast to the classic FedAvg [18], DFL is more robust to failure of message passing among the nodes and staleness of transmitting data packages. Also, DFL has the nature of having low communication overheads and keeping the data confidential during the data transmission stage, as there is no central server that requests the model parameters from all the devices. For example, in a health medical system, the patients' data and information are private, so they are not shareable over either hospitals or doctors. However, note that there is still a need that a machine learning model can extract the critical latent space structures through a sufficiently large dataset to remove the outliers. It has been shown that DFL is one of the most promising strategies to improve communication efficiency and model performance through aggregating electronic health records over multiple data resources [17].

In practice, the global model might not be unique in the sense that there could be multiple global models, each possibly containing different features of data due to the heterogeneity of data distributions. Selecting the correct memberships for the local models to each global model is not trivial, which would result in a combinatorial problem. One of the most straightforward ways is to try different global models for fitting the local data and select the best one at each iteration, which is called an

Federated Learning. https://doi.org/10.1016/B978-0-44-319037-7.00018-1

iterative federated clustering algorithm and proposed in [6]. However, this way is time-consuming as it needs all the global models to traverse all the local data sets. As the data distributions possess a cluster structure, a K-means type of algorithm is appropriate for clustering the local models based on the similarity among the nodes. In [24], federated stochastic expectation maximization (FeSEM) is proposed based on measuring the distance between the two model parameters in which one is the local model parameter and the other is the weighted mean of the parameters of the neighboring models selected by the EM algorithm. It turns out that FeSEM can learn the memberships of the local model and optimize the local loss values in an alternative way, and achieve state-of-the-art results.

Inspired by the hierarchical learning strategy, a bilevel optimization based FL model was recently proposed, which considers the membership selection (or more general feature representation) and local data adaptation as two levels of an optimization problem. In such a way, the upper level (UL) model can integrate domain knowledge into the FL model, while the lower level (LL) model can use this information for adapting the local data personally. For example, the graph knowledge about the similarity among the nodes would be proportional to the heterogeneity of data features, which can be used for enhancing the generalization performance of FL models. Despite a line of graph learning-related works that mostly focus on aggregating graph neural networks (GNNs) [10], the graph information in these studies only appears in the respective local models rather than incorporating any global graph structure information. To the best of our knowledge, the scenario in which FL clients are organized into graph embedding is rarely investigated. Under this setting, we will introduce the bilevel optimization enhanced graph-aided federated learning, which applies the graph embedding techniques to capture inherent information over the topology of FL clients.

In this chapter, we will address the heterogeneity issue of the FL systems, and bring in the GFL models and corresponding algorithms, as well as their theoretical and numerical justifications.

10.2 Decentralized federated learning

When clients are connected over a graph, the communication only happens between two neighboring nodes. In this setting, we consider a communication graph denoted by $\mathcal{G} \triangleq \{\mathcal{V}, \mathcal{E}\}$, where $\mathcal{V}$ denotes the set of the vertices in this graph and $\mathcal{E}$ stands for the edges. We use n to represent the total number of nodes, i.e., $|\mathcal{V}|$, in this graph, and subsequently $i \in [n]$ as the index of each node. The optimization problem of the distributed learning system can be mathematically formulated as follows:

$$(\mathbb{P}1) \quad \min_{\boldsymbol{\theta}_i \in \mathbb{R}^d, \forall i} \frac{1}{n} \sum_{i=1}^{n} \mathbb{E}_{\xi_i \sim \mathcal{D}_i} F_i(\boldsymbol{\theta}_i; \xi_i) \text{ such that } \boldsymbol{\theta}_i = \boldsymbol{\theta}_j, \quad j \in \mathcal{N}_i, \forall i, \quad (10.1)$$

where $\mathcal{N}_i$ represents the set of node i neighbors, $F_i(\boldsymbol{\theta}_i; \xi_i)$ denotes the (possible non-convex) loss function at the ith node, ξ_i is the data sample collected at node i and following a certain distribution $\mathcal{D}_i$. The goal of this model in Eq. (10.1) is to learn a global model $\boldsymbol{\theta} \in \mathbb{R}^d$ such that the sum of total loss functions $\{F_i(\boldsymbol{\theta}; \xi_i), \forall i\}$ is minimized based on the datasets $\{\mathcal{D}_i, \forall i\}$ sampled over graph $\mathcal{G}$.

There are many existing algorithms that can solve this problem in a distributed way, including distributed stochastic gradient descent [2], primal–dual algorithms [12,13], (variance-reduced) gradient tracking [16,20], etc. The main idea is to update each local optimization variable by aggregating its neighbor models' parameters, followed by one step of stochastic gradient descent type of update. The issue here is that each round of the model aggregation would incur a large number of parameters sent over the network, which might not be feasible or incur heavy delays in the model update. Therefore, communication-efficient transmission schemes are motivated and proposed for reducing the overload of passing model parameters per round [11].

To present the DFL algorithms, we first define the mixing matrix $\mathbf{W}$ which represents the connectivity of the nodes as follows: 1) $w_{ij} > 0$ if $(i, j) \in \mathcal{E}$ and 0 otherwise; 2) $\mathbf{W}$ is doubly stochastic, i.e., $\mathbb{1}^T \mathbf{W} = \mathbb{1}^T$ and $\mathbf{W}\mathbb{1} = \mathbb{1}$, where w_{ij} denotes the (i, j)th entry of matrix $\mathbf{W}$ and $\mathbb{1}$ stands for the all one vector. Typical rules that satisfy these two properties include the Laplacian, Metropolis–Hasting, and maximum-degree weights [23]. Let the gradient estimate of the loss function at point $\boldsymbol{\theta}$ be defined by

$$\widehat{\nabla} f_i(\boldsymbol{\theta}) \triangleq m^{-1} \sum_{k=1}^{m} \nabla F_i(\boldsymbol{\theta}; \xi_{ik}), \qquad (10.2)$$

where ξ_{ik} denotes the kth data sample at node i and m is the mini-batch size. Then, the local update of the model parameter is

$$\boldsymbol{\theta}_i^{t+1} = \boldsymbol{\theta}_i^t - \alpha^t \widehat{\nabla} f_i(\boldsymbol{\theta}_i^t), \qquad (10.3)$$

where t denotes the index of iteration and α^t is the step size. Similar as the classic FL scheme, for every τ iterations, we additionally perform one round of communication based on the local update, i.e.,

$$\boldsymbol{\theta}_i^{t+1} = \sum_{j \in \mathcal{N}_i} \mathbf{W}_{ij} \boldsymbol{\theta}_j^t - \alpha^t \widehat{\nabla} f_i(\boldsymbol{\theta}_i^t) \quad \text{if } \mathrm{mod}(t, \tau) = 0, \qquad (10.4)$$

where the step $\sum_{j \in \mathcal{N}_i} \mathbf{W}_{ij} \boldsymbol{\theta}_j^t$ refers to the model aggregation and $1/\tau$ refers to the communication frequency. The model update by Eq. (10.3) followed by Eq. (10.4) per every τ steps is a straightforward extension from classic distributed stochastic gradient descent (DSGD) to SGD-based DFL. Here, we call this algorithm DFL-SGD. It is not hard to see that DFL-SGD tries to balance the trade-off between the iterates' convergence and communication efficiency. Intuitively, the local update optimizes the individual model without sharing the data samples, and the model aggression step enforces the consensus among the distributed model parameters so that the learned model can leverage the networked data to reduce the variance of the local stochastic gradient estimate.

The DFL-SGD algorithm performs well when the network is homogeneous. When the heterogencity of data distributions $\{\mathcal{D}_i, \forall i\}$ increases, it is well known that performance of distributed SGD (DSGD) algorithm decreases as the discrepancy term of the data distributions will show up at the denominator of the convergence rate of DSGD [21]. As DFL-SGD inherits from DSGD, this issue remains. A more advanced technique, stochastic gradient tracking, is proposed to approximate the global gradient estimate locally and improve the numerical performance of DSGD deployed in the heterogeneous networks [16]. When the communication efficiency is taken into account, the local updates of the model are as follows:

$$\boldsymbol{\theta}_i^{t+1} = \boldsymbol{\theta}_i^t - \alpha^t \boldsymbol{\vartheta}_i^t, \tag{10.5a}$$

$$\boldsymbol{\vartheta}_i^{t+1} = \boldsymbol{\vartheta}_i^t + \widehat{\nabla} f_i(\boldsymbol{\theta}_i^{t+1}) - \widehat{\nabla} f_i(\boldsymbol{\theta}_i^t), \tag{10.5b}$$

where $\boldsymbol{\vartheta}_i^t$ is called gradient tracker and initialized as vector $\mathbf{0}$. It can be seen that the gradient tracking based local update Eq. (10.5a) is analogous to Eq. (10.3) with the difference being only the gradient estimate. In Eq. (10.3), the local stochastic gradient estimate is directly used for the model update, while in Eq. (10.5a) an auxiliary variable is adopted instead. From the theory perspective, $\boldsymbol{\vartheta}_i^t$ can keep tracking the network total stochastic gradient $n^{-1} \sum_{i=1}^{n} \widehat{\nabla} f_i(\boldsymbol{\theta}_i^t)$ through the update rule Eq. (10.5b). Similar to DFL-SGD, gradient tracking based DFL (DFL-GT) also conducts the model aggregation after every τ local update steps as follows:

$$\boldsymbol{\theta}_i^{t+1} = \sum_{j \in \mathcal{N}_i} \mathbf{W}_{ij} \boldsymbol{\theta}_j^t - \alpha^t \boldsymbol{\vartheta}_i^t \quad \text{if mod}(t, \tau) = 0, \tag{10.6a}$$

$$\boldsymbol{\vartheta}_i^{t+1} = \sum_{j \in \mathcal{N}_i} \mathbf{W}_{ij} \boldsymbol{\vartheta}_j^t + \widehat{\nabla} f_i(\boldsymbol{\theta}_i^{t+1}) - \widehat{\nabla} f_i(\boldsymbol{\theta}_i^t) \quad \text{if mod}(t, \tau) = 0. \tag{10.6b}$$

This DFL algorithm has been studied in [17] for decentralized learning of electronic health records. Under the mild assumption on the gradient Lipschitz continuity of the loss function, it has been established in [14] that DFL-GT algorithm can find the first-order stationary points (FOSPs) with a convergence rate of $\mathcal{O}(1/\sqrt{nT})$ in the sense that both the first-order stationarity in terms of the gradient size of the loss function in the consensus space, i.e., $\mathbb{E}\|n^{-1} \sum_{i=1}^{n} \nabla f_i(\bar{\boldsymbol{\theta}}^t)\|^2$, and the consensus violation, i.e., $\mathbb{E}[n^{-1} \sum_{i=1}^{n} \|\boldsymbol{\theta}_i^t - \bar{\boldsymbol{\theta}}^t\|^2]$, are shrinking with the speed of $\mathcal{O}(1/\sqrt{nT})$, where $f_i(\boldsymbol{\theta}_i) \triangleq \mathbb{E}_{\xi_i \sim \mathcal{D}_i} F_i(\boldsymbol{\theta}_i; \xi_i)$, $\bar{\boldsymbol{\theta}} = n^{-1} \sum_{i=1}^{n} \boldsymbol{\theta}_i$, and the expectation is taken over both the randomness of data samples and the index of the iterations. Moreover, it has been also proven in [14] that τ can be chosen as large as $\mathcal{O}(T^{1/4})$ (i.e., the communication efficiency of DFL-GT is $\mathcal{O}(T^{3/4})$ rather than $\mathcal{O}(T)$ required in the classic DSGD), and this class of algorithms is also extendable to solve problems in time-varying directed graphs.

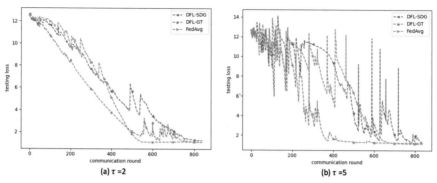

(a) τ =2   **(b) τ =5**

FIGURE 10.1

Loss value v.s. communication rounds on a synthetic dataset (testing loss).

The general DFL framework with algorithms DFL-SGD and DFL-GT is summarized in Algorithm 1.

Algorithm 1 Decentralized federated learning framework (DFL).

1: Initialize step size sequence α^t
2: **for** $t = 0, 1, 2, \ldots, T$ **do**
3:     Randomly sample m data points locally
4:     Estimate gradient of the local loss function by Eq. (10.2)
5:     Perform local model update by Eq. (10.3) or Eq. (10.5a)   ▷ at each node in parallel
6:     **if** t is a multiple of τ, i.e.,   mod $(t, \tau) = 0$ **then**
7:         Update model parameters by Eq. (10.4) or Eq. (10.6a) and Eq. (10.6b)
8:     **end if**
9: **end for**

We set up a simple topology of five nodes, using the same groundtruth weights, which are then multiplied by inputs belonging to various intervals of uniform distribution (including $[-30, 30]$, $[40, 100]$, $[-50, -55]$, $[-1, 1]$, $[-0.1, 0.1]$) with different five nonlinear functions (tanh, sigmoid, ReLu, sine, and cosine) to generate different heterogeneous data.

The numerical results of comparing FedAvg, DFL-SGD, and DFL-GT are shown in Fig. 10.1, where we use a three-layer nonlinear multilayer perceptron to regress these data, and use the same step size scheduling rule (i.e., $15/\sqrt{t}$) for DFL-SGD and DFL-GT. It can be seen that FedAvg converges the fastest because it aggregates the model completely for each round. DFL-GT converges faster than DFL-SGD as the gradient tracker over the graph can approximate the full gradient as the iterates proceed.

10.3 Multi-center federated learning

Besides the advanced algorithms designed for heterogeneous FL networks, cluster-structured models are also considered for tackling the issues of non-i.i.d. data distributions over distributed networks. The underlying assumption is that there exist K global models and the scattered local models only belong to one of these global ones. In FeSEM [24], a multi-center model aggregation model is used for FL, where all the local models are partitioned into K clusters, denoted as $\{C_k, k \in [K]\}$. Aside from minimizing the consensus errors and regression loss function, an assignment of each model to its nearest cluster is also included in the learning process. Specifically, the overall problem is formulated as follows:

$$(\mathbb{P}2) \quad \min_{\theta_i, \bar{\theta}_k, r_{ik}, \forall i, k} \frac{1}{n} \sum_{i=1}^{n} \mathbb{E}_{\xi \sim \mathcal{D}_i} F_i(\theta_i; \xi) + \frac{\lambda}{n} \sum_{k=1}^{K} \sum_{i=1}^{n} r_{ik} \mathrm{dist}(\theta_i, \bar{\theta}_k), \quad (10.7)$$

where λ controls the trade-off between the supervised loss and multi-center based model discrepancy, $\mathrm{dist}(\cdot, \cdot)$ denotes the distance between two model parameter spaces, $\bar{\theta}_k$ represents the kth center of cluster C_k, and r_{ik} is the binary assignment variable that indicate whether the ith model is classified to the kth cluster or not. The regularization term measures the distance between each local model to its nearest global model.

For the multi-center FL model, the expectation-maximization (EM) method is one of the most standard techniques for solving clustering related problems. Combining with a local supervised learning update, a stochastic block coordinate descent type of algorithm is proposed for the FL setting, called federated stochastic EM (FeSEM), in [24]. The main idea of FeSEM is adapting the EM algorithm in searching for the multiple centers $\bar{\theta}_k$ while fixing local model parameters $\{\theta_i, \forall i\}$, and then performing local updates of θ_i for τ steps to minimize the local loss function values while keeping the assignment of every model to each cluster learned from the previous step unchanged. More detailed procedures of FeSEM are shown in Algorithm 2 and explained as follows:

E-Step. The first step of each model is to look for the nearest clusters based on the distance between the local model parameter θ_i^t and the existing centers $\{\bar{\theta}_j^t, j \in [K]\}$ and obtain the assignment variable by

$$r_{ik}^t = \begin{cases} 1, & \text{if } k = \arg\min_j \mathrm{dist}(\theta_i^t, \bar{\theta}_j^t), \\ 0, & \text{otherwise.} \end{cases} \quad (10.8)$$

M-Step. Then, the center of each cluster is calculated by

$$\bar{\theta}_k^t = \frac{1}{\sum_{i=1}^{n} r_{ik}} \sum_{i=1}^{n} r_{ik}^t \theta_i^t \quad (10.9)$$

while fixing model parameters and current center assignments.

Algorithm 2 FeSEM – Federated Stochastic EM [24].

1: Initialize K, $\{\boldsymbol{\theta}_i^0\}$, $\{\bar{\boldsymbol{\theta}}_k^t\}$
2: **for** $t = 0, 1, 2, \ldots, T$ **do**
3:     **E-Step**
4:         Calculate distance $d_{ik}^t = \text{dist}(\boldsymbol{\theta}_i^t, \bar{\boldsymbol{\theta}}_k^t), \forall i, k$
5:         Update r_{ik}^t using d_{ik}^t by Eq. (10.8)
6:     **M-Step**
7:         Group devices to $\mathcal{C}_k^t$ using r_{ik}^t
8:         Update $\bar{\boldsymbol{\theta}}_k^t$ using r_{ik}^t and $\boldsymbol{\theta}_i^t$ by Eq. (10.9)   ▷ Compute the new center
9:         **for** each cluster $k = 1, \ldots, K$ **do**
10:             **for** $i \in \mathcal{C}_k^t$ **do**
11:                 Send $\bar{\boldsymbol{\theta}}_k^t$ to device i
12:                 $\boldsymbol{\theta}_i^{t+1} \leftarrow$ **Local_Update**$(i, \bar{\boldsymbol{\theta}}_k^t)$
13:             **end for**
14:         **end for**
15: **end for**

Local models. Given the multi-centers, each local device will fine-tune the model for individual data distribution by minimizing the regression loss function and the dissimilarity between the local and assigned global model parameters, which means that each $\boldsymbol{\theta}_i$ needs solving the following problem:

$$\min_{\theta_i} \mathbb{E}_{\xi \sim \mathcal{D}_i} F_i(\boldsymbol{\theta}_i; \xi) + \lambda \sum_{k=1}^{K} r_{ik} \text{dist}(\boldsymbol{\theta}_i, \bar{\boldsymbol{\theta}}_k). \tag{10.10}$$

Here, Eq. (10.10) is an unconstrained optimization problem. The model parameters can be updated efficiently by multiple steps of SGD, which corresponds to the local SGD update in the standard FL scenario. Finally, iterating the above three steps results in the FeSEM algorithm for solving the multi-center FL problem.

Algorithm 3 Local_Update.

1: **Input**: i – device index, $\bar{\boldsymbol{\theta}}_k^t$
2: **Output**: $\boldsymbol{\theta}_i^{t+1}$ – updated local model
3: Initialize $\boldsymbol{\theta}_i^t$ by $\bar{\boldsymbol{\theta}}_k^t$
4: **for** τ local training steps **do**
5:     Update $\boldsymbol{\theta}_i$ by any efficient algorithm with data $\mathcal{D}_i$ ▷ needed for Eq. (10.10)
6: **end for**
7: Return $\boldsymbol{\theta}_i$

10.4 Graph-knowledge based federated learning

Even though the multi-center FL takes the cluster structure into consideration, Fe-SEM still assumes that there is no overlap among the global models, which might not be true or restrict for practical heterogeneous networks. Actually, FeSEM can be considered as a special case of the two levels of the optimization problem, where one level is minimizing the regularization term in Eq. (10.7) for searching the cluster structure and the other is minimizing the supervised loss for data feature extraction. Mathematically, the class of multi-task learning problems can be formulated as a bilevel optimization as follows [12]:

$$\min_{\boldsymbol{\varphi}} \ell(\boldsymbol{\varphi}) \triangleq f\left(\boldsymbol{\varphi}, \{\boldsymbol{\theta}_i^*(\boldsymbol{\varphi})\}\right) \tag{10.11a}$$

$$\text{such that } \boldsymbol{\theta}_i^*(\boldsymbol{\varphi}) \in \arg\min_{\boldsymbol{\theta}_i} \mathbb{E}_{\xi \in \mathcal{D}_i} G_i(\boldsymbol{\varphi}, \boldsymbol{\theta}_i; \xi), \ \forall i \in [n], \tag{10.11b}$$

where $\boldsymbol{\varphi}$ is the UL decision variable, $\{\boldsymbol{\theta}_i, \forall i\}$ denote the LL model parameters, $f(\cdot, \cdot)$ and $G_i(\cdot, \cdot)$ respectively represent the UL and LL loss functions, and $\{\boldsymbol{\theta}_i^*(\boldsymbol{\varphi}), \forall i \in [n]\}$ stand for the optimal solutions of the LL optimization variables. This model can cover a wide range of hierarchical FL learning problems, e.g., federated acoustic speech recognition [3], personalized meta-learning [4], multi-agent actor–critic schemes in reinforcement learning [15], etc.

Note that the structured graph knowledge is related to all the local models, so the LL optimization variables would be coupled. One example is the multi-center FL case as shown in Eq. (10.10), where the kth center involved in the LL problem is calculated based on all $\boldsymbol{\theta}_i$s. Therefore, a more generalized bilevel optimization enhanced GAFL, or BiG-FL in short, is proposed in [25], by formulating the LL optimization problem as a competitive game as follows:

$$(\mathbb{P}3) \quad \min_{\boldsymbol{\varphi}} \ell(\boldsymbol{\varphi}) = f\left(\boldsymbol{\varphi}, \{\boldsymbol{\theta}_i^*(\boldsymbol{\varphi})\}\right) \tag{10.12a}$$

$$\text{such that } \boldsymbol{\theta}_i^*(\boldsymbol{\varphi}) = \arg\min_{\boldsymbol{\theta}_i} \mathbb{E}_{\xi \in \mathcal{D}_i} G_i\left(\boldsymbol{\varphi}, \boldsymbol{\theta}_i, \boldsymbol{\theta}_{-i}^*(\boldsymbol{\varphi}); \xi\right), \ \forall i \in [n], \tag{10.12b}$$

where $\boldsymbol{\theta}_{-i}^*(\boldsymbol{\varphi})$ denotes $\{\boldsymbol{\theta}_{-i}^*(\boldsymbol{\varphi}) | \boldsymbol{\theta}_j^*(\boldsymbol{\varphi}), j \neq i, \forall j \in \mathcal{N}_i\}$. From this model, we can see that the UL optimization problem is targeted at minimizing the globally shareable parameter $\boldsymbol{\varphi}$ while the LL problem is used for integrating the UL knowledge and adapting the local data distributions. In the following, we provide one way of applying the BiG-FL to a GNN-embedded FL system.

10.4.1 Applications of BiG-FL

Inspired by graph embedding learning for link prediction [7], BiG-FL can take the connectivity of FL clients/devices (i.e., edge information in the global graph structure) as a guide in the UL optimization process and maps this topology information to weigh the similarity of neighboring clients' models.

Let $\boldsymbol{\theta}^*(\boldsymbol{\varphi}) \in \mathbb{R}^{n \times d}$ denote the concatenation of all the LL optimal solutions. Constructing the embedding matrix $\mathbf{H}$ via linear message passing in GNNs yields:

$$\mathbf{H} = \mathbf{L}\boldsymbol{\theta}^*(\boldsymbol{\varphi})\boldsymbol{\varphi}, \tag{10.13}$$

where $\mathbf{L} \in \mathbb{R}^{n \times n}$ is a Laplacian matrix (e.g., $\mathbf{L} \triangleq \widetilde{\mathbf{D}}^{-\frac{1}{2}}\widetilde{\mathbf{A}}\widetilde{\mathbf{D}}^{-\frac{1}{2}}$, where $\widetilde{\mathbf{A}} = \mathbf{A} + \mathbf{I}$ and $\widetilde{\mathbf{D}}_{ii} = \sum_j \widetilde{\mathbf{A}}_{ij}$, which are commonly used in graph convolution networks (GCNs) [8]), $\boldsymbol{\theta}^*(\boldsymbol{\varphi})$ is learned from local models, and $\boldsymbol{\varphi} \in \mathbb{R}^{d \times d}$ denotes the UL parameters acting as the weights in GNN with a shape of $d \times d$.

UL loss function. With this graph-based representation, we can formulate the UL objective function using the cosine embedding loss as

$$f(\boldsymbol{\varphi}, \boldsymbol{\theta}^*(\boldsymbol{\varphi})) \triangleq \frac{1}{n}\sum_{i=1}^{n}\sum_{j \in \mathcal{N}_i}\left(1 - \cos(\mathbf{H}_i, \mathbf{H}_j)\right)$$

$$+ \frac{1}{n}\sum_{i=1}^{n}\mathbb{E}_{j \sim P_i}\max\left(0, \cos(\mathbf{H}_i, \mathbf{H}_j)\right) + \frac{\lambda}{2}\|\boldsymbol{\varphi} - \mathbf{I}\|^2, \tag{10.14}$$

where i and j are indices of the nodes (i.e., FL clients/devices),

$$\cos(\mathbf{H}_i, \mathbf{H}_j) \triangleq \frac{\mathbf{H}_i^T\mathbf{H}_j}{\|\mathbf{H}_i\|\,\|\mathbf{H}_j\|}, \tag{10.15}$$

and $\mathcal{P}_i$ denotes the negative sampling distribution at client i [7].

The UL objective function for BiG-Fed in Eq. (10.14) utilizes the cosine embedding loss to calculate both the client-pair embedding similarity of all linked clients and the client-pair embedding dissimilarity of negative samples. As the embedding is derived from the local model weights, Eq. (10.14) couples local learning tasks with the graphical link prediction task at the server side.

It is worth noting that the link prediction model learns the relative relationships among the local models. In addition, we expect that the optimized UL model can maintain the centroid of the overall weight distribution, so we initialize $\boldsymbol{\varphi}$ by the identity matrix $\mathbf{I}$, and add a regularity term on $\boldsymbol{\varphi}$ with the identity matrix $\mathbf{I}$ at the UL loss function.

LL loss function. The local LL learning tasks of BiG-FL at each device are finding the Nash equilibrium of the following problem:

$$\boldsymbol{\theta}_i^*(\boldsymbol{\varphi}) = \arg\min_{\boldsymbol{\theta}_i} g_i\left(\boldsymbol{\varphi}, \boldsymbol{\theta}_i, \boldsymbol{\theta}_{-i}^*(\boldsymbol{\varphi})\right), \forall i \in [n], \tag{10.16}$$

where $g_i(\boldsymbol{\varphi}, \boldsymbol{\theta}_i, \boldsymbol{\theta}_{-i}^*(\boldsymbol{\varphi})) \triangleq \mathbb{E}_{\xi \sim \mathcal{D}_i} G_i(\boldsymbol{\varphi}, \boldsymbol{\theta}_i, \boldsymbol{\theta}_{-i}^*(\boldsymbol{\varphi}); \xi)$. In this case, the UL weight $\boldsymbol{\varphi}$ is introduced into the LL learning task to penalize the distance between the aggregation of neighboring weights and the local one, as we assume that the neighboring clients share a similar latent space. Hence, for each client, the loss function $g_i(\cdot)$

includes both the supervised learning error and distance between the local model parameter and the centroid learned from the UL graph knowledge:

$$g_i\left(\boldsymbol{\varphi}, \boldsymbol{\theta}_i, \boldsymbol{\theta}^*_{-i}(\boldsymbol{\varphi})\right) \triangleq \frac{1}{2}\mathbb{E}_{(X_i, Y_i)\sim\mathcal{D}_i} \|Y_i - h_{\boldsymbol{\theta}_i}(X_i)\|^2$$

$$+ \frac{\lambda}{2} R_i\left(\boldsymbol{\varphi}, \boldsymbol{\theta}_i, \boldsymbol{\theta}^*_{-i}(\boldsymbol{\varphi})\right) + \frac{\kappa}{2}\|\boldsymbol{\theta}_i\|^2, \forall i \in [n], \qquad (10.17)$$

where $h_{\boldsymbol{\theta}_i}(\cdot) : X_i \to Y_i$ denotes the nonlinear mapping parametrized by a neural network with weight $\boldsymbol{\theta}_i$, X_i and Y_i respectively represent the data and labels owned by the ith client, $\mathcal{D}_i$ denotes the joint distribution of X_i and Y_i, regularization term $\kappa\|\boldsymbol{\theta}_i\|^2$ is used for stabilizing the LL learning process with $\kappa > 0$, and $R_i(\boldsymbol{\varphi}, \boldsymbol{\theta}_i, \boldsymbol{\theta}^*_{-i}(\boldsymbol{\varphi}))$ denotes the distance based regularization term,

$$R_i(\boldsymbol{\varphi}, \boldsymbol{\theta}_i, \boldsymbol{\theta}^*_{-i}(\boldsymbol{\varphi})) = \left\|(\mathbf{L}_{i,:} - \mathbf{L}_{i,i})\boldsymbol{\theta}^*(\boldsymbol{\varphi})\boldsymbol{\varphi} + \mathbf{L}_{i,i}\boldsymbol{\theta}_i\boldsymbol{\varphi} - \boldsymbol{\theta}_i\right\|^2. \qquad (10.18)$$

Furthermore, $\mathbf{L}_{i,:}$ denotes the ith row of Laplacian matrix $\mathbf{L}$. Note that term $(\mathbf{L}_{i,:} - \mathbf{L}_{i,i})\boldsymbol{\theta}^*(\boldsymbol{\varphi})\boldsymbol{\varphi} + \mathbf{L}_{i,i}\boldsymbol{\theta}_i\boldsymbol{\varphi}$ is the weight embedding, where $(\mathbf{L}_{i,:} - \mathbf{L}_{i,i})\boldsymbol{\theta}^*(\boldsymbol{\varphi})\boldsymbol{\varphi}$ does not involve current node's weight $\boldsymbol{\theta}_i$ and can be approximated by the FL server in advance.

The penalization on the difference between the current weight and the weight embedding in each LL task, together with the fact that the UL variable learns the relationship of each weight embedding simultaneously via $\boldsymbol{\varphi}$, allows us to leverage the graph information to improve the generalization of the model by integrating the prior knowledge of similarity among the nodes. Next, we will introduce an algorithm for solving Eq. (10.12).

10.4.2 Algorithm design for BiG-FL

Solving Eq. (10.17) exactly to get the optimal solution is not practical. Instead, following the FL algorithms, we apply SGD for several steps and obtain an approximate solution of the LL problem. To be more specific, the LL optimization variable is updated by

$$\boldsymbol{\theta}_i^{k+1} = \boldsymbol{\theta}_i^k - \frac{\beta^t}{m}\sum_{j=1}^{m}\nabla_{\boldsymbol{\theta}_i} G_i(\boldsymbol{\varphi}^t, \boldsymbol{\theta}_i^k, \boldsymbol{\theta}_{-i}^k; \xi_j), \quad \forall i \in [n], \qquad (10.19)$$

where k denotes the index of the inner loop by initializing $\boldsymbol{\theta}_i^0 = \boldsymbol{\theta}_i^t$, β^t is the LL step size, and $\nabla G_i(\boldsymbol{\varphi}^t, \boldsymbol{\theta}_i^k, \boldsymbol{\theta}_{-i}^k; \xi_j)$ represents the gradient of the ith BiG-FL LL empirical loss function evaluated at the point $(\boldsymbol{\varphi}^t, \boldsymbol{\theta}_i^k, \boldsymbol{\theta}_{-i}^k)$ with the jth data sample (i.e., $\xi_j \triangleq (X_j, Y_j) \sim \mathcal{D}_j$). After consecutive τ steps of the inner loop update, we set $\boldsymbol{\theta}_i^{t+1} = \boldsymbol{\theta}_i^\tau$.

Algorithm 4 Bilevel optimization enhanced GFL (BiG-FL).

1: Initialize the UL and LL step sizes α^0, β^0, and model parameters $\boldsymbol{\varphi}^0$, $\{\boldsymbol{\theta}_i^0\}$
2: **for** round $t = 0, 1, 2, \ldots, T$ **do**
3:     **for** node $i = 0, 1, 2, \ldots, n$ **do**
4:         Receive $(\mathbf{L}_{i,:} - \mathbf{L}_{i,i})\boldsymbol{\theta}^t$, $\boldsymbol{\varphi}^t$, and $\mathbf{L}_{i,i}$ from FL Server
5:         Calculate the gradient of term $R_i(\boldsymbol{\varphi}^t, \boldsymbol{\theta}_i^t, \boldsymbol{\theta}_{-i}^*(\boldsymbol{\varphi}^t))$ by Eq. (10.18)
6:         Update $\boldsymbol{\theta}_i^{t+1}$ by Eq. (10.19) $\triangleright$ needed for Eq. (10.17)
7:         Send $\boldsymbol{\theta}_i^{t+1}$ to the FL Server
8:     **end for**
9:     Receive $\{\boldsymbol{\theta}_i^{t+1}\}$ from clients
10:    Complete message passing with Eq. (10.13) to generate $\mathbf{H}$
11:    Update $\boldsymbol{\varphi}^{t+1}$ by Eq. (10.20) $\triangleright$ needed for Eq. (10.14)
12:    Distribute $\boldsymbol{\varphi}^{t+1}$, $(\mathbf{L}_{i,:} - \mathbf{L}_{i,i})\boldsymbol{\theta}^{t+1}$, and $\mathbf{L}_{i,i}$ to each node
13: **end for**

Similarly, the LL variable is updated by SGD with computing the hyper-gradient [5] as follows:

$$\boldsymbol{\varphi}^{t+1} = \boldsymbol{\varphi}^t - \frac{\alpha^t}{m} \sum_{j=1}^{m} \left(\nabla_\varphi F_j^t - \nabla_{\varphi\theta}^2 G_j^t \left(\nabla_{\theta\theta}^2 G_j^t \right)^{-1} \nabla_\theta F_j^t \right), \tag{10.20}$$

where α^t denotes the UL step size, $\nabla_\varphi F_j^t$ (the abbreviation of $\nabla_\varphi F(\boldsymbol{\varphi}^t, \{\boldsymbol{\theta}_i^t\}; \xi_j)$) is the gradient of the UL empirical loss function evaluated at point $(\boldsymbol{\varphi}^t, \{\boldsymbol{\theta}_i^t\})$ with the jth tail node of the negative sample for head node i (i.e., $j \sim \mathcal{P}_i$), $\nabla_{\varphi\theta}^2 G_j^t$ and $(\nabla_{\theta\theta}^2 G_j^t)^{-1}$ respectively stand for the stochastic approximation of the Jacobian matrix of the LL loss function with respect to both $\boldsymbol{\varphi}$ and $\{\boldsymbol{\theta}_i\}$ and the inverse of Hessian matrix of the LL loss function. Here, we assume that the LL loss functions are strongly convex (e.g., if κ is sufficiently large), implying that $\nabla_{\theta\theta}^2 G_j^t$ is invertible. The complete implementation of BiG-FL is shown in Algorithm 4, where $\boldsymbol{\theta}$ is the concatenation of $\{\boldsymbol{\theta}_i, \forall i\}$.

The convergence guarantees of bilevel optimization algorithms have been investigated in recent works [5,12]. For the BiG-FL problem, it has been shown in [25] that when the UL and LL step sizes α^t and β^t are chosen on the order of $1/\sqrt{T}$, under the Lipschitz continuity of the UL loss function, as well as its Jacobian and Hessian, plus the strong convexity of the LL loss functions, Algorithm 4 needs $\mathcal{O}(1/\epsilon^4)$ iterations to reach the FOSPs of Eq. (10.12) in the sense that both the first-order stationarity of the UL optimization variable $\boldsymbol{\varphi}$, i.e., $\mathbb{E}\|\nabla \ell(\boldsymbol{\varphi}^t)\|^2$, and the distance between $\boldsymbol{\theta}_i^t$ and its optimal counterpart, i.e., $\mathbb{E}\|\boldsymbol{\theta}_i^t - \boldsymbol{\theta}_i^*(\boldsymbol{\varphi}^t)\|^2$, $\forall i$, are $\mathcal{O}(\epsilon)$, where the expectation is taken over both the randomness of data samples and the index of the iterations.

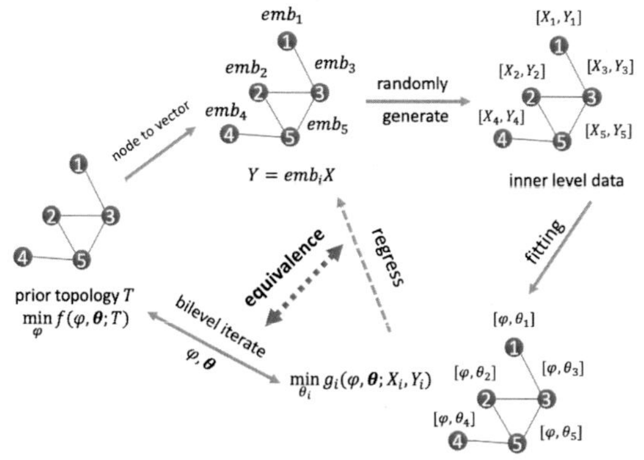

FIGURE 10.2

Homologous graph generation and data synthesis.

10.5 Numerical evaluation of GFL models

In this section, we provide numerical experiments for testing the performance of these GFL models and algorithms with a comparison with the benchmark FedAvg [18] on both synthetic and real data, which were partially shown in [25].

10.5.1 Results on synthetic data

To generate a heterogeneous network with respect to local model parameters, topology-based groundtruth weights (embedding) are generated based on a predefined graph, where inputs $\{X_i\}$ are randomly generated, and the outputs $\{Y_i\}$ are obtained by following our model in Eq. (10.13), which is further illustrated in Fig. 10.2. In order to evaluate the generalization performance of the models, we need to generate two homologous graphs so that graphs adopted in training and testing share the same distribution. To be specific, we generate two graphs that follow homologous distributions. Each of them has 50 nodes and consists of the same mixture of three standard normal distributions. The range of the centers of these distributions is $[-0.5, 0.5]$, and the standard deviation of all these distributions is 0.5. We use the four closest neighboring nodes to build the graph. The dimension of the generated samples is 64, which is used as the groundtruth weight (reshaped to 8×8) of the model for each client. For data synthesis, both training and testing sets are independently generated for the 50 LL learning tasks with uniformly distributed samples (100×8) in the range of $[-60, 60]$ as the input. The output is obtained by matrix multiplication of the input and the groundtruth weights. Parameters used in the synthetic data experiment are shown in Table 10.1.

The multi-layer perception followed by the sigmoid activation functions is used in the LL learning model, and the total number of layers of θ_i is 3 with shapes of 8×16, 16×16, and 16×8, respectively. The UL task is link-prediction based on

Table 10.1 Synthetic experiment setting.

Common Mixture Distribution	Distribution Type	Gaussian
	Number of Center	3
	Range of Center	$[-0.5, 0.5]$
	Standard Deviation	0.5
	Dimension	64
Homologous Graph Generation	Number of Neighbor Connections	4
	Node Dimension	64
	Node Number of Train Graph	50
	Node Number of Test Graph	50
Node Data Synthesis	Shape of Ground Truth Weight	8×8
	Shape of Input	100×8
	Range of Input Distribution	$[-60, 60]$
	Shape of Input	8×100
Node (Lower Level) Model	Number of Layer	3
	Activation Function	Sigmoid
	Shape of Layers	$[8 \times 16, 16 \times 16, 16 \times 8]$
Upper Level Model	Shape of GNN weight	512×512

negative sampling. For each head node, we randomly sample 10 tail nodes from all negative edges and use the DGL package with a GCN layer [22] to generate the graph embedding for learning the edge similarity. The GCN layer is used in the UL task, where φ of dimension 512×512 serves as the graph convolution kernel of the GCN layer. Each uploaded LL weight θ_i acts as the node input representative, which is flattened into a shape of 1×512 and fitted into the cosine embedding loss function after message passing. As FeSEM requires prior knowledge about the number of clustering centers, we set $K = 3$ to reflect the setting of the three mixed Gaussian distributions.

The numerical results are shown in Fig. 10.3. It can be observed that the consensus-based models perform the worst in comparison with the cluster or graph embedding based ones, as there are three mixture Gaussian data samples over the graph. FeSEM improves the performance of classic FedAvg and DFL as the EM algorithm is able to find the three centers and tailor the model to fit different kinds of data distributions. BiG-FL shows the best performance among all the models in this case, which justifies the power of the UL learning task for extracting embedding through the graph information and transferring this similarity to the testing phrase.

10.5.2 Results on real-world data for NLP

A large lookup weight table related to the number of words in the corpus plays a central role in natural language processing (NLP) tasks. Each row of the table corre-

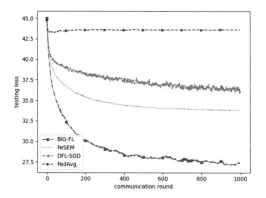

FIGURE 10.3

Performance comparison (local testing loss).

sponds to a word which is involved in the current task (i.e., word embedding). These word embeddings are trainable weights and are non-i.i.d. due to textual word data originating from different domains, and have different dimensions and interleaved weight spaces due to the differences in corpus words.

We adopt the datasets from [9] which consist of 16 different domains of review data. As shown in Table 10.2, the datasets differ in terms of review category, the average length of the review sentences, and the number of unique words. The goal of this task is to train a multi-domain next word prediction model. Here, we use the GloVe embedding vectors [19], which are commonly applied for embedding initialization to act as a global representation. We group the non-i.i.d. embeddings from multiple domains and project them into this global vector space. For the LL model, we use the classic neural probabilistic language model [1] for word embedding, where the embedding layer (i.e., a big lookup table) is with a dimension of 63144×100, a fully-connected hidden layer is with a dimension of 100×200 followed by a tanh function, and a decoder layer has a size of 200×63144. The length of the sliding window for the next word prediction task is 35 and the batch size is 100. The UL model is identical to the synthetic data case. We also set the dimension of the embedding layer for each client equal to the size of the total number of tokens for the purpose of alignment. If the current client contains a word, we set the corresponding row of the lookup table matrix of the embedding layer as trainable, and the row that does not have a corresponding word as 0. The total number of trainable rows per client is shown in the last column of Table 10.2.

The results are shown in Fig. 10.4. It can be observed that the testing losses are consistent with the synthetic dataset case. Although the testing curve of BiG-FL has some fluctuations at the early stage of the convergence, it achieves the lowest loss eventually. The reason might be due to the competition among the LL learning models, which affects the embedding search progress in the UL problem, and once the graph structure is learned, BiG-FL will showcase a stable convergence behavior. This example verifies the importance of leveraging the similarity among the word embed-

Table 10.2 Statistics of multi-domain datasets.

Dataset	Sentences	Avg Length	Unique/Total words
Books	2000	159	19,013/63,144
Electronics	1998	101	8799/63,144
DVD	2000	173	20,308/63,144
Kitchen	2000	89	9188/63,144
Apparel	2000	57	6655/63,144
Camera	1997	130	7657/63,144
Health	2000	81	8721/63,144
Music	2000	136	16,459/63,144
Toys	2000	90	8341/63,144
Video	2000	156	18,437/63,144
Baby	1900	104	8424/63,144
Magazine	1970	117	11,552/63,144
Software	1915	129	5788/63,144
Sports	2000	94	9816/63,144
IMDN	2000	269	25,195/63,144
MR	2000	21	7315/63,144

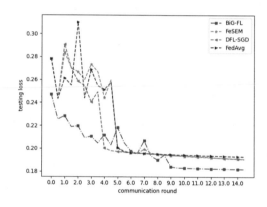

FIGURE 10.4

Real-data experiment results (testing loss).

dings in the multi-task FL problem and superiority of BiG-FL for solving this class of problems.

10.6 Summary

In this chapter, we introduced three major classes of the GFL framework, including decentralized FL, multi-center FL, and bilevel optimization enhanced FL. Each

FL model is mainly applicable for different practical FL scenarios, where DFL is designed for data samples collected in a decentralized way over a graph, multi-center FL is used for the clustered data structures, and BiG-FL is superior for integrating general topology information with adaptation to local learning tasks. Given the unique features of these GFL models, we further studied efficient gradient-based algorithms for solving the corresponding optimization problems in an FL way. It is concluded that the graph structure oriented FL systems can improve the classic FedAvg FL in terms of both learning efficiency and generalization performance.

References

[1] Yoshua Bengio, Réjean Ducharme, Pascal Vincent, A neural probabilistic language model, Advances in Neural Information Processing Systems 13 (2000).

[2] Tsung-Hui Chang, Mingyi Hong, Hoi-To Wai, Xinwei Zhang, Songtao Lu, Distributed learning in the nonconvex world: from batch data to streaming and beyond, IEEE Signal Processing Magazine 37 (3) (2020) 26–38.

[3] Xiaodong Cui, Songtao Lu, Brian Kingsbury, Federated acoustic modeling for automatic speech recognition, in: Proceedings of IEEE International Conference on Acoustics, Speech and Signal Processing (ICASSP), 2021, pp. 6748–6752.

[4] Alireza Fallah, Aryan Mokhtari, Asuman Ozdaglar, Personalized federated learning with theoretical guarantees: a model-agnostic meta-learning approach, in: Proceedings of Advances in Neural Information Processing Systems (NeurIPS), 2020.

[5] Saeed Ghadimi, Mengdi Wang, Approximation methods for bilevel programming, arXiv: 1802.02246, 2018.

[6] Avishek Ghosh, Jichan Chung, Dong Yin, Kannan Ramchandran, An efficient framework for clustered federated learning, in: Proceedings of Advances in Neural Information Processing Systems (NeurIPS), 2020, pp. 19586–19597.

[7] Will Hamilton, Zhitao Ying, Jure Leskovec, Inductive representation learning on large graphs, in: Proceedings of Advances in Neural Information Processing Systems (NeurIPS), 2017.

[8] Thomas N. Kipf, Max Welling, Semi-supervised classification with graph convolutional networks, arXiv:1609.02907, 2016.

[9] Pengfei Liu, Xipeng Qiu, Xuanjing Huang, Adversarial multi-task learning for text classification, arXiv:1704.05742, 2017.

[10] Rui Liu, Han Yu, Federated graph neural networks: overview, techniques and challenges, arXiv:2202.07256, 2022.

[11] Wei Liu, Li Chen, Wenyi Zhang, Decentralized federated learning: balancing communication and computing costs, IEEE Transactions on Signal and Information Processing over Networks 8 (2022) 131–143.

[12] Songtao Lu, Xiaodong Cui, Mark S. Squillante, Brian Kingsbury, Lior Horesh, Decentralized bilevel optimization for personalized client learning, in: Proceedings of IEEE International Conference on Acoustics, Speech and Signal Processing (ICASSP), 2022, pp. 5543–5547.

[13] Songtao Lu, Jason D. Lee, Meisam Razaviyayn, Mingyi Hong, Linearized ADMM converges to second-order stationary points for non-convex problems, IEEE Transactions on Signal Processing 69 (2021) 4859–4874.

[14] Songtao Lu, Chai Wah Wu, Decentralized stochastic non-convex optimization over weakly connected time-varying digraphs, in: Proceedings of IEEE International Conference on Acoustics, Speech and Signal Processing (ICASSP), 2020, pp. 5770–5774.

[15] Songtao Lu, Siliang Zeng, Xiaodong Cui, Mark S. Squillante, Lior Horesh, Brian Kingsbury, Jia Liu, Mingyi Hong, A stochastic linearized augmented Lagrangian method for decentralized bilevel optimization, in: Proceedings of Advances in Neural Information Processing Systems (NeurIPS), 2022.

[16] Songtao Lu, Xinwei Zhang, Haoran Sun, Mingyi Hong, GNSD: A gradient-tracking based nonconvex stochastic algorithm for decentralized optimization, in: Proceedings of IEEE Data Science Workshop (DSW), 2019, pp. 315–321.

[17] Songtao Lu, Yawen Zhang, Yunlong Wang, Decentralized federated learning for electronic health records, in: Proceedings of the 54th Annual Conference on Information Sciences and Systems (CISS), 2020.

[18] Brendan McMahan, Eider Moore, Daniel Ramage, Seth Hampson, Blaise Aguera y Arcas, Communication-efficient learning of deep networks from decentralized data, in: Proceedings of International Conference on Artificial Intelligence and Statistics (AISTATS), 2017, pp. 1273–1282.

[19] Jeffrey Pennington, Richard Socher, Christopher D. Manning, GloVe: global vectors for word representation, in: Proceedings of Empirical Methods in Natural Language Processing (EMNLP), 2014, pp. 1532–1543.

[20] Haoran Sun, Songtao Lu, Mingyi Hong, Improving the sample and communication complexity for decentralized non-convex optimization: joint gradient estimation and tracking, in: Proceedings of International Conference on Machine Learning, 2020, pp. 9217–9228.

[21] Hanlin Tang, Xiangru Lian, Ming Yan, Ce Zhang, Ji Liu, D^2: decentralized training over decentralized data, in: Proceedings of International Conference on Machine Learning (ICML), 2018, pp. 4848–4856.

[22] Minjie Wang, Da Zheng, Zihao Ye, Quan Gan, Mufei Li, Xiang Song, Jinjing Zhou, Chao Ma, Lingfan Yu, Yu Gai, Tianjun Xiao, Tong He, George Karypis, Jinyang Li, Zheng Zhang, Deep graph library: a graph-centric, highly-performant package for graph neural networks, arXiv:1909.01315, 2019.

[23] Lin Xiao, Stephen Boyd, Sanjay Lall, A scheme for robust distributed sensor fusion based on average consensus, in: Proceedings of the Fourth International Symposium on Information Processing in Sensor Networks, 2005, pp. 63–70.

[24] Ming Xie, Guodong Long, Tao Shen, Tianyi Zhou, Xianzhi Wang, Jing Jiang, Multi-center federated learning, arXiv:2005.01026, 2020.

[25] Pengwei Xing, Songtao Lu, Lingfei Wu, Han Yu, BiG-Fed: Bilevel optimization enhanced graph-aided federated learning, IEEE Transactions on Big Data (2022).

Vertical asynchronous federated learning: algorithms and theoretic guarantees

11

Tianyi Chen[a], Xiao Jin[a], Yuejiao Sun[b], and Wotao Yin[c]

[a]*Rensselaer Polytechnic Institute, Troy, NY, United States*
[b]*University of California, Los Angeles, CA, United States*
[c]*Alibaba Group, Bellevue, WA, United States*

11.1 Introduction

Most of the existing federated learning (FL) methods consider the scenario where each client has data of a different set of subjects, but their data share many common features. Therefore, they can collaboratively learn a joint mapping from the feature space to the label space. This setting is also referred to data-partitioned or horizontal FL [20,25]. Unlike the data-partitioned setting, in many learning scenarios, multiple clients handle data about the same set of subjects, but each client has a unique set of features. This case arises in e-commerce, financial, and healthcare applications [15]. For example, an e-commerce company may want to predict a customer's credit using her/his historical transactions from multiple financial institutions; and a healthcare company wants to evaluate the health condition of a particular patient using his/her clinical data from various hospitals [35]. In these examples, data owners (e.g., financial institutions and hospitals) have different records of those users in their joint user base. By combining their features, they can establish a more accurate model. We refer to this setting as feature-partitioned or vertical FL [43].

Compared to the relatively well-studied horizontal FL setting, the vertical FL setting has its unique features and challenges. In horizontal FL, the global model update at a server is an additive aggregation of the local models, updated by each client using its data. In contrast, the global model in vertical FL is the concatenation of local models, which are coupled by the loss function, so updating a client's local model requires the information of the other clients' models. Stronger model dependence in the vertical setting leads to challenges on privacy protection and communication efficiency.

Federated Learning. https://doi.org/10.1016/B978-0-44-319037-7.00020-X

11.1.1 This chapter

The present chapter puts forth an optimization method for vertical FL, which has three main components:

1. A *general optimization formulation* for vertical FL that consists of a global model and one local embedding model for each client. The local embedding model can be linear or nonlinear, or even nonsmooth. It maps raw data to compact features and, thus, reduces the number of parameters that need to be communicated to and from the global model.
2. Flexible *federated learning algorithms* that allow intermittent or even strategic client participation, uncoordinated training data selections, and data protection by differential-privacy based methods (for specific loss functions, one can instead apply multiple-party secure computing protocols).
3. *Rigorous convergence analysis* that establishes the performance lower bound and the privacy level.

From an optimization perspective, to the best of our knowledge, our method is the first that lets multiple clients upload their local models using uncoordinated SGD samples. The method also aggregates local model updates in an asynchronous, block-coordinate gradient fashion. We have also numerically validated our vertical FL algorithms and their analyses on federated logistic regression and deep learning. Tests on image and medical datasets demonstrate the competitive performance of our algorithms relative to centralized and synchronous FL algorithms.

11.1.2 Related work

Since the seminal work [19,25], there has been a large body of studies on FL covering diverse settings; see also a recent survey [21]. The most common FL setting is the horizontal setting, where a large set of data are partitioned among clients that share the same feature space [20]. To account for the personalization, multi-task FL has been studied in [32] that preserves the specialty of each client while also leveraging the similarity among clients. Horizontal FL with local representation learning has been empirically studied in [24]. Communication efficiency has been an important issue in FL. Popular methods aim to: (c1) reduce the number of bits per communication round, including [2,3,31,33,34], to list a few; and (c2) save the number of communication rounds [8,22,38,46].

More recently, feature-partitioned vertical FL has gained popularity in the financial and healthcare applications [15,18,27,43]. Unlike the aggregated gradients in the horizontal case, the local gradients in the vertical FL may involve raw data of those features owned by other clients, which raises additional concerns on privacy. Data privacy has been an important topic since decades ago [37,44]. But early approaches typically require expensive communication and signaling overhead when they are applied to the FL settings. Recently, the notion of differential privacy becomes popular because (i) it is a quantifiable measure of privacy [1,11,13], and (ii) many existing learning algorithms can achieve differential privacy via simple modifications. In the context of learning from multiple clients, it has been studied in [5,14]. But all these approaches are not designed for the vertical FL models and the flexible client update protocols.

As FL is distributed, communication is expensive and can cause delays, so one often applies asynchronous and parallel optimization methods. For the feature-partitioned vertical FL setting in this chapter, it is particularly related to the block coordinate descent (BCD) method [29,41,45]. Asynchronous BCD and its stochastic variant have been developed under the condition of bounded delay in [7,23,28]. The recent advances in this direction aim to establish convergence under weaker assumptions on delays [36,39]. VAFL uses some proof techniques from [36,39] but is also significantly different from them in the following ways:

(C1)   VAFL uses a distributed dataset and stochastic gradients. However, [36,39] use shared memory and deterministic gradients.

(C2)   VAFL has improves data privacy as it lets the workers keep their data but has provable differential privacy guarantees. However, [36,39] use a centralized dataset and do not discuss data privacy.

(C3)   While [36,39] directly require a smooth objective, we use means to guarantee it is and also provides smoothness estimates for neural networks.

VAFL is the first distributed algorithm that provably allows different agents to be uncoordinated and use their own i.i.d. mini-batches, which is an important feature for federated learning.

11.2 Vertical federated learning

In this section, we introduce the formulation of vertical FL, and present our private and asynchronous algorithm.

11.2.1 Problem statement

Consider a set of M clients, $\mathcal{M} := \{1, \ldots, M\}$. A dataset of N samples, $\{\mathbf{x}_n, y_n\}_{n=1}^{N}$, is maintained by M local clients, where each client m maintains $x_{n,m} \in \mathbb{R}^{p_m}$ for $n = 1, \ldots, N$. Vector $x_{n,m}$ is also the mth block of sample vector $\mathbf{x}_n := [x_{n,1}^\top, \ldots, x_{n,M}^\top]^\top$ at client m. Suppose the nth label y_n is stored at the server.

To preserve the privacy of data, the client data $x_{n,m} \in \mathbb{R}^{p_m}$ are not shared with other clients as well as the server. Instead, each client m learns a local (linear or nonlinear, possibly nonsmooth) embedding h_m parameterized by θ_m that maps the high-dimensional vector $x_{n,m} \in \mathbb{R}^{p_m}$ to a low-dimensional one $h_{n,m} := h_m(\theta_m; x_{n,m}) \in \mathbb{R}^{\underline{p}_m}$ with $\underline{p}_m \ll p_m$. Ideally, the clients and the server want to collaboratively solve the following problem:

Algorithm 1 Vertical asynchronous federated learning.

1: **initialize:** θ_0, $\{\theta_m\}$, datum index n, client index m
2: **while** not convergent **do**
3:    **when** a **Client** m is activated, **do:**
4:       †select private datum (or data mini-batch) $x_{n,m}$
5:       †**upload** secure information $h_{n,m} = h_m(\theta_m; x_{n,m})$
6:       **query** $\nabla_{h_{n,m}} \ell(\theta_0, h_{n,1}, \ldots, h_{n,M}; y_n)$ from Server
7:       update local model θ_m
8:    **when Server** receives $h_{n,m}$ from Client m, **do:**
9:       compute $\nabla_{\theta_0} \ell(\theta_0, h_{n,1}, \ldots, h_{n,M}; y_n)$
10:      update server's local model θ_0
11:   **when Server** receives a query from Client m, **do:**
12:      compute $\nabla_{h_{n,m}} \ell(\theta_0, h_{n,1}, \ldots, h_{n,M}; y_n)$
13:      **send** it to Client m
14: **end while**

†We can let Step 5 also send $h_{n,m}$ for those n *not* selected in Step 4. We can reorder Steps 4–7 as 6, 7, *then* 4, and 5. They reduce information delay, yet the analysis is unchanged.

Algorithm 2 Vertical t-synchronous federated learning.

1: **Initialize:** θ_0, $\{\theta_m\}$, datum index n, client index m, integer $1 \leq t \leq M$
2: **while** not convergent **do**
        Algorithm 1, Lines 3–7
8:    **when Server** receives $h_{n,m}$'s from t Clients, **do:**
        Algorithm 1, Lines 9 and 10
11:   **when Server** receives queries from t Clients, **do:**
        Algorithm 1, Lines 12 and 13 for each of t clients
14: **end while**

$$F(\theta_0, \boldsymbol{\theta}) := \frac{1}{N} \sum_{n=1}^{N} \ell\left(\theta_0, h_{n,1}, \ldots, h_{n,M}; y_n\right) + \sum_{m=1}^{M} r(\theta_m),$$

$$\text{with} \quad h_{n,m} := h_m(\theta_m; x_{n,m}), \quad m = 1, \ldots, M, \tag{11.1}$$

where θ_0 is the global model parameter kept at and learned by the server, and $\boldsymbol{\theta} := [\theta_1^\top, \ldots, \theta_M^\top]^\top$ concatenates the local models kept at and learned by local clients, ℓ is the loss capturing the accuracy of the global model parameters $\theta_0, \theta_1, \ldots, \theta_M$, and r is the per-client regularizer that confines the complexity of or encodes the prior knowledge about the local model parameters.

For problem (11.1), the local information of client m is fully captured in the embedding vector $h_{n,m}$, $\forall n = 1, \ldots, N$. Hence, the quantities that will be exchanged between server and clients are $\{h_{n,m}\}$ and the gradients of $\ell(\theta_0, h_{n,1}, \ldots, h_{n,M}; y_n)$ with respect to (w.r.t.) $\{h_{n,m}\}$. See a diagram for VAFL implementation in Fig. 11.1.

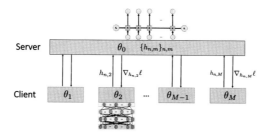

FIGURE 11.1

A diagram for VAFL implementation.

A standard optimization method to solve (11.1) is the (synchronous) block-wise stochastic gradient method [42]. Specifically, at iteration k, the server performs

$$\theta_0^{k+1} = \theta_0^k - \frac{\eta_0^k}{N_k} \sum_{n \in \mathcal{N}_k} \nabla_{\theta_0} \ell\left(\theta_0^k, h_{n,1}^k, \ldots, h_{n,M}^k; y_n\right), \qquad (11.2)$$

where $h_{n,m}^k := h_m(\theta_m^k; x_{n,m})$, $\mathcal{N}_k$ is a mini-batch randomly selected at iteration k with the sample size $N_k = |\mathcal{N}_k|$, and η_0^k is the stepsize at iteration k. With the *same* mini-batch of data $\mathcal{N}_k$, the model update at each local client m is

$$\theta_m^{k+1} = \theta_m^k - \frac{\eta_m^k}{N_k} \sum_{n \in \mathcal{N}_k} \nabla_{\theta_m} h_{n,m}^k \nabla_{h_{n,m}} \ell\left(\theta_0^k, h_{n,1}^k, \ldots, h_{n,M}^k; y_n\right) - \eta_m^k \nabla r\left(\theta_m^k\right),$$

$$(11.3)$$

where η_m^k is the step size at iteration k. When r is nonsmooth and a proximal mapping, we can replace $-\eta_m^k \nabla r(\theta_m^k)$ by an extra proximal step. Implementing updates (11.2) and (11.3) requires all the clients to use the same mini-batch of data to update their local model simultaneously. In FL, however, clients (e.g., devices) participate in the learning process only when they are available (plugged in, waked up, and/or connected with unmetered WiFi) and thus it is difficult to obtain the up-to-date information of all clients at any time. Moreover, the local embedding vectors and the local gradients exchanged between server and clients still have risk of privacy leakage.

11.2.2 Asynchronous client updates

For FL, we consider solving (11.1) without coordination among clients. Asynchronous optimization methods have been used to solve such problems. However, state-of-the-art methods cannot guarantee (i) the convergence when the mapping $h_{n,m}$ is nonlinear (thus the loss is nonsmooth), and (ii) the privacy of the update which is at the epicenter of the FL paradigm. On a high level, we describe our vertical asynchronous federated learning (VAFL) algorithm as follows. During the learning process, from the server side, it waits until receiving a message from an active client

m, which is either (i) **a query** of the loss function's gradient w.r.t. to the embedding vector $h_{n,m}$; or (ii) **a new embedding vector** $h_{n,m}$ calculated using the updated local model parameter θ_m.

To response to the query (i), the server calculates the gradient for client m using its current $\{h_{n,m}\}$, and sends it to the client; and, upon receiving (ii), the server computes the new gradient w.r.t. θ_0 using the embedding vectors it currently has from other clients and updates its model θ_0. For each interaction with server, each *active* client m randomly selects a datum $x_{n,m}$, queries the corresponding gradient w.r.t. $h_{n,m}$ from server, and then it securely uploads the updated embedding vector $h_{n,m}$, and then updates the local model θ_m. The mechanism that ensures secure uploading will be described in Section 11.4. Without introducing cumbersome iteration, client, and sample indexes, we summarize the asynchronous client updates in Algorithm 1.

Specifically, since clients update the model without external coordination, we thereafter use k to denote the global counter (or iteration), which increases by one whenever i) the server receives the new embedding vector $h_{n,m}$ from a client, calculates the gradient, and updates the server model θ_0; and ii) the corresponding client m obtains the gradient w.r.t. $h_{n,m}$, and updates the local model θ_m. Accordingly, we let m_k denote the client index that uploads at iteration k, and n_k denote the sample index used at iteration k.

For notation brevity, we use a single datum n_k for each uncoordinated update in the subsequent algorithms, but the algorithm and its analysis can be easily generalized to a mini-batch of data $\mathcal{N}_k$. Let $\hat{g}_0^k$ denote the stochastic gradients of the loss at n_kth sample w.r.t. server model θ_0 as

$$\hat{g}_0^k = \nabla_{\theta_0}\ell\left(\theta_0^k, h_{n_k,1}^{k-\tau_{n_k,1}^k}, \ldots, h_{n_k,M}^{k-\tau_{n_k,M}^k}; y_{n_k}\right) \tag{11.4a}$$

and the gradients w.r.t. the local model θ_m as

$$\hat{g}_m^k = \nabla_{\theta_m}\ell\left(\theta_0^k, h_{n_k,1}^{k-\tau_{n_k,1}^k}, \ldots, h_{n_k,M}^{k-\tau_{n_k,M}^k}; y_{n_k}\right) \tag{11.4b}$$

$$= \nabla_{\theta_m} h_{n_k,m}^k \nabla_{h_{n_k,m}}\ell\left(\theta_0^k, h_{n_k,1}^{k-\tau_{n_k,1}^k}, \ldots, h_{n_k,M}^{k-\tau_{n_k,M}^k}; y_{n_k}\right).$$

The delay for client m and sample n will increase via

$$\tau_{n,m}^{k+1} = \begin{cases} 1, & m = m_k, n = n_k, \\ \tau_{n,m}^k + 1, & \text{otherwise.} \end{cases} \tag{11.5}$$

With the above short-hand notation, at iteration k, the **server-side** update is

$$\theta_0^{k+1} = \theta_0^k - \eta_0^k \hat{g}_0^k. \tag{11.6}$$

For the **active local client** m_k at iteration k, its update is

$$\theta_{m_k}^{k+1} = \theta_{m_k}^k - \eta_{m_k}^k \hat{g}_{m_k}^k - \eta_{m_k}^k \nabla r\left(\theta_{m_k}^k\right), \tag{11.7a}$$

and for the **other clients** $m \neq m_k$, the update is

$$\theta_m^{k+1} = \theta_m^k, \tag{11.7b}$$

where η_m^k is the step size and m_k is the index of the client for the kth update.

11.2.3 Types of flexible update rules

As shown in (11.4), the stochastic gradients are evaluated using delayed local embedding information $h_m^{k-\tau_{n_k,m}^k}$ from each client m, where $\tau_{n_k,m}^k$ is caused by both asynchronous communication and stochastic sampling. Unexpected delays can cause the divergence of the algorithm. To ensure convergence, we consider several flexible update protocols:

1. *Uniformly bounded delay.* During the training process, whenever the delay of $\tau_{n_k,m}^k$ exceeds $D\,(>0)$, the server must query fresh $h_{n,m}$ from client m before continuing the server update process.
2. *Stochastic unbounded delay.* In this case, the activation of each client is a stochastic process. The delays is determined by the hitting times of the stochastic processes. For example, if the activation of all the clients follows independent Poisson processes, the delays will be geometrically distributed.
3. *t-synchronous update, $t > 0$.* While fully asynchronous update is most flexible, t-synchronous update is also commonly adopted. In this case, the server computes the gradient w.r.t. θ_0 until receiving $\{h_{n,m}\}$ from t different clients, and then updates the server's model using the newly computed gradient. The t-synchronous updates have more stable performance empirically, which is listed in Algorithm 2.

In this chapter, we do not consider dishonest and malicious clients and server, but it is possible to incorporate robust learning techniques into our vertical FL algorithms based on recent works [4,10].

11.3 Convergence analysis

We present the convergence results of our vertical asynchronous federated learning (VAFL) method for the nonconvex and strongly convex cases, and under different update rules. Due to space limitation, this section mainly presents the convergence rates for fully asynchronous version of VAFL (Algorithm 1). The proofs and the convergence results for t-synchronous one (Algorithm 2) can be also found in the online version [9].

To analyze the performance of Algorithm 1, we first make the following assumptions on sampling and smoothness.

Assumption 11.1. *Sample indexes $\{n_k\}$ are i.i.d. from $\{1, \ldots, N\}$ and $\mathbb{P}(n_k = n) = 1/N$. And the variance of gradient follows*

$$\mathbb{E}\left[\left\|g_m^k - \nabla_{\theta_m} F\left(\theta_0^k, \boldsymbol{\theta}^k\right)\right\|^2\right] \le \sigma_m^2, \quad m = 0, \ldots, M, \tag{11.8}$$

where g_m^k is the stochastic gradient $\hat{g}_m^k$ without delay, e.g.,

$$g_m^k = \nabla_{\theta_m} \ell\left(\theta_0^k, h_{n_k,1}^k, \ldots, h_{n_k,M}^k; y_{n_k}\right).$$

Assumption 11.2. *The optimal loss is lower bounded, $F^* > -\infty$. The gradient ∇F is L-Lipschitz continuous, and $\nabla_{\theta_m} F$ is L_m-Lipschitz continuous.*

Assumption 11.1 is common in analyzing SGD [6]. Generally, Assumption 11.2 cannot be satisfied under our general vertical FL formulation with *nonsmooth* local embedding functions such as neural networks. However, techniques will be introduced to enforce smoothness in Section 11.4. To handle asynchrony, we need the following standard assumption in the analysis of asynchronous BCD.

Assumption 11.3. *The uploading client index m_k is random, independent of $m_0, \ldots, m_{k-1}$, and satisfies*

$$\mathbb{P}(m_k = m) = q_m > 0. \tag{11.9}$$

A simple scenario satisfying this assumptions is that the activation of all clients follows independent Poisson processes. That is, if the time difference between two consecutive activations of client m follows an exponential distribution with parameter λ_m, then the activation of client m is a Poisson process with $q_m = \lambda_m^{-1}/\sum_{j=1}^{M}\lambda_j^{-1}$. We first present the convergence results for bounded $\tau_{n_k,m}^k$.

11.3.1 Convergence under bounded delay

We make the following assumption *only* for this subsection.

Assumption 11.4 (Uniformly bounded delay). *For each client m and each sample n, the delay $\tau_{n,m}^k$ at iteration k is bounded by a constant D, i.e., $\tau_{n,m}^k \le D$.*

To handle the delayed information, we leverage the following Lyapunov function for analyzing VAFL:

$$V^k = F\left(\theta_0^k, \boldsymbol{\theta}^k\right) + \sum_{d=1}^{D} \gamma_d \left\|\boldsymbol{\theta}^{k-d+1} - \boldsymbol{\theta}^{k-d}\right\|^2, \tag{11.10}$$

where $\{\gamma_d\}$ are a set of constants to be determined later.

Lemma 11.1. *Under Assumptions 11.1–11.4, for $\eta_0^k \leq \frac{1}{4L}$, $\eta_m^k \leq \frac{1}{4(L+2\gamma_1)}$, it follows that (with $\gamma_{D+1} = 0$)*

$$\mathbb{E}V^{k+1} - \mathbb{E}V^k$$

$$\leq -\left(\frac{\eta_0^k}{2} - L(\eta_0^k)^2\right)\mathbb{E}\left[\left\|\nabla_{\theta_0}F\left(\theta_0^k, \boldsymbol{\theta}^k\right)\right\|^2\right]$$

$$- \sum_{m=1}^{M} q_m \left(\frac{\eta_m^k}{2} - L(\eta_m^k)^2 - 2\gamma_1(\eta_m^k)^2\right)\mathbb{E}\left[\left\|\nabla_{\theta_m}F\left(\theta_0^k, \boldsymbol{\theta}^k\right)\right\|^2\right]$$

$$+ \sum_{d=1}^{D}\left(Dc^k + D\gamma_1 \max_m 2\left(\eta_m^k\right)^2 L_m^2 + \gamma_{d+1} - \gamma_d\right)\mathbb{E}\left[\left\|\boldsymbol{\theta}^{k+1-d} - \boldsymbol{\theta}^{k-d}\right\|^2\right]$$

$$+ L\left(\eta_0^k\right)^2\sigma_0^2 + \sum_{m=1}^{M} q_m\left(L + 2\gamma_1\right)\left(\eta_m^k\right)^2\sigma_m^2. \tag{11.11}$$

If $\{\gamma_d\}$ are chosen properly as specified in the supplementary materials, the first three terms on the right-hand side of (11.11) are negative. By carefully choosing $\{\eta_0^k, \eta_m^k\}$, we can ensure the convergence of Algorithm 1. We first present the convergence for the nonconvex case.

Theorem 11.1. *Under the assumptions of Lemma 11.1, if $\eta_0^k = \eta_m^k = \min\{\frac{1}{4(1+D)L}, \frac{c_\eta}{\sqrt{K}}\}$ with $c_\eta > 0$, we have*

$$\frac{1}{K}\sum_{k=0}^{K-1}\mathbb{E}\left[\left\|\nabla F\left(\theta_0^k, \boldsymbol{\theta}^k\right)\right\|^2\right] = \mathcal{O}\left(1/\sqrt{K}\right). \tag{11.12}$$

Under the additional strong convexity, the convergence rate is improved.

Theorem 11.2. *Assume F is μ-strongly convex. Under the same assumptions of Lemma 11.1, if $\eta^k = \frac{4}{\mu \min_m \sqrt{q_m}(k+K_0)}$ with $K_0 = \frac{4(4(D+1)L + \mu \min_m \sqrt{q_m}D)}{\mu \min_m \sqrt{q_m}}$, then*

$$\mathbb{E}F\left(\theta_0^K, \boldsymbol{\theta}^K\right) - F^* = \mathcal{O}\left(1/K\right). \tag{11.13}$$

It is worth mentioning that, under the assumption of bounded delay, without even coordinating clients' gradient samples and local model updates, our algorithm achieves the same order of convergence as that of block-wise SGD in both nonconvex and strongly convex cases [42]. In addition, the convergence rate in Theorems 11.1 and 11.2 depends on the number of workers M through the maximum delay D, which is typically $D = \mathcal{O}(M)$. Specifically, the condition on step sizes in Theorem 11.1 depends on D, and the condition on step sizes in Theorem 11.2 depends on D through K_0. Therefore, step sizes need to decrease as D increases, otherwise the error will increase as D increases.

11.3.2 Convergence under stochastic unbounded delay

We next present the convergence results for the case where $\tau^k_{n_k,m}$ is unbounded but stochastic. We make the following assumption *only* for this subsection.

Assumption 11.5 (Stochastic unbounded delay). *For each client m, delay $\tau^k_{n_k,m}$ is a random variable with unbounded support. There exists $\bar{p}_m, \rho > 0$ such that*

$$\mathbb{P}\left(\tau^k_{n_k,m} = d\right) \le \bar{p}_m \rho^d. \tag{11.14}$$

Under Assumption 11.5, we obtain the convergence rates of the same order as those the under bounded delay.

Theorem 11.3. *Under Assumptions 11.1–11.3 and 11.5, if $\eta^k_0 = \eta^k_m = \min\left\{\frac{1}{4(1+\min_m \sqrt{c_m})L}, \frac{c_\eta}{\sqrt{K}}\right\}$, we have*

$$\frac{1}{K} \sum_{k=0}^{K-1} \mathbb{E}\left[\left\|\nabla F\left(\theta^k_0, \theta^k\right)\right\|^2\right] = \mathcal{O}\left(1/\sqrt{K}\right). \tag{11.15}$$

Additionally, assuming strong convexity, the convergence rate is improved.

Theorem 11.4. *Assume that F is μ-strongly convex in (θ_0, θ). Then under Assumptions 11.1–11.3 and 11.5, if $\eta^k_0 = \eta^k_m = \frac{2}{\nu(k+K_0)}$ where $K_0 = \frac{4(1+\max_m \sqrt{c_m})L}{\nu}$ and ν is a positive constant depending on μ, L, $\bar{p}_m$, ρ, then it follows that*

$$\mathbb{E}F\left(\theta^K_0, \theta^K\right) - F^* = \mathcal{O}\left(1/K\right). \tag{11.16}$$

11.4 Perturbed local embedding for smoothness

In this section, we introduce a local perturbation technique that is applied by each client to smooth the otherwise non-smooth mapping of local embedding so the convergence analysis in Section 11.3 can be applied.

11.4.1 Local perturbation

Recall that h_m denotes a local embedding function of client m with the parameter θ_m which embeds the information of local data $x_{n,m}$ into its outputs $h_{n,m} := h_m(\theta_m; x_{n,m})$. When h_m is linear embedding, it is as simple as $h_m(\theta_m; x_{n,m}) = x^\top_{n,m}\theta_m$. To further account for nonlinear embedding such as neural networks, we represent $h_{n,m}$ in the following form:

$$u_0 = x_{n,m}, \tag{11.17a}$$

$$u_l = \sigma_l(w_l u_{l-1} + b_l), \quad l = 1, \ldots, L, \tag{11.17b}$$

$$h_{n,m} = u_L, \qquad (11.17c)$$

where σ_l is a linear or nonlinear function, and w_l, b_l corresponds to the parameter θ_m of h_m, e.g., $\theta_m := [w_1, \ldots, w_L, b_1, \ldots, b_L]^\top$. Here we assume that σ_l is $L_{\sigma_l}^0$-Lipschitz continuous. Specially, when h_m is linear, the composite embedding (11.17) corresponds to $L = 1$, $\sigma_1(z) = z$.

We perturb the local embedding function h_m by adding a random neuron with output Z_l at each layer l (cf. (11.17b))

$$u_l = \sigma_l(w_l u_{l-1} + b_l + Z_l), \quad l = 1, \ldots, L, \qquad (11.18)$$

where $Z_1, \ldots, Z_L$ are independent random variables. With properly chosen distributions of $Z_l, l = 1, \ldots, L$, we show below h_m is smooth and enables differential privacy. While it does not exclude other options, our choice of the perturbation distributions is

$$Z_L \sim \mathcal{N}\left(0, c^2\right), \qquad (11.19a)$$

$$Z_l \sim \mathcal{U}[-\sqrt{3}c_l, \sqrt{3}c_l], \quad l = 1, \ldots, L - 1, \qquad (11.19b)$$

where $\mathcal{N}\left(0, c^2\right)$ denotes the Gaussian distribution with zero mean and variance c^2, and $\mathcal{U}[-\sqrt{3}c_l, \sqrt{3}c_l]$ denotes the uniform distribution over $[-\sqrt{3}c_l, \sqrt{3}c_l]$.

11.4.2 Enforcing smoothness

We now connect the perturbed local embedding technique with the convergence theories in Section 11.3.

The convergence results in Section 11.3 hold under Assumption 11.2 which requires the smoothness of the overall loss function. Inspired by the randomized smoothing technique [12,26], we are able to smooth the objective function by taking expectation with respect to the random neurons. Intuitively this follows the fact that the smoothness of a function can be increased by convolving with proper distributions. By adding random neuron Z_l, the landscape of σ_l will be smoothed in expectation with respect to Z_l. And by induction, we can show the smoothness of local embedding vector h_m. Then so long as the loss function ℓ is smooth w.r.t. the local embedding vector h_m, the global objective F is smooth by taking expectation with respect to all the random neurons.

We formally establish this result in the following theorem.

Theorem 11.5. *For each embedding function h_m, if the activation functions follow $\sigma_l = \sigma$, $\forall l$, and the variances of the random neurons follow (11.19), and we assume $\|w_l\|$ is bounded, then with $\mathbf{Z} = [Z_1^\top, \ldots, Z_L^\top]^\top$, the perturbed loss satisfies Assumption 11.2, given by*

$$F_c\left(\theta_0, \theta\right) = \mathbb{E}_{\mathbf{Z}}\left[F(\theta_0, \theta; \mathbf{Z})\right]. \qquad (11.20)$$

Starting from $L_{b_L}^h = L_\sigma^0 d/c$, *the smoothness constants of the local model* θ_m *denoted as* $L_{\theta_m}^{F_c}$ *satisfy the following recursion* $(l = 1, \ldots, L - 1)$:

$$L_{b_l}^h = L_{b_{l+1}}^h \|w_{l+1}\| (L_\sigma^0)^2 + L_\sigma^0 \|w_L\| \cdots L_\sigma^0 \|w_{l+1}\| L_{\tilde{\sigma}}(c_l),$$
$$L_{w_l}^h = \mathbb{E}\left[\|u_{l-1}\|\right] L_{b_l}^h,$$
$$L_{\theta_m}^{F_c} = L_{h_m}^\ell (L_{h_m}^0)^2 + L_\ell^0 \sum_{l=1}^{L} (L_{w_l}^h + L_{b_l}^h) + L_{\theta_m}^r, \qquad (11.21)$$

where $L_{\theta_m}^r$ *is the smoothness constant of the regularizer w.r.t.* θ_m; $L_{b_l}^h$ *and* $L_{w_l}^h$ *are the smoothness constants of the perturbed local embedding* h *w.r.t. the bias* b_l *and weight* w_l; *and* $L_{\tilde{\sigma}}(c_l) = 2\sqrt{d}L_\sigma^0/c_l$ *is the smoothness constant of the neuron at the lth layer under the uniform perturbation.*

Theorem 11.5 implies that the perturbed loss is smooth w.r.t. the local model θ_m, and a large perturbation (large c_l or c) leads to a smaller smoothness constant.

11.5 Numerical tests

To evaluate the performance of our proposed VAFL method, numerical tests have been conducted on both federated logistic regression and neural network models on multiple datasets. We benchmark the fully asynchronous version of VAFL (**async**) in Algorithm 1, and t-synchronous version of VAFL (**t-sync**) in Algorithm 2 with the synchronous block-wise SGD (**sync**), which requires synchronization and sample index coordination among clients in each iteration. To simulate the client asynchrony, we use multiple threads as local clients and add random delay to each client.

11.5.1 VAFL for federated logistic regression

Data allocation. The datasets we choose are CIFAR-10, Parkinson Disease, MNIST, and Fashion MNIST. The batch size is selected to be approximate 0.01 fraction of the entire training dataset. The data are uniformly distributed among $M = 8$ clients for CIFAR-10, $M = 3$ for Parkinson Disease, and $M = 7$ for both MNIST and Fashion MNIST.

The step size is $\eta = 1 \times 10^{-2}$ for Parkinson Disease, $\eta = 2 \times 10^{-4}$ for CIFAR-10, and $\eta = 1 \times 10^{-4}$ for both MNIST and Fashion MNIST.

Parameters. The random delay follows a Poisson distribution with client-specific parameters to reflect heterogeneity. The delay on each worker m follows the Poisson distribution with parameter $2m$ and scaled by $1/2M$, where M is the number of workers and m is the worker index. The expectation of maximum worker delay is one second.

The noise added to the output of each local client follows the Gaussian distribution of each task is $\mathcal{N}(0, 0.01)$ for CIFAR-10, MNIST, and Fashion MNIST, and $\mathcal{N}(0, 1)$

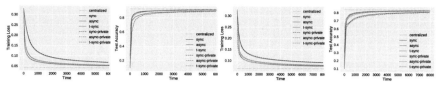

FIGURE 11.2

Training loss and testing accuracy versus clock time (s) in MNIST (left two) and Fashion-MNIST (right two) datasets.

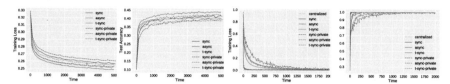

FIGURE 11.3

Training loss and testing accuracy versus clock time (s) in CIFAR10 (left two) and Parkinson disease (right two) datasets.

for Parkinson Disease. For each task, we run the algorithms sufficiently many epochs and record the training loss. Testing accuracy and clock time are recorded at the end of epoch.

We first conduct logistic regression on MNIST, Fashion-MNIST, CIFAR10, and Parkinson disease [30] datasets. The l_2-regularizer coefficient is set as 0.001. We select $M = 7$ for MNIST and MNIST, $M = 8$ for CIFAR10, and $M = 3$ for PD dataset. The training loss and testing accuracy versus wall-clock time are reported in Figs. 11.2 and 11.3. The dashed horizontal lines represent the results trained on the centralized (non-federated) model, and the dashed curves represent private variants of considered algorithms with variance $c = 0.1$. In all cases, the VAFL algorithms learn a federated model with accuracies comparable to that of the centralized model that requires collecting all raw data. And async and t-sync VAFL algorithms have a $2\times$ speed-up in most cases.

11.5.2 VAFL for federated deep learning
11.5.2.1 Training on ModelNet40 dataset
We train a convolutional neural network-based model consisting of two parts: the local embedding models and the server model. Each local model is a 7-layer convolutional neural network. The server part is a centralized 3-layer fully connect neural network. The data we chose is ModelNet40, and we vertically distributed images of the objects in the dataset from 12 angles and assigned to each local client. Each client deals with the data assigned by its local convolutional network and generates a vector whose dimension is 512 as local output.

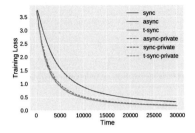

FIGURE 11.4

Training loss of VAFL with nonlinear local embedding on *ModelNet40* dataset.

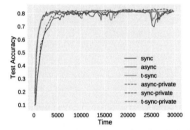

FIGURE 11.5

Testing accuracy of VAFL with local embedding on *ModelNet40* dataset.

Parameters. The random delay follows an exponential distribution with client-specific parameters to reflect heterogeneity. For each worker m, the delay follows the exponential distribution with parameter m. We use ReLU as the local embedding activation function. We add a random noise on the output of each local embedding convolutional layer. The noises follow the following distributions: $\mathcal{U}(-0.1, 0.1)$ (the first two layers), $\mathcal{U}(-0.01, 0.01)$ (the other convolutional layers except for the last layer), and $\mathcal{N}(0, 1)$ (the last convolutional layer). The server then combines the 12 vectors and passes them into the three-layer fully connected neural network and classify into 40 classes. The number of nodes of each layer is 256, 100, and 40. The step size of the local update η_m is 10^{-3} and the server step size $\eta_0 = \frac{\eta_m}{M}$ where M is the number of workers.

We first train a neural network modified from MVCNN with 12-view data [40]. We use $M = 4$ clients, and each client has 3 views of each object and uses a 7-layer CNN as local embedding functions, and the server uses a fully connected network to aggregate the local embedding vectors. Results are plotted in Figs. 11.4 and 11.5. The centralized model in this multi-view learning case coincides with sync, and is omitted. Again async and t-sync have sizable speed-up relative to sync, and private async (with $c = 1$) does not sacrifice much in accuracy.

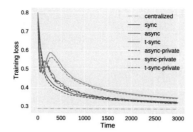

FIGURE 11.6

Training loss of VAFL with local LSTM embedding on *MIMIC-III* dataset.

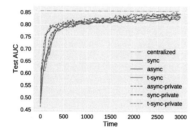

FIGURE 11.7

AUC curve of VAFL with local LSTM embedding on *MIMIC-III* dataset.

11.5.2.2 Training on MIMIC-III dataset

We further test our VAFL algorithm on MIMIC-III—an open dataset comprising de-identified health data [17]. The data are allocated to 4 workers having different feature dimensions. The local embedding part is a two-layer LSTM model and the server part is a fully connected layer. The first layer is a bidirectional LSTM, and the number of units is 16. The second layer is a normal LSTM layer, and the number of units is also 16. The random delay follows an exponential distribution with client-specific parameters to reflect heterogeneity. A random noise following Gaussian distribution $\mathcal{N}(0, 10^{-4})$ is also added to the output of each local embedding layer. We perform the in-hospital mortality prediction as in [16] among $M = 4$ clients. Each client uses LSTM as the embedding function. In Figs. 11.6 and 11.7, we can still observe that async and t-sync VAFL learn a federated model with accuracy comparable to that of the centralized model, and require less time relative to the synchronous FL algorithm. We conduct an ablation study to demonstrate how the convergence rate is affected by different number of clients. Since in the vertical FL scenarios, clients are financial institutions and healthcare companies, the number of which is usually not large, in Figs. 11.8 and 11.9, we report the training loss and the test AUC of VAFL for the number of clients $M = 6, 8, 10$. From these two figures, we can observe that when the number of clients increases, the actual runtime needed to achieve given training loss and test AUC does not decrease. This is because adding more clients in vertical

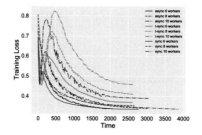

FIGURE 11.8

Training loss of VAFL with local LSTM embedding on *MIMIC-III* critical care dataset under different number of clients.

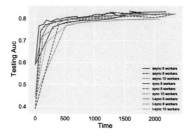

FIGURE 11.9

AUC curve of VAFL with local LSTM embedding on *MIMIC-III* clinical care dataset under different number of clients.

FL does not increase the batch size or reduce the effective variance, and, in contrast, it introduces additional asynchrony that may even impede the learning process. This is different from the *linear speedup* in the horizontal FL setting.

Acknowledgments

This work was supported by National Science Foundation CAREER Award 2047177, and the Rensselaer-IBM AI Research Collaboration (http://airc.rpi.edu), part of the IBM AI Horizons Network (http://ibm.biz/AIHorizons).

References

[1] Martin Abadi, Andy Chu, Ian Goodfellow, H. Brendan McMahan, Ilya Mironov, Kunal Talwar, Li Zhang, Deep learning with differential privacy, in: Proc. ACM SIGSAC Conf. Computer and Communications Security, Vienna, Austria, October 2016, pp. 308–318.
[2] Alham Fikri Aji, Kenneth Heafield, Sparse communication for distributed gradient descent, in: Proc. Conf. Empirical Methods Natural Language Process., Copenhagen, Den-

mark, Sep. 2017, pp. 440–445.

[3] Dan Alistarh, Demjan Grubic, Jerry Li, Ryota Tomioka, Milan Vojnovic, QSGD: communication-efficient SGD via gradient quantization and encoding, in: Proc. Advances in Neural Info. Process. Syst., Long Beach, CA, Dec. 2017, pp. 1709–1720.

[4] Arjun Nitin Bhagoji, Supriyo Chakraborty, Prateek Mittal, Seraphin Calo, Analyzing federated learning through an adversarial lens, in: Proc. Intl. Conf. Machine Learn., Long Beach, CA, Jun. 2019, pp. 634–643.

[5] Keith Bonawitz, Vladimir Ivanov, Ben Kreuter, Antonio Marcedone, H. Brendan McMahan, Sarvar Patel, Daniel Ramage, Aaron Segal, Karn Seth, Practical secure aggregation for privacy-preserving machine learning, in: Proc. ACM Conf. on Comp. and Comm. Security, Dallas, TX, Oct. 2017, pp. 1175–1191.

[6] Léon Bottou, Frank E. Curtis, Jorge Nocedal, Optimization methods for large-scale machine learning, arXiv:1606.04838, Jun. 2016.

[7] Loris Cannelli, Francisco Facchinei, Vyacheslav Kungurtsev, Gesualdo Scutari, Asynchronous parallel algorithms for nonconvex big-data optimization: model and convergence, arXiv:1607.04818, July 2016.

[8] Tianyi Chen, Georgios Giannakis, Tao Sun, Wotao Yin, LAG: lazily aggregated gradient for communication-efficient distributed learning, in: Proc. Advances in Neural Info. Process. Syst., Montreal, Canada, Dec. 2018, pp. 5050–5060.

[9] Tianyi Chen, Xiao Jin, Yuejiao Sun, Wotao Yin, VAFL: a method of vertical asynchronous federated learning, arXiv:2007.06081, Jun. 2020.

[10] Yudong Chen, Lili Su, Jiaming Xu, Distributed statistical machine learning in adversarial settings: Byzantine gradient descent, in: Proc. of the ACM on Measurement and Analysis of Computing Systems, New York, NY, 2017, pp. 1–25.

[11] Jinshuo Dong, Aaron Roth, Weijie J. Su, Gaussian differential privacy, arXiv:1905.02383, May 2019.

[12] John C. Duchi, Peter L. Bartlett, Martin J. Wainwright, Randomized smoothing for stochastic optimization, SIAM Journal on Optimization 22 (2) (2012) 674–701.

[13] Cynthia Dwork, Aaron Roth, et al., The algorithmic foundations of differential privacy, Foundations and Trends in Theoretical Computer Science 9 (3–4) (2014) 211–407.

[14] Jihun Hamm, Yingjun Cao, Mikhail Belkin, Learning privately from multiparty data, in: Proc. Intl. Conf. Machine Learn., New York, NY, Jun. 2016, pp. 555–563.

[15] Stephen Hardy, Wilko Henecka, Hamish Ivey-Law, Richard Nock, Giorgio Patrini, Guillaume Smith, Brian Thorne, Private federated learning on vertically partitioned data via entity resolution and additively homomorphic encryption, arXiv:1711.10677, Nov. 2017.

[16] Hrayr Harutyunyan, Hrant Khachatrian, David C. Kale, Greg Ver Steeg, Aram Galstyan, Multitask learning and benchmarking with clinical time series data, Scientific Data 6 (1) (2019) 96.

[17] Alistair E.W. Johnson, Tom J. Pollard, Lu Shen, H. Lehman Li-wei, Mengling Feng, Mohammad Ghassemi, Benjamin Moody, Peter Szolovits, Leo Anthony Celi, Roger G. Mark, MIMIC-III, a freely accessible critical care database, Scientific Data 3 (160035) (2016).

[18] Peter Kairouz, H. Brendan McMahan, Brendan Avent, Aurélien Bellet, Mehdi Bennis, Arjun Nitin Bhagoji, Keith Bonawitz, Zachary Charles, Graham Cormode, Rachel Cummings, et al., Advances and open, problems in federated learning, arXiv:1912.04977, Dec. 2019.

[19] Jakub Konečný, H. Brendan McMahan, Daniel Ramage, Peter Richtárik, Federated optimization: distributed machine learning for on-device intelligence, arXiv:1610.02527, Oct. 2016.

[20] Jakub Konečný, H. Brendan McMahan, Felix X. Yu, Peter Richtárik, Ananda Theertha Suresh, Dave Bacon, Federated learning: strategies for improving communication efficiency, arXiv:1610.05492, Oct. 2016.

[21] Li Tian, Anit Kumar Sahu, Ameet Talwalkar, Virginia Smith, Federated learning: challenges, methods, and future directions, IEEE Signal Processing Magazine 37 (3) (May 2020) 50–60.

[22] Weiyu Li, Yaohua Liu, Zhi Tian, Qing Ling, Communication-censored linearized ADMM for decentralized consensus optimization, IEEE Transactions on Signal and Information Processing over Networks 6 (December 2019) 18–34.

[23] Xiangru Lian, Ce Zhang, Huan Zhang, Cho-Jui Hsieh, Wei Zhang, Ji Liu, Can decentralized algorithms outperform centralized algorithms? A case study for decentralized parallel stochastic gradient descent, in: Proc. Advances in Neural Info. Process. Syst., Long Beach, CA, Dec. 2017, pp. 5330–5340.

[24] Paul Pu Liang, Terrance Liu, Liu Ziyin, Ruslan Salakhutdinov, Louis-Philippe Morency, Think locally, act globally: federated learning with local and global representations, arXiv:2001.01523, Jan. 2020.

[25] Brendan McMahan, Eider Moore, Daniel Ramage, Seth Hampson, Blaise Aguera y Arcas, Communication-efficient learning of deep networks from decentralized data, in: Proc. Intl. Conf. Artificial Intell. and Stat., Fort Lauderdale, FL, Apr. 2017, pp. 1273–1282.

[26] Yurii Nesterov, Vladimir Spokoiny, Random gradient-free minimization of convex functions, Foundations of Computational Mathematics 17 (2) (2017) 527–566.

[27] Chaoyue Niu, Fan Wu, Shaojie Tang, Lifeng Hua, Rongfei Jia, Chengfei Lv, Zhihua Wu, Guihai Chen, Secure federated submodel learning, arXiv:1911.02254, Nov. 2019.

[28] Zhimin Peng, Yangyang Xu, Ming Yan, Wotao Yin, ARock: an algorithmic framework for asynchronous parallel coordinate updates, SIAM Journal on Scientific Computing 38 (5) (Sept. 2016) 2851–2879.

[29] Meisam Razaviyayn, Mingyi Hong, Zhi-Quan Luo, A unified convergence analysis of block successive minimization methods for nonsmooth optimization, SIAM Journal on Optimization 23 (2) (Jun. 2013) 1126–1153.

[30] C. Okan Sakar, Gorkem Serbes, Aysegul Gunduz, Hunkar C. Tunc, Hatice Nizam, Betul Erdogdu Sakar, Melih Tutuncu, Tarkan Aydin, M. Erdem Isenkul, Hulya Apaydin, A comparative analysis of speech signal processing algorithms for Parkinson's disease classification and the use of the tunable q-factor wavelet transform, Applied Soft Computing 74 (2019) 255–263.

[31] Frank Seide, Hao Fu, Jasha Droppo, Gang Li, Dong Yu, 1-bit stochastic gradient descent and its application to data-parallel distributed training of speech DNNs, in: Proc. Conf. Intl. Speech Comm. Assoc., Singapore, Sept. 2014.

[32] Virginia Smith, Chao-Kai Chiang, Maziar Sanjabi, Ameet S. Talwalkar, Federated multi-task learning, in: Proc. Advances in Neural Info. Process. Syst., Long Beach, CA, Dec. 2017, pp. 4427–4437.

[33] Sebastian U. Stich, Jean-Baptiste Cordonnier, Martin Jaggi, Sparsified SGD with memory, in: Proc. Advances in Neural Info. Process. Syst., Montreal, Canada, Dec. 2018, pp. 4447–4458.

[34] Nikko Strom, Scalable distributed DNN training using commodity GPU cloud computing, in: Proc. Conf. Intl. Speech Comm. Assoc., Dresden, Germany, Sept. 2015.

[35] Chang Sun, Lianne Ippel, Johan van Soest, Birgit Wouters, Alexander Malic, Onaopepo Adekunle, Bob van den Berg, Ole Mussmann, Annemarie Koster, Carla van der Kallen, et

al., A privacy-preserving infrastructure for analyzing personal health data in a vertically partitioned scenario, Studies in Health Technology and Informatics 264 (2019) 373–377.

[36] Tao Sun, Robert Hannah, Wotao Yin, Asynchronous coordinate descent under more realistic assumptions, in: Proc. Advances in Neural Info. Process. Syst., Long Beach, CA, Dec. 2017, pp. 6183–6191.

[37] Latanya Sweeney, k-anonymity: a model for protecting privacy, International Journal of Uncertainty, Fuzziness and Knowledge-Based Systems 10 (05) (2002) 557–570.

[38] Jianyu Wang, Gauri Joshi, Cooperative SGD: a unified framework for the design and analysis of communication-efficient SGD algorithms, arXiv:1808.07576, Aug. 2018.

[39] Tianyu Wu, Kun Yuan, Qing Ling, Wotao Yin, Ali H. Sayed, Decentralized consensus optimization with asynchrony and delays, IEEE Transactions on Signal and Information Processing over Networks 4 (2) (Apr. 2017) 293–307.

[40] Zhirong Wu, Shuran Song, Aditya Khosla, Fisher Yu, Linguang Zhang, Xiaoou Tang, Jianxiong Xiao, 3D ShapeNets: a deep representation for volumetric shapes, in: Proceedings of the IEEE Conference on Computer Vision and Pattern Recognition, 2015, pp. 1912–1920.

[41] Yangyang Xu, Wotao Yin, A block coordinate descent method for regularized multiconvex optimization with applications to nonnegative tensor factorization and completion, SIAM Journal on Imaging Sciences 6 (3) (2013) 1758–1789.

[42] Yangyang Xu, Wotao Yin, Block stochastic gradient iteration for convex and nonconvex optimization, SIAM Journal on Optimization 25 (3) (2015) 1686–1716.

[43] Qiang Yang, Yang Liu, Tianjian Chen, Yongxin Tong, Federated machine learning: concept and applications, ACM Transactions on Intelligent Systems and Technology 10 (2) (Jan. 2019).

[44] Andrew C. Yao, Protocols for secure computations, in: Annual Symposium on Foundations of Computer Science, Chicago, Illinois, 1982, pp. 160–164.

[45] Bicheng Ying, Kun Yuan, Ali H. Sayed, Supervised learning under distributed features, IEEE Transactions on Signal Processing 67 (4) (Nov. 2018) 977–992.

[46] Hao Yu, Sen Yang, Shenghuo Zhu, Parallel restarted SGD with faster convergence and less communication: demystifying why model averaging works for deep learning, in: Proc. AAAI Conf. Artificial Intell., vol. 33, 2019, pp. 5693–5700.

Hyperparameter tuning for federated learning – systems and practices

12

Syed Zawad[a] **and Feng Yan**[b]

[a]*University of Nevada, Reno, NV, United States*
[b]*University of Houston, Houston, TX, United States*

12.1 Introduction

Machine learning models have two types of parameters that directly influence the performance of the model. The parameters of the first type are directly integrated within the model itself (such as weights and biases of neurons in neural networks) and are initialized and updated through the data learning process called fitting model parameters. The other parameters are called hyperparameters and cannot be directly updated through learning. These hyperparameters are used to mainly to configure models for training. The most commonly discussed in the deep learning setting are the *batch size*, *optimizer* and *learning rate* parameters, but others such as *momentum* and *dropout ratios* also exist. One of the main challenges of building effective machine learning models is to tune the hyperparameters to get the best possible model parameters. The values for hyperparameters vary significantly across models and datasets with rarely any transferable intuitions between them, making the hyperparameter tuning (or hyperparameter optimization, HPO for short) a largely trial-and-error based time-consuming process.

For traditional centralized model training, the hyperparameters are tuned towards a singular goal – the highest possible model performance. While resource consumption and time to converge are still concerns, they are secondary goals due to the expectations that hardware capabilities tend to improve over time and the ML engineers have full control over them [25,35]. As such, there has been much work in the literature that focused on providing guidelines for tuning them [17,23,31,36], while another large area of study is the automation of the tuning process [35]. Both areas have resulted in significant advances in the scope of hyperparameter tuning.

The cross-device federated learning (FL) paradigm was introduced as a means of training on large amounts of user data in a privacy-preserving and communication efficient manner. It does so through a distributed learning paradigm that addresses the privacy concerns while supporting collaborative learning across different data owners (also known as clients) [16,32]. In FL, a shared global model is managed by a central server, and different client devices perform local learning with on-device data. The client then sends the local learning model parameters to the centralized server for aggregation (also known as aggregator). Finally, the global model parameters are sent back to the client devices. In this process, since the user data never needs to migrate from mobile devices to the client device, data privacy is preserved. Although federated learning offers support on privacy and security, it comes at the cost of introducing several new practical challenges [19]. For our scope, we focus on three specific properties. First, due to the training process being offloaded to the actual client hardware, we lose much control over the training resources. The client devices can vary significantly in training capacities (a problem dubbed *resource heterogeneity*) resulting in varying amounts of consumption and training times. Second, the devices can also be expected to have extremely limited hardware capabilities. For example, IoT devices such as sensor arrays [14] may not be capable of fitting more than a batch size of 1 in their local memory, constraints are also posed due to the finite energy and availability of roaming clients such as mobile phones. Therefore, traditional hyperparameter settings may not be efficient for such highly constrained training environments. Lastly, a cross-device FL system [24] introduces additional hyperparameters such as local epochs, number of clients to select each round, device timeouts, etc., which require further tuning and directly impact the convergence rate, time, and resources.

These additional properties for FL systems require special considerations when designing an efficient training system. In fact, it can be argued that training efficiency is more important for FL systems than for traditional systems due to the fact that much less control is provided to us under a much more constrained environment. For example, training a deep neural network on a mobile device must be done in such a way that it does not interfere with the user's experience while at the same time trying to train as much as possible with the limited energy and computational capacity. Since the largest determinants of resource consumption, apart from the model size, are the hyperparameters themselves, special care must be taken to design them for cross-device FL frameworks.

For this chapter, we focus on the nuances of hyperparameter tuning in cross-device federated learning from the system's perspective. Specifically, we start by listing the various resource types that must be taken into consideration when designing an efficient cross-device FL system. We discuss briefly how they are impacted and why they are important, especially in the FL setting. We then go into in-depth discussions about the different hyperparameters that are involved in the FL training process for the state-of-practice FL system [2,24] by breaking them down into two groups: hyperparameters on the server side (which are unique to FL) and those on the client side. We discuss how each group impacts the learning process, as well as the resource costs, and explain how there often exists a trade-off between them. We then discuss the system challenges of trying to design an efficient FL training system for hyperparameter tuning. We will talk about each of the challenges at length and provide explanations as to why they are relevant to FL hyperparameter tuning in general and how they impact resource costs. Lastly, we will discuss some of the most relevant state-of-practice and state-of-the-art works that try to address these issues.

We will talk about how they affect the overall resource of efficiency and where they are lacking. In doing so, we will highlight how they all fail to consider the resource perspective, which leaves room for exploring open problems that still exist in this setting.

12.2 Systems resources

For this section, we provide the list of system resources that need to be considered when designing the state-of-practice FL framework proposed in [16,24]. We give a brief overview of what each of these resources mean and why they are significant in the cross-device FL setting. For the rest of the chapter, we will use the following metrics in the appropriate context and discuss the impact of hyperparameter value choices on these resources:

- **Computation** – This is the fundamental type of resource provided by the hardware for training by the processing units of a device that performs the basic arithmetic operations required for the execution of the training procedure. There are many variations of computational resources such as CPUs, GPUs, TPUs, etc., and further varieties within each of them which are too many to list. These variations result in different amounts of time and energy consumed for the same computation, and since there can be a large variety of them in a cross-device FL system, they can be hard to manage and make efficient use of. The simplest measure of computation consumption is the number of floating-point operations (FLOPS) used.
- **Memory** – Memory is measure of how many operations can be held at any one time to be available for computation. It is a direct limitation in that machine learning models that are above a certain size and cannot fit within the memory will not be available for training. There are also a wide variety of memory types such as L1 and L2 caches, RAM, ROM, etc. We must try to limit the amount of memory consumed since in cross-device FL systems, the memory is shared among many different applications within each device and therefore how much memory is consumed for training can determine whether we can train the model at all without interfering with the device's normal functionality. It is measured in bytes.
- **Energy** – It is the basic resource for all computational systems: the less energy used, the more efficient a system. In terms of cross-device FL, devices can be running on battery power and so have limited time to function. As such, designing systems that reduce energy consumption enables training for longer periods as well as reduces costs. It is measured in watts and joules.
- **Bandwidth** – The amount of memory that can be transferred within a time limit is defined as the device's bandwidth. In edge-devices, bandwidth is severely limited due to the lack of high-powered hardware as well as its intermittent availability. It also directly impacts the time and energy consumed during training and so must

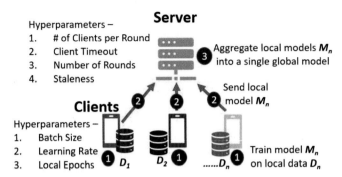

FIGURE 12.1

Cross-Device Federated Learning System Diagram, showing the training steps in a cross-device FL system and the hyperparameters to be tuned on the server and client sides.

also be used efficiently. It is measured in bits per second (b/s) or total bits transferred.

12.3 Cross-device FL hyperparameters

Next we provide the list of hyperparameters that are available by default for all baseline cross-device FL frameworks, which is based on the system proposed in [16,24]. We break down the hyperparameters into two parts: 1) *Client-side* – used for local on-device training, and 2) *Server-side* – used to control the complete training system. The full system diagram and its corresponding hyperparameters are shown in Fig. 12.1.

12.3.1 Client-side hyperparameters

The client-side (device) hyperparameters directly impact the local training process. The local training process determines the amount of computation, memory and energy used, and so they must be tuned carefully.

12.3.1.1 Batch size

This is the total number of datapoints that are used for one training pass and it determines a significant portion of the training time. With larger batch sizes, higher amounts of memory are used and therefore there is an upper-bound to it. At the same time, there are certain computational devices that reduce training time per datapoint with larger batch sizes, thereby reducing the overall training times and sometimes energy as well. However, this is not true for all computational devices and there are also diminishing returns for those that do benefit from batching. Additionally, there have been works that show that larger batch sizes may be beneficial for training [30] so it is in our best interest to use large batch sizes. For low-powered edge devices, which makes up a majority of use cases for the cross-device FL systems, however, this may not be possible or there may be a point above which the advantages become too costly. For FL systems such as FedSGD [24], it also determines the amount of bandwidth consumed. As such, the local training batch size must be chosen very carefully.

12.3.1.2 Learning rate

The learning rate is the magnitude of the step a model takes towards a direction in search for the optima. While this does not directly impact resources, it is one of the most important determinants of how fast a model converges to the optima which determines how long the training takes and thus the total amount of resources consumed. Too aggressive tuning will result in sub-par models but take less time to converge, and vice-versa. Learning rate scheduling mechanisms, in addition to optimizers, are extremely influential to the efficient training of models and therefore must be carefully tuned.

12.3.1.3 Local epochs

This is the total number of times the local model is trained on the full local dataset. It determines the total time and resources required for one FL training round and the frequency of communication with the server since a higher number of local epochs means more training is done per round on the local device and more time is spent between sending models to the server. More local epochs result in better local training and faster convergence, but too many could mean overfitting on local data and overall worse model performance along with more local resources consumed. As such, there are trade-offs to keep in mind while tuning this hyperparameter.

12.3.2 Server-side hyperparameters

The server-side hyperparameters provide control over the overall training procedure such as how many clients to train and for how long, which are also strong determinants to the overall training resources consumed.

12.3.2.1 Clients per round

Cross-device FL systems usually have a large number of clients/devices acting as data siloes. This hyperparameter determines how many are selected in each round of training. More clients selected can result in better convergence rates and better model performance depending on the underlying data distributions. However, more clients per round also mean more overall local resources being consumed for training. Also, in some cases increased number of clients per round do not cause any significant boost in performance and therefore more is not always better. More clients selected also mean that there are higher chances of selecting devices that can drop out of the training process in the middle, which causes a waste of resources and time.

12.3.2.2 Client timeout / client participation ratio

In cross-device FL, it is expected that clients have intermittent availability and can even end up not participating even if chosen for training [2]. The client timeout determines how long to wait for a client's response before determining that it has dropped out of the training process for this round, while the client participation ratio means waiting for a certain percentage of the clients to respond before moving on to the next round (both perform the same basic function of having a cutoff limit on client participation). A longer cutoff time/ratio means the amount of training time per round increases due to having to wait longer while a too short timeout can cause wasted resources as the slower clients end up throwing away their local models due to not meeting the limits.

12.3.2.3 Number of rounds

This is the total number of rounds that are spent training for the full FL process. A higher number of rounds can result in a final model with better performance, but it can also result in a larger amount of total resource consumed and longer training times.

12.3.2.4 Staleness

For asynchronous FL systems, the server does not wait for devices to return their local models before aggregating to a new global model and moving on to a new round. As such, stale updates from clients too far back in the training procedure may worsen the overall model performance or result in longer convergence rates [7]. The staleness hyperparameter determines how old of a local model should be used for updating to a new model. Too high of a staleness will result in worse models, while a too low value will result in wasted local resources.

While other hyperparameters exist, they do not directly impact FL resources and so are out of the scope of this chapter. Also, recent works have proposed more complex methods of aggregation which introduce extra hyperparameters, requiring further discussions, which we provide briefly at the end of the chapter.

12.4 System challenges in FL HPO

In this section, we discuss the system challenges of tuning hyperparameters in the cross-device FL setting and point out some of the most important works that perform hyperparameter tuning. While more works such as these exist, we limit ourselves to the papers that have seen applications as state-of-practice, those that have served as seminal works and have inspired further research in this area, and those that provide unique insights into the hyperparameter choices' impact. We provide discussions from the hyperparameter tuning's impact on system resources perspective.

12.4.1 **Data privacy**

One of the major reasons for the popularity of FL is its data privacy property. Ideally, user data on which we train the global model should not be observable. While this is good news for privacy and security, it makes hyperparameter tuning much more challenging since the machine learning engineers have no method of controlling or even observing the data they train their model on. As a result, the tuning method must be done blindly which can result in sub-par model performance.

Such a problem can be addressed by having custom tuning on each device and/or creating a singular set of hyperparameters, but doing so would require tuning on-device since the data cannot be moved to the aggregator. This has severe implications on resource usage since instead of being able to tune on a high-powered server system, we have to rely on edge devices over whose systems we have little control. This can result in wildly varying and unpredictable levels of resource consumption.

12.4.2 **Data heterogeneity**

Data heterogeneity is a property of cross-device FL where the data distributions can be vastly different between each device. This is a challenging problem to tackle as well since having to maintain the privacy means we cannot determine the data distribution variations directly. As such, a set of training hyperparameters that works well for one client may not be good for another. One popular example is the case of overfitting on biased data [2,10,20,33,39]. Here, the hyperparameter tuning is done on a single device which contains a specific type of data, which is why the client-side hyperparameters can be tuned to give good performance on the test set for that client's local data. However, since we are unaware of the other local datasets, we inadvertently end up with a singular set of hyperparameters that have varying degrees of effectiveness on the different local datasets. Papers such as [10,26] show that such singular methods of tuning can result in biased models as well.

This diversity of data means there is a need for a diverse set of hyperparameters as well. However, since we are unable to directly observe this diversity, we have to resort to tuning on each individual client separately in order to find the best possible hyperparameter for a specific data distribution. In the best case where there is no significant data heterogeneity, we can use a single set of hyperparameters for all devices. In the worst case where each device has a completely different data distribution, we need to tune them all individually. However, in some privacy constraint definitions [37] even knowledge of the underlying data distribution can be a violation, in which case we may have to assume the worst case possibility and simply tune on each device. This leads to the obvious problem of having to use up significantly more overall resources than if we had to tune on a single device only and so reducing edge device resource usage becomes challenging.

12.4.3 **Resource limitations**

A majority of use cases in cross-device FL involves training on edge devices [2] which usually contain limited resources. Of the resource types pointed out in Section 12.2, computation and bandwidth lead to longer local training times, while energy and memory impose hard limits on the training capacity. Some edge devices can be so limited that a single pass on relatively smaller deep neural networks can take a few seconds [21]. For devices which can have better hardware resources such as modern mobile phones, resource constraints must still be imposed since the hardware is shared by other tenant applications which must not be interfered with so as not to inhibit the user experience.

Even the state-of-the-art automated hyperparameter tuning techniques for centralized deep learning systems [1,12,13] require an initial trial-and-error process (sometimes called the *exploration* phase) whereby it can gain some prior knowledge of the range of possible hyperparameters. This trial-and-error process involves multiple training runs with different sets. As mentioned above, even a single training pass can be highly costly to perform for an edge device, so doing multiple passes becomes infeasible in some cases. As such, we need to make efficient resource utilization or offload as much of the computation to the server as possible without having to tune on-device. However, as mentioned above, data cannot be transferred to the server due to privacy concerns and so developing a system which can transfer the resource usage for tuning from the device to the server without violating privacy is a strong technical challenge.

12.4.4 Scalability

The need for tuning on each individual device also raises the question of the scale at which hyperparameters must be tuned. In traditional centralized training systems, the data is homogeneous and controllable, along with residing on the server. This allows the usage of a singular set of hyperparameters to be used for a single model. Additionally, since the server hardware is expected to be more powerful than edge devices, the ML engineers have much more control over the resources, which allows for the possibility of predictable and efficient usage. While much of the focus on hyperparameter tuning is on the reduction of the search space [13,18,35], in order to reduce time and cost of exploration, one significant advantage they have is that they generally need to find only one set of hyperparameters for a single model, the scalability is defined in terms of how many hyperparameters there are to tune. For a federated learning system, there is the possibility of having multiple sets of hyperparameters since each individual client can have its own custom local hyperparameter set. This means that the tuned hyperparameters must scale with the number of devices in addition to the ranges of the hyperparameter values. As such, in the worst case scenario, the number of hyperparameter sets that need to be generated can be directly proportional to the number of clients involved in the FL process. Given that this number can range in the thousands, hyperparameter tuning resource consumption can quickly become a highly expensive process. Developing techniques that can scale well (such as a method of transferable hyperparameter sets, reducing exploration phases, offloading computation to the server, etc.) is a challenge here since it requires some level of control over the resources and information on the data, which are limited in FL systems.

12.4.5 **Resource heterogeneity**

Resource heterogeneity is the phenomenon where different devices have different sets of hardware for local training. This results in different training times and resource usage for the same model which leads to unpredictability in the system, making it hard to design a resource efficient framework. The server-side hyperparameters are particularly affected by this property.

In an FL system where client device latencies for training can vary by magnitudes [2,3,5], a single training round can have significantly varying training times depending on the number of clients selected per round and the timeout hyperparameters. The higher the number of clients per round, the higher the probability of selecting slow clients in a round. Since the time per round is upper-bounded by the slowest client selected in that round, the mean time per round will increase, which results in an overall longer training period for the same number of rounds. Several practical problems arise from this. First, it results in client and server resources remaining idle while waiting for the slower clients to respond. Second, waiting during a time window may result in missing out on client availability. To elaborate, clients in an FL system may not always be available for training due to certain criteria they must fulfill in order to be eligible for training such as having enough battery power left, in sleep mode, and so on [2]. Therefore, the intermittently trainable clients are usually selected opportunistically to get the most out of every client's data. This may become hampered due to excessively long waiting times since the server may end up missing out on the available clients within a time period. Thirdly, longer time periods for training also mean more resources are being used over time.

One simple solution in this case is to keep the number of clients per round to a minimum. However, that poses several problems as well. The most significant problem is that fewer clients can result in slower rates of convergence, i.e., more rounds of training are required to achieve good model performance. This has the implication of requiring more time to train and more resources used. Additionally, fewer clients per round also mean that intermittently available clients may not get chosen during the full training process due to the probability of selection being too low. Less clients per round also means that there may not be enough clients chosen for participation to cover all available local data resulting in sub-par training. Therefore, tuning this hyperparameter quickly becomes a balancing act between resource and model performance tradeoffs, and is highly sensitive to the underlying available resources for the specific system. Keeping all these tradeoffs in mind and tuning this hyperparameter accordingly is quite challenging.

Another significant server-side hyperparameter here is the client timeout or participation ratio. This value acts as a hard cutoff on the upper time limit of a round since it assumes the clients above the cutoff period or ratio will not be participating any more and the system moves on to the next round. In a highly heterogeneous system, this value can reduce the overall training time significantly, and consequently the total amount of resources used as well. A high value here will mean that the server waits for longer times between each round and has the same problems as having a high number of clients per round. However, too low of a value here will mean that some slower clients will never participate at all, leading to sub-par training. It will also mean that a high proportion of clients that get selected will end up training locally only to end up having the server discard it due to taking too long to respond, which leads to waste of already constrained resources.

One way to avoid the above problems is to design an asynchronous FL system such as in [4,7]. However, doing so introduces the staleness hyperparameter in lieu of the others, which also suffers from the same problems. Too high of a staleness value will mean a slower rate of convergence since the training process becomes noisy due to older local models, which results in more time and resources consumed. Low staleness values will result in a waste of resources due to throwing out older models. As such, all the server side hyperparameters must be tuned very specifically by keeping the overall resource heterogeneity in mind. Considering the variety of heterogeneity possibilities, it becomes very challenging to tune these hyperparameters without compromising between resource use and waste.

12.4.6 Dynamic data

Another unique property of FL systems is that the underlying client data changes over time. Cross-device FL relies on user generated data, and so as applications are used for longer more and more data gets generated on the same device. As such, the FL training process is somewhat dynamic due to the constantly changing data distributions. A such, since client-side hyperparameters need to be tuned based on local data, the question arises of *how frequently should we tune the hyperparameters?* In centralized systems, the data is static and so a single set will suffice over time. However, since that is not the case with FL, it may be necessary to tune over time due to the changing data distributions. As explained previously, hyperparameter tuning in FL is already quite challenging. Having to do it multiple times for the same global model further exacerbates the problems and makes it an even more challenging to solve. Additionally, the server-side hyperparameter of total rounds is directly related to this problem since rapidly shifting local datasets would require more training rounds to converge while consuming more resources at the same time. Thus, determining the frequency of hyperparameter tuning such that it conserves the limited resources while getting good model performance is a challenging problem.

12.4.7 Participation fairness and client dropouts

Lastly, another major hurdle to designing good FL frameworks is the unpredictability of participation of the clients themselves. As mentioned before, clients can end up dropping out within a training round or be unavailable for training when the server is starting a new round. This results in skewed client participation, i.e., some clients have datapoints that are not selected for training at all which can result in bias and fairness issues in the global model [26]. Additionally, it may also lead to unfair resource usage. Since training is done on client hardware, due to hyperparameters such as timeouts, participation ratios, and number of clients per round, the server may end up using some clients' hardware more than others. As such, some devices will see more resource usage while others will see less (or sometimes none at all) while still reaping the benefits of the well-trained global model. As such, resource cost is skewed in favor of one client, while other clients end up paying more. A resource-efficient system should also take in to account a fair distribution of resource usage, which is challenging to do since we have little to no control over the participation rates of the devices.

12.5 **State-of-the-art**

Now that we have discussed the overarching system challenges in hyperparameter tuning for cross-device FL, we next move on to giving an overview of the current literature in this scope. We point out the most recent relevant works that focus on tuning hyperparameters in the FL space, and discuss their implications for practical FL scenarios. This leads us to highlight many shortcomings of current frameworks which leaves room for future research opportunities.

HANF [29]. Hyperparameter and Neural Architecture Search in Federated Learning (HANF) is the latest work that aims at solving both neural architecture search [9] and hyperparameter tuning in the cross-device FL space. It does so in two steps – search and evaluation. In the search stage, it performs hyperparameter optimization and neural architecture search alternatively. It does so by leveraging the multi-armed bandit game where the initial neural architecture and its initialized model weights reflect the environment that is used to derive the reward, and the hyperparameters are defined as a set of discrete actions an agent can choose from. After choosing a set of hyperparameters, the initial model is trained, and the validation loss increase of the network before and after the training steps is used to compute the loss. In the evaluation phase, the standard differentiable, cell-based neural architecture search is performed (as was first proposed in DARTs [22]) by keeping the best hyperparameter set found from the previous search phase. All of this exploration is performed on the client's hardware, and the authors limit themselves to only exploring the client-side hyperparameters. After the search and exploration phases are done by the clients, each client sends his/her individual trained differentiable architectures to the server for aggregation to generate a new global differentiable architecture.

The main focus of this paper is to enable hyperparameter tuning and NAS at the same time in cross-device FL systems. This helps generate both model and hyperparameters suitable for each individual device, ensuring an overall better global model performance after aggregation. Their results show that they clearly outperform other approaches. However, it is clear that their method is highly costly for edge devices. While the differentiable architecture search can be made one-shot so as to reduce its cost to as much as a single round of training for the evaluation phase, the search phase adds significant extra computational overhead since it has to choose a set of hyperparameters, train for a few steps, generate the reward, and move back to exploring other hyperparameters. This requires significantly extra computation, as well as a lot longer training time in a round which consequently leads to higher energy usage as well. Differentiable architectures are also heavier in size than single models, meaning they also take up much more on-device memory and bandwidth per round. Since it takes longer to train per round, it is also possible that edge devices with high rates of intermittent availability may drop out in the middle of training and thus waste resources. Additionally, scalability is also an issue since this search phase must be done on a large portion of the available clients. This framework is effective in terms of performing NAS and hyperparameter tuning, but is only feasible for cross-device systems which have an abundance of resources and time. The authors barely discuss the resource efficiency parts, and we point out here that there is much room for exploration for it.

FLoRA [40]. FLoRA performs a single-shot, client-side, and on-device hyperparameter tuning to generate a single set of hyperparameters for the FL training process. Once found, the FL training proceeds as normal. The authors start with the hypothesis that if the same set of hyperparameter performs well for a single task on a significant portion of the clients' local datasets, then it is a strong candidate for overall FL training. For their method, they start by having each client perform hyperparameter tuning locally with any adaptive scheme. The clients do so asynchronously and each generates combinations of explored hyperparameters and their corresponding loss values to be sent to the server aggregator. These sets are then used to generate an aggregated loss surface upon which a regressor method such as a Gaussian process regressor [28] is trained to do a one-shot prediction of as single set of hyperparameters best suited for the task.

There are some advantages of this method from the system perspective. First, it performs the hyperparameter exploration asynchronously for each client, meaning that there is little to no bottleneck due to slower clients. Second, it only sends the hyperparameter set and its corresponding loss values to the server, which consumes negligible bandwidth compared to transferring full models. Lastly, this method can be used on a subset of clients instead of each client since the final output is a single set of hyperparameters. This may result in sub-par tuning, but it is still a feasible approach for extremely resource-constrained systems.

While some aspects of this framework conserves resources somewhat, it still requires a lot of computational overhead on the client-side. The work proposes the use of adaptive optimization methods, such as Bayesian optimization, which are expensive exploration/exploitation-based search algorithms. While less costly than naive methods such as grid-search, they are still quite expensive and time consuming since the initial steps are randomized trial-and-error processes. In fact, depending on the range of hyperparameters explored, this may end up costing significantly more during tuning than the actual training time itself. This method requires little bandwidth, but has the cost of significant computation overhead, time, and energy expense.

FedTune [38]. The paper "FedTune: Automatic Tuning of Federated Learning Hyper-Parameters from System Perspective" is the only work in the current literature that takes a direct interest in developing resource-efficient hyperparameter tuning. It focuses on tuning two hyperparameters, clients per round and local epochs. The paper first defines resource usage into 4 metrics: 1) computational load, 2) computational time, 3) communication load, and 4) communication time. The authors first perform an empirical study to demonstrate that the choice of the two hyperparameters significantly impacts the overall resource consumption and therefore give reasons that they must be tuned to minimize overhead as much as possible. They first make an assumption that multiple good sets of client-side hyperparameters are known. They first try one such set of hyperparameters and measure the cost in terms of the above 4 metrics while trying to predict how long it will take to converge with the current set of client-side hyperparameters. They develop an equation where each of the 4 resource metrics is provided with a static coefficient which determines its importance compared to the other 3 metrics. In this way, users can choose which metric to prioritize for minimization. They solve this equation to get the predicted amount of resource usage given a certain value of clients per round and local epochs, and choose the values which minimize the 4 resources. This is done online during the actual training process.

This framework does a good job of reducing the mentioned resources in the controlled environment the authors run their setup on. They also tackle the challenge of scalability well by not requiring hyperparameter exploration on the client-side and not requiring extra phases for hyperparameter tuning, which reduces resource cost significantly. However, they make some assumptions that do not hold in practical settings. For example, they require resource homogeneity in order to have predictable outcomes, which is a strong limitation for real-world use cases. They completely ignore timeout and participation ratios, as well as assume that no clients will drop out in the middle of the training phase. They also assume data distribution will remain constant throughout the whole training process and that all clients will be available at all times. This work demonstrates that it is possible to create resource-aware hyperparameter tuning for cross-device FL, and is a great first step in this direction. However, their required criteria are hard to meet in real-world scenarios and so there is room for exploration into frameworks which can work with less constraints.

FedEx [15]. This paper is one of the first works in FL that tackle the hyperparameter tuning challenge in FL. Their focus is on reducing the amount of time spent exploring client-side hyperparameters by parallelizing the search phase. They start with a set of hyperparameter sets they wish to explore, and send different sets to different clients selected for a round of training. The clients train locally as normal and return their weights and losses to the server. On the server side, a gradient is calculated using the difference between the weights of the local models and a baseline model, and the gradients are used with a server-side learning rate to update the global model weights. In this way, multiple hyperparameters can be tried during the training process. The purpose is not find good hyperparameters, but to train well with multiple hyperparameters at different clients.

While this paper does not directly perform hyperparameter tuning and has no considerations for resource usage, it is still a relevant work for our case since it shows that it is possible to achieve good results with different hyperparameters for each client. It also performs optimization of the hyperparameter search space during the training, requiring no extra resources. However, this process is resource-oblivious. For example, assignment of high batch size values and number of local steps could be a burden to slower clients, and there were no considerations given to the server-side hyperparameters which are highly influential to the overall resource consumption. Also, it is not clear if by performing optimization during training increases the overall rounds required to converge.

Other works. While these works are the latest and most relevant to the hyperparameter tuning in the cross-device FL setting, there exist other works that are also tangentially related, and we go over them briefly. One such work is the paper "*On Large-Cohort Training for Federated Learning*" [6] where the authors explore how the number of clients sampled at each round affects FL training, but completely gloss over the resource efficiency parts. "*Federated Learning with Hyperparameter-based Clustering for Electrical Load Forecasting*" [11] is another paper that tries to predict power loads, but does not discuss the challenges of resource heterogeneity. The paper "*Robust Federated Learning through Representation Matching and Adaptive Hyperparameters*" [27] uses the REINFORCE algorithm [34] to perform online hyperparameter tuning, which has very costly exploration/exploitation phases, and the work "*Federated Bayesian Optimization via Thompson Sampling*" [8] uses Bayesian optimization on-device, which is also very costly. In summary, while there has been some work in hyperparameter optimization in FL, few authors have talked in depth about the implications of resource cost on FL.

12.6 Conclusion

In this chapter, we talked about the problem of hyperparameter optimization in cross-device FL from a system's perspective. We first listed and explained the relevant quantifiable resources to consider. We then enumerated the hyperparameters on the client and server sides, and explained their impact of training and resource consumption. We discussed the challenges in FL and their impact in terms of resource cost, and pointed out the most relevant works in the current relevant literature. Discussions of these works revealed that much work has yet to be done on designing resource-efficient hyperparameter optimization techniques for cross-device federated learning.

References

[1] Takuya Akiba, Shotaro Sano, Toshihiko Yanase, Takeru Ohta, Masanori Koyama, Optuna: a next-generation hyperparameter optimization framework, in: Proceedings of the 25th ACM SIGKDD International Conference on Knowledge Discovery & Data Mining, 2019, pp. 2623–2631.
[2] Keith Bonawitz, Hubert Eichner, Wolfgang Grieskamp, Dzmitry Huba, Alex Ingerman, Vladimir Ivanov, Chloe Kiddon, Jakub Konečný, Stefano Mazzocchi, Brendan McMa-

han, et al., Towards federated learning at scale: system design, in: Proceedings of Machine Learning and Systems, vol. 1, 2019, pp. 374–388.

[3] Zheng Chai, Ahsan Ali, Syed Zawad, Stacey Truex, Ali Anwar, Nathalie Baracaldo, Yi Zhou, Heiko Ludwig, Feng Yan, Yue Cheng, TiFL: a tier-based federated learning system, in: Proceedings of the 29th International Symposium on High-Performance Parallel and Distributed Computing, 2020, pp. 125–136.

[4] Zheng Chai, Yujing Chen, Ali Anwar, Liang Zhao, Yue Cheng, Huzefa Rangwala, FedAT: a high-performance and communication-efficient federated learning system with asynchronous tiers, in: Proceedings of the International Conference for High Performance Computing, Networking, Storage and Analysis, 2021, pp. 1–16.

[5] Zheng Chai, Hannan Fayyaz, Zeshan Fayyaz, Ali Anwar, Yi Zhou, Nathalie Baracaldo, Heiko Ludwig, Yue Cheng, Towards taming the resource and data heterogeneity in federated learning, in: 2019 USENIX Conference on Operational Machine Learning (OpML 19), 2019, pp. 19–21.

[6] Zachary Charles, Zachary Garrett, Zhouyuan Huo, Sergei Shmulyian, Virginia Smith, On large-cohort training for federated learning, Advances in Neural Information Processing Systems 34 (2021) 20461–20475.

[7] Yujing Chen, Yue Ning, Martin Slawski, Huzefa Rangwala, Asynchronous online federated learning for edge devices with non-iid data, in: 2020 IEEE International Conference on Big Data (Big Data), IEEE, 2020, pp. 15–24.

[8] Zhongxiang Dai, Bryan Kian Hsiang Low, Patrick Jaillet, Federated Bayesian optimization via Thompson sampling, Advances in Neural Information Processing Systems 33 (2020).

[9] Thomas Elsken, Jan Hendrik Metzen, Frank Hutter, Neural architecture search: a survey, Journal of Machine Learning Research 20 (1) (2019) 1997–2017.

[10] Alireza Fallah, Aryan Mokhtari, Asuman Ozdaglar, Personalized federated learning: a meta-learning approach, arXiv:2002.07948, 2020.

[11] Nastaran Gholizadeh, Petr Musilek, Federated learning with hyperparameter-based clustering for electrical load forecasting, Internet of Things 17 (2022) 100470.

[12] Lars Hertel, Julian Collado, Peter Sadowski, Jordan Ott, Pierre Baldi Sherpa, Robust hyperparameter optimization for machine learning, SoftwareX 12 (2020) 100591.

[13] Ali HeydariGorji, Siavash Rezaei, Mahdi Torabzadehkashi, Hossein Bobarshad, Vladimir Alves, Pai H. Chou, HyperTune: dynamic hyperparameter tuning for efficient distribution of DNN training over heterogeneous systems, in: 2020 IEEE/ACM International Conference on Computer Aided Design (ICCAD), IEEE, 2020, pp. 1–8.

[14] Ji Chu Jiang, Burak Kantarci, Sema Oktug, Tolga Soyata, Federated learning in smart city sensing: challenges and opportunities, Sensors 20 (21) (2020) 6230.

[15] Mikhail Khodak, Tian Li, Liam Li, M. Balcan, Virginia Smith, Ameet Talwalkar, Weight sharing for hyperparameter optimization in federated learning, in: Int. Workshop on Federated Learning for User Privacy and Data Confidentiality in Conjunction with ICML 2020, 2020.

[16] Jakub Konečnỳ, H. Brendan McMahan, Felix X. Yu, Peter Richtárik, Ananda Theertha Suresh, Dave Bacon, Federated learning: strategies for improving communication efficiency, arXiv:1610.05492, 2016.

[17] Aitor Lewkowycz, Yasaman Bahri, Ethan Dyer, Jascha Sohl-Dickstein, Guy Gur-Ari, The large learning rate phase of deep learning: the catapult mechanism, arXiv:2003.02218, 2020.

[18] Lisha Li, Kevin Jamieson, Giulia DeSalvo, Afshin Rostamizadeh, Ameet Talwalkar, Hyperband: a novel bandit-based approach to hyperparameter optimization, Journal of Machine Learning Research 18 (1) (2017) 6765–6816.

[19] Li Tian, Anit Kumar Sahu, Ameet Talwalkar, Virginia Smith, Federated learning: challenges, methods, and future directions, IEEE Signal Processing Magazine 37 (3) (2020) 50–60.

[20] Li Tian, Anit Kumar Sahu, Manzil Zaheer, Maziar Sanjabi, Ameet Talwalkar, Virginia Smith, Federated optimization in heterogeneous networks, arXiv:1812.06127, 2018.

[21] Wei Yang Bryan Lim, Nguyen Cong Luong, Dinh Thai Hoang, Yutao Jiao, Ying-Chang Liang, Qiang Yang, Dusit Niyato, Chunyan Miao, Federated learning in mobile edge networks: a comprehensive survey, IEEE Communications Surveys and Tutorials 22 (3) (2020) 2031–2063.

[22] Hanxiao Liu, Karen Simonyan, Yiming Yang, DARTS: Differentiable architecture search, in: International Conference on Learning Representations, 2018.

[23] Liyuan Liu, Haoming Jiang, Pengcheng He, Weizhu Chen, Xiaodong Liu, Jianfeng Gao, Jiawei Han, On the variance of the adaptive learning rate and beyond, in: International Conference on Learning Representations, 2019.

[24] Brendan McMahan, Eider Moore, Daniel Ramage, Seth Hampson, Blaise Aguera y Arcas, Communication-efficient learning of deep networks from decentralized data, in: Artificial Intelligence and Statistics, PMLR, 2017, pp. 1273–1282.

[25] Rasmiranjan Mohakud, Rajashree Dash, Survey on hyperparameter optimization using nature-inspired algorithm of deep convolution neural network, in: Intelligent and Cloud Computing, Springer, 2021, pp. 737–744.

[26] Mehryar Mohri, Gary Sivek, Ananda Theertha Suresh, Agnostic federated learning, in: International Conference on Machine Learning, PMLR, 2019, pp. 4615–4625.

[27] Hesham Mostafa, Robust federated learning through representation matching and adaptive hyper-parameters, arXiv:1912.13075, 2019.

[28] Eric Schulz, Maarten Speekenbrink, Andreas Krause, A tutorial on Gaussian process regression: modelling, exploring, and exploiting functions, Journal of Mathematical Psychology 85 (2018) 1–16.

[29] Jonas Seng, Pooja Prasad, Devendra Singh Dhami, Kristian Kersting, HANF: hyperparameter and neural architecture search in federated learning, arXiv:2206.12342, 2022.

[30] Samuel L. Smith, Pieter-Jan Kindermans, Chris Ying, Quoc V. Le, Don't decay the learning rate, increase the batch size, arXiv:1711.00489, 2017.

[31] Samuel L. Smith, Pieter-Jan Kindermans, Chris Ying, Quoc V. Le, Don't decay the learning rate, increase the batch size, in: ICLR (Poster), 2018.

[32] Virginia Smith, Chao-Kai Chiang, Maziar Sanjabi, Ameet Talwalkar, Federated multitask learning, arXiv:1705.10467, 2017.

[33] Hao Wang, Zakhary Kaplan, Di Niu, Baochun Li, Optimizing federated learning on non-iid data with reinforcement learning, in: IEEE INFOCOM 2020-IEEE Conference on Computer Communications, IEEE, 2020, pp. 1698–1707.

[34] Ronald J. Williams, Simple statistical gradient-following algorithms for connectionist reinforcement learning, Machine Learning 8 (3) (1992) 229–256.

[35] Li Yang, Abdallah Shami, On hyperparameter optimization of machine learning algorithms: theory and practice, Neurocomputing 415 (2020) 295–316.

[36] Kaichao You, Mingsheng Long, Jianmin Wang, Michael I. Jordan, How does learning rate decay help modern neural networks?, arXiv:1908.01878, 2019.

[37] Syed Zawad, Ahsan Ali, Pin-Yu Chen, Ali Anwar, Yi Zhou, Nathalie Baracaldo, Yuan Tian, Feng Yan, Curse or redemption? How data heterogeneity affects the robustness of federated learning, arXiv:2102.00655, 2021.

[38] Huanle Zhang, Mi Zhang, Xin Liu, Prasant Mohapatra, Michael DeLucia FedTune, Automatic tuning of federated learning hyper-parameters from system perspective, arXiv:2110.03061, 2021.

[39] Yue Zhao, Meng Li, Liangzhen Lai, Naveen Suda, Damon Civin, Vikas Chandra, Federated learning with non-iid data, arXiv:1806.00582, 2018.

[40] Yi Zhou, Parikshit Ram, Theodoros Salonidis, Nathalie Baracaldo, Horst Samulowitz, Heiko Ludwig, FLoRA: single-shot hyper-parameter optimization for federated learning, arXiv:2112.08524, 2021.

Hyper-parameter optimization in federated learning

13

Yi Zhou, Parikshit Ram, Theodoros Salonidis, Nathalie Baracaldo, Horst Samulowitz, and Heiko Ludwig

IBM Research, Yorktown Heights, NY, United States

13.1 Introduction

Despite the unique advantages federated learning or FL brings forth, there are many open problems in the FL domain [18,20], one of which is hyper-parameter optimization for FL. Existing FL systems require a user (or all participating clients) to pre-set (agree on) multiple hyper-parameters (HPs) (i) for the model being trained (such as number of layers and batch size for neural networks or tree depth and number of trees in tree ensembles), and (ii) for the aggregator (if such hyper-parameters exist). Hyper-parameter optimization (HPO) for FL is important because the choice of HPs can have dramatic impact on performance [26]. While HPO has been widely studied in the centralized ML setting, it comes with unique challenges in the FL setting. In this chapter, we will take a deep look at the FL-HPO problem which is the problem of performing HPO in an FL setup. Before describing the different challenges that arise with FL-HPO, we will first describe the FL-HPO problem in detail.

13.1.1 FL-HPO problem definition

In the centralized machine learning setting, we would consider a model class $\mathcal{M}$ and its corresponding learning algorithm $\mathcal{A}$ parameterized collectively with a hyper-parameter (HP) configuration $\boldsymbol{\theta} \in \boldsymbol{\Theta}$, and given a training set D, we can learn a single model $\mathcal{A}(\mathcal{M}, \boldsymbol{\theta}, D) \to \mathbf{w} \in \mathcal{M}$. The HP configuration can include (i) model-specific hyper-parameters such as the number of layers in a neural network and the number of neurons in each layer, and (ii) learning-algorithm-specific hyper-parameters such as the learning rate or weight decay. Here, we will consider both these classes of hyper-parameters collectively.

Given some predictive loss $\mathcal{L}(\mathbf{w}, D')$ of any learned model $\mathbf{w} \in \mathcal{M}$ evaluated on some held-out dataset D', the centralized hyper-parameter optimization or HPO problem can be stated as

$$\min_{\boldsymbol{\theta} \in \boldsymbol{\Theta}} \mathcal{L}(\mathcal{A}(\mathcal{M}, \boldsymbol{\theta}, D); D').$$

(13.1)

Federated Learning. https://doi.org/10.1016/B978-0-44-319037-7.00022-3

In the most general federated learning or FL setting, we have n clients $P_1, \ldots, P_n$ each with their private local training dataset $D_m, m \in [n]$ where $[n]$ denotes the index set $\{1, 2, \ldots, n\}$. Let $D := \bigcup_{m=1}^{n} D_m$ denote the aggregated training dataset and $\overline{D} := \{D_m\}_{m \in [n]}$ denote the set of per-client datasets. Each model class (and corresponding learning algorithm) is parameterized by global HPs $\theta_G \in \Theta_G$ shared by all clients and per-client local HPs $\theta_L^{(m)} \in \Theta_L, m \in [n]$ with $\Theta := \Theta_G \times \Theta_L$. FL systems usually include an aggregator with its own set of HPs $\phi \in \Phi$. We make this separation between the hyper-parameter type to highlight the novel aspects of the FL-HPO problem. We use $\theta \in \Theta$ to denote HPs that are part of the learning that is present both in the centralized and FL settings, while we use $\phi \in \Phi$ to denote HPs that only arise in the FL setting.

Example 13.1. With a neural network model, HPs such as the number of layers in a neural network or the activation function or learning rate would be HPs we consider as being part of θ, while HPs such as the number of sampled clients or the gradient compression rate are examples of HPs that only appear in an FL setting and we denote these with ϕ. With $\theta \in \Theta$, we further differentiate between global HPs θ_G shared across all clients such as the architectural HPs for the network (depth, width, activation), and per-client local HPs $\theta_L^{(m)}, m \in [n]$ that can be different between clients such as the learning rate or batch size.

Example 13.2. Such a distinction also exists for other machine learning models such as gradient boosted tree ensembles like XGBoost [5]. HPs such as the ensemble size, tree depth, and discretization level are present even in the centralized setting and hence we denote them as $\theta \in \Theta$. HPs such the histogram merging strategy [29] are unique to XGBoost in the FL setting and would correspond to ϕ. The ensemble HPs such as number of trees and tree depth would constitute θ_G while discretization level can constitute the per-client local HP $\theta_L^{(m)}, m \in [n]$, allowing the model to account for the potential heterogeneity in the per-client data distributions

Finally, we have an FL algorithm $\mathcal{F}$ that takes as input the model class, learning algorithm, HPs and the per-client datasets, and outputs a model $\mathbf{w}$:

$$\mathcal{F}\left(\mathcal{M}, \phi, \theta_G, \left\{\theta_L^{(m)}\right\}_{i \in [n]}, \mathcal{A}, \overline{D}\right) \to \mathbf{w} \in \mathcal{M}. \tag{13.2}$$

In this case, the FL-HPO problem can be stated in the two following ways depending on the desired goals:
(i) For a global holdout dataset D' (also known as validation set, possibly from the same distribution as the aggregated dataset D), the target problem is

$$\min_{\substack{\phi \in \Phi, \theta_G \in \Theta_G, \\ \theta_L^{(m)} \in \Theta_L, m \in [n]}} \mathcal{L}\left(\mathcal{F}\left(\mathcal{M}, \phi, \theta_G, \left\{\theta_L^{(m)}\right\}_{m \in [n]}, \mathcal{A}, \overline{D}\right); D'\right). \tag{13.3}$$

(ii) An alternative FL-HPO problem would involve per-client holdout datasets $D'_m, m \in [n]$ as follows:

$$\min_{\substack{\phi \in \Phi, \theta_G \in \Theta_G, \\ \theta_L^{(m)} \in \Theta_L, m \in [n]}} \mathrm{Agg} \left\{ \mathcal{L} \left(\mathcal{F} \left(\mathcal{M}, \phi, \theta_G, \left\{ \theta_L^{(m)} \right\}_{m \in [n]}, \mathcal{A}, \overline{D} \right); D'_m \right) \right\}_{m \in [n]}, \quad (13.4)$$

where $\mathrm{Agg}: \mathbb{R}^n \to \mathbb{R}$ is some aggregation function (such as weighted average or maximum) that scalarizes the n per-client predictive losses.

Contrasting problem (13.1) to problems (13.3) and (13.4), we can see that the FL-HPO is significantly more complicated than the centralized HPO problem. In the ensuing presentation, we focus on problem (13.3) although much of it also applies to problem (13.4). The problems (13.3) and (13.4) differ in the objective they wish to optimize – one optimizes for the performance on a global data distribution while the other optimizes for an aggregate over the performances on the per-client distribution.

13.1.2 Challenges and goals

HPO in the centralized setting has been studied extensively [32] and it might seem intuitive to explore the direct applicability in the FL setting. However, there are some basic technical issues that make it infeasible.

- Existing HPO techniques to solve problem (13.1) with centralized training often make use of the entire dataset (not only a centralized training dataset but also a centralized validation dataset), which is not available in FL.
- Centralized HPO schemes train a vast variety of models for a large number of HP configurations which would be prohibitively expensive in terms of communication and training time in FL settings.
- Personalization of models have received wide attention in FL [8,18,22]. However, personalization of models as well as personalization of HPs adds another level of complexity to the whole FL-HPO problems (13.3); whether to personalize or not can itself be a hyper-parameter for each client!
- It is not clear how existing centralized HPO schemes can handle the different kinds of HPs in FL-HPO problem (13.3) that do not exist in the centralized HPO problem (13.1).

Another important challenge that has not been adequately explored in FL literature is the support for tabular data, which are widely used in enterprise settings [23,24]. One of the best models for this setting is based on gradient boosting tree algorithms [11] which are different from the stochastic gradient descent algorithm used for neural networks. Recently, a few approaches have been proposed for FL-HPO, however, they focus on handling HPO using personalization techniques [20] and neural networks [19], and we will provide a detailed review of these approaches in Section 13.2. To the best of our knowledge, there is no HPO approach for FL systems to train non-neural network models, such as XGBoost [5] that is particularly common in the enterprise setting. In this chapter, we first provide an overview of the FL-HPO literature and discuss how these different existing schemes fare against the above technical challenges in solving problem (13.3). Then, we consider a version of the FL-HPO problem (13.3) and present the FLoRA algorithm [41,42] in Section 13.3. This algorithm has the following unique properties we will discuss in detail:

- (**C1**) It can be applied to any machine learning model such as tree ensembles, kernel machines, as well neural networks and linear models.
- (**C2**) It can **perform "single-shot" FL-HPO**, and hence is useful in situations where we have *limited* resources (in the form of computation and communication overhead), requiring only a single model via federated learning (that is, a single HP configuration).
- (**C3**) It does not *assume that clients have independent and identically distributed (IID) data distributions* and hence is able to handle heterogeneity between the per-client data distributions.

13.2 State-of-the-art FL-HPO approaches

In this section, we provide a general overview of the recent advance in FL-HPO approaches.

One of the main challenges in FL is achieving high accuracy and low communication overhead. FedAvg [25] is a predominant algorithm used for training in FL and several optimization schemes build on it. It is executed in multiple global rounds. At each round, the clients perform stochastic gradient descent (SGD) updates on their parameters based on their local objective functions. They subsequently send their updates to the server, which averages them and transmits their mean back to the clients. Several approaches have been devised for optimizing the communication performance of FL systems. Initially, communication optimizations included performing multiple SGD local iterations at the clients and randomly selecting a small subset of the clients to compute and send updates to the server [25]. Subsequently, compression techniques were used to minimize the size of model updates to the server. It has been shown that the accuracy and communication performance of these techniques depend highly on their HPs [25].

Recent optimization approaches adapt HPs such as the local learning rate at each client [21,27,31], and the number of local SGD iterations (which affect the frequency of server updates) [36]. In [6,7], Dai et al. address federated Bayesian optimization. Although considering HPO with multiple HPs, the problem setup is quite different from federated learning: they focus on a single client using information from other clients to accelerate its own Bayesian optimization, instead of building a model for all clients. Federated network architecture search (FNAS) approaches search for architectural HPs of deep learning CNN models by running NAS algorithms locally and then aggregating the NAS architecture weights and model weights using FedAvg [12,15,39]. These approaches have shown empirical gains but lack theoretical guarantees. Inspired from the NAS technique of weight-sharing, [19,20] proposed FedEx, an FL-HPO framework to accelerate a general HPO procedure, i.e., the successive halving algorithm (SHA) [17], for many SGD-based FL algorithms. FedEx focuses on building personalized models for clients by tuning local HPs of the clients. Combining with SHA, FedEx can also tune global HPs, such as global learning rate and client selection ratio, etc. They provide a theoretical guarantee for a special case of tuning a single HP (local learning rate) in a convex online learning setting. To optimize global HPs, FedEx requires multiple rounds of communication, and hence is not single-shot FL-HPO [19,20]. Note that these above techniques are multi-shot, leveraging both the idea of weight-sharing and multi-fidelity HPO for improving the communication efficiency of FL-HPO. The FedHPO-B benchmark [40] primarily focuses on neural-networks and multi-fidelity FL-HPO and is useful to evaluate the above schemes across various problems.

As most existing FL-HPO approaches focus on SGD-based algorithms and neural networks, one major limitation they share is that they do not support tree-based models, such as gradient boosted trees [11], a popular model for enterprise setting. These models provide explanability for predictions which is required for financial and healthcare FL use-cases. As laid out in a policy paper by the OECD, numerous regulations of member countries govern the use of analytics and data [28]: GDPR, for example, requires decision-making models for financial services and insurance to be explainable, which is mostly achieved using traditional models such as decision tree variants [14]. Outside consumer finance, governance rules require explanability of portfolio and risk management for auditing purposes [13]. Again, deep neural networks are not satisfactory from a current regulatory point of view and, thus, the financial services and insurance sectors rely on more explainable models (such as tree-based ones), also in federation.

Recently, Federated Loss SuRface Aggregation (FLoRA), proposed in [41,42], is a single-shot FL-HPO approach that allows the aggregator to optimize hyperparameters via constructing a unified loss surface based on collected local per-client HPO results. Moreover, it is agnostic to both model type and data modality. In the next few sections, we will present a overview of FLoRA.

13.3 FLoRA: a single-shot FL-HPO approach

In this section, we will formally present FLoRA developed in [41,42]. Before we walk you through the details of the approach, we will first go over the specific FL-HPO problem FLoRA addresses.

We simplify the FL-HPO problem in the following ways: (i) we assume that there is no personalization so there are no per-client local HPs $\theta_L^{(m)}$, $m \in [n]$, (ii) we only focus on the model class HPs θ_G, deferring HPO for aggregator HPs ϕ for future work, and (iii) we assume there is a global holdout/validation set D' which is only used to evaluate the final global model's performance but *cannot be accessed* during HPO process. Hence the problem we will study is stated for a fixed aggregator HP ϕ

as follows:

$$\min_{\theta_G \in \Theta_G} \mathcal{L}\left(\mathcal{F}\left(\mathcal{M}, \phi, \theta_G, \mathcal{A}, \overline{D}\right); D'\right). \tag{13.5}$$

This problem appears similar to the centralized HPO problem (13.1). However, note that the main challenges in (13.5) is (i) the need for a federated training for each set of HPs θ_G, and (ii) the need to evaluate the trained model on the global validation set D' for each θ_G (which is not available in usual FL-HPO setting). Hence it is not practical (from a communication overhead and functional perspective) to apply existing off-the-shelf HPO schemes to problem (13.5). In the subsequent discussion, for simplicity purposes, we will use θ to denote the global HPs, dropping the "G" subscript.

13.3.1 The main algorithm: leveraging local HPOs

While it is impractical to apply off-the-shelf HPO solvers (such as Bayesian optimization (BO) [32], Hyperopt [3], SMAC [16], etc.), FLoRA leverages local and asynchronous HPOs in each of the clients. The design of FLoRA follows a simple, but intuitive hypothesis underlying various meta-learning schemes for HPO [33,38]: *if an HP configuration θ has good performance for all clients independently, then θ is a strong candidate for federated training.*

With this hypothesis, we present **FLoRA** in Algorithm 1. FLoRA allows each client P_m to perform HPO locally and asynchronously with some adaptive HPO scheme such as BO using its local training and validation sets D_m and D'_m respec-

---

Algorithm 1 Single-shot FL-HPO with federated loss surface aggregation (FLoRA).

1: **Input:** $\Theta, \mathcal{M}, \mathcal{A}, \mathcal{F}, \{(D_m, D'_m)\}_{m \in [n]}, T$
2: **for** each client $P_m, m \in [n]$ **do**
3:     Run HPO to generate T (HP, loss) pairs

$$E^{(m)} = \left\{(\theta_t^{(m)}, \mathcal{L}_t^{(m)}), t \in [T]\right\}, \tag{13.6}$$

    where $\theta_t^{(m)} \in \Theta$, $\mathcal{L}_t^{(m)} := \mathcal{L}(\mathcal{A}(\mathcal{M}, \theta_t^{(m)}, D_m); D'_m)$.
4: **end for**
5: Collect all $E = \{E^{(m)}, m \in [n]\}$ in aggregator
6: Generate a unified loss surface $\widehat{\ell} : \Theta \to \mathbb{R}$ using E
7: Select best HP candidate

$$\widehat{\theta}^{\star} \leftarrow \arg\min_{\theta \in \Theta} \widehat{\ell}(\theta). \tag{13.7}$$

8: Invoke federated training to get $\mathbf{w} \leftarrow \mathcal{F}(\mathcal{M}, \widehat{\theta}^{\star}, \mathcal{A}, \overline{D})$
9: **Output:** FL model $\mathbf{w}$

---

tively (line 3). Then, at each client $m \in [n]$, we collect all the attempted T HPs $\theta_t^{(m)}, t \in [T] = \{1, 2, \ldots, T\}$ and their corresponding predictive loss $\mathcal{L}_t^{(m)}$ into a set $E^{(m)}$ (line 3, Eq. (13.6)). Then the aggregator collects these per-client sets of (HP, loss) pairs $E^{(m)}$ (line 5). This operation has at most $O(nT)$ communication overhead (note that the number of HPs are usually much smaller than the number of columns or number of rows in the per-client datasets). These sets containing clients' (HP, loss) pairs are used to generate an aggregated loss surface $\widehat{\ell} : \Theta \to \mathbb{R}$ (line 6) which will then be used to make the final single-shot HP recommendation $\widehat{\theta}^{\star} \in \Theta$ (line 7) for the federated training to create the final model $m \in \mathcal{M}$ (line 8).

We will discuss the generation of the aggregated loss surface in detail in Section 13.3.2. Before that, we briefly want to discuss the motivation behind some of the choices in FLoRA.

13.3.1.1 Why adaptive HPO?

HPO (centralized) schemes can be categorized into two groups: (i) adaptive schemes such as Bayesian optimization [32], where the predictive performance of previously evaluated HPs in the HPO process drive the choice of the future HPs, and (ii) non-adaptive schemes such as random search [2] and grid-search where the performance of the previously evaluated HPs has no effect on the choice of the future HPs. FLoRA uses adaptive HPO schemes instead of non-adaptive schemes such as random search or grid search. This is because adaptive HPO schemes allow FLoRA to efficiently approximate the local loss surface more accurately (and with more certainty) in regions of the HP space where the local performance is favorable instead of trying to approximate the loss surface well over the complete HP space. This has advantages both in terms of computational efficiency and loss surface approximation.

13.3.1.2 Why asynchronous HPO?

In FLoRA, each client executes HPO asynchronously, without coordination with HPO results from other clients or with the aggregator. This is in line with the objective of FLoRA to minimize communication overhead and relies on the implicit assumption that the performance of the hyper-parameter configuration is not radically different performance-wise among clients. Although there could be strategies that involve coordination between clients they could involve many rounds of communication. We can see later in Section 13.4 that experimental results show that asynchronous HPO is effective for the datasets we evaluated for.

An alternate way to build an aggregated loss surface is via a coordinated synchronous HPO involving all clients – the aggregator would be executing the HPO for T rounds by (i) recommending a HP θ_t for all clients, (ii) then receiving the per-client loss $\mathcal{L}_t^{(m)}, m \in [n]$ for this HP (each client trains and scores its local model using its local training set D_m and validation set D_m', respectively), and (iii) aggregating/scalarizing the per-client losses to allow the HPO scheme to propose the next HP θ_{t+1} and go back to step (i). While the overall communication overhead would still be $O(nT)$ like FLoRA, this would involve T **rounds of communication** instead of a **single round of communication** involved in **FLoRA**. This increased number of rounds of communication may exacerbate the issue of stragglers and would implicitly rely on the condition that all clients involved are able to train and score their local models in approximately the same amount of time. However, synchronous HPO may generate loss surfaces that better approximate the true loss function.

13.3.2 Loss surface aggregation

Given the sets of (HP, loss) pairs $E^{(m)} = (\theta_t^{(m)}, \mathcal{L}_t^{(m)})$, $m \in [n]$, $t \in [T]$ at the aggregator, FLoRA constructs a loss surface $\widehat{\ell} : \Theta \to \mathbb{R}$ that best emulates the (relative) performance loss $\widehat{\ell}(\theta)$ one would observe when training the model on $\overline{D}$. Based on the aforementioned hypothesis, the loss surfaces would have a relatively low $\widehat{\ell}(\theta)$ if θ has a low loss for all clients simultaneously. However, because of the asynchronous and adaptive nature of the local HPOs, for any HP $\theta \in \Theta$, the algorithm would not have the corresponding losses from all the clients. For that reason, FLoRA models the loss surfaces using regressors that try to map any HP to their corresponding loss. In the following, we present four ways of constructing such loss surfaces in [41]:

Single global model (SGM). In SGM, one merges all the sets $E = \bigcup_{m \in [n]} E^{(m)}$ and uses it as a training set for a regressor $f : \Theta \to \mathbb{R}$, which considers the HPs $\theta \in \Theta$ as the covariates and the corresponding loss as the dependent variable. For example, one can train a random forest regressor [4] on this training set E, then define the loss surface $\widehat{\ell}(\theta) := f(\theta)$. While this loss surface is simple to obtain, it may not be able to handle non-IID client data distribution well: it is actually overly optimistic – under the assumption that every client generates unique HPs during the local HPO, this single global loss surface would assign a low loss to any HP θ which has a low loss at any one of the clients. This implies that this loss surface would end up recommending HPs that have low loss in just one of the clients, but not necessarily on all clients.

Single global model with uncertainty (SGM+U). Given the merged set $E = \bigcup_{m \in [n]} E^{(m)}$, one can train a regressor that provides uncertainty quantification around its predictions (such as Gaussian process regressor [37]) as $f : \Theta \to \mathbb{R}$, $u : \Theta \to \mathbb{R}_+$, where $f(\theta)$ is the mean prediction of the model at $\theta \in \Theta$ while $u(\theta)$ quantifies the uncertainty around this prediction $f(\theta)$. SGM+U defines the loss surface as $\widehat{\ell}(\theta) := f(\theta) + \alpha \cdot u(\theta)$ for some $\alpha > 0$. This loss surface does prefer HPs that have a low loss even in just one of the clients, but it penalizes an HP if the model estimates high uncertainty around this HP. Usually, a high uncertainty around an HP would be either because the training set E does not have many samples around this HP (implying that many clients did not view the region containing this HP as one with low loss), or because there are multiple samples in the region around this HP but clients do not collectively agree that this is a promising region for HPs. Hence this makes SGM+U more desirable than SGM, giving us a loss surface that estimates low loss for HPs that are simultaneously thought to be promising to multiple clients.

Maximum of per-client local models (MPLM). Instead of a single global model on the merged set E, one can instead train a regressor $f^{(m)} : \Theta \to \mathbb{R}$, $m \in [n]$ with each of the per-client set $E^{(m)}$. Given this, one can construct a loss surface as $\widehat{\ell}(\theta) :=$ $\max_{m \in [n]} f^{(m)}(\theta)$. This can be seen as a much more pessimistic but also robust loss surface, assigning a low loss to an HP only if it has a low loss estimate across all clients, making it less sensitive to non-IID client data distributions.

Average of per-client local models (APLM). A less pessimistic version of MPLM would be to construct the loss surface as the average of the per-client regressors $f^{(m)}$, $m \in [n]$ instead of the maximum, defined as $\widehat{\ell}(\theta) := 1/n \sum_{m=1}^{n} f^{(m)}(\theta)$. This is also less optimistic than SGM since it will assign a low loss for a HP only if its average across all per-client regressors is low, which implies that all clients observed a relatively low loss around this HP.

Intuitively, we believe that loss surfaces such as SGM+U or APLM would be the most promising while the extremely optimistic and pessimistic SGM and MPLM respectively would be relatively less promising, with MPLM being superior to SGM because of its robustness to non-IID client distributions.

In the following section, we present the sub-optimality gap established in [42] that theoretically quantify the performance guarantees for SGM, MPLM, and APLM.

13.3.3 Optimality guarantees for FLoRA

Consider the objective in (13.5) with the aggregated training set $\overline{D}$, and the global validation set D' sampled from a distribution $\mathcal{D}(\mathbf{x}, c)$ as an estimate $\tilde{\ell}(\theta, \mathcal{D})$ of the true loss of the model (obtained via federated training with HP θ with aggregated training set $\overline{D}$), where the true loss is defined as follows:

$$\ell(\theta, \mathcal{D}) := \mathbb{E}_{D' \sim \mathcal{D}} \mathcal{L}\left(\mathcal{F}\left(\mathcal{M}, \phi, \theta_G, \mathcal{A}, \overline{D}\right); D'\right). \tag{13.8}$$

Let us define the optimal HP $\theta^{\star}$ for this estimated loss as

$$\theta^{\star} \in \arg\min_{\theta \in \Theta} \tilde{\ell}(\theta, \mathcal{D}). \tag{13.9}$$

We are interested in providing a bound for the following *optimality gap*:

$$\tilde{\ell}(\widehat{\theta}^{\star}, \mathcal{D}) - \tilde{\ell}(\theta^{\star}, \mathcal{D}), \tag{13.10}$$

where $\widehat{\theta}^{\star}$ denotes the set of HP selected by FLoRA (see (13.7)). We state the main results in Theorem 13.1. Informally speaking, Theorem 13.1 shows how to bound the optimality gap by picking the 'worst-case' HP setting that maximizes the combination of 1-Wasserstein distances [35] of the per-client data distributions $\mathcal{D}_m(\mathbf{x}, c)$ and actual quality of local HPO approximation across clients.

Theorem 13.1 ([42, Theorem 4.5]). *Consider the optimality gap defined in (13.10), where $\widehat{\theta}^{\star}$ is selected by FLoRA with each client $m \in [n]$ collecting T (HP, loss) pairs*

$\left\{ (\theta_t^{(m)}, \mathcal{L}_t^{(m)}), t \in [T] \right\}$ *during the per-client local HPO. For a target data distribution* $\mathcal{D} = \sum_{m=1}^n w_m \mathcal{D}_m(\mathbf{x}, c)$, *where* $\{\mathcal{D}_m(\mathbf{x}, c), m \in [n]\}$ *are the per-client local data distributions and* $w_m \in [0, 1]$, $\forall m \in [n]$, *we have*

$$\tilde{\ell}(\widehat{\theta}^\star, \mathcal{D}) - \tilde{\ell}(\theta^\star, \mathcal{D})$$

$$\leq 2 \max_{\theta \in \Theta} \sum_{m \in [n]} \alpha_m(\theta) \left\{ \tilde{\beta} \sum_{j \neq m \in [n]} w_j \mathcal{W}_1(j, m) + \left(\tilde{L}_m + \widehat{L}_m \right) \Delta_m(\theta) + \delta_m \right\},$$

(13.11)

where (i) $\mathcal{W}_1(j, m)$ *is the 1-Wasserstein distance between the jth client distribution* $\mathcal{D}_j(\mathbf{x}, c)$ *and the mth client distribution* $\mathcal{D}_m(\mathbf{x}, c)$, *(ii)* $\Delta_m(\theta) := \min_{t \in [T]} d(\theta, \theta_t^{(m)})$ *is the distance of* θ *to the closest HP tried at client m for a distance metric* $d : \Theta \times \Theta \to \mathbb{R}_+$, *(iii)* δ_m *is the maximum per sample training error for the local loss surface* $f^{(m)}$, *i.e.,* $\delta_m := \max_{t \in [T]} |\mathcal{L}_t^{(m)} - f^{(m)}(\theta_t^{(m)})|$, *(iv)* $\tilde{\beta}$ *and* $\tilde{L}_m$ *are the Lipschitz constants of* $\tilde{\ell}$ *with respect to* θ *and* $\mathcal{D}$, *respectively, (v)* $\widehat{L}_m$ *is the Lipshitz constant of the local loss surface* $f^{(m)}$ *with respect to* θ, *and (vi)* $\alpha_m(\theta)$ *are the per-client weights in the aggregated loss surface.*

In particular, when all clients have IID local data distributions, (13.11) reduces to

$$\tilde{\ell}(\widehat{\theta}^\star, \mathcal{D}) - \tilde{\ell}(\theta^\star, \mathcal{D}) \leq 2 \max_{\theta \in \Theta} \sum_{m=1}^n \alpha_m(\theta) \left\{ \left(\tilde{L}_m + \widehat{L}_m \right) \Delta_m(\theta) + \delta_m \right\}.$$

Note that the above sub-optimality holds under mild Lipschitz smoothness assumptions of the loss estimates, i.e., the loss estimate $\tilde{\ell}$ and the unified loss surface $\hat{\ell}$ are Lipschitz continuous (see [42]) regardless of the convexity of the loss function and the clients' (possibly heterogeneous) local data distributions. Moreover, if we define the global loss surface $\hat{\ell} : \Theta \to \mathbb{R}$ as

$$\widehat{\ell}(\theta) = \sum_{m=1}^n \alpha_m(\theta) \cdot f^{(m)}(\theta), \quad \alpha_m(\theta) \in [0, 1], \quad \sum_{m=1}^n \alpha_m(\theta) = 1,$$

(13.12)

then

i) If $\alpha_m(\theta) = 1/n$, $\forall m \in [n]$, $\theta \in \Theta$, then $\widehat{\ell}$ reduces to APLM loss surface.

ii) If $\alpha_m(\theta) = \mathbb{I}\left(f^{(m)}(\theta) = \max_{m' \in [n]} f^{(m')}(\theta) \right)$, then $\widehat{\ell}$ reduces to the MPLM loss surface (assuming all $f^{(m)}(\theta)$ values are unique).

iii) If $\alpha_m(\theta) = \mathbb{I}\left(f^{(m)}(\theta) = \min_{m' \in [n]} f^{(m')}(\theta) \right)$, then $\widehat{\ell}$ reduces to the SGM loss surface (assuming all $f^{(m)}(\theta)$ values are unique and all $\theta_t^{(m)}$ are unique $\forall m \in [n]$, $t \in [T]$).

We now make some detailed observations regarding Theorem 13.1. Firstly, the first term in our bound characterizes the errors incurred by the differences among clients' local data distributions, i.e., the magnitude of non-IID-ness in an FL system. In particular, we can see it vanish under the IID setting. Secondly, the last two terms measure the quality of the local loss surfaces $f^{(m)}$, which can be reduced if a good loss surface is selected. Thirdly, $\Delta_m(\boldsymbol{\theta}) := \min_{t \in [T]} d(\boldsymbol{\theta}, \boldsymbol{\theta}_t^{(m)})$ indicates that the optimality gap depends only on the HP trial $\boldsymbol{\theta}_t^{(m)}$ that is closest to the optimal HP setting. Finally, if we assume each client's training dataset D_m is of size $|D_m|$ sampled as $D_m \sim \mathcal{D}_m(\mathbf{x}, c)$, we can view $w_m = \frac{|D_m|}{\sum_{m' \in [n]} |D'_m|}$, i.e., with probability w_m the desired data distribution $\mathcal{D}$ is sampled from $\mathcal{D}_m(\mathbf{x}, c)$.

In fact, FLoRA improves on some existing approaches in several ways. 1) **It is more general**, as it can tune multiple HPs and is applicable to non-SGD-training settings such as gradient boosting trees. This is achieved by treating FL-HPO as a black-box HPO problem, which has been addressed in centralized HPO literature using grid search, random search [2], and Bayesian optimization approaches [32]. The key challenge is the requirement to perform computationally intensive evaluations on a large number of HPO configurations, where each evaluation involves training a model and scoring it on a (global) validation dataset. In the distributed FL setting this problem is exacerbated because validation sets are local to the clients (no global validation set usually available) and each FL training and score evaluation is communication intensive. Therefore a brute force application of centralized black-box HPO approaches that select hyper-parameters in an outer loop and proceed with FL training evaluations is not feasible. 2) **It yields minimal HPO communication overhead.** This is achieved by building a loss surface from local asynchronous HPO at the clients that yields a single optimized HP configuration used to train a global model with a single FL training. 3) **It is the first that theoretically characterizes the optimality gap in an FL-HPO setting**, for the case it focuses in this section (creating a global model by tuning multiple global HPs).

13.4 Empirical evaluation

In this section, we evaluate FLoRA with different loss surfaces for the FL-HPO on a variety of ML models – histograms based gradient boosted (HGB) decision trees [11], support vector machines (SVM) with RBF kernel, and multi-layered perceptrons (MLP) (using their respective `scikit-learn` implementation [30]) on OpenML [34] classification problems. First, we fix the number of clients $n = 3$ and compare FLoRA to a baseline on 7 datasets. Then we study the effect of increasing the number of clients from $n = 3$ up to $n = 100$ on the performance of our proposed scheme on 3 datasets. The data is randomly split across clients. We also evaluate FLoRA with different parameter choices, in particular, the number of local HPO rounds T and the communication overhead in the aggregation of the per-client (HP, loss) pairs. Finally, we evaluate FLoRA in a real FL testbed IBM FL [24] using its default HP setting as a baseline. More experimental details and results can be found in [42].

Single-shot baseline. To appropriately evaluate this single-shot FL-HPO scheme, we need to select a meaningful single-shot baseline. For this, we choose the default HP configuration of `scikit-learn` as the single-shot baseline for two main reasons: (i) the default HP configuration in `scikit-learn` is set manually based on expert prior knowledge and extensive empirical evaluation, and (ii) these are also used as the defaults in the Auto-Sklearn package [9,10], one of the leading open-source AutoML python packages, which maintains a carefully selected portfolio of default configurations.

Dataset selection. For our evaluation of single-shot HPO, we consider 7 binary classification datasets of varying sizes and characteristics from OpenML [34] such that there is at least a significant room for improvement over the single-shot baseline performance. We consider datasets which have at least > 3% potential improvement in balanced accuracy for HGB. Note that this only ensures room for improvement for HGB, while highlighting cases with no room for improvement for SVM and MLP as we see in our results.

Implementation. We consider two implementations for our empirical evaluation. In our first three sets of experiments, we emulate the final FL (Algorithm 1, line 8) with a centralized training using the pooled data. We chose this implementation because we want to evaluate the final performance of any HP configuration (baseline or recommended by FLoRA) in a statistically robust manner with multiple train/validation splits (for example, via 10-fold cross-validation) instead of evaluating the performance on a single train/validation. This form of evaluation is extremely expensive to perform in a real FL system and generally not feasible, but allows us to evaluate how the performance of FLoRA's single-shot HP recommendation fairs against that of the best-possible HP found via a full-scale centralized HPO.

Evaluation metric. In all datasets, we consider the balanced accuracy as the metric we wish to maximize. For the local per-client HPOs (as well as the centralized HPO we execute to compute the regret), we maximize the 10-fold cross-validated balanced accuracy. In Tables 13.1,13.2, we report the *relative regret*, computed as $(a^\star - a)/(a^\star - b)$, where $a^\star$ is the best metric obtained via the centralized HPO, b is the result of the baseline, and a is the result of the HP recommended by FLoRA. The baseline has a relative regret of 1 and smaller values imply better performance. A value larger than 1 implies that the recommended HP performs worse than the baseline.

Comparison to single-shot baseline. In our first set of experiments for 3-client FL-HPO ($n = 3$), we compare our proposed scheme with the baseline across different datasets, machine learning models and FLoRA loss surfaces. The aggregated results are presented in Table 13.1. For each of the three methods, we report the aggregate performance over all considered datasets in terms of (i) inter-quartile range, (ii) Wins/Ties/Losses of FLoRA with respect to the single-shot baseline, and (iii) a one-sided Wilcoxon signed rank test of statistical significance with the null hypothesis that the median of the difference between the single-shot baseline and FLoRA is positive against the alternative that the difference is negative (implying FLoRA improves over the baseline). Finally, we also report an "Overall" performance, further aggregated across all ML models.

Table 13.1 Comparison of different loss surfaces (the 4 rightmost columns) for FLoRA relative to the baseline for single-shot 3-client FL-HPO in terms of the *relative regret* (lower is better).

ML Method	SGM	SGM+U	MPLM	APLM
HGB	[0.30, 0.47, 0.68]	[0.27, 0.54, 0.64]	[0.25, 0.43, 0.67]	[0.25, 0.50, 0.65]
SVM	[0.04, 0.38, 1.11]	[0.04, 0.48, 1.07]	[0.38, 0.91, 2.41]	[0.23, 0.54, 0.76]
MLP	[0.36, 0.80, 0.97]	[0.48, 0.99, 1.01]	[0.47, 0.89, 1.00]	[0.46, 0.79, 0.95]
Overall	[**0.22**, **0.53**, 0.97]	[0.32, 0.55, 1.01]	[0.36, 0.61, 0.99]	[0.36, 0.57, **0.79**]

(a) Regret Inter-quartile range.

ML Method	SGM	SGM+U	MPLM	APLM
HGB	6/0/1	6/0/1	7/0/0	7/0/0
SVM	4/0/2	4/0/2	3/0/3	5/0/1
MLP	6/0/1	4/1/2	5/1/1	6/0/1
Overall	16/0/4	14/1/5	15/1/4	**18/0/2**

(b) FLoRA Wins/Ties/Losses.

ML Method	SGM	SGM+U	MPLM	APLM
HGB	(26, 0.02126)	(27, 0.01400)	(28, 0.00898)	(28, 0.00898)
SVM	(18, 0.05793)	(17, 0.08648)	(9, 0.62342)	(15, 0.17272)
MLP	(21, 0.11836)	(15, 0.17272)	(18, 0.05793)	(24, 0.04548)
Overall	(174, 0.00499)	(164, 0.00272)	(141, 0.03206)	(**183.5, 0.00169**)

(c) Wilcoxon Signed-Rank Test 1-sided (statistic, p-value).

   All FLoRA loss surfaces show strong performance with respect to the single-shot baseline, with significantly more wins than losses, and 3rd-quartile relative regret values less than 1 (indicating improvement over the baseline). All FLoRA loss surfaces have a *p*-value of less than 0.05, indicating that we can reject the null hypothesis. Overall, APLM shows the best performance over all loss surfaces, both in terms of Wins/Ties/Losses over the baseline as well as in terms of the Wilcoxon signed rank test, with the highest statistic and a p-value close to 10^{-3}. APLM also has significantly lower 3rd-quartile than all other loss surfaces. MPLM appears to have the worst performance but much of that is attributable to a couple of very hard cases with SVM (see [42][Appendix B] for detailed discussion). Otherwise, MPLM performs second best both for FL-HPO with HGB and MLP.

Effect of increasing number of clients. In the second set of experiments, we study the effect of increasing the number of clients in the FL-HPO problem on 3 datasets and HGB. For each data set, we increase the number of clients n up until each client has at least 100 training samples. We present the relative regrets in Table 13.2. It also displays $\gamma_n := \left(1-\min_{m\in[n]} \mathcal{L}_\star^{(m)}\right)/\left(1-\max_{m\in[n]} \mathcal{L}_\star^{(m)}\right)$, where $\mathcal{L}_\star^{(m)} = \min_{t\in[T]} \mathcal{L}_t^{(m)}$ is the minimum loss observed during the local asynchronous HPO at client i. This ratio γ_n is always greater than 1, and highlights the difference in the observed performances across the clients. A ratio closer to 1 indicates that all the clients have relatively similar performances on their respective training data, while a ra-

Table 13.2 Effect of increasing the number of clients on FLoRA with different loss surfaces for HGB.

Data	n	γ_n	SGM	SGM+U	MPLM	APLM
EEG Eye State	3	1.01	0.14	0.12	0.11	0.12
14980 samples	6	1.01	0.07	0.00	0.07	0.09
	10	1.03	0.08	0.00	0.16	0.01
	25	1.08	0.35	0.92	0.17	0.04
	50	1.20	0.20	0.23	0.67	0.12
Electricity	3	1.01	0.17	0.14	0.09	0.12
45312 samples	6	1.01	0.25	0.21	0.18	0.13
	10	1.02	0.03	0.06	0.32	0.14
	25	1.04	0.40	0.42	1.42	0.89
	50	1.07	1.57	1.57	0.89	1.13
	100	1.14	1.45	1.47	0.48	1.11
Pollen	3	1.02	0.43	0.54	0.43	0.69
3848 samples	6	1.10	1.02	0.91	0.54	0.56
	10	1.16	1.05	0.73	0.75	1.12

tio much higher than 1 indicating significant discrepancy between the per-client performances, implicitly indicating the difference in the per-client data distributions.

We notice that increasing the number of clients does not have a significant effect on γ_n for the Electricity dataset until $n = 100$, but significantly increases for the Pollen dataset earlier (making the problem harder). For the EEG eye state, the increase in γ_n with increasing n is moderate until $n = 50$. The results indicate that, with low or moderate increase in γ_n (EEG eye state, Electricity for moderate n), the proposed scheme is able to achieve low relative regret – the increase in the number of clients does not directly imply degradation in performance. However, with significant increase in γ_n (Pollen, Electricity with $n = 50$, 100 and EEG Eye State with $n = 50$), we see a significant increase in the relative regret (eventually going over 1 in a few cases). In this challenging case, MPLM (the most pessimistic loss function) has the most graceful degradation in relative regret compared to the remaining loss surfaces.
Effect of different choices in FLoRA. In this set of experiments, we consider FLoRA with the APLM loss surface, and ablate the effect of different choices in FLoRA on two datasets, each for SVM and MLP. First, we study the impact of the thoroughness of the per-client local HPOs, quantified by the number of HPO rounds T in Fig. 13.1a. The results indicate that for really small T (< 20) the relative regret of FLoRA can be very high. However, after that point, the relative regret converges to its best possible value.

We also study the effect of the communication overhead of FLoRA for fixed level of local HPO thoroughness. We assume that each client performs $T = 100$ rounds of local asynchronous HPO. However, instead of sending all T (HP, loss) pairs, we

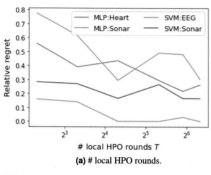 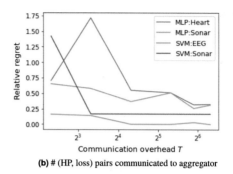

(a) # local HPO rounds.   (b) # (HP, loss) pairs communicated to aggregator

FIGURE 13.1

Effect of different choices on FLoRA with the APLM loss surface for different methods and datasets.

Table 13.3   Performance of FLoRA with the IBM-FL system in terms of the *balanced accuracy* on a holdout test set (higher is better). The baseline is still the default HP configuration of `HistGradientBoostingClassifier` in `scikit-learn`.

Data	n	$|D_m| \forall m \in [n]$	Baseline	SGM	SGM+U	MPLM	APLM
Oil spill	3	200	0.59	**0.74**	0.59	0.71	0.73
EEG eye state	3	3,000	0.89	0.92	0.92	**0.93**	0.92
Electricity	6	4,000	0.85	0.86	**0.86**	0.86	0.86

consider sending $T' < T$ of the "best" (HP, loss) pairs – that is, (HP, loss) pairs with the T' lowest losses. Changing the value of T' trades off the communication overhead of the FLoRA step where the aggregators collect the per-client loss pairs (Algorithm 1, line 5). The results for this study are presented in Fig. 13.1b, and indicate that, for really small T', the relative regret can be really high. However, for a moderately high value of $T' < T$, FLoRA converges to its best possible performance.

Federated learning testbed evaluation. We now conduct experiments for histrogram boosted tree model in an FL testbed, utilizing IBM FL library [24,29], More specifically, we reserved 40% of oil spill and electricity and 20% of EEG eye state as global hold-out set only for evaluating the final FL model performance. Each client randomly sampled from the rest of the original dataset to obtain their own training dataset. We report the balanced accuracy of any HP (baseline or recommended by FLoRA) on a single train/test split. Given balanced accuracy as the evaluation metric, we utilize (1 − balanced accuracy) as the loss $\mathcal{L}_t^{(m)}$ in Algorithm 1. Each client will run HPO to generate $T = 500$ (HP, loss) pairs and use those pairs to generate loss surface either collaboratively or by their own according to different aggregation procedures described in Section 13.3.2. Once the loss surface is generated, the aggregator uses Hyperopt [3] to select the best HP candidate and train a federated

XGBoost model via the IBM FL library using the selected HPs. Table 13.3 summarizes the experimental results for 3 datasets, indicating that FLoRA can significantly improve over the baseline in IBM FL testbed.

13.5 Conclusion

How to effectively select hyper-parameters in FL settings is a challenging problem. In this chapter, we have introduced a general definition of FL-HPO problems and discussed a few FL-HPO approaches in this new field. Moreover, we have presented FLoRA, a single-shot FL-HPO algorithm that can be applied to a variety of ML models and provided a theoretical analysis which includes a bound on the optimality gap incurred by the hyper-parameter selection by FLoRA. Some preliminary experimental evaluation shows that FLoRA can effectively produce hyper-parameter configurations that outperform the baseline with just a single shot.

The FL-HPO solutions discussed in this chapter have their own limitations. Some of them are limited to only SGD-based FL algorithms, such as FedAvg, some of them can only tune neural network architecture. One limitation of FLoRA is that it cannot handle HPs that are not active during any local HPO. These would include aggregator-specific and some FL-training-specific HPs. It is unlikely that such HPs can be handled in single-shot FL-HPO without any additional information or structure. Therefore, one of the current challenges for FL-HPO is to explore how single-shot approaches can be extended to handle such HPs in "few-shot" FL-HPO and in conjunction with some form of multi-fidelity HP evaluations.

Beyond FL-HPO, there exists a need to effectively address the FL combined algorithm selection and hyper-parameter optimization (CASH) problem of jointly optimizing for the training algorithm and its HPs. FL-CASH poses additional challenges to FL-HPO due to the increase of the search space dimensionality and the fact that each training algorithm has a different set of HPs. We have recently made initial steps to address the FL-CASH problem in [1].

References

[1] Md Alam, Koushik Kar, Theodoros Salonidis, Horst Samulowitz, DASH: decentralized CASH for federated learning, in: International Workshop on Federated Learning: Recent Advances and New Challenges (FL-NeurIPS'22) in Conjunction with NeurIPS, 2022.

[2] James Bergstra, Yoshua Bengio, Random search for hyper-parameter optimization, Journal of Machine Learning Research 13 (Feb 2012) 281–305.

[3] James S. Bergstra, Rémi Bardenet, Yoshua Bengio, Balázs Kégl, Algorithms for hyper-parameter optimization, in: Advances in Neural Information Processing Systems, 2011, pp. 2546–2554.

[4] Leo Breiman, Random forests, Machine Learning 45 (1) (2001) 5–32.

[5] Tianqi Chen, Carlos Guestrin, XGBoost: A scalable tree boosting system, in: Proceedings of the 22nd ACM SIGKDD International Conference on Knowledge Discovery and Data Mining, KDD'16, ACM, New York, NY, USA, 2016, pp. 785–794.

[6] Z. Dai, B.K.H. Low, P. Jaillet, Federated Bayesian optimization via Thompson sampling, Advances in Neural Information Processing Systems 33 (2020).

[7] Z. Dai, B.K.H. Low, P. Jaillet, Differentially private federated Bayesian optimization with distributed exploration, Advances in Neural Information Processing Systems 34 (2021).

[8] Alireza Fallah, Aryan Mokhtari, Asuman Ozdaglar, Personalized federated learning with theoretical guarantees: a model-agnostic meta-learning approach, Advances in Neural Information Processing Systems 33 (2020) 3557–3568.

[9] Matthias Feurer, Katharina Eggensperger, Stefan Falkner, Marius Lindauer, Frank Hutter, Auto-sklearn 2.0: the next generation, arXiv:2007.04074 [cs.LG], 2020.

[10] Matthias Feurer, Aaron Klein, Katharina Eggensperger, Jost Springenberg, Manuel Blum, Frank Hutter, Efficient and robust automated machine learning, in: Advances in Neural Information Processing Systems, 2015, pp. 2962–2970.

[11] Jerome H. Friedman, Greedy function approximation: a gradient boosting machine, The Annals of Statistics (2001) 1189–1232.

[12] Anubhav Garg, Amit Kumar Saha, Debo Dutta, Direct federated neural architecture search, arXiv:2010.06223, 2020.

[13] Gary Gensler, Lily Bailey, Deep learning and financial stability, 2020, Available at SSRN 3723132.

[14] Bryce Goodman, Seth Flaxman, European Union regulations on algorithmic decision-making and a "right to explanation", AI Magazine 38 (3) (2017) 50–57.

[15] Chaoyang He, Murali Annavaram, Salman Avestimehr, Towards non-i.i.d. and invisible data with FedNAS: federated deep learning via neural architecture search, arXiv:2004.08546, 2020.

[16] Frank Hutter, Holger H. Hoos, Kevin Leyton-Brown, Sequential model-based optimization for general algorithm configuration, in: International Conference on Learning and Intelligent Optimization, Springer, 2011, pp. 507–523.

[17] Kevin Jamieson, Ameet Talwalkar, Non-stochastic best arm identification and hyperparameter optimization, in: Artificial Intelligence and Statistics, 2016, pp. 240–248.

[18] Peter Kairouz, H. Brendan McMahan, Brendan Avent, Aurélien Bellet, Mehdi Bennis, Arjun Nitin Bhagoji, Kallista Bonawitz, Zachary Charles, Graham Cormode, Rachel Cummings, et al., Advances and open, problems in federated learning, arXiv:1912.04977, 2019.

[19] Mikhail Khodak, Tian Li, Liam Li, M. Balcan, Virginia Smith, Ameet Talwalkar, Weight sharing for hyperparameter optimization in federated learning, in: Int. Workshop on Federated Learning for User Privacy and Data Confidentiality in Conjunction with ICML 2020, 2020.

[20] Mikhail Khodak, Renbo Tu, Tian Li, Liam Li, Maria-Florina Balcan, Virginia Smith, Ameet Talwalkar, Federated hyperparameter tuning: challenges, baselines, and connections to weight-sharing, arXiv:2106.04502, 2021.

[21] A. Koskela, A. Honkela, Learning rate adaptation for federated and differentially private learning, arXiv:1809.03832, 2019.

[22] Li Tian, Shengyuan Hu, Ahmad Beirami, Virginia Smith, Ditto: fair and robust federated learning through personalization, in: International Conference on Machine Learning, PMLR, 2021, pp. 6357–6368.

[23] Yang Liu, Tao Fan, Tianjian Chen, Qian Xu, Qiang Yang, FATE: an industrial grade platform for collaborative learning with data protection, Journal of Machine Learning Research 22 (226) (2021) 1–6.

[24] Heiko Ludwig, Nathalie Baracaldo, Gegi Thomas, Yi Zhou, Ali Anwar, Shashank Rajamoni, Yuya Ong, Jayaram Radhakrishnan, Ashish Verma, Mathieu Sinn, et al., IBM federated learning: an enterprise framework white paper v0. 1, arXiv:2007.10987, 2020.

[25] B. McMahan, E. Moore, D. Ramage, S. Hampson, B.A. Arcas, Communication-efficient learning of deep networks from decentralized data, in: Proc. International Conference on Artificial Intelligence and Statistics, Ft. Lauderdale, FL, 20–22 Apr. 2017, pp. 1273–1282.

[26] Brendan McMahan, Eider Moore, Daniel Ramage, Seth Hampson, Blaise Aguera y Arcas, Communication-efficient learning of deep networks from decentralized data, in: Artificial Intelligence and Statistics, PMLR, 2017, pp. 1273–1282.

[27] H. Mostafa, Robust federated learning through representation matching and adaptive hyper-parameters, arXiv:1912.13075, 2019.

[28] OECD, Artificial intelligence, machine learning and big data in finance: Opportunities, challenges, and implications for policy makers, 2021.

[29] Yuya Jeremy Ong, Yi Zhou, Nathalie Baracaldo, Heiko Ludwig, Adaptive histogram-based gradient boosted trees for federated learning, arXiv:2012.06670, 2020.

[30] F. Pedregosa, G. Varoquaux, A. Gramfort, V. Michel, B. Thirion, O. Grisel, M. Blondel, P. Prettenhofer, R. Weiss, V. Dubourg, J. Vanderplas, A. Passos, D. Cournapeau, M. Brucher, M. Perrot, E. Duchesnay, Scikit-learn: machine learning in Python, Journal of Machine Learning Research 12 (2011) 2825–2830.

[31] S.J. Reddi, Z. Charles, M. Zaheer, Z. Garrett, K. Rush, J. Konecny, S. Kumar, H.B. McMahan, Adaptive federated optimization, in: International Conference on Learning Representations, 2020.

[32] Bobak Shahriari, Kevin Swersky, Ziyu Wang, Ryan P. Adams, Nando De Freitas, Taking the human out of the loop: a review of Bayesian optimization, Proceedings of the IEEE 104 (1) (2015) 148–175.

[33] Joaquin Vanschoren, Meta-learning: a survey, arXiv:1810.03548, 2018.

[34] Joaquin Vanschoren, Jan N. van Rijn, Bernd Bischl, Luis Torgo, OpenML: networked science in machine learning, SIGKDD Explorations 15 (2) (2013) 49–60.

[35] Cedric Villani, Topics in optimal transportation (books), OR/MS Today 30 (3) (2003) 66–67.

[36] Shiqiang Wang, Tiffany Tuor, Theodoros Salonidis, Kin Leung, Christian Makaya, Ting He, Kevin Chan, Adaptive federated learning in resource constrained edge computing systems, IEEE Journal on Selected Areas in Communications (2019).

[37] Christopher K. Williams, Carl Edward Rasmussen, Gaussian Processes for Machine Learning, vol. 2, MIT Press, Cambridge, MA, 2006.

[38] Martin Wistuba, Nicolas Schilling, Lars Schmidt-Thieme, Scalable Gaussian process-based transfer surrogates for hyperparameter optimization, Machine Learning 107 (1) (2018) 43–78.

[39] Mengwei Xu, Yuxin Zhao, Kaigui Bian, Gang Huang, Qiaozhu Mei, Xuanzhe Liu, Federated neural architecture search, arXiv:2002.06352, 2020.

[40] Wang Zhen, Weirui Kuang, Ce Zhang, Bolin Ding, Yaliang Li, FedHPO-B: a benchmark suite for federated hyperparameter optimization, 2022.

[41] Yi Zhou, Parikshit Ram, Theodoros Salonidis, Nathalie Baracaldo, Horst Samulowitz, Heiko Ludwig, FLoRA: single-shot hyper-parameter optimization for federated learning,

in: 1st Workshop on New Frontiers in Federated Learning: Privacy, Fairness, Robustness, Personalization and Data Ownership at NeurIPS'21, 2021.

[42] Yi Zhou, Parikshit Ram, Theodoros Salonidis, Nathalie Baracaldo, Horst Samulowitz, Heiko Ludwig, Single-shot general hyper-parameter optimization for federated learning, in: International Conference on Learning Representations, 2023.

Federated sequential decision making: Bayesian optimization, reinforcement learning, and beyond

Zhongxiang Dai[a]**, Flint Xiaofeng Fan**[a]**, Cheston Tan**[c]**, Trong Nghia Hoang**[d]**, Bryan Kian Hsiang Low**[a]**, and Patrick Jaillet**[b]

[a]*National University of Singapore, Singapore, Singapore*
[b]*Massachusetts Institute of Technology, Cambridge, MA, United States*
[c]*Institute for Infocomm Research, A*STAR, Singapore, Singapore*
[d]*Washington State University, Pullman, WA, United States*

14.1 Introduction

Classic federated learning (FL) is designed for supervised learning, i.e., multiple agents/clients collaborate to train a supervised learning model such as a neural network (NN) [54] or a decision tree-based model [44,45]. However, in addition to supervised learning, many other machine learning methods which are *sequential decision-making* problems in nature, such as the celebrated methods of *Bayesian optimization* (BO) [28] and *reinforcement learning* (RL) [71], also find important applications in the federated setting. For example, BO has been the most popular method for tuning the hyperparameters of ML models, and hence hyperparameter tuning of ML models in the federated setting naturally calls for algorithms for *federated BO* (FBO); RL has been widely adopted for clinical decision support, and therefore collaborative clinical treatment recommendation among multiple hospitals is a natural and important application for *federated RL* (FRL). Therefore, extending these classic sequential decision-making algorithms (such as BO and RL) into the federated setting holds considerable promise for more widespread applications of FL.

However, the extension of these classic algorithms into the federated setting is non-trivial and faced with significant challenges. First of all, these classic sequential decision-making algorithms need to be modified to satisfy the core principles of FL. As a prime example, an important principle in FL is that the raw data of an agent can never be transmitted [35]. Similarly, during federated sequential decision-making, the raw data of an agent, such as the history of observations in BO and the raw trajectories

Federated Learning. https://doi.org/10.1016/B978-0-44-319037-7.00023-5

in RL, must also be retained by the agent and hence never shared with others. This requirement, as well as other requirements stemming from the core principles of FL, may necessitate non-trivial problem-dependent algorithmic designs. Moreover, when modifying these sequential decision-making algorithms for the federated setting, it is challenging to preserve their rigorous theoretical guarantees (e.g., the sub-linear regret upper bound of classic BO algorithms and the sample complexity of classic policy gradient algorithms for RL) and at the same time consistently improve their empirical performances by exploiting the federation of multiple agents. In recent years, a number of works have tackled these challenges and hence introduced federated versions of classic sequential decision-making algorithms, such as FBO [14,15] and FRL [26] algorithms.

The works of [15] and [14] have proposed FBO algorithms. The work of [15] has introduced the first FBO algorithm, named *federated Thompson sampling* (FTS), which addressed several important challenges in FBO. Specifically, the FTS algorithm is free from the requirement to transmit the observations of BO, requires a small number of parameters to be exchanged, and is theoretically guaranteed to be no-regret despite agent heterogeneity [15]. The more recent work of [14] has extended the FTS algorithm of [15] to incorporate a rigorous privacy guarantee and to further improve its practical performance via the method of distributed exploration. Regarding FRL, the recent work of [26] has introduced the first FRL framework with a theoretically guaranteed convergence. Specifically, building on the classic policy gradient algorithm, [26] only requires the agents to exchange their policy gradients instead of their raw trajectories and has achieved low sample complexity by leveraging variance-reduced optimization techniques. Moreover, [26] has also achieved theoretically guaranteed robustness against Byzantine agents (i.e., caused by random failures or adversarial attacks), which is another important consideration in FL. These recent works on FBO [14,15] and FRL [26] have been shown to be both theoretically grounded and practically effective, and we will discuss them in more detail in Sections 14.2 and 14.3, respectively. In addition to FBO and FRL, another line of recent works has extended *multi-armed bandits* [40], which is another classic sequential decision-making problem, to the federated setting and hence introduced federated bandits [16,22,66]. These recent works on federated bandits mostly focus on the theoretical perspective, and we will discuss them in Section 14.4.3.

In the remainder of this chapter, we will separately discuss FBO (Section 14.2) and FRL (Section 14.3), including their background, representative existing works, algorithms/frameworks, as well as theoretical and empirical results. Subsequently, in Section 14.4, we will briefly review other recent related works on FBO (Section 14.4.1), FRL (Section 14.4.2) and federated bandits (Section 14.4.3). Lastly, we will discuss open problems and potential future directions in the area of federated sequential decision-making (Section 14.5).

14.2 Federated Bayesian optimization

In this section, we firstly present some technical background on BO (Section 14.2.1) and FBO (Section 14.2.2). Next, we give an overview of the representative existing works on FBO [14,15] (Section 14.2.3), and then discuss their algorithms (Section 14.2.4) as well as their theoretical and empirical results (Section 14.2.5).

14.2.1 Background on Bayesian optimization

Bayesian optimization (BO) aims to use sequential queries to maximize an objective function $f : \mathcal{X} \to \mathbb{R}$, i.e., to find $\mathbf{x}^* \in \arg\max_{\mathbf{x} \in \mathcal{X}} f(\mathbf{x})$, in which $\mathcal{X} \subset \mathbb{R}^d$ is a discrete subset of the d-dimensional domain.[1] The function f is usually black-box (i.e., non-differentiable and hence only available through queries) and costly to evaluate. A typical example is hyperparameter tuning for deep neural networks (DNNs), in which $\mathbf{x} \in \mathcal{X}$ is a hyperparameter configuration for training a DNN (e.g., the learning rate, regularization parameter, etc.) and $f(\mathbf{x})$ represents the validation accuracy obtained after training the DNN using the hyperparameter configuration $\mathbf{x}$. Specifically, in iteration $t = 1, \ldots, T$ of BO, an input $\mathbf{x}_t \in \mathcal{X}$ is selected and queried, yielding an output observation $y_t \triangleq f(\mathbf{x}_t) + \zeta$ where ζ is sampled from a zero-mean Gaussian noise with a variance of σ^2, $\zeta \sim \mathcal{N}(0, \sigma^2)$. To select the input queries $\mathbf{x}_t$'s intelligently, BO uses a *Gaussian process* (GP) [60] as a surrogate to model the function f.

A GP $\mathcal{GP}(\mu(\cdot), k(\cdot, \cdot))$ is characterized by its mean function μ and kernel function k. We assume without loss of generality that $\mu(\mathbf{x}) = 0$ and $k(\mathbf{x}, \mathbf{x}') \leq 1, \forall \mathbf{x}, \mathbf{x}' \in \mathcal{X}$, and we mainly focus on the widely used *squared exponential* (SE) kernel here [14,15]. In iteration $t + 1$ of BO, given the first t observed input–output pairs, the GP posterior is given by $\mathcal{GP}(\mu_t(\cdot), \sigma_t^2(\cdot, \cdot))$ where

$$\mu_t(\mathbf{x}) := \mathbf{k}_t(\mathbf{x})^\top (\mathbf{K}_t + \lambda \mathbf{I})^{-1} \mathbf{y}_t,$$
$$\sigma_t^2(\mathbf{x}, \mathbf{x}') := k(\mathbf{x}, \mathbf{x}') - \mathbf{k}_t(\mathbf{x})^\top (\mathbf{K}_t + \lambda \mathbf{I})^{-1} \mathbf{k}_t(\mathbf{x}'), \tag{14.1}$$

where $\mathbf{k}_t(\mathbf{x}) := (k(\mathbf{x}, \mathbf{x}_\tau))_{\tau=1,\ldots,t}^\top$ is a t-dimensional column vector, $\mathbf{y}_t := (y_\tau)_{\tau=1,\ldots,t}^\top$ is also a t-dimensional column vector, $\mathbf{K}_t := (k(\mathbf{x}_\tau, \mathbf{x}_{\tau'}))_{\tau,\tau'=1,\ldots,t}$ is a $t \times t$-dimensional matrix and $\lambda > 0$ is a regularization parameter [10]. In iteration $t + 1$, the GP posterior (14.1) is used to calculate an *acquisition function*, which is then maximized to select the next query $\mathbf{x}_{t+1}$. For example, the classic *Thompson sampling* (TS) [10] algorithm first samples a function f_{t+1} using the GP posterior (14.1) and then uses it as the acquisition function to chooses $\mathbf{x}_{t+1} = \arg\max_{\mathbf{x} \in \mathcal{X}} f_{t+1}(\mathbf{x})$. BO algorithms are usually analyzed in terms of *regrets* [70]. A hallmark for well-performing BO algorithms is to be asymptotically *no-regret*, which requires the *cumulative regret* $R_T := \sum_{t=1}^{T} (f(\mathbf{x}^*) - f(\mathbf{x}_t))$ to grow sub-linearly so that the simple regret $S_T := \min_{t=1,\ldots,T} (f(\mathbf{x}^*) - f(\mathbf{x}_t)) \leq R_T/T$ goes to 0 asymptotically.

---

[1] We assume $\mathcal{X}$ to be discrete for simplicity, but the extension to a continuous domain is straightforward using well-known techniques [14].

To reduce the computational cost of GP posterior inference (14.1), *random Fourier features* (RFFs) [59] is commonly adopted to approximate the kernel function k using M-dimensional random features ϕ: $k(\mathbf{x}, \mathbf{x}') \approx \phi(\mathbf{x})^\top \phi(\mathbf{x}')$. RFFs offers a high-probability guarantee on the approximation quality, i.e., we have that $\sup_{\mathbf{x},\mathbf{x}' \in \mathcal{X}} |k(\mathbf{x}, \mathbf{x}') - \phi(\mathbf{x})^\top \phi(\mathbf{x}')| \leq \varepsilon$, in which $\varepsilon = \mathcal{O}(M^{-1/2})$ [59]. Of note, RFFs makes it particularly convenient to approximately sample a function from the GP posterior (14.1). Specifically, define $\mathbf{\Phi}_t := (\phi(\mathbf{x}_\tau))_{\tau \in [t]}^\top$ (i.e., a $t \times M$-dimensional matrix), $\mathbf{\Sigma}_t := \mathbf{\Phi}_t^\top \mathbf{\Phi}_t + \lambda \mathbf{I}$, and $\mathbf{v}_t := \mathbf{\Sigma}_t^{-1} \mathbf{\Phi}_t^\top \mathbf{y}_t$. To sample a function $\widetilde{f}$ from the GP posterior with the approximate kernel $\widetilde{k}(\mathbf{x}, \mathbf{x}') \approx \phi(\mathbf{x})^\top \phi(\mathbf{x}')$, we only need to sample an M-dimensional vector

$$\boldsymbol{\omega} \sim \mathcal{N}(\mathbf{v}_t, \lambda \mathbf{\Sigma}_t^{-1}) \tag{14.2}$$

and then set $\widetilde{f}(\mathbf{x}) = \phi(\mathbf{x})^\top \boldsymbol{\omega}, \forall \mathbf{x} \in \mathcal{X}$. Refer to [15] for more details on RFF approximations of GP.

14.2.2 Background on federated Bayesian optimization

Here we present the problem setting of *federated BO* (FBO), which follows the works of [14] and [15]. FBO involves a central server and N agents/clients $\mathcal{A}_1, \dots, \mathcal{A}_N$. Every agent $\mathcal{A}_n$ attempts to maximize its own objective function $f^n : \mathcal{X} \to \mathbb{R}$, i.e., to find $\mathbf{x}_*^n \in \arg\max_{\mathbf{x} \in \mathcal{X}} f^n(\mathbf{x})$, by querying $\mathbf{x}_t^n$ and observing $y_t^n, \forall t = 1, \dots, T$. As a representative motivating example, N mobile phone users (agents) who use DNNs for next-word prediction in a smart keyboard application may wish to collaboratively tune the hyperparameters of their DNNs. In this application, agent (mobile phone user) $\mathcal{A}_n$ sequentially queries the hyperparameter configurations $\mathbf{x}_t^n \in \mathcal{X}$, $\forall t = 1, \dots, T$ in order to maximize its validation accuracy denoted by the function $f^n : \mathcal{X} \to \mathbb{R}$. As another example, a hospital can use BO to select the patients to perform a medical test to assess the possibility of readmission [81], and multiple hospitals may wish to collaborate to achieve better patient selection strategies. In this case, the input query $\mathbf{x}_t^n \in \mathcal{X}$ selected by hospital $\mathcal{A}_n$ in iteration t corresponds to the features representing the selected patient, and the corresponding value of the objective function $f^n(\mathbf{x}_t^n)$ represents the test score for the selected patient $\mathbf{x}_t^n$.

As a common ground for the collaboration among different agents, we assume that all participating agents share the same set of random features $\phi(\mathbf{x}), \forall \mathbf{x} \in \mathcal{X}$. Similar to BO discussed above, in FBO, every agent $\mathcal{A}_n$ aims to minimize its own cumulative regret, $R_T^n \triangleq \sum_{t=1}^T (f^n(\mathbf{x}_*^n) - f^n(\mathbf{x}_t^n))$. Without loss of generality, when presenting the theoretical results in Section 14.2.5, we focus on the perspective of agent $\mathcal{A}_1$. That is, we derive an upper bound on the cumulative regret of agent $\mathcal{A}_1$ denoted as R_T^1. We characterize the similarity between agents $\mathcal{A}_1$ and $\mathcal{A}_n$ by $d_n := \max_{\mathbf{x} \in \mathcal{X}} |f^1(\mathbf{x}) - f^n(\mathbf{x})|$ such that $d_1 = 0$ and a smaller d_n indicates a larger degree of similarity (or equivalently, a smaller degree of heterogeneity) between $\mathcal{A}_1$ and $\mathcal{A}_n$. In the theoretical analysis, we assume that the objective functions of all agents have a bounded norm induced by the *reproducing kernel Hilbert space* (RKHS) associated with the kernel k, i.e., $\|f^n\|_k \leq B, \forall n \in [N]$. This essentially assumes that the objective functions are smooth and is a common assumption in the analysis of BO algorithms [10].

Core principles and challenges of FBO. Since FBO needs to follow the core principles of FL, it also inherits a number of important challenges of the federated setting. Firstly, the raw data (e.g., the history of queried hyperparameter configurations and observed validation accuracies during BO) of every agent can never be shared with others. Secondly, the heterogeneity among different agents is another crucial challenge of FBO. For example, since different mobile phone users may have distinct typing habits, the optimal hyperparameters of their DNNs for next-word prediction may vary significantly. In addition, same as FL, there are also other important challenges in FBO, such as communication efficiency (i.e., the total number of exchanged parameters), rigorous privacy guarantees for the agents, decentralized communication, fairness among different agents, etc. As we will discuss in detail in Section 14.2.3, the works of [14,15] have tackled a number of these challenges (e.g., retaining the raw data, agent heterogeneity, communication efficiency and rigorous privacy guarantees), whereas the others are still important open problems for FBO.

14.2.3 Overview of representative existing works on FBO

The work of [15] has introduced the *federated Thompson sampling* (FTS) algorithm, which is the first algorithm for FBO. The FTS algorithm [15] has mainly tackled three of the major challenges faced by FBO (Section 14.2.2).

The first challenge results from the requirement to retain (hence not transmit) the raw data, which is a unique challenge faced by FBO yet not FL. Specifically, the information about a BO task is contained in its GP surrogate model (Section 14.2.1). However, unlike DNNs in standard FL for supervised learning, GPs are *nonparametric* [60]. Therefore, a BO task has no parameters (except for the raw data of BO) that can represent the GP surrogate and thus be exchanged among agents, while the raw data of BO should never be transmitted [39]. To overcome this challenge, the work of [15] has exploited RFFs (Section 14.2.1) to approximate a GP, which naturally yields parameters that contain the information about the approximate GP surrogate and can thus be communicated among the agents without exchanging the raw data. The second challenge concerns the communication efficiency, for which [15] has adopted TS as the acquisition function (Section 14.2.1), which reduces the number of exchanged parameters while maintaining competitive performances. The third challenge is caused by the potential heterogeneity among different agents, which is an important practical consideration in FL since different agents can have highly distinct properties [48]. In FBO, heterogeneity arises because different agents may have disparate objective functions. To address this challenge, [15] has derived a theoretical convergence guarantee to ensure that their FTS algorithm is asymptotically no-regret even when all agents have highly different objective functions.

More recently, the work of [14] has extended the FTS algorithm [15] by additionally addressing the challenge of rigorous privacy guarantees (Section 14.2.2) through the classic method of *differential privacy* (DP) [24]. Specifically, [14] has incorporated the general DP framework adopted by the DP-SGD [1] and DP-FedAvg [55]

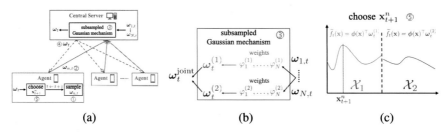

FIGURE 14.1

(a) DP-FTS algorithm without distributed exploration; (b)–(c) replacing steps (3) and (5) in (a) with that in (b) and (c) to derive the DP-FTS-DE algorithm ($P = 2$ sub-regions).

algorithms into (a modified version of) the FTS algorithm [15], to protect the *user-level privacy* of the agents in FBO. By achieving a guarantee on the user-level privacy, [14] guarantees that an adversary, even with arbitrary side information, cannot infer whether an agent has participated in FBO, hence assuring every agent that its participation will not reveal its sensitive information. In addition, to compensate for the performance loss due to privacy preservation, [14] has proposed the technique of *distributed exploration* (DE) to further improve the practical performance (i.e., utility) of their algorithm. Intuitively, the DE technique is based on the idea of local modeling in GP [25] and is incorporated into the general DP framework in a seamless way thanks to the flexibility of the framework to model multiple parameter vectors [53].

Since the method introduced by [14], named DP-FTS-DE, is the state-of-the-art algorithm for FBO, we will introduce the details of the DP-FTS-DE algorithm in the next section (Section 14.2.4), and then discuss its theoretical guarantees and empirical performances in Section 14.2.5.

14.2.4 Algorithms for FBO

For ease of understanding, in this section, we will firstly introduce the DP-FTS algorithm without the DE technique, and then describe how DP-FTS can be modified to incorporate DE to derive the DP-FTS-DE algorithm.

The DP-FTS algorithm. Fig. 14.1(a) illustrates the DP-FTS algorithm. Every iteration t of DP-FTS consists of the following steps:

Steps ① and ② by the agents. Every agent $\mathcal{A}_n$ samples a vector $\omega_{n,t}$ following equation (14.2) using its own current history of t input–output pairs (step ①), and then sends $\omega_{n,t}$ to the central server – step ②.

Steps ③ and ④ by the central server. Next, the central server processes the N received vectors $\{\omega_{n,t}\}_{n=1,...,N}$ using a sub-sampled Gaussian mechanism – step ③ – which consists of four steps:

A. Selecting a random subset of agents $\mathcal{S}_t \subset \{1, \ldots, N\}$ by choosing each agent with probability q,

B. Clipping the vector $\omega_{n,t}$ of every selected agent such that its L_2 norm is upper-bounded by S, $\widehat{\omega}_{n,t} = \omega_{n,t} / \max(1, \|\omega_{n,t}\|_2 / S)$,

C. Calculating a weighted average of the clipped vectors with $\{\varphi_n\}_{n=1,\ldots,N}$, $\omega_t = (q)^{-1} \sum_{n \in \mathcal{S}_t} \varphi_n \widehat{\omega}_{n,t}$, and

D. Adding noise $\epsilon \sim \mathcal{N}(0, (zS\varphi_{\max}/q)^2)$ to ω_t where $\varphi_{\max} = \max_{n=1,\ldots,N} \varphi_n$ and z is a parameter controlling the privacy-utility trade-off. The final vector ω_t is then broadcast to all agents – step (4).

Step (5) by the agents. After an agent $\mathcal{A}_n$ receives the vector ω_t from the central server, it can choose its next query $\mathbf{x}_{t+1}^n$ (step (5)). Choose $\delta \in (0, 1)$ and define $\beta_t := B + \sigma\sqrt{2(\gamma_{t-1} + 1 + \log(4/\delta))}$, in which B is an upper bound on the RKHS norm of the objective functions f^n's (Section 14.2.2), σ is the noise standard deviation (Section 14.2.1), and γ_{t-1} is the maximum information gain about f^n from any set of $t - 1$ queries [70].

Then, with probability of $p_{t+1} \in (0, 1]$, $\mathcal{A}_n$ chooses $\mathbf{x}_{t+1}^n$ using standard TS by sampling a function f_{t+1}^n from its posterior of $\mathcal{GP}(\mu_t^n(\cdot), \beta_{t+1}^2 \sigma_t^n(\cdot, \cdot)^2)$ (14.1) and then choosing $\mathbf{x}_{t+1}^n = \arg\max_{\mathbf{x} \in \mathcal{X}} f_{t+1}^n(\mathbf{x})$. Otherwise, with probability of $1 - p_{t+1}$, $\mathcal{A}_n$ chooses $\mathbf{x}_{t+1}^n$ using ω_t received from the server, $\mathbf{x}_{t+1}^n = \arg\max_{\mathbf{x} \in \mathcal{X}} \phi(\mathbf{x})^\top \omega_t$. The sequence $(p_t)_{t \in \mathbb{Z}^+}$ is chosen as a monotonically increasing sequence such that $p_t \in (0, 1]$, $\forall t$ and $p_t \to 1$ as $t \to \infty$. This ensures that, when $1 - p_t$ is large, an agent can leverage the information from the other agents (via ω_t) to improve its convergence by accelerating its exploration.

After choosing $\mathbf{x}_{t+1}^n$ and observing y_{t+1}^n, the agent $\mathcal{A}_n$ adds $(\mathbf{x}_{t+1}^n, y_{t+1}^n)$ to its history of observations and then samples a new vector $\omega_{n,t+1}$ – step (1). Next, $\mathcal{A}_n$ sends $\omega_{n,t+1}$ to the central server – step (2) – and the algorithm is repeated.

The DP-FTS-DE algorithm. The DP-FTS-DE algorithm is obtained by incorporating the technique of DE into DP-FTS described above.

Specifically, DE divides the entire domain $\mathcal{X}$ into $P \geq 1$ disjoint sub-regions $\mathcal{X}_1, \ldots, \mathcal{X}_P$, and the incorporation of DE requires three major modifications to DP-FTS. Firstly, during the initialization stage, every agent only explores a local sub-region $\mathcal{X}_i$ instead of the entire domain $\mathcal{X}$.

Next, instead of a single vector ω_t, the central server produces and broadcasts P vectors $\{\omega_t^{(i)}\}_{i=1,\ldots,P}$, each corresponding to a different sub-region $\mathcal{X}_i$ and using a different set of weights $\{\varphi_n^{(i)}\}_{n=1,\ldots,N}$. Interestingly, the different privacy-preserving transformations performed by the central server to produce P vectors can be interpreted as a single sub-sampled Gaussian mechanism producing a single joint vector $\omega_t^{\text{joint}} \triangleq (\omega_t^{(i)})_{i \in [P]}$ (Fig. 14.1(b)).

Then, if agent $\mathcal{A}_n$ uses the vector $\omega_t^{\text{joint}} = (\omega_t^{(i)})_{i \in [P]}$ received from the central server to choose the next query $\mathbf{x}_{t+1}^n$ (with probability $1 - p_{t+1}$), it chooses $\mathbf{x}_{t+1}^n$ by maximizing the reconstructed functions for all sub-regions, as illustrated in Fig. 14.1(c). Refer to the work of [14] for a more complete description of the DP-FTS-DE algorithm.

14.2.5 Theoretical and empirical results for FBO

The work of [14] has provided theoretical guarantees on both the privacy and utility of DP-FTS-DE. The privacy guarantee is given by the proposition below:

Proposition 14.1. *There exist constants c_1 and c_2 such that for fixed q and T and any $\epsilon < c_1 q^2 T$, $\delta > 0$, DP-FTS-DE is (ϵ, δ)-DP if $z \geq c_2 q \sqrt{T \log(1/\delta)}/\epsilon$.*

The following theorem gives a guarantee on the utility/performance of DP-FTS-DE in terms an upper bound on R_T^1 (Section 14.2.2), in which all notations have been defined in Sections 14.2.1, 14.2.2 and 14.2.4:

Theorem 14.1 (Informal). *With high probability,*

$$R_T^1 = \tilde{\mathcal{O}}\left(\left(B + 1/p_1\right) \gamma_T \sqrt{T} + \sum_{t=1}^{T} \psi_t + B \sum_{t=1}^{T} \vartheta_t \right),$$

where $\psi_t := \tilde{\mathcal{O}}((1 - p_t) P \varphi_{\max} q^{-1}(\Delta_t + z S \sqrt{M}))$, and $\Delta_t := \sum_{n=1}^{N} \tilde{\mathcal{O}}(\varepsilon B t^2 + B + \sqrt{M} + d_n + \sqrt{\gamma_t})$. $\vartheta_t := (1 - p_t) \sum_{i=1}^{P} \sum_{n \in \mathcal{C}_t} \varphi_n^{(i)}$, $\mathcal{C}_t := \{n \in [N] \mid \|\boldsymbol{\omega}_{n,t}\|_2 > S/\sqrt{P}\}$.

The first interesting insight from Theorem 14.1 is that agent $\mathcal{A}_1$ is asymptotically *no-regret* even if all other agents are heterogeneous, i.e., all other agents have significantly different objective functions from $\mathcal{A}_1$. This ensures that DP-FTS-DE is robust against the heterogeneity of agents, which is a significant challenge in FBO (Section 14.2.2).

Moreover, Theorem 14.1, when interpreted together with Proposition 14.1, also reveals some interesting theoretical insights regarding the **privacy–utility trade-off**. Firstly, a larger z (i.e., larger variance for the added Gaussian noise, Section 14.2.4) improves the privacy guarantee (Proposition 14.1), yet results in a worse utility since it leads to a worse regret upper bound (through ψ_t). Secondly, a larger q (i.e., more selected agents in each iteration, Section 14.2.4) improves the utility since it tightens the regret upper bound (by reducing the value of ψ_t) at the expense of a worse privacy guarantee (Proposition 14.1). The value of the clipping threshold S affects the regret upper bound (hence the utility) through two conflicting effects: a smaller S (1) reduces the value of ψ_t (hence, the regret bound) but is also likely to enlarge the cardinality of the set $\mathcal{C}_t$ which increases the value of ϑ_t and hence, the regret bound (Theorem 14.1). Refer to Section 4 of [14] for a more detailed discussion on the theoretical guarantees of DP-FTS-DE, as well as the associated insights.

Empirical results. The work of [14] has also demonstrated the practical effectiveness of DP-FTS-DE using three real-world experiments on landmine detection, human activity recognition, and EMNIST image classification. Some of the experimental results are displayed in Fig. 14.2, which show that FTS (from the work of

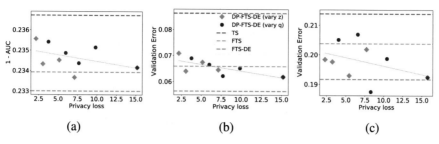

FIGURE 14.2

Scatter plots showing the trade-off between privacy loss and performance after 60 iterations for (a) the landmine detection, (b) human activity recognition, and (c) EMNIST experiments. In the above plots, plotted points leaning more towards the *left* (*bottom*) correspond to trade-off that favors privacy (utility), respectively.

[15]) consistently outperforms standard (non-federated) TS whereas FTS-DE (with the DE technique) further improves the performance of FTS. Moreover, Fig. 14.2 shows that with small privacy losses (in the single digit range [1]), DP-FTS-DE achieves a competitive performance (utility) and significantly outperforms standard TS in all settings. Furthermore, the figure also reveals a clear privacy–utility trade-off, i.e., a smaller privacy loss (more to the left) generally results in a worse utility (larger vertical value). Refer to Section 5 of the work of [14] for more details on the experimental settings, as well as more experimental results and discussions.

14.3 Federated reinforcement learning

In this section, we will first present some technical background on RL (Section 14.3.1) and FRL (Section 14.3.2). Next, we will briefly overview the representative existing works on FRL (Section 14.3.3) and discuss its framework (Section 14.3.4), as well as its corresponding theoretical and empirical results (Section 14.3.5).

14.3.1 Background on reinforcement learning

Reinforcement learning (RL) considers a discrete-time Markov decision process (MDP) [71], $M \triangleq \{\mathcal{S}, \mathcal{U}, \mathcal{P}, \mathcal{R}, \gamma, \rho\}$, in which $\mathcal{S}$ and $\mathcal{U}$ represent the state space and action space, respectively, $\mathcal{P}(s'|s, a)$ defines the transition probability from state s to s' after taking action a, $\mathcal{R}(s, a) : \mathcal{S} \times \mathcal{U} \to \mathbb{R}$ is the reward function for each state–action pair (s, a), $\gamma \in (0, 1)$ is the discount factor, and ρ is the initial state distribution. The behavior of an agent is controlled by a policy π, where $\pi(a|s)$ defines the probability that the agent chooses action a at state s. We consider episodic MDPs with trajectory horizon H. A trajectory $\tau \triangleq \{s_0, a_0, s_1, a_1, \ldots, s_{H-1}, a_{H-1}\}$ is a sequence of state–action pairs traversed by an agent following any stationary policy, where $s_0 \sim \rho$; $\mathcal{R}(\tau) \triangleq \sum_{t=0}^{H-1} \gamma^t \mathcal{R}(s_t, a_t)$ gives the discounted cumulative reward along τ.

Policy gradient (PG) methods have achieved impressive successes in model-free RL [63,64, etc.]. Compared with deterministic value function-based methods such as Q-learning [56], PG methods are generally more effective in high-dimensional problems and enjoy the flexibility of stochasticity. In PG, we use π_{θ} to denote the policy parameterized by $\theta \in \mathbb{R}^d$ (e.g., a neural network), and $p(\tau|\pi_{\theta})$ to represent the trajectory distribution induced by the policy π_{θ}. For brevity, we use θ to denote the corresponding policy π_{θ}. The performance of a policy θ can be measured by $J(\theta) \triangleq \mathbb{E}_{\tau \sim p(\cdot|\theta)}[\mathcal{R}(\tau)|M]$. Taking the gradient of $J(\theta)$ with respect to θ gives

$$\nabla_{\theta} J(\theta) = \int_{\tau} \mathcal{R}(\tau) \nabla_{\theta} p(\tau \mid \theta) d\tau = \mathbb{E}_{\tau \sim p(\cdot|\theta)}\left[\nabla_{\theta} \log p(\tau \mid \theta) \mathcal{R}(\tau) \mid M\right]. \quad (14.3)$$

Then, the policy θ can be optimized using gradient ascent. Since computing (14.3) is usually prohibitive, stochastic gradient ascent is typically used. In each iteration, we sample a batch of trajectories $\{\tau_i\}_{i=1}^B$ using the current policy θ, and update the policy by $\theta \leftarrow \theta + \eta \widehat{\nabla}_B J(\theta)$, where η is the step size and $\widehat{\nabla}_B J(\theta)$ is an estimate of (14.3) using the sampled trajectories $\{\tau_i\}_{i=1}^B$, $\widehat{\nabla}_B J(\theta) = \frac{1}{B} \sum_{i=1}^B \nabla_{\theta} \log p(\tau_i \mid \theta) \mathcal{R}(\tau_i)$. The commonly used policy gradient estimator, namely GPOMDP [6], can be expressed as

$$\widehat{\nabla}_B J(\theta) = \frac{1}{B} \sum_{i=1}^B g(\tau_i|\theta),$$

$$g(\tau_i|\theta) = \sum_{h=0}^{H-1} \left[\sum_{t=0}^h \nabla_{\theta} \log \pi_{\theta}\left(a_t \mid s_t\right)\right]\left(\gamma^h r(s_h, a_h) - C_{b_h}\right), \quad (14.4)$$

in which $\tau_i = \{s_0^i, a_0^i, s_1^i, a_1^i, \ldots, s_{H-1}^i, a_{H-1}^i\}$ and $g(\tau_i|\theta)$ is an *unbiased* estimation of $\nabla_{\theta} \log p(\tau_i \mid \theta) \mathcal{R}(\tau_i)$ [58,77].

To improve the sample efficiency of the estimation of (14.4), *stochastic variance-reduced gradient* (SVRG) [4,34,61,75] has recently been adopted to reduce the variance of policy gradient estimators. The work of [58] has adapted the theoretical analysis of SVRG to PG to introduce the *stochastic variance-reduced policy gradient* (SVRPG) algorithm. More recently, [77] has refined the analysis of SVRPG [58] and shown that SVRPG enjoys a sample complexity of $O(1/\epsilon^{5/3})$.

14.3.2 Background on federated reinforcement learning

It is well established that RL systems suffer from poor sample efficiency in real-world applications [23,42], which has motivated the development of *federated RL* (FRL) [86]. Here, we present the problem statement of FRL following the work of [26]. In FRL, K distributed agents/computing nodes $\mathcal{A}^{(1)}, \ldots, \mathcal{A}^{(K)}$ are operating in separate copies of the same underlying MDP with random initial state distributions $\rho^{(k)}$'s.

Each agent independently runs an RL algorithm by interacting with its environment. Like FBO, FRL involves a central server which is assumed to be trustworthy and governs the federation process. The objective/incentive for agents to participate in the federation is to obtain a well-performing policy θ^* with *fewer* agent-environment interactions compared to independent learning on their own. As a representative motivating example, K hospitals, each of which only possesses a limited number of admission records, who apply RL algorithms to provide clinical decision support may wish to collaboratively discover better treatment protocols for the same disease. To improve the sample efficiency of this application, in every iteration, each agent (hospital) $\mathcal{A}^{(k)}$ interacts with its environment following a parameterized policy (clinical trial protocols) $\theta^{(k)}$ and then shares some information with the trustworthy server (e.g., government), who aggregates all received information and then broadcasts it back to all agents to improve their subsequent decision making.

FRL assumes that all participating RL agents share the same sets of states $\mathcal{S}$ and actions $\mathcal{U}$ as a common ground for collaboration. In addition, an FRL system is concerned with only a single task (e.g., treatment for a single disease), and hence the underlying MDP M (i.e., the transition probability $\mathcal{P}$ and reward function $\mathcal{R}$) is assumed to be the same for all agents. Similar to RL discussed above, every agent $\mathcal{A}^{(k)}$ in FRL aims to maximize the objective function $J^{(k)} \triangleq \mathbb{E}_{\tau \sim p(\cdot|\theta^{(k)})}[\mathcal{R}(\tau)|M]$ with *fewer* interactions with the environment compared with independent learning. That is, to reach a certain performance threshold, the required total number of trajectories $|\tau^{(k)}|$ of agent-environment interactions of agent $\mathcal{A}^{(k)}$ should be smaller than that of independent learning on its own. In other words, the agent aims to improve its sample efficiency by joining the federation. To ensure that FRL leads to a speedup in sample efficiency with a larger number of agents, [26] has presented a convergence guarantee for their proposed federated policy gradient framework and derived an upper bound on the average number of trajectories required by each agent for the policy to reach an ϵ-stationary performance point (Section 14.3.5). In their theoretical analysis, the objective function $J(\theta)$ is assumed to be L-smooth, which is a commonly adopted assumption in non-convex optimization [4,61] and recent convergence results of policy gradient [58,77]. Furthermore, the initial states of the agents are assumed to be uniformly distributed, i.e., the $\rho^{(k)}$'s are uniform distributions.

Core principles and challenges of FRL. In addition to the fundamental challenge of retaining the raw data (i.e., the trajectories of agent–environment interactions $\tau^{(k)}$ shall never be shared), FRL is faced with a few other critical challenges. Firstly, with N agents independently interacting with their own copy of the environment, does FRL theoretically guarantee the convergence and proportionally improved sampled efficiency thanks to the federation? Unlike FL where the training data can be collected offline, FRL requires every agent to sample trajectories online by interacting with the environment, which can be slow and expensive. Therefore, theoretical guarantees on the convergence and sample efficiency speedup provide assurance and incentives for practical applications. Secondly, FRL systems need to account for fault tolerance, which is a critical challenge in practical decision-making applications since distributed systems are likely to fail periodically. Being fault-tolerant allows the

FRL system to continue operating properly without interruption when one or more of its agents fail. Furthermore, the heterogeneity among different agents (e.g., the difference in their initial state distributions, computational budgets, etc.) is another crucial challenge for FRL. For example, since different hospitals may administer patients from distinct geographic locations, their initial state distributions may vary significantly. Similarly, hospitals may possess different computational budgets and hence can adopt disparate policy parameterization schemes and optimization methods. Moreover, FRL is also faced with other challenges which plague FL in general, such as rigorous privacy guarantees, decentralized communication, fairness, etc. The representative work of [26], which we will discuss in Section 14.3.3, has tackled a number of these challenges (e.g., retaining the raw data, guaranteed convergence and proportional sample efficiency speedup, and fault tolerance), whereas the others remain important open problems for FRL.

14.3.3 Overview of representative existing works on FRL

Firstly introduced by [86], FRL has been applied to a number of practical applications [50,51,57, etc.]. The first general-purpose framework for FRL is the *federated policy gradient with Byzantine resilience* (FedPG-BR) framework introduced by [26]. The FedPG-BR framework [26] has mainly addressed three of the aforementioned challenges faced by FRL (Section 14.3.2). For brevity, we defer the details of the FedPG-BR algorithm to Section 14.3.4, followed by discussions on its theoretical guarantees and empirical performances in Section 14.3.5.

The first challenge addressed by [26] is regarding the theoretical guarantees on the convergence and sample efficiency improvements. To this end, [26] has adopted the *stochastically controlled stochastic gradient* (SCSG) algorithm [41], which is a variant of SVRG (Section 14.3.1), in the federated policy gradient framework, which provides a refined control over the variance of the gradient estimation. Their theoretical analysis has shown that their proposed framework is guaranteed to converge and enjoys a proportional sample efficiency speedup with respect to the number of agents. The second challenge results from the fact that distributed systems are vulnerable to random failures or adversarial attacks coming from the distributed agents, which may slow down or completely disrupt the convergence of the FRL systems. These random failures and adversarial attacks are modeled as *Byzantine faults*, which is the most stringent fault formalism in distributed computing [7,52]. Byzantine faults consider a distributed computing system with up to half of the computing nodes being random failures or adversarial attackers. They are hard to detect when the raw data of the agents is not accessible to the server, which makes them a considerable practical challenge in FL [79]. To address this challenge, [26] has designed a gradient-based Byzantine filter on top of their proposed federated policy gradient framework, in order to remove those gradients that are likely sent by Byzantine agents with high probability. This has enabled the algorithm of [26] to be tolerant to Byzantine faults when less than half of the agents are Byzantine agents.

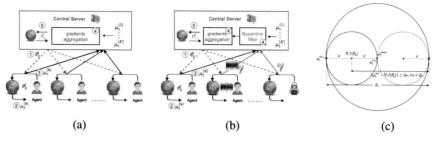

FIGURE 14.3

Workflows of (a) the federated policy gradient algorithm (without fault tolerance) and (b) the federated policy gradient algorithm with Byzantine resilience filter (i.e., the FedPG-BR framework); and (c) visualizing diagram of the concentration bound constructed by the BR filter.

14.3.4 Frameworks and algorithms for FRL

In this section, we will describe the details of the FedPG-BR framework [26], which consists of the *federated policy gradient* (FedPG) algorithm and the *Byzantine resilience* (BR) filter.

The FedPG algorithm. Fig. 14.3(a) illustrates the FedPG algorithm. Every iteration t of FedPG includes the following steps:

Step ① by the central server. FedPG starts with a randomly initialized parameter $\tilde{\boldsymbol{\theta}}_0$ at the server. At the beginning of the tth iteration, the server keeps a snapshot of its parameter from the previous iteration (i.e., $\boldsymbol{\theta}_0^t \leftarrow \tilde{\boldsymbol{\theta}}_{t-1}$) and broadcasts this parameter to all agents.

Step ② and ③ by the agents. Every agent $\mathcal{A}^{(k)}$ samples B_t trajectories $\{\tau_{t,i}^{(k)}\}_{i=1}^{B_t}$ using the policy $\boldsymbol{\theta}_0^t$, computes a gradient estimate $\mu_t^{(k)} \triangleq 1/B_t \sum_{i=1}^{B_t} g(\tau_{t,i}^{(k)}|\boldsymbol{\theta}_0^t)$ following equation (14.4) – step ② – and sends $\mu_t^{(k)}$ back to the server – step ③.

Steps ④ and ⑤ by the central server. The server computes the batch gradient μ_t by averaging the received gradient estimates – step ④ – and updates the policy parameters $\boldsymbol{\theta}_0^t$ via the following semi-stochastic gradient – step ⑤ – according to SCSG optimization [41], $v_n^t \triangleq \frac{1}{b_t} \sum_{j=1}^{b_t} \left[g(\tau_{n,j}^t|\boldsymbol{\theta}_n^t) - g(\tau_{n,j}^t|\boldsymbol{\theta}_0^t) \right] + \mu_t$, in which b_t trajectories are sampled *independently* by the server on a separate copy of the MDP M and the number N_t of optimization steps is sampled from a geometric distribution with the parameter $\frac{B_t}{B_t+b_t}$. The server then stores a new snapshot of the updated parameter, and the algorithm is repeated.

The BR filter. Fig. 14.3(b) demonstrates the complete FedPG-BR framework, which is obtained by incorporating the Byzantine resilience filter (Fig. 14.3(c)) into the FedPG algorithm described above. After receiving all the gradients, the server applies the BR filter (step ④), which is designed based on the following assumptions:

firstly, at any given iteration t, there are less than $K/2$ Byzantine agents; secondly, the gradient estimates sent by the good (non-Byzantine) agents should concentrate in a region containing the true analytical gradient defined in (14.3). In particular, the work of [26] has assumed that there exists a constant σ such that $\|g(\tau|\boldsymbol{\theta}) - \nabla J(\boldsymbol{\theta})\| \leq \sigma$ for any $\tau \sim p(\cdot|\boldsymbol{\theta})$ and any policy $\pi_{\boldsymbol{\theta}}$, which implies that the discrepancy between any two gradient estimates is at most 2σ in the Euclidean space. Therefore, the BR filter computes the pair-wise Euclidean distances of all gradients[2] and selects a set of gradients $S_2 \triangleq \{\mu_t^{(k)}\}$ that are close (within 2σ in Euclidean distance) to more than $K/2$ other gradients. Any gradient $\mu_t^{(\tilde{k})}$ that is the closest to the mean of S_2 will be noted as the mean of median vector of all received gradients, denoted as μ_t^{mom}. Thereafter, the BR filter removes any received gradient $\mu_t^{(k')}$ whose distance to μ_t^{mom} is more than 2σ from the gradients aggregation step (step ④). Essentially, the BR filter constructs a concentration bound such that the server aggregates only those gradient estimates that are not far away from the true analytical gradient. Refer to the work of [26] for a more complete description of the FedPG-BR framework.

14.3.5 Theoretical and empirical results for FRL

The work of [26] has provided theoretical guarantees on the convergence of FedPG-BR:

Theorem 14.2 (Informal). *The output of FedPG-BR, $\tilde{\boldsymbol{\theta}}$, satisfies*

$$\mathbb{E}[\|\nabla J(\tilde{\boldsymbol{\theta}}_a)\|^2] \leq \frac{2\Psi\left[J(\tilde{\boldsymbol{\theta}}^*) - J(\tilde{\boldsymbol{\theta}}_0)\right]}{TB^{1/3}} + \frac{8\sigma^2}{(1-\alpha)^2KB} + \frac{96\alpha^2\sigma^2V}{(1-\alpha)^2B},$$

where α denotes the ratio of Byzantine agents such that $0 \leq \alpha < 0.5$ and $\tilde{\boldsymbol{\theta}}^*$ is a global maximizer of J; Ψ is a smoothness constant and V is another constant used to refine the concentration bound of the BR filter. For brevity, readers are referred to [26] for the detailed definitions of Ψ and V.

This theorem leads to many interesting insights, such as the sample complexity (of each agent in FedPG-BR) to reach an ϵ-stationary point which is summarized in Table 14.1. The table reveals that the sample complexity of FedPG-BR in the single-agent setting matches that of SVRPG derived by [77]. In addition, when $K > 1$, $\alpha = 0$, Table 14.1 shows that the total number of trajectories required by each agent is upper-bounded by $O(1/(\epsilon^{5/3}K^{2/3}))$. This result gives us the theoretical grounds to encourage more agents to participate in the federation since the number of trajectories each agent needs to sample decays at a rate of $O(1/K^{2/3})$. Furthermore, for a more realistic system where an α-fraction ($\alpha > 0$) of the agents are Byzantine agents, the results in Table 14.1 assure us that the total number of trajectories required by each

---

[2] It can be implemented using the Euclidean distance matrix trick [3].

Table 14.1 Sample complexities of relevant works to achieve $\mathbb{E}\|\nabla J(\boldsymbol{\theta})\|^2 \leq \epsilon$.

Settings	Methods	Complexity
$K = 1$	REINFORCE [74]	$O(1/\epsilon^2)$
	GPOMDP [6]	$O(1/\epsilon^2)$
	SVRPG [58]	$O(1/\epsilon^2)$
	SVRPG [77]	$O(1/\epsilon^{5/3})$
	FedPG-BR	$O(1/\epsilon^{5/3})$
$K > 1, \alpha = 0$	**FedPG-BR**	$O(\frac{1}{\epsilon^{5/3}K^{2/3}})$
$K > 1, \alpha > 0$	**FedPG-BR**	$O(\frac{1}{\epsilon^{5/3}K^{2/3}} + \frac{\alpha^{4/3}}{\epsilon^{5/3}})$

agent will be increased by *only an additive term of* $O(\alpha^{4/3}/\epsilon^{5/3})$, the impact of which vanishes when $\alpha \to 0$.

Empirical results. The work of [26] has also demonstrated the practical effectiveness of FedPG-BR using standard RL benchmarks including CartPole balancing [5], LunarLander, and the 3D continuous locomotion control task of HalfCheetah [21]. The experimental results shown in Fig. 14.4 suggest that the performance of FedPG-BR is comparable to SVRPG in the single-agent training setting ($K = 1$), and is improved significantly with the federation of $K = 3$ and $K = 10$ agents. This corroborates our theoretical insights implying that the sample efficiency of FedPG-BR is guaranteed to improve proportionally with the number of agents K. Furthermore, Fig. 14.5 shows another experiment on the HalfCheetah task with $K = 10$ agents, among which 3 are Byzantine agents.

The Byzantine agents are simulated using the following three schemes: *random noise (RN)*: each Byzantine agent sends a random vector to the server; (b) *random action (RA)*: every Byzantine agent ignores the policy from the server and takes actions randomly, which is used to simulate random system failures (e.g., hardware failures); and (c) *sign flipping (SF)*: each Byzantine agent computes the correct gradient but sends the scaled negative gradient, which is used to simulate adversarial attacks aiming to manipulate the direction of policy updates at the server. The three subplots show that the existence of only 3 Byzantine agents causes the performance of federated policy gradient systems (GPOMDP and SVRPG) to be worse than that in the single-agent setting. In contrast, our FedPG-BR is robust against all three types of Byzantine failures. That is, FedPG-BR ($K = 10$, $B = 3$) with 3 Byzantine agents still significantly outperforms the single-agent setting, and more importantly, *performs comparably to FedPG-BR ($K = 10$) with 10 good agents* (shown in the rightmost subplot in Fig. 14.4). These results demonstrate that even in practical systems with random failures or adversarial attacks, FedPG-BR is still able to deliver superior performances, providing an assurance on the reliability of the framework to promote its practical deployment and significantly improving the practicality of FRL.

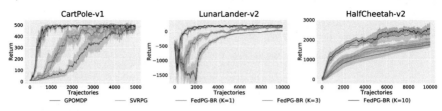

FIGURE 14.4

Performance of FedPG-BR in ideal systems with $\alpha = 0$ for the three tasks.

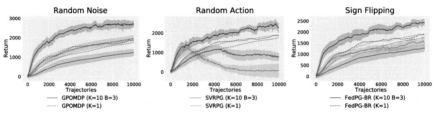

FIGURE 14.5

Performance of FedPG-BR in practical systems with $\alpha > 0$ for HalfCheetah. Each subplot corresponds to a different type of Byzantine failure exercised by the 3 Byzantine agents.

14.4 Related work

14.4.1 Federated Bayesian optimization

To the best of our knowledge, the works of [14,15] (Section 14.2.3) are the only works on FBO to date. However, a number of previous works on BO have considered similar settings to the FBO setting, which we review here.

The work of [68] has also considered collaborative BO involving multiple agents. However, since their method is not designed for the FBO setting, they did not address the important challenges faced by FBO (e.g., they have assumed that all agents share the same objective function and hence did not consider the issue of heterogeneity), but have instead focused on the issue of fairness among the agents [68]. Furthermore, a number of works such as [13,65] have studied BO in the multi-agent setting from the perspective of *game theory*. FBO also shares similarities with *batch/parallel BO*, which has seen a large body of works in recent years [12,18,20,27,30,37,72]. However, batch BO has many important differences with FBO. For example, batch BO aims to maximize a single objective function whereas FBO allows different agents to have different objective functions, and the sharing of the raw observations in batch BO is not prohibited. Another popular line of works on BO which is also related to FBO is *multi-fidelity BO* [17,36,83,84]. This is because, from the point of view of an agent in FBO, the information from the other agents (received via the central server) can be considered as low-fidelity information.

14.4.2 Federated reinforcement learning

FRL was initially introduced by [86] which studied how to collaboratively learn two Q-networks when one of the two agents does not receive rewards from the MDP. Thereafter, FRL has been applied to a number of practical applications, such as autonomous driving [50,62], fast personalization [57], robots navigation [51], traffic sign control [80], and resource management in networking [82]. Despite their promising applications, these works were not equipped with theoretical guarantees and hence did not provide theoretical understandings to the important challenges faced by FRL we have discussed in Section 14.3.2.

The work of [26] has presented the first federated policy gradient framework in the FRL setting which guarantees a proportional sample efficiency improvement with respect to the number of agents and achieves robustness against faulty (Byzantine) agents, hence tackling the challenges of theoretical guarantees and fault tolerance (Section 14.3.2). Regarding the challenge of the heterogeneity among different agents, the work of [76] has defined the heterogeneity in FRL as the data heterogeneity resulting from the difference in the initial state distributions and environment dynamics among different agents. As a result, [76] has proposed an FRL framework to tackle such heterogeneity in FRL by penalizing the Kullback–Leibler (KL) divergence (i.e., encouraging the similarity) between the local policies and the global policy.

FRL also bears close similarity to another line of works on distributed and parallel RL [2,8,31,38], because some of the challenges faced by FRL (Section 14.3.2), such as theoretical guarantees and fault tolerance, are also important considerations for these works. However, there are also substantial differences between these settings and FRL, since FRL also poses some unique challenges such as the requirement to retain the raw data. One representative work in distributed and parallel RL is [9], which has proposed the Byzantine-robust mean estimation technique for both online and offline distributed RL.

14.4.3 Federated bandits

Multi-armed bandits is another popular sequential decision-making problem [40] with important applications such as recommender systems. A growing number of recent works have introduced federated versions of classic bandit algorithms.

Some works have focused on federated K-armed bandits where the number K of arms is finite and the arms are not associated with feature vectors. The works of [46] and [47] have focused on federated K-armed bandits with rigorous privacy guarantees, and have considered both centralized and decentralized communication. The work of [66] has proposed a setting for federated K-armed bandits in which the goal is to minimize the regrets of a global bandit model, which has the same set of arms as the agents. The reward of every arm for the global bandit model is the average of the rewards of the corresponding arm from all agents. The more recent work of [67] has extended [66] to incorporate personalization such that every agent attempts to maximize a weighted combination between the global and its local rewards. After that, subsequent works have focused on other aspects of federated K-armed bandits, such as decentralized communication via the gossiping algorithm [85], the security of federated K-armed bandits through cryptographic techniques [11], uncoordinated exploration [78], and robustness against Byzantine attacks [19].

In addition, a number of works have considered the problem of federated linear contextual bandits. The work of [73] has proposed a distributed linear contextual bandit algorithm that allows every agent to use the observations from the other agents without requiring them to share their raw data. Subsequently, the work of [22] has extended the method from [73] to incorporate differential privacy and decentralized communication. The work of [32] has considered a setting of federated linear contextual bandits where every agent is associated with a unique context vector. The works of [29,43] have both focused on extending the method from [73] in order to allow asynchronous communication. The work of [33] has focused on the robustness of federated linear contextual bandits against Byzantine attacks. A few recent works have relaxed the assumption of a linear reward function adopted by linear contextual bandits to consider non-linear reward functions. The work of [16] has introduced the first *federated neural bandit* algorithm which is able to exploit neural networks to learn the reward function. Moreover, the works of [49] and [69] have, respectively, extended χ-armed bandits and combinatorial bandits to the federated setting.

14.5 Open problems and future directions

As we have discussed in this chapter, extending classic sequential decision-making algorithms (e.g., BO and RL) into the federated setting holds enormous potential, yet is also faced with immense challenges. Some of these challenges have been addressed by recent works, such as the works of [14,15] for FBO (Section 14.2.3) and the work of [26] for FRL (Section 14.3.3). However, some other challenges remain to be tackled and are hence still important open problems.

For FBO, note that the theoretical analyses from the works of [14,15] have focused on the robustness against agent heterogeneity. Therefore, it remains an open problem to theoretically show the benefit of the federation when the agents are in fact homogeneous (or when the degree of heterogeneity is low), i.e., to show that a larger number of agents lead to better regret upper bounds. Furthermore, extending FBO algorithms to cater to other important considerations of the federated setting also represents important future directions in order to make FBO algorithms more practical. For example, allowing decentralized and asynchronous communication in FBO is an important challenge and a meaningful extension, since it allows FBO to work under more flexible communication protocols. Ensuring fairness among different agents in FBO is another significant open problem, since societal issues such as fairness have been receiving growing concerns and are hence crucial considerations for the real-world deployment of FBO algorithms. To this end, the method from [68], which has studied fairness in collaborative BO among multiple agents, may provide interesting inspirations.

For FRL, although the work of [26] has managed to avoid the transmission of the raw data (i.e., RL trajectories) of the agents, they have not provided a rigorous privacy guarantee. Therefore, it is an intriguing future direction to equip FRL systems with rigorous privacy guarantees (e.g., via differential privacy) in order to protect the privacy of the participating agents in a principled way. In addition, the theoretical analysis of [26] has focused on improving the sample efficiency for homogeneous agents. Therefore, a natural future extension is to derive theoretical guarantees when the agents are in fact heterogeneous and to study situations under which the benefits of the federation can be guaranteed in the presence of heterogeneity. Furthermore, designing decentralized FRL systems and achieving fairness among different FRL agents also represent promising future directions for FRL.

Acknowledgments

This research is part of the programme DesCartes and is supported by the National Research Foundation, Prime Minister's Office, Singapore, under its Campus for Research Excellence and Technological Enterprise (CREATE) programme.

References

[1] Martin Abadi, Andy Chu, Ian Goodfellow, H. Brendan McMahan, Ilya Mironov, Kunal Talwar, Li Zhang, Deep learning with differential privacy, in: Proceedings of the 2016 ACM SIGSAC Conference on Computer and Communications Security, 2016, pp. 308–318.

[2] Mridul Agarwal, Bhargav Ganguly, Vaneet Aggarwal, Communication efficient parallel reinforcement learning, in: Uncertainty in Artificial Intelligence, PMLR, 2021, pp. 247–256.

[3] Samuel Albanie, Euclidean distance matrix trick, Technical report, 2019.

[4] Zeyuan Allen-Zhu, Elad Hazan, Variance reduction for faster non-convex optimization, in: International Conference on Machine Learning, 2016, pp. 699–707.

[5] Andrew G. Barto, Richard S. Sutton, Charles W. Anderson, Neuronlike adaptive elements that can solve difficult learning control problems, IEEE Transactions on Systems, Man and Cybernetics 5 (1983) 834–846.

[6] Jonathan Baxter, Peter L. Bartlett, Infinite-horizon policy-gradient estimation, Journal of Artificial Intelligence Research 15 (2001) 319–350.

[7] Miguel Castro, Barbara Liskov, Practical Byzantine fault tolerance, in: OSDI, vol. 99, 1999, pp. 173–186.

[8] Tianyi Chen, Kaiqing Zhang, Georgios B. Giannakis, Tamer Başar, Communication-efficient policy gradient methods for distributed reinforcement learning, IEEE Transactions on Control of Network Systems 9 (2) (2021) 917–929.

[9] Yiding Chen, Xuezhou Zhang, Kaiqing Zhang, Mengdi Wang, Xiaojin Zhu, Byzantine-robust online and offline distributed reinforcement learning, arXiv:2206.00165, 2022.

[10] Sayak Ray Chowdhury, Aditya Gopalan, On kernelized multi-armed bandits, in: Proc. ICML, 2017, pp. 844–853.

[11] Radu Ciucanu, Pascal Lafourcade, Gael Marcadet, Marta Soare, SAMBA: a generic framework for secure federated multi-armed bandits, Journal of Artificial Intelligence Research (2022).

[12] Emile Contal, David Buffoni, Alexandre Robicquet, Nicolas Vayatis, Parallel Gaussian process optimization with upper confidence bound and pure exploration, in: Proc. ECML/PKDD, 2013, pp. 225–240.

[13] Zhongxiang Dai, Yizhou Chen, Bryan Kian Hsiang Low, Patrick Jaillet, Teck-Hua Ho, R2–B2: recursive reasoning-based Bayesian optimization for no-regret learning in games, in: Proc. ICML, 2020.

[14] Zhongxiang Dai, Bryan Kian Hsiang Low, Patrick Jaillet, Differentially private federated Bayesian optimization with distributed exploration, in: Proc. NeurIPS, vol. 34, 2021.

[15] Zhongxiang Dai, Kian Hsiang Low, Patrick Jaillet, Federated Bayesian optimization via Thompson sampling, in: Proc. NeurIPS, 2020.

[16] Zhongxiang Dai, Yao Shu, Arun Verma, Flint Xiaofeng Fan, Bryan Kian Hsiang Low, Patrick Jaillet, Federated neural bandits, in: Proc. ICLR, 2023.

[17] Zhongxiang Dai, Haibin Yu, Bryan Kian Hsiang Low, Patrick Jaillet, Bayesian optimization meets Bayesian optimal stopping, in: Proc. ICML, 2019, pp. 1496–1506.

[18] Erik A. Daxberger, Bryan Kian Hsiang Low, Distributed batch Gaussian process optimization, in: Proc. ICML, 2017, pp. 951–960.

[19] Ilker Demirel, Yigit Yildirim, Cem Tekin, Federated multi-armed bandits under byzantine attacks, arXiv:2205.04134, 2022.

[20] Thomas Desautels, Andreas Krause, Joel W. Burdick, Parallelizing exploration–exploitation tradeoffs in Gaussian process bandit optimization, Journal of Machine Learning Research 15 (2014) 3873–3923.

[21] Yan Duan, Xi Chen, Rein Houthooft, John Schulman, Pieter Abbeel, Benchmarking deep reinforcement learning for continuous control, in: International Conference on Machine Learning, 2016, pp. 1329–1338.

[22] Abhimanyu Dubey, AlexSandy' Pentland, Differentially-private federated linear bandits, in: Proc. NeurIPS, vol. 33, 2020, pp. 6003–6014.

[23] Gabriel Dulac-Arnold, Daniel Mankowitz, Todd Hester, Challenges of real-world reinforcement learning, arXiv:1904.12901, 2019.

[24] Cynthia Dwork, Aaron Roth, et al., The algorithmic foundations of differential privacy, Foundations and Trends in Theoretical Computer Science 9 (3–4) (2014) 211–407.

[25] David Eriksson, Michael Pearce, Jacob Gardner, Ryan D. Turner, Matthias Poloczek, Scalable global optimization via local Bayesian optimization, in: Proc. NeurIPS, 2019.

[26] Flint Xiaofeng Fan, Yining Ma, Zhongxiang Dai Wei Jing, Cheston Tan, Bryan Kian Hsiang Low, Fault-tolerant federated reinforcement learning with theoretical guarantee, in: Proc. NeurIPS, 2021.

[27] Javier Garcia-Barcos, Ruben Martinez-Cantin, Fully distributed Bayesian optimization with stochastic policies, in: Proc. IJCAI, 2019.

[28] Roman Garnett, Bayesian Optimization, Cambridge University Press, 2022.

[29] Jiafan He, Tianhao Wang, Yifei Min, Quanquan Gu, A simple and provably efficient algorithm for asynchronous federated contextual linear bandits, arXiv:2207.03106, 2022.

[30] José Miguel Hernández-Lobato, James Requeima, Edward O. Pyzer-Knapp, Alán Aspuru-Guzik, Parallel and distributed Thompson sampling for large-scale accelerated exploration of chemical space, in: Proc. ICML, 2017.

[31] Dan Horgan, John Quan, David Budden, Gabriel Barth-Maron, Matteo Hessel, Hado Van Hasselt, David Silver, Distributed prioritized experience replay, arXiv:1803.00933, 2018.

[32] Ruiquan Huang, Weiqiang Wu, Jing Yang, Cong Shen, Federated linear contextual bandits, in: Proc. NeurIPS, vol. 34, 2021.

[33] Ali Jadbabaie, Haochuan Li, Jian Qian, Yi Tian, Byzantine-robust federated linear bandits, arXiv:2204.01155, 2022.

[34] Rie Johnson, Tong Zhang, Accelerating stochastic gradient descent using predictive variance reduction, in: Advances in Neural Information Processing Systems, 2013, pp. 315–323.

[35] Peter Kairouz, H. Brendan McMahan, Brendan Avent, Aurélien Bellet Mehdi Bennis, Arjun Nitin Bhagoji, Keith Bonawitz, Zachary Charles, Graham Cormode, Rachel Cummings, et al., Advances and open, problems in federated learning, arXiv:1912.04977, 2019.

[36] Kirthevasan Kandasamy, Gautam Dasarathy, Junier B. Oliva, Jeff Schneider, Barnabás Póczos, Gaussian process bandit optimisation with multi-fidelity evaluations, in: Proc. NeurIPS, 2016, pp. 992–1000.

[37] Kirthevasan Kandasamy, Akshay Krishnamurthy, Jeff Schneider, Barnabás Póczos, Parallelised Bayesian optimisation via Thompson sampling, in: Proc. AISTATS, 2018, pp. 133–142.

[38] R. Matthew Kretchmar, Parallel reinforcement learning, in: The 6th World Conference on Systemics, Cybernetics, and Informatics, Citeseer, 2002.

[39] Matt Kusner, Jacob Gardner, Roman Garnett, Kilian Weinberger, Differentially private Bayesian optimization, in: Proc. ICML, 2015, pp. 918–927.

[40] Tor Lattimore, Csaba Szepesvári, Bandit Algorithms, Cambridge University Press, 2020.

[41] Lihua Lei, Cheng Ju, Jianbo Chen, Michael I. Jordan, Non-convex finite-sum optimization via SCSG methods, in: Advances in Neural Information Processing Systems, 2017, pp. 2348–2358.

[42] Sergey Levine, Aviral Kumar, George Tucker, Justin Fu, Offline reinforcement learning: tutorial, review, and perspectives on open problems, arXiv:2005.01643, 2020.

[43] Chuanhao Li, Hongning Wang, Asynchronous upper confidence bound algorithms for federated linear bandits, in: Proc. AISTATS, 2022.

[44] Qinbin Li, Zeyi Wen, Bingsheng He, Practical federated gradient boosting decision trees, in: Proc. AAAI, 2020, pp. 4642–4649.

[45] Qinbin Li, Zhaomin Wu, Zeyi Wen, Bingsheng He, Privacy-preserving gradient boosting decision trees, in: Proc. AAAI, 2020, pp. 784–791.

[46] Tan Li, Linqi Song, Privacy-preserving communication-efficient federated multi-armed bandits, IEEE Journal on Selected Areas in Communications (2022).

[47] Tan Li, Linqi Song, Christina Fragouli, Federated recommendation system via differential privacy, in: 2020 IEEE International Symposium on Information Theory (ISIT), IEEE, 2020, pp. 2592–2597.

[48] Li Tian, Anit Kumar Sahu, Ameet Talwalkar, Virginia Smith, Federated learning: challenges, methods, and future directions, arXiv:1908.07873, 2019.

[49] Wenjie Li, Qifan Song, Jean Honorio, Guang Lin, Federated $\mathcal{X}$-armed bandit, arXiv:2205.15268, 2022.

[50] Xinle Liang, Yang Liu, Tianjian Chen, Ming Liu, Qiang Yang, Federated transfer reinforcement learning for autonomous driving, arXiv:1910.06001, 2019.

[51] Boyi Liu, Lujia Wang, Ming Liu, Lifelong federated reinforcement learning: a learning architecture for navigation in cloud robotic systems, IEEE Robotics and Automation Letters 4 (4) (2019) 4555–4562.

[52] Nancy A. Lynch, Distributed Algorithms, Morgan Kaufmann Publishers Inc., San Francisco, CA, USA, 1996.

[53] H. Brendan McMahan, Galen Andrew, Ulfar Erlingsson, Steve Chien, Ilya Mironov, Nicolas Papernot, Peter Kairouz, A general approach to adding differential privacy to iterative training procedures, in: Proc. NeurIPS Workshop on Privacy Preserving Machine Learning, 2018.

[54] H. Brendan McMahan, Eider Moore, Daniel Ramage, Seth Hampson, et al., Communication-efficient learning of deep networks from decentralized data, in: Proc. AISTATS, 2017.

[55] H. Brendan McMahan, Daniel Ramage, Kunal Talwar, Li Zhang, Learning differentially private recurrent language models, in: Proc. ICLR, 2018.

[56] Volodymyr Mnih, Koray Kavukcuoglu, David Silver, Alex Graves, Ioannis Antonoglou, Daan Wierstra, Martin Riedmiller, Playing Atari with deep reinforcement learning, arXiv:1312.5602, 2013.

[57] Chetan Nadiger, Anil Kumar, Sherine Abdelhak, Federated reinforcement learning for fast personalization, in: 2019 IEEE Second International Conference on Artificial Intelligence and Knowledge Engineering (AIKE), IEEE, 2019, pp. 123–127.

[58] Matteo Papini, Damiano Binaghi, Giuseppe Canonaco, Matteo Pirotta, Marcello Restelli, Stochastic variance-reduced policy gradient, in: Proceedings of ICML, PMLR, 10–15 Jul 2018, in: Proceedings of Machine Learning Research, vol. 80, 2008, pp. 4026–4035.

[59] Ali Rahimi, Benjamin Recht, Random features for large-scale kernel machines, in: Proc. NeurIPS, 2008, pp. 1177–1184.

[60] C.E. Rasmussen, C.K.I. Williams, Gaussian Processes for Machine Learning, MIT Press, 2006.

[61] Sashank J. Reddi, Ahmed Hefny, Suvrit Sra, Barnabas Poczos, Alex Smola, Stochastic variance reduction for nonconvex optimization, in: International Conference on Machine Learning, 2016, pp. 314–323.

[62] Thomas Rudolf, Tobias Schürmann, Matteo Skull, Stefan Schwab, Sören Hohmann, Data-driven automotive development: federated reinforcement learning for calibration and control, in: 22. Internationales Stuttgarter Symposium, Springer, 2022, pp. 369–384.

[63] John Schulman, Sergey Levine, Pieter Abbeel, Michael Jordan, Philipp Moritz, Trust region policy optimization, in: International Conference on Machine Learning, 2015, pp. 1889–1897.

[64] John Schulman, Filip Wolski, Prafulla Dhariwal, Alec Radford, Oleg Klimov, Proximal policy optimization algorithms, arXiv:1707.06347, 2017.

[65] Pier Giuseppe Sessa, Ilija Bogunovic, Maryam Kamgarpour, Andreas Krause, No-regret learning in unknown games with correlated payoffs, in: Proc. NeurIPS, 2019.

[66] Chengshuai Shi, Cong Shen, Federated multi-armed bandits, in: Proc. AAAI, 2021.

[67] Chengshuai Shi, Cong Shen, Jing Yang, Federated multi-armed bandits with personalization, in: Proc. AISTATS, PMLR, 2021, pp. 2917–2925.

[68] Rachael Hwee Ling Sim, Yehong Zhang, Bryan Kian Hsiang Low, Patrick Jaillet, Collaborative Bayesian optimization with fair regret, in: Proc. ICML, PMLR, 2021, pp. 9691–9701.

[69] Sambhav Solanki, Samhita Kanaparthy, Sankarshan Damle, Sujit Gujar, Differentially private federated combinatorial bandits with constraints, arXiv:2206.13192, 2022.

[70] Niranjan Srinivas, Andreas Krause, Sham M. Kakade, Matthias Seeger, Gaussian process optimization in the bandit setting: no regret and experimental design, in: Proc. ICML, 2010, pp. 1015–1022.

[71] Richard S. Sutton, Andrew G. Barto, Reinforcement Learning: An Introduction, MIT Press, 2018.

[72] Arun Verma, Zhongxiang Dai, Bryan Kian Hsiang Low, Bayesian optimization under stochastic delayed feedback, in: Proc. ICML, PMLR, 2022, pp. 22145–22167.

[73] Yuanhao Wang, Jiachen Hu, Xiaoyu Chen, Liwei Wang, Distributed bandit learning: near-optimal regret with efficient communication, in: Proc. ICLR, 2020.

[74] Ronald J. Williams, Simple statistical gradient-following algorithms for connectionist reinforcement learning, Machine Learning 8 (3–4) (1992) 229–256.

[75] Lin Xiao, Tong Zhang, A proximal stochastic gradient method with progressive variance reduction, SIAM Journal on Optimization 24 (4) (2014) 2057–2075.

[76] Zhijie Xie, S.H. Song, FedKL: tackling data heterogeneity in federated reinforcement learning by penalizing KL divergence, arXiv:2204.08125, 2022.

[77] Pan Xu, Felicia Gao, Quanquan Gu, An improved convergence analysis of stochastic variance-reduced policy gradient, in: Uncertainty in Artificial Intelligence, PMLR, 2020, pp. 541–551.

[78] Zirui Yan, Quan Xiao, Tianyi Chen, Ali Tajer, Federated multi-armed bandit via uncoordinated exploration, in: ICASSP 2022-2022 IEEE International Conference on Acoustics, Speech and Signal Processing (ICASSP), IEEE, 2022, pp. 5248–5252.

[79] Qiang Yang, Yang Liu, Yong Cheng, Yan Kang, Tianjian Chen, Han Yu, Federated learning, Synthesis Lectures on Artificial Intelligence and Machine Learning 13 (3) (2019) 1–207.

[80] Yutong Ye, Wupan Zhao, Tongquan Wei, Shiyan Hu, Mingsong Chen, FedLight: federated reinforcement learning for autonomous multi-intersection traffic signal control, in: 2021 58th ACM/IEEE Design Automation Conference (DAC), IEEE, 2021, pp. 847–852.

[81] Shipeng Yu, Faisal Farooq, Alexander Van Esbroeck, Glenn Fung, Vikram Anand, Balaji Krishnapuram, Predicting readmission risk with institution-specific prediction models, Artificial Intelligence in Medicine 65 (2) (2015) 89–96.

[82] Shuai Yu, Xu Chen, Zhi Zhou, Xiaowen Gong, Di Wu, When deep reinforcement learning meets federated learning: intelligent multi-timescale resource management for multi-access edge computing in 5G ultra dense network, IEEE Internet of Things Journal (2020).

[83] Yehong Zhang, Zhongxiang Dai, Bryan Kian Hsiang Low, Bayesian optimization with binary auxiliary information, in: Proc. UAI, 2020, pp. 1222–1232.

[84] Yehong Zhang, Trong Nghia Hoang, Bryan Kian Hsiang Low, Mohan Kankanhalli, Information-based multi-fidelity Bayesian optimization, in: Proc. NeurIPS Workshop on Bayesian Optimization, 2017.

[85] Zhaowei Zhu, Jingxuan Zhu, Ji Liu, Yang Liu, Federated bandit: a gossiping approach, in: Abstract Proceedings of the 2021 ACM SIGMETRICS/International Conference on Measurement and Modeling of Computer Systems, 2021, pp. 3–4.

[86] Hankz Hankui Zhuo, Wenfeng Feng, Qian Xu, Qiang Yang, Yufeng Lin, Federated reinforcement learning, arXiv:1901.08277, 2019.

Data valuation in federated learning

15

Zhaoxuan Wu[a], Xinyi Xu[a], Rachael Hwee Ling Sim[a], Yao Shu[a], Xiaoqiang Lin[a], Lucas Agussurja[a], Zhongxiang Dai[a], See-Kiong Ng[a], Chuan-Sheng Foo[b], Patrick Jaillet[c], Trong Nghia Hoang[d], and Bryan Kian Hsiang Low[a]

[a]*National University of Singapore, Singapore, Singapore*
[b]*Agency for Science, Technology and Research, Singapore, Singapore*
[c]*Massachusetts Institute of Technology, Cambridge, MA, United States*
[d]*Washington State University, Pullman, WA, United States*

15.1 Introduction

In recent years, there has been increasing interests in assessing the value of data in many real-world machine learning applications. Broadly speaking, in collaborative machine learning (CML), data valuation (DV) offers a trustworthy way of attributing rewards among participating clients and identifying potentially malicious ones in the learning effort. Federated learning (FL) is one of the most widely practiced CML frameworks, but its distinguishing data communication, fusion, and learning characteristics from the canonical machine learning framework necessitate tailored designs to effectively evaluate data contributed by various participating clients. For example, the server has no access to the raw data and the learning happens in an iterative round-wise manner. These characteristics pose challenges for developing effective and efficient methods.

More interestingly, different variants of FL based on the types of data partition follow vastly different learning pipelines and thus require distinct data valuation methods. FL can be typically categorized into horizontal and vertical variants. In horizontal FL (HFL), multiple clients contribute data samples that share a common feature space. For example, it can involve a large number of distributed mobile devices under a complex network. On the other hand, in vertical FL (VFL), clients contribute distinct features corresponding to the same data samples. VFL is commonly used among financial institutions and e-commerce platforms to learn models for a common set of customers.

This chapter provides an overview of data valuation methods for FL, starting with several representative data valuation methods in non-federated collaborative machine learning in Sections 15.3 and 15.4. We then discuss the possibilities for extending those established methods to the federated scenario in Section 15.5. Concrete data valuation approaches specially designed for VFL and HFL are discussed in detail in Sections 15.6 and 15.7, respectively. Finally, we briefly introduce a vastly different

Federated Learning. https://doi.org/10.1016/B978-0-44-319037-7.00024-7

approach from the other methods, learning-based valuation methods, in Section 15.8 and conclude the chapter with potential future directions in Section 15.9.

15.2 Data valuation: motivations and incentives

The essence of FL involves aggregating data resources from multiple distributed clients to collaboratively learn a better-performing machine learning model. For example, credit rating companies may collaborate with e-commerce platforms and mobile service providers for relevant data (e.g., shopping habits and phone bills) in improving their credit rating model. However, the clients may be self-interested and unwilling to participate in the federated effort unless their contributions are accurately recognized and fairly compensated. In such situations, data valuation can be useful in performing contribution evaluations and even guiding client selections, which are related to incentives in FL that will also be discussed later in this book. As such, data valuation methods are essential in facilitating collaboration among clients where data from a large group of participating clients are utilized together in a principled, efficient and fair manner.

Data valuation offers interpretability to machine learning models and decision-making. It attributes the model predictions to the most responsible training sample or feature. It also quantifies the importance of datasets (i.e., clients in FL) in achieving the final global model. More practically, the valuation can be utilized to price each client's participation and thus determine whether it is worthwhile to involve a particular client.

Other applications of data valuation include data summarization, noise detection, domain adaptation, etc. When resource constraints pose a major challenge in practice, we can utilize data valuation to select the most valuable data samples that achieve the best model performance given the limited budget [20,23]. Similarly, data valuation can guide more efficient model learning by training on the most valuable dataset first. Conversely, low values detected by valuation methods signal low-quality samples that could potentially improve model performance when removed [7,21]. Finally, data valuation facilitates domain adaptation by valuing the training data in the context of the target validation data, which could have a significantly different distribution from the training data [4,25].

15.3 Simple valuation methods

"How valuable is a dataset?"

While the whole chapter aims to address this difficult question in the context of FL, we could start to examine this problem from a more intuitive viewpoint:

"Can we identify properties that characterize a valuable dataset?"

To answer this question, we first present several intuitive valuation concepts that do not depend on model or validation dataset.

Data quantity. Quantity can be one of the most intuitive measures of data value. Roughly speaking, we expect a larger dataset to have a relatively higher value than a smaller one. Take the LibriSpeech [13] corpus data as an example, a data subset that contains 360 hours of speech is likely to have a higher value than a subset that only contains 100 hours of speech. More formally, we define the following utility to quantify the value of a dataset based on its size:

$$v(D_m) = |D_m|, \qquad (15.1)$$

where $|D_m|$ is the size of client m's data. However, the utility is often insufficient to quantify the contribution value of the data because it overlooks the presence of other clients' data in the collaboration. For example, adding the dataset from client m to an existing collaboration with limited data will create a significant impact, but adding it to a collaboration which has already acquired a significantly larger amount of data might only generate a marginal impact. Thus, to create a more informative quantification metric, we can pair the *utility* function with a simple *valuation function* to account for such relative effects (RE),

$$\phi_m^{RE} = \frac{v(D_m)}{\sum_{i=1}^{n} v(D_i)}, \qquad (15.2)$$

where n is the total number of clients. One can imagine this valuation metric to be reliable in the scenario where data samples from all n clients are independently and identically distributed (i.i.d.). We can regard this metric to be implicitly *performance-driven* because it is commonly recognized in modern machine learning that a larger dataset typically leads to a model with better performance.

Data variety. Quantity sometimes may not reveal the full picture. An extreme example is that one can replicate a single data sample for an infinite number of times to create an infinitely large dataset but the worth of the resulting dataset should not scale infinitely. More broadly, large datasets that lack data variety tend to have a lot of redundant information and might be less valuable than other datasets with a smaller size but higher variety. Therefore, data valuation also needs to account for the variety in data (i.e., diversity), often in the forms of input and target coverage of the population. For instance, the range of values for an input feature (e.g., containing only ages 0–10 instead of the whole demographic) and the number of target classes (e.g., containing only example images of digit 0 instead of the whole set of digits from the MNIST dataset) are all reflective of data variety. More concretely, let variety(m) be the variety of the dataset owned by client m, then the relative value of D_m is expressed as

$$v(D_m) = \frac{\text{variety}(m)}{\sum_{i=1}^{n} \text{variety}(i)} \quad \text{and} \quad \phi_m^{RE} = \frac{v(D_m)}{\sum_{i=1}^{n} v(D_i)}, \qquad (15.3)$$

where the exact measure for data variety requires more in-depth investigation. For example, the relative data variety is often connected to the similarity measure of distributions. If we assume a target reference distribution is sufficiently diverse (i.e., possibly covers the entire population), a dataset closer in distribution to the reference distribution is more diverse and hence, more valuable. More details will be studied in the rest of this chapter.

Communication effort. This property is related to data quantity and is unique to FL. The number of rounds of communications τ_m that a client m participated in could be a contribution indicator. More participation probably means more data quantity and also contribution in various phases of FL. The relative value of D_m can thus also be expressed as

$$v(D_m) = \frac{\tau_m}{\sum_{i=1}^{n} \tau_i} \quad \text{and} \quad \phi_m^{\text{RE}} = \frac{v(D_m)}{\sum_{i=1}^{n} v(D_i)}. \tag{15.4}$$

Overall, the three valuation metrics we introduced in this section can be simplistic at the first glance, but they can act as important guiding principles in more sophisticated data valuation method designs. We will frequently revisit these principles for the rest of this chapter.

15.4 Related work: conventional data valuation

Data valuation reflects how much each client contributes to the performance of the final global model. We first introduce data valuation methods in the canonical supervised learning setting without federated clients. In this setting, multiple clients contribute their dataset D_m to collectively learn a predictive model f. We define a coalition to be a subset of clients $C \subseteq A \triangleq \{1, \ldots, n\}$. We denote the aggregated dataset from all n clients to be $D_A = \{D_m\}_{m=1}^{n}$ where D_m is the local training dataset of client m. We overload the notation and let $D_C = \{D_m\}_{m \in C}$.

In this convention, data valuation requires an utility function $v : \mathcal{P}(D_A) \to \mathbb{R}$ and a valuation function $\phi(D_m, D_A, v)$, where $\mathcal{P}(D_A)$ denotes the power set of D_A. Different designs on the utility and valuation function yield data valuation of different properties. The utility function v aims to produce a data utility, which will be used by valuation functions ϕ to output the final value depending on the existence of other clients' data in FL. To offer an overview before delving into the details, we categorize the methods we will discuss in the rest of the chapter in Table 15.1.

15.4.1 Utility functions

A utility function v assigns a real-value utility to any coalition C formed among the participating clients. Intuitively, utility measures the "usefulness" of a coalition, which are used in valuation functions (see Section 15.4.2) to evaluate data. We present several representative utility functions next.

Table 15.1 List of data valuation methods we discuss in this chapter. Methods in black are conventional data valuation methods applicable to FL. Methods in blue (mid gray in print version) are methods developed in the FL context.

	VFL	HFL
Performance-driven	VP DAVINZ SHAP	ORC FedSV ComFedSV
Variety-driven	RV	
Similarity-driven	MMD DAVINZ	CGSV FedFAIM
Information-driven	IG CMI	
Learning-based		DVRL F-RCCE

15.4.1.1 Performance-driven

Performance-driven utility functions award data coalitions that achieve high model performance.

Validation performance (VP). VP is the most straightforward surrogate for model usefulness, adopted in Data Shapley [7]. Usually measured on a pre-defined validation set D_{val} of interest (or mutually agreed by the server and clients), we define

$$v(D_m) = -\ell(\mathbf{w}_m; D_{\mathrm{val}}), \tag{15.5}$$

where $\mathbf{w}_m$ is the model trained on D_m and ℓ denotes the loss function. Sometimes, validation accuracy is used as an alternative for negated validation loss in Eq. (15.5). This utility function is related to the performance-driven *data quantity* introduced in Section 15.3. As discussed, a larger dataset typically leads to a better-performing model, which means a lower validation loss and a higher value. However, each evaluation of the VP on a coalition requires computationally expensive model training, which could be prohibitively slow for deep neural network models. This limits the complexity of models that can be considered due to practical constraints.

Data valuation at initialization (DAVINZ). Motivated to value data in complex deep neural network (DNN) applications while completely avoiding model training, Wu et al. [21] theoretically derive a domain-aware generalization bound to estimate the generalization performance of DNNs without model training. Specifically, the utility function considers both in-domain DNN generalization error characterized by the neural tangent kernel (NTK) matrix $\mathbf{\Theta}_0$ at neural network initialization and the generalization error caused by train-validation domain divergence $d_{\mathcal{H}}(D_m, D_{\mathrm{val}})$. We have

$$v(D_m) = -\kappa\sqrt{\hat{\mathbf{y}}\Theta_0^{-1}\hat{\mathbf{y}}/|D_m|} - d_{\mathcal{H}}(D_m, D_{\text{val}}), \qquad (15.6)$$

where each element in $\hat{\mathbf{y}}$ is defined as the residual on initialized network $\hat{\mathbf{y}} = y - f(\mathbf{x}, \mathbf{w}^{(0)})$, $\mathcal{H}$ is a proper function space to evaluate domain divergence and κ is regarded as an balancing hyper-parameter. Intuitively, the first in-domain term can be interpreted as a complexity measure of D_m, whereas the second takes care of domain shifts. The authors adopt maximum mean discrepancy (MMD) for domain discrepancy in practice. Overall, DAVINZ addresses the computational efficiency problem of utility evaluation with an accurate estimate. The practical limitation lies in the determination of the hyper-parameter κ that balances the effort of in-domain and out-of-domain errors.

15.4.1.2 Variety-driven

Variety-driven utility functions examine the variety or diversity of data in coalitions as a surrogate for utility.

Robust volume (RV). Xu et al. [23] propose a new perspective that attributes data value to intrinsic characteristics of a dataset itself regardless of tasks or models. To quantify the utility of a dataset in a machine learning task, the authors propose to use volume to measure the diversity of data samples in it and established theoretical connections between a high diversity dataset and a good learning performance. This formulation thus follows the *data variety* principle and theoretically connects to model performance considered in *performance-driven* methods. Let p_m be the number of data samples in D_m and d be the feature dimension. The volume of a data matrix $D_m \in \mathbb{R}^{p_m \times d}$ is defined as

$$v(D_m) = \sqrt{\det(D_m^\top D_m)}, \qquad (15.7)$$

where $\det(\cdot)$ denotes the determinant of a matrix. RV, a robust variant of volume in Eq. (15.7), is also proposed in [23] to address the data replication issue in valuation. Overall, RV provides a viable alternative to VP-driven data valuation techniques, decoupling valuation from validation and circumventing the challenges associated with selecting a suitable validation set. The method is computationally efficient because it is training-free (i.e., no training is required). However, the disadvantage is that the theoretical performance guarantee applies to regression tasks only.

15.4.1.3 Similarity-driven

Different from methods driven by performance, similarity-driven methods inspect a dataset against a representative and trusted reference to determine values. Simply put, a dataset more similar to the aggregated data or a reference target distribution is assigned a high value.

MMD. Tay et al. [17] propose to use $D_A \cup G_A$ as the reference set where G_A represents a synthetic dataset generated from a generative model (e.g., variational autoencoder, generative adversarial networks, etc.) trained using D_A. MMD is utilized to efficiently measure the distributional similarity between two sampled datasets. Specifically, we express

$$v(D_m) = -\text{MMD}_u^2(D_m, D_{\mathcal{A}} \cup G_{\mathcal{A}}), \qquad (15.8)$$

where MMD_u is an unbiased MMD estimate. The work also discusses kernel selection for MMD and extension to incentivizing CML via synthetic data rewards, which will be discussed further in the following chapter on incentives for federated learning.

DAVINZ. Relatedly, the DAVINZ framework that we introduced earlier in Eq. (15.6) has elements of a similarity-driven metric in the out-of-domain term. Accounting for domain shifts is especially important in CML and FL because clients normally have heterogeneous local data distributions which might not be identical to the target distribution at test time.

15.4.1.4 Information-driven

Information theory provides an alternative to quantifying the "usefulness" of a model through uncertainty associated with the model. This measure is independent of the validation dataset, thus circumventing the need of choosing an appropriate validation dataset for data valuation and associated biases.

Information gain. Sim et al. [15] propose to measure the quality of a dataset D_m via the amount of uncertainty reduction in the trained model parameters $\mathbf{w}_m$ after training on D_m. Following the notions of information theory, the entropy of a random variable reflects the amount of "information" or "uncertainty" pertaining to the variable's outcome. Thus, using the prior entropy $H(\mathbf{w}_m)$ and posterior $H(\mathbf{w}_m | D_m)$ to represent the uncertainty associated with $\mathbf{w}_m$ before and after training, data value based on information gain (IG) can be expressed as

$$v(D_m) = H(\mathbf{w}_m) - H(\mathbf{w}_m \mid D_m) . \qquad (15.9)$$

To interpret, a more valuable dataset results in a greater uncertainty reduction during model training. Interestingly, IG is related to performance-driven methods because it can be regarded as a predictive performance surrogate with unknown validation [9, 10]. However, the valuation method requires a Bayesian treatment of $\mathbf{w}_m$ (and D_m) and IG may be expensive to compute for some models such as multi-layer Bayesian neural networks.

15.4.2 Valuation functions

Valuation functions operate on utilities calculated from the utility functions on multiple coalitions $\mathcal{C}$ with datasets $D_{\mathcal{C}} \subseteq D_{\mathcal{A}}$. While we usually consider coalitions of clients in $\mathcal{C}$, note that the value for each individual data sample is also well-defined under the same formulation. In this section, we discuss valuation functions with any arbitrary utility function v.

15.4.2.1 Leave-one-out (LOO)

LOO contribution test finds its root in robust statistics, where Cook [3] uses it to study the influence of individual data points in linear regression. Intuitively, it computes the distance between the model fitted on the complete data and the model fitted on data with the mth point or client deleted. In the context of data valuation, we employ

$$\phi_m^{\text{LOO}} = v(D_{\mathcal{A}}) - v(D_{\mathcal{A}\setminus\{m\}}), \qquad (15.10)$$

where v is an arbitrary utility function (some examples are given in Section 15.4.1). LOO only considers the marginal utility improvement of data to the grand coalition (excluding itself).

15.4.2.2 Shapley value (SV)

Several game-theoretic solution concepts have proved their usefulness in data valuation, including Shapley value (SV) [7], Banzhaf value [19], and least core [24]. We focus on SV here as it is an unique solution that satisfies *efficiency, symmetry, linearity,* and *null player* properties [5].

The SV of a client m is defined as the average marginal contribution of m to all coalitions $\mathcal{C} \subseteq \mathcal{A} \setminus \{m\}$,

$$\phi_m = \frac{1}{|\mathcal{A}|} \sum_{\mathcal{C} \subseteq \mathcal{A}\setminus\{m\}} \frac{1}{\binom{|\mathcal{A}|-1}{|\mathcal{C}|}} \left[v(D_{\mathcal{C}\cup\{m\}}) - v(D_{\mathcal{C}}) \right]. \qquad (15.11)$$

SV is more comprehensive than LOO as it considers marginal contributions to every possible coalition. SV is the most popular choice of valuation function to pair with the utility functions such as VP, RV, DAVINZ, MMD, IG, etc.

15.5 Extending to the federated setting: does it work?

Data valuation in the canonical supervised learning setting above requires (1) full access to the raw data and (2) a central server. This poses potential challenges when executing DV in FL.

HFL. We first recall the procedure of HFL: (1) The server broadcasts the latest global model $\mathbf{w}^{(t)}$ to all clients; (2) Clients perform local updates using their respective local datasets; (3) Server selects clients and aggregates their gradients (or updated local models) to update the global model. The three steps are repeated until convergence. Unfortunately, extending conventional DV methods to HFL is nontrivial because raw data is never shared. Instead, the server only receives the gradient information or the locally updated model. The utility functions in Section 15.4.1 would not work with aggregated gradients. Therefore, we need to develop specialized DV methods for HFL (refer to Section 15.7).

VFL. We recall the general procedure of VFL. Overall, the model is divided into multiple client-owned bottom models and a server-owned top model as shown in

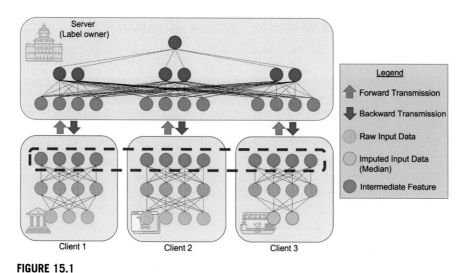

FIGURE 15.1

Intermediate representation valuation in VFL with 3 clients.

Fig. 15.1. The intermediate representations produced by the bottom models are subsequently passed as inputs to the top model for prediction or inference. We present the key steps below: (1) Before learning, a set of data samples with common identifiers are aligned across the participating clients; (2) Every client transmits the intermediate representation of the data using the respective bottom model; (3) Top and bottom models are updated through forward and backward propagation. Steps 2 and 3 are then repeated until convergence. A unique property of VFL is that each client separately owns a part of the grand model. Additionally, intermediate data representations based on the local models are shared with the server, which is usually the label owner in VFL. Therefore, DV in VFL can be regarded as valuating the contribution of data in the form of intermediate representations. Specifically, we show an example with 3 clients in Fig. 15.1. The dataset D_C with $C = \{1, 2\}$ is the concatenation of intermediate features from all 3 local models, where clients 1 and 2 output intermediate features with original local raw input data and client 3 outputs features with imputed median input data (or other reasonable imputation methods). To interpret, D_C only includes meaningful data from clients in coalition C. With this modified data representation, all utility functions and valuation functions introduced in Section 15.4 can be used in VFL.

Overall, depending on the information received by the server, data valuation in FL involves feature and gradient valuations. Conventional data valuation methods are still applicable to VFL with slight modifications on data representation. However, gradient evaluation in HFL requires a new approach. In the next section, we describe methods specially developed for data valuation in VFL and HFL, respectively.

15.6 Vertical data valuation: feature valuation

As discussed in Section 15.5, data valuation in VFL can be viewed as grouped feature attribution since each client holds part of the federated model that contributes partial intermediate feature representations. We name data valuation in VFL as *vertical data valuation* and next discuss feature evaluation methods in the context of VFL.

15.6.1 Feature importance and attribution

Shapley additive explanations (SHAP) is a popular explainable artificial intelligence (XAI) tool that attributes the model prediction of an instance **x** to each feature of **x** [12]. Interestingly, we can adapt SHAP into our data valuation formulation by using the final model output of an input instance as the utility function and SV as the valuation function. Note that SHAP, in its original form, considers single-instance multi-feature explanations. Therefore, Section 15.5 and Fig. 15.1 provide us with a more suitable and flexible approach to vertical data valuation for sets of input data. Wang et al. [18] have proposed a similar method for vertical data valuation.

15.6.2 Information-driven valuation

Han et al. [8] propose to use conditional mutual information (CMI), a commonly used metric for feature selection [1], as the data valuation metric. CMI is very similar to the information gain (IG) metric introduced in Section 15.4.1.4, except that CMI is conditioned on an additional task dataset D_{task} by the label owner in VFL. The task dataset is unique to the FL setting and the label owner holds corresponding task labels Y. Thus, [8] propose the DV metric based on the mutual information between the input set D_m and label Y conditioned on the task dataset D_{task}. Specifically,

$$v(D_m) = I(D_m; Y|D_{\text{task}}). \tag{15.12}$$

The computation of CMI above requires further *federated computations* since D_m and D_{task} are typically stored separately and privately, which is outside the scope of DV discussion here. Remarkably, different from model-dependent methods like SHAP, such an information-driven metric can evaluate federated data in the absence of a pre-determined model.

15.7 Horizontal data valuation: gradient valuation

In HFL, gradients instead of raw data are shared with the central server. However, conventional data valuation techniques require full access to the raw data. Intuitively, if the contribution of each gradient to the global model can be evaluated, it will indirectly reflect the client's contribution.

15.7.1 **Gradient contributions**

A straightforward data valuation method for HFL utilizes the gradient information readily available in the FL training procedure. Wei et al. [16] propose *one-round contribution* (ORC) to reconstruct trained models by aggregating local gradients throughout the training. The method effectively keeps track of $O(2^n)$ models (or equivalently, gradients information uploaded by clients) for each $C \subseteq A$, which are later used to evaluate the VP of a global model trained with data from C. Specifically, for each coalition C, we use the aggregated gradients of clients from this coalition C to update the corresponding model. Note that although subset models are of interest, we still only compute the gradients in each round using the global model. VP is used as the utility function v in data valuation.

However, gradients on the global model are used each round even when we are concerned with a subset model trained using only data from clients from the coalition C. Subset models can thus be different from the actual ones and affect the effectiveness of gradient values. To solve this issue, we can rely on the linearity property of Shapley value and regard each training round as a cooperative game. The overall SV is simply the sum of SV from all training rounds.

As such, *federated SV* (FedSV) [20] is proposed for valuing decentralized and sequential data in FL. The updated model performance conditioned on the existing global model is used as the utility function. Specifically, $v(C; \mathbf{w}^{(t)})$ is defined to be the VP of the updated global model additionally trained using the aggregated gradients of C from the existing global model $\mathbf{w}^{(t)}$. Following the Shapley formulation, the federated SV in a round t is defined as

$$\phi_m^{(t)} = \begin{cases} \frac{1}{|I_t|} \sum_{C \subseteq I_t \setminus \{m\}} \frac{1}{\binom{|I_t|-1}{|C|}} [v(C \cup \{m\}; \mathbf{w}^{(t)}) - v(C; \mathbf{w}^{(t)})] & \text{if } m \in I_t, \\ 0 & \text{otherwise,} \end{cases} \quad (15.13)$$

where I_t is the set of selected clients in round t. Then, the overall federated SV is the sum of all training rounds,

$$\phi_m = \sum_{t=1}^{\tau} \phi_m^{(t)}. \quad (15.14)$$

This requires τ rounds of SV computation to calculate the final FedSV. The above formulation can be generalized in two ways.

First, the weights of all coalitions are not necessarily equal. We can replace the coefficient $\frac{1}{|I_t|}$ in Eq. (15.13) with a general factor α_C that depends on specific formulations of C. For example, *Beta Shapley* [11] uses a beta distribution to weight coalitions based on their cardinalities such that the effect of noises in the utility evaluations can be reduced. Note that Beta Shapley reduces the SV to a semivalue without the *efficiency* axiom.

Second, we can vary the importance of different learning rounds. A significant drawback of ORC and FedSV is that they treat gradients from all training rounds equally. Mixing gradients from different training rounds together for gradient valuation may obfuscate essential gradients in the learning process. Therefore, Eq. (15.14) can be generalized and normalized into

$$\phi_m = \sum_{t=1}^{\tau} \beta^{(t)} \left[\frac{\phi_m^{(t)}}{\sum_{i=1}^{n} \phi_i^{(t)}} \right]. \tag{15.15}$$

Here, we may introduce a decay factor $\lambda \in (0, 1)$ to account for the diminishing effect of the gradients, such that $\beta^{(t)} = \lambda^t$. We decrease the importance of the later training iterations as they usually take smaller gradient steps and influence the predictions to a smaller extent [16]. In addition, we may upweigh rounds that lead to higher performance (i.e., accuracy). This stems from the observation that improvements over models with high accuracy are much harder than randomly initialized ones. To this end, we can set $\beta^{(t)} = \lambda^t \cdot \text{Perf}(\mathbf{w}^{(t)})$ where $\text{Perf}(\mathbf{w}^{(t)})$ denotes the validation performance of the global model at round t.

15.7.1.1 *Improving on FedSV*

An innate problem with Eq. (15.13) is that the unselected clients in a specific training round receive *zero* utility, regardless of their datasets. This raises potential unfairness because, for example, two clients with the same data can receive different FedSV due to the sampling process. Fan et al. [6] empirically shows that randomly selecting 3 out of 10 clients for 10 rounds can cause larger than 50% relative FedSV difference 65% of the times.

Fan et al. [6] propose *completed federated SV* (ComFedSV) to improve fairness by imputing the missing entries of intermediate FedSV. ComFedSV collects round-wise Shapley value of all possible coalitions into a utility matrix $\mathbf{U}$ with τ rows. Then, it imputes the missing values via low-rank matrix completion [2]. Intuitively, this method is effective because $\mathbf{U}$ should be approximately low-rank. On the one hand, similar data shared across clients can lead to similar utilities and thus columns of $\mathbf{U}$. On the other hand, utilities of the same coalition should be similar between successive rounds. Moreover, ComFedSV also gives a theoretical guarantee for a fair data valuation and demonstrates convincing empirical performance.

15.7.2 **Similarity-driven gradient valuation**

When the subject of interest changes from data to gradients in HFL, similarity-driven utility functions are still versatile enough to be applicable. Since clients usually send gradients to the server which will be aggregated later, similarity metrics more tailored for gradient comparisons have been proposed.

Xu et al. [22] propose to capture the contribution of gradient uploaded by a client using gradient vector alignment. Intuitively, the closer the gradient is to the aggregated gradient from all clients, the more contribution it has made. The aggregated gradient is the direction in which the loss value of the global model decreases fastest. From this perspective, a (directionally) similar gradient would be more effective in reducing loss. Specifically, let the parameter update from client m in iteration t be $\Delta \mathbf{w}_{m,t} \triangleq -\eta_t \nabla g_m(\mathbf{w}_m^{(t)})$ where η_t is the learning rate for iteration t and $g_m(\mathbf{w}_m^{(t)})$ is the mth client's local training loss with respect to $\mathbf{w}_m^{(t)}$. The server normalizes and aggregates the gradients as $\mathbf{u}_{m,t} \triangleq \Gamma \Delta \mathbf{w}_{m,t}/||\Delta \mathbf{w}_{m,t}||$, $\mathbf{u}_{C,t} \triangleq \sum_{m \in \mathcal{C}} r_m \mathbf{u}_{m,t}$, where Γ is a normalization coefficient used to prevent gradient explosion and r_m is an optional importance weight factor. Under this formulation, gradient alignment can be measured via the *cosine similarity* and the utility function is defined as follows:

$$v(D_m) = \cos(\mathbf{u}_{m,t}, \mathbf{u}_{A,t}) = \frac{\langle \mathbf{u}_{m,t}, \mathbf{u}_{A,t} \rangle}{||\mathbf{u}_{m,t}|| \cdot ||\mathbf{u}_{A,t}||}. \tag{15.16}$$

Note that the above utility function can be applied to data D_C from a coalition of clients $\mathcal{C}$. We use (15.16) with (15.13) and (15.14) to obtain the respective Shapley values for data. This method is named cosine gradient Shapley value (CGSV). It enable us to perform data valuation on contributed gradients without any auxiliary dataset. Notably, Shi et al. [14] share the same perspective and propose a similar formulation for gradient contribution assessment named FedFAIM. On top of the cosine similarity in (15.16), they additionally consider quality detection and filtering of low-quality local gradients.

15.8 Learning-based valuation

In this section, we deviate from game-theoretic solution concepts, which can be inefficient when the number of clients is large despite existing approximation efforts. *Can we directly model the data value or the scoring function using advances in deep learning and reinforcement learning?*

Yoon et al. [25] first came up with the idea of data valuation using reinforcement learning (DVRL). It integrates data valuation with the training process of the target predictive model and utilizes reinforcement signals to train a network for data valuation. Most specifically, an evaluator $g_\psi : (\mathbf{x}, c) \to \omega$ maps training samples to a selection probability ω, which represents the probability of using the sample in a training iteration. The target predictor model is denoted as f_θ. In a training iteration, the evaluator first estimates the selection probabilities ω for a batch of training samples $\{(\mathbf{x}^{(i)}, c^{(i)})\}_{i=1}^{B_s}$ of size B_s. Sample selection is then performed stochastically based on ω, and we obtain a selection vector $\mathbf{S} = [s_1, \ldots, s_{B_s}]$ where $s_i \in \{0, 1\}$. Here, 0 and 1 represent discarding or including the sample, respectively. Selected samples continue to train the predictor f_θ whose validation loss compared to the moving average δ of previous losses is then used as a reward signal to train the evaluator via reinforcement learning. After the convergence of the evaluator network, the selection probabilities serve as a surrogate of relative contribution (i.e., data value) in this learning effort.

The above idea has been applied to FL by Zhao et al. [26]. Instead of data samples, we consider contribution or value at the granularity of clients. Federated REIN-

FORCE client contribution evaluation (F-RCCE) modifies the evaluator to take in gradients (or equivalently, local model at the end of the communication round) as input, i.e., $g_\phi : \mathbf{w}_m^{(t)} \to \omega$. Similar to DVRL, $\mathbf{S}^{(t)} \in \{0, 1\}^n$ and the reward function is defined as

$$r(\mathbf{S}^{(t)}) = \frac{1}{n_{\text{val}}} \sum_{k=1}^{n_{\text{val}}} \ell\left(\mathbf{w}^{(t)}; \mathbf{x}_{\text{val},k}, c_{\text{val},k}\right) - \delta, \qquad (15.17)$$

where ℓ is the loss of the global model on the validation set $\{(\mathbf{x}_{\text{val},k}, c_{\text{val},k})\}_{k=1}^{n_{\text{val}}}$ and δ is a moving average of the previous losses. The evaluator's model parameter ψ is updated with learning rate α,

$$\psi^{t+1} \leftarrow \psi^t - \alpha r(\mathbf{S}^{(t)}) \nabla_\psi \log p(\mathbf{S}^{(t)}|\psi)|_{\psi^t}. \qquad (15.18)$$

Note that in this framework, the evaluator and the global target model are first fully trained before fixing the evaluator to measure contributions in another fresh round of target model re-training. In this case of FL, the selection probability at an iteration t is interpreted as the relative contribution of the client in communication round t. Overall, similar to (15.14), the value of a client m's data is the summation of its selection probability over all the rounds.

DVRL and F-RCCE are relatively efficient as they only require one complete training of the valuation network (i.e., evaluator). However, the method now measures how likely a datum or a client will be used in training the predictive model, which cannot draw a direct parallel to the relative contributions in learning. Consequently, the above papers [25,26] only perform experiments based on the ranks, rather than relative data values. Notably, the desirable properties and axioms of an equitable and fair data valuation achieved by Shapley value are not guaranteed by DVRL or F-RCCE.

15.9 Conclusion and future work

Motivated by the growing interest in assessing the value of data in machine learning applications, this chapter presents an overview of data valuation methods in collaborative machine learning with a primary focus on federated learning. Data valuation offers an interpretable contribution attribution method for datasets in collaborative learning scenarios. However, it is important to notice the limitations of the existing methods and open problems for future research.

First, the current vertical data valuation methods are not tailored to the iterative learning process of FL. It is debatable whether we should perform feature valuations on the final model or consider round-wise valuations like those in horizontal data valuation. Second, learning-based valuation has only been applied to HFL. It would be interesting to investigate the applicability of learning-based valuations on VFL. Third, properties like communication bandwidth, computational power, honesty and availability of clients are additional aspects of client contribution to FL, which can potentially constitute a more complete client valuation framework. The list of open problems is certainly not comprehensive and we invite interested readers to conduct further research on this growing field of practical significance.

To conclude, we have discussed extensions of the conventional data valuation methods to the federated setting and described horizontal and vertical data valuation methods specially developed for FL. This chapter serves as a guideline for a versatile suite of tools that empower FL practitioners to apply data valuation in various scenarios.

Acknowledgments

This research/project is supported by the National Research Foundation Singapore and DSO National Laboratories under the AI Singapore Programme (AISG Award No: AISG2-RP-2020-018).

References

[1] Gavin Brown, Adam Pocock, Ming-Jie Zhao, Mikel Luján, Conditional likelihood maximisation: a unifying framework for information theoretic feature selection, Journal of Machine Learning Research 13 (1) (2012) 27–66.

[2] Wei-Sheng Chin, Bo-Wen Yuan, Meng-Yuan Yang, Yong Zhuang, Yu-Chin Juan, Chih-Jen Lin, LIBMF: a library for parallel matrix factorization in shared-memory systems, Journal of Machine Learning Research 17 (86) (2016) 1–5.

[3] R. Dennis Cook, Detection of influential observation in linear regression, Technometrics 19 (1) (1977) 15–18.

[4] Soumi Das, Manasvi Sagarkar, Suparna Bhattacharya, Sourangshu Bhattacharya, CheckSel: Efficient and accurate data-valuation through online checkpoint selection, 2022.

[5] P. Dubey, On the uniqueness of the Shapley value, International Journal of Game Theory 4 (3) (1975) 131–139.

[6] Zhenan Fan, Huang Fang, Zirui Zhou, Jian Pei, Michael P. Friedlander, Changxin Liu, Yong Zhang, Improving fairness for data valuation in horizontal federated learning, in: Proc. ICDE, 2022, pp. 2440–2453.

[7] Amirata Ghorbani, James Zou, Data Shapley: equitable valuation of data for machine learning, in: Proc. ICML, 2019, pp. 2242–2251.

[8] Xiao Han, Leye Wang, Junjie Wu, Data valuation for vertical federated learning: an information-theoretic approach, arXiv:2112.08364, 2021.

[9] Andreas Krause, Carlos Guestrin, Nonmyopic active learning of Gaussian processes: an exploration-exploitation approach, in: Proc. ICML, 2007, pp. 449–456.

[10] John K. Kruschke, Bayesian approaches to associative learning: from passive to active learning, Learning & Behavior 36 (3) (2008) 210–226.

[11] Yongchan Kwon, James Zou, Beta Shapley: a unified and noise-reduced data valuation framework for machine learning, in: Proc. AISTATS, 2022.

[12] Scott M. Lundberg, Su-In Lee, A unified approach to interpreting model predictions, in: Proc. NeurIPS, 2017, pp. 4768–4777.

[13] Vassil Panayotov, Guoguo Chen, Daniel Povey, Sanjeev Khudanpur, LibriSpeech: an ASR corpus based on public domain audio books, in: Proc. ICASSP, 2015, pp. 5206–5210.

[14] Zhuan Shi, Lan Zhang, Zhenyu Yao, Lingjuan Lyu, Cen Chen, Li Wang, Junhao Wang, Xiang-Yang Li, FedFAIM: a model performance-based fair incentive mechanism for federated learning, IEEE Transactions on Big Data (2022) 1–13.

[15] Rachael Hwee Ling Sim, Yehong Zhang, Mun Choon Chan, Bryan Kian Hsiang Low, Collaborative machine learning with incentive-aware model rewards, in: Proc. ICML, 2020, pp. 8927–8936.

[16] Tianshu Song, Yongxin Tong, Shuyue Wei, Profit allocation for federated learning, in: Proc. IEEE Big Data, 2019, pp. 2577–2586.

[17] Sebastian Shenghong Tay, Xinyi Xu, Chuan Sheng Foo, Bryan Kian Hsiang Low, Incentivizing collaboration in machine learning via synthetic data rewards, in: Proc. AAAI, 2022.

[18] Guan Wang, Charlie Xiaoqian Dang, Ziye Zhou, Measure contribution of participants in federated learning, in: Proc. IEEE Big Data, 2019, pp. 2597–2604.

[19] Jiacheng Wang, Ruoxi Jia, Data Banzhaf: a data valuation framework with maximal robustness to learning stochasticity, in: Proc. AISTATS, 2023.

[20] Tianhao Wang, Johannes Rausch, Ce Zhang, Ruoxi Jia, Dawn Song, A principled approach to data valuation for federated learning, in: Federated Learning, Springer, 2020, pp. 153–167.

[21] Zhaoxuan Wu, Yao Shu, Bryan Kian Hsiang Low, DAVINZ: data valuation using deep neural networks at initialization, in: Proc. ICML, 2022.

[22] Xinyi Xu, Lingjuan Lyu, Xingjun Ma, Chenglin Miao, Chuan Sheng Foo, Bryan Kian Hsiang Low, Gradient driven rewards to guarantee fairness in collaborative machine learning, in: Proc. NeurIPS, 2021, pp. 16104–16117.

[23] Xinyi Xu, Zhaoxuan Wu, Chuan Sheng Foo, Bryan Kian Hsiang Low, Validation free and replication robust volume-based data valuation, in: Proc. NeurIPS, 2021, pp. 10837–10848.

[24] Tom Yan, Ariel D. Procaccia, If you like Shapley then you'll love the core, in: Proc. AAAI, 2021, pp. 5751–5759.

[25] Jinsung Yoon, Sercan O. Arik, Tomas Pfister, Data valuation using reinforcement learning, in: Proc. ICML, 2020, pp. 10842–10851.

[26] Jie Zhao, Xinghua Zhu, Jianzong Wang, Jing Xiao, Efficient client contribution evaluation for horizontal federated learning, in: Proc. ICASSP, 2021, pp. 3060–3064.

Applications & ethical considerations

3

Incentives in federated learning

16

Rachael Hwee Ling Sim[a], **Sebastian Shenghong Tay**[a], **Xinyi Xu**[a], **Yehong Zhang**[b],
Zhaoxuan Wu[a], **Xiaoqiang Lin**[a], **See-Kiong Ng**[a], **Chuan-Sheng Foo**[c],
Patrick Jaillet[d], **Trong Nghia Hoang**[e], and **Bryan Kian Hsiang Low**[a]

[a]*National University of Singapore, Singapore, Singapore*
[b]*Peng Cheng Laboratory, Shenzhen, People's Republic of China*
[c]*Agency for Science, Technology and Research, Singapore, Singapore*
[d]*Massachusetts Institute of Technology, Cambridge, MA, United States*
[e]*Washington State University, Pullman, WA, United States*

16.1 Overview and motivation

Federated learning requires clients to contribute data and resources and seeks to collaboratively train a global model with higher utility, e.g., validation accuracy. In this chapter, we will discuss *incentives* required to encourage more clients to participate, increase their contribution and address the concerns of the global server (or model owner).

To begin, a key concern in adopting federated learning in practice is that clients might be hesitant to participate considering their significant resources and costs incurred to collect data, compute model updates as well as the risk of losing data privacy while sharing information with the others. For example, a bank may be cautious about collaborating with other organizations as it may leak sensitive information about its customers and business. Furthermore, in most cases, the bank will need a guaranteed profit to participate meaningfully in a contribution: the benefit must outweigh the incurring cost and resources. On the other hand, the global server (or model owner) seeks to maximize the global model utility but may be constrained by a limited budget to compensate the clients. These concerns and desires will be formally described as incentives in Section 16.3.

Incentivization addresses these concerns through three main components: (1) *contribution evaluation*, valuing the (potential) contribution of each client; (2) *client selection*, selecting a subset of potential clients; and (3) *reward allocation* to the clients, deciding the target value of the rewards and realizing the target value by giving out different monetary payments, collaboratively trained models or outputs (such as predictions and generated dataset). Importantly, the non-monetary rewards described above are *freely replicable*: Like digital goods, they can be replicated at zero marginal cost for more clients.

Federated Learning. https://doi.org/10.1016/B978-0-44-319037-7.00026-0

These main components will be discussed in Sections 16.4–16.6. Subsequently, we will discuss how incentives are achieved in the monetary reward (Section 16.8) and the freely replicable non-monetary reward settings (Section 16.9).

16.2 Problem setting

In this chapter, we consider a global server (model owner) S and n clients. As described in the previous chapter on data valuation, the utility of any coalition (or their collaboratively trained model) is measured with the same utility function v. Each client m may contribute a resource C_m. The resource C_m can be client m's dataset $\mathcal{D}_m$ in the non-FL setting; the corresponding weight/gradient updates or computational resources used in the FL setting; and predictions on query dataset in the *federated prediction* setting. Simultaneously, each client m expects to receive at least a minimum reward or cost $\chi_m(\cdot)$ in return. Client m's minimum reward can be the utility of the model trained using C_m, i.e., $v(\mathbf{w}^m)$, and cost $\chi_m(C_m, \gamma_m)$ may be client m's total cost to collect data or compute weight updates. Each client may have a different cost function χ_m and cost type γ_m (which can be defined as the cost per unit of C_m). The main goal of incentivization is to get each client m to contribute C_m and increase his contribution, for example, by computing the gradients based on a larger local dataset, removing noise and participating in more iterations.

To achieve incentives outlined in Section 16.3, we require the 3 main components. During *contribution evaluation*, we will assign each client m's contribution C_m a value $\phi(C_m)$ which may depend on the utility function v. During the *reward allocation* phase, each selected client's value $\phi(C_m)$ is used to determine his reward value r_m. Sometimes, we need an intermediate step of *client selection* to select a subset of n clients, S, to maximize the utility of the global model, $\mathbf{w}^S$, $v(\mathbf{w}^S)$ and ensure that the global server's total budget $B(\cdot)$ can cover the selected clients total rewards, $\sum_{m \in S} r_m$. The budget $B(\cdot)$ may be fixed or dependent on the aggregated contribution C_m across every client $m \in S$.

16.3 Incentives

In this section, we will describe what the global server (model owner) and clients intuitively desire as formal properties. In particular, the global server requires:

Feasibility (F).   The reward r_m allocated to each client m is limited by the maximum reward available, such as the server's fixed budget $B(\cdot)$.

Truthfulness (T).   Each client m should truthfully report information about his cost, $\chi_m(C_m, \gamma_m)$ and his contributions, C_m. For example, it is undesirable if any client m over-reports their data quantity or submits false data to increase their reward r_m and decrease those of others.

Each client m requires:

Privacy (P). Each client m might be concerned about the global server or other clients accessing and inferring its sensitive data through his contribution, C_m. Furthermore, if the global server is untrustworthy or may exclude clients due to its limited budget, each client m risks benefiting others without getting a reward for his contribution and costly effort, e.g., to collect data and compute model weight updates. Under this risk, any client m, such as a bank, may be unwilling to submit its customers' data or other C_m to improve the credit rating or loan predictions for other banks before receiving a reward.

Collaborative fairness (CF). A client m should *fairly* receive a higher $\phi(C_m)$ than another client j if his contribution C_m is more valuable than client j's C_j such as when m share gradient updates from a larger and more informative dataset. In particular, a free-rider with a zero-valued contribution should get no reward.

Individual rationality (IR). Each client m must have non-negative profits: The client's benefit must at least balance its costs, i.e. $r_m \geq \chi_m(C_m, \gamma_m)$.

Moreover, to maximally incentivize both clients and server, we should consider:

Group welfare (GW). The reward scheme should maximize the total welfare, i.e., profits, of the server and all clients. For example, if a client is selected and submits his contribution C_m, his profit will be the reward received less his cost $r_m - \chi_m(C_m, \gamma_m)$. As another example, the server's benefit from the collaboration and profit increases as the utility of the collaboratively trained global model, $v(\mathbf{w}^S)$, increases.

As an overview, *privacy* and *truthfulness* are addressed during *contribution evaluation*. *Fairness* is addressed during *contribution evaluation* and special care is needed to maintain it during *reward allocation*. To ensure *feasibility*, *individual rationality* and maximize *group welfare* simultaneously, we control the reward value r_m for each client m and consider selecting a subset of clients S. The incentives will be further elaborated as part of each component. Moreover, additional but less common incentives are discussed in Section 16.7.

16.4 Contribution evaluation

In this section, we will discuss how to assign each client m's contribution, C_m, a value, $\phi(C_m)$, to address the privacy, fairness, and truthfulness incentives.

For **collaborative fairness (CF)**, a client m should *fairly* receive a higher value $\phi(C_m)$ than another client j if his contribution C_m is more valuable than client j's C_j. Similarly, client m's new value $\phi(C_{m'})$ should increase when his new contribution $C_{m'}$ is more valuable than C_m (*strict monotonicity*). See the previous chapter on data valuation for federated learning for a detailed discussion on how existing works define and evaluate more "valuable" formally through a utility function v. The definition can be as simple as the data quantity or dependent on the FL model (e.g., supervised vs. generative) and validation set(s).

For **privacy (P)**, each client m can limit the extent that the global server and other clients can infer about his dataset $\mathcal{D}_m$ by using *differential privacy* to protect his contribution. [5] consider the setting where each client m decides his own privacy budget and perturbs and protects his contribution C_m by adding random noise before sending C_m to the server.

Moreover, to address the problem that clients might be unwilling to share their contributions before receiving their rewards, the server can require each client to declare the value of $\phi(C_m)$ instead, such as during auctions [2], or estimate $\phi(C_m)$ in round t based on contributions from earlier rounds [3]. However, the lack of access to client m's contribution C_m limits the choice of $\phi(C_m)$. For example, if the model utility v (e.g., validation accuracy) of coalitions with multiple clients cannot be computed, we cannot use the *Shapley value* to define $\phi(C_m)$.

The **truthfulness (T)** incentive is related to **incentive compatibility (IC)**. A mechanism, such as an auction to decide the reward values, is IC when it is optimal (individually profit-maximizing) for all clients to truthfully declare their cost, $\chi_m(C_m, \gamma_m)$ (or cost type γ_m) and contribution value, $\phi(C_m)$. Separately, to incentivize clients to submit true and high-quality information instead of false and adversarial ones, the server can assign and consider each client's reputation and values in earlier rounds [10] or define $\phi(C_m)$ using the correlation in clients' predictions [8] or model updates [9].

16.5 Client selection

In this section, we will discuss how selecting a subset of clients, $\mathcal{S}$, out of all n clients can address the rationality, group welfare and truthfulness incentive. Client selection is especially important when the server has a limited budget $B(\cdot)$ and cannot afford to pay the total costs across all clients, $\sum_m \chi_m(\cdot)$, due to **feasibility (F)** constraint.

For **individual rationality (IR)**, any client with negative profits, i.e., $r_o < \chi_o(\cdot)$, should be excluded and not selected for the collaboration. For any unselected client o, his cost and reward (hence profits) is zeroed, i.e., $r_o = \chi_o(\cdot) = 0$.

To maximize **group welfare (GW)**, the global server should select clients that increase the global model's utility $v(\mathbf{w}^{\mathcal{S}})$ at a lower total cost to selected clients, $\sum_{m \in \mathcal{S}} \chi_m(\cdot)$. If costs are ignored, the global server can rank each client m based on their contribution value $\phi(C_m)$, defined using utility functions from the previous chapter on data valuation in federated learning. There are more specific strategies to increase group welfare. For example, the work of [15] uses deep reinforcement learning to intelligently choose clients to participate in each round of FL to counterbalance the bias introduced by non-IID data and improve the utility of the global model with fewer communication rounds.

To simultaneously encourage **truthfulness (T) / incentive compatibility**, the authors of [10] propose that the global server assigns a *reputation score* for each client based on past validation set performance and selects clients with the highest reputation in each round.

16.6 Reward allocation

This section further discusses how to set the reward values $(r_m)_{m \in S}$ using the contribution value $(\phi(C_m))_{m \in S}$ to maintain fairness and maximize group welfare. In addition, we also discuss how the value r_m can correspond to monetary rewards or non-monetary rewards. The incentive conditions may differ slightly in the two settings.

For monetary rewards, each selected client m receives monetary payment r_m from the global server's budget $B(\cdot)$ and can optionally get the same global model $\mathbf{w}^S$. A negative r_m implies that client m should pay the global server instead. Using monetary rewards for incentives is convenient to implement: after the payment to each client is decided, it is easy to realize and pay each client the exact amount. However, the global server and clients must agree on the monetary value per unit change in the contribution value $\phi(C_m)$ or the utility function v. The global server's profit is the monetary value of the model less the total monetary payments, $v(\mathbf{w}^S) - \sum_{m \in S} r_m$. For each selected client m, the profit is the payment received less cost $r_m - \chi_m(C_m, \gamma_m)$. The incentive conditions for monetary rewards that must be simultaneously satisfied are:

Feasibility (F).   The reward scheme must ensure **budget balance**: the total monetary rewards should not exceed the budget, i.e., $\sum_{m \in S} r_m \leq B(\cdot)$.
Individual rationality (IR).   Each client m must be paid a reward r_m which is at least his cost $\chi_m(\cdot)$, i.e., $r_m \geq \chi_m(\cdot)$.
Group welfare (GW).   The total welfare/profit of the server and clients to maximize is $v(\mathbf{w}^S) - \sum_{m \in S} \chi_m(C_m, \gamma_m)$.

Additionally, to maximize the welfare of clients only and incentivize their participation, the server should fully use the budget, i.e., $B(\cdot) = \sum_{m \in S} r_m$ (**efficiency**).

For non-monetary rewards, each selected client m will not receive any monetary payment but may receive a different model, $\mathbf{w}^{m,r}$ or additional data $\mathcal{D}_m^r$. Non-monetary rewards may be preferable when there is no available budget to compensate clients (e.g., due to legal restrictions or financial constraints). Moreover, we focus on non-monetary rewards that are *freely replicable*: Like digital goods, we can replicate a model, its outputs or data at zero marginal cost for more clients. This increases the profits for all clients and is hence preferable to monetary rewards setting where increasing the reward r_m (and profit) for client m requires a decrease in reward r_j for another client j when the budget is fully utilized. However, non-monetary rewards might be less convenient to implement:

For each client m, how do we efficiently generate a reward model or data worth some arbitrary value r_m and ensure that a higher reward value r_m would correspond to a higher utility measured by v?

The global server's profit is simply the value of the global model $v(\mathbf{w}^S)$. For each selected client m, the profit is the reward value less the minimum expected reward (i.e., cost) $r_m - \chi_m(\cdot)$. If the reward value r_m is defined as the utility of the rewarded model, $v(\mathbf{w}^{m,r})$, it would be more appropriate if the "cost" is similarly defined using the utility. The incentive conditions for non-monetary rewards that must be simultaneously satisfied are as follows:

Feasibility (F).   No client m can get more than the most valuable model or dataset derived using the aggregated contribution of clients in S. Formally, if the utility measured with v does not decrease as clients are added, we require $r_m \le v(\mathbf{w}^S)$.

Individual rationality (IR).   Each client m may expect the utility of his rewarded model, r_m, to be at the least the utility the model he can build without participating in FL, i.e., $\chi_m(\cdot) = v(\mathbf{w}^m)$.

Group welfare (GW).   The total welfare/profit of the server and clients to maximize is $v(\mathbf{w}^S) + \sum_{m \in S} r_m - \sum_{m \in S} \chi_m(C_m, \gamma_m)$. As the rewards are *freely replicable*, increasing r_m does not cost the global server and will improve group welfare. Group welfare is maximized when all clients get the most valuable model, e.g., $\mathbf{w}^S$. However, there will be no fairness. A weakened desirable condition is **weak efficiency** – the most valuable client k should fully utilize the contributions, i.e., $r_k = v(\mathbf{w}^S)$.

To preserve the **collaborative fairness (CF)** incentive, a higher contribution value $\phi(C_m)$ should translate to a higher reward value r_m. This is achieved by the naive solution of rewarding each client m with their contribution value, i.e., $r_m = \phi(C_m)$. However, the **IR** and **efficiency/weak efficiency** conditions may not be satisfied. They can be satisfied when the reward for each client is determined by some monotonically increasing function $r : \phi(C_m) \mapsto r_m \in \mathbb{R}$. If client m has a higher contribution evaluation than client k, client m should have a higher reward. Formally, if $\phi(C_m) > \phi(C_k)$ then $r_m > r_k$. To disincentivize free-riders, a client m with zero-valued contribution, $\phi(C_m) = 0$, should get no reward, $r_i = 0$, thus, we require $r(0) = 0$. A valid function for r is $r(x) = (ax)^\rho$ with $a, \rho > 0$, $x \ge 0$. Later, we will discuss how these incentives are satisfied for monetary (Section 16.8) and non-monetary (Section 16.9) rewards.

16.7 Other incentives

From existing surveys [14,17], there may be other requirements for the client selection and reward allocation:

Nash equilibrium [11].   Any client m and the server S cannot *unilaterally* increase their profits, $r_m - \chi_m(C_m, \gamma_m)$ and $v(\mathbf{w}^S) - \sum_{m \in S} r_m$, respectively by changing their decisions, e.g., on C_m and $B(\cdot)$ respectively, when others' decisions are fixed. A Nash equilibrium provides stability and predictability of outcomes as neither any client nor the server has an incentive to change their decision.

Computational efficiency.   For resource-constrained scenarios, e.g., FL on mobile devices, it may not be suitable to use computationally costly approaches for contribution evaluation (e.g., Shapley values without approximation), client selection, and reward decision and realization.

Robustness to adversarial contributors.   The model owner should filter out or discount adversarial updates.

Robustness to replication.   A client m cannot increase his total profits or rewards by duplicating himself and participating as more clients such as m'. Han et al. [4] analyze existing cooperative game theory solution concepts and propose a replication-robust reward distribution.

Stability of $\mathcal{S}$.   If clients are free to form alternative coalitions and the rewards available depend on the aggregated contribution C_m for $m \in \mathcal{S}$, an additional incentive is that the coalition $\mathcal{S}$ is stable. There must exist some client $m \in \mathcal{S}$ who has no incentive to form another coalition, i.e., all coalitions would not increase client m's profits. Sim et al. [12] discuss the stability of the grand coalition for freely replicable model rewards.

16.8 Monetary rewards

In the basic setting where any client m does not incur costs or expect a minimum reward to participate, i.e., $\chi_m(\cdot) = 0$, we can reward each selected client a share of the global server budget $B(\cdot)$ proportional to its contribution value $\phi(C_m)$. For **efficiency** and **collaborative fairness**, each client m's reward should be $\frac{\phi(C_m)}{\sum_{j \in \mathcal{S}} \phi(C_j)} \times B(\cdot)$. In the more complex setting where each client expects some minimum reward to participate, it is apt to use economic theory solutions to decide the monetary reward r_m for every potential client m and achieve incentives.

When the server and clients have perfect information but binding agreements are not possible (e.g., client m can always alter C_m), *non-cooperative game theory* is appropriate. Each participant optimizes his/her individual profit while anticipating the actions of other profit-maximizing participants. In the non-cooperative setting, such as the Prisoner's Dilemma game, the resulting solution will be a **Nash equilibrium** that may have lower group welfare than a cooperative outcome. We can consider a simultaneous game or Stackelberg game where the leader, e.g., the model owner, moves first and declares its decision Φ after using backward induction to predict the actions of the followers, e.g., clients as in [5,18].

When binding agreements are possible (e.g., a legal contract states that enforce a reward function), each client m may be willing to submit his/her contribution C_m before receiving reward. We can apply *cooperative game theory* (CGT) [1] to achieve higher group welfare. The most basic and studied form of cooperative games is a *characteristic function game* (CFG) defined by the set of clients and a characteristic function v that maps coalitions (or their contributions) to a value. Note that CFG sets the minimum expected reward $\chi_m(\cdot) = v(\{m\})$ and does not support arbitrarily defining the cost $\chi_m(C_m, \gamma_m)$. The solution to a CFG is a partition of clients into a coalition structure and a reward vector, which distributes the value of each coalition among its members. As CFG implicitly assumes the participation of all clients and that the total reward available $B(\cdot)$ is proportional to $v(\cdot)$, further **client selection** step is needed to ensure **budget balance** when the budget is a limited constant. Solution concepts, such as the Shapley value and core, can ensure **fairness** and **stability**. However, the Shapley value does not always ensure **individual rationality** for all games/clients and the core may be empty (i.e., no viable solutions). Moreover, there is no consideration of **truthfulness**. These incentives have to be addressed in additional steps such as through the reward mapping function and future solutions.

Auction theory and *contract theory* are useful tools to incentivize clients to share private information about their data quality and cost types truthfully with the global server (model owner). They explicitly consider **incentive compatibility**, **individual rationality** as constraints, support arbitrarily defined costs and **client selection**. However, both tools may not enforce *fairness* – clients with the same contribution but different declared costs may get different rewards. In a reverse auction, multiple bidders (clients) want to sell their contribution C_m and declare its value $\phi(C_m)$ and cost type γ_m to the buyer (server) with a budget $B(\cdot)$. Auction design involves explicitly setting rules for selecting winning bidders (clients) $\mathcal{S}$ and deciding the monetary payment $(r_m)_{m \in \mathcal{S}}$ to optimize the *group welfare* while satisfying IC/IR and **budget balance** constraints. For example, *Vickrey auction/mechanism* incentivizes each client m to truthfully share his/her private and true cost/data quality with the server by setting m's reward r_m only based on the valuation/total profits of *others* and independent of client m's declared values. The authors of [2,3,6] use auctions to incentivize clients. Alternatively, the server can design specific contracts (which specify the payment for the contribution, i.e., mapping from $\phi(C_m) \mapsto r_m$) for clients with different cost types to maximize the server's profits. Each client m will choose and sign none/one of the provided contracts which ensures its profit is non-negative and maximized. If the client does not contribute C_m, the server can withhold payment. See [7] for a contract theory in an FL example.

16.9 Non-monetary rewards

For freely-replicable non-monetary rewards, such as model and data derivatives, existing CGT literature is largely inapplicable as CGT assumes the constraint of limited rewards. Without this constraint, one can naively decide to allocate the maximum possible reward to all clients to maximize **group welfare**. However, this violates **collaborative fairness** which demands that a client m with a higher contribution value $\phi(C_m)$ get a strictly more valuable reward. This raises the following two questions:

- First, how should we decide the reward value to increase **group welfare (GW)** further while still maintaining other desired incentives such as **collaborative fairness (CF)**? Is there a parameter that can control *altruism* and the tradeoff between **GW** and **CF**, while ensuring **weak efficiency**?
- Second, how can we flexibly and efficiently control the reward value? Before considering the FL setting, we will first study some non-FL setting examples to cover some general strategies.

16.9.1 Non-FL setting

Existing works have considered rewarding clients with different informativeness of data or model for fairness. Hence, it is natural that the reward value of client m is set to exactly the utility of the non-monetary reward measured using ν, i.e., $r_m = \nu(\cdot)$. However, instead of rewarding client m with $r_m = \phi(C_m)$, using alternatives, such as the ρ-**Shapley value** [12] which sets $r_m^* \triangleq (\phi(C_m)/\max_j \phi(C_j))^\rho \times \nu(\mathbf{w}^S)$, $\rho \in (0, 1]$ and where ϕ is the Shapley value, can increase the reward further and is **fairness-preserving** and *weakly efficient*. By selecting a smaller ρ, we increase altruism, **group welfare** and give higher reward values to weaker contributors. Setting $\rho = 0$ assigns the best possible reward $\nu(\mathbf{w}^S)$ to all clients. While this maximizes **group welfare**, **fairness** is lost.

The next challenge is to efficiently achieve the target reward value $(r_m^*)_{m \in S}$ and some solutions are discussed below:

Model rewards, adding noise to data. In [12], each client m will get a different rewarded model $\mathbf{w}_m^r$ trained on data with additional noise injected to the training labels $\mathbf{y}$. For example, in Bayesian regression models, Gaussian noise of different variance σ_m^2 can be added and optimized by root finding. Higher variance σ^2 reduces the information gained on the model parameters and log-likelihood of the validation set. A more general approach can add noise to other quantities, such as FL gradients.

Synthetic data rewards, controlling number of data samples. In [13], each client m participates in the collaborative training of a generative model and is rewarded with a synthetic dataset drawn from the generative model that augments their original dataset. Stronger contributors will have an augmented dataset with a lower maximum-mean discrepancy (MMD) to a reference data distribution. This reference distribution is approximated with all clients' data together with a large pool of synthetic data. Tay et al. [13] use a modified version of the ρ-Shapley value from [12] to compute rewards that achieve similar incentives such as fairness. The structure of the problem allows a group welfare-maximizing set of parameters to be found with linear optimization. The synthetic reward dataset is generated by greedily sampling synthetic data points from the generative model's data distribution G until the target reward value is reached. The sampling probability of a synthetic data x point is set using the softmax function and proportional to $\exp[\beta \bar{\Delta}_x^m]$ where $\bar{\Delta}_x^m$ is the scaled marginal improvement in ν of client m due to x. A larger β will sample points with a higher marginal improvement, resulting in a higher similarity to G but a smaller synthetic dataset. This sampling algorithm stops when the target reward value is reached.

16.9.2 FL setting

During conventional FL, the global server will share the current model weights with each selected client and request the clients to compute weight updates. Thus, if we view trained models as rewards to achieve incentives, conventional FL unfairly gives each selected client the same reward, the latest $v(\mathbf{w}^S)$ in each iteration, to sustain federated learning. Hence, the authors of [16] reward clients with different training-time gradients/weight updates. A weaker contributor will be rewarded with a more sparsified gradient vector with more components zeroed out. However, this results in clients subsequently reporting weight updates from different locations in the weight space for the server aggregation.

Additionally, if the reward value r_m is exactly the utility of the non-monetary reward measured using v, it may be challenging or inefficient to solve for the weight updates to achieve the desired v, e.g., validation accuracy at every iteration. A simpler approach lets r_m represent a quantity that correlates to higher utility, e.g., the number of unsparsified gradient components. Formally, a client m with aggregated gradients contribution valued at $\phi(C_m)$ will be rewarded with a gradient component that retains the top $r_m = \tanh(\beta\phi(C_m))/\max_j \tanh(\beta\phi(C_j))$ fraction of the components with the largest magnitude. A larger β sparsifies fewer components, leading to less fairness but higher group welfare; β corresponds to an altruism factor. This causes the client's converged model parameters and predictive performance to diverge more from the global server's.

16.10 Conclusion and future work

This chapter gives a preview of incentives in FL, its main components (contribution evaluation, client selection, and reward allocation) and some existing works that strive to achieve these incentives using monetary and non-monetary rewards. Next, we briefly describe open problems to be addressed in future work.

First, how can we better achieve the **truthfulness** incentive during contribution evaluation and identify if clients are giving real, high-quality data or contribution C_m? Second, during client selection, instead of maintaining a single coalition of selected clients, S, can clients be partitioned into multiple coalitions to improve group welfare? Last, during reward allocation, what are other ways we can control the non-monetary, e.g. model, reward value in FL? Possible considerations include non-iterative and non-gradient rewards such as the number of rounds participated or updates received.

Acknowledgments

This research/project is supported by the National Research Foundation Singapore and DSO National Laboratories under the AI Singapore Programme (AISG Award No: AISG2-RP-2020-018).

References

[1] G. Chalkiadakis, E. Elkind, M. Wooldridge, Computational aspects of cooperative game theory, in: Synthesis Lectures on Artificial Intelligence and Machine Learning, 2011.

[2] Mingshu Cong, Han Yu, Xi Weng, Jiabao Qu, Yang Liu, Siu Ming Yiu, A VCG-based fair incentive mechanism for federated learning, arXiv:2008.06680, 2020.

[3] Yongheng Deng, Feng Lyu, Ju Ren, Yi-Chao Chen, Peng Yang, Yuezhi Zhou, Yaoxue Zhang, FAIR: quality-aware federated learning with precise user incentive and model aggregation, in: Proc. IEEE INFOCOM, IEEE, 2021, pp. 1–10.

[4] Dongge Han, Michael Wooldridge, Alex Rogers, Olga Ohrimenko, Sebastian Tschiatschek, Replication robust payoff allocation in submodular cooperative games, IEEE Transactions on Artificial Intelligence (2022).

[5] Rui Hu, Yanmin Gong, Trading data for learning: incentive mechanism for on-device federated learning, in: Pric. IEEE GLOBECOM, IEEE, 2020, pp. 1–6.

[6] Yutao Jiao, Ping Wang, Dusit Niyato, Bin Lin, Dong In Kim, Toward an automated auction framework for wireless federated learning services market, IEEE Transactions on Mobile Computing 20 (10) (2020) 3034–3048.

[7] Jiawen Kang, Zehui Xiong, Dusit Niyato, Han Yu, Ying-Chang Liang, Dong In Kim, Incentive design for efficient federated learning in mobile networks: a contract theory approach, in: Proc. APWCS, 2019, pp. 1–5.

[8] Yang Liu, Jiaheng Wei, Incentives for federated learning: a hypothesis elicitation approach, arXiv:2007.10596, 2020.

[9] Hongtao Lv, Zhenzhe Zheng, Tie Luo, Fan Wu, Shaojie Tang, Lifeng Hua, Rongfei Jia, Chengfei Lv, Data-free evaluation of user contributions in federated learning, in: Proc. WiOpt, IEEE, 2021, pp. 1–8.

[10] Lingjuan Lyu, Yitong Li, Karthik Nandakumar, Jiangshan Yu, Xingjun Ma, How to democratise and protect ai: fair and differentially private decentralised deep learning, IEEE Transactions on Dependable and Secure Computing (2020).

[11] John Nash, Non-cooperative games, Annals of Mathematics 54 (2) (1951) 286–295.

[12] Rachael Hwee Ling Sim, Yehong Zhang, Mun Choon Chan, Bryan Kian Hsiang Low, Collaborative machine learning with incentive-aware model rewards, in: Proc. ICML, 2020, pp. 8927–8936.

[13] Sebastian Shenghong Tay, Xinyi Xu, Chuan Sheng Foo, Bryan Kian Hsiang Low, Incentivizing collaboration in machine learning via synthetic data rewards, in: Proc. AAAI, 2022.

[14] Xuezhen Tu, Kun Zhu, Nguyen Cong Luong, Dusit Niyato, Yang Zhang, Juan Li, Incentive mechanisms for federated learning: from economic and game theoretic perspective, IEEE Transactions on Cognitive Communications and Networking (2022).

[15] Hao Wang, Zakhary Kaplan, Di Niu, Baochun Li, Optimizing federated learning on non-iid data with reinforcement learning, in: Proc. IEEE INFOCOM, IEEE, 2020, pp. 1698–1707.

[16] Xinyi Xu, Lingjuan Lyu, Xingjun Ma, Chenglin Miao, Chuan Sheng Foo, Bryan Kian Hsiang Low, Gradient driven rewards to guarantee fairness in collaborative machine learning, in: Proc. NeurIPS, vol. 34, 2021.

[17] Rongfei Zeng, Chao Zeng, Xingwei Wang, Bo Li, Xiaowen Chu, A comprehensive survey of incentive mechanism for federated learning, arXiv:2106.15406, 2021.

[18] Yufeng Zhan, Peng Li, Zhihao Qu, Deze Zeng, Song Guo, A learning-based incentive mechanism for federated learning, IEEE Internet of Things Journal 7 (7) (2020) 6360–6368.

Introduction to quantum federated machine learning

17

Samuel Yen-Chi Chen and Shinjae Yoo

Brookhaven National Laboratory, Upton, NY, United States

17.1 Introduction

Quantum computing (QC) has the potential to solve certain difficult computational tasks, such as unstructured database search [36] or large number factoring [74], with quadratic or exponential speedup over classical computers [37,61]. In addition, certain quantum algorithms have shown they can provide advantages over classical algorithms on problems such as combinatorial optimization [31]. Recently, the development of quantum hardware by large technology companies and startups, including Google [4], IBM [23], and IonQ [26], sheds light on the deployment of these advanced algorithms and the pursuit of even more potential applications.

Meanwhile, classical machine learning development has demonstrated tremendous success in nearly every aspect, including computer vision [39,45,48,76,83], natural language processing [21,82], speech recognition [34,35,66,67], medical diagnosis [25], recommendation systems [91], and complex sequential decision making (e.g., playing video games [58] or board games like *Go* [75]).

With the useful progress made in classical machine learning and the recent development of QC, it is natural to consider combining the two, namely as *quantum machine learning* (QML). The QML field has grown significantly since the inception of variational quantum algorithms (VQA) [9,11] and quantum circuit learning [57]. These frameworks provide for the possibilities of building a parameterized quantum circuit [7] architecture that can be trained or optimized and make QML possible.

Modern machine learning methods, either quantum or classical, rely on large-scale training datasets. Although there are several publicly available datasets for benchmarking studies, effective machine learning models of commercial interest still depend on a consequential amount of data being collected from users that may contain personal or sensitive data. This is especially concerning as there may be compromised channels in between during the transmission of these data.

With these challenges in mind, it is time to think about how to avoid data leakage in the QML era. Combining federated learning (FL) and QML is one potential direction worth exploring. This chapter introduces the basics of modern QML and current developments involving federated or distributed QML.

Federated Learning. https://doi.org/10.1016/B978-0-44-319037-7.00027-2

17.2 Quantum federated learning

Federated learning [56] is an emerging research field arising as people became more concerned about using large-scale datasets and cloud-based deep learning [72]. The high-level idea of FL consists of a *central node* and several *client nodes* as shown in Fig. 17.1. The *central node*'s mission is to collect the trained local models from client nodes, which may be cell phones or Internet of Things (IoT) devices, just to name a few, then perform an *aggregation* process to generate the *global model*. The resulting global model then is shared with all the client nodes. The client nodes will further train the model they received with their own *local* data. In general, the data amount each client node possesses is only a small portion of the entire dataset.

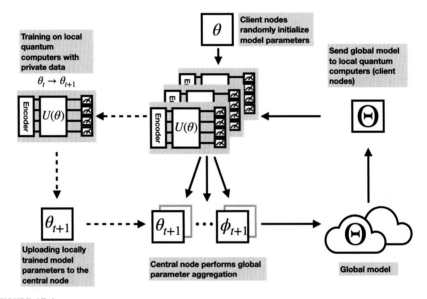

FIGURE 17.1

Quantum Federated Learning. In quantum FL, there is a *central node* and several *client nodes*. The central node's mission is to collect trained model parameters from the client nodes and perform a specific *aggregation* process to generate the new *global model*, which is shared with all of the client nodes. The client nodes usually initial their own model parameters randomly and train the model with their own private data. After the client nodes receive the aggregated global model from the central node, they will further train the model with their dataset and upload the model to the central node. This figure is prepared based on the work in [19].

By knowing what classical FL is, generalizing such an idea to the quantum regime is worth considering. Imagine an array of quantum computers located at different client sites. These devices may have various computing capabilities. However, for this proposed case, presume they share the same specification, such as the number of qubits. There is an agreed common task to achieve, which may be something like medical image classification or financial data modeling. These tasks likely will rely heavily on a proprietary data. Each client has specific sensitive or private data that should not be shared, yet none can successfully train such a model due to the relatively small data volume. Training the QML model collaboratively without sharing the data is where federated QML can help. Here, the requirement is to share the trained quantum models. Because the quantum models actually are parameterized quantum circuits with some parameters, what we need is to share those circuit parameters and they are just "classical" numbers that can be transmitted easily with existing communication infrastructures.

In the near term, available quantum computers may have a limited number of qubits, meaning that input data with large dimensions may not be able to be encoded into quantum states directly. Therefore, it is necessary to have a method to compress the data we want to proceed with. One possible way is to use classical neural networks to perform a *dimensional reduction*. For example, in an image classification task, we can employ a powerful pre-trained convolutional neural network (CNN) [76] to extract valuable features from the data of interest [64]. This method can be seen as a kind of *transfer learning* from classical to quantum, which was first introduced into the field in [53]. Fig. 17.2 shows the generic architecture of such hybrid quantum-classical transfer learning.

Recently, many groups around the world have been working on federated QML to advance privacy-preserving capabilities [12,19,27,40,46,47,49,88–90,92], and most share some common features, e.g., the underlying circuits. The next section introduces the variational quantum circuit, or VQC, the building block of QML.

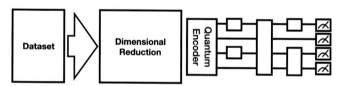

FIGURE 17.2

Hybrid Quantum-Classical Transfer Learning. This diagram shows the generic structure of hybrid quantum-classical transfer learning first introduced in [53]. This setting features a dataset consisting of classical data entries with large dimensions that cannot be processed by a near-term quantum computer directly. Such entries need to be compressed or dimensionality reduced first before they can be loaded into a quantum circuit. There are various ways to achieve this goal. For example, using a classical neural network to compress the data or more traditional ways such as down-sampling or principal component analysis (PCA). A more efficient way is to use large pre-trained models, such as pre-trained CNNs, to extract important features. For example, in [19], the authors use pre-trained VGG16 [76] to compress the large dimensional images into 4 dimensional vectors, which are suitable for quantum simulation.

17.3 **Variational quantum circuits**

Quantum FL should be based on existing QML methods. In the near term, quantum computers have a limited number of qubits and can only execute shallow circuits. This means it is not practical to perform sophisticated machine learning algorithms purely on existing quantum devices. Instead, a *hybrid quantum-classical computing paradigm* is designed to leverage today's noisy intermediate-scale quantum (NISQ) devices (Fig. 17.3). The main concept behind such a paradigm involves splitting the computational task into two parts. One part that can benefit from using a quantum computer will be deployed on the device, while the other part, which is more suited to being solved classically, will be run on a classical computer. As a starting point, Fig. 17.4 depicts the simplest parameterized quantum circuit. This single-qubit

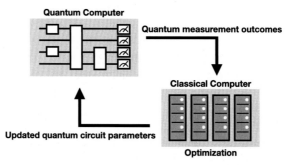

FIGURE 17.3

Hybrid Quantum-Classical Computing. This diagram introduces the hybrid quantum-classical paradigm, which is suitable for currently available NISQ devices [63]. The idea is certain parts of the calculations are performed on the quantum computer, while the optimization procedure is carried out on a classical computer. With this method, people can easily apply the optimization methods developed by the classical machine learning community.

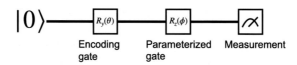

FIGURE 17.4

Simplest Parameterized Quantum Circuit Example. This simple example of a parameterized (variational) quantum circuit model includes important basic components such as *encoding gate*, *parameterized (variational) gate*, and *measurement*. The quantum system is initialized as the $|0\rangle$ state, and the state will go through the encoding and variational gates, which are controlled by the parameter θ and ϕ, respectively. The parameter θ is based on the input data and is not subject to *training*, while the ϕ is the one that will be optimized. The final measurement operation will retrieve the information from the quantum circuit as classical values that can be further processed.

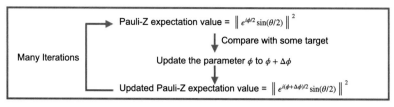

FIGURE 17.5

Concept of Updating a Parameterized Quantum Circuit.

system initialized at state $|0\rangle$ then goes through the *encoding gate*, which is parameterized by a parameter θ. The parameter θ depends on what a user wants to encode (e.g., pixel values from an image). Then, the quantum state will go through the *parameterized gate* – also called a *variational gate* – that is parameterized by ϕ. The ϕ parameter is the element to be trained or learned. After passing through the $R_y(\theta)$ and $R_z(\phi)$ gates, the quantum state should now in the form

$$
\begin{bmatrix} e^{-i\phi/2} & 0 \\ 0 & e^{i\phi/2} \end{bmatrix}
\begin{bmatrix} \cos(\phi/2) & -\sin(\phi/2) \\ \sin(\phi/2) & \cos(\phi/2) \end{bmatrix}
\begin{bmatrix} 1 \\ 0 \end{bmatrix}
$$

$$
= \begin{bmatrix} e^{-i\phi/2}\cos(\theta/2) \\ e^{i\phi/2}\sin(\theta/2) \end{bmatrix} = e^{-i\phi/2}\cos(\theta/2)|0\rangle + e^{i\phi/2}\sin(\theta/2)|1\rangle,
$$

(17.1)

where $R_y(\phi) = e^{-i\phi\sigma_y/2} = \begin{bmatrix} \cos(\phi/2) & -\sin(\phi/2) \\ \sin(\phi/2) & \cos(\phi/2) \end{bmatrix}$ and $R_z(\phi) = e^{-i\phi\sigma_z/2} =$

$\begin{bmatrix} e^{-i\phi/2} & 0 \\ 0 & e^{i\phi/2} \end{bmatrix}$.

If performing the measurement via a computational basis, there is a probability of getting state $|0\rangle$ as $P(\text{state} = |0\rangle) = \left\| e^{-i\phi/2}\cos(\theta/2) \right\|^2$ and state $|1\rangle$ as $P(\text{state} = |1\rangle) = \left\| e^{i\phi/2}\sin(\theta/2) \right\|^2$. However, each measurement will only give either $|0\rangle$ or $|1\rangle$. To obtain knowledge of this probability distribution, the quantum circuit must be prepared and measured numerous times. Such repetition is known as the number of *shots*. Given enough shots, the number of $|0\rangle$ and $|1\rangle$ can be very close to the theoretical prediction $P(\text{state} = |0\rangle)$ and $P(\text{state} = |1\rangle)$ shown herein. Therefore, the *expectation value* of this qubit can be deduced as $P(\text{state} = |1\rangle) = \left\| e^{i\phi/2}\sin(\theta/2) \right\|^2$. The expectation value is the actual output from the quantum model that can be used as the *prediction* in the learning task. For example, this output can be the prediction of a time series or function approximation. However, the quantum model needs to be *trained* akin to what usually is done in classical machine learning. The output from the quantum model must be compared with some target values, and updates to the circuit parameters will be made. As shown in Fig. 17.5, the iterative process is similar to classical machine learning. The only difference is that this time, quantum circuit parameters are updated rather than the neural network weights. Fig. 17.6 shows the

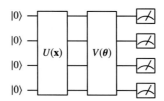

FIGURE 17.6

Generic Architecture for Variational Quantum Circuits. Here $U(\mathbf{x})$ is the quantum circuit block for encoding the (classical) input data $\mathbf{x}$ into a quantum state, and $V(\boldsymbol{\theta})$ is the variational circuit block with tunable or learnable parameters $\boldsymbol{\theta}$ that will be optimized via gradient-based or gradient-free methods. A quantum measurement over some or all of the qubits follows. The measured results are classical values and can be further processed via quantum or classical components.

general form of a VQC. Usually, a VQC includes an *encoding circuit* to load the data into the system; the *variational circuit*, which is the portion that actually is trained; and the final *measurement* to retrieve information from the quantum system.

In the QML field, applications of VQCs to standard machine learning tasks have achieved varying degrees of success. Notable examples include function approximation [20,57], classification [2,7,15–17,29,32,38,41,50,53,55,57,68,70,79,81,86], generative modeling [24,59,77,80,94], deep reinforcement learning [13,14,18,42,43, 52,78,87], sequence modeling [6,20,84], speech recognition [88], metric and embedding learning [51,60], transfer learning [53], and FL [12,19,88]. The following details common operations in a VQC.

17.3.1 Quantum encoder

The quantum gates operate only on quantum states. For a quantum circuit to operate on a classical dataset, the critical first step is to define the *encoding* method, which is to transform the classical vector or an array of values into a quantum state. The encoding scheme is important as it is related to the efficiency of hardware implementation and potential quantum advantages. In the NISQ era, the number of qubits and the circuit depth are limited. Therefore, the classical values must be encoded with a small number of qubits yet without too many quantum operations or pronounced circuit depth. For a more in-depth introduction to various encoding methods used in QML, refer to [71]. A general N-qubit quantum state can be represented as

$$|\psi\rangle = \sum_{(q_1,q_2,...,q_N)\in\{0,1\}^N} c_{q_1,...,q_N} |q_1\rangle \otimes |q_2\rangle \otimes |q_3\rangle \otimes \cdots \otimes |q_N\rangle, \qquad (17.2)$$

where $c_{q_1,...,q_N} \in \mathbb{C}$ is the *amplitude* of each quantum state and $q_i \in \{0, 1\}$. The square of the amplitude $c_{q_1,...,q_N}$ is the *probability* of measurement with the post-measurement state in $|q_1\rangle \otimes |q_2\rangle \otimes |q_3\rangle \otimes \cdots \otimes |q_N\rangle$, and the total probability should

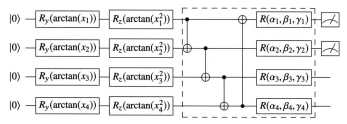

FIGURE 17.7

Variational Quantum Circuit. The VQC includes three components: *encoder, variational layer*, and *quantum measurement*. Here, the VQC shown is used in the work from [19]. The encoder consists of several single-qubit gates $R_y(\arctan(x_i))$ and $R_z(\arctan(x_i^2))$, which represent rotations along the y- and z-axis by the given angle $\arctan(x_i)$ and $\arctan(x_i^2)$, respectively. These rotation angles are derived from the input values x_i and are not subject to iterative optimization. The variational or parameterized layer consists of CNOT gates between each pair of neighboring qubits, which are used to entangle quantum states from each qubit and general single-qubit unitary gates $R(\alpha, \beta, \gamma)$ with three parameters α, β, γ. Parameters labeled α_i, β_i, and γ_i denote the iterative optimization. The quantum measurement component will output the Pauli-Z expectation values of designated qubits. The variational layer demonstrated here is not the only possible configuration. For example, the R gate can be changed to any other rotation gate such as R_x, R_y, R_z, or any combination thereof. The CNOT configuration (e.g., entangling more distant qubits) also can be changed. The number of qubits and of measurements can be adjusted to fit the problem of interest. In [19], the authors use the VQC as the final classifier layer. Therefore, the number of qubits equals the latent vector size, which is 4, and only the measurements on the first two qubits are considered for binary classification. The grouped box in the VQC may repeat several times to increase the number of parameters (subject to the capacity and capability of the available quantum computers or simulation software used for the experiments). In [19], the grouped box repeats 2 times.

be summed to 1, i.e.,

$$\sum_{(q_1,q_2,...,q_N)\in\{0,1\}^N} ||c_{q_1,...,q_N}||^2 = 1. \tag{17.3}$$

For example, in [19], the authors use a *variational encoding* scheme to encode classical values (e.g., pixel values or compressed representations) into a quantum state. The basic idea behind this encoding scheme is to use the input values or their transformation as rotation angles for the quantum rotation gate. As shown in Fig. 17.7, the encoding parts consist of single-qubit rotation gates R_y and R_z and use $\arctan(x_i)$ and $\arctan(x_i^2)$ as the corresponding transformations.

17.3.2 **Quantum gradients**

The hybrid quantum-classical model can be trained in an end-to-end manner, following the common back-propagation method used in training classical deep neural networks. *Parameter-shift* method is employed to calculate the gradients of quantum functions. The method described in [8,69] can be used to derive the analytical gradient of the quantum circuits. The idea behind the parameter-shift rule is that given the knowledge of calculating the expectation of certain observable quantum functions, the quantum gradients can be calculated without using the finite difference method. For example, given the knowledge about how to calculate the expectation value of an observable $\hat{P}$ on a quantum function,

$$f(x; \theta_i) = \left\langle 0 \left| U_0^\dagger(x) U_i^\dagger(\theta_i) \, \hat{P} U_i(\theta_i) \, U_0(x) \right| 0 \right\rangle = \left\langle x \left| U_i^\dagger(\theta_i) \, \hat{P} U_i(\theta_i) \right| x \right\rangle, \quad (17.4)$$

where x is the input value (e.g., pixel values or other classical inputs loaded into the quantum circuit); $U_0(x)$ is the state preparation routine to transform or encode x into a quantum state; i is the circuit parameter index for which the gradient is to be evaluated; and $U_i(\theta_i)$ represents the single-qubit rotation generated by the Pauli operators X, Y, and Z. It can be shown [57] that the gradient of this quantum function f with respect to the parameter θ_i is

$$\nabla_{\theta_i} f(x; \theta_i) = \frac{1}{2} \left[f\left(x; \theta_i + \frac{\pi}{2}\right) - f\left(x; \theta_i - \frac{\pi}{2}\right) \right]. \quad (17.5)$$

Having the gradient of the quantum function, the next step is to update the actual parameters. The simplest way is to perform the classic gradient-descent update, which can be written as

$$\theta \leftarrow \theta - \eta \nabla_\theta L(x; \theta), \quad (17.6)$$

where the θ is the model parameter, L is the loss function, and η is the learning rate. This simple form of gradient-descent sometimes does not work well. For example, the model may get "stuck" in local optimum [65]. Various gradient-based optimization methods have been proposed and shown to be quite successful [44,85]. Although gradient-based methods have proven to be more popular recently, it must be emphasized that gradient-free methods, such as evolutionary optimization, also can be used to optimize quantum circuit parameters as shown in [14].

17.4 Demonstration

Armed with the knowledge that a classically pre-trained CNN can extract important features of an image and then be put into the quantum circuit for classification, all the components can be brought together. The experiments described here are from the work in [19] with the following setup:

- Central node C receives the uploaded circuit parameters θ_i from each local machine N_i, aggregates them into a global parameter Θ, and distributes to all local machines.

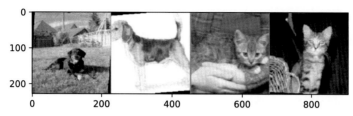

FIGURE 17.8

Cats vs. Dogs Dataset. The dataset from [30] is used in [19].

- Training points are equally distributed to the local machines, and the testing points are on the central node to evaluate the aggregated global model.
- Individual local machines N_i each have a distinct part of the training data and will perform E epochs of the training locally with the batch size B.

The authors of [19] perform the binary classification on the classic cats vs. dogs dataset [30]. Each image in this dataset has slightly different dimensions. A pre-processing routine makes all of the training and testing samples in the dimension of 224×224. Some examples from the dataset are shown in Fig. 17.8. In total, there are 23,000 training data and 2000 testing data samples. The testing data are on the central node, which will be used to evaluate the aggregated model (global model) after each training round. The training data are equally distributed to the 100 local machines N_i, where $i \in \{1, \dots, 100\}$. Therefore, in each local machine, there are 230 training points. In each training round, 5 local machines will be randomly selected, and each will perform 1, 2, or 4 epochs of training with its own training points. The batch size is $S = 32$. The trained model then will be sent to the central node for aggregation. The aggregation method used in this experiment is the collected model average. Then, the aggregated model (global model) will be shared to all of the local machines. The hybrid model used in this experiment consists of a pre-trained VGG16 model and a 4-qubit VQC as shown in Fig. 17.7. The original classifier layer in the VGG16 model is replaced with the one shown in Table 17.1 to fit the input dimension of the VQC layer. The dashed-box in the quantum circuit repeats twice, consisting of $4 \times 3 \times 2 = 24$ quantum circuit parameters. The VQC receives four-dimensional compressed vectors from the pre-trained VGG model to perform the classification task. The non-federated training uses the same hybrid VGG-VQC architecture as the one employed for the federated training. The authors perform 100 training rounds, and the results are presented in Fig. 17.9. The authors also compare the performance of FL with non-FL using the same hybrid quantum-classical architecture and dataset.

The left three sub-figures of Fig. 17.9 show the results of training the hybrid quantum model via federated settings with a different number of local training epochs. Because the training data are distributed across different clients, only the testing accuracy with the aggregated global model is considered. In the Cats vs. Dogs dataset, it can be observed that both the testing accuracy and testing loss reach a comparable level as the non-federated training. It also is evident that the training loss, which

Table 17.1 The trainable layer in the modified VGG model used in [19].

	Linear	ReLU	Dropout($p = 0.5$)	Linear	ReLU	Dropout($p = 0.5$)	Linear
Input	25088			4096			4096
Output	4096			4096			4

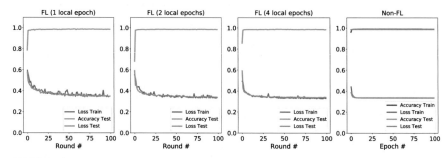

FIGURE 17.9

Results: Cats vs. Dogs. The federated training versus non-FL results from the work in [19].

Table 17.2 Comparison of performance in different training schemes with the Cats vs. Dogs dataset.

	Training Loss	Testing Loss	Testing Accuracy
Federated Training (1 local epoch)	0.3506	0.3519	98.7%
Federated Training (2 local epochs)	0.3405	0.3408	98.6%
Federated Training (4 local epochs)	0.3304	0.3413	98.6%
Non-Federated Training	0.3360	0.3369	98.75%

is the average from clients, fluctuates compared to non-federated training (shown in Table 17.2). The underlying reason may be that in each training round, different clients are selected. Therefore, the training data used to evaluate the training loss differ. Yet, the training loss still converges after 100 rounds of training. In addition, the testing loss and accuracy converge to comparable levels with the non-federated training – regardless of the local training epochs. Notably, it can be observed that a single epoch in local training is sufficient to train a well-performed model. In each round of the federated training, the model updates are based on the samplings from 5 clients with 1 local training epoch. The computing resources used are linear with $230 \times 5 \times 1 = 1150$ in total. While for a full epoch of training within a non-federated setting, the computing resources used are linear with 23,000. These results imply the potential of more efficient training on QML models with distributed schemes. This particularly benefits the training of quantum models when using a high-performance simulation platform or an array of small NISQ devices, where the communication overhead is moderate.

17.5 **Advanced settings**

In the experiments described in this chapter, the data are classical. One interesting question to pose is whether or not actual quantum data can be input into such an FL setting. In this context, there are multiple issues. First, which kind of quantum data can be used? To date, it is nearly impossible to store the actual quantum information on quantum hardware for a reasonably long time compared with a hard drive. Another question is how to communicate between different client nodes. In [12], the authors proposed a quantum FL framework to tackle the first issue – quantum data. Although it is impractical to directly store and transmit quantum data or states, it is possible to store the *quantum circuit parameters* used to generate the quantum state or the description of the quantum circuit itself. The authors demonstrate the effectiveness of quantum FL with a quantum convolutional neural network (QCNN) model as described in [22]. In addition, the authors also show via numerical simulation that their proposed framework can handle both independent and identically distributed (IID) and non-IID data. Yet, in this paper, the communication channel remains the classical one, such as a classical wireless communication channel. Another work, [40], also proposes using quantum data and demonstrates quantum advantage using quantum tensor network classifiers.

Federated or distributed QML also can be considered in another setting. For example, in the work [49], the authors consider a *blind quantum computing* protocol to carry out QML. *Blind quantum computing* [10] is a QC protocol that allows the client, "Alice," to delegate her computational task to an (untrusted) quantum server, "Bob," without revealing the details of her task, such as inputs, outputs, and computation to Bob. In [10], the authors propose a framework that consists of several clients holding private and sensitive data and a centralized quantum server to do the learning task. Within this framework, N clients work collaboratively to train a shared VQC on the quantum server. The advantage of this framework is the clients do not need to host sophisticated quantum devices. This is a desirable property for many institutions that collect and maintain sensitive data, such as hospitals and banks.

In the real world, the communication between each participant in FL may not be ideal due to environmental dynamics, such as time-varying communication channel conditions and energy constraints [54]. To overcome such challenges, the authors of [90] propose a *slimmable quantum FL* framework, which is inspired by the classical slimmable NN (SNN) architecture described in [5]. The main idea behind slimmable NN is not only can the entire model parameters be trained but a portion of the parameters also can be separately trained and used [90]. In quantum FL, the leading models are based on QNN, which is conceptually similar to classical NNs. Thus, these quantum circuit parameters can be separated into different chunks. In [90], the authors propose the following separation of quantum parameters: angle parameters of the VQC(PQC) [parameterized quantum circuit] and pole parameters of the measurement basis. In this framework, the local training consists of the following two parts: *pole training* and *angle training* for training pole and angle parameters, respectively. The communication channel condition dictates if both or part of the parameters will be transmitted. Using numerical simulation, the authors show their proposed framework can provide 11.7% higher accuracy than a traditional quantum FL setting.

For additional comparison between various quantum FL proposals, refer to [46,47]. For theoretical studies of convergence rates of these distributed or federated QML, refer to [27].

17.6 Discussion

17.6.1 Integration with other privacy-preserving mechanisms

This chapter only considers FL, meaning the trained models are shared among participants. However, the communication channels between each party may be compromised, so adversaries can obtain the models. In addition, the possibility that a malicious user joins the network cannot be ruled out, which will provide access to the aggregated global model directly without the need to attack the exchanging channels. A previous study has shown that the model parameters can be used to deduce the training data of that model [28]. In addition, it has been shown that trained machine learning models can be used to recover a training dataset [33]. Furthermore, it is also possible for adversaries to find out if a specific entry is used in the training process [73]. These possibilities raise serious concerns about applying QML models in the context of private and sensitive data. One potential solution is to train the model with *differential privacy* (DP) [1]. With DP, it is possible to share the trained model and still keep the training data information private.

Indeed, certain federated QML methods include DP features in their construction. For example, in the work described in [49], the authors show that by including DP, their framework can resist gradient attacks [93]. Another method to prevent attacks on trained quantum circuit model parameters is *quantum secure aggregation* (QSA), described in [92]. The scheme can protect the private model parameters from being disclosed to unauthorized parties by utilizing qubits to represent model parameters. When there is any attempt to eavesdrop on the private model, it will be detected immediately.

17.6.2 Various aggregation methods

While the average client models can provide good training results, more realistic situations must be considered, such as when clients upload corrupt model parameters or the communication channel is interfered by noise, leading to the global model being compromised. Several recent works present advanced aggregation schemes to address this issue [3,62]. The implementation of these advanced protocols with QML offers an interesting direction for future work.

17.7 Conclusion

This chapter introduced the basic concept of quantum federated machine learning. Initially, it explained how modern QML is based on VQC, a special kind of quantum circuit equipped with parameters trained by classical optimization algorithms. It also described how in the NISQ era, classically pre-trained CNNs can be used to extract important features and compress an image if the data dimensions exceed the available quantum computer capabilities. Such hybrid quantum-classical machine learning models can be trained in a federated manner and achieve accuracy comparable to non-federated ones. Finally, more recent quantum FL developments were described, such as learning from quantum data directly or sharing model parameters under limited communication channels. Other quantum FL formats also were shared, such as vertical FL or blind QC, which may further improve privacy-preserving features. The development of quantum FL still is in its infancy, and there are many questions left to answer, including those related to the efficient combination of other privacy mechanisms, secure communication between participants, quantum FL in the context of quantum communication channels, and several more areas to explore.

References

[1] Martin Abadi, Andy Chu, Ian Goodfellow, H. Brendan McMahan, Ilya Mironov, Kunal Talwar, Li Zhang, Deep learning with differential privacy, in: Proceedings of the 2016 ACM SIGSAC Conference on Computer and Communications Security, 2016, pp. 308–318.

[2] Zainab Abohashima, Mohamed Elhosen, Essam H. Houssein, Waleed M. Mohamed, Classification with quantum machine learning: a survey, arXiv:2006.12270, 2020.

[3] Fan Ang, Li Chen, Nan Zhao, Yunfei Chen, Weidong Wang, F. Richard Yu, Robust federated learning with noisy communication, IEEE Transactions on Communications 68 (6) (2020) 3452–3464.

[4] Frank Arute, Kunal Arya, Ryan Babbush, Dave Bacon, Joseph C. Bardin, Rami Barends, Rupak Biswas, Sergio Boixo, Fernando G.S.L. Brandao, David A. Buell, et al., Quantum supremacy using a programmable superconducting processor, Nature 574 (7779) (2019) 505–510.

[5] Hankyul Baek, Won Joon Yun, Yunseok Kwak, Soyi Jung, Mingyue Ji Mehdi Bennis, Jihong Park, Joongheon Kim, Joint superposition coding and training for federated learning over multi-width neural networks, in: IEEE INFOCOM 2022-IEEE Conference on Computer Communications, IEEE, 2022, pp. 1729–1738.

[6] Johannes Bausch, Recurrent quantum neural networks, Advances in Neural Information Processing Systems 33 (2020) 1368–1379.

[7] Marcello Benedetti, Erika Lloyd, Stefan Sack, Mattia Fiorentini, Parameterized quantum circuits as machine learning models, Quantum Science and Technology 4 (4) (2019) 043001.

[8] Ville Bergholm, Josh Izaac, Maria Schuld, Christian Gogolin Carsten Blank, Keri McKiernan, Nathan Killoran, PennyLane: automatic differentiation of hybrid quantum-classical computations, arXiv:1811.04968, 2018.

[9] Kishor Bharti, Alba Cervera-Lierta, Thi Ha Kyaw, Tobias Haug, Sumner Alperin-Lea, Abhinav Anand, Matthias Degroote, Hermanni Heimonen, Jakob S. Kottmann, Tim Menke, et al., Noisy intermediate-scale quantum algorithms, Reviews of Modern Physics 94 (1) (2022) 015004.

[10] Anne Broadbent, Joseph Fitzsimons, Elham Kashefi, Universal blind quantum computation, in: 2009 50th Annual IEEE Symposium on Foundations of Computer Science, IEEE, 2009, pp. 517–526.

[11] Marco Cerezo, Andrew Arrasmith, Ryan Babbush, Simon C. Benjamin, Suguru Endo, Keisuke Fujii, Jarrod R. McClean, Kosuke Mitarai, Xiao Yuan, Lukasz Cincio, et al., Variational quantum algorithms, Nature Reviews Physics 3 (9) (2021) 625–644.

[12] Chehimi Mahdi, Walid Saad, Quantum federated learning with quantum data, in: ICASSP 2022-2022 IEEE International Conference on Acoustics, Speech and Signal Processing (ICASSP), IEEE, 2022, pp. 8617–8621.

[13] Chih-Chieh Chen, Koudai Shiba, Masaru Sogabe, Katsuyoshi Sakamoto, Tomah Sogabe, Hybrid quantum-classical Ulam–von Neumann linear solver-based quantum dynamic programming algorithm, in: Proceedings of the Annual Conference of JSAI, vol. JSAI2020, 2020, p. 2K6ES203.

[14] Samuel Yen-Chi Chen, Chih-Min Huang, Chia-Wei Hsing, Hsi-Sheng Goan, Ying-Jer Kao, Variational quantum reinforcement learning via evolutionary optimization, Machine Learning: Science and Technology 3 (1) (2022) 015025.

[15] Samuel Yen-Chi Chen, Chih-Min Huang, Chia-Wei Hsing, Ying-Jer Kao, Hybrid quantum-classical classifier based on tensor network and variational quantum circuit, arXiv:2011.14651, 2020.

[16] Samuel Yen-Chi Chen, Tzu-Chieh Wei, Chao Zhang, Haiwang Yu, Shinjae Yoo, Hybrid quantum-classical graph convolutional network, arXiv:2101.06189, 2021.

[17] Samuel Yen-Chi Chen, Tzu-Chieh Wei, Chao Zhang, Haiwang Yu, Shinjae Yoo, Quantum convolutional neural networks for high energy physics data analysis, Physical Review Research 4 (1) (2022) 013231.

[18] Samuel Yen-Chi Chen, Chao-Han Huck Yang, Jun Qi, Pin-Yu Chen, Xiaoli Ma, Hsi-Sheng Goan, Variational quantum circuits for deep reinforcement learning, IEEE Access 8 (2020) 141007–141024.

[19] Samuel Yen-Chi Chen, Shinjae Yoo, Federated quantum machine learning, Entropy 23 (4) (2021) 460.

[20] Samuel Yen-Chi Chen, Shinjae Yoo, Yao-Lung L. Fang, Quantum long short-term memory, in: ICASSP 2022-2022 IEEE International Conference on Acoustics, Speech and Signal Processing (ICASSP), IEEE, 2022, pp. 8622–8626.

[21] Kyunghyun Cho, Bart Van Merriënboer, Caglar Gulcehre, Dzmitry Bahdanau, Fethi Bougares, Holger Schwenk, Yoshua Bengio, Learning phrase representations using RNN encoder-decoder for statistical machine translation, arXiv:1406.1078, 2014.

[22] Iris Cong, Soonwon Choi, Mikhail D. Lukin, Quantum convolutional neural networks, Nature Physics 15 (12) (2019) 1273–1278.

[23] Andrew Cross, The IBM Q experience and QISKit open-source quantum computing software, in: APS March Meeting Abstracts, vol. 2018, 2018, p. L58-003.

[24] Pierre-Luc Dallaire-Demers, Nathan Killoran, Quantum generative adversarial networks, Physical Review A 98 (1) (2018) 012324.

[25] Jeffrey De Fauw, Joseph R. Ledsam, Bernardino Romera-Paredes, Stanislav Nikolov, Nenad Tomasev, Sam Blackwell, Harry Askham, Xavier Glorot, Brendan O'Donoghue, Daniel Visentin, et al., Clinically applicable deep learning for diagnosis and referral in retinal disease, Nature Medicine 24 (9) (2018) 1342–1350.

[26] Shantanu Debnath, Norbert M. Linke, Caroline Figgatt, Kevin A. Landsman, Kevin Wright, Christopher Monroe, Demonstration of a small programmable quantum computer with atomic qubits, Nature 536 (7614) (2016) 63–66.

[27] Yuxuan Du, Yang Qian, Xingyao Wu, Dacheng Tao, A distributed learning scheme for variational quantum algorithms, IEEE Transactions on Quantum Engineering 3 (2022) 1–16.

[28] Cynthia Dwork, Aaron Roth, et al., The algorithmic foundations of differential privacy, Foundations and Trends in Theoretical Computer Science 9 (3–4) (2014) 211–407.

[29] Philip Easom-McCaldin, Ahmed Bouridane, Ammar Belatreche, Richard Jiang, Towards building a facial identification system using quantum machine learning techniques, arXiv:2008.12616, 2020.

[30] Jeremy Elson, John Douceur, Jon Howell, Jared Saul Asirra, A CAPTCHA that exploits interest-aligned manual image categorization, in: Proceedings of 14th ACM Conference on Computer and Communications Security (CCS), Association for Computing Machinery, Inc., Oct. 2007.

[31] Edward Farhi, Jeffrey Goldstone, Sam Gutmann, A quantum approximate optimization algorithm, arXiv:1411.4028, 2014.

[32] Edward Farhi, Hartmut Neven, Classification with quantum neural networks on near term processors, arXiv:1802.06002, 2018.

[33] Matt Fredrikson, Somesh Jha, Thomas Ristenpart, Model inversion attacks that exploit confidence information and basic countermeasures, in: Proceedings of the 22nd ACM SIGSAC Conference on Computer and Communications Security, 2015, pp. 1322–1333.

[34] Alex Graves, Navdeep Jaitly, Towards end-to-end speech recognition with recurrent neural networks, in: International Conference on Machine Learning, PMLR, 2014, pp. 1764–1772.

[35] Alex Graves, Abdel-rahman Mohamed, Geoffrey Hinton, Speech recognition with deep recurrent neural networks, in: 2013 IEEE International Conference on Acoustics, Speech and Signal Processing, IEEE, 2013, pp. 6645–6649.

[36] Lov K. Grover, A fast quantum mechanical algorithm for database search, in: Proceedings of the Twenty-Eighth Annual ACM Symposium on Theory of Computing, 1996, pp. 212–219.

[37] Aram W. Harrow, Ashley Montanaro, Quantum computational supremacy, Nature 549 (7671) (2017) 203–209.

[38] Vojtěch Havlíček, Antonio D. Córcoles, Kristan Temme, Aram W. Harrow, Abhinav Kandala, Jerry M. Chow, Jay M. Gambetta, Supervised learning with quantum-enhanced feature spaces, Nature 567 (7747) (2019) 209–212.

[39] Kaiming He, Xiangyu Zhang, Shaoqing Ren, Jian Sun, Deep residual learning for image recognition, in: Proceedings of the IEEE Conference on Computer Vision and Pattern Recognition, 2016, pp. 770–778.

[40] Rui Huang, Xiaoqing Tan, Qingshan Xu, Quantum federated learning with decentralized data, IEEE Journal of Selected Topics in Quantum Electronics 28 (4) (2022) 1–10.

[41] Ben Jaderberg, Lewis W. Anderson, Weidi Xie, Samuel Albanie, Martin Kiffner, Dieter Jaksch, Quantum self-supervised learning, arXiv:2103.14653, 2021.

[42] Sofiene Jerbi, Casper Gyurik, Simon Marshall, Hans J. Briegel, Vedran Dunjko, Variational quantum policies for reinforcement learning, arXiv:2103.05577, 2021.

[43] Sofiene Jerbi, Lea M. Trenkwalder, Hendrik Poulsen Nautrup, Hans J. Briegel, Vedran Dunjko, Quantum enhancements for deep reinforcement learning in large spaces, PRX Quantum 2 (1) (2021) 010328.

[44] Diederik P. Kingma, Jimmy Ba, Adam: a method for stochastic optimization, arXiv:1412.6980, 2014.

[45] Alex Krizhevsky, Ilya Sutskever, Geoffrey E. Hinton, ImageNet classification with deep convolutional neural networks, in: Advances in Neural Information Processing Systems, 2012, pp. 1097–1105.

[46] Yunseok Kwak, Won Joon Yun, Jae Pyoung Kim, Hyunhee Cho, Minseok Choi, Soyi Jung, Joongheon Kim, Quantum heterogeneous distributed deep learning architectures: models, discussions, and applications, arXiv:2202.11200, 2022.

[47] Harashta Tatimma Larasati, Muhammad Firdaus, Howon Kim, Quantum federated learning: remarks and challenges, in: 2022 IEEE 9th International Conference on Cyber Security and Cloud Computing (CSCloud)/2022 IEEE 8th International Conference on Edge Computing and Scalable Cloud (EdgeCom), IEEE, 2022, pp. 1–5.

[48] Yann LeCun, Léon Bottou, Yoshua Bengio, Patrick Haffner, Gradient-based learning applied to document recognition, Proceedings of the IEEE 86 (11) (1998) 2278–2324.

[49] Weikang Li, Sirui Lu, Dong-Ling Deng, Quantum federated learning through blind quantum computing, Science China Physics, Mechanics & Astronomy 64 (10) (2021) 1–8.

[50] Weikang Li, Zhide Lu, Dong-Ling Deng, Quantum neural network classifiers: a tutorial, arXiv:2206.02806, 2022.

[51] Seth Lloyd, Maria Schuld, Aroosa Ijaz, Josh Izaac, Nathan Killoran, Quantum embeddings for machine learning, arXiv:2001.03622, 2020.

[52] Owen Lockwood, Mei Si, Reinforcement learning with quantum variational circuit, in: Proceedings of the AAAI Conference on Artificial Intelligence and Interactive Digital Entertainment, vol. 16, 2020, pp. 245–251.

[53] Andrea Mari, Thomas R. Bromley, Josh Izaac, Maria Schuld, Nathan Killoran, Transfer learning in hybrid classical-quantum neural networks, Quantum 4 (2020) 340.

[54] Yoshitomo Matsubara, Davide Callegaro, Sameer Singh, Marco Levorato, Francesco Restuccia, Bottlefit: learning compressed representations in deep neural networks for effective and efficient split computing, arXiv:2201.02693, 2022.

[55] Denny Mattern, Darya Martyniuk, Henri Willems, Fabian Bergmann, Adrian Paschke, Variational quanvolutional neural networks with enhanced image encoding, arXiv:2106.07327, 2021.

[56] Brendan McMahan, Eider Moore, Daniel Ramage, Seth Hampson, Blaise Aguera y Arcas, Communication-efficient learning of deep networks from decentralized data, in: Artificial Intelligence and Statistics, PMLR, 2017, pp. 1273–1282.

[57] Kosuke Mitarai, Makoto Negoro, Masahiro Kitagawa, Keisuke Fujii, Quantum circuit learning, Physical Review A 98 (3) (2018) 032309.

[58] Volodymyr Mnih, Koray Kavukcuoglu, David Silver, Andrei A. Rusu, Joel Veness, Marc G. Bellemare, Alex Graves, Martin Riedmiller, Andreas K. Fidjeland, Georg Ostrovski, Stig Petersen, Charles Beattie, Amir Sadik, Ioannis Antonoglou, Helen King, Dharshan Kumaran, Daan Wierstra, Shane Legg, Demis Hassabis, Human-level control through deep reinforcement learning, Nature 518 (7540) (2015) 529–533.

[59] Kouhei Nakaji, Naoki Yamamoto, Quantum semi-supervised generative adversarial network for enhanced data classification, arXiv:2010.13727, 2020.

[60] Nhat A. Nghiem, Samuel Yen-Chi Chen, Tzu-Chieh Wei, Unified framework for quantum classification, Physical Review Research 3 (3) (2021) 033056.

[61] Michael A. Nielsen, Isaac Chuang, Quantum computation and quantum information, 2002.

[62] Krishna Pillutla, Sham M. Kakade, Zaid Harchaoui, Robust aggregation for federated learning, arXiv:1912.13445, 2019.

[63] John Preskill, Quantum computing in the NISQ era and beyond, Quantum 2 (2018) 79.

[64] Ricardo Ribani, Mauricio Marengoni, A survey of transfer learning for convolutional neural networks, in: 2019 32nd SIBGRAPI Conference on Graphics, Patterns and Images Tutorials (SIBGRAPI-T), IEEE, 2019, pp. 47–57.

[65] Sebastian Ruder, An overview of gradient descent optimization algorithms, arXiv:1609. 04747, 2016.

[66] Haşim Sak, Andrew Senior, Françoise Beaufays, Long short-term memory based recurrent neural network architectures for large vocabulary speech recognition, arXiv: 1402.1128, 2014.

[67] Haşim Sak, Andrew Senior, Kanishka Rao, Françoise Beaufays, Fast and accurate recurrent neural network acoustic models for speech recognition, arXiv:1507.06947, 2015.

[68] Abhijat Sarma, Rupak Chatterjee, Kaitlin Gili, Ting Yu, Quantum unsupervised and supervised learning on superconducting processors, arXiv:1909.04226, 2019.

[69] Maria Schuld, Ville Bergholm, Christian Gogolin, Josh Izaac, Nathan Killoran, Evaluating analytic gradients on quantum hardware, Physical Review A 99 (3) (2019) 032331.

[70] Maria Schuld, Alex Bocharov, Krysta Svore, Nathan Wiebe, Circuit-centric quantum classifiers, arXiv:1804.00633, 2018.

[71] Maria Schuld, Francesco Petruccione, Information encoding, in: Supervised Learning with Quantum Computers, Springer International Publishing, Cham, 2018, pp. 139–171.

[72] Reza Shokri, Vitaly Shmatikov, Privacy-preserving deep learning, in: Proceedings of the 22nd ACM SIGSAC Conference on Computer and Communications Security, 2015, pp. 1310–1321.

[73] Reza Shokri, Marco Stronati, Congzheng Song, Vitaly Shmatikov, Membership inference attacks against machine learning models, in: 2017 IEEE Symposium on Security and Privacy (SP), IEEE, 2017, pp. 3–18.

[74] Peter W. Shor, Algorithms for quantum computation: discrete logarithms and factoring, in: Proceedings 35th Annual Symposium on Foundations of Computer Science, IEEE, 1994, pp. 124–134.

[75] David Silver, Aja Huang, Chris J. Maddison, Arthur Guez, Laurent Sifre, George Van Den Driessche, Julian Schrittwieser, Ioannis Antonoglou, Veda Panneershelvam, Marc Lanctot, et al., Mastering the game of go with deep neural networks and tree search, Nature 529 (7587) (2016) 484–489.

[76] Karen Simonyan, Andrew Zisserman, Very deep convolutional networks for large-scale image recognition, arXiv:1409.1556, 2014.

[77] Haozhen Situ, Zhimin He, Lvzhou Li, Shenggen Zheng, Quantum generative adversarial network for generating discrete data, arXiv:1807.01235, 2018.

[78] Andrea Skolik, Sofiene Jerbi, Vedran Dunjko, Quantum agents in the Gym: a variational quantum algorithm for deep Q-learning, Quantum 6 (2022) 720.

[79] Samuel A. Stein, Betis Baheri, Ray Marie Tischio, Yiwen Chen, Ying Mao, Qiang Guan, Ang Li, Bo Fang, A hybrid system for learning classical data in quantum states, arXiv: 2012.00256, 2020.

[80] Samuel A. Stein, Betis Baheri, Ray Marie Tischio, Ying Mao, Qiang Guan, Ang Li, Bo Fang, Shuai Xu, QuGAN: a generative adversarial network through quantum states, arXiv:2010.09036, 2020.

[81] Samuel A. Stein, Ying Mao, Betis Baheri, Qiang Guan, Ang Li, Daniel Chen, Shuai Xu, Caiwen Ding, QuClassi: a hybrid deep neural network architecture based on quantum state fidelity, arXiv:2103.11307, 2021.

[82] Ilya Sutskever, Oriol Vinyals, Quoc V. Le, Sequence to sequence learning with neural networks, Advances in Neural Information Processing Systems 27 (2014).

[83] Christian Szegedy, Wei Liu, Yangqing Jia, Pierre Sermanet, Scott Reed, Dragomir Anguelov, Dumitru Erhan, Vincent Vanhoucke, Andrew Rabinovich, Going deeper with convolutions, in: Proceedings of the IEEE Conference on Computer Vision and Pattern Recognition, 2015, pp. 1–9.

[84] Yuto Takaki, Kosuke Mitarai, Makoto Negoro, Keisuke Fujii, Masahiro Kitagawa, Learning temporal data with a variational quantum recurrent neural network, Physical Review A 103 (5) (2021) 052414.

[85] T. Tieleman, G. Hinton, Lecture 6.5 – RmsProp: Divide the Gradient by a Running Average of Its Recent Magnitude, COURSERA: Neural Networks for Machine Learning, 2012.

[86] Jindi Wu, Zeyi Tao, Qun Li, Scalable quantum neural networks for classification, arXiv: 2208.07719, 2022.

[87] Shaojun Wu, Shan Jin, Dingding Wen, Xiaoting Wang, Quantum reinforcement learning in continuous action space, arXiv:2012.10711, 2020.

[88] Chao-Han Huck Yang, Jun Qi, Samuel Yen-Chi Chen, Pin-Yu Chen, Sabato Marco Siniscalchi, Xiaoli Ma, Chin-Hui Lee, Decentralizing feature extraction with quantum convolutional neural network for automatic speech recognition, in: ICASSP 2021–2021 IEEE International Conference on Acoustics, Speech and Signal Processing (ICASSP), IEEE, 2021, pp. 6523–6527.

[89] Chao-Han Huck Yang, Jun Qi, Samuel Yen-Chi Chen, Yu Tsao, Pin-Yu Chen, When bert meets quantum temporal convolution learning for text classification in heterogeneous computing, in: ICASSP 2022–2022 IEEE International Conference on Acoustics, Speech and Signal Processing (ICASSP), IEEE, 2022, pp. 8602–8606.

[90] Won Joon Yun, Jae Pyoung Kim, Soyi Jung, Jihong Park, Mehdi Bennis, Joongheon Kim, Slimmable quantum federated learning, arXiv:2207.10221, 2022.

[91] Shuai Zhang, Lina Yao, Aixin Sun, Yi Tay, Deep learning based recommender system: a survey and new perspectives, ACM Computing Surveys (CSUR) 52 (1) (2019) 1–38.

[92] Yichi Zhang, Chao Zhang, Cai Zhang, Lixin Fan, Bei Zeng, Qiang Yang, Federated learning with quantum secure aggregation, arXiv:2207.07444, 2022.

[93] Ligeng Zhu, Zhijian Liu, Song Han, Deep leakage from gradients, Advances in Neural Information Processing Systems 32 (2019).

[94] Christa Zoufal, Aurélien Lucchi, Stefan Woerner, Quantum generative adversarial networks for learning and loading random distributions, npj Quantum Information 5 (1) (2019) 1–9.

Federated quantum natural gradient descent for quantum federated learning

Jun Qi[a] and Min-Hsiu Hsieh[b]

[a]*Fudan University, Shanghai, China*
[b]*Hon Hai (Foxconn) Quantum Computing Research Center, Taipei, Taiwan*

18.1 Introduction

Deep learning (DL) technologies have been successfully applied in many machine learning tasks such as speech recognition (ASR) [17], natural language processing (NLP) [14], and computer vision [34]. The bedrock of DL applications highly relies on the hardware breakthrough of the graphic processing unit (GPU) and the availability of a large amount of training data [25,26]. However, the advantages of large-size DL models, such as GPT-3 [3] and BERT [10], are faithfully attributed to the significantly powerful computing capabilities that are only privileged to big companies equipped with numerous costly and industrial-level GPUs. With the rapid development of noisy intermediate-scale quantum (NISQ) devices [12,13,24], the quantum computing hardware is expected to speed up the classical DL algorithms by creating novel quantum machine learning (QML) approaches like quantum neural networks (QNN) [4,11,15,16] and quantum kernel learning (QKL) [16]. The VQC-based QNN seeks to parameterize a distribution through some set of adjustable model parameters, and the QKL methods utilize quantum computers to define a feature map that projects classical data into the quantum Hilbert space. Both QML methods have advantages and disadvantages in dealing with different machine learning tasks and it could not be simply claimed which one is the most suitable choice. However, two obstacles prevent the NISQ devices from applying to QML in practice. The first challenge is that the classical DL models cannot be deployed on NISQ devices without model conversion to quantum tensor formats [5,28]. For the second challenge, the NISQ devices admit a few physical qubits such that insufficient qubits could be spared for the quantum error correction [2,12,13]. More significantly, the representation power of QML is quite limited to the small number of currently available qubits [29] and the increase of qubits may lead to the problem of Barren Plateaus [22].

To deal with the first challenge, in this chapter, we introduce a variational quantum algorithm, namely a variational quantum circuit (VQC), to enable QNN to be

Federated Learning. https://doi.org/10.1016/B978-0-44-319037-7.00028-4

329

simulated on the currently available NISQ devices. The VQC-based QNNs have attained even exponential advantages over the DL counterparts on exclusively many tasks like ASR [27,36], NLP [37], and reinforcement learning [6]. As for the second challenge, distributed QML systems, which consist of local quantum machines, can be set up to enhance the quantum computing power. One particular distributed QML architecture is called quantum federated learning (QFL), which aims to build a decentralized computing model derived from a classical FL.

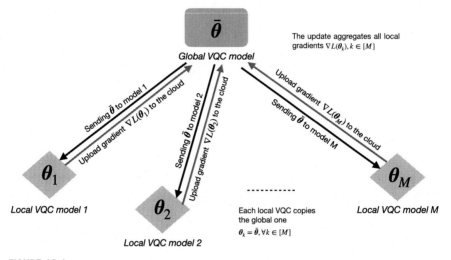

FIGURE 18.1

An illustration of quantum federated learning. The global VQC parameter $\bar{\theta}$ is first transmitted to local VQCs θ_k. Then, the updated gradients $\nabla \mathcal{L}(\theta_k)$ based on the participants' local data are sent back to the centralized server and then they are aggregated to update the parameters of the global VQC.

Konečný et al. [19] first proposed the FL strategies to improve the communication efficiency of a distributed computing system, and McMahan et al. [23] set up the FL systems with the concerns in the use of big data and a large-scale cloud-based DL [31]. The FL framework depends on the advances in hardware progress, making tiny DL systems practically powerful. For example, an ASR system on the cloud can transmit a global acoustic model to a user's cell phone and then send the updated information back to the cloud without collecting the user's private data on the centralized computing server. As shown in Fig. 18.1, the QFL system is similar to a classical FL system and differs from distributed learning in several ways as follows: (a) the datasets in the framework of QFL are not necessarily balanced; (b) the data in QFL are not assumed to be generated from an independent and identical (i.i.d.) distribution.

Chen et al. [7] demonstrates the QFL architecture that is built upon the classical FL paradigm, where the central node holds a global VQC and receives the trained VQC parameters from participants' local quantum devices. Therefore, the QFL model, which inherits the advantages of the FL framework, can unite tiny local quantum devices to generate a powerful global one. This methodology helps to build a privacy-preserving QML system and leverages quantum computing to further boost the computing power of the classical FL. As shown in Fig. 18.1, our proposed QFL and FL differ in the models utilized in federated learning systems, where QFL employs VQC models instead of their classical DL counterparts for FL. More specifically, the QFL comprises a global VQC model deployed on the cloud, and there are M local VQC models assigned to users' devices. The training process of QFL involves three key procedures: (1) the parameters of global VQC model $\bar{\theta}$ are transmitted to K local participants' devices; (2) each local VQC first adaptively trains its own model based on the local users' data, and then separately sends the model gradients $\nabla \mathcal{L}(\theta_k)$ back to the centralized platform; (3) the uploaded gradients from local participants are averagely aggregated to create a global gradient to update further the global model parameters $\bar{\theta}$.

Despite the advantages of QFL in practice, an inherent bottleneck of QFL is the communication overhead among different VQC models, which bounds up with the performance of QFL. To reduce the cost of communication overhead, we expect a more efficient training algorithm to speed up the convergence rate such that fewer counts of global model updates can be attained. Based on the above analysis, in this chapter, we put forth a federated quantum learning algorithm, namely federated quantum natural gradient descent (FQNGD), for the training of QFL. The FQNGD algorithm, developed from the quantum natural gradient descent (QNGD) algorithm, admits a more efficient training process for a single VQC [32]. In particular, Stokes et al. [32] first claimed that the Fubini–Study metric tensor could be employed for the QNGD. Besides, compared with the work [7], the gradients of VQC are uploaded to a global model rather than the VQC parameters of local devices such that the updated gradients can be collected without being accessed to the VQC parameters as shown in [7].

18.2 **Variational quantum circuit**

An illustration of VQC is shown in Fig. 18.2, where the VQC model consists of three components: (a) tensor product encoding (TPE); (b) parametric quantum circuit (PQC); and (c) measurement. The TPE initializes the input quantum states $|x_1\rangle, |x_2\rangle, \ldots, |x_U\rangle$ from the classical inputs $x_1, x_2, \ldots, x_U$, and the PQC operator transforms the quantum states $|x_1\rangle, |x_2\rangle, \ldots, |x_U\rangle$ into the output quantum states $|z_1\rangle, |z_2\rangle, \ldots, |z_U\rangle$. The outputs correspond to the expected observations $\langle z_1\rangle, \langle z_2\rangle, \ldots, \langle z_U\rangle$ arise from the measurement of the Pauli-Z operators. We present the three components in detail next.

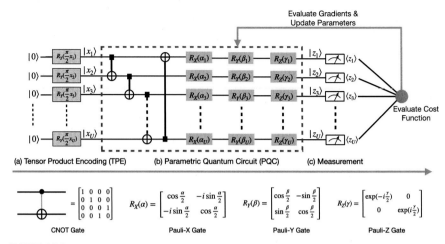

FIGURE 18.2

The VQC is composed of three components: (a) TPE; (b) PQC; (c) Measurement. The TPE utilizes a series of $R_Y(\frac{\pi}{2}x_i)$ to transform classical inputs into quantum states. The PQC consists of CNOT gates and single-qubit rotation gates R_X, R_Y, R_Z with trainable parameters α, β, and γ. The CNOT gates are non-parametric and impose the property of quantum entanglement among qubits, and R_X, R_Y, and R_Z are parametric gates and can be adjustable during the training stage. The PQC model in the green dash square (dark gray in print version) is repeatedly copied to build a deep model. The measurement converts the quantum states $|z_1\rangle, |z_2\rangle, \ldots, |z_U\rangle$ into the corresponding expectation values $\langle z_1\rangle, \langle z_2\rangle, \ldots, \langle z_U\rangle$. The outputs $\langle z_1\rangle, \langle z_2\rangle, \ldots, \langle z_U\rangle$ is connected to a loss function and the gradient descent algorithms can be used to update the VQC model parameters. Besides, both CNOT gates and R_X, R_Y, and R_Z correspond to unitary matrices as shown below the VQC framework.

The TPE model was first proposed in [33]. It aims to convert a classical vector $\mathbf{x}$ into a quantum state $|\mathbf{x}\rangle$ by setting up a one-to-one mapping as

$$
\begin{aligned}
|\mathbf{x}\rangle &= \left(\otimes_{i=1}^{U} R_Y\left(\frac{\pi}{2}x_i\right)\right)|0\rangle^{\otimes U} \\
&= \begin{bmatrix}\cos(\frac{\pi}{2}x_1)\\\sin(\frac{\pi}{2}x_1)\end{bmatrix} \otimes \begin{bmatrix}\cos(\frac{\pi}{2}x_2)\\\sin(\frac{\pi}{2}x_2)\end{bmatrix} \otimes \cdots \otimes \begin{bmatrix}\cos(\frac{\pi}{2}x_U)\\\sin(\frac{\pi}{2}x_U)\end{bmatrix},
\end{aligned}
\tag{18.1}
$$

where $R_Y(\cdot)$ refers to a single-qubit quantum gate rotated across Y-axis and each x_i is constrained to the domain of [0, 1], which results in a reversely one-to-one conversion between $\mathbf{x}$ and $|\mathbf{x}\rangle$.

Moreover, the PQC is equipped with the CNOT gates for quantum entanglement and learnable quantum gates, i.e., $R_X(\alpha_i)$, $R_Y(\beta_i)$, and $R_Z(\gamma_i)$, where the qubit angles α_i, β_i, and γ_i are tuned in the training process. The PQC framework in the green dash square (dark gray in print version) is repeatedly copied to set up a deep model, and the number of the PQC frameworks is called the depth of the VQC. The operation of the measurement outputs the classical expected observations $|z_1\rangle, |z_2\rangle, \ldots, |z_U\rangle$ from the quantum output states. The expected outcomes are used to calculate the loss value and the gradient descents [30], which are used to update the VQC model parameters by applying the back-propagation algorithm [35] based on the stochastic gradient descent (SGD) optimizer.

18.3 Quantum natural gradient descent

As shown in Eq. (18.2), at step t, the standard gradient descent minimizes a loss function $\mathcal{L}(\boldsymbol{\theta})$ with respect to the parameters $\boldsymbol{\theta}$ in a Euclidean space,

$$\boldsymbol{\theta}_{t+1} = \boldsymbol{\theta}_t - \eta \nabla \mathcal{L}(\boldsymbol{\theta}_t), \tag{18.2}$$

where η is the learning rate.

The standard gradient descent algorithm conducts each optimization step in a Euclidean geometry on the parameter space. However, since the form of parameterization is not unique, different compositions of parameterizations are likely to distort the distance geometry within the optimization landscape. A better alternative method is to perform the gradient descent in the distribution space, namely natural gradient descent [1], which is dimension-free and invariant for different parameterization forms. Each optimization step of the natural gradient descent chooses the optimum step size for the update of parameter $\boldsymbol{\theta}_t$, regardless of the choice of parameterization. Mathematically, the standard gradient descent is modified as

$$\boldsymbol{\theta}_{t+1} = \boldsymbol{\theta}_t - \eta F^{-1} \nabla \mathcal{L}(\boldsymbol{\theta}_t), \tag{18.3}$$

where F denotes the Fisher information matrix, which acts as a metric tensor that transforms the steepest gradient descent in the Euclidean parameter space to the steepest descent in the distribution space.

Since the standard Euclidean geometry is sub-optimal for optimizing quantum variational algorithms, a quantum analog has the following form:

$$\boldsymbol{\theta}_{t+1} = \boldsymbol{\theta}_t - \eta g^+(\boldsymbol{\theta}_t) \nabla \mathcal{L}(\boldsymbol{\theta}_t), \tag{18.4}$$

where $g^+(\boldsymbol{\theta}_t)$ refers to the pseudo-inverse and is associated with the specific architecture of the quantum circuit. The coefficient $g^+(\boldsymbol{\theta}_t)$ can be calculated using the Fubini–Study metric tensor, which it then reduces to the Fisher information matrix in the classical limit [21].

The Fubini–Study metric is the natural metric for the geometrization of quantum mechanics, and much of the peculiar behavior of quantum mechanics including quantum entanglement can be attributed to the peculiarities of the Fubini–Study metric.

In this chapter, the Fubini–Study metric tensor is typically defined in quantum mechanics' notations of mixed states. To explicitly equate this notation to the homogeneous coordinates, let

$$|\psi\rangle = \sum_{k=0}^{K} Z_k |e_k\rangle = [Z_0 : Z_1 : \ldots : Z_K], \tag{18.5}$$

where $\{|e_k\rangle\}$ is a set of orthonormal basis vectors for Hilbert space, and the Z_k are complex numbers; $Z_\alpha = [Z_0 : Z_1 : \ldots : Z_K]$ is the standard notation for a point in the projective space of homogeneous coordinates. Then, given two points $|\psi\rangle = Z_\alpha$ and $|\phi\rangle = W_\alpha$ in the space, the distance between $|\psi\rangle$ and $|\phi\rangle$ is

$$\gamma = \arccos \sqrt{\frac{\langle\psi|\phi\rangle\langle\phi|\psi\rangle}{\langle\psi|\psi\rangle\langle\phi|\phi\rangle}}. \tag{18.6}$$

18.4 Quantum natural gradient descent for VQC

Before employing the QFNGD for a quantum federated learning system, we concentrate on the use of QNGD for a single VQC. For simplicity, we leverage a block-diagonal approximation to the Fubini–Study metric tensor for composing QNGD into the VQC training on the NISQ quantum hardware.

We set an initial quantum state $|\psi_0\rangle$ and a PQC with L layers. For $l \in [L]$, we separately denote $\mathbf{W}_l$ and $\mathbf{V}_l(\boldsymbol{\theta}_l)$ as the unitary matrices associated with non-parameterized quantum gates and parameterized quantum ones, respectively. (See Fig. 18.3.)

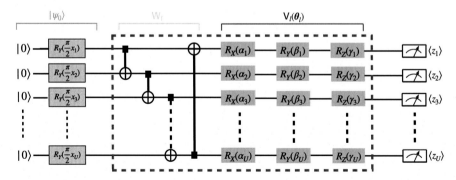

FIGURE 18.3

An illustration of unitary matrices associated with the non-parametric and parametric gates. For all $l \in [L]$, the matrices $\mathbf{W}_l$ correspond to the non-parametric gates, the matrices $\mathbf{V}_l(\boldsymbol{\theta}_l)$ are associated with the parametric ones, and $|\psi_0\rangle$ refers to the initial quantum state that is derived from the operation of the TPE.

Let us consider a variational quantum circuit given by

$$U(\boldsymbol{\theta})|\psi_0\rangle = \mathbf{V}_L(\boldsymbol{\theta}_L)\mathbf{W}_L \cdots \mathbf{V}_l(\boldsymbol{\theta}_l)\mathbf{W}_l \cdots \mathbf{V}_1(\boldsymbol{\theta}_1)\mathbf{W}_1|\psi_0\rangle. \quad (18.7)$$

Furthermore, any unitary quantum parametric gates can be rewritten as $\mathbf{V}_l(\boldsymbol{\theta}_l) = \exp(i\boldsymbol{\theta}_l H_l)$, where H_l refers to the Hermitian generator of the gate $\mathbf{V}_L$. The approximation to the Fubini–Study metric tensor admits that for each parametric layer l in the variational quantum circuit, the $n_l \times n_l$ block-diagonal submatrix of the Fubini–Study metric tensor $g_{l,i,j}^+$ is calculated by

$$g_{l,i,j}^+ = \langle\psi_l|H_l(i)H_l(j)|\psi_l\rangle - \langle\psi_l|H_l(i)|\psi_l\rangle\langle\psi_l|H_l(j)|\psi_l\rangle, \quad (18.8)$$

where

$$|\psi_l\rangle = \mathbf{V}_l(\boldsymbol{\theta}_l)\mathbf{W}_l \cdots \mathbf{V}_1(\boldsymbol{\theta}_1)\mathbf{W}_1|\psi_0\rangle. \quad (18.9)$$

Note that $|\psi_l\rangle$ in Eq. (18.9) denotes the quantum state before the application of the parameterized layer l. Fig. 18.4 illustrates a simplified version of a VQC, where $\mathbf{W}_1$ and $\mathbf{W}_2$ are related to non-parametric gates, and $\mathbf{V}_1(\theta_0, \theta_1)$ and $\mathbf{V}_2(\theta_2, \theta_3)$ correspond to the parametric gates with adjustable parameters, respectively. Since there are two layers, each of which owns two free parameters, the block-diagonal approximation is composed of two 2×2 matrices, g_1^+ and g_2^+, which can be respectively expressed as

$$g_1^+ = \begin{bmatrix} \langle z_0^2\rangle - \langle z_0\rangle^2 & \langle z_0 z_1\rangle - \langle z_0\rangle\langle z_1\rangle \\ \langle z_0 z_1\rangle - \langle z_0\rangle\langle z_1\rangle & \langle z_1^2\rangle - \langle z_1\rangle^2 \end{bmatrix} \quad (18.10)$$

and

$$g_2^+ = \begin{bmatrix} \langle y_1^2\rangle - \langle y_1\rangle^2 & \langle y_1 x_2\rangle - \langle y_1\rangle\langle x_2\rangle \\ \langle y_1 x_2\rangle - \langle y_1\rangle\langle x_2\rangle & \langle x_2^2\rangle - \langle x_2\rangle^2 \end{bmatrix}. \quad (18.11)$$

The elements of g_1^+ and g_2^+ compose $g^+(\boldsymbol{\theta})$ as

$$g^+(\boldsymbol{\theta}) = \begin{bmatrix} g_1^+ & 0 \\ 0 & g_2^+ \end{bmatrix}. \quad (18.12)$$

Then, we employ Eq. (18.4) to update the VQC parameter $\boldsymbol{\theta}$.

18.5 Federated quantum natural gradient descent

A QFL system can be built by setting up VQC models in an FL manner, given the dataset S composed of subsets $S_1, S_2, \ldots, S_K$, the objective of QFL can be formulated as

$$\min_{\boldsymbol{\theta}} \sum_{k=1}^{K} w_k g_k^+(\boldsymbol{\theta})\mathcal{L}(\boldsymbol{\theta}; S_k), \quad (18.13)$$

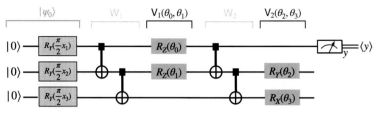

(a) The Fubini-Study metric tensor approximation to VQC

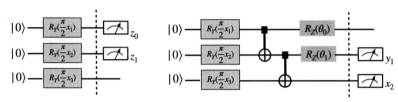

(b) the measurement of z_0, z_1 for $|\psi_0\rangle$ (c) the measurement of y_1, x_2 for $|\psi_1\rangle$

FIGURE 18.4

A demonstration of the VQC approximation method based on the Fubini–Study metric tensor: (a) A block-diagonal approximation to VQC based on the Fubini–Study metric tensor; (b) a measurement of z_0, z_1 for $|\psi_0\rangle$; (c) measurement of y_1, x_2 for $|\psi_1\rangle$.

Algorithm 1 Iterative approximation.
___
1. Given the dataset $S = S_1 \cup S_2 \cup \cdots \cup S_K$.
2. Initialize global parameter $\bar{\theta}$ and broadcast it to participants $\theta_0^{(k)}$.
3. Assign each participant with the subset S_k.
4. For each global model update at epoch $t = [T]$ do
5.   For each participant $k \in [K]$ **in parallel** do
6.   Attain $g^+(\theta_t^{(k)}; S_k)\nabla\mathcal{L}(\theta_t^{(k)})$ for the kth VQC.
7.   Send local gradient $g^+(\theta_t^{(k)})\nabla\mathcal{L}(\theta_t^{(k)}; S_k)$ to the coordinator.
8.   End for
9.   The coordinator aggregates the received gradients.
10.   The coordinator updates the global model by Eq. (18.15).
11.   Broadcast the updated global $\bar{\theta}_{t+1}$ to all participants.
12. End for
___

where w_k refers to the coefficient assigned to the kth gradient participant, and each w_k can be estimated as

$$w_k = \frac{|S_k|}{|S|} = \frac{|S_k|}{\sum_{k=1}^{K} |S_k|}. \tag{18.14}$$

The QNGD algorithm is applied for each VQC and the uploaded gradients of all VQCs are aggregated to update the model parameters of the global VQC. The

Table 18.1 The simulation results of a binary classification in terms of accuracy.

Methods	SGD	AdaGrad	Adam	FQNGD
Acc.	98.48	98.81	98.87	99.32

Table 18.2 The simulation results of a ternary classification in terms of accuracy.

Methods	SGD	AdaGrad	Adam	FQNGD
Acc.	97.86	98.63	98.71	99.12

FQNGD can be mathematically summarized as

$$\bar{\boldsymbol{\theta}}_{t+1} = \bar{\boldsymbol{\theta}}_t - \eta \sum_{k=1}^{K} \frac{|S_k|}{|S|} g_k^+(\boldsymbol{\theta}_t^{(k)}) \nabla \mathcal{L}(\boldsymbol{\theta}_t^{(k)}; S_k), \qquad (18.15)$$

where $\bar{\boldsymbol{\theta}}_t$ and $\boldsymbol{\theta}_t^{(k)}$ respectively correspond to the model parameters of the global VQC and the kth VQC model at epoch t, and N_k represents the amount of training data stored in the participant k, and the sum of K participants' data is equivalent to N.

Compared with the SGD counterparts used for QFL, the FQNGD algorithm admits adaptive learning rates for the gradients such that the convergence rate could be accelerated according to the VQC model status.

18.6 Experimental results

To demonstrate the FQNGD algorithm for QFL, we perform the binary and ternary classification tasks on the standard MNIST dataset [9], with digits $\{2, 5\}$ for the binary task and $\{1, 3, 7\}$ for the ternary one. There are 11379 training data and 1924 test data for the binary classification, and 19138 training data and 3173 test data are assigned for the ternary classification. As for the setup of QFL in our experiments, the QFL system consists of 6 identically local VQC participants, each of which owns the same amount of training data. The test data are stored in the global part and are used to evaluate the classification performance.

We compare our proposed FQNGD algorithm with other three optimizers: the naive SGD optimizer, the AdaGrad optimizer [20], and the Adam optimizer [18]. The AdaGrad optimizer is a gradient descent optimizer with a past-gradient-dependent learning rate in each dimension. The Adam optimizer refers to the gradient descent method with an adaptive learning rate as well as adaptive first and second moments. (See Tables 18.1 and 18.2.)

As shown in Fig. 18.5, our simulation results suggest that our proposed FQNGD method can achieve the fastest convergence rate compared with other optimization approaches. It means that the FQNGD algorithm can lower the communication cost

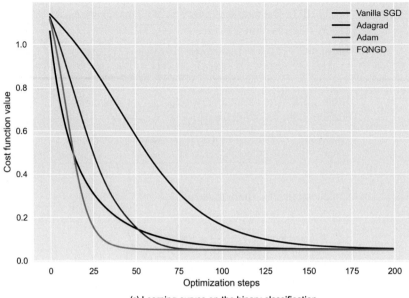

(a) Learning curves on the binary classification

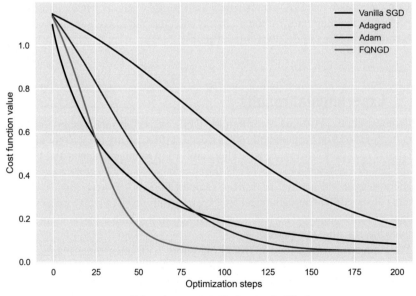

(b) Learning curves on the ternary classification

FIGURE 18.5

Simulation results of binary and ternary classification on the training set of the MNIST database: (a) the learning curves of various optimization methods for the binary classification; (b) the learning curves of various optimization methods for the ternary classification.

and also maintain the baseline performance of both binary and ternary classification on the MNIST dataset. Moreover, we evaluate the QFL performance in terms of classification accuracy. The FQNGD method outperforms the other counterparts with the highest accuracy values. In particular, the FQNGD is designed for the VQC model and is capable of attaining better empirical performance than the Adam and AdaGrad methods with adaptive learning rates over epochs.

18.7 Conclusion and discussion

This work focused on the design of the FQNGD algorithm for the QFL system in which multiple local VQC models are applied. The FQNGD was derived from training a single VQC based on QNGD, which relies on the block-diagonal approximation of the Fubini–Study metric tensor to the VQC architecture. We put forth the FQNGD method to train the QFL system. Compared with other SGD methods such as Ada-Grad and Adam optimizers, our experiments of the classification tasks on the MNIST dataset demonstrated that the FQNGD method attains better empirical results than other SGD methods, while the FQNGD exhibits a faster convergence rate than the others, which implies that our FQNGD method is capable of reducing the communication cost and maintaining the baseline empirical results.

Although this chapter focused on the optimization methods for the QFL system, the decentralized deployment of a high-performance QFL system for adapting to the large-scale dataset is left for our future investigation. In particular, it is essential to consider how to defend against malicious attacks from adversaries and also boost the robustness and integrity of the shared information among local participants. Besides, the deployment of other quantum neural networks like quantum convolutional neural networks (QCNN) [8] are worth further attempts to compose a QFL system and to alleviate the problem of Barren Plateaus.

References

[1] Shun-Ichi Amari, Natural gradient works efficiently in learning, Neural Computation 10 (2) (1998) 251–276.
[2] Philip Ball, Real-time error correction for quantum computing, Physics 14 (2021) 184.
[3] Tom Brown, et al., Language models are few-shot learners, in: Proc. Advances in Neural Information Processing Systems, vol. 33, 2020, pp. 1877–1901.
[4] Marco Cerezo, et al., Variational quantum algorithms, Nature Reviews Physics 3 (9) (2021) 625–644.
[5] Samuel Yen-Chi Chen, Chih-Min Huang, Chia-Wei Hsing, Ying-Jer Kao, An end-to-end trainable hybrid classical-quantum classifier, Machine Learning: Science and Technology 2 (4) (2021) 045021.
[6] Samuel Yen-Chi Chen, Chao-Han Huck Yang, Jun Qi, Pin-Yu Chen, Xiaoli Ma, Hsi-Sheng Goan, Variational quantum circuits for deep reinforcement learning, IEEE Access 8 (2020) 141007–141024.

[7] Samuel Yen-Chi Chen, Shinjae Yoo, Federated quantum machine learning, Entropy 23 (4) (2021) 460.

[8] Iris Cong, Soonwon Choi, Mikhail D. Lukin, Quantum convolutional neural networks, Nature Physics 15 (12) (2019) 1273–1278.

[9] Li Deng, The MNIST database of handwritten digit images for machine learning research, IEEE Signal Processing Magazine 29 (6) (2012) 141–142.

[10] Jacob Devlin, Ming-Wei Chang, Kenton Lee, Kristina Toutanova, BERT: pre-training of deep bidirectional transformers for language understanding, arXiv:1810.04805, 2018.

[11] Yuxuan Du, Min-Hsiu Hsieh, Tongliang Liu, Shan You, Dacheng Tao, Learnability of quantum neural networks, PRX Quantum 2 (4) (2021) 040337.

[12] Laird Egan, et al., Fault-tolerant control of an error-corrected qubit, Nature 598 (7880) (2021) 281–286.

[13] Qihao Guo, Yuan-Yuan Zhao, Markus Grassl, Xinfang Nie, Guo-Yong Xiang, Tao Xin, Zhang-Qi Yin, Bei Zeng, Testing a quantum error-correcting code on various platforms, Science Bulletin 66 (1) (2021) 29–35.

[14] Julia Hirschberg, Christopher D. Manning, Advances in natural language processing, Science 349 (6245) (2015) 261–266.

[15] Hsin-Yuan Huang, Michael Broughton, Masoud Mohseni, Ryan Babbush, Sergio Boixo, Hartmut Neven, Jarrod R. McClean, Power of data in quantum machine learning, Nature Communications 12 (1) (2021) 1–9.

[16] Hsin-Yuan Huang, et al., Quantum advantage in learning from experiments, Science 376 (6598) (2022) 1182–1186.

[17] Xuedong Huang, James Baker, Raj Reddy, A historical perspective of speech recognition, Communications of the ACM 57 (1) (2014) 94–103.

[18] Diederik P. Kingma, Jimmy Ba, Adam: a method for stochastic optimization, in: Proc. International Conference on Representation Learning, 2015.

[19] Jakub Konečný, H. Brendan McMahan, Felix X. Yu, Peter Richtárik, Ananda Theertha Suresh, Dave Bacon, Federated learning: strategies for improving communication efficiency, arXiv:1610.05492, 2016.

[20] Agnes Lydia, Sagayaraj Francis, AdaGrad – an optimizer for stochastic gradient descent, International Journal of Information and Computing Science 6 (5) (2019) 566–568.

[21] Sam McArdle, Tyson Jones, Suguru Endo, Ying Li, Simon C. Benjamin, Xiao Yuan, Variational ansatz-based quantum simulation of imaginary time evolution, NPJ Quantum Information 5 (1) (2019) 1–6.

[22] Jarrod R. McClean, Sergio Boixo, Vadim N. Smelyanskiy, Ryan Babbush, Hartmut Neven, Barren plateaus in quantum neural network training landscapes, Nature Communications 9 (1) (2018) 4812.

[23] Brendan McMahan, Eider Moore, Daniel Ramage, Seth Hampson, Blaise Aguera y Arcas, Communication-efficient learning of deep networks from decentralized data, in: Proc. Artificial Intelligence and Statistics, 2017, pp. 1273–1282.

[24] John Preskill, Quantum computing in the NISQ era and beyond, Quantum 2 (Aug. 2018) 79.

[25] Jun Qi, Jun Du, Sabato Marco Siniscalchi, Chin-Hui Lee, A theory on deep neural network based vector-to-vector regression with an illustration of its expressive power in speech enhancement, IEEE/ACM Transactions on Audio, Speech and Language Processing 27 (12) (2019) 1932–1943.

[26] Jun Qi, Jun Du, Sabato Marco Siniscalchi, Xiaoli Ma, Chin-Hui Lee, Analyzing upper bounds on mean absolute errors for deep neural network-based vector-to-vector regression, IEEE Transactions on Signal Processing 68 (2020) 3411–3422.

[27] Jun Qi, Javier Tejedor, Classical-to-quantum transfer learning for spoken command recognition based on quantum neural networks, in: Proc. IEEE International Conference on Acoustics, Speech and Signal Processing, 2021.

[28] Jun Qi, Chao-Han Huck Yang, Pin-Yu Chen, QTN-VQC: an end-to-end learning framework for quantum neural networks, Physica Scripta 99 (1) (2024) 015111.

[29] Jun Qi, Chao-Han Huck Yang, Pin-Yu Chen, Min-Hsiu Hsieh, Theoretical error performance analysis for variational quantum circuit based functional regression, NPJ Quantum Information 9 (1) (2023) 4.

[30] Sebastian Ruder, An overview of gradient descent optimization algorithms, arXiv:1609.04747, 2016.

[31] Reza Shokri, Vitaly Shmatikov, Privacy-preserving deep learning, in: Proc. ACM SIGSAC Conference on Computer and Communications Security, 2015, pp. 1310–1321.

[32] James Stokes, Josh Izaac, Nathan Killoran, Giuseppe Carleo, Quantum natural gradient, Quantum 4 (2020) 269.

[33] Edwin Stoudenmire, David J. Schwab, Supervised learning with tensor networks, in: Proc. Advances in Neural Information Processing Systems, vol. 29, 2016.

[34] Athanasios Voulodimos, Nikolaos Doulamis, Anastasios Doulamis, Eftychios Protopapadakis, Deep learning for computer vision: a brief review, Computational Intelligence and Neuroscience (2018) 2018.

[35] Paul J. Werbos, Backpropagation through time: what it does and how to do it?, Proceedings of the IEEE 78 (10) (1990) 1550–1560.

[36] Chao-Han Huck Yang, Jun Qi, Samuel Yen-Chi Chen, Pin-Yu Chen, Sabato Marco Siniscalchi, Xiaoli Ma, Chin-Hui Lee, Decentralizing feature extraction with quantum convolutional neural network for automatic speech recognition, in: Proc. IEEE International Conference on Acoustics, Speech and Signal Processing, 2021, pp. 6523–6527.

[37] Chao-Han Huck Yang, Jun Qi, Samuel Yen-Chi Chen, Yu Tsao, Pin-Yu Chen, When BERT meets quantum temporal convolution learning for text classification in heterogeneous computing, in: Proc. IEEE International Conference on Acoustics, Speech and Signal Processing, 2022, pp. 8602–8606.

Mobile computing framework for federated learning

19

Xiang Chen[a], Fuxun Yu[b], and Zirui Xu[c]

[a]*George Mason University, ECE, Fairfax, VA, United States*
[b]*Microsoft, Seattle, WA, United States*
[c]*CVS Health, Richmond, VA, United States*

19.1 Federated learning on mobile platforms

As the number of intelligent mobile hardware units, such as smartphones, wearables, and automobiles, will increase from 610M in 2019 to 1.56B in 2024, with a market value of $1.98B, the mobile AI software market size will also grow from $590M in 2020 to $1.84B in 2026. An ambitious vision of pervasive mobile AI systems has been largely promoted – the future AI application will provide ubiquitous AI inference services while profiling a user's or a scenario's characteristics and preferences from all angles. In such a vision, mobile-based deep learning frameworks become the key technique.

The traditional mobile-based deep learning framework is usually conducted with all data pre-collected locally and then gathered/trained in a central server, i.e., centralized training [8]. However, with more and more data generated from end-users, such as personal photos in users' mobile phones (i.e., "data islands"), centralized training for daily applications becomes highly infeasible due to many issues including communication overheads, privacy issues, etc. As a result, a lot of attention is paid to "training on edge" where the data is generated.

As one of the most well-recognized edge training techniques, federated learning (FL) expects to unit multiple resource-constrained mobile devices to collaboratively train identical neural network models with their local dataset without being uploaded [17]. By aggregating the parameter updates from each device, a global model can be collaboratively trained efficiently and securely [11].

19.2 Challenge in mobile-based federated learning

Although more mobile platforms start to support federated learning, significant issues of heterogeneity emerge in the actual learning process and require dedicated

Federated Learning. https://doi.org/10.1016/B978-0-44-319037-7.00029-6

343

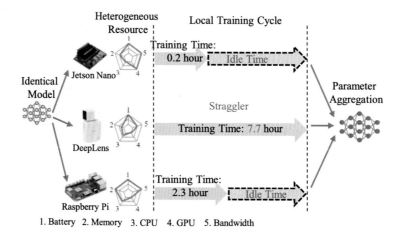

FIGURE 19.1

The straggler issue in original FL.

coordination solutions. Take data heterogeneity as an example: Different users' local data can be distinct in semantics and quantity (e.g., user photos). Thus, the locally trained models can diverge from each other in both training convergence and training speed. Another example is the heterogeneous device and resource. Each mobile device trains the same model structure and identical workload in federated learning but they may have distinct computation resources (e.g., memory capacity/bandwidth, CPU/GPU arithmetic intensity, etc.).

Like the "shortest board in a barrel," the devices with extremely weak computation capacities will take a much longer time for local training. These devices are referred to as stragglers in FL and cause challenges for device coordination in federated learning. One example is demonstrated by Fig. 19.1: with synchronous FL aggregation setting, stronger collaboration nodes (*Jetson Nano* and *Rasberry Pi*) have to keep an idle status to wait for the straggler (*DeepLens*) in every cycle and prolong the training cycle from 2.3 to 7.7 hours. Such an example illustrates the hardness of coordination in current FL frameworks.

There are many recent mobile-based federated learning frameworks that aim to improve deep learning training effectiveness and efficiency. Based on the coordination characteristics, these methods could be divided into two major categories:

- *Synchronous Methods.* These works leverage local training optimization methods to accelerate stragglers' training cycles so as to achieve synchronous aggregation [6,7]. Jiang et al. used model pruning to compress the original models to smaller ones that can satisfy the given constraints [7]. Jeong et al. reduced the model size in edge nodes based on knowledge distillation [6]. However, due to the permanent model structure loss, the information capacity of stragglers will decrease and may face convergence degradation. As shown in [15], when introducing models with diverged structures, the global model accuracy would drop as much as 10%.

- *Asynchronous Methods.* These works only aggregate parameters of stragglers at certain cycles when they become available instead of forcing synchronization [2, 3,10,12]. Nishio et al. proposed an optimized FL protocol (i.e., FedCS) to kick out straggled devices from the learning collaboration [10]. Wang et al. introduced a dedicated collaboration method to reduce the training loss introduced by the asynchronous stragglers [12].

Intuitively, changing the synchronous FL aggregation into an asynchronous manner can directly kick out the stragglers from most aggregation cycles and accelerate the training cycles [3,4,9,13,14]. However, in FL settings where most local datasets are non-identically distributed (non-IID), the stragglers may learn unique and critical information. And dramatically asynchronous collaboration may defect both local and global convergence performance [5,16]. Therefore, in order to address the coordination challenge, it is essential to eliminate stragglers' delay while preserving their learned information in the FL process.

19.3 Helios: a self-coordinated federated learning framework for mobile platform

To solve the FL straggler issue, we propose *Helios*, a heterogeneity-aware FL framework. *Helios* identifies the stragglers regarding the collaborative training pace and specifies the expected neural network model training volumes. For straggling devices, a "soft-training" method is proposed to dynamically compress the original identical training model into the expected volume through a rotating neuron training approach. With extensive algorithm analysis and optimization schemes, the stragglers can be accelerated while retaining the convergence for local training and federated collaboration.

19.3.1 Framework overview

The overall concept of the proposed *Helios* is shown in Fig. 19.2. In order to accelerate stragglers, the proposed framework is aiming to optimize the model training on stragglers.

Initialized stragglers identification. Since the straggler issue is caused by devices' heterogeneous resources, we propose two straggler identification approaches for various FL deployment contexts to improve framework flexibility, which will be discussed later.

Optimization target determination. The initialized stragglers' optimization targets (i.e., the expected model volumes) are further determined, which can reduce models' training consumption and achieve acceleration.

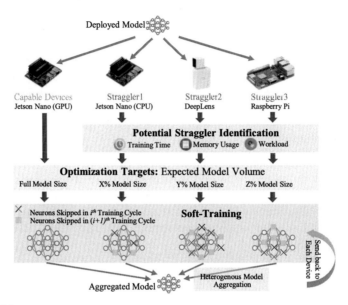

FIGURE 19.2

The *Helios* framework overview.

Soft-training. Guided by the expected model structure volumes, the "soft-training" method is introduced. In each training cycle, the proposed method can let different parts of model parameters (e.g., neurons) alternately join the training, which maintains a complete model parameter updating for collaboration. As Fig. 19.2 shows, in the ith training cycle, neurons indicated by red crosses (dark gray in print version) are skipped to achieve training acceleration. However, in the $(i+1)$th training cycle, a different set of neurons (yellow (light gray in print version) squares) are skipped. Such a training method can guarantee each model parameter on stragglers has opportunities to make a contribution to the collaboration.

Optimizations for soft-training. We further propose several dedicated optimization schemes, which can enhance the overall convergence performance and collaboration scalability based on extensive algorithm analysis and proof.

19.3.2 Straggler identification in heterogeneous collaboration

Since the straggler has a much longer training time cost than the normal devices ($35\times$ in Fig. 19.1), identifying it only after the FL process will introduce a high time overhead. Therefore, the potential stragglers need to be initially detected by comparing the computation resources of each device.

In most practical scenarios, partial/all devices' hardware configurations cannot be obtained. Therefore, we leverage the proposed time-based approximation to fast identify the stragglers. In this case, our approach will assign each device with a lightweight test bench (only train a few iterations) and quickly record their training time cost. Then the approach will rank all devices based on their training time cost values and obtain an approximate index $T = \{T_1, T_2, \ldots, T_N\}$, where T_1 represents the longest time cost. Based on FL requirements, the top-k devices in the index are identified as potential stragglers.

19.3.3 Optimization target determination

After finding the potential stragglers, it is important to identify the optimization target, namely, the expected model volumes of stragglers in each training cycle to achieve acceleration. The expected model volume can be selected with a pre-defined volume or adapted to a specific value according to the resource constraints.

For the former, we can define multiple model volume levels in advance and assign each straggler with a model volume level according to the training time cost index T. The model volume will be dynamically adjusted to an optimal point during the first several training cycles in the FL process.

19.3.4 Soft-training on straggling mobile devices

With identified potential stragglers and corresponding model volumes from initialization, we propose a "soft-training" scheme to adapt the optimized model to specific resource constraints while guaranteeing convergence effectiveness. Fig. 19.3 shows the entire "soft-training" flow, and we take neurons as our minimum model parameter structure. The algorithm can be divided into three steps:

Step 1. Straggler model shrinking. In order to achieve acceleration, we only select a set of neurons from stragglers' models to join the training cycle, thereby can meet the optimization targets (the expected model volume). As aforementioned, methods in Section 19.3 only approximately identify stragglers and their expected mode volume. Therefore, *Helios* needs the first few training cycles to finalize the stragglers and model volumes by dynamically adjusting the model volumes to accommodate normal devices *with respect to* training time cost.

During the partial training, two types of neurons are selected to achieve an optimized convergence performance: the neurons with the higher contributions to the collaboration convergence (primary converge guarantee) and some other random neurons (further converge optimization). Then we define the contribution metric by leveraging the assumption in [1] that the neurons with larger weight parameter changing values will provide larger impacts to the global model. We assume the weight parameters of the jth neuron in the ith layer after training epoch S_k as $\theta_{s,r,n}^{ij}(S_k)$, and the neuron's collaboration contribution $U^{ij}(S_k)$ will be calculated by summing the changes in the current training cycle as

$$U^{ij}(S_k) = \theta_{s,r,n}^{ij}(S_k) - \theta_{s,r,n}^{ij}(S_{k-1}), \tag{19.1}$$

where a larger U^{ij} represents the target neuron, demonstrating a higher collaboration contribution. We will elaborately show how to select these two types of neurons in each training cycle in Steps 2 and 3.

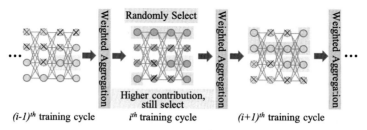

FIGURE 19.3

Soft-training scheme flow.

Step 2. Neuron rotation for model integrity. With partial training in Step 1, model training consumption on stragglers can be adapted to the specific device resource constraints. Some previous methods leverage fixed model pruning to achieve partial training [6,7]. However, without an optimized training algorithm to keep a rather complete model structure, the pruned model parameters will permanently lose their contribution to the collaboration, thereby inevitably hurting convergence accuracy and speed.

Therefore, in our "soft-training," we solve the conflict between the optimization targets and model integrity by letting different parts of model parameters (i.e., neurons) alternately join training cycles. As Fig. 19.3 illustrates, in the ith training cycle, we first choose P_s proportion of neurons[1] which have the highest changing values U^{ij} and randomly select the other $(1 - P_s)P_i n_i$ neurons from the remaining $(n_i - P_s P_i n_i)$ neurons which have relatively lower contributions. The discussions of how to choose value of P_s can be found in Section VI.A in our full paper.[2] Therefore, the total parameter changing on a straggler is

$$\Theta(S_k) - \Theta(S_{k-1}) = TopK(U^{ij}) \cup Rand(U^{ij}), \text{ where } K = P_s P_i n_i, \qquad (19.2)$$

where $\Theta(S_k)$ represent the model parameter of the straggler and *Rand* operation is randomly selecting $(1 - P_s)P_i n_i$ neurons' U^{ij}. Next, in the $(i + 1)$th training cycle, since the neurons with the highest contribution do not change, we still select them in the training to provide the primary converge guarantee. On the contrary, a different set of neurons with lower contributions will be selected. By alternately joining each training cycle, every neuron on a straggler has opportunities to keep model integrity to the global model convergence.

Step 3. Aggregation and local model updating. After finishing a local training cycle, each local mobile device will upload the gradients of the selected neurons to the global device during the aggregation cycle. Meanwhile, the global device will average the uploaded model parameters to update the global model. The discussions of

---

[1] We empirically evaluate the overhead of such sorting operation and find it can be ignored compared to the training cost (e.g., 18 ms vs. 12 min).
[2] https://arxiv.org/pdf/1912.01684.pdf.

Table 19.1 4 stragglers with heterogeneous resource.

Constraints	Nano (CPU)	Raspberry	DeepLens (GPU)	DeepLens (CPU)
Computation Workload (GFLOPS)	7	6	5.5	4.5
Memory Usage (MB)	252	150	100	110
Time Cost (min)	20.6	23.8	27.2	34

the global average convergence proof can be found in Section VI.B in our full paper. Once the new global model parameters are obtained, they will be sent to each local device for local model updating and the local mobile devices can start the next training cycle.

With the above three steps, models on the stragglers adapted to the optimization targets while still maintaining a rather complete model structure and balanced contribution, thereby guaranteeing the global model convergence performance.

Optimizations with neuron rotation regulation. One important condition requirement in the proposed soft-training is that neurons should not be inactivated for the long term, which may introduce 0 p_i and stale parameter issues. In order to satisfy this requirement, we pull the long-term skipped neurons back to training cycles timely. Specifically, during aggregation, each straggler will send its partial updated gradients index to the global device. The global device will record all currently skipped neurons and update their skipped cycles value C_s. In every aggregation cycle, *Helios* will inquire C_s. Once a certain neuron's C_s exceeds a pre-defined threshold (we set it to $1 + \frac{m}{\sum p_i n_i}$), the global device will inform the corresponding straggler and the targeted neuron will rejoin the training.

19.4 Performance evaluation

We evaluate *Helios* in terms of the converge accuracy and speed. Specifically, we first profile several mobile devices' resource configurations. Then, by adjusting the configuration of CPU/GPU bandwidth and memory availability, we can simulate these mobile devices' training performance on multiple Nvidia Jetson Nano development boards and let them as stragglers with different resource capabilities. The details of these straggler settings when running *AlexNet* on *CIFAR-10* are shown in Table 19.1. Three CNN models are used as our testing targets, namely, *LeNet*, *AlexNet*, and *ResNet-18*. The above three CNN models are trained on *MNIST*, *CIFAR-10*, and *CIFAR-100*, respectively.

In order to exhibit the superiority of *Helios*, we re-implement five other FL schemes for comparison: (1) *Synchronized FL (Syn. FL)*: All devices (including stragglers) update their parameters synchronously; (2) *Asynchronous FL (Asyn. FL)*: Normal mobile devices update their parameters immediately after local training without waiting for stragglers; (3) *Random [2]*: In each training, the stragglers randomly select a partial model with the expected model structure volume; and (4) *AFO [14]*:

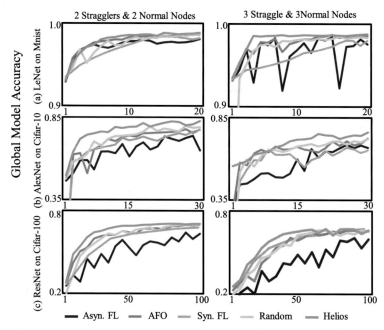

FIGURE 19.4

Soft-training effectiveness evaluation.

An optimized asynchronous method aiming to reduce the staleness issue of stragglers.

19.4.1 General helios performance evaluation

As shown in Table 19.1, there are two straggler settings involved: (1) Four devices join in the FL with two capable devices and two straggled devices as Strag. 1 and Strag. 2; (2) Six devices join in the FL with three capable and three straggled devices as Strag. 1, Strag. 2, and Strag. 3.

Accuracy evaluation. Fig. 19.4 illustrates the experimental results on converge accuracy. The x-axis represents the aggregation cycles of capable mobile devices. We can find that *Asyn. FL* always achieves the lowest accuracy due to information degradation. As for *Syn. FL*, since its training cycle is determined by the stragglers, it shows a much lower aggregation speed than other methods, resulting in lower accuracy. *Helios* always shows the best accuracy compared to all the baseline methods. Specifically, for *LeNet* on *MNIST*, *Helios* achieves at most 0.24% accuracy improvement on two kinds of straggler settings. For *AlexNet* on *CIFAR-10*, *Helios* has at most 4.64% accuracy improvement. For *ResNet18* on *CIFAR-100*, *Helios* improves the accuracy by at most 2.11%.

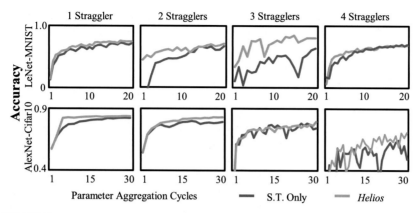

FIGURE 19.5

Model aggregation optimization evaluation.

Convergence speed evaluation. It is clear that *Asyn. FL* has the worst converge speed, and even fails to converge due to the staleness parameters and information loss. Although *AFO* optimizes the asynchronous updates, its convergence is still affected by the staleness parameters of stragglers. On the contrary, *Helios* shows the fastest convergence speed, especially for the FL with more stragglers. For the experiments of 6 nodes on *MNIST*, *CIFAR-10*, and *CIFAR-100*, *Helios* approaches convergence after 4, 12, and 40 aggregation cycles, respectively, while other methods require at least 10, 18, and 50 aggregation cycles.

19.4.2 Model aggregation optimization evaluation

In this part, the effectiveness of the model aggregation optimization scheme is also evaluated under the same setting (stragglers are increasing from 1 to 4). We use soft-training without aggregation optimization as the baseline, which is represented as *S.T. Only*. Fig. 19.5 illustrates the comparison results between *Helios* and *S.T. Only*. We can see that *Helios* achieves at most 17.37% accuracy improvement and reduces the accuracy variance caused by partial model aggregation while the accuracy curve of *S.T. Only* still has obvious fluctuations.

19.5 Conclusion and future directions

In this chapter, we demonstrated that training coordination will be a main challenge for mobile-based federated learning due to resource heterogeneity across different mobile devices. A resource-aware federated learning framework was further introduced to provide a potential solution. Considering the continually increasing scale and diversity of pervasive mobile AI systems, the coordination issue will become more critical for the future mobile-based federated learning. Therefore, applying efficient training methods (e.g., distillation) and developing new federated learning aggregation topologies (e.g., hierarchical FL) will be attractive solutions.

References

[1] Dan Alistarh, Torsten Hoefler, Mikael Johansson, Nikola Konstantinov, Sarit Khirirat, Cédric Renggli, The convergence of sparsified gradient methods, in: Advances in Neural Information Processing Systems, 2018, pp. 5973–5983.

[2] Sebastian Caldas, et al., Expanding the reach of federated learning by reducing client resource requirements, arXiv:1812.07210, 2018.

[3] Y. Chen, et al., Asynchronous online federated learning for edge devices, arXiv:1911.02134.

[4] Yang Chen, Xiaoyan Sun, Yaochu Jin, Communication-efficient federated deep learning with asynchronous model update and temporally weighted aggregation, arXiv:1903.07424, 2019.

[5] Ido Hakimi, Saar Barkai, Moshe Gabel, Assaf Schuster, Taming momentum in a distributed asynchronous environment, arXiv:1907.11612, 2019.

[6] Eunjeong Jeong, Seungeun Oh, Hyesung Kim, Jihong Park, Mehdi Bennis, Seong-Lyun Kim, Communication-efficient on-device machine learning: federated distillation and augmentation under non-iid private data, arXiv:1811.11479, 2018.

[7] Yuang Jiang, Shiqiang Wang, Bong Jun Ko, Wei-Han Lee, Leandros Tassiulas, Model pruning enables efficient federated learning on edge devices, arXiv:1909.12326, 2019.

[8] Mu Li, Li Zhou, Zichao Yang, Aaron Li, Fei Xia, David G. Andersen, Alexander Smola, Parameter server for distributed machine learning, in: Big Learning NIPS Workshop, vol. 6, 2013.

[9] Umair Mohammad, Sameh Sorour, Adaptive task allocation for asynchronous federated mobile edge learning, arXiv:1905.01656, 2019.

[10] T. Nishio, et al., Client selection for federated learning with heterogeneous resources in mobile edge, in: ICC'19, 2019.

[11] V. Smith, et al., Federated multi-task learning, in: NIPS'17, 2017.

[12] S. Wang, et al., Adaptive Federated Learning in Resource Constrained Edge Computing Systems, IEEE Journal on Selected Areas in Communications (2019).

[13] W. Wu, et al., SAFA: a semi-asynchronous protocol for fast federated learning with low overhead, arXiv:1910.01355.

[14] Cong Xie, Sanmi Koyejo, Indranil Gupta, Asynchronous federated optimization, arXiv:1903.03934, 2019.

[15] Binhang Yuan, et al., Distributed learning of deep neural networks using independent subnet training, arXiv:1910.02120, 2019.

[16] Wei Zhang, Suyog Gupta, Xiangru Lian, Ji Liu, Staleness-aware Async-SGD for distributed deep learning, arXiv:1511.05950, 2015.

[17] Y. Zhao, et al., Federated learning with non-IID data, arXiv:1806.00582.

Federated learning for privacy-preserving speech recognition

20

Chao-Han Huck Yang[a] **and Sabato Marco Siniscalchi**[b,c]

[a]*Nvidia Research, Taipei, Taiwan*
[b]*University of Enna, Enna, Italy*
[c]*Norwegian University of Science and Technology, Trondheim, Norway*

20.1 From voice protection to federated assistant

Human speech data contains a rich set of information [49] that represents gender, accent, and speaking environment, and further empower ubiquitous computing of virtual assistant (e.g., Alexa, Siri, and Google Assistant) toward human life. With the increasing concern about acoustic data privacy issues [38], it is important to understand virtual assistant architectures satisfy the requirements of new privacy-preservation regulations, e.g., GDPR [61]. Federated learning (FL) [70] is one potential strategy for data protection by decentralizing an end-to-end deep learning framework and separating feature extraction from the virtual assistant inference engine. Meanwhile, deploying high-performance speech applications [2,37,51] often requires a large amount of training speech data, which are often collected from end-users. Protecting data privacy is indeed a rising concern when speech data are employed to deploy commercial speech applications **through the deployment of federate architectures**. We will briefly review some recent regulation that is highly related to the design of federated learning based speech processing.

20.1.1 Introduction of automatic speech recognition

Automatic speech recognition (ASR) [51,52,72] is emerging as a technology widely used in spoken language processing applications in human society, including smart device control [40], speech transcription [56], intelligent human-machine dialogue [36,59], and spoken language understanding [2]. To build ASR systems, a large collection of user speech [45] is often required for training high-performance acoustic models. Protecting information privacy, such as whether data from a specific user is used for model training, is becoming a critical issue for service providers. Recent research efforts to federated learning enhanced ASR system can be categorized into two groups: (i) systemic, such as distributed training [38], data isolation [24,68], and (ii) algorithmic, mainly differential private federated learning [1,11]. Federated architectures [17,38,68] have been studied in the speech processing community to increase privacy protection. For example, the average gradient method [17] was used to update the learning model for decentralized training [50]. Next, we will review how the data protection regulation related to federated speech processing.

20.1.2 New data regulation and federated speech processing

In recent years, public regulations, such as European Union's General Data Protection Regulation (GDPR) [26,61] and California Consumer Privacy Act (CCPA) [57], have been proposed to establish new guidelines related to data privacy measurement and identity protection in end-user applications.

Different from the existing efforts for voice coding [21,33] and encryption [58] in speech processing, these data regulations further provide concrete refinements on privacy measurement and data protection when deploying a large-scale prediction model or system from users' data. We illustrate the related data regulatory requirements below:

Privacy measurement: *"Controllers and processors of personal data must put in place appropriate technical and organizational **measures** to implement the data protection principles."* (stated in Article 4 of [61])

Limited access of using data: *"The data subject shall have the right to obtain from the controller confirmation as to whether or not personal data concerning him or her are being processed, and, where that is the case, **access to the personal data** and the following information..."* (stated in Article 15 of [61])

Unsuccessful privacy protection examples have been reported and associated with large amounts of financial punishments, which include Google's 50 million euros fine in 2019 [22] and Amazon's 746 million euros fine in 2021 [41] related to insufficient data protection and privacy measurement on their deployed advertisement models and **federated speech recognition** systems against GDPR. Moreover, recent works on model inversion attacks [7,23] highlighted the importance of data privacy when the original data profile (e.g., facial images) could be recovered from a machine learning model by using query-free optimization techniques. Meanwhile, there exist successful cases on investigating advanced privacy-preserving mechanisms in commercial services to protect user information with high-performance machine learning algorithms, such as Apple's differential privacy budgets for language modeling and **Google's federated keyboard modeling system** [71].

With the aforementioned concerns about user privacy in speech applications and model parameter protection, it is becoming an emerging research topic in designing **federated machine learning models** to prevent privacy interference from model parameters and meet certain privacy measurement constraints. This chapter focuses on studying a general algorithmic approach to measure and protect data privacy and provides some systems approaches that could connect to federated architectures for large-scale industrial systems.

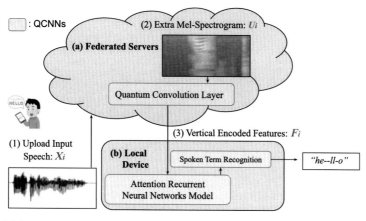

FIGURE 20.1

A vertical federated learning based acoustic modeling (AM) architecture [68] in with competitive performance including (a) a quantum convolution layer on Noisy Intermediate-Scale Quantum (NISQ) servers or cloud API; and (b) a local model (e.g., second-pass model [11,67]) for speech recognition tasks.

20.1.3 Distributed training and federated approaches

Federated architectures [17,38,68] have been studied in the speech processing community to increase privacy protection. For example, the average gradient method [17] was used to update the learning model for decentralized training [50]. Heterogeneous computing architectures [12,68] show advantages in acoustic feature extraction for vertical federate learning. There exist also some algorithmic efforts on investigating privacy-preserving speech processing by using cryptographic encryption [5,24], and computation protocols [48]. Meanwhile, these encryption algorithms and protocols barely cover the training sample-level privacy protection, which plays a major role in deploying large-scale machine learning models. More recent works on federated keyword spotting [38] and federated n-gram language [11] marked the importance of privacy-preserving learning under the requirement of acoustic and language data protection.

20.1.3.1 Vertical and horizontal federated learning for speech

We first discuss two basics setup for federated speech processing, vertical federated learning (VFL) and horizontal federated learning (HFL). As shown in Fig. 20.1, one major vertical federated acoustic modeling (AM) scheme is based on decentralized feature extraction and quantum encoded convolutional neural network (QCNN) [29] by combining a variational quantum circuit (VQC) learning paradigm [43], and a deep neural network [31] (DNN). VQC refers to a quantum algorithm with a flexible designing accessibility, which is resistant to noise [28,43] and adapted to NISQ hardware with light or no requirements for quantum error correction. Based on the advantages of VQC under VFL, a quantum-enhanced data processing scheme can

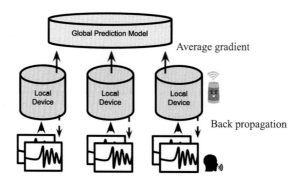

FIGURE 20.2

A horizontal federated learning based acoustic modeling (AM) architecture, which has been used in the federated keyboard [11] for Google assistant. The central idea is to use an average gradient to update the model information and avoid accessing data directly.

Table 20.1 An overview of how vertical federated leaning [70] (VFL) machine learning could empower quantum machine learning based speech processing. CQ stands for a hybrid classical-quantum (CQ) [4] model used in this paper. QA stands for quantum advantages [28], which are related to computational memory and parameter protection. VQC indicates the variational quantum circuit. DNN stands for deep neural network.

Approach	Input	Learning Model	Output	Properties
Classical	bits	DNN and more	bits	Easy implementation
Quantum	qubits	VQC and more	qubits	QA but limited resources
hybrid CQ	bits	VQC + DNN	bits	Accessible QA over VFL

be realized with fewer entangled encoded qubits [3,4] to assure model parameters protection, and lower computational complexity. As shown in Table 20.1, VFL has played a big role in the **first** work to combine quantum circuits and DNNs and build a new QCNN [29] for ASR. To provide a secure data pipeline and reliable quantum computing, we introduced the VFL architecture for decentralized ASR tasks [67], where remote NISQ cloud servers are used to generate quantum-based features, and ASR decoding is performed with a local model. Empirically, evaluated on the Google Speech Commands dataset with machine noises incurred from quantum computers, federated based decentralized quantum-based ASR framework [68] attains a competitive 95.12% accuracy on isolated word recognition. For horizontal federated learning, Google [11] and IBM [14] have explored different solutions for federated training parallel stochastic gradient. One major advantage is the direct connection to on-device voice assistant servers that can speed up the learning progress by large-scale decentralization as shown in Fig. 20.2.

20.1.4 **Differential privacy and federated speech assistant**

After understanding the foundation of federated speech model design, we will connect to the privacy-preserving federated speech modeling that could incorporate the new data regulation requirements providing measurable privacy loss through a reliable federated system. More specifically, we focus on differential privacy [1,18] (DP) preserving federated learning framework, where federated learning with DP aims at offering a quantitative privacy measure. DP satisfies some of the requirements specified in the GDPR guidelines because of its advantages in protecting both data privacy (e.g., user identity) and model parameters (e.g., weights and gradient information). DP algorithms [1,20] is aiming to provide quantitative guarantees and further prevent identity (e.g., accent) inference. We define a mathematical formation of differential privacy and investigate potential impacts on speech processing in the following discussion, where differential privacy mechanism [18] has been recognized as an established standard to deploy algorithms with a target privacy guarantee.

We will introduce some recent developments on extending and developing the Renyi divergence [42,62] measurement from the definition of local differential privacy to the context of speech processing and provide a theoretical justification on some advantages of combining an ensemble learning framework for DP-preserving speech processing.

We first elaborate ε-DP for supervised speech recognition, where ε denotes a privacy budget forming from a random noise mechanism deploying on the training speech dataset. A smaller ε indicates a large noisy distortion in a space with ℓ_p-norm bounded ($p \geq 1$) distance [64]. We define a mathematical formation of differential privacy and investigate potential impacts on speech processing in the following discussion, where differential privacy mechanism [18] has been recognized as an established standard to deploy algorithms with a target privacy guarantee.

Definition 20.1. A randomized algorithm $\mathcal{M}$ with domain $\mathcal{D}$ and range $\mathcal{R}$ is (ε, δ)-differentially private if for any two neighboring inputs (e.g., speech data) $d, d' \in \mathcal{D}$ and for any subset of output predictions (e.g., labels) $S \subseteq \mathcal{R}$, the following stands:

$$\Pr[\mathcal{M}(d) \in S] \leq e^\varepsilon \Pr[\mathcal{M}(d') \in S] + \delta. \tag{20.1}$$

The definition above produces a notion of privacy that can be explained as a measure of the probabilistic difference of a specific outcome by a multiplicative factor, e^ε, and an additive amount, δ. The DP mechanism with post-processing [1] (e.g., batch-wise training) is under a general Renyi-divergence [42] measurement with order $\alpha \in (1, \infty)$, called RDP_α, for all neighboring data sets d, d':

$$\mathrm{RDP}_\alpha\left(\mathcal{M}(d) \| \mathcal{M}(d')\right) = \frac{1}{\alpha - 1} \log S_{\theta \sim \mathcal{M}(d')}\left[\left(\frac{p_{\mathcal{M}(d)}(\theta)}{p_{\mathcal{M}(d')}(\theta)}\right)^\alpha\right] \leq \varepsilon. \tag{20.2}$$

As $\alpha \to \infty$, RDP_α converges to the standard $(\varepsilon, 0)$-DP. Both ε and δ should be positive or equal to zero. Considering $\delta \to 0$ with only minor relaxation, a smaller value of ε indicates a stronger $(\varepsilon, 0)$-differentially private guarantee. In other words, nearly equal probabilities in (20.1) would be given from the neighboring inputs d and d', which makes data identity much hard to infer. Moreover, learning from post-processing features (e.g., Mel-spectrum [6,16]) based on the speech data could also be differentially private, which has been shown by the theorem given in [1,18]. We aim to further study a performance trade-off between the additive DP-noise and robustness of neural network based models in this proposal, which remains an open problem to design high-performance DP-preserving speech models and understand their limits. As one popular deep neural network based DP-preserving baseline, we provide a review of differentially private stochastic gradient descent (DPSGD) [65]. DPSGD is based on stochastic gradient descent (SGD) [30], which is an iterative optimization method for solving the convex optimization problem. SGD starts with an starting point w_0, and at step t, updates the iterate as

$$w_{t+1} = w_t - \eta_t \left(\lambda w_t + \nabla \ell \left(w_t, x_t, y_t \right) \right), \tag{20.3}$$

where η_t denotes learning rate, and the (sub)gradient $\nabla \ell \left(w_t, x_t, y_t \right)$ is computed based on a single input x_t and label y_t. To introduce DP-noises, a DPSGD update is defined as

$$w_{t+1} = w_t - \eta_t \left(\lambda w_t + \nabla \ell \left(w_t, x_t, y_t \right) + Z_t \right), \tag{20.4}$$

where each Z_t is a random noise vector in $\mathbb{R}^d$ drawn independently from the density of $\rho(z) \propto e^{-(\alpha/2)\|z\|}$. DPSGD have been recently [15] introduced into large-scale optimization machine learning backbone to replace SGD for training a model under DP measurement. However, both direct database-level DP perturbation and DPSGD will largely degrade model performance. When ASR and voice assistant production are still performance-driven tasks, we will introduce some recent federated training methods to enhance ASR performance.

20.1.5 Teacher-student learning for federated ASR

How to reduce the privacy budget and deploy a performance-driven ASR system is one challenging topic. To reduce the privacy cost over the standard data-independent bound, Papernot et al. [46] have provided a theoretical analysis of a general data-dependent upper bound through **ensemble learning** with deep neural networks, which needs with less cost of a predicting loss to achieve a targeted DP-privacy budget (ε). We could extend the random privacy-preserving algorithm $\mathcal{M}$ (introduced in (20.1)) under ε-DP, where ε is equal to 2γ [1] with an ensemble learning model (τ), $\tau \geq \Pr\left[\mathcal{M}(d) \neq o^*\right]$ for some prediction outcome (o^*). Let $l, \gamma \geq 0$ and $\tau < \frac{e^{2\gamma}-1}{e^{4\gamma}-1}$. Then for any neighbor datasets d' of d, $\mathcal{M}$ satisfies with private moment accoun-

---

[1] For instance, at each step, we use an aggregation mechanism with noise $\text{Lap}\left(\frac{1}{\gamma}\right)$ which is $(2\gamma, 0)$-differential privacy. Therefore, over T steps, we attain $\left(4T\gamma^2 + 2\gamma\sqrt{2T \ln \frac{1}{\delta}}, \delta\right)$-differential privacy.

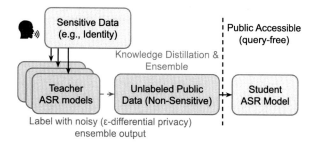

FIGURE 20.3

Utilizing private aggregation teacher ensemble (PATE) to train end-to-end **federated ASR** with ε differential privacy, where an ensemble of the teacher models could be trained in a distributed setting. Teacher-student learning process could be done in different computing instances for vertical federated learning with data isolation.

tant [1] (α) for privacy cost measurement:

$$\alpha\left(l; d, d'\right) \leq \log\left((1 - \tau)\left(\frac{1-\tau}{1 - e^{2\gamma}\tau}\right)^l + \tau e^{(2\gamma l)}\right). \tag{20.5}$$

Bound (20.5) is built upon a foundation of composition theorem [19] over aggregation methods for ε-DP. We refer to Theorem 1, and Theorem 3 in [46] for more details.

We now describe the private aggregation of teacher ensembles (PATE) [46,47] based acoustic modeling to empower ε-DP in the federated settings. First, an ensemble of teacher models is built by partitioning the training dataset into I disjoint subsets, $\mathcal{D}_1, \ldots, \mathcal{D}_I$. Next, these are used to train I teacher models independently, $\mathcal{T}_1, \ldots, \mathcal{T}_I$. They are employed to generate acoustic model scores [8] to be combined as an effective way for teacher-student learning in order to aggregate frame-level predictions of the teachers by taking a weighted average of context-dependent state posteriors from ASR models. For each frame of audio x, the final aggregated teacher model produces a vector of posteriors, $\mathcal{T}_{\mathrm{ens}}(s \mid x)$, over context-dependent states s computed as follows:

$$\mathcal{T}_{\mathrm{ens}}(s \mid x) = \sum_{i=1}^{I} w_i \mathcal{T}_i(s \mid x), \tag{20.6}$$

where $\mathcal{T}_i(s \mid x)$ is the posterior from the ith model, and w_i is its weighting coefficient. The corresponding states from individual teacher models have the same dimension J before the output alignment (e.g., considering a special silent character before alignment).

To ensure ε-DP under the PATE method, a random perturbation was introduced into the individual teachers' predictions ($\mathcal{T}_i$). We revise (20.6) to obtain a final en-

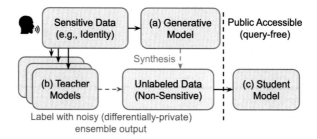

FIGURE 20.4

Private aggregation of teachers ensemble (PATE) learning: (a) the teacher prediction models training from sensitive data; (b) a joint generative model (e.g., adversarial autoencoder for audio synthesis in this study); and (c) student prediction model training from non-sensitive data.

semble from noisy teachers:

$$\mathcal{T}_{\text{PATE}}(x, \lambda) = \sum_{i=1}^{I} w_i \left(\mathcal{T}_i(x) + Y_j(\lambda) \right), \tag{20.7}$$

where $Y_1, \ldots, Y_m$ are i.i.d. Laplacian or Gaussian random variables with location 0 and scale λ^{-1}, where λ refers to a privacy parameter that influences (ϵ, δ)-DP guarantees and for which a bound has been proven under composition theorems applicable to model aggregation [46,47].

As shown in Fig. 20.3, the next PATE step is a process of knowledge transfer, where the noisy ensemble output is used to relabel a non-sensitive data set, having a total sample number equal to K, which in turn is deployed to train a student model, $\mathcal{S}$. Both the prediction outputs and the trained student model's internal parameters are free from querying requests, which allows the only privacy cost to be associated with acquiring the training data for the student model. The researchers have evaluated two noisy aggregation processes, Gaussian NoisyMax (GNMax) and Laplacian NoisyMax (LNMax) presented in previous studies [46,47]. Under this setup, the student model is $(\varepsilon, 10^{-3})$-DP guaranteed using λ from an analysis in [46,47]. According to (20.7), a large λ refers to a **smaller ε providing a stronger privacy guarantee**, but degrades the accuracy of the labels from the noisy maximum prediction output of the PATE function.

20.2 Federated speech recognition with synthetic data

The aforementioned PATE privacy-preserving federated training method and its improved version [47] were proven useful in reducing the model accuracy drop through a voting process during the noisy ensemble. Nonetheless, the teacher–student learning process highly depends on a hypothesis [32,46,47] that there exists a sufficient

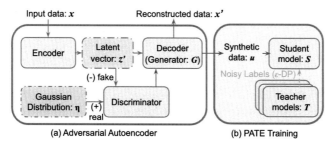

Input data: x Reconstructed data: x'

(a) Adversarial Autoencoder   (b) PATE Training

FIGURE 20.5

The PATE-AAE [69] vertical training framework does not require sufficient non-sensitive data to train a DP-preserving speech model, where its AAE module has been recognized as a generative modeling process without text labels and speech data.

amount of public (non-sensitive) data to train the model. PATE-GAN [32] tries to overcome this issue by incorporating a generative block jointly trained with the PATE block; the goal is to provide enough synthetic data to train deep models effectively. PATE-GAN does not work well for high-dimensional data synthesis (e.g., images), as demonstrated in recent studies [9,27]. Moreover, generating speech samples is a challenging task, as shown in recent studies about neural vocoders [44,54]. We introduce an adversarial autoencoder [39] (AAE) based model into PATE to improve the generative process for privacy-preserving speech classification. PATE-AAE first adapts an autoencoder to minimize a reconstruction loss, training on sensitive data. As shown in Fig. 20.4(a), the generative model produces synthetic data as non-sensitive samples. Meanwhile, the training data are divided into I isolated subsets to train individual teacher classifiers. For instance, I is equal to 3 in Fig. 20.4(b). The teacher classifiers then undergo an output aggregation process to generate noisy labels, which ensures the ε-differentially private protection. Finally, a student classifier uses the labeled synthetic samples (non-sensitive data) for training its model. The proposed PATE-AAE framework is assessed with the Google Speech Commands Dataset Version II [63]. Our experimental evidence demonstrates competitive results in terms of synthetic sample quality and classification accuracy with a strong ε-DP guarantee ($\varepsilon < 1$) considering established privacy-preserving learning (PPL) works [32,66]. To the best of the authors' knowledge, this is the **first** attempt to introduce the PATE architecture with generative models into a speech classification task. Moreover, the proposed solution benefits from adversarial autoencoder block, with advantages over existing GAN solutions [23,32] of having a better test-likelihood estimation. The proposed method consists of AAE and PATE models with feature encoders [13]. We focus on the application of PATE for speech processing, which is often in shortage of non-sensitive human voice data and more severe than in the original PATE [46]. It should be noted that PATE-GAN has succeeded in synthesizing low-dimensional data (e.g., short sequences of EEG) but has failed when dealing with high-dimension data (e.g., images). This could be due to its difficulties of using a random noise generator to match *input data* distribution from *sample* discriminator in standard GAN [25] training.

20.2.0.1 Vertical training with adversarial autoencoder (AAE)

We introduce AAE training as follows. Instead of training the noisy generator as in GAN, AAE leverages an autoencoder-based regression model to minimize a reconstruction loss between input data (x) and decoded output (x'). The bottleneck vector (latent space z) is modeled as variational autoencoder [34] but uses a discriminator to refine z closing to a real vector (η) sampling from a fixed Gaussian distribution as shown in Fig. 20.5(a). This discriminative training resulted in a better test-likelihood on synthetic samples [13,39]. Let x and z be the input and the bottleneck latent vector of an encoder-decoder model, respectively. The universal approximator posterior $q(z)$ introduced [39] is

$$q(z \mid x) = \int_\eta q(z \mid x, \eta) p_\eta(\eta) d\eta \tag{20.8}$$

$$\Rightarrow q(z) = \int_x \int_\eta q(z \mid x, \eta) p_d(x) p_\eta(\eta) d\eta dx, \tag{20.9}$$

where the stochasticity in $q(z)$ comes from both the data distribution x and the random noise η with a fixed Gaussian distribution at the input of the encoder. The adversarial training procedure can match $q(z)$ to $p(z)$ by back-propagation through the encoder network directly. The encoder encodes an input data x into latent vector, $z_i' \sim \mathcal{N}(\mu_i(\mathbf{x}), \sigma_i(\mathbf{x}))$, by variational inference used in [34]. Therefore, a training objective for reconstructing input x is computed by minimizing the following upper-bound on the negative log-likelihood of x,

$$E_x \left[E_{q(z|\mathbf{x})} [-\log(p(x \mid z))] + E_x[\mathrm{KL}(q(z \mid x) \| p(z))]. \tag{20.10}$$

Makhzani et al. [39] further introduce a discriminative update into the second terms of (20.10) that makes $q(z)$ to match to the distribution of $p(z)$ to train an AAE. The discriminative training objective between the latent vector z' (denoted as a fake sample as 0) and the sampling noise η is computed by BCE loss and back-propagated gradients to input data (x) for updating encoder's parameters (Fig. 20.5 (a)).

Next, for training teacher models, we partition the sensitive dataset into n subsets, $\mathcal{D}_1, \ldots, \mathcal{D}_I$, with $|\mathcal{D}_i| = \frac{|\mathcal{D}|}{I}$ for $\forall q$. Each teacher model (T_i) is training with discriminator loss,

$$\mathcal{L}_{T_i} = - \left(\sum_{q \in \mathcal{D}} \log T_i\left(q(z)\right) + \sum_{j=1}^{I} \log\left(1 - T_i\left(q\left(z'_j\right)\right)\right) \right). \tag{20.11}$$

To generate synthetic samples for training student model, we take I samples of Gaussian distribution, $\eta_1, \ldots, \eta_I$ using the trained AAE decoder network (G) to synthesize sample $\hat{\mathbf{u}}_j = G(\eta_j)$ for each class. Following the PATE mechanism for knowledge

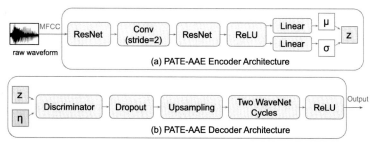

FIGURE 20.6

A privacy-preserving joint voice synthesis architecture introduced in [69].

transfer, the aggregated noisy output from the teachers models in (20.11) labels the synthetic data for training a differentially private student model, where noisy label refers $r_j = \text{PATE}\left(\hat{\mathbf{u}}_j, \lambda\right)$ from (20.7). Finally, we train the student model to maximize the standard cross-entropy loss on this teacher-labeled data:

$$\mathcal{L}_S = \sum_{j=1}^{I} r_j \log S\left(\hat{\mathbf{u}}_j\right) + \left(1 - r_j\right) \log \left(1 - S\left(\hat{\mathbf{u}}_j\right)\right).
\qquad (20.12)$$

We train $G, T_1, \ldots, T_I$, and S iteratively, with each iteration of G consisting of first performing gradient updates on all teachers, then performing gradient updates of the student. The major difference between proposed PATE-AAE and PATE-GAN [32] is on the generative process. The proposed AAE method uses a regression autoencoder architecture to reconstruct the input samples and use a random variable for the refined latent space as the decoder (generator) input for generating new synthetic samples. Instead, PATE-GAN adapts discriminator on the sample generator directly to refine the learning process from random noise to synthetic data, which produces worse test-likelihood on high-dimensional data from previous studies [9,10] related to the convergence properties [35] of GAN. To conduct privacy-preserving speech processing frameworks, we select PATE-GAN [32] and DP-GAN [66] as baselines in our studies motivated by the condition of without any available non-sensitive audio dataset. The previous work [69] carefully build our encoder–decoder upon a WaveNet-based autoencoder presented in [13,55,60], which has shown competitive performance for speech synthesis tasks as shown in (20.6). PATE-AAE decoder applied a randomized dropout layer from an output of the discriminator, which is selected from a latent vector (z) or a random vector (η). The previous work [69] followed μ-law compounding transformation [44,53] with 256 quantization levels to generate raw 16k Hz audio. For the spoken command classification task, classification accuracy is used to evaluate the student model.

20.3 Conclusion

In this chapter, we have discussed some design strategies to be adopted when deploying a speech recognition system that has to comply with critical data protection guidelines and public regulations, such as European Union's General Data Protection Regulation (GDPR) and California Consumer Privacy Act (CCPA). In fact, rich information encompassing gender, accent, speaking environment, and other speaker characteristics contained in the speech signal could be recovered by sophisticated machine learning techniques, such as model inversion attacks. Therefore, specific mechanisms to protect critical information embedded in speech data are needed.

Both horizontal and vertical federated learning strategies for data protection in speech recognition and general acoustic processing were presented. In particular, we have described one of the major vertical federated acoustic modeling (AM) schemes, which is based on a decentralized feature extraction block, and a quantum-encoded convolutional neural network. The experimental results reported on the Google Speech Commands dataset with machine noises incurred from quantum computers were useful to demonstrate that federation-based decentralized quantum-based ASR framework could attain a competitive accuracy of 95.12%. On the other hand, a major advantage of horizontal federated learning is the possibility of a direct connection to on-device voice assistant servers that can speed up the learning progress by large-scale decentralization.

Next, motivated by the recent review of data protection requirements, we have also reviewed the basic elements of *differential privacy* (DP) and how federated learning with DP can offer a quantitative privacy measure. Finally, we have presented (i) a novel private aggregation teacher ensemble (PATE) to train end-to-end federated ASR with differential privacy, and (ii) a federated speech recognition system leveraging synthetic data obtained with an adversarial autoencoder.

References

[1] Martin Abadi, Andy Chu, Ian Goodfellow, H. Brendan McMahan, Ilya Mironov, Kunal Talwar, Li Zhang, Deep learning with differential privacy, in: Proceedings of the 2016 ACM SIGSAC Conference on Computer and Communications Security, 2016, pp. 308–318.

[2] Janet M. Baker, Li Deng, James Glass, Sanjeev Khudanpur, Chin-Hui Lee, Nelson Morgan, Douglas O'Shaughnessy, Developments and directions in speech recognition and understanding, part 1 [dsp education], IEEE Signal Processing Magazine 26 (3) (2009) 75–80.

[3] Ville Bergholm, Josh Izaac, Maria Schuld, Christian Gogolin, Carsten Blank, Keri McKiernan, Nathan Killoran, PennyLane: automatic differentiation of hybrid quantum-classical computations, arXiv:1811.04968, 2018.

[4] Jacob Biamonte, Peter Wittek, Nicola Pancotti, Patrick Rebentrost, Nathan Wiebe, Seth Lloyd, Quantum machine learning, Nature 549 (7671) (2017) 195–202.

[5] Ferdinand Brasser, Tommaso Frassetto, Korbinian Riedhammer, Ahmad-Reza Sadeghi, Thomas Schneider, Christian Weinert, VoiceGuard: secure and private speech processing, in: Interspeech, vol. 18, 2018, pp. 1303–1307.

[6] John S. Bridle, Michael D. Brown, An experimental automatic word recognition system, JSRU Report 1003 (5) (1974) 33.

[7] Nicholas Carlini, Florian Tramer, Eric Wallace, Matthew Jagielski, Ariel Herbert-Voss, Katherine Lee, Adam Roberts, Tom Brown, Dawn Song, Ulfar Erlingsson, Alina Oprea, Colin Raffel, Extracting training data from large language models, in: USENIX Security Symposium, 2021.

[8] Yevgen Chebotar, Austin Waters, Distilling knowledge from ensembles of neural networks for speech recognition, in: Interspeech, 2016, pp. 3439–3443.

[9] Dingfan Chen, Tribhuvanesh Orekondy, Mario Fritz, GS-WGAN: a gradient-sanitized approach for learning differentially private generators, Neural Information Processing Systems (NeurIPS) (2020).

[10] Dingfan Chen, Ning Yu, Yang Zhang, Mario Fritz, GAN-Leaks: a taxonomy of membership inference attacks against generative models, in: Proceedings of the 2020 ACM SIGSAC Conference on Computer and Communications Security, 2020, pp. 343–362.

[11] Mingqing Chen, Ananda Theertha Suresh, Rajiv Mathews, Adeline Wong, Cyril Allauzen, Françoise Beaufays, Michael Riley, Federated learning of n-gram language models, arXiv:1910.03432, 2019.

[12] Samuel Yen-Chi Chen, Shinjae Yoo, Federated quantum machine learning, Entropy 23 (4) (2021) 460.

[13] Jan Chorowski, Ron J. Weiss, Samy Bengio, Aäron van den Oord, Unsupervised speech representation learning using wavenet autoencoders, IEEE/ACM Transactions on Audio, Speech and Language Processing 27 (12) (2019) 2041–2053.

[14] Xiaodong Cui, Songtao Lu, Brian Kingsbury, Federated acoustic modeling for automatic speech recognition, arXiv:2102.04429, 2021.

[15] Testuggine Davide, Mironov Ilya, Opacus, Sept. 2020.

[16] Steven Davis, Paul Mermelstein, Comparison of parametric representations for monosyllabic word recognition in continuously spoken sentences, IEEE Transactions on Acoustics, Speech, and Signal Processing 28 (4) (1980) 357–366.

[17] Dimitrios Dimitriadis, Kenichi Kumatani, Robert Gmyr, Yashesh Gaur, Sefik Emre Eskimez, A federated approach in training acoustic models, in: Proc. Interspeech, 2020.

[18] Cynthia Dwork, Differential privacy: a survey of results, in: International Conference on Theory and Applications of Models of Computation, Springer, 2008, pp. 1–19.

[19] Cynthia Dwork, Aaron Roth, et al., The algorithmic foundations of differential privacy, Foundations and Trends in Theoretical Computer Science 9 (3–4) (2014) 211–407.

[20] Cynthia Dwork, Guy N. Rothblum, Salil Vadhan, Boosting and differential privacy, in: 2010 IEEE 51st Annual Symposium on Foundations of Computer Science, IEEE, 2010, pp. 51–60.

[21] D. Esteban, C. Galand, Application of quadrature mirror filters to split band voice coding schemes, in: ICASSP'77, IEEE International Conference on Acoustics, Speech, and Signal Processing, vol. 2, IEEE, 1977, pp. 191–195.

[22] Chris Fox, Google hit with $57M GDPR fine, BBC News, 2019.

[23] Matt Fredrikson, Somesh Jha, Thomas Ristenpart, Model inversion attacks that exploit confidence information and basic countermeasures, in: Proceedings of the 22nd ACM SIGSAC Conference on Computer and Communications Security, 2015, pp. 1322–1333.

[24] Cornelius Glackin, Gerard Chollet, Nazim Dugan, Nigel Cannings, Julie Wall, Shahzaib Tahir, Indranil Ghosh Ray, Muttukrishnan Rajarajan, Privacy preserving encrypted phonetic search of speech data, in: International Conference on Acoustics, Speech and Signal Processing (ICASSP), IEEE, 2017, pp. 6414–6418.

[25] Ian J. Goodfellow, Jean Pouget-Abadie, Mehdi Mirza, Bing Xu, David Warde-Farley, Sherjil Ozair, Aaron C. Courville, Yoshua Bengio, Generative adversarial nets, in: NIPS, 2014.

[26] Nils Gruschka, Vasileios Mavroeidis, Kamer Vishi, Meiko Jensen, Privacy issues and data protection in big data: a case study analysis under GDPR, in: 2018 IEEE International Conference on Big Data (Big Data), IEEE, 2018, pp. 5027–5033.

[27] Kazi Nazmul Haque, Rajib Rana, Björn W. Schuller, High-fidelity audio generation and representation learning with guided adversarial autoencoder, IEEE Access 8 (2020) 223509–223528.

[28] Vojtěch Havlíček, Antonio D. Córcoles, Kristan Temme, Aram W. Harrow, Abhinav Kandala, Jerry M. Chow, Jay M. Gambetta, Supervised learning with quantum-enhanced feature spaces, Nature 567 (7747) (2019) 209–212.

[29] Maxwell Henderson, Samriddhi Shakya, Shashindra Pradhan, Tristan Cook, Quanvolutional neural networks: powering image recognition with quantum circuits, Quantum Machine Intelligence 2 (1) (2020) 1–9.

[30] Geoffrey Hinton, Li Deng, Dong Yu, George E. Dahl, Abdel-rahman Mohamed, Navdeep Jaitly, Andrew Senior, Vincent Vanhoucke, Patrick Nguyen, Tara N. Sainath, et al., Deep neural networks for acoustic modeling in speech recognition: the shared views of four research groups, IEEE Signal Processing Magazine 29 (6) (2012) 82–97.

[31] Sepp Hochreiter, Jürgen Schmidhuber, Long short-term memory, Neural Computation 9 (8) (1997) 1735–1780.

[32] James Jordon, Jinsung Yoon, Mihaela Van Der Schaar, PATE-GAN: generating synthetic data with differential privacy guarantees, in: International Conference on Learning Representations, 2019.

[33] Biing-Hwang Juang, D. Wong, A. Gray, Distortion performance of vector quantization for LPC voice coding, IEEE Transactions on Acoustics, Speech, and Signal Processing 30 (2) (1982) 294–304.

[34] Max Welling Kingma, P. Diederik, Auto-encoding variational Bayes, in: The International Conference on Learning Representations (ICLR), 2014.

[35] Naveen Kodali, Jacob Abernethy, James Hays, Zsolt Kira, On convergence and stability of GANs, 2017.

[36] H.-K.J. Kuo, Chin-Hui Lee, Discriminative training of natural language call routers, IEEE Transactions on Speech and Audio Processing 11 (1) (2003) 24–35.

[37] Chin-Hui Lee, Qiang Huo, On adaptive decision rules and decision parameter adaptation for automatic speech recognition, Proceedings of the IEEE 88 (8) (2000) 1241–1269.

[38] David Leroy, Alice Coucke, Thibaut Lavril, Thibault Gisselbrecht, Joseph Dureau, Federated learning for keyword spotting, in: ICASSP 2019-2019 IEEE International Conference on Acoustics, Speech and Signal Processing (ICASSP), IEEE, 2019, pp. 6341–6345.

[39] Alireza Makhzani, Jonathon Shlens, Navdeep Jaitly, Ian Goodfellow, Brendan Frey, Adversarial autoencoders, arXiv:1511.05644, 2015.

[40] Ian McGraw, Rohit Prabhavalkar, Raziel Alvarez, Montse Gonzalez Arenas, Kanishka Rao, David Rybach, Ouais Alsharif, Haşim Sak, Alexander Gruenstein, Françoise Beaufays, et al., Personalized speech recognition on mobile devices, in: 2016 IEEE Interna-

tional Conference on Acoustics, Speech and Signal Processing (ICASSP), IEEE, 2016, pp. 5955–5959.

[41] Chavi Mehta, EU hits Amazon with record-breaking $887M GDPR fine over data misuse, Reuters (2021).

[42] Ilya Mironov, Rényi differential privacy, in: 2017 IEEE 30th Computer Security Foundations Symposium (CSF), IEEE, 2017, pp. 263–275.

[43] Kosuke Mitarai, Makoto Negoro, Masahiro Kitagawa, Keisuke Fujii, Quantum circuit learning, Physical Review A 98 (3) (2018) 032309.

[44] Aaron van den Oord, Sander Dieleman, Heiga Zen, Karen Simonyan, Oriol Vinyals, Alex Graves, Nal Kalchbrenner, Andrew Senior, Koray Kavukcuoglu, WaveNet: a generative model for raw audio, arXiv:1609.03499, 2016.

[45] Vassil Panayotov, Guoguo Chen, Daniel Povey, Sanjeev Khudanpur, LibriSpeech: an ASR corpus based on public domain audio books, in: Proc. IEEE ICASSP, IEEE, 2015, pp. 5206–5210.

[46] Nicolas Papernot, Martín Abadi, Ulfar Erlingsson, Ian Goodfellow, Kunal Talwar, Semi-supervised knowledge transfer for deep learning from private training data, in: ICLR, 2017.

[47] Nicolas Papernot, Shuang Song, Ilya Mironov, Ananth Raghunathan, Kunal Talwar, Ulfar Erlingsson, Scalable private learning with pate, in: International Conference on Learning Representations, 2018.

[48] Manas A. Pathak, Bhiksha Raj, Privacy-preserving speaker verification and identification using Gaussian mixture models, IEEE Transactions on Audio, Speech, and Language Processing 21 (2) (2012) 397–406.

[49] Manas A. Pathak, Bhiksha Raj, Shantanu D. Rane, Paris Smaragdis, Privacy-preserving speech processing: cryptographic and string-matching frameworks show promise, IEEE Signal Processing Magazine 30 (2) (2013) 62–74.

[50] Jun Qi, Chao-Han Huck Yang, Javier Tejedor, Submodular rank aggregation on score-based permutations for distributed automatic speech recognition, in: ICASSP 2020-2020 IEEE International Conference on Acoustics, Speech and Signal Processing (ICASSP), IEEE, 2020, pp. 3517–3521.

[51] Lawrence R. Rabiner, Ronald W. Schafer, Introduction to Digital Speech Processing, vol. 1, Now Publishers Inc., 2007.

[52] L.R. Rabiner, B-H. Juang, C-H. Lee, An overview of automatic speech recognition, Automatic Speech and Speaker Recognition (1996) 1–30.

[53] CCITT Recommendation, Pulse code modulation (PCM) of voice frequencies, in: ITU, 1988.

[54] Dario Rethage, Jordi Pons, Xavier Serra, A wavenet for speech denoising, in: 2018 IEEE International Conference on Acoustics, Speech and Signal Processing (ICASSP), IEEE, 2018, pp. 5069–5073.

[55] Olaf Ronneberger, Philipp Fischer, Thomas Brox, U-Net: convolutional networks for biomedical image segmentation, in: International Conference on Medical Image Computing and Computer-Assisted Intervention, Springer, 2015, pp. 234–241.

[56] Frank Seide, Gang Li, Dong Yu, Conversational speech transcription using context-dependent deep neural networks, in: Twelfth Annual Conference of the International Speech Communication Association, 2011.

[57] Sanford Shatz, Susan E. Chylik, The California consumer privacy act of 2018: a sea change in the protection of California consumers, The Business Lawyer 75 (2020).

[58] S. Sridharan, E. Dawson, B. Goldburg, Fast Fourier transform based speech encryption system, in: IEE Proceedings I-Communications, Speech and Vision, vol. 138(3), 1991, pp. 215–223.

[59] Andreas Stolcke, Klaus Ries, Noah Coccaro, Elizabeth Shriberg, Rebecca Bates, Daniel Jurafsky, Paul Taylor, Rachel Martin, Carol Van Ess-Dykema, Marie Meteer, Dialogue act modeling for automatic tagging and recognition of conversational speech, Computational Linguistics 26 (3) (2000) 339–373.

[60] Ashish Vaswani, Noam Shazeer, Niki Parmar, Jakob Uszkoreit, Llion Jones, Aidan N. Gomez, Lukasz Kaiser, Illia Polosukhin, Attention is all you need, in: NIPS, 2017.

[61] Paul Voigt, Axel Von dem Bussche, The EU General Data Protection Regulation (GDPR). A Practical Guide, vol. 10, 1st ed, Springer International Publishing, Cham, 2017, p. 3152676.

[62] Yu-Xiang Wang, Borja Balle, Shiva Prasad Kasiviswanathan, Subsampled Rényi differential privacy and analytical moments accountant, in: The 22nd International Conference on Artificial Intelligence and Statistics, PMLR, 2019, pp. 1226–1235.

[63] Pete Warden, Speech commands: a dataset for limited-vocabulary speech recognition, arXiv:1804.03209, 2018.

[64] G.R. Wood, B.P. Zhang, Estimation of the Lipschitz constant of a function, Journal of Global Optimization 8 (1) (1996) 91–103.

[65] Xi Wu, Arun Kumar, Kamalika Chaudhuri, Somesh Jha, Jeffrey F. Naughton, Differentially private stochastic gradient descent for in-RDBMS analytics, CoRR, arXiv:1606.04722 [abs], 2016.

[66] Liyang Xie, Kaixiang Lin, Shu Wang, Fei Wang, Jiayu Zhou, Differentially private generative adversarial network, arXiv:1802.06739, 2018.

[67] Chao-Han Huck Yang, Linda Liu, Ankur Gandhe, Yile Gu, Anirudh Raju, Denis Filimonov, Ivan Bulyko, Multi-task language modeling for improving speech recognition of rare words, arXiv:2011.11715, 2020.

[68] Chao-Han Huck Yang, Jun Qi, Samuel Yen-Chi Chen, Pin-Yu Chen, Sabato Marco Siniscalchi, Xiaoli Ma, Chin-Hui Lee, Decentralizing feature extraction with quantum convolutional neural network for automatic speech recognition, in: ICASSP 2021–2021 IEEE International Conference on Acoustics, Speech and Signal Processing (ICASSP), IEEE, 2021, pp. 6523–6527.

[69] Chao-Han Huck Yang, Sabato Marco Siniscalchi, Chin-Hui Lee, PATE-AAE: incorporating adversarial autoencoder into private aggregation of teacher ensembles for spoken command classification, in: Proc. Interspeech 2021, 2021, pp. 881–885.

[70] Qiang Yang, Yang Liu, Tianjian Chen, Yongxin Tong, Federated machine learning: concept and applications, ACM Transactions on Intelligent Systems and Technology (TIST) 10 (2) (2019) 1–19.

[71] Timothy Yang, Galen Andrew, Hubert Eichner, Haicheng Sun, Wei Li, Nicholas Kong, Daniel Ramage, Françoise Beaufays, Applied federated learning: improving Google keyboard query suggestions, arXiv:1812.02903, 2018.

[72] Victor W. Zue, The use of speech knowledge in automatic speech recognition, Proceedings of the IEEE 73 (11) (1985) 1602–1615.

Ethical considerations and legal issues relating to federated learning

21

Warren Chik and Florian Gamper

Singapore Management University, Singapore, Singapore

21.1 Introduction

The development of AI for organizations to enhance productivity, gain new insights and create new products or services to drive new business models or revenue streams for a vibrant digital economy is based on the trusted use of data assets. Businesses and organizations are recognizing that pooling data together, or getting access to external sources of data, can generate greater value. However, establishing trust between data asset providers can be complex, with various interconnected considerations of business, law, and technology. Federated learning (**FL**) has emerged as a promising new method to facilitate data sharing across a diverse group of business and organizations.

This chapter analyzes the legality of FL, the legal issues that must be resolved for it to be operationalized, and the importance of establishing trust and understanding between businesses that partake in data sharing collaborations. FL is a method of training machine learning (**ML**) models, and therefore, legal and ethical issues relevant for ML and artificial intelligence (**AI**) will also apply to FL. This chapter focuses on the issues which are specific to FL. Relatively extensive literature on the legality and ethics of ML and AI already exists, and the reader may want to consult this literature in tandem with this chapter. Herein, the more general issues relating to ML and AI will only be analyzed to the extent necessary to analyze their legal and ethical issues in relation to FL.

First, this chapter will describe the general ethical principles governing data sharing as well as AI and how they translate into law and practice. It is important to appreciate the particular challenges involved for FL. In the subsequent parts of the chapter, we will highlight the most relevant areas of law and the challenges that must be considered in each context. One such challenge is that models created through FL are potentially less transparent than models created by standard ML. This is an significant issue because transparency is an important principle for ethical AI. Another important area is data protection and privacy legislation. Since FL is intrinsically linked to data – in particular, the collection, use, storage, conversion, and dissemination of it – the current data regimes are important. This is particularly so if the FL is meant to be operationalized across borders (which is likely the case). Intellectual

Federated Learning. https://doi.org/10.1016/B978-0-44-319037-7.00032-6

property (**IP**) rights are also an important issue, not least to establish the rights and liabilities of the stakeholders, vis-à-vis one another and third parties. Finally, where not otherwise covered by the current laws and frameworks, governance and internal rules to govern the robustness and integrity of the FL processes will be considered.

At the time of writing, FL is still relatively new, and thus far no standardized FL terminology has emerged. Therefore, before starting the analysis, it is important to clarify some terminology and assumptions. In its basic form, FL consists of a central server and various data sets. For simplicity, it will be assumed that the same entity that controls the server is also the entity that sends out the initial model, receives back the models trained on the local data sets (the **Local Data Sets**) and aggregates the models into one model (the **Final Model**). A model trained on the Local Data Sets before it is aggregated into the Final Model will be referred to as the Local Model (the **Local Model**). The Final Model can then be sent back to the Local Data Sets for further training and be aggregated yet again into the Final Model, this can be done repeatedly (ad infinitum). Further, it will be assumed that there is only one such entity and this entity also structures, organizes, and is overall in charge of the FL process. This entity will be referred to as the Aggregator (the **Aggregator**). The person who controls a Local Data Set will be referred to as the Controller (the **Controller**). The Aggregator and Controllers collectively are referred to as the Participants (the **Participants**).[1] The entire FL process (e.g., sending out the model, aggregating the models, etc.) will be referred to as the FL Project (the **FL Project**).

21.2 Global trends and ethical guidelines for trustworthy AI and the universal fundamental principles

FL is a way to train ML models, and training ML models involves data gathering. Therefore, two sets of ethical principles are particularly relevant to FL: principles for ethical data sharing and principles for ethical AI/ML.

21.2.1 Principles for ethical data sharing

Data has special characteristics that give rise to a distinct set of issues. On the one hand, the disadvantages of data use may be experienced not by the person who makes the decision of how the data is used but by the data subject. In other words, using economics jargon, there are externalities involved. For instance, a healthcare provider may sell access to medical records to an insurance company, and the insurance company may use this information to charge patients higher premiums. Here, the disclosure of the medical records was decided by the healthcare provider, but the

---

[1] The term Participant should not be confused with the term stakeholder, as the latter is wider in coverage than the former. A Participant is either the Aggregator or the Participant, whereas a stakeholder is every entity who has a stake or interest in the FL project.

disadvantage is borne by the patients (in the form of higher premiums). Another distinct characteristic of data is that it is 'non-rival,'[2] meaning that the use of data by one party does not diminish its use by another party. Therefore, in theory data could be used an infinite number of times, which can lead to substantial economic and social benefits. According to the OECD, analyzing different studies:

> [D]ata access and sharing can help generate social and economic benefits worth between 0.1% and 1.5% of gross domestic product (GDP) in the case of public-sector data, and between 1% and 2.5% of GDP (in a few studies up to 4% of GDP) when also including private-sector data."[3]

However, simply because there are substantial economic and social gains from data sharing does not explain why special ethical consideration should apply to it or why government initiatives are needed to facilitate data sharing. If the data use by one person does not diminish the use of data by another person, then it may be thought that the free market would provide enough incentives for data sharing and government intervention is not required. However, there are various obstacles preventing effective data sharing.[4] The first important obstacle is a lack of understanding, which may result in many businesses being unaware that data sharing can be a profitable strategy.[5]

Another problem is businesses not knowing how to share data in a legally compliant manner, or how to create a mechanism for data sharing. Indeed, many governmental initiatives in this area aim specifically at providing education on data sharing. For instance, in Singapore, the Infocomm Media Development Authority (**IMDA**) published the *Trusted Data Sharing Framework* specifically to provide such guidance.[6] A second important obstacle is that data sharing often requires trust. Although data is non-rival, disclosing data often entails risks. For instance, a group of banks may benefit from sharing customer data to detect fraud. However, each bank may be reluctant to share customer data out of concern that the other banks may use the data to poach clients. A third obstacle is that data is difficult to value, and people may be reluctant to share data because they do not know what the fair value of the data is.[7] A further

---

[2] See, e.g., Charles I. Jones and Christopher Tonetti, Nonrivalry and the Economics of Data, American Economic Review 2020, 110(9):2819–2858; [14].

[3] OECD, Enhancing Access to and Sharing of Data – Reconciling Risks and Benefits for Data Re-use across Societies (2019), Chap. 3, Economic and social benefits of data access and sharing, available at [18].

[4] Note that the focus of this chapter is on what may be called *Pareto-efficient data sharing* (i.e., through data sharing at least one party is made better off and no party is made worse off). A case of non-Pareto-efficient data sharing is when a business may not want to share the valuation of a company the business wants to acquire because this could result in other companies trying to buy the company.

[5] See, for instance, Singapore's Trusted Data Sharing Framework, available at [2].

[6] See Singapore's Trusted Data Sharing Framework *supra* at Note [6]. See also, Australia's 'Privacy Preserving Data Sharing Frameworks – People, Projects, Data and Output', available at [1].

[7] Another problem is that the marginal cost of using data may be close to zero but the average costs are not, which may make data sharing not cost effective. This could, for instance, be the case if data sharing

important obstacle is that if they disclose data, businesses may be concerned that it will constitute a breach of customers' trust.

These two special properties of data (i.e., externalities, and non-rivalry) have given rise to two countervailing regulatory tendencies. On the one hand, there is data protection legislation limiting the use of data. Examples are the EU's General Data Protection Regulation (**GDPR**) and Singapore's Personal Data Protection Act (**PDPA**) setting limits on the use of personal data; and the US' Health Insurance Portability and Accountability Act (**HIPAA**) setting limits on the use of medical records. On the other hand, because data sharing can lead to substantial economic benefits, many governments are crafting guidelines and regulatory frameworks to facilitate data sharing between organizations.[8] This clash of the countervailing tendencies of data sharing as both restricted and encouraged make FL an exciting development. FL has the potential of restricting data sharing while training models on large amounts of data. Concurrently, it is important to appreciate that the benefits of FL are not restricted to potentially enabling regulatory-compliant data sharing. FL has the ability to addresses the non-regulatory obstacles, which currently make data sharing difficult. As FL does not require the sharing of the Local Data Sets, there is less risk in sharing the data. FL also has the potential of making it easier to agree on each Controller's reward for contributing the data at the outset (i.e., data valuation and incentivization). Therefore, even if FL does not provide any benefits in relation to data protection regulation, FL could still provide important advantages for data sharing.

21.2.2 Principles for ethical AI/ML

Many regional groupings and countries have developed AI regulation. Much of this is based on general guidelines and general oversight rather than legal mechanisms and requirements; although some, such as the EU, have gone on to produce and propose more concrete legislation to regulate AI, viz. the proposed Artificial Intelligence Act (**AIA**).[9] The aim is to provide a conducive environment for AI innovation and for businesses involved in AI development so that they can establish themselves in a manner that invigorates the economy, whilst developing a social environment that encourages trust and use of products and services that leverage on the benefits of AI. The best example of a regional initiative is the EU's human-centric approach to AI, encapsulated first in the Ethics Guidelines for Trustworthy Artificial Intelligence (produced by a High-Level Expert Group on Artificial Intelligence that was set up by the European Commission) that was developed in 2018 and refined in 2019[10];

---

costs a certain amount of money to set-up, but once that is done, the sharing of data does not involve further costs.

[8] This chapter deals with what may be considered as Pareto-efficient data sharing (i.e., at least one party is made better off without making another party worse off).

[9] See the EU's proposed Artificial Intelligence Act, available at [19].

[10] See European Commission, White Paper on Artificial Intelligence: A European Approach to Excellence and Trust, 19 February 2021, available at [25].

followed by the European Commission's White Paper on Artificial Intelligence – A European Approach to Excellence and Trust, which favors a risk-based approach (using sector and application-specific risk assessment).[11] Similarly, in 2019, Singapore's IMDA published the Artificial Intelligence Governance Framework, one of the earliest of such frameworks in Asia.[12] The objective was to propound a balanced approach: On the one hand, facilitating innovation and the digital healthcare economy, while, on the other hand, building consumer trust and protecting the individual's interest. It had the further goal of providing a 'common global reference point' and to lead the way in the Asian region.

Although the different guidelines around the world emphasize different aspects of AI ethics, some common themes can be identified. The common themes are that AI should be human centric, fair, and transparent.[13] *Human centric* can be considered as the overarching value, and simply means that AI 'should augment rather than reduce human potential.'[14] The values of fairness and transparency are ways to substantiate *human centricity*. Fairness relates to the idea that AI decisions should be free from unethical or illegal biases or discrimination. The authors would add that for AI to be fair, it is important the AI decisions are free from error (as far as reasonably possible). Transparency means that AI systems *should be capable of being understood and their decisions capable of being explained*. This is important because it allows humans to be make a meaningful decision on whether or not to use AI. The value of fairness and transparency have also been recognized in legislation.

In relation to the processing of personal data, the GDPR requires processing to be *lawfully, fairly and in a transparent manner*,[15] as well as requiring that personal data shall be *accurate, and where necessary up to date*.[16] Similarly, by way of comparison, Singapore's PDPA contains an obligation for organizations to 'make a reasonable effort to ensure that personal data [...] is accurate and complete.'[17] The proposed AIA in the EU requires from 'high-risk AI systems' that 'training, validation, and testing data sets be relevant, representative, free of errors and complete,'[18] and that '[t]raining, validation, and testing data sets be subject to appropriate data governance and management practices.'[19] That training data is accurate and free from bias also

---

[11] See European Commission, White Paper on Artificial Intelligence: A European Approach to Excellence and Trust, 19 February 2021, available at [7]. Note that the EU have also produced other reports that focus on data strategy, safety, and liability.

[12] Infocomm Media Development Authority, Personal Data Protection Commission Singapore, Artificial Intelligence Governance Framework Model, Second Edition, 21 January 2021, available at [4].

[13] See, e.g., the Artificial Intelligence Governance Framework, *supra*. Note [13].

[14] Simon Chesterman, We, the Robots?: Regulating Artificial Intelligence and the Limits of the Law, Cambridge University Press, 2021, Chap. 7, [6].

[15] Article 5.1(a) of the GDPR (see [8]).

[16] Article 5.1(b) of the GDPR.

[17] Section 23 of the PDPA (see [16]).

[18] Article 10(3) of the AIA.

[19] Article 10 of the AIA.

has potential implications with regards to anti-discrimination legislation[20] where a user of an AI system is sued for discrimination, it may well be an issue of whether the data on which the AI system was trained was biased.

The requirements for fairness and transparency pose special problems for FL because access to the underlying data sets is strictly limited or not possible at all in FL systems.[21] Truong et al. summarize the issues as follows:

> Furthermore, the nature of preventing service providers from accessing the original training dataset as well as the inability to inspect individuals' locally trained ML model [...] amplifies the lack of transparency and fairness in FL systems. As a result, an FL system finds it problematic to transparently execute the training operations as well as to ensure any automated decisions from the system are impartially performed. This, consequently, induces impracticality for any FL systems and fails to fully comply with the GDPR requirements of fairness and transparency.

This issue is compounded by the problem that FL may be subject to *poison attacks*, which are aimed *at manipulating the training process by feeding poisoned local model updates to a coordination server.*[22] The problem is that if a poison attack cannot be detected then the FL model created will potentially be biased and inaccurate. It is important to emphasize that data quality is also an issue for standard ML and any kind of statistical analysis. However, FL developers need to be aware that this issue is especially acute for FL. The challenge is to create an FL structure which ensures that the data is *relevant, representative, free of errors, and complete*, and establishing appropriate data governance with the limitation of not being able to directly examine the underlying data sets.

It may be said that this is less of a problem because to establish the accuracy of the Final Model it is not necessary to examine the Local Data Sets, as all that is needed is to check the accuracy of the Final Model itself. However, although the accuracy of the Final Model is, of course, crucial, it does not mean that the quality of the underlying data is unimportant. The Final Model may be tested by using a validation set; however, what ultimately matters is how the model performs in the *real world*.[23] And it may be challenging to ascertain whether a model makes accurate predictions in the real world. One problem is that it may take considerable time to establish if a model

[20] See Philipp Hacker, A Legal Framework for AI Training Data – From First Principles to the Artificial Intelligence Act, Law, Innovation and Technology (2021), available at SSRN (accessed 8 Aug. 2022), pages 12–15; [12].
[21] See, for instance, Nguyen Truong, Kai Sun, Siyao Wang, Florian Guitton, YiKe Guo, Privacy Preservation in Federated Learning: An Insightful Survey from the GDPR perspective, Computer & Security 110 (2021); Rossello, Morales, and Muñoz-González, Data Protection by Design in AI? The Case of Federated Learning, Computerrecht 2021/116 (2021), [39]; see also [33].
[22] Truong et al., supra. Note [25], pages 10–11. See also Rossello, Morales, and Muñoz-González, supra. Note [25], part 2.3.
[23] See Hacker, supra. Note [24], page 20.

makes accurate predictions in the real world. Developers will also not always receive the relevant feedback on how the models have been performing (i.e., from users of their models). Further, if one waits to check the accuracy of 'real world' predictions, the damage the model may cause may already be done. It is also important to note that the proposed AIA specifically focuses on data quality by requiring that the training and validation sets are 'relevant, representative, free of errors and complete.' In other words, it is not just the Final Model that matters. Lastly, in order to check whether a model is biased for the purpose of anti-discrimination, it may be necessary to analyze the data the model was trained on.

How to assure data quality in FL and how to guard against poison attacks is currently a very active area of research in computer science.[24] Current research seems to suggest that while it is possible to prevent poison attacks which aim to jeopardize the entire system, more targeted attacks are more difficult to prevent. Technical solutions may provide some assistance with this problem, however, they are unlikely to solve the issue in its entirety. It is also important to keep the above-mentioned point regarding externalities in mind. FL developers *may* be able to solve the data quality issue to the extent necessary for users of their models to be satisfied with the accuracy of their model. Nevertheless, this alone is not enough. FL developers also need to take into account the persons impacted by the ML model and not only think of the users of the model. However, it is important to recognize that AIA requires only *appropriate data governance* (emphasis added). *Appropriate* should be interpreted in the context in which the AI system is likely to be used. For example, this would mean that the development of an AI system for hiring decisions requires different data governance than an AI system suggesting music playlists.

In summary, it is important to recognize that FL has great potential to overcome the challenges posed by data sharing. However, FL has disadvantages in relation to AI ethics. The trade-off between these two competing considerations may be reducible through improved technology and good governance structure, however, it is unlikely that it can be completely eradicated.

Although governments have largely encouraged the development and use of AI to be done according to general ethical principles to allay concerns of trust and to maintain the 'human focus' of such innovation, we are starting to see more concrete rules and regulations of AI emerging. This may be the start of a trend towards stronger regulation of AI. For example, as noted previously, on 21 April 2021, the European Union released its proposal for the AIA with a stronger set of rules for the development and use of AI – from regulation to prohibition – according to the risk that the AI poses. The Regulation, if it comes to pass, will mainly require compliance with rules in an organization's internal processes such as data governance, record-keeping, transparency, and user access to information, human oversight, and maintaining a robust, accurate, and secure database.

High risk AI must meet conformity requirements before they can be launched or used, and there is a post-market monitoring system to detect problems and to mitigate

---

[24] Rossello, Morales, and Muñoz-González, supra. Note [25], page 6.

them. This is the start of what will likely become more regulation (and forms of regulation) of AI in the years to come. There is also a new Machinery Regulation requiring use of AI-capable machinery to conduct a conformity assessment. Less than a year later, on 23 February 2022, the European Commission also proposed new rules for the access and use of data that is generated in the EU for the economic sector to maintain fair competition. It is likely that other regional groups or countries will follow suit in a bid to pre-empt issues in the use of AI and to ensure its viability, hence any FL projects should keep track of any legislative requirements that may be mandatory to avoid the consequences and liabilities for non-compliance.

21.3 Privacy and personal data rights and the international data protection regime

A key benefit that FL is intended to provide is to enable data sharing in compliance with privacy and data protection regulations.[25] When analyzing the extent to which FL is compliant with this legislation, it is important to remember that the type of data one is dealing with will have ramifications on any conclusions that can be drawn. For instance, financial data will be treated differently than medical data, which again will be treated differently from national security data. In some cases, these categories of data may not be mutually exclusive as well. The analysis in this chapter will be limited to an overview of the main issues relating to FL and personal data in relation to the EU's GDPR (in addition, some references to Singapore's PDPA will also be made for comparison).

21.3.1 Does federated learning involve the processing of data?

One of the GDPR's central provisions is that processing of personal data is only allowed if one (or multiple) of the conditions set out in Article 6(1) are met (e.g., the data subject consents[26] or it is necessary for the performance of a contract[27]). The key question is whether conducting an FL project qualifies as a *processing* for the purposes of GDPR. There is no explicit regulatory guidance or judicial determination on this point, and, thus far, this question has also not received much attention in the legal literature. However, some commentators have analyzed this point and come to the conclusion that *[t]here is little doubt that, if the raw training data provided by the data holder(s) qualifies as personal data, the operations performed on such data in the context of the federated learning process will fall under the material scope of the GDPR.*[28] If this view is correct, then it would be incorrect to hold that GDPR does

---

[25] For instance, the GDPR, PDPA, and HIPAA (see [40]).

[26] Article 6(1)(a) GDPR.

[27] Article 6(1)(b) GDPR.

[28] Rossello, Morales, and Muñoz-González, supra. Note [25], page 9.

not apply to FL, which would mean that FL projects could only be conducted if the FL system meets at least one of the conditions in Article 6(1), or one of the other conditions on re-use of personal data in Article 6(4) is met. However, it is important to stress again that, as of the time of writing, there is no specific judicial or regulatory guidance on this point. Further, the definition of processing in GDPR Article 4(2) does not mention *analyzing data*, which may suggest that FL does not constitute processing the data. On the other hand, Article 4(2) states that the 'use' of data falls within the definition of processing, which may make the definition broad enough to encompass FL. It is interesting to compare the definition of processing in the GDPR with the relevant concepts in the PDPA. PDPA requires consent for the *collection, use, and disclosure* of personal data.[29] *Collection, use, and disclosure* is not defined in the PDPA. However, in advisory guidance, it is stated that *these terms would apply as they are commonly understood*[30] and that *use refers to any act or set of acts by which an organization employs personal data.* This could potentially mean that FL processing falls within meaning of *collection, use, and disclosure.*

Certainly, if there is a way to conduct research without involving personal data at any stage of the process (e.g., differential privacy), that removes the problem entirely. The question of whether something does or does not constitute personal data may be more complex than one might think. For instance, the use of anonymized data may not exempt the data controller from legal responsibility (and liability), depending on when it was anonymized, whether there are tools to de-anonymize or re-identify, and access to other data that, together with the anonymized data, may re-identify an individual. Once personal data is used, the next question is whether there can nevertheless be a way to reduce the administrative burden and impediments to data collection, use or disclosure. Although data protection laws differ in the level of protection accorded to personal data, all have some form of exception to the obligations under the law, acknowledging conflicting interests and other public policy concerns that require some exemptions to strict compliance with these rules.

Returning to the GDPR, even if FL is considered processing, GDPR provides that *processing [...] for statistical purposes shall [...] not be considered incompatible with the initial purposes.*[31] However, it should be noted that even if the statistical purpose exemption applies, GDPR requires that processing for statistical purposes must be done with 'appropriate safeguards,' for instance, data minimization and pseudonymization.[32] There is no definition of 'statistical purposes' in the main text of GDPR, however, Recital 162 states that it refers to 'any operation of collection and the processing of personal data necessary for statistical surveys or for the production of statistical results.' However, Recital 162 further states that the result from the statistics are not to be 'used in support of measures or decisions regarding

---

[29] Section 13 PDPA.
[30] Personal Data Protection Commission Singapore, Advisory Guidelines on Key Concepts in the Personal Data Protection Act, Issued 23 September 2013, revised 1 October 2021, section 7, page 31, [31].
[31] Article 6(1)(b) GDPR.
[32] Article 89(1) GDPR.

any particular natural person.' Therefore, if the FL process trains a model which will be used to make decisions regarding any natural person, then the statistical purpose exemption cannot be used. It is submitted that this means that many FL projects will fall outside GDPR's statistical purpose exemption. Hence, this exemption may have limited implications for FL.

Under the data protection regime, the obligation to seek consent to the collection, use and disclosure of personal data can be onerous and costly. Many data protection laws have exceptions based on public policy bases. In the EU and some other countries such as Singapore, there is an exception based on *legitimate interest*. Recital 47 of the GDPR states that:

> *The legitimate interests of a controller, including those of a controller to which the personal data may be disclosed, or of a third party, may provide a legal basis for processing, provided that the interests or the fundamental rights and freedoms of the data subject are not overriding, taking into consideration the reasonable expectations of data subjects based on their relationship with the controller.*

This requires a balancing of the legitimate interest of the data controller (and the importance of the processing in question) against the fundamental rights and freedoms of data subjects (including possible harmful effects). As far as research is concerned as a basis, research that is valuable to the controller, and especially to society in general, will carry a higher weight in such an assessment.

In the case of the GDPR, the 'reasonable expectation' or the fairness and foreseeability of the personal data processing is key to the exception, which is quite narrow as compared to a legitimate interest that is based on other grounds or considerations such as whether the legitimate interest simply outweighs any adverse effects on the individual.[33]

Some countries' data protection legislation has a more specific exception from the consent obligation for personal data for the purpose of research. It is noteworthy that the Singapore PDPA provides for just such an exception, but only in relation to use and disclosure (and not collection).[34] The research exception in the PDPA is not limited to, for example, business improvements. It allows for wider research purposes and objectives such as academic, historical, and statistical research. There are conditions, however, involving reasonableness of use and practicableness of disclosure (without seeking consent), public benefits, the impact on the individual and non-publication of identifiable information.[35]

---

[33] Schedule 1, Part 3(1) of the PDPA.
[34] Schedule 2, Parts 2 and 3, Div. 3 of the PDPA.
[35] See PDPC, *Advisory Guidelines on Key Concepts in the Personal Data Protection Act, supra.* Note [38]. See also [32].

21.3.2 **Other issues in relation to the GDPR**

It is thought that FL is particularly useful in a cross-border setting by facilitating the training of a model on data sets held in different jurisdictions. This is an important issue because of Chapter 5 of the GDPR, which imposes special requirements on transfers of personal data outside the EU/EEA. A similar regime is created by PDPA which imposes special restrictions on transferring data out of Singapore.[36] *Transfer* is not explicitly defined in the GDPR. However, the European Data Protection Board (**EDPB**) issued guidance that transfer means *[disclosure] by transmission or otherwise makes personal data.*[37] FL clearly does not disclose data by transmission, but it may make 'data available.' As with the previous question, there is no authoritative guidance on this point. However, the authors submit that the answer to the question will depend on how the FL Project is structured. If the Aggregator is granted full access to the Local Data sets without any restrictions, then it this should count as making the data available. However, if the Aggregator only sends a specific model to the Controllers, and the Controller allows that model to conduct analysis on the Local Data Set, it should not count as making the data available.

Another important question is whether a model or algorithm can be personal data for the purposes of the GDPR. If a model itself can be personal data, then GDPR could not only apply to the Local Data Sets but also to the models created by the FL process. This would, for instance, mean that the Aggregator would need to comply with GDPR in relation to the further use of the models. According to the GDPR, data is personal data if it relates to an *identifiable natural person*.[38] Identifiability needs to be assessed based on *all the means reasonably likely to be used*.[39] There are studies, which suggests that, under certain circumstances, it may be possible to reveal the underlying personal data from a model.[40] The argument in favor of holding that models can be personal data is that if it is reasonably likely that a natural person can be identified from the model, the model should count as personal data. A counterargument is that in practice to reverse engineer is *much harder than the empirical studies proving certain attack strategies seem to imply*.[41] Furthermore, in the case of *Breyer*, the Court of Justice of the European Union (**CJEU**) held that *all means reasonably likely to be used* does not include illegal means.[42] *Leiser and Dechense* argue that to *reverse engineer* from a model to the underlying personal data is illegal under GDPR, and therefore, following *Breyer*, this possibility should not be taken into account in assessing whether a model is personal data, which means that models cannot

---

[36] Section 26 of the PDPA.

[37] The European Data Protection Board, Guidelines 05/2021 on the Interplay between the application of Article 3 and the provisions on international transfers as per Chapter V of the GDPR Guidelines, adopted 18 Nov. 2021, page 4, available at [5].

[38] Article 4(1) of the GDPR.

[39] Recital 26 of the GDPR.

[40] See, for instance, M. Veale, R. Binns and L. Edwards, Algorithms That Remember: Model Inversion Attacks and Data Protection Law, Phil. Trans. R. Soc. A 376 2018, pages 1–15, [41].

[41] Hacker, supra. Note [24], page 7.

[42] CJEU, Patrick Breyer vs. Bundesrepublik Deutschland, 19 Oct. 2016 Case C-582/14, [20] *(Breyer)*.

be personal data.[43] However, the authors of this chapter agree with *Hacker*'s analysis that a rigid application of the illegality criterium is not warranted.[44] Illegality is not mentioned in the GDPR (neither in the main text nor in the recitals) and applying the illegality criterium strictly may lead to the undesirable outcome of leaving data subjects without a remedy under GDPR if the data was processed illegally.[45] It seems more in line with the overall purpose of the GDPR to regard models as personal data if it is reasonably like that a natural person can be identified from it. However, as stated above, in practice it may not happen all that often that a natural person can be identified from a model. However, FL developers need to be aware that if the model does qualify as personal data, the requirements for personal data set out in GDPR will apply. Among other things, this means that the so-called *right to be forgotten* (as set out in Article 16 of GDPR) will apply, which may in turn mean that the Final Model needs to unlearn the contribution made by a particular Local Data Set.

The above analysis may give the impression that FL has only limited benefits in relation to the GDPR. However, FL has a number of important advantages over standard ML in relation to GDPR. Article 25 of GDPR requires *data protection by design*, stating that the data controller shall *implement appropriate technical and organizational measures, such as pseudonymization, which are designed to implement data-protection principles, such as data minimization, in an effective manner and to integrate the necessary safeguards.*[46] Standard ML may require data to be copied (e.g., data is copied to a central server). However, this is not necessary with FL, because the models are trained on the Local Data Sets. Therefore, FL leads to data minimization, which is an important goal of GDPR. Another advantage of FL is that, as the data is not held at a central server, this arguably reduces the risk of the data being hacked.[47] Again, this may be considered a form of *data protection by design*. Therefore, FL has clear benefits with regards to data protection by design because it minimizes data, and provides better protection against hacks than standard ML. However, the extent to which data protection regulation like GDPR or PDPA apply to FL in practice is unclear. One of the issues is clearly that the many of the relevant statues were drafted before FL emerged or the drafters did not have FL in mind when writing the legislation. It is also important to remember that data protection regulation is not the only issues for effective data sharing. As was stated above, lack of trust is an important obstacle to effective data sharing, and in this respect FL has clear advantages over standard ML.

---

[43] Leiser and F. Dechesne, Governing Machine-Learning Models: Challenging the Personal Data Presumption, International Data Privacy Law (10) 2020, pages 187–200, [17].

[44] Hacker, supra. Note [24], pages 6–9.

[45] *Ibid.*

[46] Article 25(1) GDPR.

[47] See Rossello, Morales, and Muñoz-González, supra. Note [25], part 7, pages 7 and following.

21.4 Intellectual property rights relating to federated learning systems

Many of the IP issues in relation to FL are similar to the IP issues in relation to standard ML. However, some special considerations apply to FL, which will be highlighted below.

21.4.1 How to protect models created by federated learning

An important question is whether there are any IP rights in the Final Model and who can claim these rights. The most common IP rights relevant for ML models are patents, copyright, and trade secrets. It is possible to receive a patent for algorithms if, to use European terminology, it involves *the use of technical means [...] or [...] its subject-matter has a technical character*.[48] What this means is easiest to illustrate through an example. A purely abstract AI model like *support vector machine* cannot be patented, but a more specific application, like the *neural network in a heart monitoring apparatus for the purpose of identifying irregular heartbeats makes a technical contribution*, may be.[49] Other jurisdictions broadly follow similar principles. For instance, in Singapore, an ML method can be patented if it *solves a specific problem in a manner that goes beyond the underlying mathematical method*.[50] It is, however, not always easy to tell whether an algorithm is sufficiently technical to be patentable. Furthermore, to be awarded a patent, an application has to be made, which can be costly and time consuming. Therefore, patents are not always the best option to protect ML models.

An alternative to patents is copyright. Copyright protects the expression of an idea, and covers things like works of literature, music, or paintings.[51] In many jurisdictions it is possible to receive copyright for computer programmes, as well as the compilation of data, provided the necessary requirements are fulfilled.[52] However, to be able to receive copyright protection, there must be a creative expression by a human author. The CJEU states that *it is both necessary and sufficient that the subject matter reflects the personality of its author, as an expression of his free and creative choices*.[53] The question is whether an ML is the creative expression of a hu-

---

[48] See European Patent Office, Guidelines for Examination, Chapter II, part 3.3. Mathematical methods, available at [23].

[49] See European Patent Office, Guidelines for Examination, Chapter II, part 3.3.1, Artificial intelligence and machine learning [24].

[50] See Intellectual Property Office of Singapore, IP and Artificial Intelligence Information Note, page 6 (highlights removed) available at [21].

[51] For more details, see, for instance, [26].

[52] For example, the UK, the USA, and Singapore.

[53] Brompton Bicycle Ltd vs. Chedech / Get2Get, 11 June 2020, Case C-833/18. For discussion, see Katarina Foss-Solbrekk, Three Routes to Protecting AI Systems and Their Algorithms under IP Law: The Good, the Bad and the Ugly, Journal of Intellectual Property Law & Practice, Volume 16, Issue 3, March 2021, Pages 247–258, at page 251, [9].

man author? There is certainly some human creativity involved in ML development. Undoubtedly, the way the model is trained is an expression of human creativity. Developers are responsible for arranging the necessary hardware, the data sets, picking the initial model, deciding how the model should be trained, etc. However, this does not mean that the model itself is an expression of human creativity. For instance, Katarina Foss-Solbrekk argues that:

> *Unsupervised learning algorithms and models are unlikely to be regarded as an author's own intellectual creation because the developer plays a small role in the algorithms' functioning. [...] Supervised learning algorithms similarly struggle to satisfy [the requirements for copyright] as they are often open source, thus not original, with predominantly technical expressions.*[54]

Not all commentators agree with this conclusion.[55] Some jurisdictions have taken steps to address this issue. In the UK, a provision was added to the Copyright, Designs and Patents Act 1988, stating that in case of computer-generated work *the author shall be taken to be the person by whom the arrangements necessary for the creation of the work are undertaken.*[56] Similar provisions were also enacted in Hong Kong (SAR), India, Ireland, and New Zealand.[57] This may be helpful for getting copyright protection for ML algorithms. However, some questions remain, especially in relation to FL.

One such question is who *the person by whom the arrangements necessary for the creation of the work are undertaken* is?[58] Another problem is that not all jurisdictions have enacted special provisions for computer-generated work, in which case developers need to rely on standard principles of copyright, which (as discussed) may not be fit for purpose in this regard. For FL developers, it is important to recognize that the issue whether an ML can be considered as an expression of human creativity is even more acute in an FL setting. As the Aggregator does not even know the content of the Local Data Sets, it is, arguably, even less of an expression of human creativity.

Another issue for FL is that there are potentially many parties who could be entitled to copyright (as well as other IP rights). Copyright, different from patents, is awarded automatically.[59] Due to the uncertainty surrounding copyright within the context of FL, it will not always be possible to determine to whom the copyright will arise. It could, for instance, be the case that it is desired that the copyright should be held by the Controller, however, it will arise to the Aggregator. To deal with this uncertainty, all Participants (i.e., the Aggregator and Controller) should enter into a

---

[54] See Katarina Foss-Solbrekk, supra. Note [61], page 251.

[55] For an alternative analysis, see Begona Gonzales Otero, Machine Learning Models Under the Copyright Microscope: Is EU Copyright Fit for Purpose?, GRUR International, 70(11), 2021, pages 1043–1055, [27].

[56] Article 9(3) of the UK Copyright, Designs and Patents Act 1988, [30].

[57] Andres Guadamuz, Artificial intelligence and copyright, WIPO Magazine, Oct, 2017, available at [11].

[58] See Guadamuz, supra. Note [65]. Section **Addressing Ambiguity**.

[59] However, some jurisdictions provide for copyright to be registrable.

contract, setting out how to deal with IP issues. In particular, the Participants should nominate who should be the holder of any copyright (if copyright indeed arises). This designated holder of the copyright can either be the Aggregator, the Controller, all Participants, or anyone else. Further, the contract should state that if any copyright (or other IP) arises to a Participant, this Participant shall assign this copyright to whoever is the designated holder of the IP rights.

Another way to protect algorithms is through trade secrets. For instance, Google, Facebook, and Yahoo use trade secrets to protect their algorithms.[60] For something to be a trade secret, it must be *commercially valuable because it is secret, be known only to a limited group of persons, and be subject to reasonable steps taken [. . .] to keep it secret*.[61] These criteria may pose a problem for FL. If the Final Model is distributed to a large number of Controllers then this will conflict with the requirement that the *secret, be known only to a limited group of persons*. Even, if the Final Model is only distributed to a small number of people, it is important that reasonable steps are taken to keep it a secret. One such step could be that Participants sign a non-disclosure agreement (**NDA**) in relation to the Final Model. However, it is important to note that a disadvantage of trade secrets is that once the trade secret becomes public (i.e., is not a secret anymore), the trade secret status is lost. This is different from patents and copyright which remain in place even if the relevant information is public. Thus, even if there is an NDA in place, if a Participant makes the algorithm public (whether or not in breach of the agreement), the trade secret will be lost.

21.4.2 Avoiding IP infringement

The FL project needs to ensure that it does not infringe any IP rights. This may happen if conducting the FL project on the local data infringes IP rights in the local data. IP right infringement is also an issue for standard ML, however, this issue is more of a problem for FL because the Aggregator does not have direct control over the data and has to the rely on the data sets provided by the Controllers. One way to deal with this issue is to do it contractually. All Participants can enter into an agreement whereby each Controller declares that conducting the FL project does not infringe any IP rights in relation to her local data set. This can be further bolstered by each Controller providing an indemnity to hold other harmless against any loss they may incur if running FL operations on the participants' data set is found to have infringed copyright.

In addition, Participants may be able to take advantage of the *fair use* doctrine. In the absence of a statutory exception for computational uses of copyrighted material, creating models through an FL Process may be *transformative* enough to constitute fair use in jurisdictions that provide protection from liability for such permitted uses. In the United States, where the open-ended fair use doctrine emerged, there is a

---

[60] See Katarina Foss-Solbrekk, supra. Note [61], page 257.
[61] See World Intellectual Property Organization, Trade Secrets – What is a Trade Secret?, available at [42].

strong line of cases that have found text and data mining practices and the creation of databases for such material to constitute fair use, particularly on the basis of the *transformative use* doctrine.

Alternatively, there are certain exemptions for text and data mining (*TDM*) under some copyright legislation. The TDM exemptions in copyright law is making inroads in many jurisdictions like the UK, the USA, EU, and Australia.[62] The European Union's Copyright Directive (Directive on Copyright in the Digital Single Market) also requires Member States to include such an exemption in their national copyright laws by June 2021.[63] The EU Directive applies to commercial and non-commercial use of TDM, however, rights holders may opt-out in case of commercial use. The UK also has a TDM exemption. Originally, the exemption was only for non-commercial use, however, in 2022 the UK government announced that the exemption will be extended to commercial use. In Singapore, the Singapore Copyright Act in 2021 (**CA**) was amended to include a new exception for computational data analysis, including text and data mining (automated analysis of big data for useful purposes such as to detect trends and patterns), including for ML. The protection extends to the storage, retention, and copying of a copyrighted work for such analysis.[64] Hence, for example, making copies of the work to give it *new meaning* (derivative data) that would normally require specific authorization (copying and adaptation),[65] can be done without having to seek the permission of the copyright owner.

Although the TDM exception is indeed helpful for collaborative research or study (especially for the purpose of sharing) and data analysis, its usefulness should not, however, be overstated. The exception will apply only where there is analysis performed on the works that have been copied and it is only an exception to copyright infringement and not all other laws protecting data. Hence, data protection laws will still apply if it involves personal data (but note the statutory exceptions that may apply there). Also, the user must have lawful access to the works in the first place if there is one (e.g., through a paid subscription to a subscription-based database) and the work is not made freely available by the copyright holder in the public domain. Rights holders can also implement reasonable measures to maintain the security and stability of their computer systems and networks and the exception does not give the user a right to hack or otherwise circumvent these systems without permission (which is an offence under the computer crime laws in many countries).

---

[62] See, e.g., Matthew Sag, The New Legal Landscape for text Mining and Machine Learning, 66 J. Copyright Soc'y USA. 291 (2019); and Matthew Sag, Copyright Law's Impact on Machine Learning in the United States and the European Union, 14 FIU L. Rev. 293 (2020), [34]; see also [35].

[63] Article 3 of Directive 2019/790 of the European Parliament and of the Council on Copyright and Related Rights in the Digital Market and Amending Directives 96/9/EC and 2001/29/EC, 2019 PE–CONS 51/19 [29]. See also, Christophe Geiger, Giancarlo Frosio, and Oleksandr Bulayenko, Text and Data Mining in the Proposed Copyright Reform: Making the EU Ready for an Age of Big Data?, 49 Int'l Rev. Intell. Prop. & Competition L. 814, 815-20 (2018), [10].

[64] Section 244(3) of the CA, [22]. See David Tan & Thomas Lee, Copying Right in Copyright Law: Fair Use, Computational Data Analysis and the Personal Data Protection Act, 33 SAcLJ 1032 (2021), [37].

[65] Section 112(1)(a)(e) of the CA.

21.5 **Governance structure**

The previous sections highlight some of the legal, cultural, and societal issues FL developers need to tackle. In contrast, this section highlights some of legal tools that can be utilized to address some of these issues. This section will sketch out how a successful governance structure can help to deal with some of the key challenges faces by FL. It is important to note that the creation of successful governance structure is not primarily a legal issue, rather it requires business and technological considerations. One problem in analyzing FL governance is that FL structures are highly diverse. An FL Project where the Aggregator has substantial bargaining power, and there are many Controllers with almost no bargaining power, requires a different governance structure than a structure where there is only a small number of Participants who all have substantial bargaining power. Also, if the FL Project is conducted across multiple companies, this will require a different governance structure than if the FL Project is conducted within a single company. Due to size constraints, this section will only analyze the situation where data sets are held by different companies, all the Participants have some bargaining power, and the number or Participants is sufficiently small that meaningful bargaining can take place.

As mentioned in the introduction, one of the key aspects of data sharing is trust. In relation to FL, this means that there needs to be a governance structure that creates trust among Participants, most importantly the Controllers have to trust the Aggregator, and the Aggregator has to trust the Controllers. While it is desirable for there to be trust among the Participants too, this is less important as the Participants do not directly interact with each other. The role of the Aggregator requires trust for several reasons. In some FL Projects, a Controller may receive a benefit in proportion to the quality of the data they contribute, and the Aggregator needs to determine the quality of the data. Another important role of the Aggregator is to distribute the initial model as well as the model updates to the Controllers. The Controller needs to trust that these models do not cause any harm and only *extract* the specific information as agreed. The Aggregator needs to trust the Controller that the Local Data Sets conform to certain parameters, and that the model updates have not been *poisoned*.

In the relevant computer science literature, it is sometimes assumed that the Aggregator can be trusted.[66] However, to make FL operational, trust cannot simply be assumed, it must be created. In order to create this trust, the first step is that the rights and obligations of all Participants are clearly defined before the FL Project starts. An effective way to do this is for the Participants to enter into a contractual agreement (the **FL Agreement**). First, the parties to the FL Agreement need to be determined. There are essentially two options. One option is to have a single FL Agreement that all Participants sign. The other option is to have bi-lateral FL Agreements that the Aggregator signs with each Controller. In the first option, each Participant has a direct contractual link with all other Participants, which means each Participant can enforce the contract. In the second option, a Controller only has a contractual link

---

[66] See, e.g., [38].

with the Aggregator, which means that this is the only contract that the Controller can enforce. Which structure is preferable will depend on the specific of the situation. For instance, if there are many Participants, then the only realistic option is for the Aggregator to enter into a separate contract with each Controller. What structure is chosen for a particular FL Project will also depend on the bargaining strength of the parties. If the Aggregator has a strong bargaining position, he/she may insist on signing separate FL agreements with each Controller because then only the Aggregator can enforce an FL agreement against a particular Controller.

21.5.1 Common contractual federated learning projects

The FL Agreement needs to set out the rights and obligations of each Participant. This will include a clause stating that the Aggregator will send the initial model and model updates to the Controllers, and that the Controller will allow the model to be trained on his/her Local Data Set. Care must be taken when drafting the clause. If the clause is drafted too widely, giving the Aggregator wide access rights to the Local Data Set, then this runs the risk that it will be considered as giving the Aggregator access to the Local Data Set for the purpose of Section V of GDPR, as well as being considered as data processing within the meaning of Article 4(1) of GDPR. If the clause is drafted very narrowly (e.g., by specifying in great detail what model the Aggregator can transmit), then even a slight change in the model could mean that the Aggregator is in breach of FL Agreement. The FL Agreement must also set out for how long the model is allowed to be trained at the Local Data Set, and whether a Controller has the right to withdraw from the FL Project. Other clauses will include obligations for the Aggregator to aggregate the Local Models received from the Controller as well to give the Controllers the agreed reward. If the reward is the Final Model and that the quality of the model received by Controllers depends on the quality of the Local Data Set, then there needs to be a clause how this is to be determined.

However, a contract is only meaningful if the contract can be enforced, and enforcement depends on the possibility of detecting breach. Therefore, it is crucial that the FL Agreement creates provisions to enable monitoring for breaches. There should be an obligation on each Participant to keep accurate and complete records in relation to the Local Data Set, to enable effective monitoring. For instance, these records should state how the data was collected, what steps were taken to ensure the data is accurate, how the data was updated, etc. In addition, there needs to be a provision that allows for inspections of these records. Depending on the situation, one can also go a step further, and put in an obligation for a data audit. Such a data audit would consist of an independent third party checking the records (and, if possible, even the Local Data Set itself) and certify that they are correct. An audit can either take place at specific intervals (e.g., once per year), or upon request if there is suspicion that the Local Data Set does not correspond to the required standard. The disadvantage of data audits is that they are costly and time consuming. Therefore, they are not suitable for all types of FL Projects. It is important to point out that record keeping and audits are not a guarantee that the data is of a stated quality because, obviously, records can be forged, and even honest records cannot guarantee that the data is accurate. However, record-keeping and audits provide an *extra layer* of assurance. It is also important to point out that in many cases Controllers will have a natural incentive to contribute data within the prescribed parameters. This is especially the case when the Controllers receive the Final Model as a reward and then it may be in the interest of the Controller to improve the Final Model.

Record keeping and the possibility to inspect these records should apply to the Aggregator too, however, with the Aggregator there are additional complexities. The Aggregator's obligations are continuous, which makes it more difficult to monitor. Furthermore, when a Controller breaches his/her obligations, realistically, only the Final Model will be affected. However, when the Aggregator breaches his/her obligations, the integrity of the Local Data Sets may be jeopardized. One way to deal with this issue is to engage an independent third party to act as an Aggregator. There are a number of commercial enterprises offering the services of an Aggregator currently in the market.[67] Engaging an independent third party has the advantage of this party being likely to have less incentive to breach the confidentiality of the Local Data Sets. For instance, a bank may be reluctant to appoint another bank as the Aggregator out of concern of disclosing valuable information to a competitor. However, the bank may be more willing to appoint a third party as Aggregator because the data will not be directly relevant the third party. Furthermore, if the third party is in the business of providing the services of an Aggregator, the third party will have an interest in preserving its long-term reputation. On the other hand, independent third parties also will be subject to commercial pressure, which may impact the level of trust. In addition to commercial enterprises, governmental (or quasi-governmental) entities may offer Aggregator Services.[68] Governmental entities have different incentive than commercial providers, which may make the former more trustworthy than the latter. However, this is not necessarily guaranteed, and of the time of writing, no such service exists.

Another important aspect that Participants should set out a complaints and dispute handling procedure in the FL Agreement. Otherwise, Participants may have to rely on the courts to resolve a dispute. Of course, even if a complaints procedure is included in the FL Agreement, enforcement still ultimately depends on the courts. However, a contractual complaint's procedure provides a way to resolve conflicts before the assistance of the courts is sought. The problem with relying on courts (or tribunals) is that it can be expensive, slow, and adversarial. Often one party suing a counterparty will end the relationship between the parties. Furthermore, including a complaint's handling procedure allows the parties to devise their own remedies. The complaint's procedure will set out what should happen if a party does not fulfill its obligation under the FL Agreement. For instance, the procedure may provide for what should happen if a Controller cannot provide a Local Data Set, or the Aggregator cannot

---

[67] See, e.g., Felt (https://feltoken.ai/); Apheris (https://www.apheris.com/platform); Owkin (https://owkin.com/collaborate); Intellegens (https://intellegens.com/products-services/ichnite/), [3,13,15,28].

[68] Singapore seems to have the ambition of building such a service. See [36].

send out the model. The procedure should also provide a mechanism for a Participant to leave the FL Project, and, possibly, for a Participant to be excluded from the FL Project under certain circumstances. Importantly, the FL Agreement should state whether the determinations of the Aggregator are final, or whether they can be appealed, and if so, how.

Lastly, the Participants should consider whether to include a provision which allows for the inspection of the Local Data Sets by another Participant in certain circumstances. As stated above, it may be necessary to examine the Local Data Sets to rebut an allegation that the model is discriminatory. Therefore, the Participants may want to consider inserting a provision that if a Participant is sued in relation to the model in a bona fide lawsuit and needs to access the Local Data Set of other Participants in order to defend the suit, access to the Local Data Set should be granted. Having this mechanism may contribute towards making FL Project more transparent and potentially safer. However, the disadvantages of such a provision is that it weakens the confidentiality of the Local Data Sets. One way to address these concerns is to make sure that access to the Local Data Set will only granted if certain requirements are fulfilled, which aim to preserve confidentiality as much as possible.

21.6 Conclusion

FL is an exciting new development, which has the potential to address many of the legal, cultural, and societal issues in relation to data sharing. There are some downsides to FL. Due to size constraints, in this chapter it was only possible to highlight some of the problems. To give a comprehensive answer, further analysis is required. As to the downsides discussed herein, first, as Local Data Sets are not accessible, the Final Models created through FL Projects are less transparent. This lack of transparency may conflict with the goal of creating AI, which is human centric, fair, and transparent. Second, there are areas of uncertainty in relation to the practical implementation of FL. It is not clear to what extent GDPR and PDPA apply to FL, and to what extent Local Models and Final Models created through FL attract copyright. Another challenge is how to establish trust in an Aggregator. The creation of an FL Agreement can go some way towards this, however, it is unlikely to resolve the issue completely. Other options include appointing an independent third party or government agency. To set out an FL Agreement, this chapter highlights some of the key clauses one would expect to find in such a contract, and the rationales thereof. Notwithstanding the uncertainties and shortcomings related to FL, it is important to stress that FL has great potential and answers many of the issues raised by ML.

Acknowledgments

This research is supported by the National Research Foundation Singapore and DSO National Laboratories under the AI Singapore Programme (AISG Award No: AISG2-RP-2020-018).

References

[1] Australia's, Privacy preserving data sharing frameworks – people, projects, data and output, Available at https://www.acs.org.au/insightsandpublications/reports-publications/privacy-preserving-data-sharing-frameworks.html. (Accessed 8 August 2022).

[2] Singapore's, Trusted data sharing framework, Available at https://www.imda.gov.sg/-/media/Imda/Files/Programme/AI-Data-Innovation/Trusted-Data-Sharing-Framework.pdf. (Accessed 8 August 2022).

[3] Apheris, Apheris platform, https://www.apheris.com/platform. (Accessed 8 August 2022).

[4] Infocomm Media Development Authority and Personal Data Protection Commission Singapore, Artificial intelligence governance framework model, Second Edition, Available at https://www.pdpc.gov.sg/-/media/Files/PDPC/PDF-Files/Resource-for-Organisation/AI/SGModelAIGovFramework2.pdf, 21 January 2021. (Accessed 8 August 2022).

[5] The European Data Protection Board. Guidelines 05/2021 on the Interplay between the application of Article 3 and the provisions on international transfers as per Chapter V of the GDPR Guidelines, November 2021, adopted 18, Available at https://edpb.europa.eu/system/files/2021-11/edpb_guidelinesinterplaychapterv_article3_adopted_en.pdf. (Accessed 8 August 2022).

[6] Simon Chesterman, We, the Robots?: Regulating Artificial Intelligence and the Limits of the Law, vol. 110(9), Cambridge University Press, 2021, Chapter 7.

[7] European Commission, White paper on artificial intelligence: a European approach to excellence and trust, Available at https://ec.europa.eu/info/publications/white-paper-artificial-intelligence-european-approach-excellence-and-trust_en, 19 February 2021. (Accessed 8 August 2022).

[8] Council of European Union, GDPR (EU): regulation (EU) 2016/679 (general data protection regulation), https://gdpr-info.eu/, 2016.

[9] Katarina Foss-Solbrekk, Three routes to protecting AI systems and their algorithms under IP law: the good, the bad and the ugly, Journal of Intellectual Property Law and Practice 16 (3) (2021) 247–258.

[10] Christophe Geiger, Giancarlo Frosio, Oleksandr Bulayenko, Text and data mining in the proposed copyright reform: making the EU ready for an age of big data?, 49 Int'l Rev. Intell. Prop. & Competition, L. 814 (2018) 815–820.

[11] Andres Guadamuz, Artificial intelligence and copyright, WIPO magazine, Available at https://www.wipo.int/wipo_magazine/en/2017/05/article_0003.html, Oct. 2017. (Accessed 8 August 2022).

[12] Philipp Hacker, A Legal Framework for AI Training Data – From First Principles to the Artificial Intelligence Act', Innovation and Technology (2021) 12–15, Available at SSRN, https://papers.ssrn.com/sol3/papers.cfm?abstract_id=3556598. (Accessed 8 August 2022).

[13] Intellegens, Ichnite: a federated learning platform that helps aggregate models trained on completely separate and private data sources, https://intellegens.com/products-services/ichnite/. (Accessed 8 August 2022).

[14] Charles I. Jones, Christopher Tonetti, Nonrivalry and the economics of data, American Economic Review 110 (9) (2020) 2819–2858.

[15] Felt Labs, Felt Token, https://www.apheris.com/platform. (Accessed 8 August 2022).

[16] Legislature of Singapore, PDPA (SG): Personal Data Protection Act 2012 (Singapore), https://sso.agc.gov.sg/Act/PDPA2012, 2012.

[17] Leiser, F. Dechesne, Governing machine-learning models: challenging the personal data presumption, International Data Privacy Law 10 (2020) 187–200.

[18] OECD, Enhancing access to and sharing of data – reconciling risks and benefits for data re-use across societies, Ch. 3 Economic and social benefits of data access and sharing, https://www.oecd-ilibrary.org/sites/90ebc73den/index.html?itemId=/content/component/90ebc73d-en, 2019. (Accessed 8 August 2022).

[19] Council of European Union, AIA (EU): proposal for a regulation of the European Parliament and of the council laying down harmonised rules on artificial intelligence (artificial intelligence act) and amending certain union legislative acts COM/2021/206 final, https://eur-lex.europa.eu/legal-content/EN/TXT/?uri=CELEX%3A52021PC0206, 2021. (Accessed 8 August 2022).

[20] Court of Justice of the European Union (CJEU), Patrick Breyer v Bundesrepublik Deutschland, 19 October 2016, Case C-582/14.

[21] Intellectual Property Office of Singapore, IP and artificial intelligence information note (highlights removed), Available at https://www.ipos.gov.sg/docs/default-source/default-document-library/ip-and-ai-info-note.pdf. (Accessed 8 August 2022).

[22] Legislature of Singapore, A(SG): Copyright Act 2021 (Singapore), https://sso.agc.gov.sg/Acts-Supp/22-2021/Published/, 2021.

[23] European Patent Office, Guidelines for examination, Chapter II, part 3.3. Mathematical methods. Available at https://www.epo.org/law-practice/legal-texts/html/guidelines/e/g_ii_3_3.htm. (Accessed 8 August 2022).

[24] European Patent Office, Guidelines for examination, Chapter II, part 3.3.1, Artificial intelligence and machine learning, Available at https://www.epo.org/law-practice/legal-texts/html/guidelines/e/g_ii_3_3_1.htm. (Accessed 8 August 2022).

[25] High-Level Expert Group on Artificial Intelligence set up by the European Commission, Ethics guidelines for trustworthy AI, https://digital-strategy.ec.europa.eu/en/library/ethics-guidelines-trustworthy-ai, 8 April 2019. (Accessed 8 August 2022).

[26] World Intellectual Property Organization, IP and artificial intelligence information note, Available at https://www.wipo.int/copyright/en/. (Accessed 8 August 2022).

[27] Begona Gonzales Otero, Machine learning models under the copyright microscope: is EU copyright fit for purpose?, GRUR International 70 (11) (2021) 1043–1055.

[28] Owkin, The AI biotech company, https://owkin.com/collaborate. (Accessed 8 August 2022).

[29] European Parliament, Directive 2019/790 of the European Parliament and of the council on copyright and related rights in the digital market and amending, Directives 96/9/EC and 2001/29/EC, 2019 PE–CONS 51/19, https://eur-lex.europa.eu/eli/dir/2019/790/oj, 2019.

[30] UK Parliament, UK copyright, designs and patents act (CDPA-UK), https://www.legislation.gov.uk/ukpga/1988/48/contents, 1988.

[31] Personal Data Protection Commission Singapore, Advisory guidelines on key concepts in the personal data protection act, Issued 23 September 2013, revised 1 October 2021, 2013/2021, https://www.pdpc.gov.sg/-/media/Files/PDPC/PDF-Files/Advisory-Guidelines/AG-on-Key-Concepts/Advisory-Guidelines-on-Key-Concepts-in-the-PDPA-1-Oct-2021.pdf?la=en.

[32] Paul Quinn, Research under the GDPR – a level playing field for public and private sector research?, Life Sciences, Society and Policy 17 (4) (2021), https://doi.org/10.1186/s40504-021-00111-z.

[33] Rossello, Morales, Muñoz-González, Data protection by design in AI? The case of federated learning, Computerrecht 116 (2021).

[34] Matthew Sag, The new legal landscape for text mining and machine learning, 66 J. Copyright Soc'y USA 291 (2019).

[35] Matthew Sag, Copyright law's impact on machine learning in the United States and the European Union, 14 FIU L. Rev. 293 (2020).

[36] AI Singapore, AI Singapore's journey into the world of federated learning, Available at https://epoch.aisingapore.org/2020/10/ai-singapores-journey-into-the-world-of-federated-learning/. (Accessed 8 August 2022).

[37] David Tan, Thomas Lee, Copying right in copyright law: fair use, computational data analysis and the personal data protection act, SAcLJ 33 (2021) 1032.

[38] Sebastian Shenghong Tay, Xinyi Xu, Chuan Sheng Foo, Bryan Kian Hsiang Low, Incentivizing collaboration in machine learning via synthetic data rewards, Proceedings of the AAAI Conference on Artificial Intelligence 36 (9) (2022) 9448–9456, https://doi.org/10.1609/aaai.v36i9.21177.

[39] Nguyen Truong, Kai Sun, Siyao Wang, Florian Guitton, YiKe Guo, Privacy preservation in federated learning: an insightful survey from the GDPR perspective, Computers & Security 110 (2021).

[40] United States Congress, HIPAA (USA)): H.R.3103 – health insurance portability and accountability, Act of 1996, https://www.congress.gov/bill/104th-congress/house-bill/3103/text, 1996.

[41] M. Veale, R. Binns, L. Edwards, Algorithms that remember: model inversion attacks and data protection law, Philosophical Transactions of the Royal Society. A 376 (2018) 1–15.

[42] World Intellectual Property Organization (WIPO), Trade secrets – What is a trade secret?, Available at https://www.wipo.int/tradesecrets/en/. (Accessed 8 August 2022).

Index

Symbols

(ϵ, δ)-differential privacy, 40
ρ-Shapley value, 307

A

Abundant data aggregation, 129
Accelerated gradient
    descent, 134
    methods, 15, 18
Acceptable performance, 164
Accuracy, 112
    adversarial, 86
    classification, 112, 361, 363
    convergence, 348
    curve, 351
    drop, 70, 71, 360
    evaluation, 350
    improvement, 99, 350, 351
    level, 134
    loss, 112, 114, 116, 118
    model, 87
    variance, 351
Acoustic
    data privacy issues, 353
    models, 353
Acoustic modeling (AM) schemes, 355, 364
Acquisition function, 259
Active
    client, 204
    server, 119
Adaptive
    attacks, 100, 119
    clipping, 36
    learning rates, 8, 337
    strategies, 50, 51
Adaptive Personalized Federated Learning (APFL), 128, 135
    algorithm, 126, 128
Adjustable model parameters, 329
Adult dataset, 152
Advanced
    aggregation schemes, 322
    settings, 321
Adversarial
    accuracy, 86
    actors, 165
    agents, 94, 95
    aggregates, 168, 169
    attacks, 91, 92, 99, 102, 162, 163, 258, 268, 271
    capabilities, 51
    clients, 97, 170, 175
    cohort, 168
    contributors, 305
    direction, 85
    examples, 83, 86, 87, 92, 111
    goal, 76, 92, 167
    local model updates, 96
    model, 51
    objective, 80, 81
    trigger, 170
    updates, 79, 83, 166, 169
    users, 101
Adversarial autoencoder (AAE), 362
    method, 363
    training, 362
Adversarial training (AT), 86, 362
Aggregated
    data, 286
    dataset, 151, 238, 284
    gradients, 155, 156, 200, 288, 291, 292, 308
    loss, 243, 246
    model update, 164
    updates, 32
    variance, 109
Aggregating
    local gradients, 291
    server, 30
Aggregation, 34
    algorithms, 102
    cycles, 345, 348, 350, 351
    federated learning, 93, 352
    function, 239
    method, 319, 322
    model, 183, 351
    nodes, 33
    private, 359
    process, 312
    results, 100
    rules, 76, 79, 84, 92, 96–98, 165, 171
    secure, 62, 65, 78, 161, 162, 164, 165, 167
    server, 94, 308
    speed, 350
Aggregator, 370
    HPs, 241
    server, 230
Algorithm design, 190

Printed in the United States
by Baker & Taylor Publisher Services